The Dress of the People

FOUNDL

ter

rks and Clo

Ribbons

JOHN STYLES

The Dress of the People

EVERYDAY *f*ASHION
IN EIGHTEENTH–CENTURY ENGLAND

*Y*ALE UNIVERSITY PRESS
NEW *H*AVEN *&* LONDON

Published with assistance from the Annie Burr Lewis Fund

Copyright © 2007 by John Styles
Third printing 2013

All rights reserved.
This book may not be reproduced, in whole or in part, in any form (beyond that copying permitted by Sections 107 and 108 of the U.S. Copyright Law and except by reviewers for the public press), without written permission from the publishers.

Designed by Gillian Malpass

Printed in China

Library of Congress Cataloging-in-Publication Data

Styles, John.
 The dress of the people : everyday fashion in eighteenth-century England / John Styles.
   p. cm.
 Includes bibliographical references and index.
 ISBN 978-0-300-12119-3 (cl : alk. paper)
 1. Clothing and dress–Great Britain–History–18th century.
 [1. Great Britain–Social life and customs–History–18th century.]   I. Title.
 GT736.S79 2007
 391.00942′09033–dc22

2007025371

A catalogue record for this book is available from
The British Library

Frontispiece 'Red Cloth' and 'spriged linen', 1759,
woollen cloth dyed red, pinned on top of linen printed with sprigs in red,
London Metropolitan Archives, A/FH/A/9/1/135, Foundling no. 12058.

10 9 8 7 6 5 4

Contents

Notes for Readers — vii

Preface — ix

Introduction: Consuming the Eighteenth Century — 1

Part I Patterns of Clothing

1 Travellers' Tales: Nation and Region — 19

2 What the People Wore — 31

3 Clothing Biographies — 57

4 Keeping up Appearances — 71

5 Changing Clothes — 85

6 Fashioning Time: Watches — 97

7 Fashion's Favourite? Cottons — 109

Part II Getting and Spending

8 Clothing Provincial England: Fabrics — 135

9 Clothing Provincial England: Garments — 153

10 Clothing the Metropolis — 167

Part III Understanding Clothes

11 The View from Above — 181

12 The View from Below — 195

13 Budgeting for Clothes — 213

Part IV People and their Clothes

14 Clothes and the Life-cycle — 229

15 Involuntary Consumption? Prizes, Gifts and Charity — 247

16 Involuntary Consumption? The Parish Poor — 257

17 Involuntary Consumption? Servants — 277

18 Popular Fashion — 303

Conclusion — 321

Appendix 1 Sources — 327

Appendix 2 Tables — 335

Notes — 359

Select Bibliography — 403

Photograph Credits — 425

Index — 426

Notes for Readers

ABBREVIATIONS

LMA	London Metropolitan Archives
NYCRO	North Yorkshire County Record Office
NYCRO, QSB	North Yorkshire County Record Office, Quarter Sessions Bundles for the North Riding of Yorkshire
OBP	Old Bailey Proceedings online
PRO	Public Record Office (National Archives)
PRO, ASSI 45	Public Record Office, Assizes, Northern Circuit depositions
WYAS	West Yorkshire Archive Service
WYAS (Wakefield), QS 1	West Yorkshire Archive Service (Wakefield), Quarter Sessions Rolls for the West Riding of Yorkshire

CURRENCY

In the pre-metric currency used throughout the book, £1 is made up of 20s. (shillings); 1s. of 12d. (pence); 1 guinea is equal to £1 1s.

Following page   Joseph Highmore, *Pamela Preparing to Go Home* (detail), 1743-4, oil on canvas, National Gallery of Victoria, Melbourne, Felton Bequest 1921, 1115-3. One of a series of paintings by Highmore illustrating Samuel Richardson's best-selling novel *Pamela*, published in 1740. In this scene, Pamela, on the right, prepares to leave her place as a servant in a grand country house and return to her poor parents in her native village. She is dressed for humble village life, in a brown stuff gown, plain white apron, simple white cap and knitted mittens turned up with white calico. In her fingers she clasps the string of a cheap straw hat decorated with a blue ribbon. Clothes play an important role at this point in the novel's plot. Pamela is showing a fellow servant three bundles into which she has divided her clothes, in the process demonstrating her unaffected virtue. The bundle she holds contains items that she considers suitable for the village, like those she is wearing. The other two contain fine clothes given to her by her master and mistress. These Pamela renounces as inappropriate to her new life. They are represented here by the silk-trimmed clothing and expensive pair of stays lying on the floor.

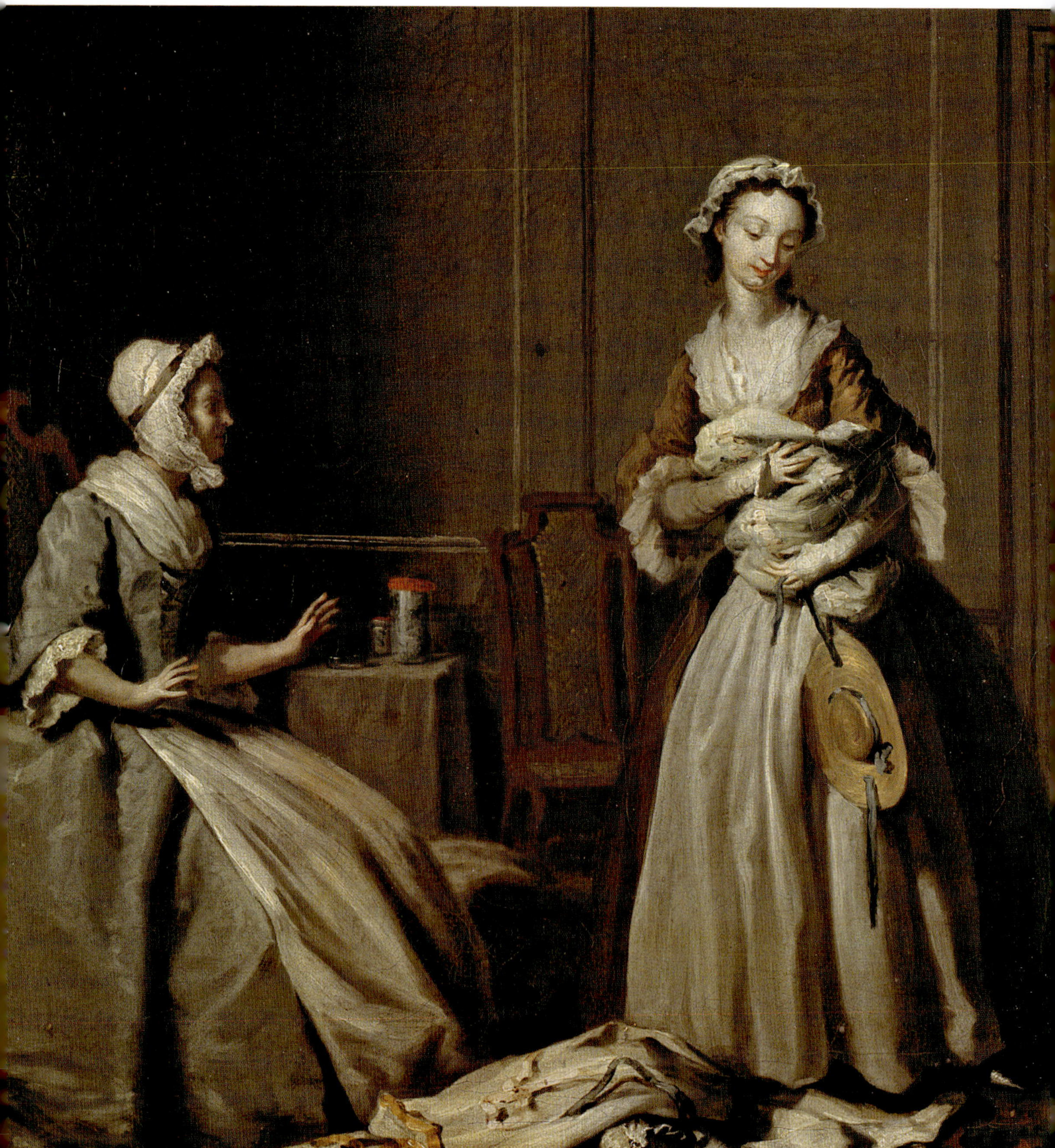

Preface

THE DRESS OF THE PEOPLE owes a great debt to my native city of Bradford, Yorkshire. That debt is primarily to the lost childhood Bradford of the 1950s and 1960s, proud capital of the worsted trade, with its busy mills, wagons laden with improbably vast bales of wool, gown shops where my mother bought stylish evening dresses for dinner dances at the Connaught Rooms, and machinery buyers calling on my grandfather at Christmas to celebrate years of doing business together. Bradford, too, was where I held my first university teaching post, as a temporary lecturer at the University of Bradford. The course I taught on the history of the British textile industries may have bemused the textile management students obliged to sit through it, but I remain grateful to them for helping me lay the intellectual foundations of this book. It was one eminent Bradfordian, my friend the late Jonathan Silver, who inspired *The Dress of the People*. Jonathan taught me to appreciate clothes: how to wear them, how to manufacture them, how to sell them. No one could have done a better job of impressing on me the inescapability of fashion, or the intellectual and aesthetic excitement of bringing fashion to ordinary people.

The book could not have been written without the support of my fellow historians. Thirty-five years ago, Roger Wells alerted me to the potential of witness statements in criminal cases as a source for studying everyday life in all its aspects, both criminal and non-criminal. I have spent a good chunk of my career endeavouring to realise that potential. I hope the results match the combination of ingenuity, rigour and imagination that he has brought to working with historical sources. Subsequently, I have incurred other intellectual debts. For references, comments and suggestions I thank Jan Albers, Dorothy Auyong, Gail Bancroft, Shelley Bennett, Elizabeth Bogdan, Christopher Breward, John Brewer, Clare Browne, Barbara Burman, Tom Cogswell, John Cross, Anthony Farrington, the late Andrew Federer, Madeleine Ginsberg, Paul Glennie, Nigel Goose, Hannah Greig, Avril Hart, Steve Hindle, Tim Hitchcock, Joanna Innes, Peter Jones, Beverly Lemire, Judith Lewis, Ann Smart Martin, David Mitchell, John Moore, Scott Myerly, Susan North, Sarah Pennell, Robert Poole, Roy Ritchie, Giorgio Riello, Kevin Rogers, Bev Sanders, Pamela Sharp, Susan Stuart, Naomi Tadmor, Alannah Tomkins, Janice Turner, Amanda Vickery, Tim Wales, Alex Werner, Jonathan White and Nuala Zahedieh. I also offer a collective 'thank you' to my former colleagues at the Victoria and Albert Museum and to my present colleagues at the University of Hertfordshire. They created two very different, but equally supportive intellectual environments which nurtured this book.

The generosity of a number of historians in sharing their data has been especially gratifying, in particular Nancy Cox, Peter Earle, Edmund Green, Tim Hitchcock, Peter King, Norma Landau, Mark Overton and Claire Walsh. I am indebted to Joan Howard-Drake and Brian Brassett for contributions to Chapter 16; to Joan Howard-Drake for allowing me to use her card index of clothes entries from the overseers' accounts for Leafield, Oxfordshire; and to Brian Brassett for making his transcripts of the overseers' accounts for Holne, Devon, available online. Working through overseers' accounts is arduous, time-consuming labour. Their hard work trawling through what are often intractable documents enabled me to extend the geographical range of my discussion of clothing under the Poor Law. More arduous still is the work of literally unravelling the tightly rolled, but un-indexed probate documents for York at the Borthwick Institute for Archives. John Smail deserves special thanks for allowing me to use his detailed list of Halifax parish wills and inventories in working on Chapters 8 and 9.

In researching the book, the greatest support came from Helen Clifford. As research assistant at the beginning of the project, she displayed a combination of imagination, skill and tenacity that would be hard to match. Subsequently, I have had research assistance from Sarah Foster, Jane Hamlett, Rachel Fuller and Cathy Strongman. I am immensely appreciative. Credit is also owed to my students on the V&A/RCA M.A. Course in the History of Design between 1982 and 2004 who wrote relevant essays and dissertations, from which I learned much. Sadly, the book's select bibliography cannot do justice to all the archives, libraries and museums across England and Wales visited in the course of researching it. Archivists, librarians and curators are the unsung heroes of a massive expansion in historical research over the last forty years, of which this book is a product.

Research was funded through the generosity of several great scholarly institutions. I started work on the book when I was awarded a Pasold Research Fund Research Readership in the History of Fashion and Clothing. I would like to express my gratitude to the Pasold Governors, to Negley Harte, former Director of the Fund, and to the committee which advised me on their behalf: Natalie Rothstein, Aileen Ribeiro, Santina Levy and the late Anne Buck. Half the book was written at the Huntington Library in California, where I held the Fletcher Jones Distinguished Chair in the Humanities for a year. I owe a personal debt of gratitude to Robert C. Ritchie, W. M. Keck Foundation Director of Research at the Huntington, now a valued friend. Finally, I would like to thank the Leverhulme Trust for awarding me a Major Research Fellowship which enabled me to complete the book. Along the way, the project also received support from the British Academy, the Annie Burr Lewis Fund, and the Victoria and Albert Museum, for which I am grateful.

Elements of Chapters 8, 9 and 17 appeared in 'Clothing the North. The Supply of Non-Elite Clothing in the Eighteenth-Century North of England', *Textile History*, 25 (1994), 139-66 and in 'Involuntary Consumers? The Eighteenth-Century Servant and

Preface

her Clothes', *Textile History*, 33 (2002), 9-21. I thank Stanley Chapman, Steven King and Christiana Payne for their helpful editorial comments. Elements of Chapters 13, 14 and 17 appeared in 'Custom or Consumption? Plebeian Fashion in Eighteenth-Century England', in Maxine Berg and Elizabeth Eger, eds, *Luxury in the Eighteenth Century: Debates, Desires and Delectable Goods* (London, 2003). My thanks to the two editors for their suggestions.

It is hard to imagine a book like this, concerned with a historical subject as visual as clothing, being published anywhere but Yale University Press, London. I am beholden to Gillian Malpass, the book's brilliant editor at Yale, for her visual discrimination and her coolness under pressure, as I am to Sarah Derry, the book's copy editor, and to Hazel Hutchison and Katie Harris, Yale's former and present publicity managers.

Living with four women who can each distinguish artificial from natural fibres at twenty paces impresses on me daily the importance of clothes. This book is dedicated to one of them, my wife, Amanda Vickery. No historian ever looked better in a little black dress.

John Styles,
London, June 2007

1 Henry Wigstead, *St James's, St Giles's*, 1794, coloured engraving, Lewis Walpole Library, Farmington, Conn., 794.1.0.4. One of many eighteenth-century prints pointing out that sartorial contrasts between rich and poor often concealed moral equivalence.

Introduction
Consuming the Eighteenth Century

> Clothes came as sluggishly as food . . . I made shift, however, with a little over-work, and a little credit, to raise a genteel suit of clothes, fully adequate to the sphere in which I moved. The girls eyed me with some attention; nay, I eyed myself as much as any of them.[1]

THUS THE BIRMINGHAM BOOKSELLER WILLIAM HUTTON recounted in old age how as a young, ill-paid, stockinger's apprentice in Nottingham in 1741 he succeeded in acquiring a new suit of clothes. It is a story that sits uneasily with those accounts of eighteenth-century labouring people which emphasise poverty, immiseration and resistance. Hutton's plebeian dandyism shows that some, at least, among the working poor did find ways to share in the transformation in material life that historians have identified as a defining feature of eighteenth-century England. His story reveals, moreover, that ordinary people's engagement with the eighteenth century's culture of consumption was not simply a matter of getting and spending. It extended to the way acquisitions were understood. Hutton's use of the pervasive eighteenth-century language of gentility to characterise his new suit alerts us to at least one of the ways working people thought about the things they laboured to acquire. And, because Hutton goes on in his autobiography to itemise the clothes he bought and the occasions on which he wore them, he shows us how this plebeian gentility was realised in everyday life.

Between the restoration of Charles II in 1660 and the Great Reform Act of 1832, ordinary English men and women enjoyed unprecedented access to novel material things. Their diet expanded to include new, exotic luxuries such as tea and sugar, the fruits of British mercantile and colonial expansion. Their homes came to be furnished with new household goods like pendulum clocks and Staffordshire pottery, the products of British manufacturing ingenuity (fig. 2). Most visibly, their bodies were clothed in new fabrics and new fashions – women in calico gowns and muslin neckerchiefs, men in wigs and silver-plated shoe buckles. Ownership of these novelties was not confined to the narrow ranks of the lords and ladies, country squires, City merchants, sleek lawyers and master manufacturers who comprised the nation's elite. *The Dress of the People* argues that it extended to the working multitude who inhabited the opposite end of the social scale – the day labourers, small farmers and petty tradespeople who

2   William Bigg, *Poor Old Woman's Comfort*, 1793, oil on canvas, Victoria and Albert Museum, London, 199-1885. The old woman's comforts include a table and chairs, a fire and a candlestick, a clock, an earthenware teapot, teacup and tea saucer, a tea caddy, a teaspoon, white bread and butter. She wears a black, full-crowned hat with a peak over a cap, a plain white bedgown and a striped yellow neckerchief. A red cloak hangs over the back of her chair.

formed the bulk of the population. Material abundance came to play a crucial part in defining what it was to be English for rich and poor alike. Working people considered themselves materially better off than their continental European neighbours. Plebeian patriots celebrated the roast beef of Old England and disparaged foreigners for wearing wooden shoes (fig. 3). These emblems of English superiority were xenophobic clichés, but they were rooted in material fact. Foreign travellers in England marvelled at the quality of ordinary people's dress. All this is not to deny deprivation, exploitation and repression in the plebeian experience, but to focus on immiseration to the exclusion of much else is to misrepresent it. Humble men and women could be beneficiaries, as well as victims, of the distinctive commercial society that emerged in eighteenth-

3   Henry Bunbury, *La Cuisine de la Poste*, 1770, watercolour, Lewis Walpole Library, Farmington, Conn., 770.0.136dr. In the kitchen of a French post house, a *curé* is wearing shoes and a postillion is wearing huge boots, but the other two male figures are shown in *sabots* or wooden clogs. Bunbury produced a number of satires of this kind playing on English stereoypes of the French, which often include men wearing clogs.

century England. Their clothes were the most blatant manifestation of the material transformation of plebeian life.

This view does not command universal assent. There has been a tendency, especially among historians whose sympathies lie with 'those whom the consumer society consumed', to deny that labouring people were much affected by those changes in consumption that Neil McKendrick famously identifies as comprising an eighteenth-century consumer revolution.[2] They contend that if the working poor were touched at all by the proliferation of new fabrics and furnishings, pots and pans, cups and saucers, knives and forks, it was mainly to their disadvantage: either their labour was exploited in manufacturing them, or their sturdy plebeian collectivism was undermined in acquiring them, corrupted by an individualistic hunger to own and accumulate. Throughout the eighteenth century, maintains Edward Thompson, 'capitalist process and non-economic customary behaviour are in active and conscious conflict, as in resistance to new patterns of consumption'.[3] It was only in the aftermath of the Industrial Revolution and its accompanying demographic revolution, well into the nineteenth century, that the 'needs' of working people were remodelled, the threshold of their material expectations raised, traditional cultural satisfactions devalued and the authority of customary expectations destroyed.[4] Others address the question of who shared in the expanding culture of consumerism more directly, insisting that consumerism was almost entirely inaccessible to the great majority of the nation's population.[5] Optimists like McKendrick, they argue, fail to realise just how far up the social scale stood the boundary between the consuming classes and those who enjoyed next-to-no choice, earning too little to provide access to anything more than the barest of necessities.[6]

On neither side of this debate have arguments regularly been grounded in close empirical research into ordinary people's acquisitions and possessions. Research has been hampered by a shortage of evidence. Yet our understanding of English patterns of consumption from the sixteenth to the early eighteenth centuries has been revolutionised by the use of probate inventories, the lists of goods drawn up after the owner's death for the purposes of inheritance. Probate inventories have proved an invaluable and flexible source for studying patterns of consumption, bringing a welcome precision to debates about changes in the accumulation of goods. Nevertheless, the inventories suffer from severe limitations. Crucially for our purposes, their social range is heavily biased towards the wealthier half of the population; after 1660 very few include detailed listings of clothes, and after 1740 they rarely survive at all.[7] In their absence, studies of everyday consumption in the eighteenth century have relied either on aggregate and usually highly approximate national estimates hard-won from intractable sources such as wage and price data, tax revenues and household budgets, or on the opinions of contemporary commentators and businessmen, who often had axes to grind.

Consequently, although powerful objections have been offered to the view that plebeian men and women enjoyed expanding choice as consumers in the eighteenth century, they have usually been couched in very general terms. Three principal lines of argument characterise these objections. The first is a straightforward denial, on economic grounds, of Neil McKendrick's influential claim, itself based purely on the views of polite commentators, that eighteenth-century consumer society extended to many of the labouring poor. His claim that 'the expansion of the market [for fashionable clothing], revealed in the literary evidence, occurred first among the domestic-servant class, then among the industrial workers, and finally among the agricultural workers' is dismissed on the grounds that working people were simply too poor.[8] The second argument reasserts an older, pessimistic view of the effects of early factory industrialisation on working-class living standards. While some improvements in working people's material lives are acknowledged, they are dismissed as inconsequential and acquired at too high a price. Edward Thompson mocks economic historians who cite improvements in working-class living standards to justify the Industrial Revolution with the comment that the 'average' working man's share in the 'benefits of economic progress' consisted of 'more potatoes, a few articles of cotton clothing for his family, soap and candles, some tea and sugar, and a great many articles in the *Economic History Review*'.[9] The third line of argument is an insistence that any increase in the threshold of material expectations among plebeian men and women inevitably clashed with their traditional customary satisfactions and defences. Consumption and custom were incompatible. Any expansion in working-class consumption faced obstacles that were cultural as well as economic.

Behind the stark opposition between optimists and pessimists lie two overlapping issues. The first concerns raw purchasing power, the second the desire to use it. Decades of research into working people's standard of living between 1760 and 1850 have concluded that aggregate gains were, at best, extremely limited, especially before the 1830s.[10] Working people's disposable incomes were low, and their real wages rose only very slowly. The vast majority of earnings was spent on foodstuffs. Food prices rose steeply in the late years of the eighteenth century – often faster than wages – as population growth took off after a period of stagnation or low growth in the first half of the century. As the population increased after 1750, the poorer half of the country undoubtedly consumed more in aggregate, because they were more numerous, but principally they consumed more of the same. What remains debatable is whether their per capita consumption increased at all. If their real wages hardly rose, it is hard to imagine they provided a rapidly deepening market for the new kinds of consumer goods that poured forth from factory and workshop.

Nevertheless, these findings have failed to undermine the optimists' case that the eighteenth century witnessed profound changes in patterns of consumption that extended to the labouring poor. Too often, attempts to measure working people's purchasing power have focused on changes in the period after 1790. The economically harsh years of the 1790s are hardly the best starting point if our concern is plebeian consumption across the previous century.[11] Studies of working people's standards of living during the classic Industrial Revolution have largely ignored developments during the three-quarters of a century before its beginning, somewhere between 1760 and 1780. Real wages in England, argues Robert Allen, himself echoing Daniel Defoe, were already the highest in Europe at the end of the seventeenth century, approached only by those in the Low Countries.[12] This earlier period, it is generally agreed, witnessed important additions to plebeian consumption, including the rapid take-up of tobacco, sugar and tea as regular purchases.[13] Already, by 1786, Lancashire calico printers insisted that '3 parts out of 4 of printed goods are consumed by the lower class of people'.[14] Some of these developments, especially the adoption of exotic groceries like sugar and tea, had a great deal to do with falling prices, but optimistic historians also emphasise the importance of changes in ordinary people's attitudes to consuming that led to them to want new things and more things. These optimists stress the capacity of novel tastes and desires to entice people out of self-sufficiency into buying more and working harder. The lures of fashion, novelty, luxury and – in the cases of gin, tea and tobacco – addiction persuaded people to rely more on purchases of marketed commodities, and less on the things they produced for themselves at home. In order to buy more, it is argued, members of plebeian households, especially the wives and daughters, devoted increasing time and effort to paid work. The Industrial Revolution was preceded, argues Jan de Vries, by an industrious revolution that took place principally within the home.[15]

Precisely what we should make of these arguments for changes in consumer expectations depends on the questions we want to pose in the first place. If our question is whether an eighteenth-century consumer revolution had the capacity to kick-start the Industrial Revolution, then the evidence regarding consumer expectations is not wholly supportive. It is hard to agree with McKendrick that the eighteenth century witnessed a consumer revolution that was sudden and unprecedented, abruptly inaugurating a new humble consumer society. It seems improbable that any remodelling of tastes and desires only began in the eighteenth century. At the start of the century, poor consumers were already strikingly dependent on money wages, market transactions and national and international as well as local circuits of commodities. This was a feature of early eighteenth-century English consumption famously emphasised by Daniel Defoe in 1726: 'Suppose the poorest Country-man wants to be cloathed, or suppose it be a Gentleman wants to cloath one of his servants, whether a footman in a livery or suppose it be any servant in ordinary apparel, yet he shall in some part employ almost every one of the manufacturing counties of *England*, for making up one ordinary suit of cloaths'.[16] Before 1700, moreover, labouring people were already responsive to accessible innovations. Indeed, the big initial rise in tobacco consumption was over by the early years of the eighteenth century; for the rest of the century, consumption of tobacco stabilised (fig.4).[17] Phenomena like fashion, endowed with the power to entice people into the marketplace, may have intensified in the course of the eighteenth century and reached more consistently down the social scale, but they were not unfamiliar to ordinary people before 1700.[18] Between the mid-sixteenth century and the early eighteenth, gowns and mantuas replaced kirtles for ordinary women; the combination of coat, waistcoat and breeches replaced doublet and hose for ordinary men; worsteds and semi-worsteds such as serge and shalloon superseded cheap woollens such as russet and frieze.

Just as we should not assume that new desires and broadening tastes were absent before 1700, equally we should beware of assuming they then proceeded to sweep all before them, revolutionising consumer demand as the eighteenth century progressed. There is no reason to believe that those who developed a taste for the latest novelty in one aspect of their material lives necessarily applied it to all the others. A visitor to Camelford in Cornwall at the start of the nineteenth century was surprised that every girl of the inferior classes 'was dressed in the pink of the mode', but found a whimsical

4 William Bigg, *The Husbandman's Enjoyment*, 1793, oil on canvas, Victoria and Albert Museum, London, 198-1885. The husbandman enjoys tobacco and beer at the cottage door. He is dressed in his working clothes – brown coat and breeches, a white shirt, and gaiters over his stockings and shoes. His round hat and red neckerchief lie on the bench beside him.

contrast 'between such fashionable attire, and the wretched hovels in which the fine folks dwelt'.[19] Prosperous skilled workers in expanding industries were much better placed to cultivate a taste for fashion and novelty than underemployed rural day labourers. Plebeian Londoners enjoyed much more direct engagement with the world of high fashion than cottagers in remote Pennine townships where there were few shops and fewer resident gentry.

Even when the expectations of ordinary consumers were sufficiently revolutionised to draw them into the commercial marketplace in new ways, we cannot assume that the results necessarily showed up in sudden increases in demand for the products of workshop or factory. Ordinary consumers who wanted to acquire the more expensive new goods may have had little option but to rely on leftovers from an expanding market among the middle and upper ranks. Beverly Lemire argues that demand in eighteenth-century Britain was two-tiered. At the top were those in the middle and upper ranks who were able to buy new furnishings, clothing, tableware and the like. Below them were those who aspired to consume more, but were limited in the range of brand new articles they could afford. Those outside the highest social levels, insists Lemire, depended on second-hand goods to access the latest modes, either by purchase, or surprisingly often, by theft. This state of affairs changed only gradually over the course of the Industrial Revolution, as new goods became available at prices they could afford.[20] If Lemire's second-hand consumerism was the norm, it may have encouraged entrepreneurs to redouble their efforts to cut manufacturing costs, but in the short term it increased demand for new products only indirectly.

Nor should we expect acquisitions driven by new tastes or fashions necessarily to show up as improvements in plebeian living standards, as conventionally measured by relating trends in wages to trends in the prices of foodstuffs and other regularly purchased necessities, or by aggregating surviving household budgets. Although some of the new, fashionable goods that ordinary people came to want were, as Lemire suggests, expensive, such as mahogany furnishings, silver watches or silk gowns, and may only have been accessible second-hand, others were far less costly. They were, moreover, of a kind whose purchase could be postponed during hard times, when harvests were bad or work in short supply. In other words, they met the desire for novelty, but they are unlikely to figure in economic historians' calculations of ordinary people's standards of living, because they were cheap and did not require regular purchase. In the third quarter of the eighteenth century, a yard of silk ribbon, enough lace to edge a cap, a chip hat or an earthenware teapot could each be bought for a shilling or less, as indeed could an ounce of tea or a pound of sugar. A printed cotton handkerchief cost under two shillings, a pair of silver-plated buckles not much more. In years of full employment and low prices, a few such purchases, if made only intermittently, need not have represented an impossibly heavy demand on the budgets of labouring families whose annual household expenditure, even in hard years, was estimated to run at between 500 and 1,000 shillings.[21] Much ink has been spent debating whether or not young women working in the fields ever really wore the fashionable black silk hats portrayed in George Stubbs's paintings *The Haymakers* and *The Reapers*, yet it is often forgotten that when labouring women in the 1780s bought such hats, as they did, they paid little more than five shillings, a large sum, but not one that was unattainable for those who were young, single and earning (figs 5, 6, 7, 18).[22]

If, however, our concern is less with the question of what drove an industrial revolution and more with the material culture of ordinary eighteenth-century men and women, then mapping their expectations and their preferences as consumers is crucial, irrespective of whether those expectations were incoherent, or financially

5 (*facing page*)   George Stubbs, *The Haymakers* (detail), 1783, oil on panel, National Trust, Upton House, 13057. The woman on the left wears a spotted red handkerchief over her shoulders and a straw hat. The woman on the right wears the black silk-covered hat fashionable in the period and sports a bright pair of buckles on her shoes.

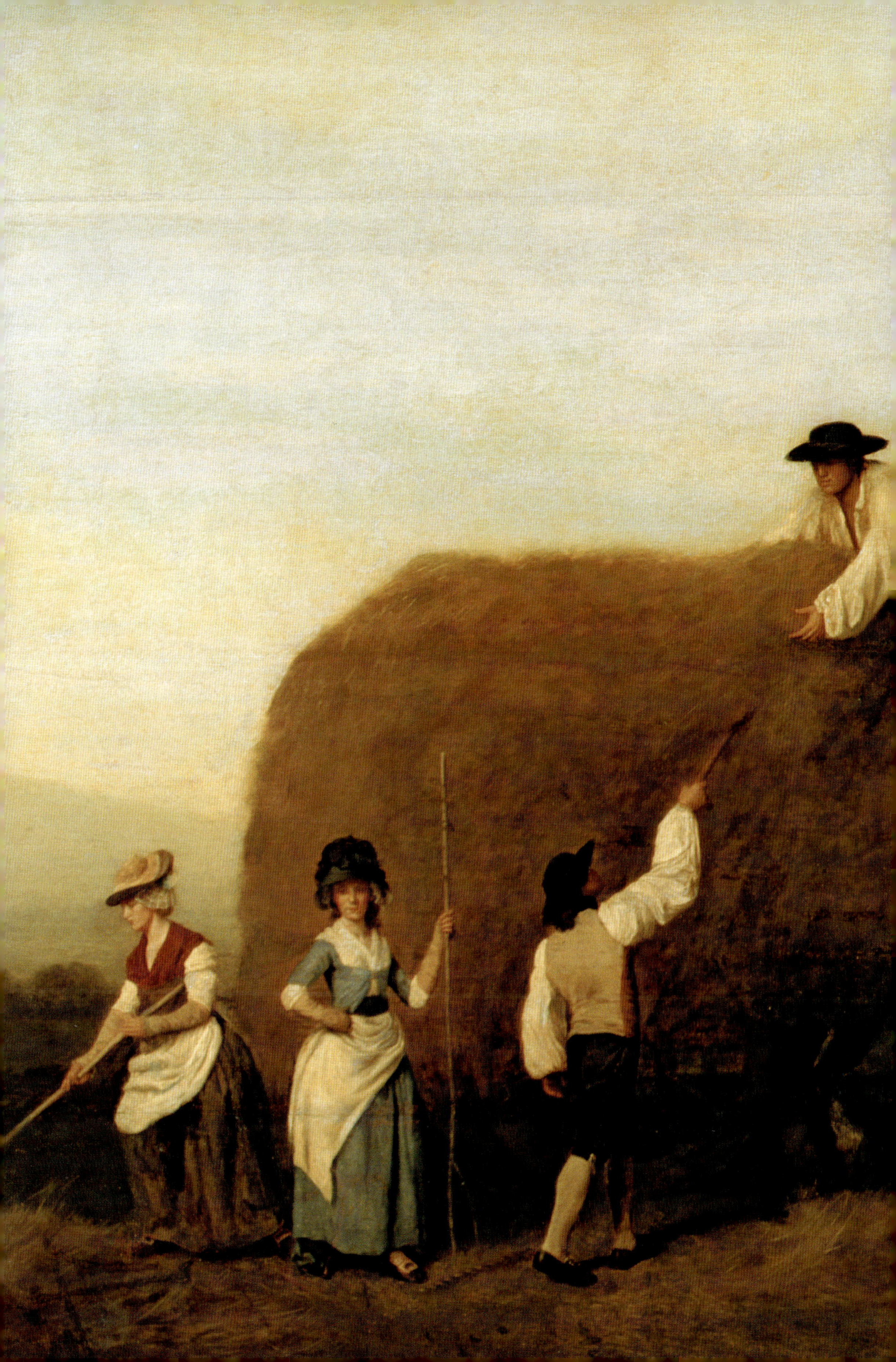

6 George Stubbs, *Haymakers* (detail), 1794, enamel on Wedgwood biscuit earthenware plaque, National Museums Liverpool, LL3682. The woman in the centre wears a black silk-covered hat. In contrast to Stubb's earlier paintings on this theme, all the men are portrayed wearing white stockings, while their breeches are in a variety of light colours, including blues and greys. Breeches worn by runaways advertised in the 1780s and 1790s were predominantly dark in colour, very rarely blue or grey, while their stockings were mainly coloured.

undemanding, or realised through cast-offs and hand-me-downs, or of little consequence for economic growth in the long run. As Sue Bowden and Avner Offer point out in their study of household appliances in the twentieth century, a direct relationship between the economic significance of a group of consumer goods and their social and cultural significance cannot be assumed: 'The outlay on domestic appliances has claimed only a tiny fraction of disposable income, rising from 0.5 percent in the U.S. in 1920 to about 2 percent in 1980. And yet the sequence of electrical and mechanical durables has altered profoundly the activities and experiences of households in America and Britain in the twentieth century.'[23] *The Dress of the People* is concerned with only one aspect of plebeian material culture in the eighteenth century – clothing – but it, too, was one that loomed large in the activities and experiences of ordinary men and women, as well as probably accounting for a higher percentage of their disposable incomes than did domestic appliances in twentieth-century America.[24]

Exploring the part clothing played in those activities and experiences requires attention to subjects that range from cleanliness to sewing, from village fairs to servants'

7 Henry Walton, *A Group of Figures with a Fruit Barrow*, 1779, oil on canvas, private collection. The small girl is portrayed in a straw hat with elaborate ribboning. The wealthy young woman who accompanies her is shown wearing an expensive, exquisitely laced, pink silk gown and a black silk hat with a high soft crown. Working women were often portrayed during the subsequent decade wearing cheaper versions of the same kind of hat.

boxes. Nevertheless, it is an exploration that inevitably returns again and again to issues regularly encountered in the debates between optimists and pessimists over consumption and the Industrial Revolution.[25] This should not surprise us. Technical innovations in textile production were crucial in propelling and defining the Industrial Revolution. Fashion, especially fashion in clothing, was central to any remodelling of consumer expectations that preceded, or accompanied revolutionary increases in production. No eighteenth-century commodity revealed differences in living standards between rich and poor more visibly than clothing. It was employed by caricaturists for that purpose over and over again (fig. 1). And, like any historical study, *The Dress of the People* is grounded in an existing literature that, for the eighteenth century, revolves around these issues.

In contrast to much of the existing literature, this book specifies the kinds of clothes characteristically worn by ordinary people in different parts of England in the eighteenth century. It identifies what they owned, what they wore, what it was made from, what it was worth and how it changed. It does so by putting to work unfamiliar and often incomplete sources, such as the records of criminal trials and advertisements for fugitives, in systematic ways (Appendix 1). At the same time, it employs engravings, paintings and textiles from the period to establish how these clothes, very few of which survive, looked and were worn. These sources enable us to pinpoint the major changes that affected the plebeian wardrobe in the course of the eighteenth century. They can provide, moreover, an essential quantitative starting point for assessing how clothing was implicated in the activities and experiences of ordinary people. What these sources do not offer is the kind of precise statistical time series beloved by historians of economic growth. They cannot provide year-on-year measurements of change in the quantity or value of everyday clothing. Nor can they supply the precise figures needed to calculate variations across the century in the proportion of gross domestic product constituted by expenditure on plebeian clothing. The evidence available for such exercises is lacking. Attempts to undertake them have usually been compromised by its shortcomings.[26]

In establishing what ordinary people wore, this book pays particular attention to differences in the quality and value of clothing, especially those differences that can be linked to fashion. Fashion, of course, can mean a number of different things. For the economist it means regular changes in visual appearance of any type of good for the purpose of stimulating sales. For the retailer it can be simply another way of saying clothes. For the dress historian it means the annual or seasonal manipulation of normative appearance specifically through clothing. For the fashion pundit it means those forms of self-conscious, avant-garde innovation in dress pursued by a social or cultural elite – the fashion of seventeenth-century royal courts, the eighteenth-century *beau monde,* or twentieth-century *haute couture.* The notion of fashion employed here combines the third and fourth of these meanings – the new modes paraded among London's *beau monde* that tended to set the fashion, and the regular changes in normative appearance expected of people who were sufficiently well off to follow them. These were not, as Hannah Greig has reminded us, precisely the same thing. For the *beau monde,* fashionability was about more than modish trendsetting in dress.[27] It was an exclusive currency of connection and self-identity among a particular metropolitan elite, one that defined them as the 'people of fashion'. It was not confined to dress and could not simply be bought. The more optimistic readings of eighteenth-century fashion in dress that present it as a site of unprecedented, radical democratisation, with all kinds of potential for unbridled emulation, are, therefore, misplaced.[28]

It was, nevertheless, new ways of dressing pioneered or at least endorsed by the *beau monde* that conventionally set the fashions disseminated season by season and year after year by milliners and drapers, by mantuamakers and tailors, and by articles in newspapers and illustrations in ladies' pocket books (fig. 8). But was their dissemination wide enough to reach the ordinary consumers who are the concern of this book? *The Dress of the People* gauges the fashionability or otherwise of plebeian dress by reference to these widely disseminated innovations, but it does so according to a broad chronology of change, not a specific seasonal or annual timetable. Everyday fashion was not necessarily right up to the minute, nor does the evidence available to track it offer great chronological precision. Most of that evidence, moreover, takes the form of verbal descriptions which identify some fashion innovations, but fail to register many others. The cut of a husbandman's coat and the tilt of a maidservant's hat remain almost entirely lost to us.

Similar evidential problems apply to identifying the ordinary men and women who are the subject of this book. Its concern is with the clothing of the poorer half of the population. These are the people who figure only marginally in existing inventory-based studies of eighteenth-century consumption, the people who, Edward Thompson insists, were victims rather than beneficiaries of consumer revolution, the people whom the Yorkshire woolstapler John Hustler identified in the famine year of 1766 as most vulnerable to high food prices: 'our manufacturers and working people, our lesser tradesmen'.[29] As John Hustler's list suggests, identifying this group is not simply a matter of distinguishing between waged workers and the rest. Those who worked with their hands for small returns in the eighteenth century included many small tradesmen who operated enterprises on their own account. Frequently they employed other family members, as well as perhaps taking on an apprentice, or even one or two waged workers, although sometimes only intermittently. They included working artisans in the manual trades, small shopkeepers, agricultural smallholders and husbandmen. Together with waged workers, apprentices, servants and parish paupers they comprised the core of those whom Edward Thompson famously labels 'plebeians', contrasting them to the patrician elite of nobles and gentry, merchants and professionals who ruled eighteenth-century England.[30]

8   *A Lady in the newest full Dress, and another in the most fashionable Undress*, 1778, printed engraving, Lewis Walpole Library, Farmington, Conn., 778.00.00 A2 L33. An illustration from a lady's pocket book showing two women, one in wide-hooped full or court dress and the other in fashionable undress, both broadly reflecting current taste among the metropolitan *beau monde*.

Thompson has been criticised for ignoring the importance of a middling group between plebeians and patricians, comprised of people with moderate but significant wealth, including yeoman farmers, prosperous retailing tradesmen, master manufacturers and lesser professional men.[31] This middling group played a dominant role in local, especially parish government in the eighteenth century. It has been singled out as the principal beneficiary of both the early eighteenth-century expansion in consumption observed in probate inventories and the late eighteenth-century consumer revolution identified by Neil McKendrick.[32] *The Dress of the People* focuses not on this middling group, but on the plebeian classes who came beneath it in the social hierarchy. The book is concerned with those who laboured with their hands on a daily basis and, except in the poorest communities, were unlikely to share prominently in governing their parishes. These core plebeians almost certainly comprised well over half the population, although it is difficult to be precise about their numbers.[33] The difficulty arises not simply because eighteenth-century statistics on social structure are few and inaccurate. It also comes about because boundary lines between the middling group and those below it were permeable and remain hard to identify. Distinctions between the manual trades and what were termed the 'clean' trades, between small country shopkeepers and leading urban retailers, between husbandmen and big farmers and between employees and employers are often unclear in sources like the trial records used repeatedly to identify plebeian clothing in this book. It consequently adopts a deliberately cautious, conservative approach when those distinctions have to be made (see Appendix 1).

These core plebeians were often treated by their social superiors as an undifferentiated mass: the common people, the poor, the vulgar, the mob. Edward Thompson's division of eighteenth-century society into two opposed and separate groups – patricians and plebeians – runs the risk of treating them in the same way. Yet, in practice, the group he terms plebeian was homogeneous neither in resources, employment nor modes of life. It incorporated such a large proportion of the nation's population that it inevitably displayed wide variations in ways of dressing, as well as attitudes to dress, although always subject to the constraint of limited disposable incomes. Indeed, variations in the quality of dress existed even among people in the same humble occupations, as elite commentators were wont to point out disapprovingly. At the King's jubilee celebrations at Wimpole Hall in Cambridgeshire in October 1809, the author Mary Berry noted that 'it was curious to observe the great and decided difference of industry and sobriety in exactly the same situation in life, some labourers with wife and two children upon twelve shillings a week, perfectly tidy, and, though darned and patched, clean and comfortable; others, on the same wages, hanging in dirty tatters'.[34] It is with variations in plebeian sartorial experience that much of this book is concerned, variations which grew out of differences of gender, age, location and employment, although not exclusively so. The one important plebeian group the book omits is children. This is a significant omission, as children accounted for about a third of the plebeian population. It is an omission that reflects the book's focus on active consumers and their engagement with fashion, a focus that grows out of the existing literature in the field and one that necessarily privileges adults.

Similarly, the book's chronological focus on the eighteenth century reflects the importance the period has been accorded by historians of consumption as a key moment of transformation, with ordinary people's clothing in the vanguard of a humble consumer revolution. Yet there are other reasons for a focus on the years from the late seventeenth century to the early nineteenth century. In this period there were marked continuities in the basic elements that went to make up a typical wardrobe, despite changes in silhouettes, materials and accessories. For men, the establishment of the three-piece suit, consisting of coat, waistcoat and breeches, took place in the late years of the seventeenth century.[35] It was to continue in this form until the early years of the nineteenth century, when trousers replaced breeches. For women, too, the basic combination of a long gown over body-forming stays and petticoat established itself in the late seventeenth century and was to persist into the nineteenth, although with changes later in the century away from open gowns towards closed gowns in an increasingly classical style.

In contrast to many other parts of Europe, moreover, eighteenth-century England had no sumptuary laws dictating what people of different ranks could and could not wear. Sumptuary legislation of this kind had been repealed a century before, in 1604, and was not revived.[36] The main legislative constraints on dress came from customs and excise duties. By the early years of the eighteenth century, most foreign manufactured goods were subject to heavy import tariffs, so high in the case of French manufactures before the Eden Treaty of 1786 that a legal import trade was almost impossible. In addition, excise duties were sometimes levied on particular items of clothing. The longest lasting was the excise on printed silk, linen and cotton fabrics, including printed handkerchiefs, first introduced in 1710, and finally repealed only in 1831.

Most excises on specific items of clothing were found, however, to be difficult to enforce and did not endure. The excise on men's hats survived less than thirty years, from 1783 to 1811, that on gloves and mittens less than a decade, from 1785 to 1794, while the excise on watches, enacted in 1797, was repealed the following year.[37] There were also a few outright prohibitions on importing and sometimes on wearing certain items, notably those imposed on printed calicoes between 1701 and 1774.[38] In combination, these various pieces of legislation were intended to protect domestic manufacturers, especially manufacturers of woollen textiles, while raising revenue in ways that favoured what governments regarded as the everyday necessities of ordinary people over superfluous luxuries. They made some of the clothes most prized by plebeian consumers more costly than they would otherwise have been, although rarely unattainably so. Even when their clothing was taxed, it tended to be at a lower rate than tea or beer. This ramshackle assemblage of overlapping tariffs, taxes and prohibitions was not wholly dismantled until well into the nineteenth century.

The study of everyday dress is important for how we understand the eighteenth century in England. Its significance for an understanding of the economy is clear. Clothing textiles were central to the new technologies of the Industrial Revolution. They and their raw materials were crucial to Britain's increasing domination of global trade. Even the small-scale, fragmented, fashion-driven characteristics of the way those textiles were made up into clothes – characteristics that at one time historians dismissed as economically backward – have recently taken on a new significance in the light of twenty-first-century enthusiasm for flexible, consumer-orientated manufacturing systems. But the study of everyday dress is also a lens for examining eighteenth-century society and its culture. The eighteenth century was obsessed with the challenge to established notions of social, moral and political order posed by the material abundance arising from Britain's commercial success. Clothing loomed large here. It helped, for instance, to define key cultural categories like gentility and politeness. It was implicated in pioneering studies into the links between luxury, labour and poverty undertaken during the eighteenth century by the first political economists. Clothing informed Georgian debates on female participation in public life, which frequently invoked arguments about feminine vanity and materialism. More broadly, the subject matter of this book reflects the new intellectual respectability the study of clothes has acquired in an era when surfaces and appearances excite as much scholarly interest as deep structures and root causes. Cultural historians now focus on the way people in the past constructed identities. In the process, they have rehabilitated scholarly interest in the very features of dress that once made it suspect as a subject of intellectual enquiry – its ephemerality, its superficiality, its variability, its loquacity.

Clothes were the brightest manifestation of the material abundance that defined what it was to be English in the eighteenth century. It was with muslin neckcloths and silver watches, silk bonnets and cotton stockings that plebeian men and women flaunted the fruits of the nation's commercial prosperity. This book retrieves the ordinary consumers of eighteenth-century England – what they wore and what it meant.

I

Patterns of Clothing

9 *Whole Length Figures of Welch Peasants*, 1797, coloured engraving, Lewis Walpole Library, Farmington, Conn., 797.0.4. The woman is shown with the man's hat, handkerchief covering the head, fringed woollen shawl, short woollen petticoat and bare feet that English visitors identified as typical of Welsh women's dress. The man, by contrast, wears little to distinguish his clothes from English common dress of the period. Even the striped stockings pulled up over his breeches and held up with garters are old-fashioned and rustic, rather than specifically Welsh.

1
Travellers' Tales: Nation and Region

'THE DRESS OF THE PEOPLE', noted the American Quaker, Jabez Fisher, when he visited Montrose on the east coast of Scotland in 1775, 'is vastly different from the English'.[1] Foreign visitors and native commentators alike agreed that ordinary English men and women dressed distinctively. Travellers' observations on clothing have often been quoted by historians looking to enliven accounts of eighteenth-century English society, but they have rarely been addressed systematically. This chapter offers a review of travellers' evaluations of ordinary people's dress, incorporating the opinions of those who compared England with continental Europe, those who compared the different parts of the British Isles, and those who compared different English regions. Their observations do not represent a reliable survey of how ordinary English people dressed. Nevertheless, they do alert us to aspects of common dress educated, cosmopolitan visitors found distinctive. These aspects of common dress merit special attention when we go on to explore what ordinary English people actually wore.

The distinctiveness of English plebeian dress did not lie in regional variations or vernacular styles. It was the high quality of everyday clothing that excited attention. Already at the end of the seventeenth century, the visiting Frenchman Henri Misson noted that 'the very Peasants are generally dressed in Cloth', a state of affairs so unfamiliar to him that he employed it to demonstrate the abundance of woollen cloth in England.[2] Half a century later, in 1750, his countrywoman Madame du Boccage explored the cottages of shepherds and the houses of farmers near Oxford: 'People of this class have their houses well furnished, are well dressed, and eat well; the poorest country girls drink tea, have bodices of chintz, straw hats on their heads, and scarlet cloaks upon their shoulders.'[3] The Swedish botanist Pehr Kalm, staying at Little Gaddesdon, Hertfordshire in 1748, concurred: 'Here it is not unusual to see a farmer's or another small personage's wife clad on Sundays like a lady of "quality" at other places in the world, and her every-day attire in proportion.' Previously he remarked: 'I believe there is scarcely a country where one gets to see so many *Peruques* as here . . . It did not, therefore, strike one as being at all wonderful to see farm-servants, clod-hoppers, day-labourers, farmers, in a word, all labouring-folk go through their usual every-day duties all with *Peruques* on the head. Few, yea, very few, were those who only wore their own hair. I had to look around a long time in a church or other gathering of people, before I saw anyone with his own hair.'[4]

Similar opinions continued to be expressed by foreign visitors during the second half of the eighteenth century. The German Pastor Karl Philipp Moritz, visiting London in June 1782, expressed 'much real pleasure, when I walk from Charing-cross up the Strand, past St. Paul's to the Royal Exchange, to meet, in the thickest crowds, persons, from the highest to the lowest ranks, almost all well-looking people and cleanly and neatly dressed. I rarely see even a fellow with a wheelbarrow, who has not a shirt on; and that too such an one, as shews it has been washed; nor even a beggar, without both a shirt, and shoes and stockings.' On leaving Oxford for Birmingham a few weeks later, he noted that 'women in general, from the highest to the lowest, wear hats, which differ from each other less in fashion, than they do in fineness', concluding, 'There is, through all ranks here, not near so great a distinction between high and low, as there is in Germany.'[5] Other late eighteenth-century German visitors agreed. Johann Wilhelm von Archenholz observed in 1789: 'The most elegant part of an English-woman's apparel is her hat, which is usually adorned with ribbands and feathers. No female, of whatever rank, dares appear in the streets of London on foot, without one of these; the very beggars wear them.'[6] Friedrich August Wendeborn concluded in 1792:

> In Germany there is a great difference as to value between the dress of different ranks of people; but in England this distinction holds in a much smaller degree. The cloathing manufactured for the poor and common people, is in small proportion to their number, and few or none of them like to wear it. Even in country places it is but little used; and in London, or the great towns, it is seldom or never to be seen. All do their best to wear fine clothes, and those who cannot purchase them new buy the old at second-hand, that they may at least have the appearance of finery.[7]

Foreigners were not insensible to the presence of people dressed in poor, ragged clothing. Pastor Moritz, who was unusual in choosing to travel far from London on foot, noted the 'dirty and tattered cloaths' worn by his guide to the caves at Castleton in Derbyshire and the 'singularly vulgar and disagreeable' dress of the colliers he met at the Navigation Inn near Nottingham.[8] Nevertheless, it was the high standard of ordinary people's clothes that prompted the majority of comments: the good quality of the materials, the wide range of the garments, the adherence to fashion, and the muted social distinctions.

English-speaking travellers addressed these issues too, but, unlike their continental counterparts, often they did so by contrasting the different parts of the British Isles. The deficiencies of the clothing typically worn by the poor of Scotland and Ireland, compared with their equivalents in England, became almost a cliché, especially the fact that so many of them went barefoot, a sure sign of impoverishment to eighteenth-century English eyes. Arthur Young, the agricultural writer, travelling through Ireland between 1776 and 1778, famously reported: 'The common Irish are in general cloathed so very indifferently, that it impresses every stranger with a strong idea of universal

10 *Economy*, c.1800, wood engraving, private collection. In this engraving, published at Alnwick in Northumberland, economy is ironically symbolised by a Scotsman wearing tartan and a kilt, but no shoes or stockings.

poverty. Shoes and stockings are scarcely ever found on the feet of the children of either sex; and great numbers of men and women are without them.' He also noted a general lack of hats among the women, although he acknowledged that there had been recent improvements and that the poor were better clothed on Sundays and holidays.[9]

Jabez Fisher, the American Quaker, travelling in Scotland the year before Young embarked on his Irish tour, observed similar deficiencies in the dress of the common people. On the road from Kilsyth to Glasgow in October 1775, he 'overtook a vast many people going to market. The road alive, the women mostly barefooted and bare legged while the men keep up the prerogative, by wearing shoes and stockings.' Arriving in England five days later near Carlisle, he was pleased to find 'the dress and manners totally different'.[10] Two decades later, Harriet Clark, great-niece of the York architect John Carr, visited Glasgow: 'The Town class of women go half naked, without Shoes and Stockings hats or Cloaks, in short, half a bedgown and small petticoat, and sometimes a little plaid, is all their dress.'[11] In 1801, Susan Sibbald, the daughter of a naval doctor, found the same shortcomings by English standards in the clothes worn by the common people at Kelso, just five miles from the English border, 'particularly in the females;– without shoes and stockings, no caps, short petticoats, and bedgowns with short sleeves' (fig. 10).[12]

English visitors to Wales placed less emphasis on the deficiencies of Welsh common dress and more on its singularity. Nevertheless, their observations shared two characteristics with those of travellers in Scotland and Ireland: first, English common dress set the standard by which local practice was judged and, second, it was the clothing worn by women that excited most attention.[13] The late eighteenth century saw wealthy English tourists flock to the Welsh mountains in search of picturesque scenery. Wales also attracted visitors because it seemed sufficiently remote to withstand the corrupting influence of metropolitan luxury. 'The people here', wrote Henry Wigstead approvingly in 1797, 'are really almost in a state of simple nature.'[14] Such views coloured tourists' evaluation of Welsh dress. Ways of dressing that might otherwise have been dismissed as badges of poverty were frequently extolled as evidence of virtuous simplicity. Mary Morgan, travelling across south Wales in 1791, identified 'an absence of vanity in the country people, and likewise a superior degree of judgement, which teaches them to prefer the warmth and plainness of their own woollen manufacture to the cold and tawdry productions of other climates'. She contrasted the 'neatness and decency' of the blue cloth jackets and petticoats worn by small farmers' wives at Llandovery in Carmarthenshire to the 'gay and tawdry cottons worn by English women of this order'.[15]

During the late years of the eighteenth century, visitors like Mary Morgan consistently identified a number of items of clothing worn by ordinary Welsh women which marked them out from their English equivalents (fig. 11). Welsh women wore short jackets or bedgowns[16] made from woollen cloth, especially striped Welsh flannel, and petticoats of the same material, often without aprons. English women, although in the late eighteenth century they sometimes wore bedgowns and jackets made from a variety of materials for work, were also accustomed to wear full-length gowns of worsted stuff or cotton over petticoats, with an apron. Welsh women wore black, low-crowned, felted hats, like those worn by men, over handkerchiefs. The English tended to wear straw or silk hats over white linen caps. Welsh women wore short woollen cloaks, or a square, untailored piece of woollen cloth, worn like a shawl. English countrywomen were expected to have long red woollen cloaks (fig. 16).

The letters of Catherine Hutton, the daughter of a successful Birmingham bookseller who visited Wales several times in the 1780s and 1790s, are particularly detailed in their descriptions of these familiar items of Welsh women's dress. At Aberystwyth on the Cardiganshire coast in 1787 she found that 'the women universally wear a petticoat, and a jacket fitting close to the waist, of striped woollen, and a man's hat. A blue cloak many of them have, but it is reserved for dress, and in common they wear a long piece of woollen cloth wrapped round the waist.' At Mallwyd, Merionethshire, in 1796 she noted: 'Here the common people speak no English. The dress of the women is entirely supplied by the sheep of the country, with the exception of two pocket handkerchiefs, one worn on the neck, the other on the head and brought to the throat, and tied behind. Over this head-dress, summer and winter, indoors and out, they wear a black hat, distinguished from the men's only by a riband tied round the crown.'

11 Julius Caesar Ibbetson, *Newcastle Emlyn Costumes*, 1792, watercolour, National Museum of Wales, Cardiff, A 17502. The women of this Carmarthenshire town wear the men's hats, head handkerchiefs, short jackets, short striped petticoats, blue cloaks and lengths of untailored cloth described by visitors to Wales.

Hutton noted differences between town and country dwellers in north Wales, but these simply served to highlight the extent to which Welsh and English practice could diverge. In 1797 she observed the guests at the wedding of a sailor to the daughter of a shoemaker at Canaervon. 'The town ladies were clad, not like the mountaineers, in woollen, but in printed cotton gowns, white petticoats, and white stockings; but they retained the beaver hat, and, as the morning was cloudy, the blue cloak, which nothing but the hottest sunshine, and sometimes not even that, could persuade them to lay aside.'[17]

Most of these distinctive features of Welsh women's dress involved the use of short lengths of cheap, coarse fabrics, locally manufactured. Nevertheless, they were interpreted by many, though not all, English commentators as evidence of simplicity and innocence rather than inaccessibility, poverty and uncouthness. More difficult for the English to justify in these terms was the practice of going barefoot frequently observed among Welsh women (fig. 9).[18] So powerful a sign of 'wretched penury' were bare feet to the English that Mary Morgan felt compelled both to dismiss the practice as a rarity and to mount a convoluted defence of it in order to sustain her assertion that Welsh women's dress was 'one of the most commodious, comfortable, and simple, that I ever saw adopted by any set of people whatsoever'.[19] Another sartorial indicator of Welsh poverty that was hard to romanticise was observed by Arthur Young when he travelled through Carmarthenshire on his return from Ireland in 1776: 'The poor people spin a good deal of wool, and weave it into flannel for their own wear, no linen is worn by them, flannel supplying the place.'[20] Washable linen undergarments were almost universal among the poor in England; the use of wool for undergarments was conventionally regarded as antiquated and unhealthy. The Reverend Gilbert White, writing about his Hampshire village of Selborne in 1789, noted: 'The use of linen changes, shirts or shifts, in the room of sordid or filthy woollen, long worn next the skin, is a matter of neatness comparatively modern, but must prove a great means of preventing cutaneous ails. At this very time, woollen instead of linen prevails among the poorer *Welch*, who are subject to foul eruptions.'[21]

Everyday dress in eighteenth-century Ireland, Scotland and Wales was neither as unchanging nor as geographically uniform as visitors' comments might suggest. Modes of dress that confounded conventional national stereotypes often went unremarked because they failed to conform to visitors' preconceptions or prejudices. Lengths of printed cotton for gowns and bedgowns were certainly among the textiles sold to servants and a shoemaker by a shopkeeper at deeply rural Penmorfa, Canaervonshire, in the 1790s, casting doubt on Catherine Hutton's conclusions about the differences between town and country dress in north Wales.[22] Felted hats appear in the painter George Morland's portrayals of poor English countrywomen at the end of the century (figs 16 and 21). Nevertheless, English visitors' observations on common dress in other parts of the British Isles do help identify precisely what they regarded as superior about the common people's clothing in England. They focused on shoes and stockings, on hats, on finer, costlier fabrics in longer lengths, whether of woollen, linen or cotton, and on a range of accessories including ribbons, caps and aprons. These were precisely the elements identified as distinctive by continental European visitors.

If travellers considered English common dress to be superior to that worn elsewhere, they were also alert to regional differences within England itself. Eighteenth-century England lacked, as Anne Buck has argued, those 'variations from the main stream of fashion which appear in many countries of Europe, called folk, peasant or regional costume'.[23] From north to south, east to west, the style of the clothing the common people wore was essentially a coarser version of contemporary high style. Nevertheless, travellers in England did find that regional variation, though muted, was not entirely absent. Susan Sibbald, for example, on her way from London to Scotland in 1801, commented: 'What a marked difference we saw even before we arrived at Newcastle, between the lower class of people as to their dress thus far North.'[24] Often, these distinctions turned on the quality or condition of the clothes worn, rather than their style. The Edinburgh-trained doctor Sylas Neville, travelling in the Midlands in 1781, judged that the people of Warwickshire 'look better and are better clothed than those of Derbyshire'.[25] Such differences were even observed within London itself. Samuel Curwen, the American loyalist, summing up the way people at Liverpool were clothed in 1780, concluded: 'Dress and looks more like inhabitants of Wapping, Shadwell, Rotherhithe than in neibourhood of Exchange or London anywhere above Tower.'[26]

In some parts of England, however, these regional variations in everyday dress extended to particular items of clothing. Three garments in particular had distinct regional associations: whittles, wooden clogs and smock frocks. In the west of England, countrywomen wore mantles or whittles – pieces of fringed woollen cloth, similar to those worn in Wales – in preference to the full cloaks that were standard women's outer wear elsewhere in England. Celia Fiennes saw them at Taunton in Somerset at the very end of the seventeenth century: 'You meete all sorts of country women wrapp'd up in the mantles called West Country rockets, a large mantle doubled together of a sort of serge, some are linsywolsey, and a deep fringe or fag at the lower end; these hang down some to their feete some only just below the wast, in the summer they are all in white garments of this sort, in the winter they are in red ones; I call them garments because they never go out without them and this is the universal fashion in Sommerset and Devonshire and Cornwall.'[27] In 1700 they were described by James Brome as 'a peculiar sort of Garment which they wear upon their Shoulders, called Whittles, they are like Mantles with fringes about the edges, without which the common sort never ride to Market, nor appear in publick'.[28] At Holne in Devon they were still being supplied by the overseers of the poor in the 1770s. What distinguished whittles was their cheapness. At Holne, one and a half yards of shag, a very cheap woollen cloth bought at 8d. per yard, was used to make a whittle for an adult, while cloaks were made from two and a half yards of Penistone, a more expensive woollen cloth at 14½d. per yard.[29]

In the north of England, travellers remarked on the wearing of clogs. In 1750 the Irish clergyman Dr Richard Pococke noted: 'In these counties of Cumberland, Westmoreland, and the north part of Lancashire, they wear shoes with wooden soles, and many on working days go without stockings.'[30] A Quaker traveller commented in 1798 that the wearing of clogs by men, women and children was 'general in the north of England'.[31] These were not the leather undershoes known as clogs, worn by wealthier women to protect their shoes in wet weather, but common people's footwear with wooden soles, often ironed or nailed, and leather uppers. They were hardly known south of Derbyshire.[32] Clogs were, of course, to become a familiar element of working women's dress in the industrial north of England in the late nineteenth century, but the eighteenth-century travellers who identified them as a northern peculiarity did not make it clear how commonly they were worn, as opposed to how widely. Clogs were certainly cheaper to buy than shoes. When the overseers of the poor at Calverley near Leeds in Yorkshire bought footwear for Matthew Johnson in 1761, his clogs cost only 9d., while his shoes cost 2s.[33] The average cost of the 22 purchases of clogs bought by the female servants of Robert Heaton, a worsted manufacturer from Haworth, Yorkshire, between 1768 and 1790 was 2s. 1d. a pair, while their 47 purchases of new shoes and pumps cost on average 3s. 11d. a pair.[34] Clogs were not only cheaper to buy; they lasted longer. Sir Frederick Eden, writing in the 1790s in his *State of the Poor*, considered clogs to be 'much cheaper, more durable, and more wholesome, than shoes'. He thought that a pair of clogs would last a labouring man a year or a year and a half, while he would need two pairs of shoes each year.[35]

Wooden shoes were signs of poverty, conventionally disparaged as the footwear worn by oppressed foreigners, especially Catholic Frenchmen, not free-born, Protestant Englishmen. 'Where *Slavery* is, there are *Wooden Shoes*,' a shoemaker insisted in a 5 November speech reported in the *Gentleman's Magazine* in 1731.[36] The clogs worn in the north of England had wooden soles with leather uppers, unlike all-wooden French rural *sabots*. Nevertheless, when a correspondent to *Annals of Agriculture* in 1793 noted that in Lancashire 'the soles of all the common people's shoes are of wood', it was as evidence of their wretchedness and impoverishment, which proceeded, he believed, 'entirely from the disproportioned unreasonable high wages, and the low price and ready temptation and supply, of spirituous liquors'.[37] Yet the purchases made by Robert Heaton's servants suggest that fewer clogs were bought than shoes, a disparity that perhaps reflects their greater durability, although they were not necessarily alternatives to each other. At least 18 of the 28 servants had both clogs and shoes. A greater disparity between clogs and shoes emerges in the purchases of footwear made for parish paupers by Yorkshire overseers of the poor, who might have been expected to be especially price sensitive. At Spofforth, an agricultural village near Knaresborough, the overseers bought 16 pairs of clogs for men, women and children between 1770 and 1799, but 128 pairs of shoes. At Thornhill, on the southern edge of the Yorkshire woollen manufacturing district near Dewsbury, the overseers bought only three pairs of clogs during the same three decades, but 90 pairs of shoes. And there were far fewer cloggers in the north than there were shoemakers. A 1787 local census of Westmorland listed only nine cloggers, but 45 cordwainers and shoemakers.[38]

Although clogs might have been practical for outdoor work, shoes seem to have been preferred. For the first two-thirds of the eighteenth century, however, conventional measures of the standard of living among the common people suggest the north was poorer than the south, and clogs had the advantage of cheapness. Samuel Finney, the Cheshire minature painter and magistrate, in his 1785 survey of Wilmslow in Cheshire, recorded that forty years previously there had been no more than two shoemakers in the parish, but 'at least a dozen wooden clog makers . . . for every body amongst the farmers, Servants, labouring and poor People, Men, Women, and Children, wore Cloggs'. The following years witnessed a rapid rise in prosperity due to the expansion of textile manufacturing in the parish. Footwear was transformed. 'There are now at least a dozen Shoemakers in the Parish, and perhaps not above two or three Cloggmakers.'[39] But this process could go into reverse. By the early nineteenth century, as leather prices rose steeply and shoes became more expensive, the overseers of the poor in one north-west Yorkshire parish, Carleton-in-Craven, began to supply clogs to paupers in preference to the shoes they had supplied previously.[40] In the north, at least, clogs offered a cheap alternative to shoes when economies had to be made.

The smock frock or round frock, the third garment with distinct regional associations, was widely worn by agricultural workers in the Midlands and the south of

12   *The Lucky Escape, or Jolly Carpenter*, 1793, mezzotint, Lewis Walpole Library, Farmington, Conn., 793.10.24.2. In this illustration to a song of Charles Dibdin's, the two men are identified by their stereotypical occupational dress. The ploughman is portrayed in a short smock frock worn over a dark coat or waistcoat, with a round hat, spotted neckerchief, breeches, striped stockings and gaiters. The sailor, a ship's carpenter, is shown in a high-crowned round hat, a short blue jacket with brass buttons, loose-fitting canvas slop breeches, blue stockings and shoes with buckles. The ploughman's wife wears a printed gown with white ruffles on the sleeves, a printed neckerchief and a white cap and apron.

England towards the end of the eighteenth century (figs 12, 16, 40). It took various forms, but was generally a loose-fitting linen garment that served as a kind of washable overall, covering and protecting the clothes beneath.[41] Its loose fit was proverbial, even in London, where in 1785 a man wearing another man's coat was told it 'fits you like a smock frock, it touches your heels'.[42] Thomas Pennant saw them in Sussex on the road from Arundel to Chichester in 1801, where 'the men had chiefly smock frocks over their clothes and were mounted on pretty ponies'.[43] When Marianne Thornton, the daughter of a merchant brought up in the countryside near Hull in Yorkshire, went to stay at the village of Lancing in Sussex in 1797 during the harvest, she reported that she had: 'never seen any peasants' dress so picturesque as these; it consists generally of a brown or light blue linen frock (for the men) with a straw hat bound with black ribbon'.[44] A less picturesque perspective was offered by an excise officer confronted with 30 men on the Dorset coast in 1788: 'seeing them ride down in their long smock-frocks, I took them to be smugglers'.[45]

Familiar earlier in the century as the dress of carters and waggoners, by its end the smock frock had become standard wear for male rural workers in the south.[46] No smock frocks appear in advertisements for runaways in the Oxford and Worcester newspapers or in the transcripts of Old Bailey trials before 1760. Between 1760 and 1799, 20 appear in the advertisements, worn by a labourer, a farmer, farmers' servants and apprentices, and they are mentioned in 72 Old Bailey trials between 1760 and 1799, especially in the 1780s and 1790s. Yet it is not surprising that Marianne Thornton, brought up in Yorkshire, was unfamiliar with them, because smock frocks were little worn in the north of England. Only five figure in runaway advertisements in the Leeds newspapers, all after 1775, and two of them were described as waggoner's frocks. Once again, an explanation for the differences between north and south can be found in the economic experiences of the common people in the different regions. Smock frocks became general wear among agricultural labourers in the Midlands and the south at precisely the period in the late eighteenth century when their real wages began to come under pressure, unemployment started to rise and living standards to decline.[47] Wages, employment and living standards did not deteriorate in the same way for agricultural labourers in the north, where industrial expansion served to keep demand for labour high. Near Horsham in Sussex in 1823, William Cobbett noted: 'The men and boys wear smock-frocks more than they do in some counties. When country people do not, they always look dirty and comfortless.'[48] Smock frocks were durable, washable and relatively cheap, retailing at 5s. 6d. to 8s. at a shop in rural Westoning, Bedfordshire in the 1790s. Conventional outer garments cost much more. When men who bought smock frocks purchased waistcoats at the same shop, they had to pay between 10s. 6d. and 14s.[49] As Anne Buck observes: 'The smock, which could be worn to protect good clothing, could also conceal poor clothing.'[50]

Whittles, wooden clogs and smock frocks were not the only regionally distinctive garments noted by eighteenth-century travellers in England, but the rest were mostly specialised items of clothing associated with local occupations like mining or fishing.

In the parts of the country where the three kinds of regionally distinctive clothing examined here were worn, they transcended occupational boundaries to a considerable extent. What they had in common was cheapness compared with the mainstream alternatives in general wear among the common people. The smock frock in particular would subsequently be romanticised as a kind of rural folk costume, in the same way that late eighteenth-century Welsh women's clothing would be re-formulated into a national costume in the nineteenth century. Reinstated in their eighteenth-century context, the cheap, geographically distinctive ways of dressing found noteworthy by travellers in Wales, Scotland, Ireland and some English regions have a different significance. They emphasise the high standard to which elite observers expected ordinary English men and women usually to be clothed. Foreign visitors shared these high expectations. The degree of unanimity is striking. Shoes and stockings, good quality fabrics and an extensive range of clothing accessories made English common dress distinctive.

13   Henry Singleton, *The Ale-House Door*, c.1790, oil on canvas, Victoria and Albert Museum, London, 1834–1900. The woman's cap, shoes and cuffs over her elbows are all in the fashion of the 1780s. She wears a fitted jacket over a plain petticoat, with a green apron and a striped neckerchief. The man wears the round hat and spotted neckerchief of common people's wear, but also a coat with the large buttons fashionable in the 1780s, over a double-breasted waistcoat.

2
What the People Wore

On a Thursday afternoon in May 1789 part of the market town of Brandon, situated in the north-west corner of Suffolk, was devastated by one of the fires that swept through settlements in eighteenth-century England with alarming frequency. Brandon stands on the Little Ouse between the Norfolk Brecklands and the Fens. On the afternoon of the fire, many of its inhabitants were at a fair in nearby Thetford. The fire destroyed a number of houses, consuming the contents. In nine cases the things burnt included almost all the clothes left at home by their inhabitants.[1] Consequently, the itemised lists later drawn up of goods destroyed represent the bulk of the clothing owned by these victims, apart from whatever they happened to be wearing on the afternoon of the fire.[2] The lists provide an exceptionally rare, detailed snapshot of the stocks of clothes owned by different sorts of people living in the same street. The fire made no distinction between the possessions of rich and poor. Those who suffered extended from members of the town's professional and mercantile elite to humble servants and artisans. As a result, we can recreate an entire community through its possessions.

The contrast between the clothes owned by rich and poor is plain (table 1). The greatest loss of clothes in aggregate was suffered by two elite families, those of William Webb, postmaster, and Francis Shanley, surgeon and apothecary. They each lost over 200 items valued at more than £75. Although Webb and Shanley were among the town's wealthiest inhabitants and evidently owned large numbers of valuable clothes, we should bear in mind that they were unlikely to have come close in either the extent of their wealth or the magnificence of their clothing to the 'great number of noblemen and gentlemen [who] reside in the neighbourhood in the sporting season'.[3] The clothes owned by the two poorest families affected by the fire were fewer in number and of less value. Mark Palmer, a blacksmith, lost 72 items valued at just over £16. John Neel, a cordwainer, lost 41 items valued at just over £7. Smaller still were the wardrobes of those working men and women who were unmarried and childless. They tended to own the least clothing. William Eagle, a servant, lost 17 items valued at under £5; Elizabeth Cooper, a mantuamaker, lost 22 items valued at only £2 13s.

In what ways did the clothes lost in the fire by rich and poor differ? The crucial differences lay in numbers, quality and value. This was true irrespective of whether our focus is outer garments, undergarments or accessories, as an examination of the women's gowns and shifts, men's shirts, and men's and women's handkerchiefs lost in the fire demonstrates. All of the nine victims lost gowns, except William Eagle, an unmarried male servant, but each of the three wealthy victims (Webb, Shanley and Warner) lost more of them than any of the six poorer victims. The postmaster William Webb lost four times more gowns (see table 2). In addition, it was only the three wealthy families where gowns made from expensive silk figure among the burnt clothing. William Webb's two silk lustring gowns were valued at £1 10s. each. The surgeon Francis Shanley's three best cotton gowns were worth less, at 15s. each, but that was still significantly more than the most expensive gown found among the losses from the poorer victims – the 'cotton gown (almost new)' belonging to the cordwainer John Neel, valued at 12s. 6d. The servant Sarah Holmes's workaday stuff gown was valued at only 4s. 6d.

If we turn to shirts and shifts, the basic eighteenth-century undergarments for men and women respectively, a similar pattern emerges (see table 3).[4] The three wealthy victims owned many more of these garments. Moreover, it is mainly among the clothes lost by the wealthy that shifts and shirts made from the finer and more expensive linens appear. Francis Shanley's four new Holland shirts were valued at 11s. 3d. each, more than twice as much as William Eagle's one new shirt at 5s., which was probably made from a standard, fairly coarse linen. The ownership of handkerchiefs, mainly worn as neckwear, but including some pocket handkerchiefs, followed the same pattern, the three wealthy victims listing far greater numbers among their losses, including more in costly fabrics like silk and muslin (see table 4). Only one silk handkerchief was lost by a poorer victim. It was the servant Mary Cooper's black silk handkerchief, valued at 2s. Francis Shanley's 'full trimmed black silk handkerchief laced etc' was worth nearly four times as much, at 7s. 6d.

Behind these differences in the number and value of the clothes owned by rich and poor, lay distinctions of quality and appearance which were readily accessible to contemporaries, but are difficult for us to recapture. It is important to recognise, however, that the crucial differences between rich and poor did not lie in the types of garments they wore. From the wealthy surgeon to the poor cordwainer, the adult victims of the Brandon fire owned broadly the same kinds of garments. We do not, of course, know what the victims were wearing at the time of the fire, but there were few items lost by the wealthy that were entirely absent from the homes of their poorer neighbours. Those few tended to be specialist accessories such as gloves, pairs of drawers, a wig, a cane and an umbrella. Some sense of how contemporaries judged differences in quality between clothing items of the same type can be derived from paintings and prints, although it remains difficult to establish the degree to which artists exaggerated or manipulated social distinctions (figs 14, 15, 19). Judgements about quality emerge also in the evidence given in criminal trials. A poor widow accused in 1751 of stealing money from a house she cleaned in London was suspected because 'she was a very miserable creature before, but now she was well dressed'. Being 'well dressed' involved wearing 'fine' versions of many of the items that constituted the normal woman's

14 *In Fashion. Out of Fashion*, 1787, coloured engraving, Lewis Walpole Library, Farmington, Conn., 787.1.18.2. The wealthy woman on the left is in the height of fashion, wearing her gown looped up over her white petticoat, a muslin or gauze shawl projecting at her breast, a wide-brimmed hat trimmed with feathers and lace, a large muff and pink stuff shoes. The poor woman on the right wears typical working woman's dress of the 1780s: a red spotted cotton or linen printed gown looped up over a red petticoat, a white apron, a red shawl, a blue spotted neckerchief, a low-crowned straw or chip hat with a ribbon over a cap, and leather shoes. The print emphasises that the dress of the poor woman includes many of the elements worn by her wealthy companion, but without the ultra-fashionable accessories or the exaggerated silhouette.

wardrobe. She 'had bought herself new cloaths, silver buckles, and fine things, a pair of tabby stays, a fine black hat, and fine shoes'. When someone of low social status wore the kind of expensive, specialist materials that were confined to the richer families at Brandon, it was the accessories that excited attention. Sophia Pringle, the daughter of a journeyman tailor living on the Ratcliffe Highway in east London, aroused suspicion at the Bank in 1787 because, having first appeared 'in the habit of a servant', she returned a week later 'in a different situation, with her muff and feathers and dress, which it seemed she could not afford'.[5] A London pawnbroker's apprentice was mistaken for a man of fortune because 'he was elegantly dressed, with a number of superfluous ornaments', including a 'very elegant diamond shirt pin'.[6]

Despite the differences in quality, materials and (where it is possible to identify them) unit values between many of the clothes owned by rich and poor at Brandon, there

15. George Morland, *The Child at Nurse*, 1789, oil on canvas, Fitzwilliam Museum, Cambridge, PD.115-1992. Both the wet-nurse and her cottage are improbably spruce. Nevertheless, her clothes are consistent with evidence from other sources about the best dress of young rural women in the 1780s. She wears a long, striped gown, either cotton or linen, over a green petticoat, a red printed neckerchief spotted with yellow, and a cap decorated with a lace edging. The wealthy mother, like the wet-nurse, has ruffles on her sleeves and a handkerchief at her neck, but of a far superior quality, consistent with her muslin gown, blue silk sash, fine black laced shawl, feathered hat, white shoes and fashionable hair.

was also considerable overlap. Silk gowns were confined to the three wealthy families, but cotton, linen and stuff gowns were owned by rich and poor alike (table 2). John Neel's 'cotton gown (almost new)' valued at 12s. 6d. was worth more than the older cotton gowns owned by Francis Shanley, or the linen and cotton gowns owned by William Webb. The same is true of stockings (see table 5). Silk stockings were confined to one of the wealthy families, but stockings made from worsted or cotton were common to rich and poor. William Webb's 15 pairs of cotton stockings were valued at 2s. a pair, the same as the mantuamaker Elizabeth Cooper's best pair. Black mourning suits were owned by both Francis Shanley the surgeon and Mark Palmer the blacksmith.

The lists drawn up of the clothing lost in the fire at Brandon not only allow us to compare the clothes of the town's rich and poor, but also enable us to examine in detail the clothes of the six poorer victims and their families. Their losses included almost all the normal elements of English popular adult dress in the eighteenth century (table 6). For the men, that meant a linen shirt, over which was worn a waistcoat, coat and breeches. This combination of under- and outer garments was accompanied by a number of accessories to complete a decent appearance – a pair of shoes with removable buckles, a pair of stockings, a hat and some kind of neckwear, usually a handkerchief or neckcloth (fig. 13). John Neel the cordwainer lost 16 items of clothing: three shirts, one man's coat, four waistcoats, two pairs of breeches, two pairs of men's stockings, a man's hat and three handkerchiefs. As his children appear to have been very young, all of these were probably his own clothes, with the exception of some of the handkerchiefs. They were worth at most £3 5s. The servant William Eagle's 17 lost items of clothing were worth more at £4 16s. He lost one shirt, two waistcoats, two pairs of breeches, two great coats and two frock coats. He also lost three pairs of stockings, a pair of shoes with buckles, a pair of boots and two hats. The 28 items of men's clothing lost by Mark Palmer the blacksmith were worth considerably more, at £11 3s. 6d. We cannot be sure that all belonged to Palmer himself, as opposed to his sons, but they included exactly the same range of clothes as those lost by Neel and Eagle.

It is important to remember that these lists exclude whatever the three men were wearing on the afternoon of the fire. In other words, they represent changes of clothes, not entire wardrobes. If we assume that each of the three was wearing a full set of clothes at the time, then the lists reveal that they all had at least one spare item of clothing in almost every category, and often more than one. But the lists also demonstrate that there was considerable variety in the clothes poorer men owned. Neel, the cordwainer, whose clothes had the lowest value among those lost by the men, does not appear to have had a change of shoes. His combination of one spare coat and four spare waistcoats suggests that he may have worked wearing his waistcoats. Palmer and Eagle's boots and buskins (a kind of half boot) were associated with work with horses. Palmer's muslin neckcloths and plated shoe buckles appear to be small luxuries, probably for best wear. Both Palmer and Eagle had great coats and surtout coats for outdoor wear and they owned breeches made from cotton fabrics as well as leather, at a time when the former was displacing the latter. Among the shirts owned by Neel and Palmer were many made from hempen cloth, a Suffolk speciality.[7]

If we turn to the women, again we find almost all the standard elements of everyday dress: a linen shift (sometimes with removable sleeves), over which were worn stays to shape the outer garments, then a petticoat and over that a gown (figs 5, 14, 15). The all-important accessories which completed the female outfit were a pair of shoes with removable buckles, a pair of stockings, an apron, a linen cap, a hat and some sort of

16 George Morland, *A Windy Day* (detail), n.d. [1790s], oil on canvas, Fitzwilliam Museum, Cambridge, PD.105-1992. The man wears a smock frock and a round hat. The woman wears a red cloak and a round hat like a man's.

neckwear, at this period usually a handkerchief or a shawl.[8] For outdoor wear, women usually wore a cloak over their gown (figs 16, 21). Most of these elements of the woman's wardrobe were represented among the losses of the two poorest women, Elizabeth Cooper, mantuamaker, and the wife of John Neel, cordwainer. Neel's wife lost 17 items of clothing: two shifts, a pair of boned jumps (a kind of leather stays), two quilted petticoats, a cotton gown, two pairs of worsted stockings, two fine linen aprons, one flowered, four caps, a gauze bonnet, a new cotton handkerchief and a fine half-shawl (fig. 17). They were worth £2 13s. 9d. The 22 items lost by Elizabeth Cooper were worth nearly the same. She lost one shift, one pair of boned stays, three petticoats, three cotton gowns, a pair of shoes and plated buckles, three pairs of cotton stockings, one muslin apron and two Irish linen aprons, four caps, a muslin handkerchief and a cloth cloak.

17 *A St. Giles's Beauty*, 1784, coloured engraving, Lewis Walpole Library, Farmington, Conn., 784.2.14.2. Seated in her St Giles's lodging room, this London prostitute is shown wearing shoes with silver or plated buckles, a white quilted petticoat, a sprigged gown with matching ruffles, a clean white apron, a trellis-pattern neckerchief and a white cap with a pink ribbon, on top of which is perched a heavily beribboned white hat. The fineness of her clothing is highlighted by the dinginess of her lodging.

As with the poorer men, the lists of clothing lost in the fire demonstrate that these five women possessed changes of clothes in almost every category, except buckles. Again we find considerable variation in the precise characteristics of the spare clothes available to different owners. The two servants, Mary Cooper and Sarah Holmes, owned more clothes than the other women. They were distinctive in losing decorative and protective items, like removable shift sleeves, ruffles to attach to gowns and caps, and pattens to keep shoes clean in the wet. But their spare clothes also included cheap stuff gowns and Sarah Holmes was the only one of the poorer women to lose a bedgown, the loose, short garment, cheaper than a full-length gown, which became a familiar article of dress, along with the closer-fitting short jacket, among working women in the second half of the eighteenth century (figs 13, 18).[9]

Looking at the poorer victims' losses in the Brandon fire in aggregate, what distinguished the clothes lost by the poorer women from those lost by the poorer men is their greater number and lower value. The women tended to have more spare clothes than the men, but the average value of each item of their clothing was less. Men's clothes were worth more than women's, especially main garments like coats and waistcoats made from woollen cloth. John Neel's good cloth coat was worth 15s., his wife's almost new cotton gown only 12s. 6d. Shirts and shoes in the larger men's sizes required more material and consequently were worth more than their female equivalents. The pair of shoes with buckles belonging to the servant William Eagle was valued at 5s., that belonging to the mantuamaker Elizabeth Cooper at only 3s. Eagle's new shirt was valued at 5s., the servant Mary Cooper's four good hemp shifts at only 3s. 3d. each. What the poorer men and women's clothes had in common was a mixture of the mundane and the showy. Alongside worsted stockings, leather breeches and stuff waistcoats, the men owned muslin neckcloths, plated buckles, velveret breeches and a shirt made from fine Irish linen. Alongside worsted stockings, stuff gowns and check aprons, the women owned the shawls that were newly fashionable in the 1780s, plated buckles, silk bonnets and aprons made from muslin, Holland and flowered lawn.

The Brandon fire provides a remarkable opportunity to examine the clothing of rich and poor as they lived cheek by jowl in neighbouring houses in a small Suffolk town. But how typical of the clothes worn by the common people across England were the losses sustained by the poorer victims of the Brandon fire? They included servants and lesser artisans and their wives, but not rural day labourers or urban street sellers. Their losses comprised stocks of spare clothes, but not the clothes they were wearing when the fire took hold. To establish broader patterns of clothes ownership among working people in the 1780s we need to turn to other evidence, in particular that offered by newspaper advertisements for runaways and criminal trials for thefts of clothes.

Both these sources provide evidence about the clothes worn by ordinary people, but they differ in the kinds of people and the kinds of clothing (for details, see Appendix 1). Newspaper advertisements for runaways listed descriptive information necessary for identifying individuals. They focused on the outer clothing actually worn by younger working men and tradesmen, with apprentices accounting for over a quarter

18 George Stubbs, *The Haymakers*, 1785, oil on panel, Tate, London, T02256. Stubbs has been criticised for the improbably fine clothes worn by the female haymakers in the different versions of this painting and its partner, *The Reapers*. The women in this version are shown wearing hats covered with black silk, of the sort that were fashionable at this period and often owned by working women. It is noticeable, however, that all three of the women wear these hats. None of them wear the cheaper plain straw hats often portrayed in other depictions of harvesting, including Stubbs's first version of the painting (fig. 5). The second woman from the left is shown wearing a bedgown over a petticoat.

of all of those advertised. Advertisements for absconding women were few and far between. The men advertised in the Leeds and the Oxford and Worcester newspapers in the 1780s dressed in similar ways to the poorer male victims of the Brandon fire, with little variation between the north and the Midlands (table 7). Overwhelmingly, their outer garments comprised the familiar combination of waistcoat, coat and breeches. These three garments were mentioned in the advertisements more than any others. As at Brandon, breeches were made from either leather or cotton. Coats were predominantly made from woollen cloth, with various shades of brown the most common colour, followed by blue, and then green. Waistcoats displayed a wider range of fabrics, including woollen cloth, worsted, linen and various cottons and a wider range of colours.

Shirts, as undergarments, were hardly mentioned at all in the advertisements, but a number of highly visible accessories appeared repeatedly, especially hats, stockings and handkerchiefs. Hats were overwhelming round rather than cocked, occasionally with a hat band and a buckle. Stockings were made from a range of yarns, like those at Brandon, including wool, worsted, thread and cotton, but not silk. Most were coloured, but a few were white. Neck handkerchiefs were the most colourful items listed. Colours included black, rose, red and white, purple and white, green and red and yellow. The majority were described as silk. This suggests an understandable tendency in the advertisements to pick out the distinctive and the unusual for purposes of identification, especially where accessories were concerned, but it also confirms the capacity of working men to acquire petty clothing luxuries. The shoe buckles listed in the advertisements also demonstrate that capacity. They included the cheap, made from iron or brass, but the majority of those described in detail were more expensive and showy, often silver-plated or 'fashionable'. Less than five percent of the clothes itemised in the advertisements were described as old, worn, faded, patched or ragged; nearly as many were described as fashionable or new.

As sources of information about clothing, the records of thefts from plebeian owners have three advantages over the advertisements. First, they include male and female clothes in broadly similar numbers, stolen mostly when they were not being worn (table 8). Second, they do not focus on the most visible and distinctive items of clothing in the way the advertisements do. Undergarments are prominent among the stolen clothes in addition to outer garments. Shirts, shifts and caps all figure prominently, partly because linen undergarments were washed regularly and were vulnerable to theft when left to dry in the open air, often on hedges. Third, they enable us to establish values for different kinds of clothing, because the law required the indictment against the accused to state a value for each stolen item. These were usually second-hand values, established by the owner and the court clerk who drew up the indictment. In practice, valuations can be inconsistent and have to be used with caution, especially when the numbers of clothes at issue is small, or the observed differences in value are slight (see Appendix 1). Nevertheless, it is reassuring that the relative values of the different items of clothing aggregated from the 1780s indictments are broadly consistent with those for clothing lost by the poorer victims of the Brandon fire in 1789.

The information provided by the criminal trial records does, however, suffer from a number of limitations. The clothes itemised in criminal indictments show a bias towards more valuable materials, reflecting, perhaps, the priorities of both thieves and prosecuting owners, although this bias is rarely so extreme that cheaper materials are completely absent. It is difficult, moreover, to establish from the criminal indictments the sex of the wearer in the case of those kinds of clothing that might be worn by either men or women, such as shoes, stockings and handkerchiefs, because the trial records do not consistently specify for which sex the garment was intended. They identify the legal owner, not the wearer. At law, the owner of a wife's or daughter's clothing was the male head of the family. It is also difficult to distinguish between adults' and children's clothing. Nevertheless, subject to these limitations, the pattern of clothes ownership observed among poorer theft victims in the trial records from

Yorkshire and London in the 1780s is similar to that which characterises the Brandon lists and the advertisements for runaways.

The combination of waistcoat, coat and breeches accounted for the vast majority of the outer garments stolen from plebeian men. In both London and Yorkshire coats were, on average, by far the most valuable element in this combination and they were noticeably more valuable than any of the main garments stolen from plebeian women. Breeches were rather more valuable than waistcoats, but both were worth considerably less than coats. As with the advertisements, coats were overwhelmingly made from plain woollen cloth, in blue, green and grey as well as brown, although blue was worn mainly by sailors. Stolen waistcoats, like those described in the advertisements, displayed a wider range of fabrics, including woollen cloth, worsteds, linens, various cottons and silk mixes. Where colours and decoration are described, the range is much wider than for coats, including some stripes. Stolen breeches were made from leather and cotton fabrics, as in the advertisements and the Brandon fire lists, but woollen and worsted fabrics also appear. The only silk breeches to appear were stolen in London and owned by servants. Male undergarments consisted entirely of shirts, all made from linen. Most of those described by colour were white, but some, owned largely by sailors, were striped blue and white. The average value ascribed in the indictments to shirts was a quarter of that of coats, and not much more than half that of waistcoats and breeches. All these valuations are broadly consistent with those for the clothes of the poorer Brandon fire victims. The other item of men's dress that can be identified in small numbers in the indictments is their hats, rarely described, but valued at over four shillings on average.

The women's outer garments that appear in the indictments of the 1780s were predominantly gowns and petticoats, just as they were among the poorer victims of the Brandon fire. Three-quarters of the gowns stolen in Yorkshire were cotton or linen, often printed and colourful. The most frequently mentioned colour combination was purple and white. Cotton gowns in these colours were owned by a sailor, a tailor and a weaver. Others were red, white, and blue and white. The fabrics of the rest of the gowns stolen in Yorkshire were either silks, silk and worsted mixes or worsted stuff. In the London theft indictments, cotton and linen fabrics also accounted for nearly three-quarters of the gowns, although colours were rarely described, and there was none made from plain worsted stuffs. The very small numbers of the cheap, workaday stuff gowns listed in the indictments, which other sources suggest were worn widely among the poorer sections of the population, may simply indicate that they were unattractive targets for thieves in both Yorkshire and London. Not surprisingly, the small number of silk gowns owned by plebeian victims of theft had the highest average valuation, but cotton gowns were not far behind, especially in Yorkshire. Cotton gowns were valued above the average for stolen plebeian gowns as a whole; stuff and linen gowns were valued well below. Evidently the popularity of cotton gowns lay in a superior appearance and ease of washing, not in their cheapness relative to gowns made from the alternative fabrics. Bedgowns were cheaper still, because they were made from shorter lengths of fabric, usually three yards, rather than the seven yards or more required for a gown.[10] The small number that appear in the theft records were all made from either linen or cotton.

Stolen petticoats displayed a greater diversity of materials than gowns, but were much less valuable. Woollen and worsted fabrics, such as calamanco, flannel and, in Yorkshire, linsey-woolsey, figured prominently alongside linens and, in London, cottons and silks. In Yorkshire, the average value ascribed to petticoats was less than a third that of gowns, although in London it was nearly two-thirds, reflecting the theft of a handful of high-value silk and calico examples. Some petticoats were decoratively patterned – a number of those described in the indictments were striped – but petticoats were not just decorative items. They were also designed for warmth. This explains the presence of warm woollen fabrics such as flannel and the fact that a number of the petticoats in lighter materials were quilted.

Stolen cloaks were far fewer in number than gowns or petticoats. They could be costly. In London their average value, pushed up by the presence of a number of high-value silk cloaks, was greater than that of gowns. The same was true for the poorer Brandon fire victims. In both Yorkshire and London, half of the stolen cloaks were made from woollen cloth, predominantly red, and half from black silk. Evidently the red cloth cloak, so often considered to be typical country wear and described by Madame du Boccage in rural Oxfordshire in 1750, was also worn in London, although it was regarded there as an indication of country origins and not genteel (fig. 16).[11] When Lucy Stockford came from Duns Tew, her north Oxfordshire village, to London in search of a service in April 1795, she was wearing her red cloak, although she also had with her in her box a black silk cloak. Unfamiliar with the city and searching for somewhere to stay, she was lured into a prostitutes' lodging in Union Street, north of Oxford Street. She reported that two girls there 'took my red cloak up, and asked me why I wore a red cloak?' They then went away, only to return with three men. 'They asked me whether I was a country girl? and I told them yes; they chucked me under the chin, and said I was a pretty country girl.'[12]

Just as stolen male undergarments consisted entirely of shirts, so stolen female undergarments consisted entirely of shifts. Like the men's shirts, they were all made from linen. Their average value was less than three-quarters of that of the shirts, being made from shorter lengths of material. Women's caps, inexpensive but considered essential to a decent appearance, were also made almost exclusively from linen materials. Caps lent themselves to relatively cheap, but highly visible decorative embellishments. Decorated caps were stolen from plebeian women of a variety of backgrounds. A woman who sold fish and fruit about the streets of London lost a lace cap, as did the wife of a husbandman at Egglestone Abbey on the River Tees in Yorkshire, while the wife of a labourer at Sharlston, near Wakefield in Yorkshire lost a sprigged lawn cap.[13]

Stays, which women wore over their shifts, could be expensive items. Although they are conspicuous by their rarity in the criminal indictments, they were crucial to achieving correct posture and silhouette. Poorer women who could not afford the more expensive boned stays wore cheaper versions in leather, like a number of the victims of the Brandon fire (figs 20, 30).[14] It seems likely that all but a few of the many women whose stolen clothes appear in the indictments would have worn some kind of stays, although it was not unknown for women to go without. The stabbed body of a forty-year-old woman who lived with a London watchman was found next to the fire in their ground floor apartment in 1770, dressed in a gown, petticoat and shift, but without a cap or stays. Asked whether the body had any stays on when he discovered it, a neighbour declared: 'I don't believe she ever wore any.'[15] The fact that so few stolen stays appear in the indictments may result from many poorer women owning only one pair, which they were wearing when the thefts took place. Alternatively, cheaper stays may have been less attractive to thieves than other garments, or when not being worn they may have been stored in ways that made them less vulnerable to opportunistic theft.

Aprons, by contrast, were frequently stolen. They were not always identified in the indictments as women's or men's, but most of them were probably women's, made not from leather, but predominantly from linen or from check, and worth on average well under two shillings. In the Yorkshire indictments, which provide information on materials and colours more frequently, most were either blue and white check, or plain white linen. Both linen and check, which could be either a cotton or a linen fabric, could be washed readily and frequently. Aprons like these served to protect women's other garments as they worked, indoors and out. It is important to bear in mind, however, that aprons were not necessarily just functional wear. They were a standard element of the female wardrobe at this period, worn by rich and poor alike. Often they were decorative as much as protective. In the criminal indictments, alongside many workaday aprons, we find a few that were more expensive and showy, made from lawn, muslin, or, in the case of one owned by a Yorkshire husbandman, black silk. When worn by servants, aprons in different materials could signal different levels in the domestic hierarchy. The American loyalist Samuel Curwen, describing the hiring fair at Waltham Abbey in Essex in 1783, reported: 'The females of the domestic kind are distinguished by their aprons, viz. Cooks in coloured, nursery maids in white linnen and the chamber and waiting maids in lawn or cambrick.'[16] The few women's hats and bonnets listed in the indictments were also made from black silk, probably at this period worn over a large straw frame, with an average value much lower than men's hats (figs 2, 18). They were, nevertheless, more valuable than the simple straw and chip hats so frequently mentioned by foreign visitors as common wear. When a scourer and dyer whose watch was stolen during a sexual assignation in 1759 apprehended the thief eight hours later, 'she had a black sattin hat on her head; I look'd at it, and said; I believe you have a piece of my watch on your head.'[17] The cheapest hats made from straw or chip were not, perhaps, worth stealing.

Among the clothing accessories that it is impossible from the trial records of the 1780s to allocate to either men or women, handkerchiefs and other neckwear were the most colourful. They were made from cotton, linen, muslin and silk, although silk did not predominate here as it did among the handkerchiefs worn by runaways, with linens and cottons outnumbering silk in London. The divergence between the advertisements and the indictments in the materials from which neckwear was made may reflect differences between men and women's purchases. Handkerchiefs made from silk were given the highest valuations, followed by muslin, then cottons and, by far the least valuable, linens. On average, handkerchiefs were worth slightly less than aprons. Colours are itemised only in Yorkshire – yellow, blue, black, white and 'chocolate', but red is the colour mentioned most often. Neckcloths and cravats identified as men's included some in white muslin, suggesting that plebeian men were not resticted to the brightly coloured neck handkerchiefs commonly associated with plebeian male dress (fig. 13). Neck handkerchiefs were not just decorative items, however. A woman who in September 1749 had recently arrived in London from hop-picking in Kent claimed she was robbed in the street of three handkerchiefs, two of which were around her neck. The next morning she encountered a man in a gin shop, and 'seeing my two handkerchiefs about his neck, I took hold of him with my hands; sirrah, said I, it is hard you should have my two handkerchiefs, and I have nothing to put on to keep me from the cold'.[18] It was expected that working women would wear a neck handkerchief. When the murdered body of Jane Brown, a middle-aged widow, was found at Newcastle in 1789, the constable made inquiries into what had become of her handkerchief, 'as the deceased had not any on her neck'.[19]

Shoes, though an indispensable element of everyday dress, appear in the indictments infrequently. All those identified as men's were leather, as were at least one pair of women's shoes, but there were also two pairs of the more fashionable women's shoes with uppers made from worsted stuffs. This pattern of plebeian women owning both leather shoes and stuff shoes is also found among the shoes lost by the poorer female victims of the Brandon fire. Stockings appear in the indictments far more often than shoes. They were made from a variety of materials, including cotton, worsted, thread, yarn and silk. In Yorkshire, more theft victims owned stockings made from the cheaper worsted than from the other materials; in London they were most likely to own the slightly more expensive cotton stockings. Consequently stockings were worth on average less in Yorkshire than in London. The colours mentioned were predominantly white or black. White stockings were considered a sign of high status. A London waterman claimed in 1741 that a prostitute had 'shew'd her white Stockings, and said, do you think these white Stockings can walk to the Gatehouse? No, D – you, I will have a Coach'.[20]

Much more expensive were the buckles and watches found in the indictments. Buckles, valued on average at over three shillings, were overwhelmingly silver or silver plated, rather than the iron or brass of the buckles worn by some of the runaways. Once again, this suggests that the theft indictments over-represent more expensive materials when compared with the advertisements. Watches, valued on average at over forty shillings, almost all silver and often with accompanying watch chain and seals, appear in the indictments almost as often as buckles, but not in the advertisements.

Other items of clothing appear in the criminal indictments and in the advertisements, but in very small numbers. Some of them, such as boots, frock coats and women's pockets also figure in the Brandon lists. Others, like jackets, smock frocks, men's aprons, trousers and regimentals do not. A number of these garments had strong occupational associations, especially the men's. Occupational dress is one of the critical ways historians of clothing have engaged with the dress of working people. Often they have treated it as a utilitarian, vernacular counterpoint to fashionable clothing, rooted in the functional imperatives of particular forms of manual labour and resistant to change. It therefore deserves particular attention.

Smock frocks were, as we have seen, worn by waggoners and, in the south and the Midlands towards the end of the eighteenth century, by a wide range of farm workers. Boots were associated with work with horses. Men in a variety of trades wore aprons to protect their other clothes as they worked (figs 19, 78, 91). The three men's aprons listed in the advertisements were worn by an apprentice clothier, a currier and a mason. When asked whether a coach harness-maker had been dressed in his working clothes when he was killed in London in 1749, his fellow workman replied 'Yes; he had his apron on.'[21] Indeed, leather aprons were proverbially the wear of poorer working tradesman. A writer in 1766, lamenting what he considered the improper interest London citizens were taking in affairs of state, complained that 'the veriest drudge, who now wears a leathern apron, can tell how far a secretary of state's power ought to extend'.[22]

Links between particular occupations and particular items or combinations of clothing were widely recognised.[23] Newspaper advertisements described a pair of shoes worn by a Yorkshire runaway as 'farmer like', two footpads in Oxfordshire as 'dressed like bargemen', and 'a changeable colour waistcoat' stolen from a Wiltshire inn as 'such as are frequently worn by Scotchmen and Pedlars'.[24] But relationships between specific occupations and garments were rarely fixed or exclusive. Take men's jackets. Jackets, which were shorter than coats, were often worn for work (fig. 94). A boy who had been working in the brickfields on the eastern edge of London spent part of four pounds he stole from a public house in 1766 on 'a coarse working jacket'.[25] Some kinds of jacket had more precise occupational associations, however. In 1775, when George Catcott descended a cave at Westbury-on-Trim in Gloucestershire, close to the Kingswood coalfield, he wore 'a large Collier's Hat, Jacket and Trowsers', and miners elsewhere wore jackets underground.[26] In London, witnesses in criminal trials at the Old Bailey referred to several different occupationally specific types of jacket: the butchering jacket, the brewer's jacket, the soldier's or regimental jacket and the sailor's jacket.[27]

It was sailors' jackets that were mentioned in the Old Bailey trials most frequently (figs 12, 20).[28] They were first identified in the printed trial records in 1725, much earlier than the other types of jacket, although they were being stolen in London long before that.[29] Short jackets, often blue, were the archetypal dress of sailors, worn by merchant and naval seamen alike, usually with loose breeches or trousers, and often

19 Johan Zoffany, *Porter with a Hare*, oil on canvas, 1760s, Herbert Art Gallery and Museum, Coventry, VA.1955.563. The porter is shown wearing a coarse apron tied over his coat with string. He wears a round hat and dark stockings but no neckcloth. The coarse materials of his apron, coat, stockings and shoes are in striking contrast to those worn by the two well-turned-out boys, one of whom is reading the delivery address on the label for him while the other points out directions.

20 Francis Wheatley, *The Sailor's Return*, 1786, oil on canvas, National Maritime Museum, London, BHC1076. The man is shown in typical sailor's dress: a short blue jacket with brass buttons and short, loose canvas trousers. He also wears a white shirt, a red neckerchief, white stockings and shoes with large, decorated buckles. In his hand he holds a round tarpaulin hat, together with the stick often shown in depictions of sailors. The young woman is dressed for indoors, with stays worn over her shift and a red petticoat (see also fig. 30). She wears an apron but no gown. Her gown may be the white garment draped over the back of her chair.

21 George Morland, *A Soldier's Return* (detail), n.d. [1790s], oil on panel, Paul Mellon Collection, Yale Center for British Art, New Haven, Conn., B2001.2.102. The man wears a soldier's uniform of red jacket with buff facings and tight white breeches, but he sports a round hat instead of his cocked and laced regimental hat, which he carries on his knapsack. He is accompanied by a woman in a blue, hooded cloak, wearing a round hat like a man's.

with blue or check shirts. The Royal Navy had no official uniform for common seamen before the mid-nineteenth century, but did supply clothes for sailors to purchase from ships' pursers. These clothes were known as 'slops', a term defined in 1733 as 'a wide sort of Breeches worn by Seamen', but used more broadly to refer to the distinctive clothing supplied by the Admiralty and worn by both naval and merchant seamen.[30] Even when on shore, sailors tended to wear finer, more elaborate versions of their on-board working dress, often, if they could afford it, with costly accessories like silver buckles. Consequently, they were highly recognisable. Smugglers observed by a customs officer at Blythborough in Suffolk in 1801 fell into two distinct groups: 'Some had the appearance of landsmen, and some sailors.'[31] A Newcastle pitman recalled seeing three men suspected of a theft in 1789: 'One of them had the appearance of a sailor, being cloathed in a short blue jacket and long dirty trowsers.' Even at Grinton in Swaledale in the Yorkshire Pennines, 35 miles from the sea, a sailor who claimed in 1731 to be travelling from Edinburgh was identified by his 'Seamans Habitt'.[32] In the Yorkshire criminal trials in the 1780s most of the jackets and trousers listed were stolen from seamen, as were most of the blue and white check shirts. But jackets were certainly not the exclusive wear of seamen. In London in 1785 only one of the stolen jackets belonged to a sailor and none of the jackets identified in the Yorkshire and Midlands runaway advertisements in the 1780s was worn by sailors, reflecting the fact that the newspapers concerned were printed in Leeds, Oxford and Worcester, all inland towns. In the advertisements, they were worn by men in a variety of occupations, but deserters from the army wearing regimental jackets figure especially prominently.

Unlike the navy, the army did provide a uniform, both to regular soldiers and to those serving in the militia (fig. 21). The uniform was paid for partly out of deductions from soldiers' pay, so they were permitted to keep the items they had notionally bought when they were discharged from service. Consequently army uniform seeped into civilian dress. The Newcastle wood engraver Thomas Bewick remembered encountering in his youth an old soldier at Ovingham in Northumberland who had fought at the battle of Minden in 1759, and 'appeared occasionally in his old Military Coat, &c as long as he lived'.[33] A Warwick ostler ran away from his wife in 1797 wearing a cast-off soldier's jacket.[34] Uniform regulations were demanding, minutely differentiated according to rank and regiment, and strictly enforced down to the smallest detail. Infantry uniforms were predominantly scarlet, those of the cavalry scarlet or dark blue. Each regiment had its own colours for facings, that is for collars, cuffs and lapels, its own headgear and its own patterns for buttons, lace and epaulettes. Senior army officers were obsessive and sometimes brutal in their determination that regular soldiers sustain a colourful and visually arresting appearance, intended to have the maximum possible impact on civilian viewers and other soldiers alike.[35] Uniforms became ever more elaborate and standards ever more demanding as the eighteenth century progressed, sometimes to the detriment of military efficiency. Prussian practice, which put special emphasis on tight fit, erect posture and decorative accessories, was influential after 1768, following the dazzling victories of the Prussian army in the Seven

22   John Collet, *The Recruiting Sergeant* (detail), 1767, oil on canvas, Hackney Art Gallery, London. A recruiting sergeant is at work outside a country inn on the Portsmouth road. The sergeant is resplendent in a uniform consisting of a red coat with buff facings, embellished with white lace and silver buttons. His cocked and laced hat sports a cockade. The drummer on the right wears the same colours, but in reverse: a buff coat with chevrons in the regimental red on his sleeves. He also wears a drummer's bearskin cap. The new recruit is simply dressed in a plain, light-coloured coat and breeches and carries a round hat. The young woman wears a quilted brown petticoat, a blue-and-white check apron and a straw hat decorated with a pink ribbon.

Years War. One arena in which the resulting sartorial spectacle played a decisive role was recruiting (fig. 22). Recruiting parties sometimes wore especially elaborate uniforms. The Oldham weaver, William Rowbottom, noted in his diary in 1794 that 'Joseph Scoles having got a recruiting order for the 57th Regiment of foot, beat up in Oldham in a superb new suit of clothes.' It was not only potential recruits who were impressed. Three weeks later he recorded: 'As a proof of the influence which the Military have over the fair sex a young woman possessed with less virtue than beauty, decamped from the Cotton Tree Oldham with one of the train of Artillery.'[36]

The specialised clothes worn by sailors and soldiers represented a significant element in adult men's dress in the eighteenth century because the numbers of men who wore them were huge. This was not simply because Britain was a trading nation, with a large merchant marine. Britain was at war for much of the century. Indeed, between 1689 and 1815 there were almost as many years of war as there were of peace. The size of both the army and the navy fluctuated enormously between wartime and peacetime. Wartime numbers of men under arms advanced from a maximum of 186,000 in 1711 during the War of Spanish Succession, to a maximum of 437,000 in 1795 during the French Revolutionary War. In peacetime, their numbers plummeted – to a mere 30,000 in 1723 and to an only slightly larger 51,000 in 1786.[37] Nevertheless, for much of the century the army and the navy were major presences in the market for adult men's clothing.

Uniforms for civilian officials were less common. The clothes provided to minor officials like parish beadles were closer to the kind of livery worn by male domestic servants than to military uniforms. Many officially licensed occupations, like London porters and watermen, simply wore a badge or a token. In the case of some officials, however, it is possible to detect a shift towards a more formal uniform in the course of the eighteenth century. In 1728, Post Office letter carriers had been issued with brass tokens bearing the King's arms to identify them, but at the end of the eighteenth century, in 1793, the London General Post letter carriers were given a full uniform consisting of a scarlet coat with blue lapels and cuffs and brass buttons with the wearer's number, and a beaver hat and blue waistcoat. Already from 1784 the guards of the new mail coaches had been issued with a scarlet uniform with blue lapels and gold braid, and a black hat with a gold band, which had decidedly military overtones. The curmudgeonly traveller John Byng remarked while at Shrewsbury in 1793: 'The guard of the mail-coach is one of the grandest and most swaggering fellows I ever beheld, dress'd in ruffles and nankeen breeches, and white stockings.'[38]

The other large group of people wearing occupationally distinct clothing consisted of footmen and other male household servants in livery. The livery was chosen and supplied by their employer. Its most distinctive element was a coat in the employer's chosen colour with contrasting, often brightly coloured linings and facings. It shared these features with army uniform, which had originated in personal livery. Tax records list nearly 50,000 male household servants in England and Wales in 1780, the majority of whom probably wore livery.[39] Despite such large numbers in the country as a whole, the only item of livery that appears in the trial records and runaway advertisements from the 1780s is a claret-coloured livery frock coat with scarlet lining, collar and cuffs, worn by an absconding servant advertised in the Oxford newspaper in 1782. Perhaps it was uncommon for liveried servants to abscond in such conspicuous clothing, while clothes in easily recognised livery colours may have had little appeal for thieves. And of course not all male servants wore livery. No livery coats were identified among the clothes lost by William Eagle, the servant who was a victim of the Brandon fire, perhaps because, as his clothes suggest, he worked mainly with horses rather than as a footman.

In exploring the relationship between occupation and clothing, it is important to bear in mind that almost any item of clothing worn by labouring people might have been required to serve as a working garment, although not one that was specific to a particular occupation. The drab fustian frock coat worn by an apprentice joiner and cabinetmaker from the West Riding of Yorkshire advertised in the *Leeds Intelligencer* in 1789 was 'dirtied with blue paint'. A hostler advertised as a runaway in *Berrow's Worcester Journal* in 1784 abandoned his family dressed in the yellow striped jacket 'which he usually did wear at his work'. The light drab coat worn by a twenty-one-year-old Shropshire peruke-maker and hairdresser advertised in the same paper in 1786 was described as his 'working dress', in contrast to his pea green cloth coat with silver-plated buttons and his corded dimity waistcoat with chintz edging, which constituted his 'best dress'.[40]

Some occupations, moreover, could require very high standards of dressing, most obviously certain categories of domestic service, but equally shop work and prostitution. At the beginning of the eighteenth century in London, female thieves trying to rob houses by deception were said to put 'themselves into a good handsome Dress, like some Exchange Girl'.[41] Exchange girls were the milliners' and seamstresses' apprentices who served customers in the fashionable shops in the New Exchange on the Strand and the Royal Exchange in the City (fig. 23). In the 1780s, the young Robert Owen, working as a shop assistant at a busy draper and haberdasher's on London Bridge which served 'customers of an inferior class', was expected to be well dressed to receive them. Each morning he, like the other shopmen, had 'the hairdresser to powder and pomatum and curl my hair'.[42]

By no means all women involved in prostitution dressed well, but it could be professionally advantageous to do so (fig. 24). In 1767 the owner of a women's clothes shop in Rosemary Lane, London sold two women 'a gown, a pair of stays, an upper petticoat, a shift, a pair of stockings, a hat, a pair of shoes, and aprons' each, for more than £6. They already had new caps and silk handkerchiefs. 'I thought they were girls of the town; such often come to clothe themselves at our shop.' Some prostitutes were supplied with appropriate clothing by the women who employed them. Ann Smith was accused in 1754 of stealing clothes from Elizabeth Ward of Spring Gardens near Charing Cross in London, including a flowered cotton gown, a laced cap, lawn ruffles, a Dresden handkerchief, a cross-barred lawn apron, a French dimity petticoat, silk stockings, a satin hat and a pair of paste earrings. Ward claimed she made her living by

23 *A Morning Ramble, or The Milliners Shop*, 1782, coloured mezzotint, Lewis Walpole Library, Farmington, Conn., 782.5.20.5. The three women working behind the counter in this milliner's shop are portrayed as extraordinarily overdressed, particularly in their high-dressed hair and laced head and neck wear. They accord with popular stereotypes of the young women employed as shop girls by fashionable milliners, who were believed to be flirtatious with male customers and a prime target for the attentions of wealthy young men about town. The man on the counter is dressed for riding, with a frock coat, boots and buckskin or nankeen breeches with strings. His companion appears from his cockade and the facings on his coat to be a manservant, albeit a well-dressed one in an elaborate wig, white stockings and well-buckled shoes.

24   *British Vessels. Described for the use of Country Gentlemen*, 1802, coloured engraving, Prints and Photographs Division, Library of Congress, Washington, D.C., PC3-1802-British vessels. Different types of prostitute are distinguished here by the quality of their dress, from the 'First Rate', dressed in the height of fashion with muff, feathers and white stockings, to the 'Fire Ship', dressed in a ragged blue gown with brown stockings and a cap tied with a ribbon, but no hat.

sewing and washing, and had hired Smith as a live-in servant. According to the constable, however, Ward kept a disorderly house. Smith, who had been wearing most of the clothes when apprehended, protested that Ward 'had lent her the things to appear in company with . . . as a lady' and had provided other girls living in the house with clothing for the same purpose. A sceptical Old Bailey judge asked Ward: 'Is this finery fit for a washerwoman?' to which Ward offered the circumspect reply: 'My lord, it is all the finery I had.'[43]

Perishable and hardly ever preserved in museums, the clothing worn by ordinary eighteenth-century people is extraordinarily difficult to retrieve. No single documentary source provides a satisfactory account. This chapter has triangulated three sources from the 1780s to delineate the characteristic features of the plebeian wardrobe during that decade. The pattern of plebeian clothing that emerges from the newspaper advertisements and trial records broadly confirms the picture derived from the 1789 Brandon fire, as well as corroborating the observations repeatedly made by travellers and foreign visitors. Plebeian men characteristically wore shirt, breeches, coat and waistcoat, supplemented by shoes, stockings, hat and neckcloth. Plebeian women wore petticoat and gown over stays and shift, supplemented by shoes, stockings, apron, cap, hat and neckcloth. Ordinary people often succeeded in owning changes of at least some items of clothing. Many possessed a mix of clothes, some of them coarse and inexpensive, but others costlier and more decorative. Regional variation was muted.

25 Paul Sandby, *London Cries: 'Last Dying Speech and Confession'*, c.1759, watercolour over graphite, Paul Mellon Collection, Yale Center for British Art, New Haven, Conn., B1975.3.225. The woman's outer garments are all ragged.

3
Clothing Biographies

ORDINARY PEOPLE IN THE EIGHTEENTH CENTURY often chalked out their lives in clothes. Garments appear again and again in their life stories as markers of maturity and achievement, or of struggle and failure. Reconstructing clothing biographies for individual men and women – tracing the timing and circumstances of acquisitions and disposals – can provide a dynamic narrative of how they clothed themselves that transcends the still image derived from criminal trials, newspaper advertisements and lists of losses by fire.

The trials, the advertisements and the fire lists capture only one moment in the personal clothing biography of any individual. They also represent certain kinds of people to the exclusion of others. Only some runaways were worth advertising. Thieves tended to target those who owned clothes that were worth stealing, or those who owned changes of clothes that were vulnerable because they were being washed or stored. None of the stolen clothes itemised in the 1780s criminal indictments was described as ragged, or even old. Some of the worst-dressed plebeians are probably, therefore, under-represented in these sources: day labourers, itinerants, beggars, parish paupers, generally those who did not have a change of clothes.

By reconstructing the clothing biographies of individual men and women, we can move beyond snapshot images and provide information about people who remain under-represented. Unfortunately the evidence available to establish individuals' clothing practices, even over short periods in their lives, is very slim for those below the level of the gentry, the larger farmers and the mercantile elite. All we have is a sparse collage, constructed from a handful of memoirs, autobiographies, diaries, account books and Poor Law records. Nevertheless, it is a collage that both deepens and extends the understanding of plebeian dress available to us from other, more systematic sources, especially in the way it enables us to capture variations and extremes of experience.

Clothes loom large in one group of plebeian autobiographies: the literally rags-to-riches stories of men like William Hutton, the Birmingham paper dealer, bookbinder and bookseller, Francis Place, the London tailor, and, to a more limited extent, James Lackington, the London bookseller. In their memoirs, these three men plot the failures and successes of their early adulthood through their struggles to accumulate and retain a decent, sometimes stylish wardrobe. William Hutton was born at Derby in 1723, the son of a wool-comber. At the age of seven he began work as an apprentice in the Derby silk mill. After seven years there he began a second apprenticeship with his uncle, a stocking-frame knitter at nearby Nottingham, which lasted until 1744. Under the terms of this second apprenticeship he was obliged to pay for his own clothes from the proceeds of whatever he could knit over and above a demanding weekly work target set by his uncle. In 1739, the year of his sixteenth birthday, he remembered:

> Clothes came as sluggishly as food. I was arriving at that age when the two sexes begin to look at each other, consequently wish to please; and a powerful mode to win is that of dress. This is a passport to the heart, a key to unlock the passions, and guide them in our favour. My resources were cut off; my sun was eclipsed. Youth is the time to dress; the time in which it is not only excusable, but laudable. I envied every new coat: I had the wish to earn one, but not the power.[1]

Two years later, in 1741, he had decided that he detested employment at the knitting frame. 'I made shift, however, with a little over-work, and a little credit, to raise a genteel suit of clothes, fully adequate to the sphere in which I moved. The girls eyed me with some attention; nay, I eyed myself as much as any of them.' Shortly after, he quarrelled with his uncle and ran away, carrying his best clothes carefully organised in two bags. He had his new suit 'neatly packed' in one. In the other he put a shirt, a pair of stockings, and his 'best wig, carefully folded, and laid at top, that, by lying in the hollow of the bag, it might not be crushed'. His 'best hat, not being properly calculated for a bag' he hung on his coat button. His only other possessions were the clothes he stood up in, a sixpenny loaf, some butter, a new Bible, a sun dial and five shillings in cash. When he arrived in the evening at Lichfield, over 30 miles from Nottingham, he opened his bags in the fields, dressed in his best clothes, 'and took a view of the city for about two hours'. He then returned to where he had hidden his bags and re-packed his prized new clothes 'in decent order'. Yet all his care was in vain. His bags were stolen when he went off to find a place to sleep. Shortly after, destitution forced him back to his uncle.[2]

The episode 'ruined me in point of dress, for I was not able to reassume my former appearance for five years. It ran me into debt, out of which I have never been to this day. Nov. 21, 1779.' Nevertheless, Hutton recorded that in 1743, 'I began to make a small figure in dress, but much inferior to that two years ago.' A fellow apprentice gave him 16 shillings for a dulcimer he had made, with which Hutton bought a coat. In 1746, now a journeyman, he borrowed money to buy his own knitting frame. At the same time he began bookbinding. 'I now purchased a tolerably genteel suit of clothes, and was so careful of them, lest I should not be able to procure another, that they continued my best for five years.' Soon the stocking trade was in recession and the master hosiers denied work to men like Hutton who owned their own frames. However, the next year he was able to buy a silver watch, which had long been his greatest ambition, although in 1750 he still did not possess a greatcoat. By 1751 he had moved to Birmingham to set up as a bookbinder and bookseller. His sartorial aspirations were as compelling as ever, but they had to be restrained, at least temporarily. 'I had been nearly a year in Birmingham, and had not indulged myself with any new clothes. My best coat now had been my best coat five years. Frederick Prince of Wales died in March; I dressed in a suit of mourning. My new clothes introduced me to some new acquaintance.'[3]

Nearly half a century later in London, the young Francis Place was equally obsessed with the way he dressed. Unlike Hutton, Place married young, at the age of 19, two years after leaving his apprenticeship, so his autobiography shows the importance clothes could hold for a young married couple. He was born in 1771, the illegitimate son of a London sponging-house keeper. Apprenticed to a breeches-maker until he was 17, he subsequently worked as a journeyman in the trade. In 1790, at the age of 18, he was preparing for marriage. 'My intended wife had a good stock of cloaths and I hoped that I should be able by working hard to increase my very scanty quantity.' He was able 'to save a trifle, not by any means enough to enable me to purchase many cloaths, but I bought as many as I could. Had my work been supplied to me regularly as it ought to have been, I should soon have been able to make a respectable appearance which as it was I could not do, to anything like the extent I wished.' Once married, the young couple 'contrived to dress ourselves respectably'. In 1793 he moved to a different master and took up making stuff breeches: 'I worked incessantly, and soon saved money enough to buy some good cloaths'. However, a strike followed and then eight months of unemployment. 'As long as we had any thing which could be pawned we did not suffer much from actual hunger, but after everything had been pawned, but "what we stood upright in," we suffered much from actual hunger.' His wife was reduced to a 'comfortless, forlorn and all but ragged condition'.[4]

Once back in work in the winter of 1793–4, Place 'bought cloaths, and bedding and other necessaries'. At the weekends he and his wife 'put on our best cloaths if the weather was fine and took a walk'. Foreseeing that the hostility he experienced from his employer's wife would eventually lead to his dismissal, 'we therefore made every effort we could to obtain money and to purchase with it as many useful articles and cloaths as would serve us for a long time and enable us to keep up our respectable appearance, a matter of the greatest importance to every working man, for so long as he is able to keep himself up in this particular, he will have resolution to struggle with, and frequently if not generally to overcome his adverse circumstances. No working man, journeman [sic] tradesman is ever wholly ruined until hope has abandoned him.' Two years later, he was in business on his own account and once again very short of money. 'The few good cloaths we had left were taken great care of, and when out of the house we always made a respectable appearance and were generally considered by those who knew us; as florishing people, who wanted for nothing.'[5]

James Lackington's memoirs contain less detail about clothes, but they play a similar role as measures of his early achievements and setbacks. Lackington was born in 1746 at Wellington in Somerset, the son of a journeyman shoemaker. He was apprenticed to a shoemaker in Taunton, worked in that trade in Bristol and subsequently moved to London. At the age of 21 at Taunton, just out of his apprenticeship, he teetered on the edge of destitution. 'I began the world with an unsuspecting heart, was tricked out of about three pounds (every shilling I was possessed of) and part of my cloaths, by some country sharpers. Having one coat and two waistcoats left, I lent my best waistcoat to an acquaintance, who left the town and forgot to return it.' By 1773 he was married and had recently moved to London, where he found plenty of work shoemaking at higher wages than in the West Country. He and his wife 'were soon enabled to procure a few cloaths. My wife had all her life before done very well with a superfine broad cloath cloak, but now I prevailed on her to have one of silk . . . I had never found out that I wanted a *great coat*, but now I made that important discovery.' However, having turned bookseller the following year, he found himself strapped for cash, so that he 'more than once pawned my watch, and a suit of clothes'.[6]

What emerges from all three autobiographies is the precariousness of the lives of young working men and the limited earnings available to them, even after they had served out their apprenticeships. Nevertheless, clothing was a key component of these young men's aspirations. Building up a stock of clothes, including some for best wear, was one of their first priorities in spending their wages. In their autobiographies, decent, stylish, 'genteel' clothes have multiple connotations. They are a sign of sexual maturity, a means of sexual attraction, a currency in both sexual competition and male bonding, an emblem of material self-advancement, a declaration of respectable status in public places, a badge of moral worth and a source of self-regarding pleasure. Clothing emerges as economically important too. All three men used their clothes as a form of capital, which might be extended by careful husbanding when there was no money to buy new clothes, or realised by sale or pawn to finance a business venture, or simply to pay for food and shelter in hard times.

We should not imagine, however, that it was only in the autobiographies of aspirational working men who made good that clothing was employed to gauge life's highs and lows. The same device was used by Mary Saxby in her *Memoirs of a Female Vagrant Written by Herself*, one of the first authentic working-class autobiographies to be published. Saxby was born in 1738, the daughter of a London silk weaver. About 1750 she ran away from home, and soon began a precarious, picaresque life in the Home Counties and the south Midlands as a travelling woman, living with gypsies, singing ballads, selling small wares and picking up work as it came along. It was to be a life characterised by many penniless, ragged episodes and precious few riches. She died in poverty, an evangelical convert. Nevertheless, clothes played an important part in the story of her life, often in the same ways and for the same reasons as they did in the lives of Hutton, Place and Lackington. Like them, she was keen to dress smartly, though she rarely managed to do so for long. Like them she treated her clothes as a store of capital to be drawn on when she fell on hard times. Like them, the way she dressed could shape her personal and professional relationships.

In the 1750s, Saxby was making a living as a ballad singer, 'a profitable trade', in Kent. 'A vessel was, at this juncture, wrecked near Sandwich; and the cargo, consisting of checks and muslins, was sold cheap; which afforded opportunity to me, and many more, to get clothed for a trifle'. Having made herself 'clean and smart', she was able to join forces with 'a decent woman' who travelled selling hardware. Some time later, she fell ill while working weeding corn. She had to sell all she had and return to her father in London, who found her medical help and clothed her. Recovered, she returned to rural Kent and Essex and fell in with a group of gypsies she already knew. 'While my clothes lasted, they used me well: but they soon took them from me; and then kept me, as it were, in a state of slavery.' Rescued by the man whom she was later to marry, she became pregnant. He left to go haymaking, so she took up her 'old trade of ballad-singing, and soon got plenty of good clothes for myself and my infant'. The baby was born, but its father did not return, having enlisted as a soldier. Saxby was then abandoned by the father's mother and sister, who took all her money, and had to rely on charity for 'money and clothes for my child'. Finally he returned and, after several years had passed and two more children had been born, they were married at Olney in Bedfordshire in 1771. Her older, evangelical self recalled this as 'a day of dissipation and vanity', the cost of which she measured in terms of clothes: 'Though we had two small children, there was as much spent on this occasion as would have gone far toward clothing them.' They subsequently lived as travellers in Northamptonshire and Bedfordshire, selling goods in the villages and living in huts in the fields. When their huts burnt down, one of Saxby's children was killed. 'We had not a garment left, to shift either ourselves or children; although before, we had some very good ones. A watch, and a large pair of silver buckles, which we had about us, was all that remained.' The family was 'obliged to go in to the hay country that summer, to earn ourselves and children some clothing'.[7]

For other plebeian autobiographers, clothes emerge as a source of conflict. The buckle-maker James Gee, who took considerable pride in his appearance, arrived in Walsall in Staffordshire from Dublin in the 1760s looking for work. Accustomed to wear a cocked hat that was smart by the standards of the Irish capital city, he was reluctantly obliged by his fellow workers to conform to what he called 'the custom of the place' and wear a round hat with a brim that flapped down over the face.[8] Francis Place remembered that in London in the 1770s 'round hats were coming into fashion', but his father evidently shared Gee's disapproval: 'My father said none but thieves and persons who were ashamed to shew their faces wore them.'[9] Place too was the victim of communal solidarities among his fellow working people which punished those who failed to conform to local sartorial practice. Shortly after marrying in 1791, Place and his wife were living in their first, cheap lodging and contriving to be 'respectably' dressed. 'We soon acquired the character of being proud and above our equals, this was the certain consequence of our having no acquaintance with any one and being better dressed than most who were similarly circumstanced, and were contemptuously called *the* Lady and Gentleman.'[10] However, it is important to stress that the local sartorial standards transgressed by the 19-year-old Place and his 17-year-old wife were not necessarily plain or modest. Place recalls the concern with dress and appearance displayed by many boys up to the ages of 18 or 20 in his part of London off the Strand, with the most obsessed among them affecting hairstyles in 'fashions of their own'. He recalled that 'a bunch of st[r]ings at the knees and about a dozen of buttons close together with white cotton or silk stocking shewed a lad who was especially knowing'.[11]

A different kind of conflict emerges in the autobiographical writings compiled by Benjamin Shaw, who worked as a mechanic in the early textile mills at Dolphinholme near Lancaster and later at Preston.[12] Shaw was born at Dent in the north-west Yorkshire Pennines in 1772. Married in 1793, he and his wife quarrelled constantly about money, particularly about money for clothes. Their arguments started early, but the issues remained the same until her death in 1828. She liked to spend liberally, running the family constantly into debt, pawning Shaw's coat, waistcoat and watch without his permission, and always making her purchases in shops or from itinerant Scotsmen, 'a ruinous concern'.[13] Yet for all her love of spending, Shaw felt she displayed insufficient pride in her clothes.

> She was very remarkable in some things, she seems to be nearly without pride, quite careless about clothes, this is strange, (I have my doubts whether I can gain credit for what I now say) but it has been a great misfortune to me, as well as to all her family, for pride is as necessary as anything that belongs to the female character, to stir them up to care and diligence, to get and to save all that they can to appear respectable, and to be independent, and free from any obligation to any, (O that my wife had had a few grains of this useful pride,) but she was quite indifferent about clothing, furniture, character, etc.[14]

We catch something of his wife's view of the matter in Shaw's recollection that early in their married life 'we had often to differ on money accounts, instead of mending the children's clothes she bought new ones, she did not like to mend, or to see them in mended clothes (her common saying was she did not like to be poor and seem so, etc.)'.[15] Evidently Shaw's wife did care about appearances. She certainly had examples to emulate, because in her youth she had worked as a servant in the houses of Lancaster's mercantile elite. What Shaw regarded as sartorial carelessness and lack of pride, appears from her point of view to have been a refusal of the constant labour involved in the upkeep of clothing, combined with an essentially throwaway, disposable approach to dress. This was not an irrational stance, since her husband was a skilled worker, earning good wages when employed, who, by his own admission, gave her a more generous allowance than most working men's wives received. Looking back to the 1790s, before they married, when his wife was a Dolphinholme mill girl, he reflected wearily:

> When she was young she never had any thing, scarce any thing of her back, she never had but one gown, all the time that before we were married I knew her, and that somebody gave her and when she had had it a little while, she was out of conceit with it, and she gave it to her mother (that is step mother) to cut for the children

frocks, etc., and when she got any thing, bedgowns, handkerchiefs, or stocking, or any article new, she gave the old ones away as soon as she got them or before, so that she never had anything – she had nothing to care for etc . . . this is her plan, she will not have any thing, she knows that it is some trouble to have any thing – and she often says that her children shall not fall out about her things for she will not have any for them to differ about.[16]

Shaw found his wife's behaviour not simply exasperating, but inexplicable. He never fully accounts for her preference for retaining only her newest clothes and disposing of the rest. Consequently we cannot be sure whether it reflected uncompromising attachment to modish novelty, an unwillingness or inability to sew, or utter indifference to materialistic accumulation. Her susceptibility to the sales patter of pedlars and credit traders suggests a fondness for whatever was showy and fashionable.

Indifference or even hostility to material accumulation was probably common enough among working people. Some late eighteenth- and early nineteenth-century memoirs and autobiographies, like those of Joseph Mayett, a Buckinghamshire soldier and labourer, and Anthony Errington, a County Durham waggonway wright, hardly mention clothing. We should not, however, take silence as proof that the subject was of no concern to them. Different autobiographers incorporated different priorities into what they wrote. Mayett, writing in his pious and impoverished old age, disapprovingly recalled being impressed by the appearance of the sergeants and corporals of the Royal Bucks Militia at church in Buckingham in 1802.[17] Yet clearly there were working men who dressed badly not because they were too poor to dress any better, but because they chose to do so. One such was Johnny Chapman, a pitman employed by the engraver Thomas Bewick's father on the banks of the Tyne in the 1750s and 1760s. Bewick describes him, not unsympathetically, in the *Memoir* he wrote towards the end of his life as 'clothed in rags . . . His living was of the poorest kind, bread, potatoes & oatmeal was the only provender he kept by him; with these & milk & water he finished his meals – When, by this mode of living, he had saved the overplus money of his wages, for a month or 6 Weeks – he then posted off to Newcastle to spend it in Beer, and this he called "*lowsening his skin*".'[18] A preference for sensual gratification over decent clothing was also commonly associated with seamen. Woodes Rogers, captain of a privateer, had noted early in the eighteenth century that 'good Liquor to Sailors is preferable to Clothing'.[19]

It is impossible to establish precisely what proportion of eighteenth-century working people were badly dressed, in the sense of having only cheap, coarse clothing, or clothes that were old and patched, shabby and threadbare, irrespective of whether the poor state of their dress was a matter of choice, or necessity. As we have seen, the evidence of the autobiographies suggests it was common enough for working men and women, at some periods in their lives, to suffer disastrous losses of clothes, to be obliged to pawn them, and to have to forgo replacements. Nevertheless, it is surprising how few of the clothes described in the runaway advertisements are described as being actually

26 Paul Sandby, *London Cries: 'Shoe Cleaner'*, c.1759, pen and brush and grey ink and watercolour over graphite, Paul Mellon Collection, Yale Center for British Art, New Haven, Conn., B1975.3.207. The shoe cleaner wears a ragged apron to protect her clothes.

ragged. Yet ragged clothes are mentioned repeatedly by the autobiographers and others in describing people who were utterly impoverished. They appear in Paul Sandby's brutally unsentimental watercolours of London street sellers in the 1750s (figs 25, 26).[20] They remained all too visible on the cold, foggy streets of London six decades later, in April 1817, when Melesina Trench, the wife of a wealthy Irish gentleman making her way home from the theatre, passed 'silent and drooping figures in the prime and middle of life, seated, shivering and dying, on the steps of houses, without stockings, without linen, in ragged clothing above that of the lower class'.[21]

The admissions registers of the St Marylebone workhouse in Paddington, London, which survive for the 1770s, provide a unique opportunity to assess the condition of the clothing worn by the helpless and destitute of the capital. People entered the workhouse because they were ill or impoverished. Out of 83 adults admitted during four months in 1770, 48 were suffering from an illness or were about to give birth, while 35 were poor, friendless or miserable.[22] Most stayed in the workhouse for only a short time, a majority for less than three months. Their average age was 39, with the men tending to be slightly younger than the women, but women outnumbered men by a ratio of nearly two to one. On admission, 'cloaths brought in' were listed in the registers for each new arrival. Here, not surprisingly, the proportion of those who wore old and ragged clothes was much higher than in the provincial runaway advertisements. The clothes worn by more than a quarter (27 percent) of those admitted were not even itemised in the registers, but simply entered as 'ragged', 'rags', or, in one case, 'cloath'd alias coverth'd with raggs only'. In addition, another 20 percent of those admitted had at least one item of clothing described as 'old'. It was women, especially older women, who were most likely to be dressed in rags. Of the women admitted, 30 percent were ragged, compared with 21 percent of men. Their average age was 46, compared with an average age for all adult women entering the workhouse of 39. Ragged men, by contrast, tended to be significantly younger than the generality of male inmates (average age 30, compared with an average of 37 for all males admitted).

If 47 percent of those admitted to the workhouse arrived wearing some clothes identified as old or ragged, the other 53 percent did not. This was a crucial distinction. 'Was it a decent person, or a ragged person?' was one of the questions put to a witness at the Old Bailey in 1789, in order to establish a suspect's identity.[23] A significant proportion of the men and women who entered the workhouse appear to have been at least adequately dressed, as far as we can judge from the descriptions in the registers, which allow us to differentiate only in terms of quantity and type. Overall, the women tended to have more clothes than the men, consistent with the pattern observed among the poorer Brandon fire victims. Twenty of the 54 female inmates (37 percent) had 12 items of clothing or more, indicating that they brought changes of some clothes with them to the workhouse, usually aprons, caps, handkerchiefs and stockings, but sometimes gowns and petticoats. Sixty-eight-year-old Hester Davis, who entered the workhouse because she was lame, had 23 items of clothing: a gown, three petticoats, two shifts, three handkerchiefs, five caps, three pairs of stockings, a pair of shoes, a hat, a cloak and a pair of stays. Another woman had even more clothes. Oddly, changes of shifts were relatively few. Of the 35 women whose clothing was itemised, 29 had hats, 22 had cloaks and 15 had stays. Almost all the 35 had the essential elements of a decent wardrobe: shoes, stockings, a shift, a handkerchief, an apron and a gown or a petticoat. Only two lacked those key indicators of sartorial decency: shoes and stockings. Aged 67 and 72 respectively, they were among the oldest inmates admitted to the workhouse. Both were ill and, if housebound, may have had little need for outdoor footwear. Among the men, changes of clothes were far less common. All the 22 with itemised clothing had shoes, stockings, breeches and a coat or a waistcoat. Most had shirts and hats. Seven even had wigs. Nevertheless, none of them had more than nine items of clothing. None of the men admitted to the St Marylebone workhouse and hardly any of the women had anything approaching the numbers of clothes lost by the poorest victims of the Brandon fire.

For some, perhaps, this state of affairs marked the culmination of weeks or months of selling off previously larger stocks of clothes in order to get by, before eventually

27 Paul Sandby, *Wine Seller* c.1759, watercolour, Ashmolean Museum, Oxford, WA1963.89.79. A drunken street seller with wine bottles and a wine glass in her basket.

seeking parish relief.[24] For others it was probably a chronic condition. The workhouse admissions registers furnish evidence of a variety of clothing trajectories among the few who were admitted again and again, although inevitably the serially destitute all eventually ended up in rags. Some experienced a progressive decline. Sarah Pooley was 40 when she was admitted at the end of 1769. Described as 'poor and troublesome', she arrived with a basic wardrobe of a bedgown, two petticoats, apron, handkerchief, shift, shoes, stockings and a hat. Six months later she was discharged to haymaking. By December 1770 she was back, with the same mix of clothes, but now including changes of shifts and handkerchiefs. Discharged after a fortnight, within a month she was back again, having spend the intervening weeks 'crying kitchen stuff in the street, drunk'. Now described as 'a very drunken, troublesome woman', she was dressed in rags. Three months later, in April 1771, she ran away, only to return in the autumn, still in rags. She was last admitted in 1772, still poor and wearing an old green gown and rags, before finally running away the next year taking a shift and a cloak that belonged to another inmate (fig. 27).

28 Paul Sandby, *London Cries: 'A Muffin Man'*, c.1759, watercolour, pen and black ink, brush and grey ink, Paul Mellon Collection, Yale Center for British Art, New Haven, Conn., B1975.3.205. The muffin man is depicted wearing a green coat, a red waistcoat and brown breeches, all in reasonably good condition.

Elizabeth Alveradoe, by contrast, started ragged and stayed that way. Described as 'an old incumbant', she was 70 when admitted in February 1770 with pain in her limbs and feet, already 'very ragged'. Admitted three more times over the next two years, she spent the intervening periods in Kent, sometimes employed at hopping. Nevertheless, every time she returned to the workhouse she was 'very ragged and filthy'. Yet another trajectory is exhibited by Mary Dole, a servant aged 18 when first admitted early in 1770 with ague and fever. She arrived with a minimal wardrobe of nine items, including a gown described as 'old'. Discharged in the summer to another service, she returned two months later, again suffering from a fever, but now in possession of an ample wardrobe of 28 items. After a fortnight she left to work as a servant for a different employer. Two years later she was re-admitted, suffering from venereal disease and dressed in rags.

The Marylebone workhouse registers afford numerous examples of destitute people dressed in old, ragged clothes, who resemble some of the most impoverished among the street sellers portrayed by Paul Sandby. Yet even among the street sellers, who

29 Paul Sandby, *London Cries: 'A Milkmaid'*, c.1759, pen and black ink, brush and grey ink and watercolour over graphite, Paul Mellon Collection, Yale Center for British Art, New Haven, Conn., B1975.3.209. The milkmaid wears a short red cloak, a large white apron and a straw hat over a red-spotted handkerchief. None of them is ragged.

included some of the poorest and most vulnerable of London's population, there existed a variety of sartorial experiences. Sandby did not portray all his street sellers as ragged (figs 28, 29). If we examine the clothes stolen from street sellers who appear as victims of theft in the trials at the Old Bailey, we find stored in their lodgings while they worked the streets many of the costlier items owned by other kinds of labouring people. Elizabeth Hicks, who lived in a second-floor room in a lodging house near Coleman Street in the City of London, sold fruit in the street. While out 'at her basket' on an April afternoon in 1780, her room was broken into and her drawers emptied. Among other things, she lost two cotton gowns, a silk crape gown, a woollen cloth cloak, a silk handkerchief and a muslin handkerchief. Esther Hudson, who got her living 'in the street at Cornhill', owned a scarlet cloth cloak and two printed calico muslin gowns. They were stolen from her lodging near London Wall in April 1785, while she was out for the day.[25] These and similar cases remind us that alongside the Sarah Pooleys, ragged and drunk crying kitchen stuff in the streets, there were also street sellers like the young Mary Saxby, for whom ballad singing was a sufficiently 'profitable trade' to get 'plenty of good clothes'.[26]

In the lives of ordinary men and women, clothes came and went, sometimes agonizingly slowly, sometimes unexpectedly and with alarming speed. Plebeian clothing biographies were marked by variability. A genteel suit of clothes, a watch, even a pair of silver buckles embodied life's possibilities; garments that were old, patched and ragged represented its perils. For many, although by no means all, smart clothing was a social, sexual, moral and economic priority, the first call on whatever money they had to spare. Even for those driven to seek refuge in the workhouse, clothes could be important. Some arrived ragged, but there were many others who, despite their privations, had succeeded in retaining the basic elements of a decent wardrobe.

30 Paul Sandby, *At Sandpit Gate: Washing Day*, n.d. [early 1750s], watercolour, Royal Collection, RL 14329. A woman washes linen in tubs in the kitchen of a house near Windsor, Berkshire, while her companion tends to a fire that is heating the water for washing. Dressed for work, the woman at the fire wears back-lacing stays over a shift and petticoat, without a gown (see also fig. 20).

4
Keeping Up Appearances

Those who went ragged did so because their clothes had worn to tatters. In 1730, Thomas Banks was known around the city of York 'by the name of Tom Tatterrags'.[1] Those who managed to avoid dressing in rags succeeded because they replaced, repaired and cleaned their clothes sufficiently often to keep them decent. Richard Dixon, a weaver from Sawrey in Furness, encountered a man on the road near Keswick in Cumberland at Christmas 1782 wearing a faded blue cotton velvet coat. The man remarked that the coat 'was farr worn and would not turn rain and that he intended to have a new one soon'.[2] The consequences of failing in the proper upkeep of clothing were summed up in a report on a Hampshire poorhouse in the 1790s: 'As no care was taken to keep the clothes in repair, nor any distinction made between old and new, they were always in rags, and yet always craving for new clothes.'[3]

In contrast to many foodstuffs, clothing was not a perishable commodity, but neither did it display the durability of goods like pewter or wooden furniture, acquired by ordinary people perhaps only two or three times in their lives, if they ever owned them at all.[4] Compared to these durables, clothing wore out relatively quickly. Eighteenth-century clothing is perhaps best thought of as a kind of semi-durable, although different garments characteristically displayed different rates of wear, depending on the sturdiness of the materials from which they were made and the frequency with which they were worn and cleaned. Prevailing notions of decency required some items of clothing to be cleaned regularly by washing, especially those worn next to the body. In order to put clothes repeatedly through the time-consuming process of washing and drying while remaining fully dressed, changes of at least some items were essential. It is in the light of these two imperatives – rates of wear that varied between garments and the need for some garments to be regularly washed – that we should judge the stocks of clothes possessed by plebeian men and women.

Lists of people's clothes, whether compiled by workhouse officials, court clerks or fire victims, cannot tell us how long the listed items had lasted, how often they were worn, or how regularly they were replaced. The lists, in other words, are silent about both turnover and frequency of wear. Rates of replacement were never simply a matter of durability, even for the working poor; propriety and fashion were important too. Nevertheless, some garments tended to be far more transient than others. Outer garments, especially men's outer garments made from sturdy woollen cloth, tended to last longest, but their longevity was measured in years, not decades. The yeoman Richard Gough, writing at the start of the eighteenth century about the inhabitants of his Shropshire village of Myddle, found it odd that Richard Wicherley, though the heir of a wealthy kinsman, 'never altered the fashion of his cloathes, for hee never had but one and the same suit during all the time that I knew him, which was about ten years'.[5] When William Hutton noted in 1751 that 'my best coat had been my best coat five years', it was to illustrate his exceptional abstemiousness.[6] Women's heavier outer garments could also be long-lasting. Catharine Sullivan, the wife of a London watchman, had her woollen cloth cloak stolen from her lodging in 1793. It was three years old, but time had taken its toll. The cloak was stained, ripped in two or three places and had broken trimmings, although a pawnbroker was still prepared to lend the thief six shillings in exchange for it.[7]

The prevailing view among patrician commentators was that the woollen outer garments worn by the labouring poor, who worked their clothes hard, characteristically wore out faster than these cases of exceptional longevity would suggest. Sir Frederick Eden estimated in the 1790s that a good foul-weather man's coat bought ready-made from a London slop shop would last 'very well' for two years, as would the 'cheapest kind of cloak' for a woman bought in the same shop. Believing that the working poor should produce more of what they wore at home, he hinted that these slop-shop purchases were less durable than the clothing made up by country tailors, but those with experience of providing clothes for the poor near London did not necessarily agree.[8] The budgets David Davies collected in his home village of Barkham, Berkshire in 1787 suggest that a man's suit and his working jacket and breeches would each last, in combination, no more than three years, and probably as little as two.[9] A pamphlet on the woollen trade published in 1736 concurred: 'The poorer and most industrious people are not cloathed above once in two years.'[10] This kind of lifespan was not confined to woollen main garments. Eden estimated that a man's hat bought at a London slop shop would last three years and the cheapest sort of woman's hat two years. The only item of clothing he identifies as likely to last longer than three years is a pair of stays bought at a London slop shop, which 'will last six years'.[11]

Other garments had much shorter lives. Eden considered a pair of slop-shop breeches would last only a year. Davies estimated that his Barkham labourers needed one new pair of 'stout shoes nailed' a year, their wives 'one pair of strong shoes'. This may, however, underestimate just how quickly working men's shoes wore out and needed to be replaced. For the general agricultural labourer, shoes were, as Peter Jones has reminded us, 'the most important tools of his trade'.[12] Eden's budgets for an Ealing, Middlesex labourer and an Epsom, Surrey gardener show them both needing to purchase two new pairs of shoes a year, although the Epsom gardener's wife acquired only one new pair. It is unlikely that these labouring men owned more than one pair of shoes at a time, so each pair must have worn out in only six months, despite being mended. The same appears to have been true of men's shirts and stockings. At Barkham, Davies recorded labourers having two new shirts and two new pairs of stockings annually, their wives one new shift and one new pair of stockings. If we assume that at any one time husband and wife each possessed two of these items of clothing, to allow one to be washed while the other was worn, then the man's shirt and stockings had a wearing life of about six months, the woman's of about a year.[13] No wonder Esther Hewlett's *Cottage Comforts*, one of many early nineteenth-century manuals on domestic economy aimed at the poor, distinguished between shoes and undergarments, which 'of necessity will always be wearing out', and outer garments, which 'are not things of every-day purchase'.[14]

How long a piece of clothing actually lasted depended on how frequently it was worn and cleaned, and for what purpose it was worn. Cloaks and coats, especially best ones, were not usually worn every day of the year. When a London coachman claimed his stolen coat 'never was worn six months', the Monmouth Street salesman who bought it from the thief responded with disbelief: 'Then, you have worn it night and day.'[15] Similarly, best gowns were not worn constantly. When Rachael Toms, a Whitechapel mantuamaker, had a blue satin gown stolen from a trunk in December 1770 while she was at work, it was three weeks since she had worn it.[16] The same was true of prized accessories. In 1793, a pair of stuff shoes with silver buckles were stolen from Penelope Reading, a widow from Hanwell in Middlesex, along with her best silk and muslin clothes, while she was at work in the fields. In court she was cross-examined about how old they were: 'How long have you had these buckles? – Near two years. Q[uestion]. Have you worn them at all? – Not much, only now and then of a Sunday, when I went to church.'[17] Other clothes, however, were worn day in, day out. Catharine Sullivan, the London watchman's wife whose old, decrepit cloak was stolen in 1793, lost a handkerchief to the same thief. She readily identified it at the Old Bailey: 'The silk handkerchief I used to wear every day.'[18] A Whitechapel Road brushmaker explained that he knew a bedgown stolen in 1794 because 'my wife has always worn it every morning for this two years back'.[19] A seaman accused of a rape in 1779 claimed he had worn the shirt he was arrested in for a week.[20] Generally, it was considered exceptional to wear the same clothes for more than three weeks without changing or cleaning them.[21]

Basic working clothes were subject to more wear and tear than best clothes. The difference Davies and Eden identified in the rate at which husbands and wives wore out shoes and shirts or shifts reflected different kinds of work, husbands being more likely to do heavy work outdoors. Davies considered that labourers' wives 'commonly begin the world with an infant, and are mere nurses for ten or twelve years after marriage, being always either with child, or having a child at breast; consequently incapable of doing much other work besides the necessary business of their families, such as baking, washing, and the like'.[22] Eden found that the wife of his Epsom gardener, 'seldom going out', needed few clothes.[23]

The lifespan of almost any item of clothing could be extended by careful upkeep. For many tailors and shoemakers, consequently, mending accounted for the majority of the orders they were commissioned to perform (fig. 31).[24] Time and time again,

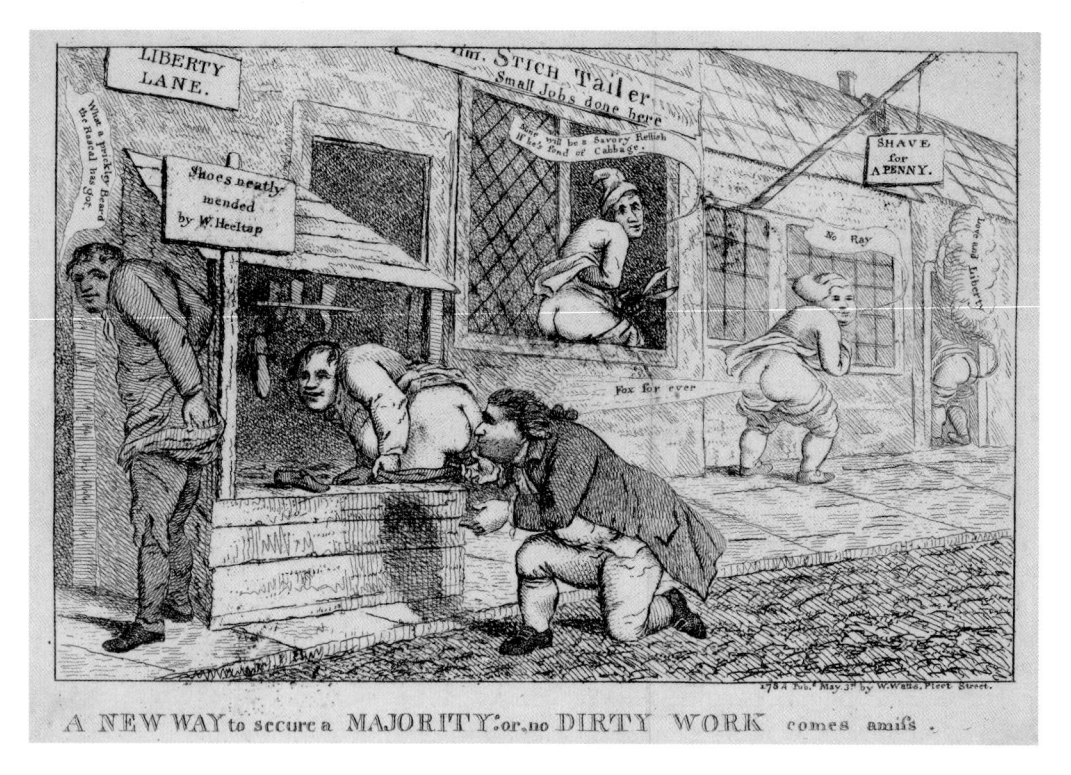

31 *A New Way to Secure a Majority: or, no Dirty Work comes amiss*, printed engraving, 1784, British Museum, London, BMSat 6572. A satire on Charles James Fox canvassing poor tradesmen while a candidate in the 1784 Westminster election. The lowly status of the cobbler and the tailor is signalled by their shabby premises and the fact they work mainly at mending. The notice fixed to the cobbler's lean-to stall says: 'Shoes neatly mended'. The tailor's shop sign reads: 'Small Jobs done here'.

witnesses in criminal trials identified otherwise unremarkable items of stolen clothing by the way they had been mended, even though patched and refurbished garments were probably less attractive to thieves. 'I know the gown, I have mended it', Ann Barnes, a parish pensioner, told the Old Bailey in 1793.[25] 'Here is a pocket handkerchief that is mine, a silk handkerchief, it is worn out and mended at the corner', announced Mary Julphs in 1784.[26] Many of the clothes ordinary people possessed were inevitably patched, faded and worn, without being actually ragged (figs 32, 33). The shirt stolen from a Moorfields, London errand lad in 1789 'was rather faded, and there was a patch put under it'.[27] A journeyman carpenter and cabinetmaker apprehended in London in 1780 was said to have 'had on a light green suit of clothes, very much faded'.[28] A Shoreditch woman whose employment was to look after a child had her printed shawl stolen in 1814: 'The shawl was worth eighteen pence. I gave nine shillings and sixpence for it; I have worn it long, the colours were all worn out; it is an old one now.'[29] A farmer from Feltham in Middlesex described his stolen handkerchief in 1808:

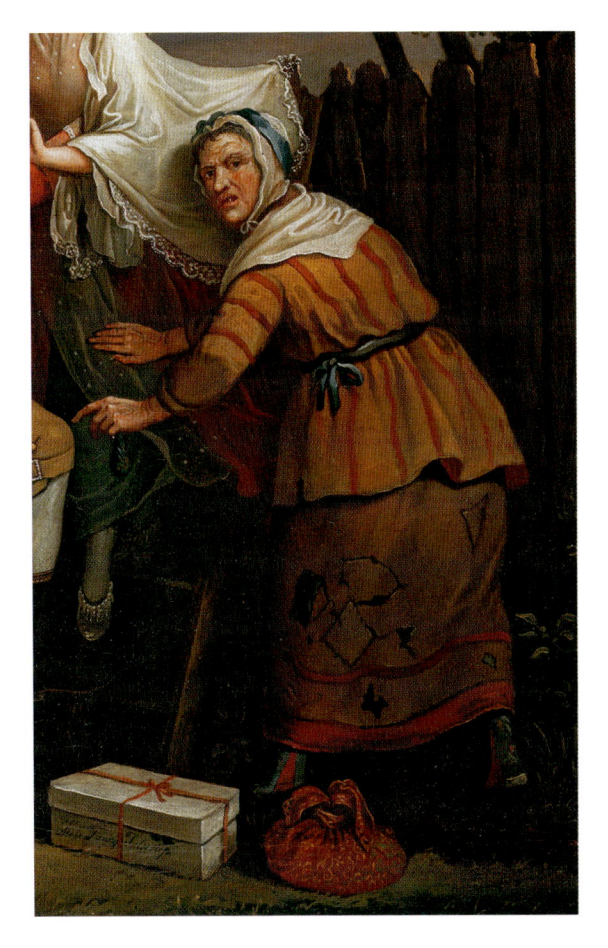

32　John Collet, *Modern Love - the Elopement* (detail), 1764, oil on canvas, The Colonial Williamsburg Foundation, Va., 1969-48, 2. The woman is meanly dressed, with a loose bedgown or jacket made from a coarse striped material, belted with a cord or apron string around the waist. Her short petticoat is heavily patched. Nevertheless, she wears stockings decorated with contrasting clocks, and a blue silk ribbon tie her cap.

'It is faded in the double by wearing it; it is faded with the sun, and wearing round my neck with the perspiration; I always wear them round my neck at home.'[30] A shift stolen from the daughter of a yeoman from Slaidburn, Yorkshire, in 1758 had holes under each armpit 'made by her stays with raking of hay', while two shirts stolen at the same time belonging to her brother were described as 'one man's shirt of brown linen much clouted and worn, and another man's shirt not much worn'.[31] Newness was defined by the absence of mending. 'I know it is mine', said Catherine Cane, the wife of a London bricklayer's labourer, identifying her stolen cotton gown in 1757, 'because it is a new one and never was mended'.[32] Indeed, there was a recognised scale of wear, which extended from the brand new, through the partly worn, to the irredeemable. A High Holborn innkeeper distinguished in 1785 between 'an old pair of white ribbed stockings . . . not worth a farthing', new stockings and a pair of stockings which 'were in the middling way, they might be darned in the heels'.[33] Hence the range of descriptive adjectives used in the Brandon fire lists, which ranged from 'new', via 'almost new', 'good' and 'mended', to 'old'.

33   Thomas Barker, *Man holding a Staff*, c.1800, oil on canvas, Paul Mellon Collection, Yale Center for British Art, New Haven, Conn., B1976.7.3. The old man, with his oaken staff, embodies English resilience. He is shown wearing a heavily patched coat coming apart at the seams, made from very coarse material, over a blue waistcoat with gilt buttons.

In addition to repair, keeping up appearances required that clothes be clean, but cleaning them was neither easy, nor cheap. Wearing silk garments posed a particular challenge to working people because they were not only expensive to buy, but also difficult to keep in good condition, whether worn in muddy country lanes or sooty, coal-fired towns. Silks were vulnerable to damage by dirt, water and sunlight, and were often too delicate to wash. They deteriorated if exposed to the rain and had to be stored with great care. Peggy Ashworth, the wife of a Halifax innkeeper, recounted how in April 1783 'about twelve o'clock at noon she was going abroad and meant to have taken her black silk cloak with her having taken it out her drawers for that purpose but thinking it likely to rain and that it might be spoil'd she wrapped it up in a crimson and white checked silk handkerchief and put it so wraped up in one of the drawers again'.[34] Hence the appeal of 'washing gowns' and other outer garments made from printed cottons and linens, which, like silks, boasted vibrant colours, but in a form that was colour-fast and washable. A month after Peggy Ashworth put her silk cloak back in its drawer at Halifax for fear that the rain would damage it, the wife of a cutler at Sheffield, 30 miles across the hills to the south, had no qualms about having her servant wash her printed cotton gown and hang it out to dry on the railings of a nearby house.[35] Washing was especially necessary in towns, where gowns could quickly become soiled. The owner of a cotton gown snatched from a washing line in London in May 1783 told the Old Bailey: 'I am a countrywoman, and wore it up to London; I had been here going on nine weeks, and the gown was very dirty, it was washed on the Monday and hung out.'[36]

Woollen clothing got just as dirty, but was much harder to clean than cotton. Simply constructed, plain items might be washed, like a flannel petticoat belonging to a filesmith's wife, stolen while drying on a wall at Sheffield in 1782.[37] But more complex woollen garments, tailored, lined and dyed in colours that might run, could not be washed easily. A dirty coat could be brushed or scraped, but if that did not produce the desired effect it had to be cleaned professionally, which usually involved scouring, and sometimes dismantling and re-dyeing.[38] David Morgan, a highwayman, stayed at the Crown Inn on Enfield Chase, north of London, for three-quarters of an hour on a wet Wednesday night in April 1761, after robbing a chaise. His soaked, dirty coat was given to a servant to clean. 'The maid scraped Morgan's coat, which was daubed when the chaise pulled him off his horse, and throwed him down in the dirt; it was not dry enough to be brushed.' Morgan and his companions then rode on into London, to Robinson's bagnio in Prince's Street, Covent Garden. A servant there recalled that Morgan's coat was still dirty. 'He desired it to be cleaned. I took it to dry by the fire, but could not get it clean, and was obliged to send it to the scowerer's.'[39] Francis Place recalled that in his youth the wives and grown daughters of tradesmen had quilted camblet petticoats that were 'worn day by day until they were rotten, and never were washed'.[40] In his late years, Place was inclined to play up the improvements in standards that had taken place since he was a boy, but his colourful description emphasises just how difficult it was to clean woollen garments.

Despite the difficulties working people faced in keeping their outer garments free of dirt, it was by the cleanliness of their appearance that they were liable to be judged when seeking accommodation, shopping or work. When Jane Field applied for a lodging in Great St Ann's Street, Westminster in 1793, the landlord remembered 'she appeared rather poor but the clothes she had on were very clean; I thought her a working person as she said she was.'[41] Hannah Sealy was observed by a London shopkeeper in 1732 wearing 'a short Mob [cap] and a wash'd Gown; you was clean dress'd, and looked like a tight Girl'.[42] John Keys, a 16-year-old accused of stealing a shirt in London in 1789, claimed in his defence that he had found it on the ground: 'I picked it up and took it home; having a dirty shirt on, I put on that I found, being clean, as I was going to my master the next morning.'[43] Wearing clean clothes may not have been a priority, or even a practical possibility for all working people, but for many it was. Elizabeth Green drank a dish of tea at an inn at Doncaster in Yorkshire after walking the 12 miles from Rotherham on a Saturday morning in November 1753. She then left the inn, 'first pulling on a clean handkerchief, apron and cap and saying she was going into the market and loved to be clean'.[44] People were expected to be consistent in the degree of sartorial cleanliness they sustained. Mixing clean and dirty items of clothing could arouse suspicion, as in the case of Joseph Wade, who worked on a wharf on the Thames near Somerset House in London in 1771. When seen at the Hat and Feather, a nearby public house where he lodged, it was noted that 'the neckcloth he had on appeared cleaner than his shirt'.[45]

The incongruity of Joseph Wade's neckcloth being cleaner than his shirt was all the greater because body linen was considered the key to personal cleanliness, at every level in society. Being clean turned first and foremost on the condition of linen undergarments and accessories, particularly men's shirts and women's shifts, but also stockings, caps, sleeves and ruffles. Their condition was much more important for perceptions of personal cleanliness than the condition of outer garments, or how often the skin was washed. This conception of cleanliness explains the German Pastor Karl Philipp Moritz's astonishment when, in 1782, he noted that the men pushing wheelbarrows through the streets of London wore shirts, and that those shirts had been washed. He was surprised that such poor people were able to be clean.[46] Defining cleanliness in this way was partly a reflection of practicalities: the linens from which undergarments were generally made could be cleaned by washing far more easily than the woollens or silks of outer garments. But it also reflected deeper cultural preoccupations with health and the body. From the late Middle Ages, regular changes of linen undergarments came to be regarded throughout western Europe as a more effective way of keeping the body clean than bathing. Clean linen was considered the best means to absorb and remove sweat, dirt and other life-threatening impurities. Received medical wisdom required bodily excretions to be removed from the skin in order to prevent them being absorbed back into the body. Failure to do this was held to cause fevers and skin disease and encourage vermin. Caring for undergarments was therefore a way of caring for the body which those undergarments encased. Putting on clean linen cleansed the skin and the body beneath. Wearing foul linen resulted in the body being literally 'poisoned with dirt'.[47] This way of thinking about bodily cleanliness had implications that were private, personal and intimate. At the same time, it turned cleanliness into a public sartorial spectacle, possessed of far greater semiotic power than if cleaning the body had been just a matter of washing the skin. A person's cleanliness could be judged simply by scrutinising their linen clothing, especially where it protruded from the overgarments at the neck, the elbows and the wrists. Clean linen became the key sign of a clean and healthy body. The whiter the linen, the cleaner it was considered to be.[48] Hence the importance accorded to whiteness in garments that touched the skin, and hence the desire to accumulate sufficient numbers of linen shirts and shifts, caps, ruffles and sleeves to permit regular washing and frequent changes.[49]

The whitest, finest linens, such as lawn, cambric and Holland, were expensive. So too were the cleaning agents and hot water required to keep them pristine. Nevertheless, most plebeian men and women did succeed in owning changes of shirts, shifts, sleeves and caps made from linen, and in washing them regularly. These kinds of body linen figure very prominently among the stored clothes lost by the poorer victims of the Brandon fire. Even among those Londoners whose circumstances were so reduced that they sought entry to the St Marylebone workhouse, a significant minority of the women owned changes of at least some body linen. Of course, the vast bulk of the body linen worn by working people was made from the cheaper, coarser varieties of flaxen and hempen cloth. It is unlikely these fabrics ever appeared brilliantly white. Often they had a distinctly brownish tinge. One was known literally as 'brown linen' (fig. 101). Yet this did not deter those who wore these fabrics from making great efforts to ensure their cleanliness. Time and time again the records of eighteenth-century criminal trials describe shifts, shirts and caps belonging to labouring people being stolen from country hedges or lines strung across city yards, where they had been left out to dry after being washed. And they were washed repeatedly. A London horse breaker accused in 1760 of the theft of a Holland shirt, insisted it was an old one that he had acquired second-hand: 'That shirt has been washed about 40 times.'[50]

How frequently body linen was washed depended on how many changes were available. Military regulations required soldiers, who were expected to have at least two shirts and to be immaculate in appearance, to change them twice a week.[51] A London day labourer claimed in 1792 that he had his linen washed once a week.[52] Mary Hardy, a Norfolk farmer's wife, washed fortnightly in 1778.[53] Esther Nicholson, a breadbaker who lived in Kendal in Westmorland and was affluent enough to employ a live-in female servant, had sufficient linen to wash only once every three weeks in the late 1780s.[54] Nicholson's servant helped her mistress with the regular wash and her own linen was probably included in it, as was usually the case for the many working people who lived as dependants in their employers' households. Consequently, even the lowliest and most put-upon of these employees could expect to have their body linen washed regularly. Ann Naylor, a 13-year-old parish apprentice employed with three others making mittens and purses in a tiny London room, was starved to death by her mistress in 1762. Denied food, she nevertheless had clean shifts 'once a week, and sometimes once a fortnight'.[55]

Washing linen clothes was time-consuming, expensive and exhausting. The fact that so many working people succeeded in having their linen washed regularly is testimony to the acute sense of shame that attached to being seen in dirty shirts and shifts. Sarah Trimmer recounted in 1787 how

> It is a most lamentable sight to enter a cottage, and behold a poor woman sitting in rags, surrounded by a set of dirty children: we are shocked, and turn away with disgust, condemning her in our hearts for sloth and untidiness; but let us stop an instant, and hear her apology. 'I am ashamed to appear before you ladies in this condition, but indeed I have not the means of cleanliness . . . we have no change of apparel – look at the bed in which my dear babes must lie naked while I wash their linen – not so much as a single sheet – nor can I purchase even a bit of sope.'[56]

This sense of shame was echoed by John Loppenburg, a Russian servant resident in London in 1740, who 'frequently used to go into the Fields to wash his Shirts, because he did not care that any Body should see them.' He went to a secluded pond at Paddington 'in order to wash a coarse dirty Shirt; I was ashamed to be seen doing it by any body, because it was torn and ragged. . . . I hung my Shirt up to dry, and walked to and fro while it was drying, and saw two Men walking about; I threw the Shirt from me least they should laugh at me.'[57]

Loppenburg seems to have washed his shirt simply by pounding it clean in the cold water of the pond without any soap or other cleaning agent. This somewhat ineffective method of washing was commonly reported from Scotland, Ireland and Wales in the eighteenth century, but rarely in England (fig. 34).[58] In England it was more usual to employ hot water in combination with a cleaning agent, which might be homemade or purchased. Stale urine could be used, or lye, a form of potash made from wood ash or ferns. Usually urine or lye was combined with soap, which had to be bought at excessive cost due to a heavy excise duty. Already, at the end of the seventeenth century, the French visitor Henri Misson was struck by the extent to which people in many parts of England used nothing but soap. 'At *London*, and in all other Parts of the Country where they do not burn Wood, they do not make Lye. All their Linnen, coarse and fine, is wash'd with soap.'[59] The social investigators David Davies and Sir Frederick Eden found that impoverished rural labouring families at the end of the eighteenth century bought soap regularly. So did parish overseers of the poor on behalf of the paupers in their care. Margaret Wilson, a weaver's wife resident in the workhouse at Ovenden, near Halifax, was accused in 1757 of stealing four balls of soap that had been given her by the master of the house 'to wash her clothes with'.[60] Sometimes blue was added to the final rinse to make whites brighter, adding a further cost.[61]

The process of washing involved water being heated over a fire and then transferred to tubs, where the linen would be soaped, beaten with a dolly, beetle or other implement, and scrubbed, if possible on a washing board (fig. 30). Boiling and rinsing would

34 Julius Caesar Ibbetson, *The Gossips*, c.1800, oil on canvas, private collection. Women wash clothes by the River Conway at Llanrwst Bridge, Denbighshire, north Wales. Water is being heated over a fire on the right.

follow, and then drying, ideally outdoors to benefit from the sun's bleaching action. Thoroughly dried body linen was considered as essential to health as regular changes. The linen might, in addition, be starched and ironed. The combination of crudely processed, inconsistent and often ineffective chemicals, boiling water and hard pounding was brutal to clothes.[62] It was also physically very demanding for the women who washed, whether as part of their domestic duties, or professionally as washerwomen. When the health of Benjamin Shaw's wife began to fail in 1827, 'she gave up washing and anything that required Strength'.[63]

Despite the cost of soap and firing, and the difficulty of drying linen, especially in cramped city lodgings, many, probably most, plebeian wives undertook the household washing themselves, often with the assistance of relatives, friends or servants, if they employed them. But a surprising number of plebeian households paid to have their linen washed, including even the households of labourers. In December 1753, for example, Martha Clark, the wife of a Bradford, Yorkshire labourer, hired a woman to wash, as did the wife of Thomas Ambler, a Sheffield labourer, in 1786.[64] Arrangements like these may often have been temporary, occasioned by ill health, pregnancy, or the demands of looking after small children, but they were common and must have represented a significant element in the work of the many women who made a living by washing. Indeed at Tynemouth in Northumberland towards the end of the eighteenth century, a farmer, James Vardy, ran a common washhouse which he rented out to washerwomen for a penny a day. It was used by women like Mary Lay from nearby North Shields, the wife of a seaman, who worked 'as a washer woman for several people in and about North Shields', including at least one wife of another seaman.[65]

Employing a washerwoman was costly, however. Eden reported that washerwomen at Sheffield in the 1790s were paid one shilling a day, plus food, while a labourer's wife in Shropshire, who had previously been a laundry maid, earned three shillings a week by washing, although it was unusual to earn so much regularly.[66] To wash for a household with children would take at least a day and drying could take much longer. George Parker, an itinerant actor, remembered being shamed by his washerwoman at Gloucester when he failed to pay her: 'Damn him . . . does he think I pay nothing for my soap and starch? I thought by his linen he was a vagabond, and I never should be paid. I wonder how the fellow gets it on; he must do it by piece-meal; a sleeve in one tub, a collar in another, and a wristband in a third'.[67] No wonder that in 1785 a 14-year-old London shop boy paid the common carrier to take his dirty linen to be washed each week at his parental home at Hanwell in Middlesex, ten miles away.[68]

Regular cleaning, mending and replacement were all essential if ordinary men and women were to keep up appearances. This has important implications for the relationship between stocks of clothes and flows of clothes; between, on the one hand, the snapshot listings of at least some of the clothes people owned at a particular moment, like those for the Brandon fire victims or the runaways advertised in the newspapers, and, on the other, the turnover in people's clothing from year to year and from decade to decade, for which the little evidence we possess is incomplete, as in the plebeian autobiographies. The effort, time and money ordinary people had to expend to stay decent shaped the relationship between stocks and flows of clothing in three significant ways.

The first concerns the rate at which they acquired new clothes. To sustain anything approaching a decent appearance, it was necessary to own changes of clothing, particularly body linen and accessories like handkerchiefs and aprons that were washable. The less changes that were owned, the more rapidly clothes wore out and the more frequently they needed replacing. The poorer the consumer, therefore, the more intense the rate at which they were likely to have to acquire clothing, if they were to stay decent.

The second concerns the asset value of clothing. Because clothes were relatively ephemeral semi-durables, they did not represent a permanent store of value; they were literally a diminishing asset. Buying second-hand represented one way of reducing the money poorer people had to lay out on each item of clothing, but second-hand clothes were already part-worn and did not last as long as new clothes. When Mary Little stole three shawls, a gown, two shifts and a bonnet belonging to an old washerwoman in London in 1811, she sold or pawned some of the stolen items, but the rest she wore out herself in less than six months.[69] The greater the reliance on second-hand clothing, therefore, the greater the frequency at which replacements had to be acquired.

The third concerns clothing as an index of economic circumstances. Clothes aged fairly quickly, but replacing them could be postponed when times were hard. In Huntingdonshire, it was reported in 1796 that some labourers' families had 'not bought clothes the last three years' because of ruinously high food prices which culminated in near-famine conditions in 1795. 'A small shop-keeper in Buckden says, that of stuff for cloaths, he sold none last year.'[70] Clothes were, consequently, a sensitive and very public indicator of fluctuations in prosperity and disparities in wealth. This was true both for individuals and for communities. Clothes did not have to be actually ragged for deterioration to become rapidly apparent. Hence the plebeian autobiographers' fixation with clothes as measures of their material success or failure. Hence, too, the close attention paid to the condition of everyday dress by patrician travellers looking for a way to gauge the standard of living of localities, regions and even whole nations.

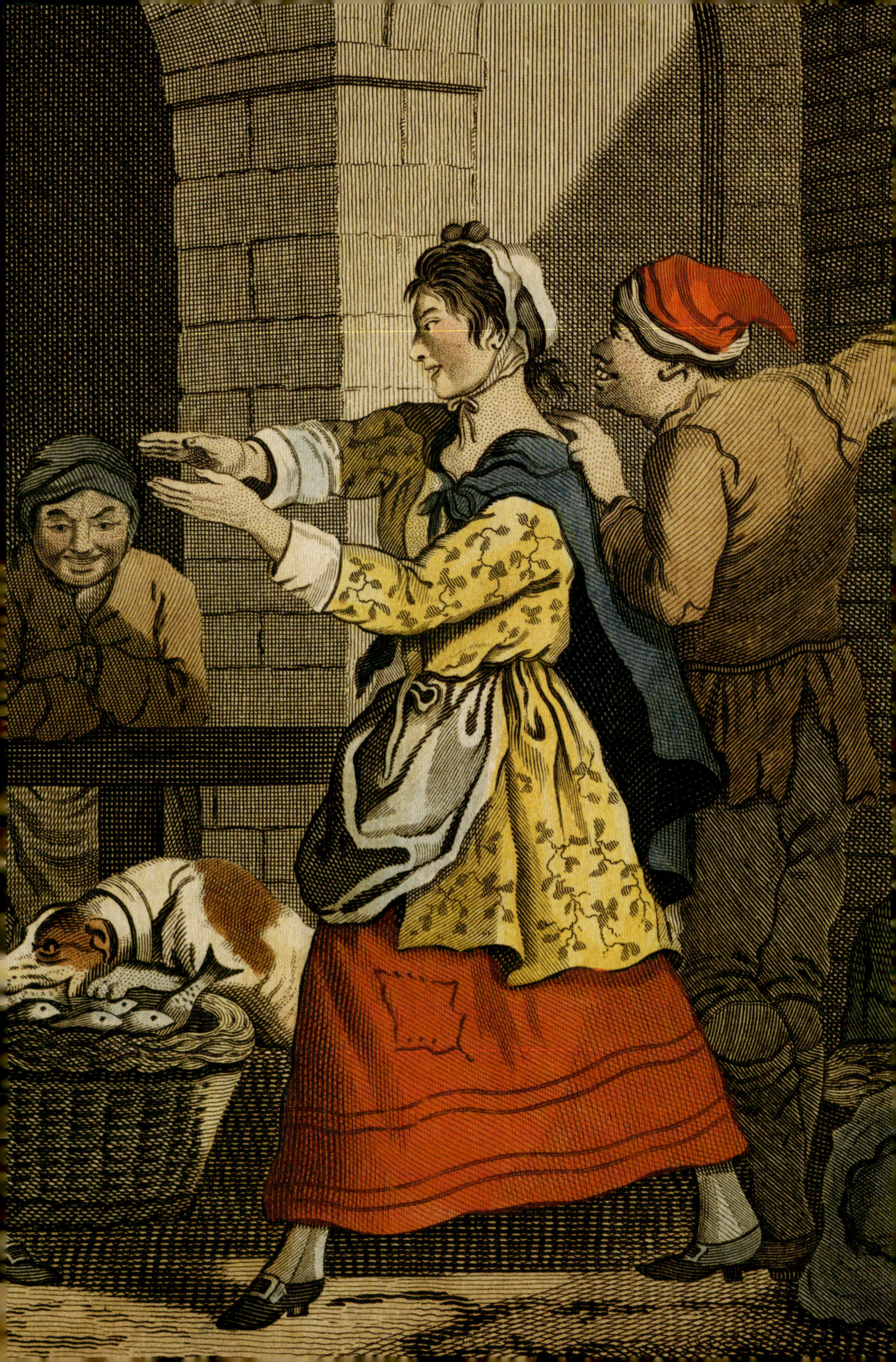

5

Changing Clothes

In September 1756, a newly made copper-coloured camblet gown, valued at six shillings, was stolen from a one-room, upstairs lodging in Gravel Lane, Aldgate, London where Cecilia Hardley lived with her husband, a weaver. 'The gown that is lost is mine', she told the court at the Old Bailey. 'I had not worn it. I hung it upon a line, intending to throw this away that I have on, being a very bad one.'[1] Those who possessed few clothes had little choice but to acquire replacements with some regularity. Replacing old, worn-out clothing could be postponed, but not indefinitely. Renewal was, therefore, an inescapable necessity, but what were its consequences? Did it simply result in more of the same, or did the need to acquire new clothes provide an opportunity to embrace change? And insofar as plebeian consumers did embrace change, what did it comprise? Was it a matter of new kinds of fabrics, or new kinds of garments, or new styles? Did plebeian sartorial innovation slavishly follow changes in the clothes worn by wealthier men and women? Eighteenth-century elite commentators made much of the power of emulation to transform the behaviour of ordinary people. Historians have gone further, identifying 'the mill girl who wanted to dress like a duchess' as a driving force propelling the Industrial Revolution.[2] Was there any connection, even of the most tenuous kind, between plebeian novelties and the shifts in high fashion paraded in the remote, exalted spheres of the royal court and the *beau monde*?

These questions can be addressed using the sources employed in Chapter 2 to examine plebeian clothing in different parts of the country in the 1780s – provincial newspaper advertisements for runaways and the records of criminal trials for theft in London and Yorkshire. The answers they provide remain, of necessity, incomplete, as a result of their shortcomings as sources (see Appendix 1). It is only for the years from the 1730s to the 1790s that we can combine the Yorkshire and London trial records and the Yorkshire and Midlands runaway advertisements to map broad changes in the dress of the people. Even in combination, these sources cannot provide a statistically balanced sample of continuities and changes in the clothing worn by the poorer part of the English population as a whole, or a decade-by-decade tabulation of changes in

35 *(facing page)* John Collet, *The Female Orators* (detail of fig. 36), 1768, coloured engraving, Lewis Walpole Library, Farmington, Conn., 768.11.20.1. Over her patched red petticoat, the female street seller is shown wearing a short bedgown with a sprigged pattern on a cream or yellow ground, probably intended to suggest a printed linen or cotton.

the numbers of clothes owned. Nevertheless, they do offer an account of change in the types, the materials and sometimes the styles of the principal items of clothing worn by significant sections of the plebeian population. They enable us to address the question of how much access ordinary people enjoyed to novelty and fashion, which has dominated debate about everyday clothing among historians.

In the case of the runaway advertisements, which date predominantly from after 1740, changes across the last sixty years of the eighteenth century are best captured by comparing the periods before and after 1770 and focusing on items of clothing that appear in substantial numbers. Working men and tradesmen accounted for the majority of those advertised, so it is their sartorial experience that predominates. Most of the significant changes in garments and fabrics can be observed in both the Yorkshire and the Midlands advertisements, suggesting that the dominant trends affected different parts of provincial England in broadly the same way.

Four garments display especially striking changes in numbers: wigs, frock coats, smock frocks and jackets (tables 9 and 10). Wigs appear frequently in descriptions of runaway men in the middle years of the century, but disappear shortly after 1770 in both the Midlands and the north. Before 1770, nearly a quarter of runaways in the Midlands whose hair-covering was described wore wigs and in Yorkshire nearly a third (table 11). The Swedish traveller, Pehr Kalm, may have exaggerated when he insisted that almost all the labouring men he saw in the Hertfordshire countryside in 1748 sported wigs, but the advertisements confirm that it was common enough at that time for working men to wear them.[3] Runaways who wore wigs included labourers, journeymen, weavers and small tradesmen, but they tended to be rather older than average and, in Yorkshire, there were no apprentices among them. After 1770, the number of runaways wearing wigs is tiny (less than 5 percent) and by the end of the 1780s wigs had entirely disappeared from the advertisements. Two aspects of this chronology are striking. First, during the middle years of the eighteenth century large numbers of plebeian men were able to acquire wigs and evidently considered them a sufficiently important element in their attire to wear them when they absconded. Second, there followed a rapid disappearance of wigs among this section of the male population after 1770. Wearing wigs died out later among elite men, despite a brief fashion for wearing natural hair in the 1760s, with its final eclipse coming only in the 1790s.[4] The discrepancy shows that, at the very least, changes in plebeian sartorial taste could enjoy a marked degree of autonomy from elite taste. It also raises the possibility that this was a case of elite fashion following plebeian fashion.

A similar, though less spectacular decline in numbers can be observed for men's frocks, which were much more frequently mentioned in the Midlands than Yorkshire. These were not the frock smocks increasingly worn as working outer garments by agricultural labourers in the Midlands and the south of England in the late eighteenth century, already discussed in Chapter 2 and prominent in the Midlands advertisements after 1770. Most smock frocks were made from linen and lacked buttons, because they did not open at the front, but over two-thirds of the garments described simply as frocks in the advertisements for which the materials are given were made from fustian or thickset, heavy mixed cotton and linen fabrics, and they often had buttons. They appear to have been a kind of frock coat, but they differed from the frock coats worn by elite men, which were usually made from woollen cloth and resembled ordinary coats, though looser (at least earlier in the century) and with a collar. Interestingly, cases mentioning fustian frocks at the Old Bailey show a similar decline in numbers to the advertisements. The fustian frocks in London were sometimes stolen from servants and others involved in work with horses, although this association does not emerge in the runaway advertisements. Precisely why the fustian frock declined is not clear, but its decline emphasises that although cotton enjoyed huge success as a clothing fabric during the eighteenth century, not all garments made from cottons increased their share of the plebeian market.[5]

The opposite chronological trajectory characterised men's jackets, although they are mentioned in the advertisements far less frequently than wigs or frocks. Before 1770 they hardly appear at all, but they become more common thereafter. Most of those identified by material were made from woollen fabrics, but a few were fustian or thickset. The newspapers from which the advertisements are drawn were printed in inland towns, so seamen account for very few of the runaways wearing jackets. Indeed, among those wearing jackets in the advertisements, deserters from the army were much more prominent than sailors, because army uniforms began to include jackets after about 1770. But jackets were also increasingly worn by civilians, especially apprentices and working men, although they never threatened the overwhelming supremacy of the coat as their normal outer wear (fig. 94). At this period the jacket enjoyed no particular currency in elite fashion, so what we are observing is the adoption of an item that originated as seamen's dress by a much wider range of plebeian men, probably as a working garment. Moreover, from the mid-1780s, another element of seamen's clothing – trousers – also begins to appear in the Yorkshire advertisements, worn by landsmen aged in their twenties, although the numbers remain very small, amounting to just six. In borrowing trousers from nautical dress, these plebeian men were prefiguring a move from breeches to trousers that would transform elite men's fashion only after the turn of the nineteenth century.

If our concern is changes in the kinds of garments worn, the plebeian male wardrobe described in the runaway advertisements exhibited some areas of dynamism, often independent of elite fashion trends, or even in advance of them. Nevertheless, it is continuity that is most striking, hardly surprising in view of the stability that prevailed from the end of the seventeenth century to the start of the nineteenth in the basic elements comprising the male wardrobe. From the earliest Midlands advertisements in the 1710s right through to the runaways described in the newspapers of the 1790s, the basic eighteenth-century male combination of coat, waistcoat and breeches plus stockings, shoes and hat reigned supreme, as it did at more elevated levels in the social hierarchy. Among both main garments and accessories, it is in materials and styles that we discover broader change, although we should beware of exaggerating it.

Among main garments, the materials used for waistcoats and breeches changed more than those used for coats. Before 1770, waistcoats were predominantly made from a variety of woollen fabrics, especially woollen cloth and flannels. In the Midlands at this earlier period less than a quarter were made from linens or cottons (and most of those were linens), and fewer still in Yorkshire. After 1770, a third were made from linens or cottons in the Midlands, and 40 percent in Yorkshire, with cotton fabrics like velveret far outnumbering linens. The trend away from woollens and linens towards cottons is unmistakable, but not overwhelming. Woollen fabrics remained the predominant materials used for waistcoats even in the 1790s, and included woollen cloths that had not appeared earlier, such as kerseymere (cassimere, patented in 1766), beaver, and Bath coating. The same pattern can be observed in breeches. Before 1770 leather was the principal material, accounting for 83 percent of breeches in the Midlands advertisements and 77 percent in Yorkshire. Most of the rest were made from woollen fabrics. After 1770, leather still predominated, but now accounted for only 74 percent of breeches in the Midlands and 54 percent in Yorkshire.[6] It was cotton fabrics, such as corduroy, velveret, fustian and thickset, that comprised most of the remainder. As with waistcoats, the preference for cottons was stronger in Yorkshire than in the Midlands. But this shift towards cottons is not exhibited in the coats described in the runaway advertisements, which in both the Midlands and Yorkshire continued after 1770 to be made overwhelmingly from woollen fabrics, especially plain woollen cloth.

The accessories worn by the runaways display a similar combination of continuity and change. The impact of cotton was surprisingly muted. The rise of British cotton manufacturing had some affect on the stockings worn by runaways after 1770, but it was a limited one. Previously, their stockings were predominantly worsted, with a few linen, and ranged in colour from white, via grey, blue and brown, to black. After 1770 cotton stockings, all white, began to be worn, but they accounted for less than 15 percent of the stockings described, which remained overwhelmingly worsted. Cotton failed to make even this limited impact on the handkerchiefs worn round the necks of runaways, which were virtually all described as silk before and after 1770. The buckles which fastened and ornamented the runaways' shoes, and sometimes their knee breeches, were much more obviously responsive to recent British innovation in manufacturing, benefiting from the invention in 1742 of Sheffield plate, a fusion of silver and copper that was almost indistinguishable from pure silver. None of the buckles worn by runaways before 1760 was silver plated by this process, and only a handful in the 1760s. During this earlier period their buckles were made chiefly from base metals like copper, brass and iron, with a couple identified as pure silver. After 1770, by contrast, in both Yorkshire and the Midlands, more than two-thirds of the buckles worn by runaways were silver-plated. Hats in the runaway advertisement are described not by materials but by style, and then very rarely before 1750. Even in the 1750s, however, cocked hats are conspicuous by their rarity, with hats described as round, slouched or flapped predominant in both Yorkshire and the Midlands (figs 36, 94). Indeed, the hat worn by a baker who eloped from his master at Evesham in Worcestershire in 1766

36 John Collet, *The Female Orators*, 1768, coloured engraving, Lewis Walpole Library, Farmington, Conn., 768.11.20.1. One of the chairmen is portrayed wearing a cocked hat with its brim turned up, while the fiddler on the right is shown in a round hat with a brim that flaps in front.

was described as 'flapped before', exactly the style the buckle-maker James Gee identified as 'the custom of place' when he arrived in the West Midlands from Dublin in the 1760s and found so uncongenial.[7] Round hats began to enjoy wide currency in elite circles only gradually from the 1770s, suggesting this was another case of elite fashion aping plebeian practice.[8]

If we turn from the clothes described in the runaway advertisements to those stolen from plebeian men in London and Yorkshire across parts of the same period, a broadly similar pattern of change emerges, although the numbers involved are smaller. Too few frocks, smock frocks or wigs appear in the indictments to establish any pattern of change, but, as in the advertisements, it is only towards the end of the eighteenth century, in the 1780s, that jackets and trousers owned by landsmen appear, and then only in very small numbers. Otherwise the types of main garments owned by plebeian men display continuity, consisting almost entirely of the basic eighteenth-century male combination of coat, waistcoat and breeches, plus the shirts that rarely appear in the advertisements because they were less distinctive and visible.

Materials in the criminal indictments exhibit a similar combination of continuity and change to that revealed in the advertisements. Coats and shirts hardly changed at all. Coats continued to be made predominantly from woollen cloth across the period.[9] Shirts were made exclusively from linen throughout. Breeches and waistcoats, by contrast, changed a good deal. As in the advertisements, they displayed a marked, though not overwhelming trend towards cotton materials. In the 1730s and 1750s, breeches were made either from leather or from woollens, with none made from cottons. By the 1780s, however, nearly half the breeches stolen were made from cotton materials, with the rest leather or woollens, although in London there were fewer breeches made from leather and, in addition, a small number made from silks – velvet and satin. Waistcoats were predominantly made from woollens in the earlier period, although a Londoner who dealt in pigeons had a laced silk waistcoat in 1756, while in the same decade two striped cotton waistcoats and one of striped linsey-woolsey were stolen in Yorkshire. By the 1780s, in both London and Yorkshire, waistcoats made from cottons slightly outnumbered those made from woollens, and in London a small number were made from silks. The fact that in London a working man such as a labourer in the East India Company's warehouse might occasionally own a silk waistcoat hints at a higher standard of plebeian dress in the capital.[10]

Unlike the advertisements, which mainly deal with men, the criminal records allow us to identify changes in the clothes worn by plebeian women. As with the men, continuity is the most striking feature of the elements that constituted their wardrobe. From the 1730s to the 1780s, there is hardly any deviation from the basic eighteenth-century female combination of shift, gown, petticoat, and, rather less frequently, cloak or hood.[11] The only exception is the bedgown, which does not appear among the clothing stolen in the 1730s and 1750s, but is present in small numbers by the 1780s. There were four bedgowns among the Yorkshire stolen clothes in the 1780s and six in London in 1785. Seven were cotton, three were linen, and their average valuation in the indictments was less than a third of that for full-length gowns made from cotton and linen at the same period.

It is in the materials employed to make these main garments that we discover change, though not uniformly so. The materials used for gowns and petticoats changed significantly, while those used for shifts and cloaks did not change at all. Shifts, like men's shirts, were made exclusively of linen throughout. Cloaks and hoods were made either from woollen cloth, usually red, or silk, usually black, with no discernible change across the period. The materials used to make gowns and petticoats, on the other hand, changed in ways that parallel men's breeches and waistcoats. Like them, petticoats displayed a trend away from woollens towards cottons, albeit a muted one. All the stolen petticoats in the 1730s and 1750s, in both Yorkshire and London, were made from woollen materials, apart from London, where one was made from silk and one from dimity, which at that date could have been either cotton or linen. By the 1780s, the small number of petticoats stolen in Yorkshire were still all made from woollens apart from one in linen, but in London in 1785 there were seven petticoats made from cotton materials, six from woollens, five from silks and two from linen. The persistence into the 1780s of woollen fabrics such as flannel for petticoats is explained by their role in keeping their wearers warm, as is the fact that a number of those in lighter materials were identified as quilted.

Decoration and colour were described in the indictments more often for gowns than for petticoats. It is not surprising, therefore, to find that gowns were more likely than petticoats to be made from lighter cotton or linen materials that could be printed. This was already the case in the middle years of the eighteenth century. In the 1730s and 1750s, in both Yorkshire and London, slightly more than half the stolen gowns were made from woollen materials, especially stuff and camblet, but cottons and more particularly linens made up most of the rest. Together linens and cottons accounted for a third of the stolen gowns identified by material in London in 1756, and well over a third in Yorkshire in the 1730s and 1750s. This proportion is significantly higher than the equivalent for men's breeches or waistcoats at the same period. Indeed, it is the highest proportion of linens and cottons among any of the stolen outer garments at this earlier period, female or male. There was only one silk gown stolen from a plebeian owner, and that was in Yorkshire. The high proportion of linens and cottons among gowns at this early date is confirmed by the provincial newspaper runaway advertisements. Gowns were the item described most frequently among the clothes worn by the small number of women who were advertised. Cottons and especially linens accounted together for nearly a third of the gowns whose fabric was itemised in the advertisements before 1770. This advertisement evidence demonstrates that the prominence of colourful, patterned cottons and linens among the stolen gowns during the middle years of the eighteenth century is not the result of any tendency in the criminal records to over-represent best gowns that were more valuable, worn infrequently, and stolen while stored (figs 35, 37). By the 1780s, cottons had triumphed as the materials for gowns. They had overtaken linens, while woollens were almost entirely eclipsed. In London in 1785, the sample of gowns stolen from plebeian women does not include a single example made from a woollen material. Cottons accounted for nearly two-thirds of the stolen gowns, silks for a quarter, and linens for the rest. In Yorkshire in the 1780s the same pattern can be observed, although it was less extreme. Cottons accounted for nearly half the stolen gowns, linens for a quarter, and silks and woollens for the rest, with silks outnumbering woollens.[12]

A number of clothing accessories in the trial records show the same marked trend towards cotton materials between the 1750s and the 1780s that we have observed among main garments. The trend towards cottons is especially marked for neckwear and stockings.[13] Cottons accounted for less than a fifth of the stolen handkerchiefs and other neckwear in the 1730s and 1750s in both Yorkshire and London, with linens predominant. By the 1780s cottons accounted for more than a third, with muslins prominent. In London, fashionable muslin shawls were stolen from a working coachmaker and a tailor. The trend towards cottons can also be observed in stockings. In the London trial records, worsted stockings outnumbered cotton by six to one in 1756, a ratio that

16

Lambs-Conduit fields
~~Hatton Garden~~, Nov. 15 - 1745 at 7

a Female Child about 3 Weeks old

Cloathing of the Child

Cap Holl'd Edged w. Cambr.k a Narrow pink
Biggin Edged
Forehead-Cloth Edged
Head-Cloth Cam
Long-Stay Cam

Hester Mathews   220

was almost reversed by 1785, with cotton outnumbering worsted by four to one. In Yorkshire too, cotton made inroads among stockings, but they were less spectacular. No stockings made from cotton appeared in the indictments from the 1730s and 1750s; by the 1780s they accounted for nearly a quarter of those stolen. Whether the different take-up of the more expensive cotton stockings in Yorkshire and London reflected differences in plebeian affluence or taste remains unclear. The evidence of buckles in the indictments suggests differences in affluence may have played a part. The Yorkshire indictments, like the provincial newspaper advertisements, show a shift from expensive pure silver buckles in the 1730s and 1750s to those made from cheaper silver plate by the 1780s, whereas in London silver buckles continued to outnumber those made from silver plate in the 1780s. Stolen watches hint at a similar differences in plebeian spending power between Yorkshire and London, at least earlier in the century. In London, the number of watches stolen from plebeian owners in 1756 was hardly any less, relative to the overall number of plebeian clothing cases, than in 1785. In Yorkshire, however, there were far fewer cases involving watches stolen from plebeian owners in the 1730s and 1750s than there were to be by the 1780s.

Change in the materials from which accessories were made was not universal. Stolen aprons, for example, continued to be overwhelmingly made from linen in the 1780s, just as they had been in the 1730s and 1750s. Moreover, the information provided by the indictments is sometimes inadequate to identify either continuity or change; materials and styles are so rarely described for stolen hats and shoes that it is impossible to judge. In the 1730s and 1750s, moreover, too few items of clothing in the sample of indictments are valued to assess whether plebeian clothes were more or less costly by the 1780s.

Nevertheless, the evidence of the indictments and the advertisements is, in combination, sufficiently robust to identify a number of important trends in plebeian clothing during the second two-thirds of the eighteenth century. The clothes worn by plebeian men and women in the eighteenth century were neither narrowly functional nor resistant to fashion. They displayed considerable dynamism, often following elite fashion, but occasionally in advance of it, perhaps even leading it. The fundamental elements of plebeian dress, both male and female, remained broadly the same up to 1800, but this was equally true higher up the social scale. Most of these fundamental elements were common to plebeian and elite wardrobes, although some distinctive features of elite dress, such as the swords often worn by wealthy men in the early decades of the century, were entirely absent among plebeian men and women.[14] Others, like watches, appeared only belatedly, at least outside London. Moreover, the minute distinctions characteristic of elite dress, between full dress and undress, for example, or between sack and fitted gown, are missing from the sources employed here. Insofar as

37 *(facing page)* 'Blue and white strip'd cotton turn'd up with purple and white linen,' 1745, woven cotton striped in blue and linen printed in blue, made up into a baby's sleeve, accompanied by a pink silk ribbon, London Metropolitan Archives, A/FH/A/9/1/3, Foundling no. 220. Colourful cotton and linen fabrics of these kinds were already becoming popular in the 1740s for ordinary women's gowns.

38 Attributed to Charles Jervas, *Catherine Douglas, Duchess of Queensberry, as a Milkmaid*, 1725–30, oil on canvas, National Portrait Gallery, London, 283. Here the duchess is portrayed in a fashionably pastoral mode as a milkmaid, dressed in an apron with her hand on a milk pail, while a cow is milked in the fields behind her. It was about the time this portrait of the duchess was painted that Beau Nash obliged her to remove her apron at the Bath assembly.

these sources allow us to judge styles of clothing, plebeian men and women appear to have worn highly simplified versions of elite styles, closest in form to the clothes worn by their social superiors when in the country or at home as morning wear. In this sense, plebeian dress followed elite fashion. It should be remembered, however, that during the eighteenth century informal modes of dressing associated with domestic and rural life were constantly gaining ground in fashionable metropolitan circles, offering an opportunity for plebeian practice to influence elite fashion.[15] Some new developments in plebeian dress, like the agricultural labourer's smock frock, were destined to remain outside the fashionable mainstream, but others, such as the round hat or leaving off wigs, pre-dated equivalent changes in high fashion. The chronology suggests these were instances where high fashion, in particular male high fashion, followed plebeian modes, rather than vice versa. Not that female high fashion was immune to this tendency. The apron, in origin an item of plebeian women's working dress, established itself as an item of fashionable elite dress in the first half of the eighteenth century. Richard 'Beau' Nash famously obliged the Duchess of Queensberry to remove her apron when attending a ball at the Bath assembly in 1721, emphasising its plebeian associations by 'observing that none but abigails appeared in white aprons', but by 1769 even Queen Charlotte was wearing a white apron for undress (fig. 38).[16]

Clothing materials, too, displayed a combination of marked continuities and radical changes, in ways that often shadowed trends in high fashion, although, of course, usually in cheaper varieties of the same material. The most striking change in plebeian wardrobes was the shift away from woollen fabrics towards lighter linens and especially cottons for a variety of male and female outer garments, in particular women's gowns and petticoats, and men's waistcoats and breeches, although in each case to different degrees. Elite dress saw a parallel shift towards linens and cottons, but it had a different trajectory, composed partly of a move away from woollens but largely of a move away from expensive silks. Silk main garments were never very widespread in plebeian circles and, although silk was much more common for plebeian accessories like neckwear, cotton made its mark here too. Continuity characterised the use of linens for the shirts and shifts of rich and poor alike, while plebeian men remained resolutely attached to sturdy woollen cloth for coatings. Plebeian men's coats reveal no evidence of the trend among elite men to forgo silk coatings for woollens, another instance of elite fashion increasingly conforming to plebeian practice. The flow of fashionable ideas was not all one way. For all the allure of modes originating among the metropolitan *beau monde*, the virility and unaffected naturalness associated with plebeian dress exercised a powerful hold of their own.

39 Pair-cased verge watch, numbered 9263, 1763, silver, steel, brass and enamel, Museum of London, 52.23/6. The watch has a silver inner case marked 'T.D' and a silver outer case with a plain back. It is an unremarkable, London-made, silver watch.

6
Fashioning Time: Watches

In 1747, William Hutton, then a 24-year-old framework knitter at Nottingham, bought a silver watch for 35 shillings. 'It had been the pride of my life, ever since pride commenced, to wear a watch', he later remembered. The watch turned out badly. 'It went ill. I kept it four years, then gave *that* and a guinea for another, which went as ill. I afterwards exchanged this for a brass one, which, going no better, I sold it for five shillings, and, to close the watch farce, gave the five shillings away and went without for thirty years.'[1] The unhappy story of Hutton's watches has three noteworthy features. First, for Hutton, who, as we have already seen, was a young working man with sartorial aspirations, it was *wearing* a watch that was the focus of pride and longing. Owning a watch was in large part about display. Second, he was able to invest lavishly in acquiring two expensive silver watches in the course of four years, but also to realise some of their value when he disposed of them. Third, the watches he bought were unreliable disappointments as timepieces, although it was many years before frustration at their functional shortcomings finally conquered his desire to make a show.

Hutton's ambition to acquire a watch was not an unusual one among working men in provincial England, but it was one that during the first half of the eighteenth century few succeeded in achieving.[2] In the provinces, cases of watch theft were almost always tried at the Assizes, the criminal court which dealt with more serious offences. There are 117 cases of watch theft among the surviving depositions from the Assizes for Yorkshire, Northumberland, Cumberland and Westmorland between 1640 and 1800 (table 12).[3] Only seven of them date from before 1750, and only one of those involved a watch stolen from someone identified as a working man – a sailor whose watch was stolen in 1749. The owners of the rest, when identified, were gentlemen. After 1770, by contrast, more than half the owners of the far greater number of stolen watches in the depositions were plebeian men, or very occasionally plebeian women.

This pattern was not confined to the north of England. In Worcestershire and Oxfordshire too, prosecutions for watch theft were infrequent in the first half of the century, only to become much more common after 1750, although it is rarely possible to identify the occupations of their owners.[4] In London, by contrast, watch thefts were already numerous earlier in the century, with the proportion of Old Bailey trials involving watches rising continuously each decade from the 1700s to the 1770s, suggesting that watch ownership was increasing rapidly (table 13). In the decade 1700–9 the ratio of watch trials to the total number of trials was 1 in 37; by 1770–9 it was 1 in 9. In other words, by the 1770s more than a tenth of the cases tried at the Old Bailey involved the theft of a watch. At the end of the seventeenth century and the start of the eighteenth, there were almost as many cases at the Old Bailey involving gold watches as silver watches, suggesting that at this period they were owned predominantly by the very wealthy. Plebeian ownership of gold watches was certainly considered unusual. In 1745, a London pawnbroker told a man he understood to be a nobleman's servant:'I think it is very odd your ambition should induce you to wear a gold watch.'[5] After the first decade of the century the proportion of gold watches among Old Bailey cases fell progressively. In 1756 plebeian owners, overwhelmingly men, accounted for a small majority of the non-watchmaker victims whose occupations are described for the Old Bailey cases of watch theft originating in Middlesex. They remained a small majority in 1785. The evidence of the criminal records suggests, therefore, that watches became widespread first in London and were adopted earlier there by plebeian men. Only later, in the second half of the eighteenth century, did watches become widespread among plebeian men in provincial England.[6]

Watches long pre-dated the eighteenth century, but they achieved reasonable accuracy as timekeepers with improvements introduced during the second half of the seventeenth century, especially the balance spring.[7] The evidence of the criminal records shows the spread of watches among plebeian men in London to have taken place in the half-century that followed these improvements, but it took longer in the provinces. The reasons for this pattern of delayed trickle-down from the metropolis to the provinces remain unclear. It may reflect greater purchasing power among sections of the common people of the capital. Alternatively it may reflect these consumers' proximity to the watchmaking workshops of London, where the British industry's final assembly and finishing stages were concentrated. Well over two-thirds of the plebeian watches in the northern depositions which were identified by place of manufacture had the names of London makers. The same was true of the watches entered in the pledge book kept for 18 months in 1777 and 1778 by George Fettes, a York pawnbroker serving mainly plebeian clients.[8] If proximity to the metropolitan centres of the watch trade was crucial to the precocious take-up of its products among London's plebeian consumers, the timing of their diffusion in provincial England would suggest that plebeian fashions originating in the capital spread only slowly elsewhere. But watches were, of course, no ordinary fashion. They were consistently the most valuable single item of wearing apparel stolen from plebeian victims in the eighteenth century. Why did such an expensive item come to be widely owned among the section of the population least able to afford it?

Watches stolen from plebeian owners were more valuable than their other most expensive clothing – their coats and waistcoats, or their cloaks and gowns – in large part because the cases which housed the watch mechanisms were made overwhelmingly from silver. William Hutton, exasperated at the unreliability of his silver watches, may have been driven to make do with a cheap brass-cased watch before giving up watches altogether, but few plebeian men were prepared to follow his example. Out of the 47 watches stolen from plebeian owners and identified by material in the northern Assize depositions, 42 had silver cases, with an average value of 44 shillings in the corresponding indictments. A few plebeian owners did own watches with cheaper cases, all Pinchbeck, an alloy of copper and zinc that looked like gold. They were valued on average at 18 shillings, but only three of them appear in the depositions. In London too, it was watches with valuable silver cases that predominated among plebeian victims of watch theft. One nobleman's servant in London in 1785 even had a gold-cased watch valued at 80 shillings. It is difficult, however, to find more than a handful of prosecutions involving watches with brass cases anywhere in the printed Old Bailey proceedings and there are relatively few involving watch cases made from other base metals. The same pattern emerges in the pledge book kept by George Fettes, the York pawnbroker. Of 176 entries for watches taken in pawn that name the material from which the cases were made, 168 were silver, four were gold and four were Pinchbeck.[9]

The records of pawnbrokers and of prosecutions for theft have a tendency to over-represent valuable items that were more attractive to pawn or to steal. Nevertheless, there were thousands of prosecutions for thefts of items of clothing worth considerably less than William Hutton's five-shilling brass watch. If the absence of brass watches and the predominance of silver in the northern Assize depositions misrepresents the mix of case materials among watches owned by the plebeian population at large, it is unlikely that it does so to any great degree. In the main, the watches increasingly acquired by plebeian owners in the eighteenth century had cases made from costly silver, despite the availability of cheaper alternatives. And silver watches were expensive. The indictment valuations, at 44 shillings on average, are second-hand values, broadly consistent with the prices quoted by the handful of victims at the Old Bailey who stated how much second-hand watches had actually cost. Purchasers of new silver watches paid much more, among Old Bailey victims well over 70 shillings, while members of clock and watch clubs in rural Leicestershire at the very beginning of the nineteenth century paid between 84 and 95 shillings for their new watches.[10] At 35 shillings, the silver watch which William Hutton was so proud to acquire in 1747 was probably a second-hand one. Moreover, the expense of a watch did not end with its purchase. As Hutton discovered, watches did not necessarily work very well. From time to time they needed professional cleaning and oiling, and parts like springs wore out and had to be replaced.[11] They also depreciated in value. Asked how much his watch was worth, a London biscuit baker declared in 1780: 'it cost me three guineas and an half; it is now worth two guineas'.[12]

Analysis of the proliferation of timepieces, including watches, in this period has revolved around Edward Thompson's argument that changes in people's inward notation of time were essential to the transformation in work disciplines associated with the coming of the factory.[13] Natural time associated with task-orientated labour in field or workshop was replaced, Thompson argues, by the tyranny of the clock, associated with time-orientated labour at the machine. Widespread ownership of clocks and watches is cited as evidence of this profound cultural shift, as well as one of its driving forces. For Thompson, 'a general diffusion of clocks and watches is occurring (as one would expect) at the exact moment that the industrial revolution demanded a greater synchronisation of labour'.[14] The shortcomings of Thompson's position have been addressed most powerfully by Paul Glennie and Nigel Thrift.[15] Thompson fails to appreciate just how widely clocks were available in both public and domestic settings well before the Industrial Revolution, indeed well before the eighteenth century. In addition, he ignores the possibility that awareness of clock time did not necessarily require the presence of clocks. As Glennie and Thrift argue, 'most facets of what we now call clock time had become naturalised well before the industrial revolution, and consequently the imbrication of a sense of clock time in the general population is not an aspect of this process'.[16] Thompson, moreover, assumes that the accuracy offered by a timekeeping technology should correspond to the temporal accuracy required in the lives of those who owned it, failing to recognise that technologies often offer capacities well in excess of what is required by most of their users.

When Thompson deals specifically with watches, especially watches owned by working people, he is more nuanced. As with clocks, he is insistent that their general diffusion did not come before the close of the eighteenth century, a view which is not supported by the evidence presented in this chapter.[17] Nevertheless, Thompson is well aware that timepieces in general, and watches in particular, were prized among working people. 'The small instrument which regulated the new rhythms of industrial life was at the same time one of the more urgent of the new needs which industrial capitalism called forth to energize its advance.'[18] He goes on to offer three reasons to explain why working people acquired watches. First, watches were utilitarian tools for measuring time, evidence that working people had internalised the new time disciplines demanded by industrial capitalism. Second, they were sources of prestige. Third, they were realisable assets, 'the poor man's bank'.[19] If our task is to explain why plebeian men came increasingly to own watches, especially silver-cased watches, earlier in the eighteenth century, are these three reasons convincing?

It was received wisdom that watches were much used by working people to raise money. 'A watch', it was observed in 1817, was 'in general the first article put off in times of distress, and the last put on again when distress is removing.'[20] Eighty years before, in 1734, a woman who lodged in a single room in London had worried about the watch hung up by the chimney being stolen, 'for if I or my Husband should be taken ill, we had nothing else that we could make a little Money of'.[21] The capacity of watches to raise money can be demonstrated from the pledge book of George Fettes, the York pawnbroker. If we list the individual items against which Fettes lent the ten largest sums of money during four weeks across the year 1778, watches accounted for half of them, more than any other type of possession.[22] A silver watch like those on which Fettes was prepared to lend an average of 15 shillings represented a far better store of value than the brass watch an exasperated William Hutton got rid of for five shillings. As we have seen, it was silver-cased watches that predominated among the timepieces Fettes took in as pledges. Nevertheless, the bare fact that silver watches were readily pawned does not, in itself, explain how working people were able to acquire them in the first place, however much it might help us understand why they acquired silver watches in preference to either cheaper watches, or valuable goods of other kinds.

Turning to the relationship between watches and time discipline, even if we agree with Thompson that ownership of a watch might be taken to imply familiarity with clock time, Glennie and Thrift demonstrate that such familiarity was already widespread in the sixteenth and seventeenth centuries. The diffusion of watches in the eighteenth century was not necessary to create such familiarity among working people, nor did their acquisition of such familiarity result immediately in their acquisition of watches. To explore the relationship between watches and time discipline further, we need to establish whether watches actually were used for timekeeping, particularly timekeeping associated with work. One way of addressing that question is to examine the occupations of those who owned watches. More than half the 52 plebeian owners of stolen watches in the northern Assize depositions between 1749 and 1799 were involved in a variety of working trades (table 14), some of them as employees, others working on their own account on a small scale. The largest single group among them was made up of seamen (nine), followed by textile workers (five), and then a diversity of trades from coal miner and gardener to tailor and cordwainer.[23] The other occupational categories among plebeian owners of stolen watches were servant, labourer, husbandman and soldier.

Significantly for Thompson's argument, none of the owners of watches worked in one of the new cotton or worsted spinning mills that proliferated in Yorkshire after 1780, despite the fact that workers in these factories do appear in the criminal records in connection with other kinds of theft.[24] Most of the workers in the early factories were women and children. Only one of the 52 plebeian watch owners was a woman, an unmarried servant. Ownership of goods by wives and daughters is, of course, concealed in eighteenth-century criminal records by the legal rules concerning couverture, but the proportion of women among plebeian owners of stolen watches in the northern depositions is tiny, even by comparison with the proportion of women among owners of stolen clothes.[25] A very low level of female watch ownership is confirmed by the records kept by George Fettes, the York pawnbroker. Out of 197 people who pawned watches with him in 1777 and 1778 there were only 11 women, yet women accounted for more than three-quarters of all the pledges he received. The most valuable items pawned by women consisted principally of gowns, especially more expensive gowns made from cotton and linen, but they did not command anything approaching the sums Fettes lent against men's watches.[26] Although this evidence may simply indicate that plebeian women chose to own combinations of cheaper goods in preference to watches, it is more likely that women could rarely afford to acquire watches and that in plebeian marriages they were treated as belonging to the husband. Limitations on female spending can be observed in the Leicestershire clock and watch clubs, where the sums subscribed by women were much smaller than those subscribed by men, sufficient to save only for sets of silver spoons costing 25 shillings or less, not for watches.[27]

The relatively small numbers of women, labourers and husbandmen among plebeian owners of stolen watches in the northern depositions and the large numbers of seamen and textile workers suggest that ownership of silver watches was greatest among men in the higher-earning manual occupations that were prospering as manufacturing and mining expanded in the north of England in the course of the eighteenth century. Younger men employed in weaving, coal mining and shipping could command substantial wages during periods of full employment, especially towards the end of the century. Wage rates in the north of England began the eighteenth century well below the national average, but by its end were above average, a shift which may account for the late but rapid take-up of watches among higher-earning working men in the north after 1750. Yet it is difficult to imagine that most of these men needed a watch for timekeeping at their work. Sailors toiled at sea to the rhythm of four-hourly watches set by the ship's master, weavers laboured at the loom to the weekly rhythms of the putting-out system, pitmen hewed coal in shifts measured by set output quotas, and even those urban journeymen whose working hours were fixed according to the different amounts of daylight available in summer and winter would have known the time of day by the chimes of their parish church clock.[28]

Very few of the stolen watches that appear in the Assize depositions were taken from their owners as they worked. In part this was because other locations were, perhaps, more propitious for theft, especially night-time bedrooms, busy inn parlours, unsupervised storage chests, lonely highways or the scene of a drunken sexual assignation. Nevertheless, in several cases the depositions make it emphatically clear that watches did not accompany their owners to work. The silver watch belonging to William Brooke, a collier from West Ardsley in Yorkshire, was stolen from his house after he had left for work early on a Friday morning in June 1789. James Groves, servant to Matthew Ridley of Heaton House, near Newcastle, hung up his silver watch on a nail at the foot of his bed in Heaton House on a Thursday night in December 1751. 'He did not take down the said watch but when he was going to bed on Friday night he looked for the said watch in order to wind it up as was his usual custom, but could not find it.' When Ambrose Bell, 'a poor labouring man', lost his silver watch on a Saturday afternoon in February 1776, it was hanging up in the room in his house at Ruswarp, near Whitby where he usually slept. At the time it was stolen, he was 'at work a little from the house' and his wife had left to go to Whitby market, locking the doors. James Stockdale, a sailor in the whale fishery, bought a silver watch only after landing at South Shields in August 1787, having returned from the long and dangerous, but lucrative summer voyage to the David Straits between Greenland and Baffin Island.[29]

There was one group of workers, however, whose work did require accurate timekeeping and whose watches were sometimes stolen at work. These were men who worked in road transport, especially drivers of coaches and carriages. They worked unsupervised and were expected to keep to timetables. Indeed, under the new mail coach system instituted in 1784, the Post Office guards who rode the mail coaches were provided with watches calibrated to London time. They were required to keep a record of arrival and departure times along the journey. The victims of watch theft in the northern Assize depositions included a mail coach driver from Shap on the road from Kendal to Carlisle and a chaise driver employed by an innkeeper at Glenwhelt on the road from Newcastle to Carlisle.[30] In addition, two watches were stolen at inns in Kendal and York from hostlers, the employees responsible for horses and stabling who were also required to be alert to the timing of arrivals and departures.[31]

It appears unlikely, however, that the generality of plebeian watch owners encountered in the northern depositions required their watches for work. The watches hanging from their bedsteads or chimney pieces may have served to wake them for the start of the working day, doing so in a more accurate and more intimate manner than the bell of a distant church clock or a night watchman crying the hour. Perhaps these watches were serving as substitutes for domestic clocks. Nevertheless, watches were first and foremost made to be carried. A majority of those encountered in the northern depositions were stolen while in their owners' pockets. Some were removed from a breeches pocket when their owners were sleeping, others when highway robbers were encountered on the road, but more were stolen when their owners were at leisure, especially in the evenings when drinking. A silver watch with a china face was picked from the pocket of James Hargreaves, a Colne tailor, as he stood near the starting post at Thornton-in-Craven races in September 1765. George Hanson, a collar maker from Aughton in Yorkshire, lost his silver watch from his watch pocket while drinking at the Black Horse in nearby Rotherham late on a Monday night in May 1782. A silver watch with a blue and white striped ribbon, 'fastened to it in order to pull it out by', was stolen from the pocket of James Harrison, servant to a Swaledale yeoman, during a fight at an inn in Richmond, Yorkshire on a weekday evening in August 1774. The next year a silver watch with 'a china face with a steel single linked chain, a brass key, [and] two seals', belonging to William Jennison, a saddletree plater, was taken from his 'watch pocket in his breeches' in a public house in Ripon, Yorkshire, between seven and eight on a Tuesday evening in February.[32]

Relieving a drunken, befuddled victim of his watch may have been especially easy work for a thief and, as a consequence, prosecutions for watch theft may tend to over-represent watches stolen under such circumstances. Nevertheless, the fact remains that watches were stolen far more often from plebeian owners when they were out enjoying their leisure at an inn or the races than when they were at work. These were evidently occasions when it was considered appropriate for watches to be worn and displayed. A watch was a very public item of clothing. Although the watch itself normally lay concealed in a breeches fob pocket, the ribbon or chain used to pull it out was usually worn hanging down below the waistcoat for all to see, often with seals and a watch key attached to it (fig. 40). Like the watch itself, these accoutrements were decorative items. Watch chains, made mostly from bright steel, were attached to 20 of

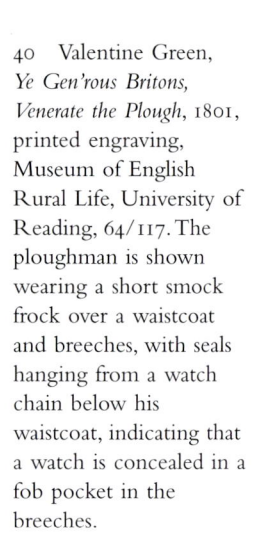

40 Valentine Green, *Ye Gen'rous Britons, Venerate the Plough*, 1801, printed engraving, Museum of English Rural Life, University of Reading, 64/117. The ploughman is shown wearing a short smock frock over a waistcoat and breeches, with seals hanging from a watch chain below his waistcoat, indicating that a watch is concealed in a fob pocket in the breeches.

the stolen watches in the northern depositions. Three more watches were stolen with coloured silk ribbons, like the blue and white striped ribbon taken with James Harrison's watch at Richmond. Fourteen of the chains and ribbons had seals fastened to them when stolen. Most were cheap steel seals, valued at one or two pennies, but a few are described as set in silver or copper, and were probably made from semi-precious stones such as cornelian or crystal.

Only a few of the depositions describe the impressions engraved or stamped on the seals. James Stockdale, returned from his whaling voyage, had a seal with an angel and the foul anchor on one side and a head on the other; another seaman had a seal with a flaming heart. The anchor might have been straightforwardly nautical in its associations, but it could also represent hope, an allegorical meaning common in late eighteenth-century jewellery, just as the flaming heart could represent passion. Nautical imagery was not confined to sailors. William Jennison, the Ripon saddletree plater, had two seals, one of which was 'half brass half steel having the impression of a ship on one side thereof and on the other side a man's head'. His other seal was a steel one 'with an impression of a cock heading a hen'. The Yorkshire servant Elizabeth Rose's

41 Guy Head, *Horatio Nelson, Viscount Nelson*, 1798–9, oil on canvas, National Portrait Gallery, London, 5101. An idealised image of Admiral Nelson, by this date a popular icon of heroic masculinity, at the Battle of the Nile, showing seals hanging from a watch chain below his waistcoat, indicating that he has a watch in a fob pocket.

seal simply had the letter E engraved on it.[33] Initial letters, heads, allegorical devices: these motifs were not confined to seals worn by plebeian owners. They probably bought them ready-made, but exactly the same sorts of devices were found on seals engraved to order for much richer men and women, although plebeian owners did not possess the seals made from precious stones or engraved with coats of arms favoured by the very wealthy.[34]

How often these seals had a practical use for their plebeian owners in sealing letters or documents is unclear. The need to do so cannot have arisen as often as it did for the wealthy, who sustained extensive correspondence and had to authorise legal documents in their management of land and inheritance. Yet only 4 of the 15 plebeian owners of watch seals were unable to sign their names, suggesting seals were not primarily owned by the illiterate as a substitute for a signature. What watch seals and the chains from which they hung undoubtedly did offer plebeian men was an important vehicle for sartorial display, just as they did for the rich, the fashionable and the famous (fig. 41). Chains and seals did not have to be worn hanging out of the fob pocket, but it was normal for them to be displayed in this way (figs 40, 42). When a silver watch

42 *The Sailor and Banker, or The Firm in Danger!* 1799, printed engraving, Lewis Walpole Library, Farmington, Conn., 799.10.28.1. The sailor is shown wearing a short blue jacket over a waistcoat and loose white trousers with two sets of seals hanging from watch chains below his jacket, indicating that two watches are concealed in fob pockets in the trousers, in the same style as Admiral Nelson in figure 41.

with a steel chain and a small silver seal set with a red stone was stolen in 1778 from Benjamin Proctor, a hawker and peddler living at Old Malton in Yorkshire, he followed the thief to Newcastle, over 60 miles away. Suspicion was aroused there when the thief, having had the chain and seal hanging out of his pocket, was seen to 'put the said chain and seal into his pocket and draw the flap of his waistcoat over it'.[35] Watches themselves were decorative items as well as sophisticated pieces of technology, despite usually being concealed when worn. Their compact size, elegant cases in shining silver, reflective watch glasses and enamelled or china dials combined many of the elements of eighteenth-century jewellery (fig. 39).[36] Showing off these features required a performative flourish as the watch was removed from the pocket, adding to the sense that these were objects to be displayed. When a London labourer, James Johnson, first tried on his expensive new suit of clothes in 1789, he 'insisted on having his watch, and a looking glass; says he, I am a fine gentleman'.[37]

Of the three reasons offered by Edward Thompson to explain why working men acquired watches, we should not underestimate their importance as practical tools for measuring time. Nevertheless, for all except a few who worked in road transport, watches were not indispensable necessities when it came to the business of everyday timekeeping. What they did offer those affluent workers who could afford them was reasonably accurate, general-purpose timekeeping in a conveniently portable package. In addition, they were, as Thompson argues, both a quickly realisable store of value and a prestigious form of male jewellery, worn frequently, perhaps especially, when enjoying convivial sociability. The particular importance of display is emphasised by the aesthetics of watch design and the ways watches were personalised by means of cheap, expressive accessories. Silver watches signalled enviable affluence combined with a suitably masculine command of technology, of the kind richer men manifested through purchases of scientific instruments and the like. Not that richer men were immune to the decorative allure of watches. 'A fool cannot withstand the charms of a toy-shop', the Earl of Chesterfield warned his son in 1749, 'snuff boxes, watches, heads of canes, etc. are his destruction'.[38] It is no wonder that for William Hutton, that most sartorially ambitious of young, provincial journeymen, to wear a watch, even a second-hand one, was the pride of his life.

Roller
Bed
Waiscoat *Dimper*
Shirt *Irish trimed*
Clout *rushey*
Pilch
Stockings
Shoes

Marks on

A G

not Christened

43 'Flowered lining', 1759, linen printed in red, blue and black, London Metropolitan Archives, A/FH/A/9/1/143, Foundling no. 12924.

7
Fashion's Favourite? Cottons

Nothing did more to change the way ordinary people dressed in the eighteenth century than the advent of cotton fabrics. During the second half of the century an ever-expanding range of textiles made wholly or partly from cotton challenged the supremacy of woollens, silks, linens and leather as materials for waistcoats and breeches, gowns and petticoats, handkerchiefs and stockings. Cotton was the fibre of industrial revolution. The new factories powered by water or steam that multiplied from the 1770s housed machines invented specifically to process cotton. From their gates poured forth hank upon hank of machine-spun cotton yarn, and later, especially from the 1820s, yard upon yard of machine-woven cotton cloth, at cheaper and cheaper prices. As prices fell, demand expanded. Over the decades between 1750 and 1850, British-manufactured cottons demonstrated a protean capacity to fulfil the terms of Saye's Law, according to which supply creates its own demand.

Recently, however, historians have insisted that cotton's success with English consumers in the eighteenth century was not simply a matter of price. Cotton, in Beverly Lemire's telling phrase, was fashion's favourite. Cotton could be printed, painted or dyed in washable, fast colours. For Lemire, it was this distinctive attribute that made cotton the midwife of popular fashion. When first imported from India towards the end of the seventeenth century, 'cotton textiles appeared to arrive suddenly and to acquire a phenomenal popularity almost overnight, overturning many of the cost restraints that previously had limited popular fashions'. Their vibrant colours and designs offered the middling and lower orders 'a cheap facsimile of the brocades and flowered silks favoured by the aristocracy'. Yet cheap facsimiles were possible, Lemire argues, only because the late seventeenth century witnessed what she sees as a democratisation of western European high fashion, with the rise of more simplified, informal and varied modes of elite dressing that were easier to replicate in alternative fabrics. Cotton was the means of that replication, bringing fashion to the people. By the early eighteenth century, cotton fabrics, sourced in India, had already become ubiquitous in England, 'popular among almost all ranks of the people' and pervading the domestic market for many different kinds of clothing. An outcry from domestic producers of woollens and silks resulted in acts of parliament that prohibited the wearing first, in 1701, of printed and painted calicoes imported from Asia and second, in 1722, of calicoes printed or painted in Britain.[1] Yet the effect of prohibition was merely to interrupt cotton's progress and divert its impact, channelling demand for decorated fabrics towards British manufacturers of printed linens and cotton-linen mixes.[2]

Lemire's attention to the importance of fashion in the rise of cotton fabrics has much to commend it. Particularly compelling is her stress on the appeal to consumers, especially perhaps plebeian consumers, of Indian techniques for patterning cloth with washable, fast colours. The silks woven with complex, colourful patterns for women's gowns at Lyon in France and Spitalfields in London constituted the summit of elite fashion during the late seventeenth century and for much of the eighteenth century. They were expensive and virtually impossible to wash, indeed difficult to clean at all. David MacPherson remarked in 1805, looking back to the gowns worn in the mid-eighteenth century, 'the common use of silk, if it were only to be worn while it retains its lustre, is proper only for ladies of ample fortune'.[3] The cottons painted or printed in India were cheaper but similarly colourful, although lacking the textured effects achieved by some silks. In addition, they could be washed, as could the cottons and linens printed with increasing sophistication in England from the 1670s, using Indian techniques. It is not surprising, therefore, to find that by the 1750s gowns were the garments most likely to be made from cottons and linens among those stolen from plebeian men and women. The gown was a key garment for women's fashion at every social level, the largest and most expensive decorated item in most plebeian women's wardrobes.

The prominence at mid-century of these light, colourful fabrics as materials for plebeian gowns goes some way to confirm cotton's role in bringing fashion to ordinary people. But questions remain about the precise terms of the developing relationship between cotton and plebeian fashion. Did the prominence of these fabrics in the middle of the eighteenth century mark a stage in the onward march of cotton, or did it represent a retreat from higher levels of penetration of the market for gowns prior to the prohibitions on printed cottons in 1701 and 1722? Was it a measure of the specific appeal of cotton as a fabric for gowns, or did it simply indicate the broad appeal of printed textiles, irrespective of whether they were cotton or linen? Did it register a radical shift in the decorative quality of gowns available to ordinary people, or were similar effects possible in other, more familiar fabrics? Did it move plebeian women's fashion closer to that of the elite, as repeated eighteenth-century complaints about emulative excesses might suggest, or did significant distinctions remain?

The evidence of the criminal records challenges the notion that Indian cottons enjoyed sudden popularity among almost all ranks of the people in the decades before the imposition of the legislative prohibitions, at least as far as gown materials are concerned. Huge quantities of Indian cotton textiles of many different kinds were imported into England by the East India Companies in the last three decades of the seventeenth century, but the majority consisted of plain rather than patterned cloths and many of them were destined for re-export.[4] It was asserted repeatedly by those paid to write in opposition to these imports on behalf of domestic woollen and silk manufacturers that Indian cottons were enthusiastically taken up as dress materials by rich and poor alike, threatening the livelihoods of those who made a living from the manufacture of other textiles in England. 'As ill weeds grow apace,' complained John Pollexfen in 1700, 'so these manufactured goods from India met with such a kind reception, that from the greatest gallants to the meanest cook-maids, nothing was thought to fit, to adorn their persons, as the Fabrick from India'.[5] Nevertheless, evidence for widespread ownership of gowns made from Indian painted and printed fabrics before 1700 at any social level is sparse. Out of 285 cases in the Old Bailey Proceedings for the 1670s, 1680s and 1690s involving gowns stolen from owners of all social classes, only two mentioned gowns made from cotton fabrics (table 15). There were only 7 cases mentioning any fabric used for any purpose described as printed or painted. By contrast, at least 62 cases involved gowns made from silk and 40 cases gowns made from various kinds of worsted stuff. If the number of stolen gowns in Indian printed and painted fabrics in the Old Bailey Proceedings was tiny, it was not because Indian cottons appeared infrequently. On the contrary, in the same decades there were 73 mentions of muslins, mainly plain white and used for various head-cloths and neck-cloths, although comprising only a minority of such items. Calicoes and chintzes, many of them probably painted or printed, also appeared, though less frequently. They were used for a variety of items of clothing, including aprons, hoods, handkerchiefs, petticoats, shirts and children's frocks, but especially for furnishings, in particular curtains, quilts and pillowcases.[6]

Evidently Indian cottons, especially muslins, made inroads during the late decades of the seventeenth century in the English markets for clothing accessories and furnishings.[7] These markets were already experiencing a tide of innovation in linens, silks and worsteds, but Indian cottons were an arresting new departure, especially those that were decorated by means of painting or printing. Nevertheless, the criminal records before 1700 show little evidence of English or European-made light fabrics being dramatically pushed aside by Indian-made decorated cottons at any level in the market for gowns, perhaps the key market for decorated main garments. Where Indian fabrics undoubtedly did make an impact was in igniting an explosion of economic pamphleteering, lavishly funded by rival mercantile interests. The calico craze of the late seventeenth century emerges less as a wholesale transformation in consumers' choices, engineered by a flood of cheap, colourful Asian imports, than as a political phenomenon generated by the mutual suspicion of a number of wealthy trading and manufacturing interests, each accustomed to support from the state and each struggling to secure it for its own advantage.

At the Old Bailey, it is only in the two decades after 1700, between the first and the second prohibition Acts, that we begin to find marked increases in the number of gowns made from cotton and increasing numbers of printed fabrics, both cotton and linen. The surviving Old Bailey Proceedings for the 1700s and 1710s include less cases involving stolen gowns of any kind than those for the three previous decades. Nevertheless, 41 of them included gowns made from cotton, far more than appeared before 1700. Imports of Indian patterned cottons were prohibited from 1701, so the fabric for whatever proportion of these stolen gowns was patterned had either been smuggled, or printed in Britain. Most likely, the decorated cotton gowns stolen in these years came to their owners from a combination of these two sources. In addition, three linen gowns appear, suggesting that as the plain Indian cottons initially used for printing in Britain were subjected to increased taxation, printers began to employ linens as an alternative, sourced in continental Europe or the British Isles.[8] Although we should not assume that all the stolen gowns described as cotton or linen were printed, it is striking that the same chronology can be observed in Old Bailey cases involving thefts of printed fabrics, suggesting a common trajectory (table 16).

Expansion in the numbers of printed fabrics and garments in these years is precisely what the opponents of the East India interest were already complaining of in 1702, shortly after the first prohibition Act. 'Though it was hoped that this prohibition would have discouraged the consumption of those goods, we find that the allowing calicoes unstained to be brought in, has occasioned such an increase of the printing and staining calicoes here, and the printers and painters have brought that art to such perfection, that it is more prejudicial to us than it was before the passing of that Act.'[9] By the early years of the eighteenth century the East India Company too was complaining that printing could be done in England at half the price charged for Indian goods and in better colours and patterns.[10]

All this suggests that what principally appealed to English consumers about these fabrics was not Indian design, or even cotton as a material, but the Indian technique of colour-fast printing on light fabrics. Already in the second half of the seventeenth century, the design of Indian chintzes for the English market was largely dictated from London.[11] Once English printers had mastered some of the Indian techniques for applying colour, keeping costs down by the use of wood-block printing rather than hand painting, they were able to produce printed fabrics at increasingly keen prices. Moreover, their designs could respond to market trends in London much more quickly than designs which had to undergo the long journey out to India and back again. Price was clearly important for consumers of these domestically printed fabrics, because the tax differentials imposed during these two decades pushed printers away from cottons and towards linens. Woollen manufacturers complained in 1707 that while the Indian painted fabrics imported before 1701 'were most used by the richer sort of people whilst the poor continued to wear and use our woollen goods', the English printed fabrics 'are so very cheap and so much the fashion that persons of all qualities and degrees clothe themselves and furnish their houses in a great measure with them'.[12] It was evidently at this period that printed cottons and linens began to offer serious competition to the light worsteds and half-silks patterned with stripes or small figures that were woven at Norwich and Spitalfields for ordinary women's gowns and petticoats.[13]

This assessment is confirmed by developments in the aftermath of the Second Prohibition Act which took effect in 1722, outlawing the wearing of prints on pure cotton cloth, as well as dyed or patterned cottons. The Act did not extend to prints on fustian, a combination of linen and cotton yarn, or on linen. At the Old Bailey in the 1720s, the Act was followed by a marked fall in the number of cases involving cotton gowns, but a large increase in those involving gowns made from linen, although the number of cases involving gowns in one or other of these fabrics remained the same as in the 1710s. The Act appears, therefore, to have succeeded in reducing purchases of pure cotton prints, but to have inflicted only a brief pause on the long-term progress of printed fabrics. After the 1720s the number of cases involving gowns described as either cotton or linen proceeded to increase decade on decade, with cottons overtaking linens in the 1730s and the number of cases involving cotton gowns overtaking those involving gowns made from either silks or worsteds in the 1740s.[14] A similar trajectory characterises cases involving printed cotton and linen fabrics, although printed linens continued to outnumber printed cottons. By the 1750s, it was not just cases involving cotton gowns, but also those involving linen gowns that had overtaken cases with gowns made from silks or worsteds. In the 1750s, as has been seen, these cotton and linen gowns had significant numbers of plebeian owners, in London and elsewhere.

At first sight it is odd that after 1722 so many of these stolen gowns went on being described in the charges at the Old Bailey as cotton, when the prohibition specifically outlawed almost every kind of patterned or coloured cotton garment. In practice, the gowns described as cotton in these and other records after that date were in the main not pure cottons, but combinations of cotton wefts and linen warps which fell within the category of fustian and were specifically exempted from the terms of the Act.[15] Despite this exemption, there is only one instance of a gown actually being described as fustian in all the eighteenth-century Old Bailey Proceedings, use of the term fustian there being almost entirely confined to the heavier mixed linen-cotton fabric used for men's breeches, frocks and waistcoats.[16] Evidently the mixed cotton-linen material used for gowns after 1722 was sufficiently distinct from both linens and traditional fustians to retain an identity among consumers as cotton. Consumers could certainly distinguish. 'Here are two gowns', observed Judith Macquire, the wife of a London milkman, in 1758, 'one cotton, one linen'.[17]

By the 1750s, as we have seen, fabrics described as cotton or linen accounted for a third or more of the gowns stolen from plebeian owners. This was merely an intermediate stage in the adoption of such fabrics by plebeian consumers of gowns, a process which lasted most of the eighteenth century. It began not with the imports of Indian decorated fabrics in the late decades of the seventeenth century, but in the early decades of the eighteenth century as Indian techniques for applying colour and pattern were harnessed by British manufacturers. It ended in the last decades of the century when pure cottons dominated ordinary women's purchases of gowns. Nevertheless, this intermediate stage is an instructive one, because all the options available to plebeian consumers can be observed in contention. As plebeian consumers gradually moved over to cottons and linens for their gowns, it was not the elaborate woven silks of elite fashion they deserted, but cheaper patterned worsteds and silk-worsted mixes.

Three reasons for preferring cottons and linens were offered in early eighteenth-century debates over prohibiting printed fabrics: washing, fashion and price. Of these, only washing was addressed in any detail. 'All those who wear Callicoe or Linen now, wou'd not wear Woollen Stuffs if there was no such thing as Printed Callicoe or Linen,' insisted one pamphleteer in 1719, 'but Dutch or Hambro' Strip'd and Chequer'd Linens, and other things of that kind, and for the same Reason that they now wear printed Callicoe or Linen, *viz* because nothing else washes near so well'.[18] Of course, cleanliness was, like fashion, a matter of appearance, as Fayrer Hall, writing in the slightly less frenzied climate of the 1730s, emphasised. 'Will any one say there is a Yard of Woollen worn the more for such Prohibition? Is there a Wench above Sixteen who does not find herself more acceptable to others when she looks clean, than when she is obliged to wear Woollen, which never looks so clean; or when dirty, can it so easily be made clean?'[19]

The pamphlets are less revealing about what rendered the alternative fabrics less fashionable, or about the way price effected the choices made by plebeian consumers. When the term fashion was used in the debates over prohibition at the beginning of the eighteenth century, it was usually in the generalised sense of printed calicoes being a new fashion, rather than referring to specific design characteristics which made calicoes fashionable.[20] To describe something as a new fashion in a diatribe appears to have been sufficiently pejorative to remove any need for elaboration. Between 1741 and 1760, however, the huge collection of textile swatches in the London Foundling Hospital billet books enables us to investigate the look and feel of the kind of decorated cottons and linens used for ordinary women's gowns, and to compare them with some of the worsted and worsted-silk alternatives. This is the largest collection of eighteenth-century textiles in Britain, and probably in the world, providing an unparalleled archive of what ordinary women wore. The textiles in the billet books represent the fabrics available to impoverished, desperate mothers whose infants were taken in by the Hospital. Most of the textiles arrived made up into infant clothing, although many would previously have been worn by adults. Swatches were retained by the Hospital authorities for identification, often accompanied by a verbal description of the fabric (see Appendix 2).

We can establish which of these surviving textiles were of the types used for gowns from the verbal descriptions of ordinary women's gowns found in the criminal records for Yorkshire in the 1730s and 1750s, London in the 1750s, and the provincial runaway advertisements before 1770 (Appendix 1). These sources detail not only the fabrics used, but sometimes also the way gowns were coloured or patterned. Cotton gowns were described as flowered, purple and white, and flowered purple and white. Linen gowns were flowered, striped, white, blue and white, and striped blue and white. Other cotton and linen gown materials were lawn, white dimity and a dark chintz. Exactly the same terms are repeatedly found in the Foundling Hospital billet books. The word 'flowered' was used by the Hospital's clerks to describe printed patterns consisting of large or small flowers printed on either cotton or linen. They could be monochrome (figs 44, 45) or polychrome (figs 43, 46). 'Flowered' could also describe much more

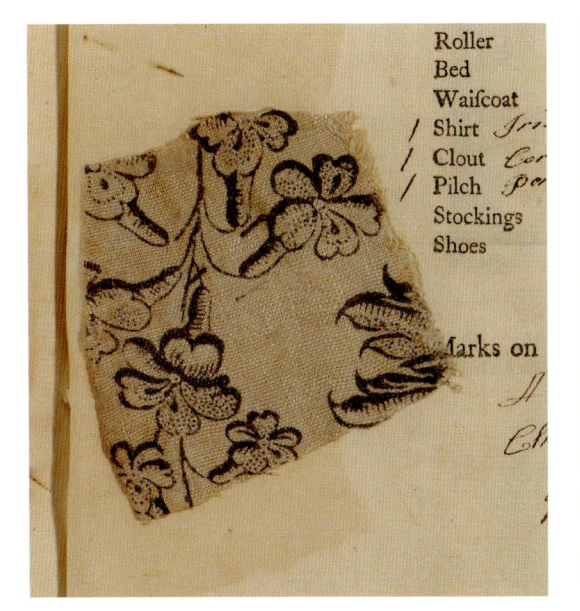

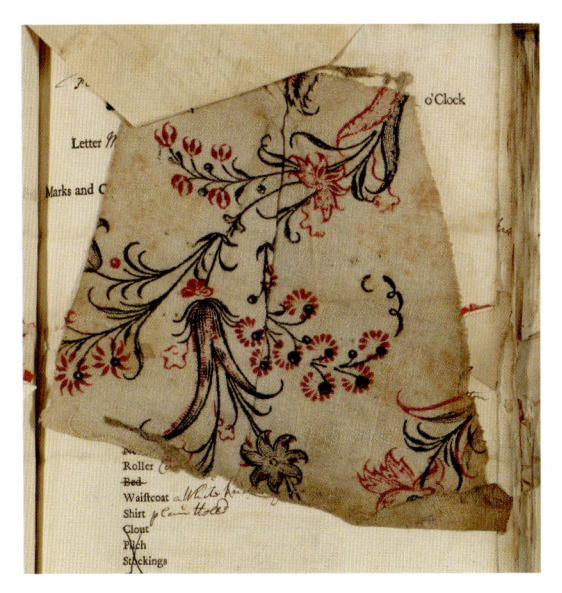

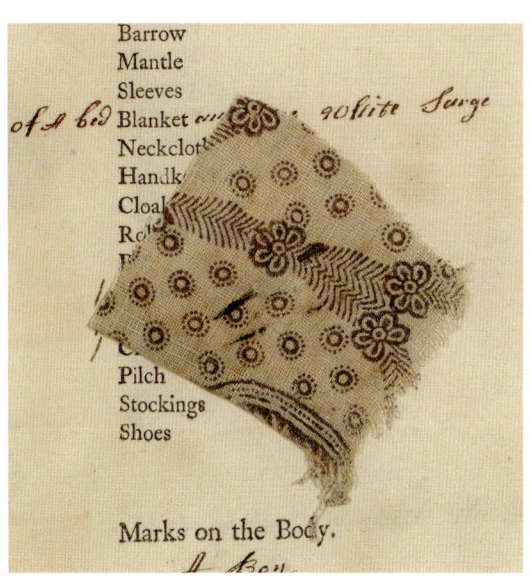

44 (*top*) 'Flowered cotten', 1759, cotton printed in purple, London Metropolitan Archives, A/FH/A/9/1/139, Foundling no. 12536.

46 (*above*) 'Flowered cotten', 1747, cotton printed in red and black, London Metropolitan Archives, A/FH/A/9/1/5, Foundling no. 374. See fig. 43 for a similar pattern on linen.

45 (*top*) 'Flowered Lining', 1759, linen printed in blue, London Metropolitan Archives, A/FH/A/9/1/133, Foundling no. 11877.

47 (*above*) 'Purpel and white flowered cotten', 1759, cotton printed in purple, London Metropolitan Archives, A/FH/A/9/1/127, Foundling no. 11337.

48 'Flowerd all over with cards', 1759, cotton or linen printed with images of playing cards in red, blue and black, London Metropolitan Archives, A/FH/A/9/1/164, Foundling no. 14922.

abstract patterns (fig. 47) and in some cases it was simply a generic term used to describe any pattern that was printed. One fabric printed with a playing-card pattern was described as 'flowerd all over with cards' (fig. 48). Cotton prints and linen prints in the billet books resemble each other in the coarseness of the yarn, the density of the weave and the register of the printing. The most striking difference is that blue and white colour combinations are found almost exclusively on linen, while purple and white combinations appear predominantly on cotton, consistent with the descriptions in the criminal records and the advertisements. The small minority of prints with dark grounds tend to be on cotton. Prints identified as linen and prints identified as cotton appear in the billet books in roughly equal numbers.

Fashion's Favourite? Cottons

Striped linens are also common among the foundling textiles, predominantly blue and white, woven rather than printed, and in a huge variety of widths and shades of stripe (figs 49, 54).[21] Far less common, as in the criminal records and the advertisements, are dimities, chintzes and lawns. The dimities are plain, but the chintzes and lawns are painted or printed (figs 50, 51). The fabric of the chintzes and lawns is of a markedly higher quality than that of the printed cottons and linens, thinner, lighter and woven from much finer yarn. All have polychrome patterns, on a dark ground in the case of one chintz from 1759, reminiscent of the dark chintz gown reported to

49 (*left*)   'Striped Lining', 1759, linen woven in blue and white stripes, London Metropolitan Archives, A/FH/A/9/1/131, Foundling no. 11954.

50 (*below left*)   'Flowered lawn', 1759, lawn printed in red, purple, blue and black, London Metropolitan Archives, A/FH/A/9/1/133, Foundling no. 11868. The yarn is much finer and the cloth thinner and lighter than the printed cottons and linens found in the Foundling Hospital books at this period.

51 (*below right*)   'Chins', 1759, chintz cotton printed or painted in blue and red on a white ground, London Metropolitan Archives, A/FH/A/9/1/149, Foundling no. 13414. Again, the yarn is much finer and the cloth thinner and lighter than other printed fabrics in the Foundling Hospital books at this period.

52 'Flowered chince', 1759, chintz printed or painted with a blue pattern on a red ground, London Metropolitan Archives, A/FH/A/9/1/153, Foundling no. 13789.

have been worn by Elizabeth Smith from Congleton in Cheshire in 1766 when she escaped from prison (fig. 52).[22]

Exactly what attracted plebeian consumers to these cotton and linen fabrics for gowns becomes clear if we compare them with the alternatives. Those mentioned most frequently in the criminal records and the advertisements were stuff and camblet. These were cloths that could be made from worsted, or silk, or a combination of the two, but in this context most were probably the cheaper worsted varieties.[23] Stuff gowns were described as green, purple, brown or just dark; one was made from a brown and white Irish checkered stuff. Camblets were described as brown, brown copper, drab, dark-coloured and brown checked; only one was light-coloured. Mentioned less frequently in these sources were other kinds of worsted gown materials: serge, calamanco and tammy. In addition there were a few gowns made from woollen cloth and from linsey-woolsey, a wool-linen mixture. There were also a handful of gowns made from silk, but far fewer than those made from worsted; one was striped, one was blue, and one was made from paduasoy, a corded silk fabric. Mixtures of silk and worsted and silk and stuff (half-silks) were rather more common, including one silk and worsted in grey. A black crape gown, worn for mourning, could have been either a silk or a worsted.

Examples of many of these fabrics are interleaved with the cottons and linens in the Foundling Hospital billet books for 1759. The worsteds, like those described in the

53 (*top*) 'Stript stuf', 1759, worsted stuff woven in purple and green stripes, London Metropolitan Archives, A/FH/A/9/1/161, Foundling no. 14629.

55 (*above*) 'Blew sarge', 1759, serge dyed blue, London Metropolitan Archives, A/FH/A/9/1/160, Foundling no. 14522.

54 (*top*) 'Striped stufe cuffed with blue and white', 1759, worsted stuff woven in brown, red, blue, yellow, white and purple stripes, attached to a linen or a cotton woven in blue and white stripes, London Metropolitan Archives, A/FH/A/9/1/125, Foundling no. 11199.

56 (*above*) 'Checkt stuf', 1759, worsted stuff woven in a check pattern in yellows, reds and browns, London Metropolitan Archives, A/FH/A/9/1/164, Foundling no. 14953.

57 'Striped Calimanker', 1759, calamanco woven in red, yellow and brown stripes, with flowered decoration in red yarn, London Metropolitan Archives, A/FH/A/9/1/144, Foundling no. 12956.

58 'Striped Linsey,' 1759, linsey-woolsey woven in blue and white stripes, London Metropolitan Archives, A/FH/A/9/1/142, Foundling no. 12808.

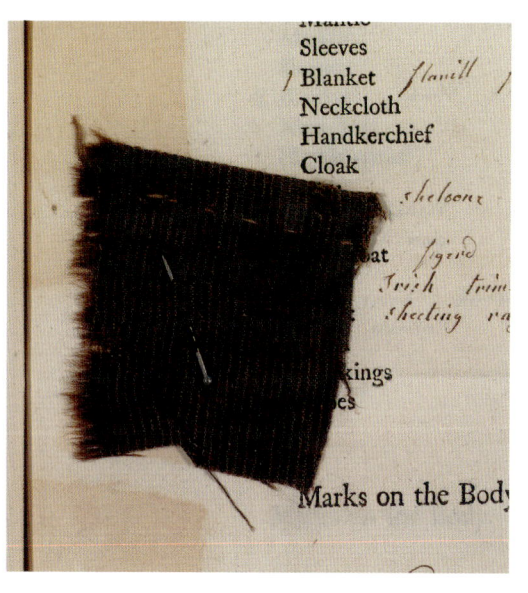

59 'Silck and stuf', 1759, silk and worsted (half-silk) woven in purple and green stripes, London Metropolitan Archives, A/FH/A/9/1/161, Foundling no. 14664.

60 'Blue silk', 1755, silk dyed blue, London Metropolitan Archives, A/FH/A/9/1/17, Foundling no. 1254.

61 'Striped Satten' and 'flowered cotten', 1759, silk woven in gold, red and white stripes over a cotton printed with dots and flowers in blue, London Metropolitan Archives, A/FH/A/9/1/149, Foundling no. 13429.

62 'Flowerd silck', 1760, silk woven in a flowered pattern in blue, pink, white and black, London Metropolitan Archives, A/FH/A/9/1/165, Foundling no. 15023.

criminal records and the advertisements, are predominantly dark in colour, though often striped (figs 53, 54, 55). A few are checked (fig. 56). The most elaborate is a striped calamanco with flowered decoration (fig. 57). Plain woollen cloth also appears, as does linsey-woolsey, in plain, checked and especially striped varieties (frontispiece, fig. 58). Some, but not all of these fabrics are noticeably heavier and coarser than the cottons and linens that fill the billet books. Their wool content means that most of them were probably warmer. But the most important difference is in their appearance. Plain or patterned, they tend to be densely coloured, in predominantly dark shades, and this is also true of the worsted-silk mixes included in the billet books (fig. 59). The bright white grounds of the cotton and linen prints and the striped linens are almost entirely missing. Where an attempt is made to produce the same effect in a striped linsey-woolsey, the result is less crisp and would have been much more difficult to keep clean (fig. 58). It was the white grounds of most of the cottons and linens that gave them the clean look that was so prized for gowns.

It was also a fashionable look in the way it reproduced colour combinations and effects characteristic of the costly striped and flowered silks of the period. The billet books contain only a handful of silks, but among them are both plain silks (fig. 60), and striped and flowered varieties (figs 61, 62). The striped satins and woven flowered silks, acquired perhaps as second-hand off-cuts by poor mothers and then used for clothing their infants, have long lost their lustre, indicating how difficult it must have been to keep the most expensive fabrics clean. Yet their once white, light grounds and formerly bright colours have much in common with the kinds of pattern characteristically found printed on the cottons and linens, despite the fact that the cottons and linens do not match the silks for sheen or delicacy (fig. 35).

If these decorated cottons and linens were fashionable in the sense that they incorporated key elements of the look of modish silks, that is not to say that they took on the seasonal changes in pattern characteristic of the most expensive Spitalfields silks, or even that they matched for quality, particularly for colourfulness, either the silks or the linens and cottons worn by wealthier women. In the Foundling Hospital billet books, the majority of the prints are executed in a single colour. There are from one and a half to two times more monochrome prints than polychrome.[24] Richer women were more likely to have multi-coloured prints. Barbara Johnson, the daughter of a prosperous Bedfordshire clergyman, kept a book containing samples of the fabrics she acquired for outer garments from the age of eight in 1746 until her death in 1825.[25] Between 1746 and 1770, eight out of 11 printed linens and cottons in the book are polychrome (fig. 63), although at this period she acquired more silks than either linens or cottons. Single colours were cheaper to print.[26] Many of the Foundling prints make extensive use of dots produced by nails hammered into the wooden printing block, one of the most economical methods of patterning a block. Yet simple, monochrome designs of this kind, though sometimes crudely executed, could sustain a fashionably rococo effect with designs featuring shell forms or botanically inspired sprigs (frontispiece, figs 64, 65).

63 A page from Barbara Johnson's album, fabrics from 1746–49, Victoria and Albert Museum, London, T.219-1973. Printed cottons, silks, a printed linen and a camblet acquired by the Bedfordshire clergyman's daughter, Barbara Johnson, in her youth.

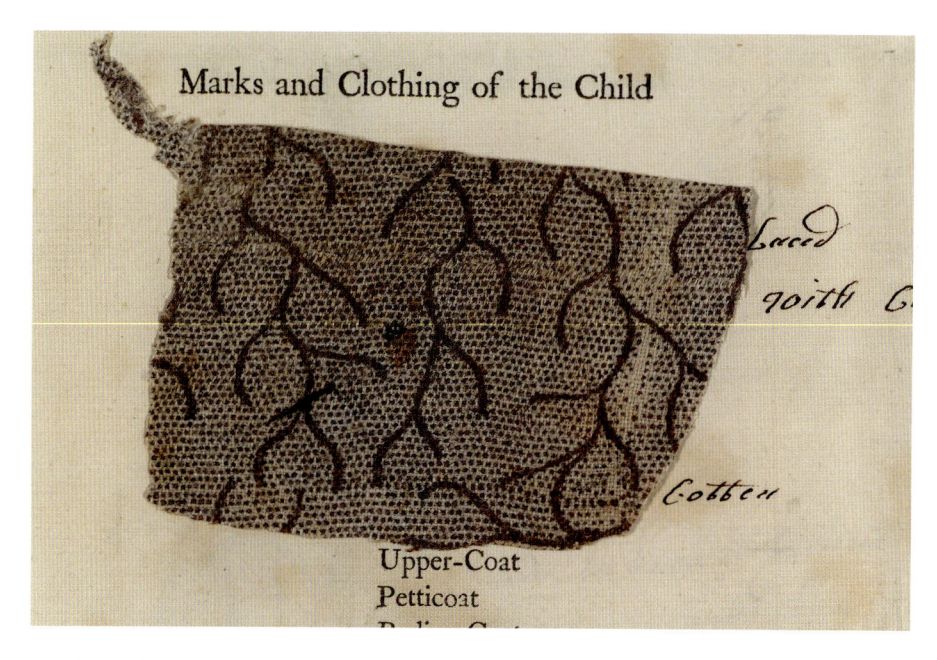

64 'Spriged cotten', 1759, cotton printed with a sprig pattern and dots in purple, London Metropolitan Archives, A/FH/A/9/1/145, Foundling no. 13287.

Even these simple prints did not come cheap. Printed fabrics may have been more affordable than silks, but they were consistently more expensive than most of the worsted stuffs used for gowns, partly because since 1712 they had borne an excise duty of three pence a yard.[27] Insofar as prints replaced stuffs, it was not because they were cheaper. Stephen Hudson kept a shop in the 1750s at Fewston, high in the Yorkshire Pennines between Skipton and Knaresborough, serving a clientele consisting overwhelmingly of poor farmers and tradespeople. In 1759 he sold a variety of cottons in gown lengths, charging 13d. or 14d. a yard for plain blue cotton and 15d. a yard for striped cottons, but asking between 24d. and 28d. a yard for printed cottons and 48d. a yard for chintz cotton.[28] The worsted stuffs he sold in gown lengths, such as calamanco, camblet, stuff and tammy – some of them figured – were much cheaper than the prints, at only 10d. to 15d. a yard. He sold hardly any silks in gown lengths, but when he did, he charged 35d. a yard for twelve yards of damask, more expensive than any of his printed fabrics apart from the costly chintz.[29] The same price differentials can be observed in the fabrics acquired by Barbara Johnson between 1746 and 1769. Her printed linens and cottons cost on average 38d. a yard. Her worsted stuffs, which included two that were printed, were considerably cheaper at 23d. a yard, but her silks cost much more, on average 78d. a yard. The same hierarchy of monetary value can be observed among the gowns stolen from plebeian owners in the Old Bailey Proceedings in the 1750s.[30] We find the few gowns made from silks valued on average

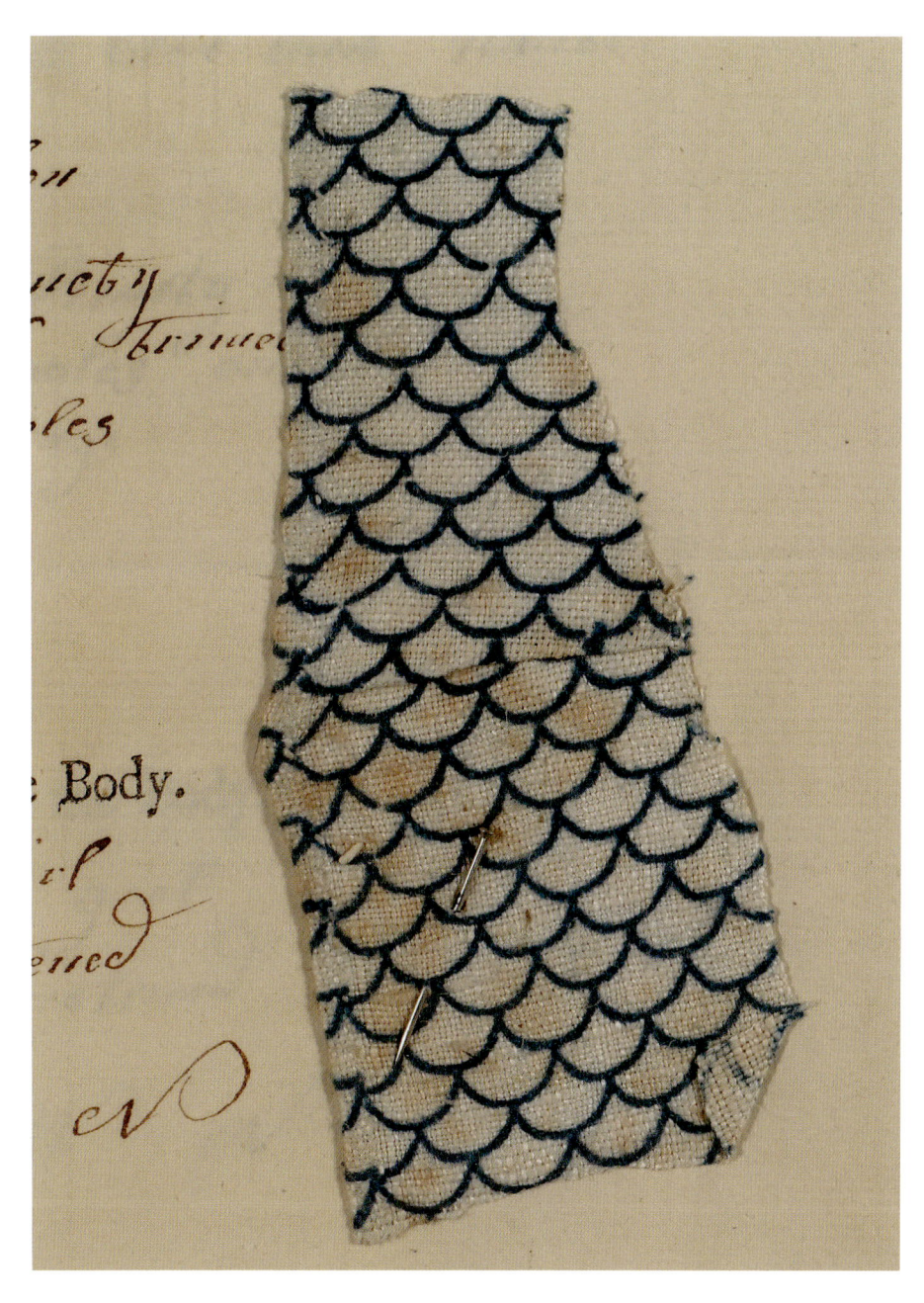

65 'Blue and white sheled', 1759, cotton or linen printed with a shell pattern in blue, London Metropolitan Archives, A/FH/A/ 9/1/125, Foundling no. 11148.

at 9s. 10d., those made from cottons or linens at 6s. 8d., and those made from camblet or serge at only 5s. 6d. In none of these cases was there any marked difference in average values between prints on linen and prints on cotton.

Despite these price differences, certain kinds of cottons and stuffs could still be treated as alternatives for each other at this period. In 1753, for example, a young female customer in Margaret Bourne's London shop selling ready-made and second-hand clothes 'asked for a striped camblet gown'. Bourne's daughter, who was serving in the shop, 'asked her whether she would have a new one or an old one; she said, a second-hand one; I told her we had never a one; but my mother called out and said, we have a second-hand cotton one'.[31] But we should bear in mind that many, perhaps most plebeian women owned more than one gown. Often they were made from different fabrics. Elizabeth Brown, a poor women who lodged in a multi-occupied room in London in 1753, had all her clothes stolen while she slept. They included her two gowns, one in purple and white flowered cotton and the other in striped linen.[32] Susannah Rogers owned a cotton gown, a linen gown and a camblet gown, all of which were stolen from her London lodging room in 1758.[33] Two gowns were stolen in 1756 from a carpenter's house at Fewston in Yorkshire, close to Stephen Hudson's shop. One was made from striped linen, the other from camblet stuff.[34] Gowns in different fabrics, with different decorative characteristics and prices, may well have been worn for different purposes. In the Old Bailey cases in the 1750s, it is noticeable that cotton and linen gowns were often stolen from lodgings and houses when their plebeian owners were out at work, wearing, perhaps, a cheaper, workaday gown while their more decorative and expensive gown was put away at home for best wear on Sundays and holidays. Cotton and linen gowns, especially prints, certainly enjoyed a cachet in plebeian circles. It was on a Sunday that Elisabeth Wills wore a linen gown she had stolen from a garret lodging near Lincoln's Inn in 1755. When a Covent Garden linen draper's servant wanted to give presents to a girl in 1758, it was printed cotton for gowns that he stole from his master's shop. And when Elizabeth Rowland wore the purple and white cotton gown she stole from a Smithfield lodging in 1752, she was described as being 'dressed very well'.[35]

By the 1780s the victory of the printed cotton gown was almost complete. Not only had printed fabrics vanquished worsteds and half-silks, but prints on cotton were eclipsing prints on linen, as they did in the many other uses to which printed fabrics were being put. The trend towards cottons and away from linens can be observed not only in plebeian women's gowns, but also in Barbara Johnson's sample book.[36] For David MacPherson, looking back from 1805, the triumph of cotton reflected the lower cost of cotton yarn compared with linen, but in the late 1770s and the 1780s cotton gowns do not appear to have been cheaper than linen gowns.[37] Indeed in criminal records, pawnbrokers pledge books and retailers' accounts alike, plebeian women's cotton gowns were consistently ascribed similar or higher values to their linen gowns (tables 17, 18, 19). At this date, the advantage enjoyed by cotton gowns was one of quality, not cheapness relative to linen. A key development here was the transformation in the cotton fabrics used for printing following the repeal in 1774 of the Acts prohibiting the wearing of pure cottons.[38] Secured by Richard Arkwright, who held the patent for the spinning frame, the repeal enabled printing to be undertaken legally on fabric with a cotton warp and weft, as opposed to the cottons with linen warps that printers had been obliged to use between 1722 and 1774. Printing on pure cottons resulted in a lighter fabric and better colour. Women quickly appreciated the change. In 1776 a Bedfordshire gentlewoman asked a friend in London to get her 'one of the *new* manufactory which are *Cotten* both ways, have sent a pattern. It is a great deal lighter than a Cotton, and the colours look more lively.'[39] The 1774 Act set the excise duty payable on the new pure cotton printed fabrics at three pence per yard, the same rate paid by printed linens and cotton-linen mixes, but lower than the rate that had been imposed on prints on imported calico in 1714. Equality of taxation would persist, apart for a brief interlude in the mid-1780s.[40]

The triumph of printed cotton as a gown material for plebeian women resulted, therefore, from its superior appearance, not its cheapness. It is significant that before 1800 cotton fabrics were virtually never supplied by overseers of the poor to paupers either for gowns or other outer garments; paupers went on having to make do with cheap woollens and worsteds.[41] Yet the good looks of the new, all-cotton prints did not guarantee fashionability. Already in the 1780s elite women's gowns were beginning to move away from printed cottons towards the lighter, more expensive white muslins, a trend which relatively few plebeian women were able to follow, in that decade at least. This is not to say that elite women entirely deserted cotton prints. Overlaps in aesthetic effect between their gowns and those worn by plebeian women continued into the early years of the nineteenth century. Yet if cotton encouraged a democratisation of fashion by providing colourful designs to poorer people on an unprecedented scale, it was a democratisation that was always in contention with the countervailing tendency in high fashion to accentuate sartorial distinctions between rich and poor.

★   ★   ★

Cotton's triumph in the late eighteenth century was not confined to printed gowns. It enjoyed huge success in all its decorated forms, whether printed and woven, as a material for many varieties of clothing and furnishing. Yet for many historians of these developments, the success of cotton was not simply a matter of appearance. Generations of scholars have proposed that cotton triumphed as quickly and as extensively in the market for unadorned, utilitarian textiles as it did in the realm of decorated fabrics. They have suggested that, in the course of the late eighteenth century, cottons replaced linens as plain fabrics for everyday use in shirts and shifts. Indeed, this assertion has been so widely accepted that reductions in mortality in the period have been ascribed to the supposed improvements in hygiene that resulted from the use of cotton as body linen.

M. C. Buer in her 1926 study *Health, Wealth and Population in the Early Days of the Industrial Revolution* argued that 'at first this industry was a luxury one, catering only for the well-to-do, but the rapid cheapening of its product by the application of machinery, soon led to production for the masses. Cotton cloth was cheap material suitable for women's dresses and for body and household linen; it wore less well than stout woollen material but that was advantageous from the health point of view since it could be cheaply renewed. Cotton washed easily and therefore its use much encouraged cleanliness.'[42] Writing in 1967, J. D. Chambers developed a similar argument as he struggled to account for the fall in mortality in Nottingham from the 1770s. He could offer no explanation except the fact that 'Nottingham, of course, was a cotton town, the first in fact'. He noted that 'by the end of the century cotton hosiery, underwear, calicoes, bed-hangings and sheets would be ousting those of wool; and cotton can be boiled, which is fatal for the typhus louse. The change to cotton would be especially beneficial to the poor of the large towns.'[43] More recently, David Landes has also emphasised the importance for hygiene of 'the introduction of cheap cotton underclothing'.[44] In the same vein, Woodruff D. Smith asserts that 'in the last years of the eighteenth century, cotton moved strongly to replace linens and mixed textiles as the favored material for shirts and undergarments at almost every income level'.[45] Curiously, these authors offer no direct, quantitative evidence for such a change. Some of them refer to the broad downward trend exhibited by price series for cotton fabrics derived from the records of institutional purchasers and wholesale dealers. Others refer to the comments on the spread of cotton clothing among the labouring poor made by the early nineteenth-century radical and inveterate social optimist Francis Place.[46] But Place's comments on the benefits of cotton clothing referred not to undergarments – shirts for men and shifts for women – but to petticoats and stays, which women wore over their shifts.[47]

A very different picture emerges if we turn to the evidence of the Old Bailey Proceedings (table 20). Cotton shirts appear there in tiny numbers very early, from the 1680s, which is consistent with what we know about the efforts of the East India Company to promote the use of Indian cottons for shirting in that decade.[48] In October 1682, the Company's Directors ordered its Madras factors to have 200,000 ready-made cotton shifts and shirts made up for sale in England. This was an enormous initial order for a new commodity which appears to have been largely untested in the market.[49] The size of the order can be judged by the fact that it represented approximately one cotton shirt or shift for every two adults in London.[50] Indeed this single order represented two percent of what Gregory King estimated to be the annual English *national* consumption of these garments in the 1680s.[51] Essentially this was a bold exercise in market manipulation, designed to undermine the established preference for linens among consumers of shirts and shifts by dumping vast quantities of ready-made cotton shifts and shirts onto the London market at artificially low prices. For Josiah Child, the Governor of the Company, it was 'the onely way I know to introduce the using of Callicoe for that purpose in all these Northern parts of the world'.[52] Indian ready-made cotton shirts and shifts, wrote the Directors, 'may be (being sold cheap in ye drapers shops) a means to introduce into more general use ye wearing of Callicoe in stead of French Holland, or Flanders Cloth'.[53]

In this new venture, the Company was determined to exploit every major segment of the market, not just the elite. Its specifications for shifts and shirts were set out with considerable care. 'Lett some of the coursest sort for Seamens and ordinary peoples use be strong blew Cloath, and some white for the like ordinary use, others white Midling, for Citizens and Middle sort of People and some fine enough for Ladies, and Gentle-women . . . take especial care that the sowing be very good and all the Cloth strong in its kind, as well fine as course.'[54] Yet despite all the attention devoted to customis-ing the product for different levels in the market, the initiative was a failure.[55] Early in 1685 the Directors wrote to Madras ordering that no more shirts or shifts should be supplied. The reason for their change of heart emerges in a stock list of goods remain-ing unsold in the Company's warehouse in December 1685, which included over 100,000 shirts and shifts, with 'send none' written alongside.[56] By comparison, the number the Company managed to sell at its regular twice-yearly London auctions was tiny. Less than five thousand were sold in 1684 and 1685, and less than ten thousand in 1686.[57] A brief attempt to revive the trade in 1690 with an order for 100,000 shifts 'strong and substantially sow'd for poor Peoples wear' also failed.[58]

The manner in which the whole exercise was conducted suggests the Company was aware it faced strong resistance to its efforts to remodel consumer taste in shifts and shirts. Such resistance was to persist for more than a century. Despite some growth in the numbers of cases involving cotton shifts and shirts at the Old Bailey in the course of the eighteenth century, they remained very few compared with those involving shirts and shifts made from linen. Even in the last two decades of the century, when cotton was trouncing linen in the market for decorated fabrics, its impact on shirts and shifts was small. As late as 1802, a London upholsterer told a servant who had claimed some suspicious cloth she found in her possession was for making shirts, 'this is cotton, this is not for shirts'.[59] After about 1800, the Old Bailey Proceedings lack information about the materials from which stolen goods were made. It is possible, however, to trace the relative fortunes of cotton and linen shirts and shifts after that date in the Yorkshire criminal records (table 21). For the period up to 1800, the results are con-sistent with the Old Bailey evidence, though the number of cases is far smaller. No cases of stolen cotton shifts or shirts appear at all. It is only in the nineteenth century that cotton shirts and shifts begin to appear, yet even in the early 1820s they accounted for only 20 percent of those stolen in the West Riding of Yorkshire, with the losses from plebeian victims including both linen and cotton.

In the 1820s, therefore, cotton was only starting to gain a foothold in the markets for plain shirting and shifting. Historians have been premature in their estimates of when cotton succeeded in these markets. Why was there such a discrepancy between the timing of the substitution of cottons for linens in the markets for fashionable, dec-orated fabrics and in the markets for these plain, utilitarian fabrics? The obvious answer is price, but, as we have seen, cotton's early success in the markets for decorated fabrics was not initially a matter of cheapness compared to decorated linens. Moreover, it is all too easy to exaggerate the extent of price reductions in finished cotton cloth in the twenty years before and after 1800, despite the dramatic technical improvements that took place in spinning.[60] Price series for linens equivalent to those for cottons are unavailable, but we know that linen spinners responded vigorously to very high flax prices during the Revolutionary and Napoleonic wars of 1793 to 1815, when trade with northern Europe was disrupted. They converted to power spinning and improved preparatory processes to increase dramatically the yarn yielded by each pound of raw flax. After 1815, when flax prices fell by nearly a third, there was a buoyant market for domestically woven light household linens, of which shirting comprised a large part.[61]

Even if price series were available for cotton and linen shirtings, direct comparison between yardage prices for the two fibres might be inappropriate. Linen is stronger than cotton and one of the complaints voiced against cotton was that it lacked durability.[62] As early as 1681, the author of *The Trade of England Revived* claimed that worsted linings like 'perpetuana or shalloon will wear out two coats', while 'glazened calico will hardly wear out one coat'.[63] In 1727 Daniel Defoe famously dismissed calico as 'ordinary, mean, low-priz'd, and soon in rags'.[64] A century later, in 1825, Esther Hewlett, the author of *Cottage Comforts with Hints for Promoting them Gleaned from Experience*, was still criticising calico in the same terms, estimating that it wore out three to four times as quickly as unbleached linen.[65] If these complaints were justified, cotton yardage prices would have needed to be well below linen yardage prices to compete successfully in a market segment where durability was crucial. In 1794 the agriculturalist Arthur Young identified 'strength and warmth' as criteria by which linen shirting was judged.[66]

Consumers at all social levels washed household linen frequently, both for hygiene and appearance, but they had little choice but to employ ineffective soaps and correspondingly aggressive washing techniques. If cottons were less hard-wearing, they would have needed a price advantage sufficiently great to cover the cost of more frequent replacement. In the 1820s the price differential, though substantial, does not appear to have been sufficient to persuade the generality of poorer purchasers to switch. In 1822 the poor members of the charitable clothing society run by the curate in the Northamptonshire villages of Creaton and Spratton used their weekly contributions to buy 1,150 yards of linen shirting at 1s. a yard and 1,540 yards of linen sheeting at 1s. 1½d. a yard, but they bought only 200 yards of calico despite its costing a mere 6d. a yard. At the end of the 1820s a similar pattern emerges at Farthinghoe, twenty miles to the south, where the members of the provident clothing society used their weekly contributions to buy 1,180 yards of linen at 7½d. a yard, but bought only 767 yards of plain calico, despite its being two-thirds the price at 4½d. and 5d. a yard.[67]

To those who had a professional interest in promoting the use of cotton, it appeared to be a fabric ideally suited to shirts and shifts. In their enthusiasm, they found it all too easy to make over-optimistic prophecies of the imminent displacement of linen in this market. A hundred years after Josiah Child expressed the belief that the East India Company's calico shirts and shifts would replace linens, Samuel Salte, London agent for the muslin manufacturer Samuel Oldknow, once again confidently predicted that 'the fashion of wearing calico shirting will obtain very much'.[68] His prophecy did eventually come true, but it took the best part of half a century. Only after 1825 did cottons really began to challenge the dominance of linens in the market for shirts and shifts. In 1829, Edward Baines, the editor of the *Leeds Mercury*, noted that the linen weavers of Barnsley in Yorkshire were suffering because 'cotton fabrics have of late come much into competition with linens, and one article in particular, cotton shirting is now very much in request'.[69] And only in the 1850s did the market for domestically produced linens actually collapse.[70]

There is a tendency in some histories of product innovation in Europe from the seventeenth century to the nineteenth century to present cotton as if it were a single product, protean and infinitely substitutable for textiles made from other materials. There is no doubt that in the long term cotton enjoyed spectacular success, much of it by capturing markets previously served by other fibres. Nevertheless, its success was uneven across the various markets for clothing textiles, especially so in the period before 1800. Adapting cotton to new uses sometimes required radical and difficult reworking of what defined it as a product. Manufacturers of other fibres were capable of responding in kind. At issue were not simply considerations of price. Much turned on the specific material characteristics and qualities of different fabrics, and on the tastes and preferences of those who wore them. Nowhere is this more evident than in the history of shirts and shifts. For well over a century, from the 1680s to the early 1800s, great efforts were made to promote the use of cotton for undergarments, by organisations and entrepreneurs with proven records as successful innovators. Yet most consumers of shirts and shifts remained unmoved.

As for the health benefits that historians have often ascribed to cotton undergarments, any benefits are unlikely to have accrued before the second quarter of the nineteenth century. Yet it is hard to see that cotton actually had the great advantage over linen in this respect that has been claimed. Buer and Chambers believed mistakenly that undergarments were previously made from wool. As we have seen, this was not the case in eighteenth-century England. Shirts and shifts, whether made from linen or from cotton, were expected to be washed frequently, even among the poor. Indeed shirts and shifts made from linen may have been kept cleaner, because they could be washed with less anxiety about wear than those made from cotton. If the cleanliness of body and household linen was crucial for improvements in hygiene, then the substitution of cotton for linen was not the key innovation. More important were increases in the levels of ownership of body and household linen of any kind, which would allow for more frequent changes of underclothing and bedding, and improvements in the effectiveness of soaps. In several parts of England, ownership of household linen, at least, seems to have undergone a long-term increase from the sixteenth to the eighteenth centuries.[71] Soaps, by contrast, changed relatively little before the introduction of chemical soda made by the Leblanc process, which became widely available in England only after the repeal of the salt duty in 1825. What remains obscure, however, is the precise nature of the linkages between clothing, cleanliness and infection and how much they actually contributed to mortality.

The life-saving power of cotton undergarments has been a cherished story, repeated again and again in accounts of the Industrial Revolution, but it is unsound. Cotton was undoubtedly the leading fibre of industrial revolution, its dazzling rise the textile phenomenon of the eighteenth century, but it did not carry all before it. The spectacular early triumph of cotton among plebeian consumers arose from its visual, decorative, fashionable qualities. Where appearance was crucial, cotton succeeded. Where utilitarian durability counted, cotton sometimes lagged behind.

II

Getting and Spending

66 Woodblock impression on paper of a design for a printed cotton, 1780–85, ink and watercolour on paper, Victoria and Albert Museum, London, E.1854–1921. This design of small red-and-white flowers on a chocolate ground with black stripes is from a book of patterns believed to have been circulated by a Carlisle printworks in the 1780s.

8
Clothing Provincial England: Fabrics

In a much-quoted passage from his *State of the Poor* of 1797, Sir Frederick Eden presented a striking contrast between northern and southern England in the way farmers, mechanics and labourers were clothed at the end of the eighteenth century.

> In the midland and southern counties, the labourer, in general, purchases a very considerable portion, if not the whole, of his cloaths, from the shop-keeper. In the vicinity of the metropolis, working-people seldom buy new cloaths: they content themselves with a cast-off coat, which may be usually purchased for about 5s. and second-hand waistcoats and breeches. Their wives seldom make up any article of dress, except making and mending cloaths for the children. In the North, on the contrary, almost every article of dress worn by farmers, mechanics, and labourers, is manufactured at home, shoes and hats excepted: that is, the linen thread is spun from the lint, and the yarn from the wool, and sent to the weaver's and dyer's: so that almost every family has its web of linen cloth annually, and often one of woollen also, which is either dyed for coats, or made into flannel, etc.[1]

In subsequent passages, Eden qualified this extremely stark contrast. He acknowledged a recent increase in the use of shop-bought textiles in the north of England. Nevertheless, he remained adamant that 'within these twenty years, a coat bought at a shop was considered as a mark of extravagance and pride, if the buyer was not possessed of an independent fortune.'[2]

When he insisted there were marked regional differences in patterns of consumption between north and south, Eden made it clear that he was referring not just to differences between far-flung, remote parts of the north and the area immediately around London, the nation's commercial metropolis, but to regional disparities within provincial, mainly rural England as a whole. It was here, in the countryside, that more than two-thirds of the population lived throughout the eighteenth century, not in London or in provincial towns.[3] Eden did not think such disparities were confined to clothing. Indeed, it was through an analysis of regional differences in diet that he developed most fully his criticism of those 'wasteful systems of domestic economy' he considered the principal impediment to material improvement among the labouring poor of the Midlands and the south.[4] Eden, of course, had an axe to grind. Deeply sceptical about the desirability of the Poor Law, he was anxious to demonstrate the potential for self-reliance among the labouring poor. He quoted approvingly John Locke's remark that the cause of the growth of the numbers of the poor 'can be nothing else but the relaxation of discipline and the corruption of manners.'[5] His comments on the clothing of the labouring poor, like those on their diet, drew on stock eighteenth-century ideas about the incompatibility of wealth and virtue. Eden presented the north of England as commercially backward. It therefore served to demonstrate the poor's capacity, under the right conditions, to exist in a state of robust and virtuous self-sufficiency. His portrayal of the Midlands and the south, by contrast, suggests that the insinuation of commercial relationships and an extended division of labour into the supply of basic commodities like clothing had resulted in unnecessary extravagance among the poor. His remarks consequently have to be treated with some scepticism as evidence of either northern sturdiness or southern degeneracy.

Eden's insistence that there were significant disparities between north and south in the supply of a range of basic commodities is echoed in recent writing on the history of eighteenth-century retailing. The north may have been the heartland of those transformations in production that constitute the classic notion of the Industrial Revolution, but it has generally been agreed that the region was not the site of major innovations in consumption. Marked differences between north and south in the staple diet of the labouring poor have frequently been noted by historians.[6] Evidence from probate inventories during the century from 1660 to 1760 suggests that levels of ownership for many goods were relatively low in Lancashire, Cumbria and the rural north-east, when compared with the south-east of England, although the goods concerned do not include clothes.[7] Studies of retailing have proposed that the north of England was characterised by a relatively few shops per head of population during the late eighteenth century.[8] Nevertheless, we should be cautious. Whatever the differences in diet between labouring people in north and those in the Midlands and the south, there were, as we have seen, few regional variations in the kind of clothes they wore. If regional differences existed in the ways their clothes were sourced, they were not ones that generated anything that could really be described as regional costume.[9]

The issue of regional variations in the way clothing was supplied to plebeian consumers is an important one for the study of eighteenth-century consumption. Undue attention has often been devoted to a few spectacular but exceptional examples of innovation in marketing, advertising and other forms of commercial propaganda, associated with a strictly limited range of products and concentrated in the capital: to Josiah Wedgwood's innovatory London pottery showroom, to James Lackington's cash-only book emporium, to the expensively engraved trade cards commissioned by retailers serving the rich, or to the narrow range of branded goods that emerged in the course of the century.[10] Examining regional variations in the supply of a basic commodity like clothing can help us avoid excessive concern with the extraordinary and the unusual, and arrive at a more balanced assessment of the relationship between the consumer and the market. If we take Eden's remarks as our starting point, we can approach this relationship not simply by considering new initiatives in marketing fabrics and fashions taken by retailers and manufacturers, but also by assessing the changing role of the household as a unit of both consumption *and* production. We can ask whether there was a significant commodification of plebeian dress in this period; whether there was a move away from clothing that was vernacular and literally homespun to a reliance on clothing acquired through retailers from distant suppliers. Where did the boundary lie between self-provisioning and market supply, between goods made or processed within the household for use by its members and those sourced from outside the household? Did this boundary mark a distinction between female and male work?[11] These are the issues raised by Eden's contrast between the supply of plebeian clothing in the north of England and the south. His remarks are the point of departure for this and the next chapter. Their concern is not primarily with the history of retailing, but rather with establishing how plebeian consumers in provincial England acquired fabrics and clothing. They focus first on the north of England, in order to assess Eden's claims for its distinctiveness, and then compare it with the Midlands and the south.

When historians of manufacturing and consumption in eighteenth-century England have sought alternatives to the attempts to measure aggregate economic growth characteristic of much recent economic history, it is to changes in the way the production and supply of goods was organised that they have turned their attention. In particular, they have sought out increases in the scale of business enterprises and intensifications of the division of labour along the supply chain.[12] These concerns often derive, of course, from a set of teleological expectations about the trajectory of economic development; about what the appropriate yardsticks would be for measuring change. The underlying assumptions are that, as an economy develops, firms should get larger, the division of labour should become more intense, and processing should increasingly move out of the domestic sphere and into the market. Analysis of economic change in terms of increases in the size of firms, in the division of labour and in the extent to which production was commodified offers considerable advantages over what has often become a sterile search for measures of aggregate economic growth in the eighteenth century. But we need to beware the Whiggish assumptions that can easily creep in here; the unspoken belief that change progresses in one direction and that what is important is that which is bigger, or more specialised, or more commodified.

The analysis that follows begins by mapping broad, structural trends in the commercial supply of clothing fabrics to plebeian consumers in the north of England between 1660 and 1800. It does so for the north alone because it is only for Yorkshire and parts of some adjacent counties that detailed probate inventories survive in large numbers for the late eighteenth century.[13] In other parts of England probate inventories exist in only very small numbers (if at all) after 1720. Consequently it is possible to undertake for parts of the north a comparison of the moveable wealth and stocks of textile and clothing suppliers across the eighteenth century of a kind that is not feasible elsewhere. The comparison is based on a combination of three samples from surviving inventories, mainly for Yorkshire. They cover the period from 1660 to 1800 and include towns and rural areas with a variety of agricultural and industrial activities.[14] The inventories allow us to assess changes in scale in the businesses of retailers who stocked the materials from which clothing was made, as well as sometimes garments or accessories. The retailers concerned were principally those described as mercer, draper, haberdasher, milliner, chapman or plain shopkeeper. Inventories of people with these occupational designations normally included some textile and clothing items among their lists of stock.

The picture that emerges from the inventories is one of a striking decline in scale between the late seventeenth and the late eighteenth centuries. The mean total value of the retailers' inventories before 1740 was £488 (n = 15). After 1740 it was £113 (n = 25). The mean stock values (not just clothing and textiles) fell from £237 to £74. This shift is accounted for mainly by the appearance after 1740 of much larger numbers of small shops selling a range of basic commodities. All but one of the 16 retailers in the samples who were described as shopkeepers appear after 1740, and their mean stock values, at £36, were markedly lower than those of the specialist textile and clothing retailers. The downward trend in stock values would have been even more marked if the retailers category had been extended to incorporate those weavers and clothiers whose inventories suggest that they operated tiny general retail businesses selling some clothing items.

The pattern of declining scale lends some support to the view that in the eighteenth-century north the numbers of shops increased and that this increase was particularly marked at the bottom of the market.[15] Probably, as Carole Shammas has argued, it was growth in the consumption of exotic groceries among the poor, especially tea, sugar and tobacco, that enabled these small shops to proliferate during the eighteenth century, not the limited range of cloth and clothing accessories they also sometimes sold.[16] However, it is also important to remember that large numbers of shops already existed in the late seventeenth-century north, selling a wide price range of fabrics and clothing. Indeed Nancy Cox, while acknowledging regional variations in the density of the retail network, has questioned the extent to which retail provision did actually decline with distance from London. She suggests that in most parts of the country people had access to a wide choice of goods by 1700, even where the number of shops was limited.[17] We certainly should not assume that the subsequent proliferation of small shops confirms Eden's picture of a shift among the northern labouring poor away from bespoke manufacture of cloth and clothing towards a reliance on shop-bought goods.[18]

The evidence of the northern inventories does not indicate, therefore, a wholesale transformation in the means by which clothes and clothing materials reached plebeian customers between the late seventeenth century and the late eighteenth century. We do not find any evidence in the retailers' inventories of the northern self-sufficiency extolled by Eden, but that would be unlikely to emerge from the records of textile suppliers. What the inventories do reveal is a well-established, pre-existing commercial retailing network being extended through a proliferation of small general stores, although the impetus for this probably had little to do with the supply of clothing.

Probate inventories suffer from numerous shortcomings as historical evidence for the supply of goods. They can be useful for a quantitative mapping of the structure of formal business activity, but retailers' inventories tell us little about the system of provision in operation.[19] They provide no evidence about household manufacturing for domestic use, little about the manufacturing of cloth on a bespoke basis for local markets, and what they have to offer on itinerant trading is restricted to the larger chapmen. Inventories in general can, of course, offer evidence about the domestic manufacture of textiles in the form of stocks of raw wool, flax or hemp, and equipment like looms and spinning wheels. It is not possible, however, to distinguish with any real confidence between materials and equipment dedicated to manufacture for household or local consumption, and materials and equipment devoted to production for distant markets. The latter was very extensive in the north of England in the eighteenth century, undertaken both by independent small producers and by waged workers under the putting-out system.

We can, however, use other kinds of evidence to supplement the inventories, showing how the supply of clothing materials actually worked in the north and also how it changed. In particular, the statements of witnesses in a sixty-year sample of criminal cases (see Appendix 1) make it clear that some of the kinds of domestic production for household or local use on which Eden laid such stress were undoubtedly pursued by plebeian men and women in the north of England. These activities need, however, to be carefully distinguished. Eden suggested that, in the north, nearly every article of dress was manufactured in whole or in part at home, shoes and hats excepted. He insisted that northern plebeian families characteristically spun both linen and woollen yarn, had it woven and dyed, and then made it into garments, including heavy garments such as coats. Criminal cases in the north of England repeatedly mention yarn spun by the women of a household being woven locally and then made up into garments for the household's use.[20] It was, however, almost always hemp or flax that was being spun to make into coarse cloth for shirts and shifts, not wool for outer garments. John Brown of Sandhutton in the North Riding of Yorkshire had four shifts stolen from a hedge in the yard at the back of his house in 1694. His wife found one of them in the back yard of George Waud in the same village, which she recognised because it was 'of her own spinning'.[21] Cases like this involving hemp or linen cloth went on appearing right through the eighteenth century, suggesting the persistence of household production.[22]

Criminal cases mentioning woollen yarn being woven into fabric for family use were conspicuous by their rarity. The only example involving a clothing fabric involved a kersey waistcoat stolen in 1734 from a labourer at Kirby Ravensworth in the North Riding of Yorkshire. It had been made from woollen yarn spun by his aunt. The aunt testified that 'what enables her to be so positive as to this waistcoat is that she this examinant spun the yarn of which the whole waistcoat was made, and sent it to the weaver to weave, and had it from his hands again, and then gave it to her nephew James Scott to make him a waistcoat with'.[23] But woollen yarn was not only woven into cloth. Knitting stockings for household use from yarn spun by members of the family was clearly commonplace enough for Joseph Eastwood, a clothier from Longwood near Huddersfield accused of stealing several pounds of white wool in 1785, to claim in his defence that he took the wool to make a pair of stockings.[24]

Knitting household-spun yarn into stockings for family use may have been widespread in northern households, but there is little evidence in the criminal records of yarn being woven into cloth in the spinner's own household. Examples of cloth for a family's own use being woven by a member of the household are confined to families where a member of the household wove for a living and described himself as a weaver. For instance, at Christmas 1782 Richard Dixon, a weaver from Sawrey in Furness, wore for his journey on foot to Keswick a striped linsey-woolsey waistcoat made from material he had woven himself.[25] Normal practice in non-weaving households was to have household-spun yarn woven on commission by a local jobbing weaver, like the Kirby Ravensworth labourer already mentioned. Throughout the north there were weavers who wove cloth for local consumption, especially linen, harden and linsey-woolsey. Sometimes they operated on a bespoke basis, working up other people's yarn into cloth on commission, in the manner already described. Cloth woven on a commission basis was not necessarily for the use of the spinner's own family, however. To raise money to enable her to marry in 1750, Margaret Kennel of Saltburn on the Yorkshire coast was said to have spun enough yarn to make 18 yards of hempen cloth, had it woven and sold it locally.[26] At other times weavers would make cloth on their own account and retail it in the locality. Thomas Walsh, a Wetherby linen weaver who in 1735 had a stall in Wetherby market where he sold linen cloth, put out his own flax to be spun by women in the town.[27] William Baldridge, a linen weaver at Easingwold in the North Riding of Yorkshire, was probably operating on a similar basis when in 1784 he sold to Ellin Bayston, an Easingwold yeoman's wife, a shirt cloth for her husband and a shift cloth for her daughter.[28] This sort of production was, of course, not confined to clothing fabrics. Ralph Watson, a linen weaver from Aiskew near Bedale in the North Riding of Yorkshire, had books of diaper and damask paper patterns, probably for tablecloths, which he circulated in the area to solicit business in the late eighteenth century (fig. 67).[29]

The criminal records enable us to establish the existence of the various kinds of household and local making of clothing fabrics that characterised the north of England, but they did not record this sort of activity systematically. Mentions of it are relatively few. To gauge the balance within the consumption decisions of plebeian men and women between clothing fabrics produced in the household or the immediate locality, and those acquired from distant manufacturers through the retailing network, we need to turn to other sources, in particular household and Poor Law accounts.[30] The few surviving account books of eighteenth-century northern husbandmen and rural trades-

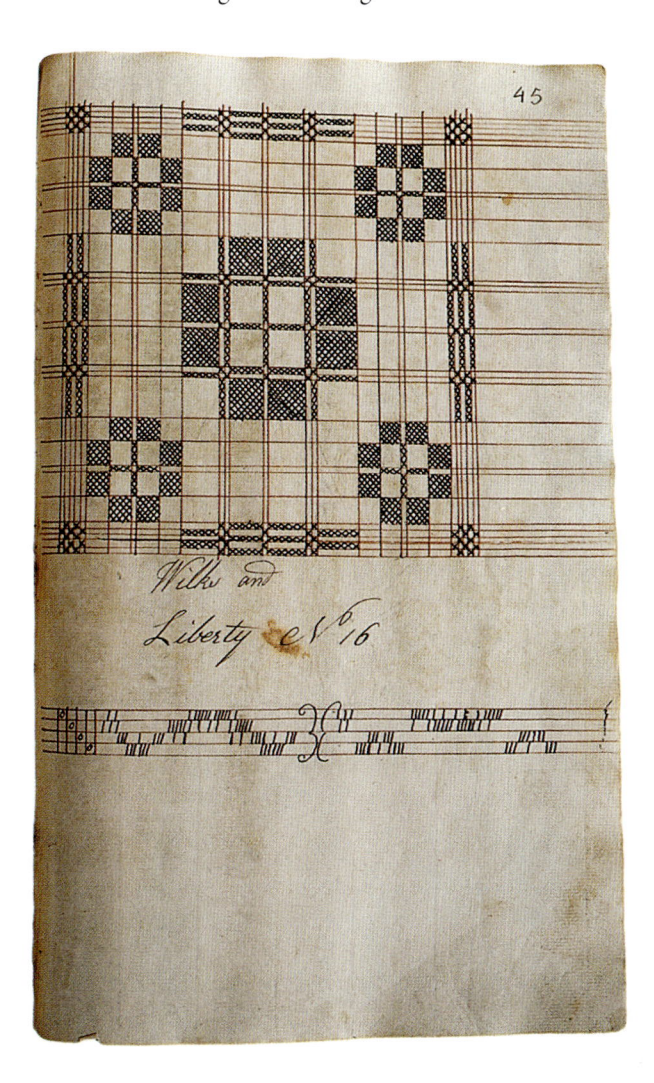

67 'Wilks and Liberty No. 16', late eighteenth century, ink on paper, North Yorkshire County Record Office, z.371.
A design for a woven linen cloth drawn by the jobbing linen weaver Ralph Watson of Aiskew near Bedale, North Yorkshire. From 'The Weaver's Guide', the book of figures he circulated among his local customers.

men are consistent with those of the gentry in suggesting that it was not uncommon for families to have cloth made up from their own fibre or yarn, or to acquire cloth woven by weavers in the immediate neighbourhood. But there is no case in the surviving accounts where fabrics of this kind accounted for the overwhelming bulk of the cloth recorded as used by the household, even at the beginning of the eighteenth century. Usually the range of such fabrics was narrow, their quality coarse, and they accounted for a minority of the cloth used for clothing (where it is possible to distinguish it).

The most humble northern family for whom a long run of household accounts is available is that of Richard Latham and his wife Nany, who farmed a smallholding of approximately 19 statute acres at Scarisbrick in west Lancashire.[31] The accounts cover all Richard Latham's married life from 1724 to his death in 1767. Between 1726 and 1741, eight children were born, seven of whom lived to adulthood. Six of the surviving children were daughters. There are a number of payments for spinning wheels and their accoutrements from the very beginning of the accounts, so it seems that spinning was performed both by Nany Latham and by her daughters as they grew beyond infancy. Payments appear in the accounts almost every year for raw flax. Raw hemp, wool and cotton were bought from time to time, but much less frequently. In the mid-1740s the Lathams bought some seed to grow flax, but we have no evidence they had done so previously. There is also good reason to believe that the women of the family undertook spinning for wages on an outwork basis. Scarisbrick was in the spinning catchment zone for both the Lancashire linen and cotton industry and the Lancashire-Yorkshire worsted industry.[32] In the late 1730s the family bought several wheels for spinning cotton, yet they subsequently bought only very small quantities of cotton wool to spin on them. The presence of the specialised wheels and a subsequent rise in the level of family expenditure suggests that cotton was being spun for wages.

It is difficult to establish precisely how the textile fibre bought or grown by the family was used, because the accounts offer little direct evidence of cloth being woven on commission from the yarn spun by the family out of its purchases of fibre. The family could certainly have sold the yarn they spun in the locality. But in the first 18 years of the accounts up to 1741, when the children were mostly young, it seems unlikely they did so to any great extent. This is the only period in the whole of the account book when the family paid to have spinning done by others, suggesting that if anything there was insufficient spinning labour available within the household to supply its own requirements. Yet the only payment for weaving recorded in the accounts during these years is for 16 yards of linsey-woolsey. In the same period less than 29 yards of plain linen cloth was bought ready-woven, much of it described as 'fine', although in addition they did regularly buy ready-woven linen in the form of handkerchiefs and occasionally aprons. It is inconceivable that a family which numbered nine by 1741 could have made do with such a small amount of plain linen, amounting to 1.6 yards per year, for clothing as well as household and farm purposes.[33] Three yards of cloth was sufficient to make only one adult man's shirt.[34]

In the same period, the family bought over 400 lbs of flax and hemp. According to contemporary calculations, to spin this fibre into yarn would have represented about eleven days unbroken work per year for an adult woman.[35] This amount of spinning was perhaps all that Nany Latham could manage, even with the assistance of her older daughters, while she was nursing young children and coping with her many other daily tasks on a farm where there were no live-in servants. Nevertheless, it was sufficient to make approximately 23 yards of relatively coarse plain linen or hempen cloth annually.[36] Not all of this would have been used for clothing. Well over a third by weight of the flax and hemp fibre bought by the family was cheap tow, consisting of shorter fibres, which would have produced a very coarse cloth probably used for household or farm purposes (sheeting, curtains, etc.) rather than for clothes. In addition some yarn may have been sold. If we assume that about half the flax and hemp fibre bought was used for clothing, this would represent approximately 12 yards a year, an amount probably sufficient in combination with the small amounts of linen purchased ready-woven to supply the requirements for linen clothing of a family with a growing number of young children, although hardly generously.

Hence, despite the absence of payments for weaving from the accounts, there are strong grounds for believing that much of the flax and hemp purchased by the family between 1724 and 1741 was spun and woven up into plain linen cloth for their own use. The weaving may have been done by jobbing weavers in the neighbourhood, paid in kind, or by work, or in money that was not recorded in the account book. It is also possible that Richard Latham did some of this relatively simple weaving himself, but if he was weaving in the years before 1741 when the children were young, it remains odd that no payments were recorded for loom equipment, which would have had to be renewed or repaired. The accounts include a number of payments for buying and repairing spinning wheels during these years.

There are no payments in the Latham account book for weaving pure woollen or worsted cloth, although the family did have small amounts of linsey-woolsey woven before and after 1741. Even if weaving was undertaken that does not appear in the accounts, it remains unlikely that the family had very much cloth woven from woollen yarn, because they bought only relatively small quantities of wool to spin.[37] Most of the yarn spun from this wool they probably knitted into stockings. They certainly owned knitting needles. In all likelihood, therefore, virtually all the woollen and worsted cloth they wore was purchased ready-woven. During the years 1724–41 the accounts record an average annual purchase of approximately 5 ¼ yards of woollen and worsted cloth per year, which was almost entirely used for the making of outer garments. If the adults followed the practice noted by Eden in various parts of the country of making do in the early and expensive years of married life with the stock of clothes acquired before marriage, then the purchases of woollen and worsted cloth recorded in the account book, in combination with a little linsey-woolsey woven from their own yarn, were probably sufficient to provide the bare minimum required for the family to clothe itself, although only by exercising the greatest austerity.[38] Nany Latham, for example, bought no gown lengths of cloth during the whole of these 18 years.[39]

We cannot know the precise ratio of household-spun to ready-woven cloth used by the Latham family in making its clothes. It seems almost certain, however, that in the financially strapped years of early marriage between 1724 and 1741 the family used more household-spun cloth than ready-woven. Indeed, if the estimates above are accurate, they used as much as two yards of household-spun for every yard of ready-woven. But this does not substantiate Eden's claim that almost every article of dress was made from home-manufactured fabric. The Latham's household-spun cloth was overwhelmingly plain, relatively coarse linen which would have been used for shirts, shifts and probably some (though by no means all) aprons. The family's outer garments and many accessories, including handkerchiefs and caps, were made from cloth bought ready-woven from retailers. Household-spun linens and ready-woven woollens were not substitutes for each other to any great extent. The yardage of household-spun cloth used to make clothes exceeded that of ready-woven fabric in these years only because the family could not afford to buy more than the barest minimum of the kinds of ready-woven cloth it required for outer garments and accessories.

After 1741, when the family's income increased, the situation changed dramatically. Ready-woven cloth eclipsed household-spun. Between 1742 and 1754 the amount of flax and hemp fibre purchased declined by 20 percent, although it was supplemented by some flax grown by the family.[40] In the same period the amount of plain linen bought ready-woven rose more than threefold to at least four yards per year, while the amount of ready-woven woollen and worsted cloth quadrupled to at least 21 yards per year. If the yardage of household-spun fabric used for clothing remained roughly the same as before 1742, the ratio of household-spun to ready-woven in their clothing was now reversed, with approximately two yards of ready-woven fabric for every yard of household-spun. Indeed so much more ready-woven cloth of all kinds was bought after 1742 that across the whole period from the start of the account book in 1724 to the time the children left home in the mid-1750s it is most unlikely the yardage of household-spun fabric used for clothing exceeded that of ready-woven cloth.[41]

Not enough accounts survive for families below the level of the gentry to establish trends over the eighteenth century, but gentry accounts suggest a decline in the proportion of household textile requirements sourced from home or local production. Late seventeenth- and early eighteenth-century northern gentry families often had significant amounts of linen and sometimes woollen cloth woven from yarn spun in their own households, although as with the Lathams cloth of this sort accounted for under half the yardage of fabric they used for clothing the family, including the male servants. As the eighteenth century progressed, the quantity of textiles secured in this manner appears to have declined and the range of cloth to have narrowed, a trend that a number of eighteenth-century commentators also noted in plebeian households.[42]

The pattern of a significant but subordinate role for home-made and locally made textiles that emerges from eighteenth-century northern household accounts re-occurs in Poor Law accounts for Cumberland, Furness and the West Riding of Yorkshire. In some Poor Law accounts, like those for Carleton, Yorkshire from 1713 to 1820, there are no payments for having cloth woven. In others, like those for Mirfield, Yorkshire between 1717 and 1795, and Calverley, Yorkshire between 1692 and 1822, flax and wool were bought for paupers to spin and some of the yarn was woven by local weavers into linen, harden or linsey-woolsey. However, such cloth generally accounted for only a minority of the fabric acquired by the overseers.[43] Exactly the same types of cloth were purchased ready-woven and by no means all such cloth was used for clothes. The bulk of the cloth used by paupers was bought ready-woven. It is difficult to determine from the accounts what proportion of this bought-in cloth was locally woven and what proportion ultimately sourced at a distance, but the range of fabrics makes it unlikely that the bulk of it was the product of local, bespoke manufacture. The one item of clothing that seems to have been made by paupers in very large quantities for their own use was stockings.[44]

There is little support then, either in the criminal depositions or in the household and Poor Law accounts, for Eden's contention that it was normal practice among plebeian families in the north to have the cloth for nearly every article of dress made at home or in the immediate locality. Some coarse linens, coarse woollens and linsey-woolseys might have been acquired in this way, but they were not all used for clothing, they provided only a minority of a household's garments, and they accounted for a particularly small proportion of adult outer garments. The evidence of gentry household accounts suggests, moreover, that this limited use of home- or locally produced cloth was in long-term decline over the eighteenth century, although it had been very widespread during the previous century.

By the 1830s, evidence from the census and official reports suggests household self-provisioning of clothing fabrics in the north of England had almost disappeared.[45] What then had sustained the combination of self-provisioning and purchase we have observed during the eighteenth century and why did self-provisioning progressively die out? Eden offered three explanations: price, quality and household income.[46] First, he claimed that in the 1790s shop-bought cloth was ousting household-spun fabric because of its low cost. The precise importance of cost in determining whether plebeian consumers used household-spun or ready-woven cloth is hard to establish. Not only is it a hazardous procedure for the historian to ascribe a cost to the spinning and other processing performed within the household, but it is also improbable that decisions in eighteenth-century plebeian families about the deployment of household labour involved minute calculations of relative costs. Moreover, it is not clear that the cost of the relevant shop-bought fabrics, whether linen or wool, did decline. Prices paid for the cheaper varieties of linen shirting, serge and flannel by northern overseers of the poor remained fairly stable for much of the eighteenth century, with if anything an upward trend towards its close. Only prices for cottons declined, yet, as we have seen, plebeian consumers demonstrated a continuing reluctance to substitute cotton for linen in shirts and shifts until the 1820s (see Chapter 7).

Second, Eden asserted that fabric made from household-spun yarn was superior because it was warmer and more durable. However, we should remember that the views of plebeian consumers on what constituted quality did not necessarily coincide with those of patrician commentators anxious to instruct them in household economy. Household-spun fabrics may well have been more durable than some of the equivalent fabrics supplied by shopkeepers, but it is also possible that such consumers judged quality less in terms of durability and more in terms of comfort, convenience or fashionability. It is striking that as their incomes rose in the 1740s the Lathams bought more ready-woven linen cloth, especially the finer varieties.

Third, Eden lamented the inability, owing to low incomes, of wage labourers to buy the raw materials necessary for spinning. Yet there is broad agreement among historians that real wages for labourers rose in the north towards the end of the eighteenth century and, if the Latham evidence can be generalised, higher incomes were more likely to be spent on increased quantities of shop-bought fabrics than on increased quantities of raw flax or wool. Moreover, the ability to pay for raw materials was only one of the ways considerations of household income might influence the deployment of a household's spinning labour.[47] In much of the north of England, such labour could be employed to earn wages, paid either in cash or in goods at the local shop. In a cash-starved economy, liquidity was attractive and the amount of spinning undertaken for household use may well have declined wherever waged spinning work was available.

Eden appears to have wilfully ignored the most obvious explanation for the decline of household self-provision in textiles in the eighteenth-century north – the rise of male wages there, combined with expansion of the more lucrative forms of waged outwork for women and children as the textile industries grew – perhaps because of his suspicion of high wages and their effects. However, this does not provide an entirely convincing explanation for the gentry's abandonment of household-spun linen. The decline in the use of household-spun woollen cloth, which appears to have taken place earlier, is instructive here.[48] The quality of locally made woollens appears to have been poor, in terms of fineness, finish, colour and range, compared with commercially sourced woollens of the same kinds made by specialist manufacturers, often for highly competitive international markets.[49] Consequently, the latter replaced the former. Increasingly, the same was coming to be true of linens. Already, at the end of the seventeenth century, a huge range of linens, both English-made and imported, could be bought from shopkeepers and itinerant salesmen.[50] By 1759, Stephen Hudson's shop at remote Fewston, high in the Yorkshire Pennines, sold eight named varieties of plain linens in different finenesses to a clientele consisting overwhelmingly of poor farmers and tradespeople. They ranged from Russia cloth at 4½d. a yard and harden at 6d., to fine Irish cloth at 22d. a yard and cambrick at 24d.[51] As Jan de Vries has suggested, women who moved from producing textiles for household use into waged work were attracted not just by a money income. Such a move was also encouraged by the ease with which they could replace fabrics woven from yarn they had spun themselves with commercially sourced textiles that were equally, or sometimes more, serviceable.

There is little doubt, therefore, that in the north in the eighteenth century the bulk of the fabric used to make garments for ordinary men and women came from retailers of various kinds, rather than being the production of the wearer's own family, although it may often have came indirectly through employers, charitable gifts or the Poor Law authorities. The criminal records provide examples of such men and women using the whole range of shops that appear in the probate inventories, as well as temporary outlets that the inventories do not record, such as stalls at markets and fairs. By the 1780s we find them patronising small village general stores, with their stocks of treacle, tea, candles and remnants of cotton velveret, where customers largely drawn from among the labouring poor could sit and pass the time of day.[52] Some of these small shops were extremely crude affairs, like that owned by John Lees at Elland near

Halifax in 1736, which consisted of a corner of his barn, partitioned off with flagstones.[53] But there are also the large urban drapers, with their rolls of cloth on shelves, their long counters, their display windows and their shop assistants. It is important to emphasise that working people, in addition to the well-to-do, patronised these larger establishments. There is certainly no indication in the criminal cases that when they came into these shops and asked to look at cotton prints or handkerchiefs their presence was automatically considered an occasion for special vigilance.

Inventories and business records make it clear that the whole range of such establishments provided credit to their retail customers. In the case of the smaller outlets, the fastest growing sector in the eighteenth century, credit appears to have been almost universal. It is curious, then, that so much emphasis has been placed in the literature on eighteenth-century consumption on the emergence of cash-only dealing in a few branches of retailing in London.[54] The assumption underlying this emphasis is presumably the Whiggish one that this was the way of the future. Yet work on twentieth-century consumption has stressed the overriding importance of new forms of credit (especially hire-purchase) for changes in patterns of acquisition, particularly of automobiles and white goods.[55] Although it is well-nigh impossible to gauge changes in the availability of shop credit in the eighteenth century, we need to acknowledge the range of sources of credit available for retail purchases, not just from shopkeepers, but from employers, relatives and neighbours. The period also saw the emergence of new devices for financing the purchase of clothing fabrics, such as the clothes club. These subscription clubs, usually organised by a draper or a tailor, were used by working people, like that run by Mr Roddam, a shopkeeper in Newcastle-on-Tyne in the late 1780s.[56]

However, there were other channels through which clothing fabrics were supplied which are not recorded in inventories. One of the most important of these was petty itinerant selling. In the sample of Yorkshire inventories there are chapmen's and hawkers' inventories, but most of them are for relatively wealthy men with total values over £50. It has been calculated from surviving licensing data that the number of licensed hawkers underwent a marked decline between the 1690s and the 1780s, but the possibility remains that this may not have been the experience of smaller, unlicensed itinerants.[57] We possess little evidence of how their numbers changed. Nevertheless, the criminal records make it clear that small-scale, usually unlicensed itinerant selling of clothing fabrics and accessories was widespread and welcomed by large numbers of respectable customers.

What has been called the 'hidden economy' of no-questions-asked dealing, so extensive in the modern world, flourished in the eighteenth-century north.[58] It could provide a cheap way of securing fabrics, including sought-after fabrics such as printed cottons. In November 1781, for example, three or four pieces of printed cotton (each 28 yards long) were stolen from the print field of Mitchel, Bell, Donald and Company at Wrayholme near Carlisle in Cumberland. In July the next year Susannah Dodgson, the wife of a Maryport seaman, was challenged in Carlisle market because she was wearing a gown made from the cloth and her child a frock made from it. Dodgson deposed that she had bought ten yards of the cloth from a man called John Byers. Dodgson recalled that

> Byers who seemed to be a labouring man and said he lived at Aspatria . . . came to the house of Hannah Brougham, mother of this informant, at Maryport . . . and offered to both this informant and her said mother ten yards of printed cotton and six yards of printed cotton of a different pattern from the said ten yards, to sell, saying that he the said Byers had a christening and wanted money to buy necessaries with.[59]

Dodgson bought the cloth at 1s. 6d. a yard (cheap, but probably not absurdly so) and her mother bought the other six yards at 17d. a yard. Dodgson had a gown and a bedgown made for herself, and a frock for her young child from the ten yards of cloth. Maryport was 27 miles from Carlisle and she was unlucky to be spotted in the market at Carlisle by someone who recognised the cloth so long after the theft. Similarly, two years earlier, Ann Brown, a farmer's wife from Stanwix outside Carlisle, bought two and a half yards of cotton printed in black on a chocolate ground from a local woman for 5s. She had it made it up into a bedgown. The fabric was a new design that had been stolen from the print field belonging to Thomas Losh and Company at Dentonholme in Carlisle. The bedgown was identified by one of Losh's workmen when she wore it on a Saturday in Carlisle market (fig. 66).[60] Again and again, offenders charged with stealing cloth or clothing said (if pleading innocence) that they got the stolen goods from a hawker, or (if confessing) that they had disposed of them, or intended to dispose of them, 'in the country'. The prices charged may have been low, but there was always a ready excuse available – a desperate need for liquidity when faced with a pressing debt, a sale of bankrupt stock, a family crisis. The acceptability of such dealing was reinforced by the large numbers of legitimate dealers selling in this way, like the West Riding clothiers who travelled the fairs of the East Riding in 1791 selling small lengths of their woollen cloth.[61]

The other important route for the supply of clothing materials to final customers that does not emerge from the inventories was through tailors and mantuamakers. No inventories were found in the sample for anyone described as a mantuamaker and tailors' inventories rarely record any stock. But shopkeepers' and drapers' business records make it clear that these tradespeople did not simply process cloth which had been bought by their customers (although this was often the case), but also arranged the purchase of the material (or at least paid for it). These stocks of material rarely appear in the tailors' inventories because they were turned over quickly. On the other hand, sometimes the relationship was reversed, the draper making the arrangements with the tailor for the cloth to be made up.[62] Arrangements of this kind were particularly easy for someone who operated both as a tailor and as a general shopkeeper.[63]

This chapter has used a critique of Frederick Eden's comments about the north of England at the end of the eighteenth century to develop a picture of the supply of plebeian clothing materials in the region between the late seventeenth and the late eighteenth centuries. Already at the beginning of the eighteenth century, most people had ready access to appropriate shops. The two developments that have emerged as most important for the supply of plebeian clothing materials are the spread of the small shop and the decline in the volume and range of cloth woven for household use from yarn spun in the household.

There is good reason to believe that the same pattern applied to much of the rest of provincial England. Small shops proliferated there, too, becoming the subject of much patrician criticism by the end of the eighteenth century.[64] Moreover, just as Eden greatly exaggerated the degree of household self-sufficiency in clothing materials in the eighteenth-century north of England, so he overstated the dependence on shop-bought fabrics in the Midlands and the south. The Board of Agriculture reports in the 1790s and early 1800s make it clear that some of the kinds of household self-provisioning Eden described for the north were widespread in the Midlands and parts of East Anglia at this period, although often, as in the north, in decline.[65] In Staffordshire, for instance, it was reported in 1794 that 'there is no considerable public manufacture of linen, but a good deal of hurden, hempen, and flaxen cloth, got up in private families', while 'a good deal of woollen cloth is got up in the country by private families, though in less quantity than formerly'.[66] Similarly, especially earlier in the eighteenth century, we find overseers of the poor having cloth woven by local weavers, often from yarn spun by paupers. This was the case at Thaxted in Essex before 1716, Eaton Socon in Bedfordshire between 1706 and 1718, and Chalfont St Peter in Buckinghamshire in 1752, although, as in the north, it was far from universal. In other well-documented southern parishes, such as Holne in Devon, there is no evidence of the practice.[67]

The same was true of families. In the 1740s, the Smedley family, which farmed at Breadsall just outside Derby, regularly bought tow to spin into linen yarn which was made into cloth for household use by a local weaver.[68] In east Suffolk, where hemp was grown and there was a buoyant commercial hemp-weaving industry, families like that of the Chediston shoemaker John Spore in the 1770s and 1780s would buy and spin hemp and have it woven into cloth in quantities that suggest it was principally intended for household use.[69] The blacksmith Mark Palmer who lost his possessions in the 1789 fire at Brandon, at the opposite end of Suffolk, owned a spinning wheel for tow.[70] Elsewhere in the Midlands and the south, in Cambridgeshire, Kent and Sussex for example, gentry and professional families followed the same practice, in the late seventeenth and early eighteenth centuries at least.[71] As in the north, there is no suggestion that the whole of these households' cloth requirements were supplied internally, but domestically produced fabrics, predominantly coarse linens, made a significant contribution. The practice may have declined rather earlier in the century in parts of the Midlands and the south than in the north.[72] Yet we should no more accept Eden's account of complete plebeian dependency on shop-bought clothing there, than his picture of northern self-sufficiency.

Whatever the empirical deficiencies of Eden's account of regional variations in the supply of clothing, it can tell us a great deal about elite attitudes to plebeian domestic economy at the end of the eighteenth century. Its rhetorical effectiveness was sustained by the way it extended to the north as a whole an image of sturdy, virtuous Cumbrian self-sufficiency that had become a stereotype by the 1790s. Neither the received image of Cumbrian self-sufficiency nor Eden's extension of it to the rest of the north of England stand up to detailed scrutiny. Eden's north was geographically elastic and ever-receding. In one passage in *The State of the Poor* he condemned what he regarded as the extravagance of labouring people in the Home Counties by contrasting it to the frugality of the labouring poor in Yorkshire, but in another it was the excesses of the poorer inhabitants of Leeds in Yorkshire that he compared unfavourably with the thrift practised by their equivalents in 'the more northern parts of England'.[73] Where clothes were concerned, Eden's general statements portrayed self-sufficiency as a characteristic of the north as a whole, but all but one of his locationally specific references to northern self-provisioning were to Cumbria.[74] When he described Cumbrian yeomen and labourers of the mid-1790s as being, or having recently been, virtually self-sufficient in clothing, Eden simply reproduced what was a stock theme in the work of those authors who contributed to the boom in topographical writing about the Lake Counties from the 1770s.[75] Thomas West in *The Antiquities of Furness*, published in 1774, said that 'within the memory of man, every family manufactured their own wearing apparel'. William Hutchinson in his *History and Antiquities of Cumberland*, published in 1794, said of the inhabitants of Carlisle in the mid-eighteenth century that 'most of the people's apparel continued to be of their own spinning'. John Housman in his *Topographical Description of Cumberland, Westmorland, Lancashire and a part of the West Riding of Yorkshire*, published in 1800, described the Cumbrians as 'almost all manufacturers in miniature, there being few families in the county who do not spin their own linen and woollen cloth; and also spin and knit their own stockings'.[76]

Passages of this kind should be treated with some caution as historical evidence. At one and the same time, they served to demonstrate the social and economic progress the region was making, while emphasising the picturesque backwardness of Lakeland yeoman families and the sterling simplicity of their manners and customs.[77] A significant corrective is provided by one of the earliest comments on the subject of Cumbrian clothing, which appeared in a letter published in the *Gentleman's Magazine* in 1766, before the boom in topographical writing about the area and in the very different context of debates on taxation. Although the letter is at pains to emphasise the extreme poverty of Cumbrian yeoman families, it does not claim they were self-sufficient in clothing. Instead, it notes a similar combination of household-spun and cheap shop-bought cloth to that which emerges in the Latham family accounts and elsewhere. 'They wear wooden shoes, shod like a horse's foot with iron, sackcloth shirts, yarn stockings, home-spun linsey, and cloth that comes about 2s. a yard, felt hats.'[78]

Exaggerating the intensity and extent of northern self-provisioning in clothing helped sustain Eden's broader argument in *The State of the Poor*. The book's shortcomings as a source for the study of clothing and textiles derive directly from the strategies Eden employed to make his case convincing to his eighteenth-century audience. Eden was critical of the Poor Law and the extravagant systems of plebeian domestic economy he associated with it. He sought to demonstrate that, under the right circumstances, the labouring poor could lead independent, self-reliant lives which would reduce the burden on the poor rates. An obvious way to have made this point would have been to use the example of Scotland, which did not have a Poor Law on the English model and where self-provisioning of the sort he extolled was widespread.[79] But for late eighteenth-century Englishmen, Scotland exemplified the worst associations of poverty – bare legs, backwardness, degradation and filth. Travellers who crossed the Solway from Dumfriesshire into Cumberland were in no doubt that dress and manners were totally different.[80] Although Eden did mention and indeed praise Scottish self-provisioning, his case was better served by his claim that plebeian self-sufficiency in clothing was a general characteristic of the north of England.[81] It allowed him to contrast virtuous plebeian frugality in the north with corrupt plebeian extravagance in the south. In this way his argument could draw on the deep eighteenth-century anxiety about the morally debilitating effects of luxury, without appearing to endorse those manifestations of poverty which the English despised among the Scots. The result was a forceful and influential intervention in the late eighteenth-century debate on the English Poor Law, but a misleading account of the supply of plebeian clothing in provincial England.

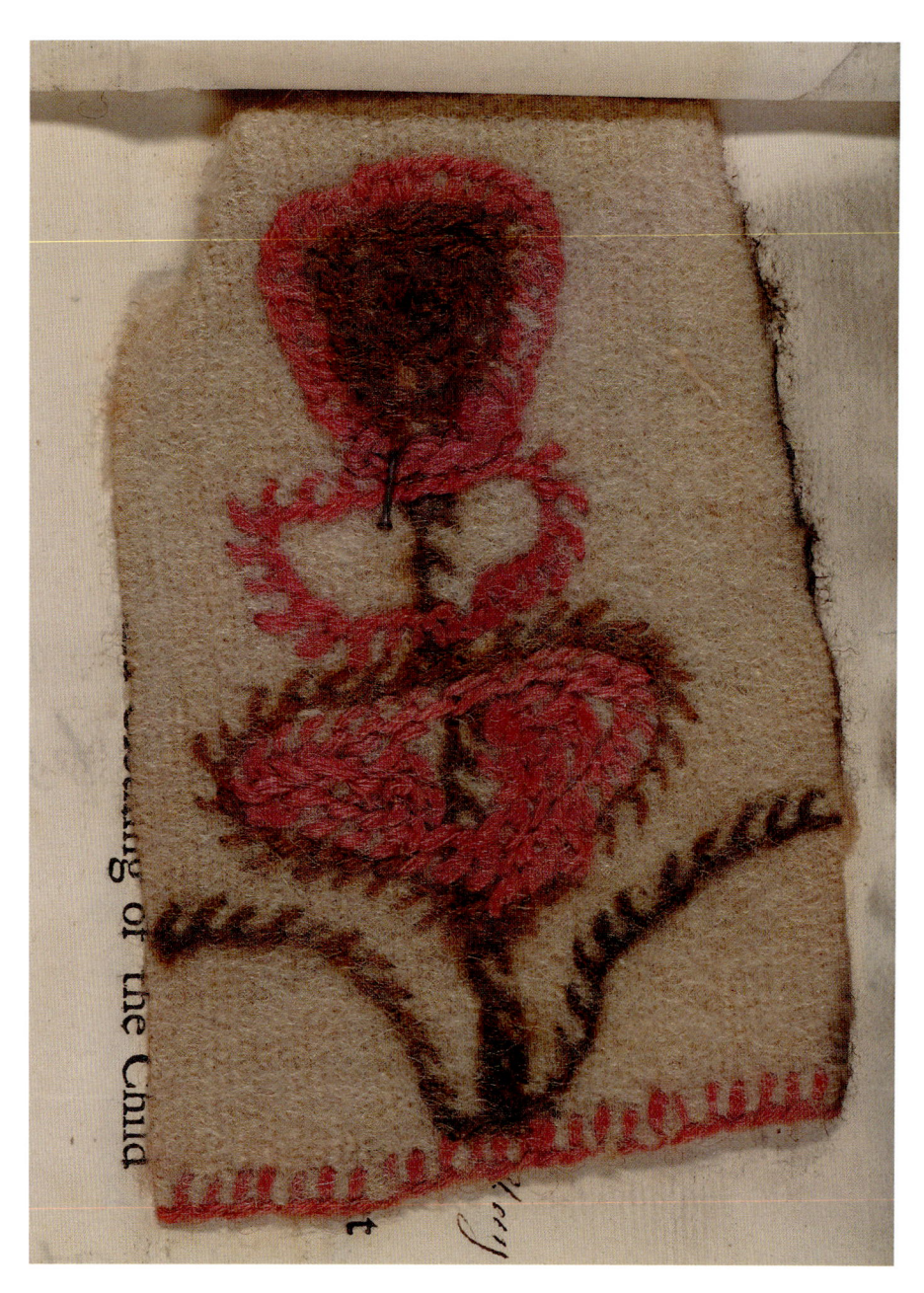

68 'Flannel the bottom worked', 1759, flannel embroidered with worsted yarn, London Metropolitan Archives, A/FH/A/9/1/143, Foundling no. 12843. Crude embroidered decoration on the bodice-coat left with an infant boy at the London Foundling Hospital.

9
Clothing Provincial England: Garments

WHEN SIR FREDRICK EDEN COMPARED LABOURERS' CLOTHING in the north and south of England in *The State of the Poor*, he was concerned not just with how they obtained clothing materials, but also with how their clothes were made and supplied.[1] Yet he had surprisingly little to say on the subject, apart from pointing to the reliance of labouring people in the immediate neighbourhood of London on ready-made and especially second-hand clothing. In the north, he insisted, almost every article of plebeian dress was manufactured at home, apart from shoes and hats, whereas in the Midlands and the south labourers bought their clothes from shopkeepers. He never specified, however, whether these purchases consisted of the materials out of which clothes were to be made on a bespoke basis, or ready-made clothes.

This is an important distinction, because the emergence of ready-made clothing, especially ready-made main garments such as gowns, suits, breeches, jackets, waistcoats and coats, has been a key preoccupation in histories of clothing.[2] It is an innovation that historians have used to gauge economic development, an intensification in the division of labour they regard as characteristic of modern economies. Neil McKendrick has gone so far as to write of the emergence of 'mass production' in this context, asserting that the eighteenth century witnessed the appearance for the first time of 'mass-produced cheap clothes'.[3] This use of the notion of 'mass production' is misleading. Clothes were not machine-cut or machine-sewn at this period, although garments and accessories made by hand were certainly sold ready-made.[4] Beverly Lemire's surveys of sellers of ready-made garments (new and second-hand) in late eighteenth-century English trade directories and insurance records demonstrate that such retailers were fairly numerous.[5]

The three linked samples of Yorkshire probate inventories employed in Chapter 8 include both retailers who sold ready-made clothes and the artisan-retailers who were the principal makers of bespoke clothing. Among the latter, the two main occupations that appear in the inventories are tailors and shoemakers.[6] Between the late seventeenth and the late eighteenth centuries, the inventories of these artisan-retailers show similar, marked increases in wealth. The average value of tailors' inventories shows an increase of 40 percent between the earlier period 1660 to 1740 and the later period 1740 to 1800.[7] The equivalent increase for shoemakers was 43 percent.[8] It is important to stress, however, that even as they became more prosperous, most of these artisan-retailers, especially in rural areas, continued to operate on a small scale. They remained far from wealthy, often living in small rural settlements where they combined their trade with some agricultural pursuit. The aggregated values of the stock in trade held by shoemakers, principally leather, show virtually no change overall, while hardly any tailors' inventories record any stock in trade at all. A few urban shoemakers carried large stocks of finished boots and shoes, but this was not a new development. The practice was already established in Yorkshire well before 1740 and had existed across the Pennines at Chester in the sixteenth century.[9] What is absent in the Yorkshire inventory samples is evidence of large stocks of ready-made or second-hand garments like those held by the salesmen (sellers of ready-made and second-hand clothes, usually a combination of the two) whose inventories survive for early eighteenth-century Kent. The 1703 inventory of Robert Amsden, a Canterbury salesman, included over 200 gowns and petticoats and nearly 400 coats, waistcoats and breeches for men and boys.[10] The tailors and other garment-makers in the Yorkshire sample carried hardly any stock. The only exception was James Robinson, a Bradford breeches-maker, who died in 1782 with 30 pairs of finished breeches in his shop valued in his inventory at £4. Drapers, mercers and shopkeepers often held a couple of cloaks, a gown or two, a petticoat or some waistcoats among their shop stock, but the numbers were always small.

This pattern was not true of clothing accessories – handkerchiefs, stockings, gloves and hats, for instance. People who described themselves as drapers, mercers or shopkeepers frequently held some of these items in large quantities, although there is no marked chronological trend. Some caution is necessary here, however, regarding what constituted a finished article. It is clear from the evidence of criminal depositions that what were described in the inventories as handkerchiefs were often not individual objects, but continuous pieces of cloth from which an individual handkerchief had to be cut and then hemmed.[11] The same may have been true of aprons and caps, and was certainly true of shirts, shifts, gowns and waistcoats. The words gown and gown-piece, shirt and shirt-piece, and waistcoat and waistcoat-piece were used interchangeably. Sometimes these terms indicate a ready-made item of clothing, but by no means always. Failure to recognise the custom can lead to exaggeration of the availability of ready-made items.[12]

The evidence of the Yorkshire inventories suggests, therefore, that the means by which clothes were made for customers in the north did not change greatly between the late seventeenth century and the late eighteenth century. The majority of artisan-retailers went on making clothes on a bespoke basis. They seem to have became more prosperous, but it is not clear that the clothes-making element in their businesses changed dramatically in scale. The availability of some ready-made articles, particularly shoes, was well established in towns, but this does not appear from the inventories to have been true of garments to any marked degree.

Precisely how, then, were plebeian garments made? The evidence of northern criminal records, along with business, personal and Poor Law accounts, suggests a broad but far from rigid division between garments made up within the family and those which outsiders were paid to make. Almost all the references to the assembly of outer garments – men's coats, waistcoats and breeches, and women's gowns and cloaks – indicate that the task was undertaken by specialists, although the specialist might execute the work in the customer's own home. It is also striking how often these specialists were male tailors, who made up women's gowns and cloaks in addition to men's garments, despite the availability of sewing skills among the female population. Male tailors made up most of the women's outer garments for the Latham household and a good deal of the business of a tailor-shopkeeper from the north Tyne valley in the 1770s involved making up women's gowns.[13]

It was only in the course of the eighteenth century that the pre-existing male near-monopoly of the making of plebeian women's outer garments was ended. For most of the sixteenth and early seventeenth centuries, it had been normal practice for outer garments for both sexes and at all social levels to be made by male tailors. But in the course of the late seventeenth century this male monopoly was challenged by the emergence in London of the female mantuamaker, making a new garment, the mantua, a loose gown, initially for a fashionable, elite clientele.[14] By the 1690s female mantuamakers were present at York. The city's Merchant Tailors Company tried to prevent these women working, initially by prosecuting them and later by promoting a nation-wide campaign for legislation to suppress them. The same threat to the male monopoly of garment-making had arisen in other provincial towns at roughly the same time and, as part of its campaign, the York Company wrote for support to tailors in towns across the country, including Pontefract, Ripon, Wakefield, Richmond, Hull and Newcastle in the north of England. However, the campaign did not succeed and in 1704 the York Merchant Tailors accepted ten pounds in exchange for permission for a Mrs Johnson to work 'no wayes further than the making of mantees and pettycoates'. Subsequently, the Company accepted other women in return for a suitable payment and these women went on to take apprentices, mainly girls.[15]

At first these women were few in number and probably made mantuas mainly for wealthy women. It was only in the course of the eighteenth century that mantuamakers became widely represented in rural areas. As they did so, and as fashion moved away from the mantua, they came to make women's gowns of all sorts, as well as cloaks and petticoats, although they retained the name mantuamaker. Unfortunately, the lack of occupational information for eighteenth-century women renders it very difficult to establish the rate at which mantuamakers spread. By the mid-century, women calling themselves mantuamakers were present even in isolated upland districts, such as Ann Wigglesworth at Thruscross near Pateley Bridge in Yorkshire in the 1750s and Sarah Crosthwaite at Threlkeld in Cumberland in 1766.[16] But it is only with the 1787 Westmorland census, which, unusually, recorded women's occupations, that it is possible to establish any sense of their distribution. Out of 13 townships for which women's occupations were consistently recorded in the census, mantuamakers were present in almost as many townships (five) as had resident tailors (six), although the number of individual tailors was far larger.[17] Even in remote, mountainous Westmorland, plebeian men and women enjoyed ready access to garment-making skills characterised by a division of labour along gender lines.

If mantuamakers were generally as widespread in the late eighteenth-century north as the Westmorland evidence suggests, it is inconceivable that their work could have been restricted to making outer garments only for wealthy women. There may have been more tailors, but tailors' work involved heavier fabrics and more time-consuming techniques, and it was not restricted to garments. Tailors went on making women's gowns well into the second half of the eighteenth century in parts of the north, but it is clear from the criminal records for the 1780s and 1790s that by the end of the century it was principally the local mantuamaker that plebeian women approached to have gowns or other outer garments made. The progressive feminisation of the assembly of women's outer garments was one of the most striking changes in the supply of clothing in the north of England in the course of the eighteenth century, calling into question the widely held view that there was a diminution in women's work opportunities in the course of the century.[18]

The question of why mantuamakers replaced tailors in the assembly of plebeian women's outer garments in the course of the eighteenth century is best approached by considering the broader issue of how tasks were divided across garment assembly in general. Eden's suggestion that all plebeian garments were assembled predominantly at home by members of the household can hardly be correct if both tailors and mantuamakers were so widespread throughout the late eighteenth-century rural north. Yet undoubtedly many items of clothing were made up at home by northern plebeian women. What were the considerations that determined whether a garment would be assembled by a member of the household or by a professional, by a woman or by a man?

Basic cutting and sewing skills were widespread among plebeian women in the eighteenth-century north of England, but they were generally applied to making inner garments and accessories, not to outer garments. There are numerous references in the criminal records to plebeian women cutting, sewing, altering and mending shirts, shifts, handkerchiefs, aprons, caps, childrens' frocks and petticoats for their own families. The vast majority of these items was probably made up at home in this manner. Such skills were largely absent among men, other than professionals like tailors, breeches-makers and shoemakers. Single adult sons had their clothes repaired and linen garments made by mothers and sisters both before and after they left home. Making shirts was seen as a fundamental female duty. When her brother James set out for Liverpool in 1781, Mary Room of Kirkpatrick near Gretna Green, widow, 'being his own sister, made and sewed part of his shirts and when finished saw the two initial letters J.R. put upon the haunch of three of the said shirts'.[19] Single men who were strangers in a locality would go to women to have shirts made, like George Fenkell, a North Shields shipwright who, when in Whitby in 1753, got two shirts made from a piece of stolen checked cotton by a widow, Mary Carter.[20] The only evidence of men sewing (other than in a professional capacity) is among soldiers and sailors, who often had to mend their own clothes. William Broadfoot, a private soldier, offered as an alibi when accused of a highway robbery at Newcastle in 1798 the fact that he stayed up late 'mending his breeches', while a North Shields sailor recognised a shirt stolen from him in 1792 because he had mended it himself at the sleeve with a piece of white cloth.[21]

Basic cutting and sewing skills may have been widespread among plebeian women, but they were far from universal. One of the most striking features of northern Poor Law accounts is the large number of women on whose behalf the overseers paid not only for linen cloth to make shifts, but also for having the cloth cut and sewn. Cutting out and sewing up a shift was a relatively simple task. Nevertheless, at Calverley, Yorkshire, in 1757–8 the overseers paid for both cloth and making for nine women, but provided cloth alone to only two. In all seven instances at Carleton in the West Riding in 1803 where shifts were provided, the overseers paid for both cloth and making. Even in a workhouse like that at Mirfield, Yorkshire in the mid-eighteenth century, where the inmates were expected to work at spinning, regular payments were made to outsiders for making up linen inner garments and accessories such as shifts and caps.[22] Whether this evidence demonstrates that the female paupers concerned lacked the appropriate sewing skills is unclear. It is possible they had possessed the skills, but were too old or infirm to use them. This seems unlikely, given the large numbers of mothers of young children on relief. Alternatively, they may have had the skills but were not encouraged to use them, because of an emphasis by the overseers on spinning, or because of a desire on the part of the overseers to channel sewing work to particular women in the parish as a means of providing them with an income. On the other hand, perhaps many plebeian women could simply not sew well enough. A survey of the poor of Chester at the end of the century found that, in one parish, three-quarters of girls aged nine to 13 'could not sew at all, and not one of them so well, as to make a single article of dress' (figs 68, 69, 70).[23]

If the women of a family were unable to cut and sew inner garments and accessories, for whatever reason, then other women were hired to do the work. It might constitute part of their duties as domestic servants, or they might undertake it on a jobbing basis. In 1792, for example, Mary Temple of the Raw, high on Elsdon Common in Northumberland, deposed that she had known Margaret Crozer, a neighbour and a small shopkeeper, for several years and that she lived under the same roof as Crozer from May 1790 to May 1791. She

> used to cut out, make, mend and wash the linnen and cloathes of the said Margaret Crozer, who was very infirm through age and that there was no part of the cloaths, linnen and wearing apparel of the said Margaret Crozer but what she the said Mary Temple was well acquainted with.[24]

Another neighbour, Elizabeth Jackson, explained how she knew a black quilted petticoat with a blue and white striped worsted lining was Margaret Crozer's.

> She helped make the aforesaid petticoat along with Mary Temple at the same time on or about Christmas last past who then lived under the same roof as Margaret

69   Fabric 'worckt with flowers cuft up with purpill and white cotten', 1759, linen or cotton embroidered with silk thread, London Metropolitan Archives, A/FH/A/9/1/155, Foundling no. 14084. Accomplished embroidered decoration, possibly professional, on the gown worn by an infant boy left at the London Foundling Hospital.

> Crozer lived at the Raw aforesaid – and also one blue and white checked apron, which this deponent cut out for the said Margaret Crozer.[25]

It was probably women whose livelihoods depended on taking in this kind of light work who were described as seamstresses in the 1787 Westmorland census. There they were almost as numerous as the mantuamakers, but were distinguished from them in the listings.[26] There is no evidence of such work being undertaken by male tailors.

As far as inner garments and many accessories were concerned, therefore, Eden's view that in the north clothing was made up by members of the household was broadly correct, if somewhat exaggerated. However, as we have seen, this was not true of outer garments, either for men or for women. Despite the wide extent of basic cutting and sewing skills among the female population, women did not make tailored garments

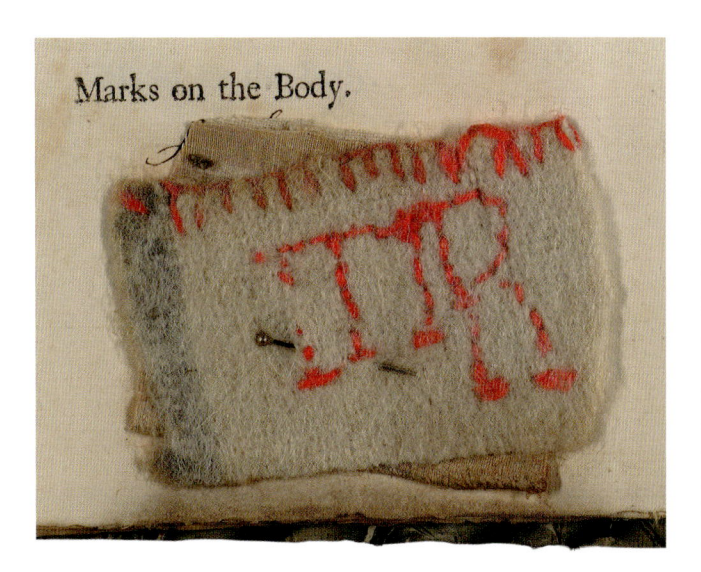

70 'Flannel marked MR and overcast with red worsted', 1759, flannel embroidered with worsted yarn, London Metropolitan Archives, A/FH/A/9/1/126, Foundling no. 11285. Very crude embroidery on clothing left with an infant boy at the London Foundling Hospital.

for their menfolk and usually went to specialists to have their own outer garments – gowns and cloaks especially, but also petticoats – made up or even altered. For example, in September 1789 Suzannah White, a labourer's wife from Rothwell near Leeds, came to the house of Sarah Hey at Rothwell and 'brought a long black silk cloak to be altered for herself which [Sarah Hey] altered and one of the said Suzannah White's children fetched the same away again'.[27]

Why did relatively poor women in the eighteenth-century north, who could often cut and sew, pay for specialists to make and alter their own outer garments? Why did the gender of those specialists change from the male tailor to the female mantuamaker? These patterns of specialisation, it is important to emphasise, were confined neither to the north of England nor to the plebeian classes. Change originated elsewhere, both geographically and socially. Mid-seventeenth-century plebeian women's outer garments had been made generally by male tailors out of woollen fabrics. Like the fashionable garments of elite women at that period, they had to be assembled in ways that required the key tailoring skill of moulding the garment to the body. With the advent of the new fashion for the loose-hanging mantua in elite circles during the second half of the seventeenth century, a different technique was needed. The essential skill required for making and fitting a mantua was that of pleating and draping the light silk fabric over a foundation of boned stays (which continued to be made by men). Male tailors may have been competent to undertake this work, but in France it was opened to women by royal decree in 1675. This new French practice of women making outer garments provided a model of fashionable women's garment-making that was swiftly taken up in elite circles in England, although male tailors continued to make elite women's riding habits and other garments that required heavy materials and traditional tailoring skills.[28]

As we have seen, the practice of women making outer garments, especially gowns, did not immediately affect non-elite women. But during the century after 1675, as plebeian women's outer garments came increasingly to be made from lighter fabrics, especially linen and cotton, their making was gradually transferred from male tailors to female mantuamakers. This transformation seems to have owed something to the change in fabric, something to the changes in technique which followed the adoption of the mantua and something to the model provided by fashionable elite practice. Price may also have been a factor. It is virtually impossible to establish precise price comparisons, but female mantuamakers, like other women workers, may well have been accustomed to accept less money than their male counterparts for equivalent work.

But why did poor women employ specialists to make their outer garments at all? In the seventeenth century, plebeian women would not have acquired the skills necessary for tailoring woollen fabrics in the course of making inner garments from linen. But the lighter fabrics increasingly used for plebeian women's outer garments during the eighteenth century were closer in character to the fabrics with which plebeian women were already familiar. Nevertheless, the skill required for making gowns was greater than that needed for making shirts and shifts, both during the period in the early eighteenth century when the fashion for loose mantua-like gowns prevailed, and in the second half of the century when gowns were more closely fitted. It would be wrong to underestimate the level and specialisation of the skills required in making plebeian women's gowns from light fabrics, although it is difficult to establish the precise character of those skills because so few of the garments concerned survive. By the late eighteenth century it may have been the way the fabric was cut that was crucial, with the distinction between what might be expected to be undertaken by a mantuamaker, as opposed to the women of a household, possibly turning on this key skill. Such appears to have been the case for two Leeds women who stole ten yards of linen near Barnsley in 1786. They took the linen to the house of Sarah Lockwood of Worsborough Dale 'and desired her to cut the same out into bed gowns . . . and they took each of them one, and gave Lockwood four yards of the said striped linen for her trouble in cutting them out'.[29] A couple of days later they were apprehended wearing the bedgowns, having evidently not required Lockwood's specialist skills for the sewing.

The dependence on specialists should not, however, be interpreted simply as testimony to the shortage of appropriate skills among the female population at large. It also reflected the quality standards which plebeian consumers applied to the clothes they acquired. The materials used for plebeian men and women's outer garments were, for them, costly; usually much more than a typical week's wage for fabric for a man's suit or a woman's gown. The overwhelming reliance on specialists for making outer garments, whether male tailors or female mantuamakers, testifies to their customers' concern to ensure that such expensive materials should not be wasted in the cutting, and should meet their criteria for style, fit and the handling of pattern. These criteria are often difficult to reconstruct, but their pursuit indicates the importance plebeian consumers attached to the way their clothes looked.

In considering how clothes were made, our concern so far has been with bespoke garments, whether made by household members, or by professionals. But was it really the case that ready-made garments, whether new or second-hand, were unimportant in the supply of plebeian clothing in the north of England? Neither Eden's *State of the Poor* nor the Yorkshire inventory samples offer evidence for the availability of ready-made main garments, in contrast to the availability of ready-made accessories – shoes, stockings, hats, buckles and the like – which is well established. A different picture emerges from the criminal records. One of the most noteworthy features of thefts of money in the eighteenth century is the frequency with which offenders spent stolen money on food, drink and especially clothing. Out of 15 examples in the 60-year sample of northern criminal cases which detail the clothing purchased with the stolen money, nine involved buying garments ready-made, and six buying cloth to make into garments. Clearly it was possible for offenders in the north of England to buy garments ready-made. Often they chose to do so, although it is usually unclear whether the clothes concerned were new or second-hand. In 1756, for example, William Wilson, the 14-year-old son of a potter from Blackwell, county Durham, was charged with stealing over £16 from a house at Masham in the North Riding of Yorkshire. At Richmond, on his way home, he was able to buy

> the coat and waistcoat which he now has on of Mrs Wrather, for which he gave her twelve shillings, and the stockings he bought of Christopher Watkin for which he gave eighteen pence and a silk handkerchief and the wigg he bought of Thomas Scott for which he gave four shillings.[30]

This evidence needs to be treated with some care, however. Offenders of this kind were usually on the run and therefore more likely than other clothes buyers to want ready-made items. Having cloth made up would have exposed them to additional risk of detection while the cloth was with the tailor or mantuamaker. Moreover, all the purchases of ready-made clothes under these circumstances took place in the largest towns – York, Newcastle, Whitehaven, Leeds, Richmond and Lancaster – even when the theft was undertaken elsewhere. This would suggest that it was much harder to come by ready-made items on demand in the countryside and the smaller market towns. Indeed, what is most noteworthy is that some of these offenders did buy cloth to be made up, rather than buying ready-made garments, and that they made such purchases not only in the countryside but also in towns like Newcastle and Barnsley. If London caricatures are to be believed, one of the reasons for preferring bespoke to ready-made garments, especially if there was no shortage of cash, was the latter's poor fit (figs 71, 74).

Take an example from 1793. Jane Boys, a female apprentice in husbandry from Stillington near York, stole several guineas from her master. She and another woman went to shops at Easingwold, four miles away, and looked 'at some small patterns for frocks and purchased eight yards of printed cotton and 7 yards of dimity' for £1 11s. 10d. The young apprentice then bought a ribbon, a pair of women's gloves, two cotton handkerchiefs, one pocket handkerchief, some tea, six and a half yards of wildbore stuff and a cheese. She and her companion subsequently bought a tin tea kettle, some wine, a tin saucepan, a pair of bellows, a japanned hand or tea board, two japanned waiters, a pair of woman's plated buckles, a pair of woman's pattens, 1 pair of box joints and two box locks, total cost 11s. 3d.[31] This list is remarkable because it includes so many of the new consumer durables and semi-durables that became available to working people (although rarely like this all at once) in the late eighteenth century. Indeed, it is almost a checklist of plebeian female consumer longing. It is striking, however, that the two women did not buy finished garments off the peg, even though Stillington was only ten miles from York, with its clothes dealers and pawnbrokers. For clothing, they bought fabric and accessories. Even in a large maritime town like Newcastle an offender of this kind might prefer to buy cloth and have it made up rather than buy finished garments. Mark Thornton, a pitman from Heaton Colliery in Northumberland, was accused in 1793 of stealing £278 from the colliery office, mainly in bank notes, but partly in cash. Shortly afterwards, he and a local tailor came to a Newcastle draper's shop where Thornton bought a cassimere waistcoat-piece with linings and trimmings and 'stuff for a pair of breeches'.[32]

Nevertheless, if we examine cases where clothes were stolen, it is clear that the market for second-hand clothing in the north of England was huge. As with dealing in fabrics, this market often operated on a purely informal basis. Just as it appears to have been reasonably unexceptionable to sell cloth door to door, so it was to sell garments in public. For example, in 1794 Thomas Dearlove, a servant in husbandry, was at work at Aickton near Wetherby in Yorkshire along with about twenty other people gathering potatoes. William Bramley and Thomas Musgrave, labourers at a corn mill at Hunsingore four miles away, came into the field and offered to sell him some clothes.

> He at first refused to buy as he did not want any, but on Musgrave's importuning and representing his distressed situation he at last consented to purchase one pair of boots and a great coat . . . for the sum of £1 3s. 6d. which he instantly took into his possession and the same evening Bernard Marshall a taylor wanted to buy them of this deponent which he refused to sell.[33]

The involvement of a tailor is significant, because tailors and innkeepers often appear in the criminal depositions as purchasers of stolen clothes. Innkeepers also operated as informal pawnbrokers, although the boundary between buying stolen clothing and offering money on their security is not a clear one.

Stolen clothes were also acquired by more specialised dealers – old-clothes sellers and pawnbrokers (despite legislation in 1757 and after designed to prevent the pawning of stolen goods and to control the sale of unredeemed pledges by pawnbrokers).[34] Such tradesmen existed in most of the large northern towns from at least the late seventeenth century, as the behaviour in 1691 of Abraham Wright, the son of a Spofforth labourer, suggests. Happening to be at Leeds, twelve miles from Spofforth, he obviously assumed there would be a dealer in old clothes in the town, although he did not know of one. He asked a stranger in the street where he could buy a coat and was directed to a broker's shop. There he acquired one for five shillings.[35] The way such dealers were used to dispose of stolen clothing is illustrated by a case a hundred years later, when their numbers had increased considerably.[36] In December 1791, three seamen stole waistcoats, trousers, two woman's bedgowns, several pair of men's stockings and a pair of blankets from a sea chest in another seaman's house at North Shields in Northumberland. They put them into two pillowcases, took them across the River Tyne and sold them to James Grey who lived at South Shields and dealt in old clothes.[37] Cases involving people described as dealers in second-hand clothing or pawnbrokers were, however, few compared to those involving informal sales or pawns of stolen clothing, and sales or pawns to tradespeople who were not so identified, particularly the owners of public houses.

Nevertheless, it is important to bear in mind just how extensive the clothes side of a specialist pawnbroker's legitimate business could be. In the late 1770s, George Fettes, the York pawnbroker, was taking in between 150 and 200 pledges a week from customers who were largely plebeian. Over three-quarters of them were female. Two-thirds of these pledges were clothes. Over 80 percent of the clothes pledged to Fettes as security were redeemed, but even this apparently low rate of default could result in the accumulation of unredeemed clothing at a rate of 30 to 40 items a week, which had to be sold off second-hand. It was predominantly women's clothing that was pawned, especially the more expensive items in plebeian women's wardrobes. In the pledge book Fettes kept for 18 months in 1777 and 1778, 1,896 gowns were entered as pledges, compared with only 199 shifts, yet women would normally expect to own more shifts than gowns. Among the gowns, 911 were made from costly cotton or linen (average pledge value 3s. 11d.), and only 235 from cheaper worsted stuff (average pledge value 2s. 7d.).[38] Like men's watches, women's gowns, especially their more expensive, best gowns, represented a store of value, not just a means of fashionable display. They were the first items of clothing to be turned into cash when these women's circumstances required, their owners presumably retaining their less valuable workaday stuff gowns to wear. Plebeian women may have prized stylish clothes, but they were the items in their wardrobes most likely to be pawned when personal circumstances changed. They were also the items most often abandoned in the pawnbroker's hands.[39] The beneficiaries were those other plebeian women who acquired items sold off as unredeemed pledges, enjoying a selection of second-hand gowns that was especially choice. In the course of a mere four weeks in 1778, Fettes took in 14 gowns as pledges that appear never to have been redeemed. Ten of them were identified by material. Five were cotton or linen, four were silk, and only one was made from worsted stuff.[40] To the extent that this pattern was characteristic of used clothes transactions in general, then an active second-hand market accelerated the circulation of the more expensive, fashionable kinds of plebeian dress.

Yet it is difficult to establish precisely how active and extensive the second-hand market was in the north of England. The criminal records reveal significant numbers of specialist dealers in second-hand clothing. Why then do inventories for those dealers not appear in the probate inventory samples, when there are so many drapers and mercers, tailors and shoemakers? The answer lies in the relatively small numbers of people who operated as specialist pawnbrokers and salesmen in the north of England, where the criminal depositions, like the trade directories, suggest they were confined to the larger towns such as York, Sheffield, Leeds, Whitby, Halifax, Hull, Beverley and Richmond.[41] The evidence of trade directories suggests they multiplied in the course of the late eighteenth century, but they remained overwhelmingly urban, their increasing numbers reflecting the very rapid growth of towns in the north, beginning from a relatively low level of urbanisation at the start of the century.[42] Only the larger towns could provide the level of demand necessary to justify carrying large stocks of second-hand or new, ready-made garments. Large stocks were necessary to ensure a sufficient variety of garments in a sufficient range of styles, fabrics, colours and sizes, to assure potential customers who would otherwise buy a personalised, bespoke garment that they could find what they wanted. This was particularly important in the second-hand trade, where prices were lower, but regular customers had to buy replacements more frequently because they were buying part-worn commodities that had a shortened life. The trade in second-hand clothes, formal and informal, was important and extensive in the eighteenth-century north, but it would be wrong to exaggerate the extent to which it was organised through specialist or semi-specialist outlets, especially in the rural areas where the bulk of the population still lived. Many plebeian men and women in the north must have bought second-hand garments from time to time, but it seems unlikely that most clothed themselves in this way regularly or systematically.

The same was probably true of most of the provincial south.[43] Levels of urbanisation were higher there in the early eighteenth century, so it is not surprising that more salesmen appear at an earlier date in probate inventories.[44] Access to London with its many clothes dealers and manufacturers was easier. Yet salesmen and others dealing in ready-made clothes, new or old, were relatively few in number outside the coastal towns of the south, such as Bristol, or Dover and Gravesend in Kent, where selling slops to seamen may have been a crucial part of their business. At Norwich between 1660 and 1730, a time when it was the largest provincial town in England, probate inventories suggest that only a few tailors held stocks of ready-made clothes – and they were not extensive.[45] For many inland southern counties, the numbers of salesmen's probate inventories surviving from the early part of the eighteenth century is tiny. In Berkshire, for instance, between 1653 and 1710 only one appears.[46] By the later years of the eighteenth century, trade directories were being compiled that provide fuller lists of those active in the clothes-dealing trades. With the exception of London and the four northernmost counties of England, disparities in numbers between north and south were not especially marked.[47] In both areas, clothes dealers were overwhelmingly urban.

Some sense of how important these dealers were in the provision of main garments to plebeian men and women in the provinces can be gained from the policies of overseers of the poor. It is striking that in neither north nor south did rural overseers make much use of them. Indeed, few parishes bought any ready-made garments, new or second-hand. Their normal practice was to buy cloth and have it made up into garments by professionals on a bespoke basis. This was the norm across the century in parishes with long runs of surviving overseers' accounts, such as Holne in Devon, Leafield in Oxfordshire, and Spofforth and Thornhill in Yorkshire (see Chapter 16). The main exception, as Eden suggested, was in the immediate vicinity of London. At Mortlake in Surrey, eight miles from London, the overseers' accounts record payments to salesmen and slop-sellers beginning in the 1770s, although cloth continued to be bought and payments went on being made to tailors.[48] London slop shops were recommended for the purchase of Sunday School boys' coats, waistcoats, jackets and breeches in 1789 by a writer from Hartingfordbury, 20 miles north of the capital.[49] In the 1790s, the overseers at Theydon Garnon in Essex, 15 miles from London, bought a whole range of different kinds of clothing, including leather stays for women, leather breeches, kersey waistcoats, boys' jackets, smock frocks, hats and stockings as well as cloth from one supplier, James Haslam. He is unlikely to have made them all up himself.[50] He could have drawn supplies from a firm like James Mills and Company, whose 'Warehouse for Cloathing Charity Schools, Workhouses, etc'. was in Bishopsgate Street in London. Mills advertised in 1789 that he could supply 'every necessary article of cloathing' for men, women or children 'either in town or country'.[51] Alternatively, there were shops selling ready-made clothes in the towns around London, such as Brentford, although it is not always clear whether their trade was in new or second-hand garments.[52]

The purchasing policies of overseers of the poor are not a perfect proxy for the behaviour of the general run of plebeian consumers. Nevertheless, the ways they sourced cloth and clothing appear to be broadly consistent with patterns of plebeian clothes-purchasing observed in other sources.[53] They register, for instance, the takeover of women's outer garment assembly by mantuamakers. What they reveal about the way main garments were sourced offers, therefore, a rough-and-ready guide to the practice of the generality of plebeian men and women in provincial England. Despite the growing availability of ready-made garments and the existence of a flourishing second-hand market, the usual procedure, except in the vicinity of London and perhaps in the largest provincial towns, was to buy cloth which was then made up into garments by professionals. For men those professionals were male tailors, but for women they became, in the course of the eighteenth century, female mantuamakers. This was a system of clothes supply that relied heavily on market transactions. It was far removed from romantic notions of rural self-sufficiency. Most fabrics were sourced commercially from distant manufacturers. Although domestic sewing of simpler undergarments and accessories was widespread, outer garments were usually made professionally on a bespoke basis. Reliance on professional specialists to make up the most valuable, complex and visually arresting items in the plebeian wardrobe suggests a determination that minimum sartorial standards for respectability, decency and fashionability should be met. The dramatic shift to specialisation by gender among those professionals suggests that those standards were rising.

71 *Monmouth Street*, 1789, coloured engraving, Lewis Walpole Library, Farmington, Conn., 789.6.9.1. The interior of a clothes shop in Monmouth Street, St Giles, London, a street renowned for dealing in ready-made and second-hand clothes. The proprietor tries to gloss over the poor fit of a second-hand coat with his sales patter.

10
Clothing the Metropolis

WHEN IT CAME TO ACQUIRING INEXPENSIVE CLOTHING, London was different from the rest of England, as befitted the largest city in eighteenth-century western Europe. It offered an extraordinary array of ways to buy, from street sellers hawking old clothes and artisan-retailers making bespoke garments in small workshops, to huge retail drapery warehouses and whole streets of shops selling ready-made and second-hand clothes such as Rosemary Lane, Houndsditch and Monmouth Street (figs 71, 72, 73). In the face of such diversity, this chapter offers a *tour d'horizon* of the means available to plebeian Londoners to acquire clothes, highlighting where they differed from provincial practices, and where they resembled them.[1]

London was the major British centre of both retailing and manufacturing. It dominated the circulation within Britain and its colonies of artefacts and information about artefacts, and it was the principal British site where fashion and taste were promulgated and contested. For an early-modern city, London's population was enormous. Already nearly 600,000 at the start of the eighteenth century, it grew to nearly 950,000 at its end. Its size was matched by its affluence, its commercialisation and its sophistication. London was a city of high wages. On average Londoners were wealthier than the rest of the population, although that average conceals extremes of wealth and poverty ranging from destitute tenants sharing shabby, two-penny Spitalfields lodging rooms to the titled owners of the grandest houses in Grosvenor Square in the West End.[2] But even London's poor depended on commercial mechanisms for the supply of basic essentials, especially food, to an extent unparalleled in rural areas.

London, moreover, was the national centre for the circulation of commercial information in printed form, which grew prodigiously, especially after the lapsing of the Licensing Act in 1695 left few official controls on the press other than fiscal ones. Within London, the density of information networks and personal interactions in which ordinary Londoners were enmeshed educated them as consumers of clothing by exposing them to fashion and novelty in a particularly intense way. London pioneered the glazed shop windows that proliferated from the late seventeenth century and became the norm in the eighteenth. Window dressing became a crucial tool in shopkeepers' promotional strategy. Gazing at those displays became a key part of eighteenth-century shopping.[3] But London offered other, more direct ways of engaging with new, fashionable things. 'On the Queen's birth day generally hairdressers go to see the present fashions; I went for that purpose only', stated a man accused of steal-

72 *High Change, Rag Fair*, 1782, aquatint, Guildhall Library, London, p749141x. The scene is Wellclose Square, Stepney, London, just beyond the eastern end of Rosemary Lane. Old clothes are being sold. Garments and hats hang from the wall of the building in the background. The woman in the left foreground is selling shoes laid out on a chair. Rosemary Lane was the site of Rag Fair, where old clothes were sold in the street each afternoon. It also housed numerous shops selling second-hand and ready-made clothes.

ing a watch in the crowd gathered in St James's on 18 January 1790 to see the nobility parade in their coaches.[4] Only in London were there opportunities of this kind for ordinary people to monitor fashion regularly.

There was an increasing tendency for manufacturing to move out of the capital after the mid-seventeenth century, but throughout the period London remained the largest manufacturing centre in the country with, by the early eighteenth century, an astonishingly wide range of industries. The concentration of such a large population of consumers in a relatively small area meant that even under conditions of hand production there was huge potential for specialisation in the manufacturing process and for product differentiation. These often went hand in hand. Subcontracting all or parts of the work to specialists, both within London and beyond, was associated with the making of

73 Henry Bunbury, *The Houndsditch Macaroni*, 1772, etching, Guildhall Library, London, p5383282. One of a series of caricatures by Bunbury published in 1772, many of them set in specific London locations, satirising the exaggerated styles worn by wealthy young men known as 'Macaronis'. The man's face is portrayed with the crude profile of stereotypical lower-class physiognomy. The reference to Houndsditch, a London street famous for clothes retailing, suggests he has acquired his Macaroni fashions second-hand or ready-made.

luxury, bespoke goods like coaches and fine silver, as well as with the production of relatively cheap ready-made clothing.[5] So large was the London market that just as the division of labour could be more intense than in provincial towns, so the scale on which enterprises conducted their business could be larger.

This tendency can be observed in retailing. London had shops that were bigger, brighter and showier than those found elsewhere. Nevertheless, what is most striking about the establishments used by plebeian customers to buy clothes and clothing materials in London is how widely they ranged in scale. At one extreme, plebeian customers buying clothing fabrics or accessories patronised large-scale drapers and the retail linen, shoe and hat warehouses that became increasingly common as the eighteenth century progressed. The word warehouse was used by London retailers from early in the century to suggest good value and often ready-made goods (fig. 74). In the shoe trade, they were associated with cash sales of cheap, ready-made shoes to plebeian customers.[6] Late on Saturday nights, London shoe warehouses in the 1760s were said to be 'fill'd with noisy and difficult Customers, especially of Nightmen, Penny-Postmen and Slaughter-House-men, who have just receiv'd their Week's Wages'.[7]

> SNIP's WAREHOUSE for Ready made CLOATHS — Great Variety of FANCY WAISTCOATS.
>
> 'Does it come up high in the Collar Mr — O! yes Sir — it sits to a charm — 'tis ease & Elegance itself — can Your Honor button it — Yes Mr but dont You think it too full — not at all Your Honor, You woud'nt wish to be pinch'd to be sure _____ (Mr Snip) And Sir I hope the Young Gentleman's Breeches will be quite to his satisfaction Sir, do ye see, tho to be sure they comes on a little stiffish or so at first — but You know Sir every thing gets easier in time as a body may say ___ I desires him to thrust himself well in, ___ and I am sure they'll do.
>
> Publish'd Decr 20 1791, by Robt Sayer & Co Fleet Street London.

74 *Snip's Warehouse for Ready made Cloaths – Great Variety of Fancy Waistcoats*, 1791, printed engraving, British Museum, London, BMSat 8036. The scene is the interior of a ready-made clothes shop which trades as a warehouse. The title plays on the way retail warehouses promoted their large and varied stocks as a selling point. The sales patter kept up by the proprietor and his wife is designed to draw the customers' attention away from the poor fit of the garments.

A sense of what these establishments were like at their busiest can be obtained from the descriptions of a Ludgate Hill draper's shop in 1808 given by witnesses at the Old Bailey. It was identified as 'the shop to which so many people are thronging to purchase goods'. On a Thursday in January, the 'shop was very much crowded with customers; and the counter was very much crowded with goods'. Some 600 customers passed through the shop in the course of the day, with up to 50 or 60 customers in the shop at one time, served by eight or nine shopmen, one of whom specialised in shawls. The business depended on a high turnover of standard goods. A poor woman seeking to buy a half-shawl was told they did not cut shawls and was immediately ordered to stand away from the counter to let the next customer through.[8] At another large-scale linen draper's in Marylebone in 1785, a customer seeking some Irish linen had to wait two hours on a February afternoon, because, as one of the shopmen said, 'we were so busy we could not serve her'.[9]

At the other extreme, there were many small general-purpose shops which served plebeian Londoners with similar goods. In 1785, for example, Barbara Richards, a labourer's wife, kept 'a small shop, some chandlery, some stockings, and some handkerchiefs' in French Alley, Spitalfields, although it was not too small to make a display of a few silk handkerchiefs on a show board (fig. 75).[10] We should not forget, however, that in between these two extremes were vast numbers of medium-sized, specialist outlets organised along the traditional lines of demarcation between trades – the

75   *The Chandler's Shop Gossips, or Wonderful News*, n.d., mezzotint, The Colonial Williamsburg Foundation, 1973-262. The scene is the interior of a small chandler's shop serving plebeian customers. The shop is presented as a site of idle gossiping, encouraged by its proprietor, Dame Prattle. Dot Drab, the customer on the right, is depicted as a poor woman with a torn apron and a bottle in her pocket.

76 Paul Sandby, *Man Selling Stockings*, c.1759, watercolour, Nottingham Castle Museum, 1966-46. The man is shown standing in front of the pillory next to the statue of Charles I at Charing Cross, London. He wears sailor's clothing in good condition: a short red jacket, a blue shirt, loose-fitting canvas slop breeches and a check neckerchief. A watch seal hangs at his waist. His own stockings are dark, but those he is selling are white. Stockings are also hung up for sale in the left background.

drapers and mercers, haberdashers and hatters that could be found in every part of the city. And, of course, new goods of much the same kind were also hawked by street sellers, including cloth, ribbons, handkerchiefs, lace and various clothing accessories (fig. 76).[11] Household self-provisioning of cloth was conspicuous by its absence.

The distinction between these different scales of retailing was not simply a matter of variety and price. Shops offering huge, well-displayed stocks at keen prices were of little practical use to cash-poor customers if they demanded ready money and refused credit (although by no means all large shops were cash-only). Shopkeepers who supplied credit tended to charge higher prices for their goods to compensate. They also required assurance that customers were credit-worthy, something not always easy to secure in a vast city like London. Most shops offered credit, but those like Barbara Richard's small shop in Spitalfields selling chandlery goods, stockings and handkerchiefs had certain advantages. It was exactly this sort of establishment that could sustain personal relationships with plebeian customers in its immediate locality, thereby cutting the risks associated with offering credit to the poor. Chandlers, moreover, sometimes doubled as pawnbrokers and second-hand dealers, providing another line of credit or cash to their customers, at the same time as securing their loyalty.[12] The difficulty plebeian men, in particular, faced in financing purchases of clothing is indicated by the emergence in late eighteenth-century London, as in the provinces, of clothing clubs. London appears to have had a particularly wide range of these subscription clubs, usually organised by a retailer or a publican, and often patronised by working men. Francis Place ran a breeches club in the 1790s.[13] From the 1760s up to the end of the century, witnesses at the Old Bailey mentioned clothes clubs, coat clubs, shoe clubs, boot clubs, hat clubs, watch clubs and even old clothes clubs.[14] A shoe club at a Westminster public house, patronised by a carpenter, soldiers and 'creditable people in the neighbourhood', was described in 1796 as 'a club for people that want shoes cheap, to pay sixpence a week, and spend twopence'. The same publican hosted a 'raffling club' with about 25 members. People joined to raffle for a watch.[15]

In the retailing of footwear in London, Giorgio Riello argues, there were two main innovations in the course of the eighteenth century. First, the emergence of shops selling standardised footwear on a large scale. Second, the practice of selling shoes along with cloth, clothes and clothing accessories in smaller general stores.[16] These trends, broadly conceived, were neither restricted to footwear, nor confined to London, although they were at their most intense in the capital. We have observed a similar trend towards selling clothing items in small shops in the samples of Yorkshire inventories, although large-scale retail warehouses do not appear. Trade directories and newspaper advertisements make it clear, however, that these new forms of large-scale cloth and clothes retailing did arrive in northern and other provincial towns in the course of the eighteenth century.[17]

If we turn from the supply of fabrics and accessories to the supply of garments, the most distinctive characteristic of the capital was the easy availability of ready-made articles. London dominated this trade. Manufacturing and retailing ready-made main garments had begun its major expansion in the capital in the second quarter of the seventeenth century. It is then that people calling themselves 'salesman' began to seek loans from the Merchant Tailors Company in large numbers and systematic complaints against their activities started to be made to the Company's officers.[18] Even in 1681, in a complaint about the damage salesmen were inflicting on other trades, it was still possible to describe their activities as 'this new Trade' and to assert that 'many remember when there were no new Garments sold in *London*, as now there are, only old Garments at second hand'. Nevertheless, by the last quarter of the seventeenth century, retailers of ready-made main garments were well established and were able, it was claimed, to supply these garments at lower prices than the bespoke tailors.[19]

This development was, of course, an instance of the wider tendency towards greater specialisation in many London trades as the city grew. In the case of ready-made main garments, the trend may have been encouraged by the large orders placed for military clothing during the Civil War, by the expansion of shipping and colonial settlement and the accompanying demand for ready-made garments for sailors, indentured servants and plantation slaves, and perhaps by a shift in some men's and women's garments to simpler styles in the late seventeenth century.[20] Nevertheless, it is important to emphasise that the rise of the salesman began before most of these developments and rested primarily on the rapid growth in the size of London as a market. Ready-made garments came to be made and sold, as we have seen, outside London, but London remained the dominant centre for their manufacture and supply through the late seventeenth and eighteenth centuries, with London salesmen marketing their wares to the provinces and provincial salesmen going to London to acquire stock.[21]

Within London, the trade became ever more specialised: slop-sellers served mainly seamen; other shops specialised by gender, like the Monmouth Street 'sale shop for women's clothes' kept by Eleanor Hawkins in 1783.[22] By the late eighteenth century making and retailing ready-made garments was a huge business, serving the well-to-do as well as working people, but it is one whose market share among poorer Londoners is hard to quantify. Aggregate sales records do not exist, while it is impossible to disentangle the sale of new ready-made garments from those that were second-hand. 'The Salesmen', declared Campbell's *London Tradesman* in 1747, 'deal in Old Cloaths, and some times in New. They trade very largely, and some of them are worth some Thousands.'[23] The trade, whether in new or second-hand garments, ranged from large sale shops with stocks of many hundreds of gowns, petticoats, coats, breeches and waistcoats, to itinerant street sellers, often women, hawking a few old clothes (fig. 77).[24]

As in the provinces, the second-hand trade was fed by, and often encompassed, pawnbrokers, formal and informal. They were, however, a much more a prominent feature of plebeian life in the capital. If trials for theft at the Old Bailey are a reliable guide, pawnbrokers were the first resort of those who stole clothing and wanted to turn it into cash, far more so than in the provinces where various informal methods of dis-

77 Paul Sandby, *Woman Selling Old Clothes*, c.1759, watercolour, Nottingham Castle Museum, 1966-50. Sandby portrays this London street seller wearing a short, red cloak and a straw hat. She carries a man's coat and a pair of shoes.

posal and sale were more common. So familiar a part of everyday life was pawning for plebeian Londoners that they were expected to have a regular pawnbroker. 'What is the name of the pawnbroker you deal with?' a London street seller was asked at the Old Bailey in 1785. 'Davis, in London Wall', she replied.[25] Clothing comprised the bulk of the pledges offered to most London pawnbrokers, as it did for the pawnbroker George Fettes at York.

With so many dealers in second-hand and ready-made garments in London, often concentrated in particular streets and districts, and with such huge quantities on sale, consumers could realistically expect to find made-up garments incorporating the features they wanted, whether in terms of style, fabric, colour, size, price or newness. This was evidently the assumption of the young woman described by a London shopkeeper's daughter in 1753, who 'came to my mother's shop, and asked for a striped camblet gown; I asked her whether she would have a new one or an old one; she said, a second-hand one'.[26] In London, therefore, it was much more feasible than in the provinces for plebeian men and women to expect to acquire a large proportion of their clothes by means of regular, repeated second-hand purchases. The ballad 'The Humours of RAG FAIR' played on this contrast between Town and Country, when it described the surprise of a countryman visiting London at finding 'a lane full of second hand Taylors' offering coats, vests, breeches, banyans, fustian frocks, shirts and 'cheap left-off cloaths for Spital-fields beaus'.[27] Indeed, in London even parish vestries resorted to regular second-hand purchases to clothe their paupers, as at St Botolph Aldgate, the parish incorporating part of Rosemary Lane, where Rag Fair was located.[28] Yet there remain indications that even brand-new ready-made clothes, though often cheaper than bespoke, were regarded as inferior. When a tailor was commissioned in 1787 to make a suit of clothes for a labourer from measurements he already had, without taking new measure, he was told, 'if I could not make them without the measure, she would buy them ready made, because they were going out of town'.[29] London caricatures of the late eighteenth century suggest ready-made garments were as notorious for the inadequacy of their fit as those who sold them were for the mendacity of their sales patter (figs 71, 74).

One way the makers of ready-made garments responded to the problem of poor fit was sizing. Human bodies vary greatly in size and shape, but main garments, which even among the poor were made almost exclusively by professionals, were expected to fit in a regularised way that conformed to contemporary notions of fashion, or at least decency. The makers of ready-made main garments had to confront problems of measurement and fit that were more complicated than those faced by most manufacturers of clothing accessories. These problems did not make standardisation of sizing essential to the successful sale of ready-made clothing; after all, a vast second-hand trade was carried on in clothing of all sorts, which, by its very nature, could not use standard sizes. Nevertheless, some sort of sizing system must have been very attractive to manufacturers, retailers and customers alike. Sizing ready-made main garments not only made the retailer's task of selecting garments for the customer easier. It also enabled retailers to place orders with manufacturers in quantities that reflected the distribution of sizes among the population.

It is not clear whether such a sizing system was introduced during the period when the making and sale of ready-made main garments emerged in seventeenth-century London. At least one of the orders for main garments placed on behalf of the New Model Army in 1645 specifies size, but only by the phrase 'the largest size', in marked contrast to the numerical system already in use in the orders to specify shoe sizes.[30] However, there is no doubt that a numerical sizing system based on a scale of 1 (small) to 10 (large) was in use in London for civilian ready-made main garments for men by the 1740s. At least one Houndsditch salesman had his orders supplied by his manufacturing tailor in nearby Shoemaker Row according to this scale.[31] What remains obscure is how much uniformity there was in sizing standards among different retailers and manufacturers at this period, and the extent to which their customers were familiar with the sizing system. By the 1780s a sizing system similar to that in use in the 1740s appears to have been common to all the London slop shops and was a matter of public knowledge.[32]

In practice, however, the division between ready-made and bespoke garments was not always clear-cut. The objective of the ready-made clothes seller was to provide a garment that looked and wore like a piece of bespoke clothing, while actually being made in a limited number of standard sizes in the interests of manufacturing efficiency. Yet even sales shops that used standardised sizing were prepared to have their makers supply fitted garments to the order of individual customers.[33] In a manufacturing system based on skilled hand labour, often in close proximity to the retail shop, such flexibility was not difficult. Yet many plebeian men continued to have garments made to fit by tailors in the traditional manner. The numbers of those described as tailors vastly outnumbered those described as salesmen. Among Westminster householders in 1784, there were over 500 tailors, resulting in a ratio of 20 tailors to every salesman.[34] Tailors were the third most numerous occupational group among the householders. Most of these tailors can have operated on only a modest scale (fig. 31). Even if much of their work involved repair, some of their time must have been taken up with making clothes, often for plebeian customers.

The same was true of the many mantuamakers who, on the evidence of trials at the Old Bailey, dominated the bespoke making of plebeian women's outer garments in London.[35] Mantuamakers like Elisabeth Murphy of Shoreditch, who in 1755 made a cheap stuff gown for a shopkeeper's servant, were readily able to identify stolen articles they had made.[36] There is little indication here of male tailors making plebeian women's outer garments at any point in the eighteenth century. As in the north of England, plebeian women often made up some clothes for themselves and their families, but their sewing skills were generally applied to inner garments and accessories, not to making outer garments. There are numerous references in evidence at the Old Bailey to plebeian women cutting, sewing, altering and mending shirts, shifts, handkerchiefs, aprons, caps, childrens' frocks, petticoats and sometimes bedgowns for their own families. The wife of an Islington dealer in old shoes, for instance, identified his stolen shirt as 'my own making, but the frill is taken off, I can safely swear to my own work'.[37] As in the north, these items were probably largely made up at home in this manner, despite the easy access the capital offered, at a price, to ready-made shirts, shifts, caps, aprons and other accessories from retailers. Yet surprisingly in a city where so many women had to survive by sewing for a living, making army uniforms, clothing for the sale shops or childbed linen for charities, there were others who could not cut or sew fabric at all.[38] They had little choice but to pay. 'Did you make the shift yourself?' Esther Hudson, a Cornhill street seller, was asked in 1785. 'No, I never makes nothing; the cloak was made at No. 2, Houndsditch, I have worn it twice.'[39]

III

Understanding Clothes

78 John Collet, *The Frenchman in London*, 1770, coloured engraving, Lewis Walpole Library, Farmington, Conn., 770.11.10.1. A pugnacious London butcher, the embodiment of English masculinity, proudly plebeian in striped butcher's jacket, coloured neckcloth and apron, is shown confronting an effete, exquisitely dressed Frenchman. The Frenchman's questionable manliness is emphasised by way the woman dressed in a sprigged gown is quizzically examining his pigtail.

11

The View from Above

Societies understand their clothes in a multiplicity of ways. They can be defences against the weather, marks of social distinction, products of successful industries, safeguards against ill health, badges of subcultural identity, tools in spiritual exercises and sources of erotic stimulation. Modern cultural theorists, like a host of eighteenth-century writers, have been powerfully attracted by the idea that dress constitutes a language, capable of being manipulated by its wearers and read by those who observe them. If so, then it is a form of language that can be exceptionally unstable, elusive and ambiguous, easy to manipulate and easier still to misinterpret. Semiotic ambiguity fuelled the anxieties surrounding dress which, it has been argued, were particularly acute in eighteenth-century Britain.[1] Clothes and fashion became obsessions with social critics in an intellectual climate where wealth and virtue were constantly juxtaposed as implacable opponents. The rise of commercial luxury was thought to jeopardise social hierarchy, public morality, military might and economic efficiency. Again and again, critics of luxury, as well as some of its defenders, found evidence of its remorseless advance in the subversion of social hierarchy by fashion, which was believed to have seduced the populace into emulating their betters by dressing above their station. At issue here was the question of whether growing national wealth debauched the people by rendering them insubordinate, soft and lazy, or improved them by stimulating their industry and refining their tastes. But also at issue was the very feasibility, in a commercial society, of judging people's moral and personal worth by their appearance. The capacity of clothes to deceive seemed to grow as fashion became ever more pervasive and people more willing and better able to engage with it. In a culture which clung to the expectation that appearance should be a legible guide to personality, this was deeply troubling.

For defenders of luxury, the code of manners known as politeness represented an important means by which the civilising influence of commerce could polish taste and improve behaviour. Politeness promoted openness and accessibility in social behaviour. It did not deny the legitimacy of social rank, but it required the different ranks to mix with each other in an agreeable manner. Defining itself as much against patrician *hauteur* as it did against plebeian vulgarity or provincial grossness, politeness aimed to create people of decorum, taste and refinement who could be agreeable in the correct way. What was demanded of them was gentility, the behaviour expected of gentlemen and ladies. Politeness did not require its followers to be genteel by birth, merely that when in company they behave in a genteel manner. Such performances could be demanding. Often they had to be learnt and many of them required the correct material props. Richard 'Beau' Nash, the Master of Ceremonies at the resort city of Bath, insisted early in the eighteenth century that nobles should treat lesser visitors with the same courtesy they usually reserved for each other. To that end he outlawed the customary prerogative among nobility and gentry of wearing swords, but at the same time he prevented the Duchess of Queensberry from wearing her apron, newly fashionable, but also plebeian, menial and vulgar in its associations, and therefore potentially impolite.[2] A gentleman should not 'trudge about in Linsey-Woolsy' insisted William Darrell in his much reprinted conduct book, written, he claimed, for the instruction of a young nobleman.[3]

Critics of politeness felt its stress on performance led to artificiality, insincerity and dishonesty, not least in matters of dress.[4] From the mid-eighteenth century it was increasingly opposed by an alternative code of manners – sensibility – which emphasised authenticity rather than display, sincerity of emotion rather than performance, rustic simplicity rather than metropolitan polish. Sensibility extolled simple dressing as a manifestation of simple, honest feelings. Yet sensibility was subject to the same criticisms as politeness. Sensibility set its face against fashion, yet it became fashionable. Simplicity could be contrived. The immodest found ways to dress modestly. Sensibility's preferred sartorial language of virtuous authenticity could, it turned out, tell lies.

These issues dominated eighteenth-century debates in pamphlet and periodical about the meanings of clothes, including ordinary people's clothes. The questions raised in such debates about the proper relationship between personal consumer choices and the public good influenced the ways plebeian dress was evaluated by rich and poor alike. They are this chapter's principal concern, although it does not claim that they represent anything approaching an exhaustive list of possible meanings that the historian of eighteenth-century plebeian clothing might explore.

The clothes worn by ordinary people were something of an obsession with the largely elite readership of eighteenth-century newspapers, periodicals and pamphlets. From the beginning of the century to its end, patrician commentators complained endlessly about the common people's desire to dress above their station. Usually they denounced it as improper and destructive. Sometimes they accepted it as a necessary evil, an incentive to labour and a spur to refinement. Often they identified the elite's own indulgence in absurd fashions and frivolous ostentation as its cause. At the start of the century, Edward Chamberlayne's *Angliae Notitia: or the Present State of England* complained that citizens, country people and servants 'appear clothed, for the most part above and beyond their Qualities, Estates or Conditions, and far more Gay than that sort of People were wont to be in former times'.[5] Bernard Mandeville famously concurred in his *Fable of the Bees*: 'The poorest laborer's wife in the Parish, who scorns to wear a strong wholesome Frize, as she might, will starve herself and her Husband to purchase a second hand Gown and Petticoat, that cannot do half the service, because, forsooth, it is more genteel.'[6] In 1725 Daniel Defoe complained about servants in similar terms. 'It is a hard Matter to know the Mistress from the Maid by their Dress, nay very often the Maid shall be the finer of the two' (fig. 79).[7]

By the second half of the century, denunciations of inappropriate finery among the poor had multiplied, along with the numbers of newspapers and periodicals, but there was no great change in their character. In 1761, the *Annual Register* was convinced that 'dress, fashion, and affectation, have put all upon an equality; so that it is difficult to tell the milliner from her ladyship, my lord from the groom, or his grace in Pall-mall from the tallow-chandler at Wapping' (fig. 23).[8] Twenty years later the same complaints prevailed. 'The very servant not only apes but rivals her mistress in every species of whim and extravagance', insisted the *European Magazine* in 1784. 'All sorts of people

79 John Collet, *High Life below Stairs*, 1763, oil on canvas, The Colonial Williamsburg Foundation, Gift of Mrs Cora Ginsburg, G1991-175. The painting illustrates James Townley's popular farce, *High Life below Stairs*, first performed in 1759, in which servants aped the nobility, holding a party while their master was away. A footman wearing a blue livery faced with red tends the hair of a well-dressed female servant. She wears a fine apron of gauze or muslin and red shoes. Her wide-brimmed, be-ribboned silk hat leans on the table. The woman on the left also has carefully styled hair, but the other two female servants are dressed for work, the one in the centre wearing a red striped handkerchief and a plain white apron over a gown printed with blue sprigs on a white ground.

are consequently confounded or melted down into one glaring mass of superfluity or absurdity. The lower orders are intirely [sic] lost in a general propensity to mimic the finery of the higher; and every woman we meet would seem by her gesture and apparel to possess at least an independent fortune.'[9] When Sarah Trimmer used her didactic novel *The Two Farmers*, published in 1787, to criticise tawdry gew-gaws prized by labouring women, such as gauze caps or handkerchiefs worn in preference to durable linen, or second-hand gowns bought from a lady's maid worn in preference to stout camblet, it was in remarkably similar terms to Bernard Mandeville's strictures on wholesome frize published some seventy years before.[10] Calls for a resurrection of sumptuary legislation to rein back the sartorial excesses of the labouring classes surfaced repeatedly.[11]

Judgements of this kind were not confined to published works. They emerged again and again in private writings. On the way to Oxford in 1781, the curmudgeonly traveller John Byng, younger son of a noble family, noted in his diary: 'I meet milkmaids on the road with the dress and looks of Strand misses.'[12] Three years earlier, the immensely wealthy Elizabeth Montagu had complained in a letter to her sister from her Berkshire village of Sandleford:

> the Farmers Daughters go to Church in hats trimmed with gauze & ribbon & flowers, & carry their caps, if not their hands, as high as ye finest ladies. These rural lasses have white silk capuchins trimmed with lace. If you were to see ye congregation at our village church on Sunday you wd not suspect I was ye richest woman in ye parish, & yet without vanity I am.[13]

It is not necessary to read far in eighteenth-century letters, diaries, periodicals and pamphlets to find complaints of this kind about plebeian sartorial extravagance, endlessly recycled and often tediously misogynistic. Stereotypical in the types of clothing they attacked and repetitive in the arguments they deployed, the ubiquity of these diatribes should not surprise us. Clothes were a very obvious manifestation of plebeian insubordination, because they covered and adorned the body in public. Smart clothes, moreover, were one of the first major consumer expenditures that many young plebeian adults chose to make as soon as they became financially able. Nevertheless, these diatribes were not an arena for original thinking about plebeian consumption. It was in the debates over gin and tea, over household budgeting and poor relief, that new ideas about the appropriate relationship between the plebeian classes and the consumer goods available in a commercial society were principally forged, not in discussions of plebeian clothing.[14] Of course, these conceptually more inventive debates might invoke clothes to support an argument, yet that argument rarely turned on dress. Clothing was not the principal subject for new lines of analysis.

Dress was sometimes brought up, for instance, in the incessant agonising during the second half of the eighteenth century about the effects of enclosure and high grain prices on the rural economy and the rural poor. It was employed in critiques of engrossing farmers as evidence that their new-found affluence was corrupt and unjustified, in ways that drew on some of the sartorial stereotypes we have already identified. 'A Country Farmer' complained in 1786: 'As to dress no one that is not personally acquainted with the opulent farmer's daughter can distinguish her from the daughter of a Duke by her dress.' In the happy days before enclosure, by contrast,

> you might view the farmer in a coat of the growth of his flock, and spun by his industrious wife and daughters, and his stockings produced from the same quarter of his industry, and his wife and daughters clad from their own hands of industry, and the growth of their own flock their best attire – their outward covering being a neat camblet, faced with a small quantity of silk in colour according to the choice of the wearer.[15]

Before-and-after narratives of this kind, bemoaning a shift from virtuous, socially inclusive self-sufficiency to selfish opulence, emerged repeatedly in analyses of changing rural life published from the 1760s to the 1830s. They offered various chronologies of degeneration, with a lost golden age located anywhere from the 1740s to the early 1800s, but it was rare for clothes to serve as the principal evidence for the moral and social superiority of the old-fashioned farmer over his new-fashioned successor. New-fangled household goods such as pianos and carpets, and fancy parlours, figured more prominently in complaints about the expanding gulf between rich farmer and impoverished labourer (figs 80, 81).[16]

Those who defended commercial farmers countered by arguing that the rural labouring poor were the authors of their own misery, through their excessive consumption of luxurious extravagances. Yet, here again, it was not clothing, but tea, tobacco, sugar, gambling, spirits, white bread and strong beer that were cited as evidence of the poor's extravagance. The most significant contributions to the wider debate came from reflections on these commodities, not clothes. Indeed, the agriculturalist Arthur Young, a prominent and early contributor to the debates, suggested that the poor's clothing suffered because of the take-up of other more attractive consumer goods. Pauper families, he claimed in 1768, 'will let their cloaths drop into pieces without being at the trouble and expence of ever *mending* them, at the very time they have every day drank their tea sweetened with nine-penny sugar'.[17]

It is important to bear in mind, however, that carping about farmers' daughters who abandoned homespun to dress like duchesses, or servant maids attired like their mistresses, was not the only way that elite commentators evaluated plebeian clothes. In the background, less shrill perhaps, but pervasive and deeply influential none the less, were other, more positive ways of thinking. We have already noted how travellers, both English and foreign, used the clothing of the common people to judge the economic condition of nations and regions. Well-dressed working people were a sign of collective prosperity and a cause for celebration. Samuel Johnson set out the reasons in 1775:

> The true state of every nation is the state of common life. The manners of a people are not to be found in the schools of learning, or the palaces of greatness, where the national character is obscured or obliterated by travel or instruction, by philos-

80 James Gillray, *Farmer Giles's Establishment – Christmas day – 1800*, 1830, coloured engraving, Lewis Walpole Library, Farmington, Conn., 830.1.10.1. At Christmas in 1800, Farmer Giles entertains his workpeople, the men in their smock frocks, at his humble kitchen table.

ophy or vanity; nor is public happiness to be estimated by the assemblies of the gay, or the banquets of the rich. The great mass of nations is neither rich nor gay: they whose aggregate constitutes the people, are found in the streets, and the villages, in the shops and farms; and from them collectively considered, must the measure of general prosperity be taken. As they approach to delicacy a nation is refined, as their conveniences are multiplied, a nation, at least a commercial nation, must be denominated wealthy.[18]

It was possible to apply this thinking to nation, locality or cottage. In 1750, Andrew Hooke supported his argument that Britain was wealthier than it had been for a century and a half by asking whether anyone could remember a time when '*Tradesmen, Farmers, Manufacturers, Artificers*, and others of inferior Rank, were ever better cloathed or fed, or maintained their Families in a more decent Manner, than at present?'[19] For Lady Louisa Stuart, the daughter of a Prime Minister, writing in 1778, the superiority of Yorkshire over Bedfordshire lay in its

81 James Gillray, *Farmer Giles's Establishment – Christmas – 1816*, 1830, coloured engraving, Lewis Walpole Library, Farmington, Conn., 830.1.0.8. Sixteen years later, at Christmas in 1816, the newly affluent Farmer Giles hosts an exclusive, elegant Christmas entertainment for fashionably over-dressed guests, who are waited on by his liveried servant.

cottages, all neatly built of stones, and seeming clean and comfortable within, the children playing about them, not the miserable, pining, ragged, poor little creatures you see in this country, but looking fat and healthy, and their fathers and mothers strong, handsome people, in general neatly dressed, and always employed.[20]

Taking pleasure in a well-clothed population did not, of course, necessarily imply approval for plebeian ostentation. Nevertheless, such pleasure could embrace some of those plebeian luxuries in dress attacked by other patrician commentators. When Tobias Smollett wanted to portray a properly paternalistic May Day celebration in his 1762 novel *Launcelot Greaves*, he wrote approvingly about country girls 'in their best apparel dight, their white hose, and clean short dimity petticoats, their gawdy gowns of printed cotton; their top-knots, kissing-strings, and stomachers, bedizened with bunches of ribbons of various colours, green, pink, and yellow'.[21] Equally, when Samuel Finney, the miniature-painter and magistrate, sought to measure the improvements in everyday life in his Cheshire parish of Wilmslow over the 40 years leading up to 1785, he did so by listing consumer goods 'unknown to former times', newly available to the common people, especially clothing textiles: 'Tea, Coffee, loaf Sugar; Spices, printed Cottons, Callicoes, Lawns, Cambricks, fine Linnens, Silks, Velverets, Silk Waistcoat pieces, Silk Cloaks, Hats, Bonnets, Shawls, laced Caps, and a Variety of other Things' (fig. 82).[22]

Two powerful tendencies in eighteenth-century social thought fuelled such positive evaluations of plebeian dress. Firstly, the conventional Christian belief in a divinely ordained hierarchy, in which the ranking of the population into different stations was regarded as God's will. Divinely ordained inequality was held to carry with it divinely ordained mutual obligations between rich and poor. Although such religious teaching rejected social levelling, it imposed on the wealthy a duty of charity and with it the expectation that the poor should enjoy at least a share in society's material comforts. In a sermon given at Bury in Lancashire in 1765, the Reverend John Smith declared: 'It is therefore a false and partial Notion, which some Men entertain, that the Poor are a Rank of inferior Beings, and entitled to none of those Comforts which the Rich enjoy.' According to the law of God, he went on, 'we are all of the same Frame, subject to the same Wants, and endowed with the same Capacities and Appetites'.[23] Hence the wording of a request made in 1755 that a Surrey parish vestry provide 'clothes in a decent Christian-like manner' to a pauper apprentice.[24] From here it was but a short step to the providential view that a nation that was clothed well was one that enjoyed God's approval. There were more secular, nationalistic versions of the same position. Even Arthur Young, not always sympathetic to the aspirations of the labouring poor, grudgingly accepted in 1768 'that the poor ought to be well fed – well cloathed – and live in that *warm* comfortable manner, requisite to *Englishmen*'.[25] Earlier, Thomas Andrews, a Wiltshire clergyman, had in 1738 linked the religious and the secular, suggesting that he could see 'no reason that can possibly incline a Christian and a Free Society, to cut off its poor, impotent Members from the common Comforts of Life'.[26]

Secondly, positive judgements of everyday dress were encouraged by the notion, ever more frequently proposed in patrician circles as the century progressed, that emulation could provide an incentive for the poor to engage in socially desirable forms of behaviour (figs 83, 84). From Dudley North in the late seventeenth century to Adam Smith in the late eighteenth, writers on economics argued that aspiration was a spur to industry, although such arguments were repeatedly qualified by the concern that the labouring poor might not respond appropriately.[27] Nevertheless, it was widely believed that a lack of emulation among the common people led to economic and social stagnation, as the experience of Ireland towards the end of the eighteenth century was held to demonstrate. 'The disadvantages of many of the poor in Ireland originate in want of education, in a total ignorance of the comforts of life, and a consequent indifference about them', wrote Thomas Bernard in the 1790s. He judged the necessary remedies to include the inculcation of 'a taste for the comforts of life, as applied to food, habitation and clothes'.[28]

82 William Bigg, *Poor Old Woman's Comfort* (detail of fig. 2). An earthenware teapot, a teacup and saucer, a tea caddy, a teaspoon, white bread and butter are among the comforts laid out on this three-legged table in an old woman's cottage. The title of Bigg's painting suggests sympathy for the deserving poor, endorsing comforts such as tea and white bread which were often condemned by patrician critics obsessed with pauper extravagance.

There was, however, another, more practical way in which the wealthy endorsed plebeian dress: they copied it. Although the rise of sensibility in the second half of the eighteenth century brought with it a new emphasis on modest dressing, especially for wealthy women, the appeal of simple modes was already well established among the

83 George Morland, *The Comforts of Industry*, 1790, oil on canvas, National Gallery of Scotland, Edinburgh, NG 1835. In this painting and its companion, *Miseries of Idleness* (fig. 84), Morland juxtaposes two cottage interiors to inculcate a stark moral lesson. Here, improbably fine clothing, along with ample provisions and well-ordered furnishings, show the benefits the rural poor were supposed to accrue by following the proper rules of domestic economy laid down by their social superiors.

fashionable in the early part of the century.[29] Plainness was regarded as a distinctive characteristic of normal English dressing, even among the nobility. Foreign visitors were especially attentive to this. In 1750, the Frenchwoman Madame du Boccage noted 'the white apron, and the pretty straw-hat' worn by grand ladies in London as informal morning and outdoor dress, which 'become them with the greatest propriety, not only in their own apartments, but at noon in St James's Park'.[30] Both derived from plebeian ways of dressing. Wealthy men, too, adopted plebeian styles. Jean Bernard Le Blanc noted with some astonishment in 1747 that at London 'masters dress like their

84 George Morland, *The Miseries of Idleness*, 1790, oil on canvas, National Gallery of Scotland, Edinburgh, NG 1836. Here ragged clothes, along with torn curtains and disarrayed furniture, show the consequences of improvidence.

valets, and dutchesses copy after their chamber-maids'. He picked out for special attention what he called the English *petit-maître*, by which he meant a genteel fop or dandy. In England, he suggested, this kind of person dressed in exactly the opposite way to his exquisite, affected French equivalent.

> A short bob wig without powder, a handkerchief round the neck instead of a cravat, a sailor's waistcoat, a strong knotty stick, a rough tone and language, an affectation of the airs and an imitation of the manners of the meanest populace; these are the characteristics of the English Petit-maitre.[31]

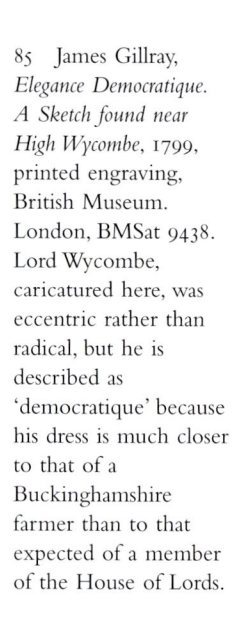

85 James Gillray, *Elegance Democratique. A Sketch found near High Wycombe*, 1799, printed engraving, British Museum, London, BMSat 9438. Lord Wycombe, caricatured here, was eccentric rather than radical, but he is described as 'democratique' because his dress is much closer to that of a Buckinghamshire farmer than to that expected of a member of the House of Lords.

English commentators noted the same phenomenon. In 1739, the *Gentleman's Magazine* criticised 'a reigning Ambition among our *young Gentlemen*, of degrading themselves in their Apparel to the Class of the *Servants* they keep'. Smart young fellows were dressing like stage-coachmen and grooms, in 'a *narrow-edg'd* Hat flapp'd down, a *plain Shirt, Buckskin-Breeches,* and an *India Handkerchief* round the Neck'.[32] Dressing down like this was not the only way that wealthy young men rebelled sartorially against their elders in the middle decades of the eighteenth century. Some affected an exaggerated aristocratic magnificence.[33] Nevertheless, those who chose to dress down were sharing in a powerful trend towards the rural, the sporting and the plebeian that surfaced repeatedly in fashionable eighteenth-century male dressing. It culminated towards the end of the century in some of the greatest nobles in the land attending the House of Lords dressed like working farmers or graziers, and, more broadly, in a general simplification of men's fashion (fig. 85).[34]

For wealthy, fashionable English men and women, the appeal of simpler, plainer ways of dressing was many-faceted. It reflected the attachment of the English elite to country

86 Henry Bunbury, *Blouzelind*, 1782, coloured engraving, Lewis Walpole Library, Farmington, Conn., 781.3.1.2+. A late eighteenth-century portrayal of Blouzelind, 'the peerless maid that did all maids excel', heroine of John Gay's burlesque pastoral poem 'The Shepherd's Week', first published in 1714.

living and country sports. It drew on literary idealisations of arcadian simplicity, peopled with unaffected shepherdesses and clean, healthy milkmaids (fig. 86). It responded to the emphasis politeness placed on moderation as a tool of sociability. It benefited from nationalistic celebrations of pugnacious, plebeian masculinity as the embodiment of English liberty (fig. 78). It drew on the idea, increasingly common as the century progressed, that virtuous women who made consumer choices that were moderate and restrained could uphold the morality of a commercial society, protecting it from its own depravity.[35] All this did not result in each and every item of dress that was distinctively plebeian being appropriated by the elite. Those items that were incorporated into the dress of the wealthy were usually subject to a process of remodelling in more expensive fabrics. Nevertheless, their incorporation was one of the most striking trends in eighteenth-century fashion.

87 Francis Wheatley, *The Return from Market*, 1789, oil on canvas, Leeds City Art Gallery. Wheatley was criticised for painting plebeian subjects dressed in improbably fine clothing, but this self-sufficient rural housewife, counting her money after a successful trip to market, is portrayed as the antithesis of luxury, dressed almost entirely in coarse, patched, probably homespun fabrics in sombre reds and browns. The poem that accompanied the engraving of the painting tells us that luxury 'was ne'er the lot of this sequestered maid', who 'must charm with simpler aid', being 'a prudent housewife, virtuous, fond and true'.

12
The View from Below

THE VIEWS OF EIGHTEENTH-CENTURY ELITES ON PLEBEIAN DRESS are readily accessible; the opinions of ordinary people on the subject are far more elusive. Nevertheless, it is possible to discern a variety of overlapping and sometimes contradictory views that found expression under different circumstances. For the common people, clothes were powerful symbols of social inequality and, consequently, of plebeian identity. Thus expensive silk clothing was, as Peter Linebaugh has insisted, a widely acknowledged sign of exalted social rank.[1] Clothes were especially likely to be invoked as badges of plebeian identity on occasions of conflict between working people and those in authority. When the armed freemen of Newcastle-on-Tyne massed to quell a grain riot in the town in 1740, they were identified by the mob as the 'White Stocking Gentlemen'.[2] The phrase captured a key distinction between the dress of rich and poor in the north of England in the first half of the eighteenth century; the distinction between the white silk or cotton stockings worn by the rich, and the coloured, usually worsted stockings worn by the poor. Yet ironically, insofar as the rioters treated their own coloured stockings as a proud badge of plebeian solidarity and rejected the white stockings worn by Newcastle's freemen, they ran the risk of aligning themselves with the most conservative among elite commentators, who believed that sartorial distinctions between the classes were sacred and immutable. 'Poor people must not stand for the colour of their stockings', asserted Hannah More in her didactic novel, *The Shepherd of Salisbury Plain*, later in the century.[3] She did so because stockings were a key object of both plebeian aspiration and plebeian shame. A man accused of a London street robbery in 1751 was said to have 'kept in the house because he was low in habit, he had no shoes or stockings'.[4] Yet in the second half of the eighteenth century increasing numbers of plebeian victims of theft owned white cotton stockings, especially in London. Such stockings were already a common subject of plebeian aspiration in 1750, when a thief and his accomplice were bantering over the counter with the proprietor of a haberdashery shop in Soho, London. One, pretending to be the other's master, offered to buy him a ribbon. Seeing a white pair of cotton stockings lying on the counter, the other replied 'I had rather you'd buy me such a pair of stockings as they are.'[5]

Plebeian men and women could be acutely sensitive to social distinctions in highly visible items of dress such as stockings. The way they employed such distinctions varied according to precisely who was doing the judging and the circumstances in which the judgement was applied. It is possible to observe here a tension between differentiation and imitation, between separation and belonging, of the kind that Georg Simmel famously argued is intrinsic to fashion.[6] It is important to stress, however, that the way sartorial distinctions were evaluated did not turn on a simple division of working people into two groups, one of which was aspirational and emulative, the other conservative and resistant to new or socially elevated wants. The same people could display very different attitudes under different circumstances. The kind of high-earning colliers who participated in the riots at Newcastle in 1740 against the 'White Stocking Gentlemen' were prominent among the northern working men who in subsequent decades liked to show off their newly acquired silver watches. None the less, the plebeian classes comprised such a vast and diverse range of people, some of whom shared little more than their restricted spending power, that it would be surprising if a variety of sometimes diametrically opposed attitudes to clothing had not coexisted among them.

Many were sartorially ambitious. From the beginning of the eighteenth century to its end, showy, fashionable and expensive clothing exercised a powerful attraction for large numbers of ordinary men and women. We have already observed how that attraction emerged in their acquisitions, and seen it expressed in their autobiographical writings. It can also be observed among their heroes. Fine clothing was an essential element in the image of the polite, gentlemanly highwayman. This image was, as Robert Shoemaker has pointed out, an eighteenth-century creation, popular with readers of newspapers and pamphlets at all social levels, calculated to encourage sympathy and even admiration for highwaymen by asserting a distinction between them and mere footpads, who were reviled as vulgar and violent.[7] Its most famous embodiment was James Maclaine, executed in 1750, who was 'called the Gentleman Highwayman, and in his Dress and Equipage very much affected the fine Gentleman' (fig. 88). How much 'a laced coat, bag-wig, and white silk stockings' actually made a gentleman out of Maclaine or the other highwaymen who dressed like him was a question often asked by sceptical commentators.[8] Nevertheless, this was a way of dressing that other less famous highwaymen frequently reproduced, at least in some of its elements. Anthony Drury wore a red coat and a laced hat when he robbed a wagon near London in 1726. He was initially mistaken by its driver for 'some Maggotty London Gentleman, that was got upon a drunken Frolick'. Henry Cook, an Essex shoemaker, apprehended for highway robbery in 1740, was overheard saying that he 'generally robb'd in a Gold laced Hat'.[9]

How were fine clothes understood by their plebeian wearers? We have seen that in the autobiographical writings of plebeian men like William Hutton and Francis Place, the best, stylish clothes they acquired as young men – clothes they sometimes referred to as 'genteel' or 'respectable' – were interpreted in a variety of overlapping ways: as signs of sexual maturity, a means of sexual attraction, a currency in both sexual competition and male bonding, emblems of material self-advancement, declarations of

88 *An Exact Representation of Maclaine the Highwayman Robbing Lord Eglington on Hounslow Heath on the 26th of June 1750* (detail), 1750, printed engraving, Lewis Walpole Library, Farmington, Conn., 750.8.13.1. James Maclaine, the 'Gentleman Highwayman', is portrayed robbing a carriage wearing a laced hat and waistcoat. He is described in the caption as 'commonly very gay in his Dress'.

respectable status in public places, badges of moral worth or sources of self-regarding pleasure. Others found the lure of stylish clothing equally irresistible, but impossible to explain. Elizabeth Wild came into a London shop in January 1716 asking for a pair of black silk gloves. 'Not liking the first (according to the Custom of such Persons) others were shown her.' She proceeded to be 'very difficult, and nothing could please, and thereupon went away'. Called back to the shop, she was found to have stolen three pairs of silk gloves worth 13s. 6d. All she could say in her defence was that 'she long'd for them, and that she knew not why else she did it, not having any occasion as she knew of for them'.[10]

Fine dressing was not, however, universally pursued in plebeian circles. Some plebeian men and women regarded it with indifference, or even hostility. There were those like Johnny Chapman, the ragged Northumbrian pitman described by the engraver Thomas Bewick, who took no interest in their clothes. There were others who could not afford to do so. There were others again who dressed according to local or communal standards that explicitly disavowed elite modes in favour of customary sartorial conventions, like the buckle-makers at Walsall who required James Gee to give up his prized cocked hat when he came to live in the Staffordshire town in the 1760s. Transgressors risked ostracism and derision of the sort heaped upon Francis Place and his wife in the early 1790s, when they earned the ironic title of '*the* Lady and Gentleman' from their London neighbours for dressing 'respectably'.[11] Yet, as Place's autobiography tells us, local, communal sartorial conventions were not necessarily plain or modest. Plebeian norms could embrace the flashy, the costly, and the competitive, reproducing and appropriating elements of elite fashion while self-consciously maintaining a distance from it. The flashiest dressers among the young plebeian men in the London of Francis Place's youth – those Place termed 'especially knowing' – affected distinctive hairstyles, white cotton or silk stockings with stripes, and breeches with unnecessarily large numbers of buttons and strings hanging at the knees. Their look had parallels in some elite ways of dressing (fig. 23), but Place gives no indication that their dress was emulative either in intention or effect; on the contrary, 'they who aimed at being thought knowing had fashions of their own'.[12] When an item or style of dress was worn first by the rich and subsequently trickled down to the poor, we should not automatically assume that, in adopting and wearing it, the poor necessarily identified themselves with the elite, or with elite taste. The white stockings worn by Place's young Londoners had very different associations, for all concerned, from those worn by the 'White Stocking Gentlemen' at Newcastle forty years earlier.

No group exemplified this kind of appropriation and reworking of showy items from elite dress into a distinctive and proudly plebeian look than sailors, despite their reputation for preferring drink to clothes. Indeed, for elite commentators such appropriations were an especially blatant manifestation of sailors' childlike irrationality. 'Having little intercourse with the world', complained Thomas Trotter, a naval doctor, in 1797, 'they are easily defrauded, and dupes to the deceitful, wherever they go: their money is lavished with the most thoughtless profusion; fine cloathes for his girl, a silver watch, and silver buckles for himself, are often the sole return for years of labour and hardship'.[13] A seaman's best, shore-going dress might include silver-plated buckles, a silver watch, even a wig or a laced waistcoat. Isaac Tulley, a seaman on a ship sailing out of Whitehaven in Cumberland in 1751, wore his wig when sent ashore in Wales to buy provisions. A London woman overheard two men in the street say in 1749: 'there is some sailor with a fine laced waistcoat, let us take it from off his back; he has been at sea and took a little prize money'.[14] It was in their flamboyant shore-going rig that sailors were often portrayed in the printed engravings of them that were so popular in the second half of the eighteenth century.[15] Nevertheless, it remained essentially a fancy version of their on-board, working dress – jacket, trousers and coloured or checked shirt. Seamen who dressed like landsmen in what were known as 'long clothes', even if it was to deceive the press gang, were mocked by their comrades. The seaman Robert Wilson, captured by the press gang in 1805 wearing landsmen's clothes, was derided as a 'Lord Mayor's-man'. The Marine Society's policy of issuing clothes to landsmen recruited for the fleet was designed partly to prevent them being ridiculed by other seamen because of their land clothes.[16]

Dressing ostentatiously was, therefore, something numerous working people aspired to do. It might have involved trying to follow the prevailing elite fashions on a limited budget. It might have entailed conforming to a set of sartorial conventions that were distinctively plebeian. Most frequently, perhaps, it involved some combination of the two. For others, however, nostalgia for plain, homespun clothing had a powerful appeal. The popular ballads of the late eighteenth and early nineteenth centuries suggest its appeal was especially strong among the increasingly impoverished rural poor. Earlier rural ballads, such as 'God speed the Plow, and bless the Corn-mow' had celebrated the agricultural labourer's simple, hard-wearing clothes.[17] They went on being reprinted throughout the eighteenth century, but in the second half of the century, newer ballads began to reproduce the criticisms of new-fashioned commercial farmers found in the debates in pamphlet and periodical over enclosure and high grain prices, including their attacks on ostentatious dressing by farmers' wives and daughters (figs 89, 90). Like the contributors to the published debates, the ballads regretted the newly wealthy farmers' rejection of older, communal lifestyles, in which the farmer's family and the labourer shared the same farmhouse, the same world view and the same simple, honest ways of dressing.

> The farmers' daughters used to work
> All at the spinning-wheel, sir;
> But now such furniture as that
> Is thought quite ungenteel, sir.
> Their fingers they're afraid to spoil
> With any such kind of sport, sir:
> Sooner than handle mop or broom,
> They'd handle a piano-forte, sir.
>
> Their dress was always plain and warm,
> When in their holiday clothes, sir;
> Besides, they had such handsome faces,
> As red as any rose, sir;
> But now they're frilled and furbelowed
> Just like a dancing monkey:
> Their bonnets and their great black veils
> Would almost fright a donkey.[18]

What was at issue here was not simply a demand for a return to fairness and justice in terms which paralleled arguments in the elite debate on the same issue. The ballads were also informed by a powerful sense of what constituted appropriate dress for farmer and labourer alike. Specifically, they attacked fashion and fine clothes, regretted the

89 *The English Farmer's Wife converted to a fine Lady during his Absence in London*, 1772, printed engraving, Lewis Walpole Library, Farmington, Conn., 772.8.0.1. The farmer is depicted as an archetypal countryman, wearing boots and a heavily caped greatcoat and carrying a riding whip. His farm servant wears a smock frock and carries a carter's whip. The farmer's wife is shown with an absurdly exaggerated hairstyle and enormous ruffles at her sleeves. One of the books she has been reading is entitled *Art of Dressing*.

decline of domestically manufactured clothing and asserted the superiority, both practical and moral, of plain, durable, homespun fabrics.

> Now the commons they are taken in, and cottages are pulled down,
> And Molly has no wool to spin her linsey-woolsey gown;
> The winter cold, and clothing thin, and blankets very few,
> Such cruelty did ne'er abound, when this old hat was new.[19]

The decline of the kind of self-provisioning with home-spun textiles regretted in the ballads coincided with the rise of the smock frock as the everyday dress of the agricultural labourers of the Midlands and the south of England, often worn to conceal clothing that was inadequate in other respects. The popularity of the ballads indicates this coincidence was not lost on the increasingly impoverished labourers.[20] Their choices as consumers of clothing were restricted. When resources were being progressively squeezed, the triumph of shop-supplied fabrics was, at best, a mixed blessing. But did this amount to anything more than nostalgic regret for a more prosperous golden age, articulated in ways that hint at the influence of sentimental poems and novels, and treatises on rural economics?

90 *Farmer Giles and his Wife showing off their daughter Betty to their Neighbours on her return from School*, 1809, coloured engraving, Lewis Walpole Library, Farmington, Conn., 809.1.1.1. The picture framed on the wall is entitled Cheese Farm. It shows a thatched roof and a cow being milked, suggesting the simpler, unpretentious lifestyle that Farmer Giles and his family have abandoned now they are wealthy enough to afford the modish neoclassical furnishings and pretentious female accomplishments that surround them at Cheese Hall.

The popularity of these ballads among the agricultural labourers can be read as evidence that wearing plain, coarse fabrics was not simply an unavoidable necessity, but had become a vehicle for expressing their bitterness at impoverishment and loss of autonomy. In other words, what we may be observing here is the assertion of a oppositional, customary sartorial standard antagonistic to the ramping up of working people's needs that Edward Thompson sees as one of the main effects of eighteenth- and early nineteenth-century capitalism.[21] Jeanette Neeson has suggested that such a stance certainly typified commoners who opposed enclosure. 'Commoners had little but they also wanted less. The result may have been that they lived well enough for themselves, but invisibly and poorly in the eyes of outsiders.'[22] What appeared to be poverty to polite observers, argues Neeson, could represent self-sufficient adequacy to those who lived on the commons. Like Thomas Barnard's Irish poor, they were impervious to the siren song of emulation.

It is entirely possible, therefore, that among the downtrodden agricultural labourers of the south and the Midlands, there were those who embraced plain dressing as a kind of customary, oppositional identity, worn in defiance of enclosing landlords, opulent farmers and oppressive parish vestrymen. Faced with the intensifying privations of rural life in the last decades of the eighteenth century and the early decades of the nineteenth, their numbers may have grown.[23] Nevertheless, some caution is necessary here. It was not only the ballads that extolled domestic self-provisioning of clothing. It was also a priority for writers on rural economics such as Sir Frederick Eden who were keen to prod working people back into virtuous self-sufficiency, not so much to restore their autonomy and prosperity, but rather to reduce the burden of the poor rates on farmers (fig. 87). Yet despite the best efforts of balladeers and economists alike, the decline of textile self-provisioning in rural families continued unabated in the late years of the eighteenth century.

What this abandonment of self-sufficiency may signify is a divergence in attitudes between men and women in those families, or even between young and old.[24] Perhaps rural working women who were responsible for spinning preferred working for money. Perhaps, too, they preferred to spend that money on colourful cotton prints for their gowns, rather than make do with coarse, drab linsey-woolsey woven from home-spun yarn, irrespective of whether they were urged to do so by their menfolk or their social superiors. This was certainly to be true of young village women in Hertfordshire in the 1860s, who made payments in weekly instalments to visiting shopkeepers from St Albans to get hold of 'a good bit of the so-called finery so carefully debarred and tabooed from the clothing clubs' where the rector's daughters policed their acquisitions.[25] Earlier, tension between female sartorial acquisitiveness and male attachment to simplicity, fuelled by nostalgia for a lost childhood world of rural self-sufficiency, was a leitmotif in the marriage of Benjamin Shaw, the Lancashire mill mechanic, as it was in popular ballads and prints (fig. 91).[26] It can be found in the diary of the Oldham weaver William Rowbottom, who lamented in 1792 that it was 'a pity that the prevailing fashion and superfluity of dress should so much attract the attention of females as to cause them to shrink from the paths of virtue and respectability. Such has been the weakness of Susan Lord of Northmoor who was this day found to have robbed her late Master.'[27] We should remember, though, that flamboyant dressing for feast and fair, especially by young adults, was as much a part of the customary world of the rural working poor as resistance to grasping farmers and penny-pinching overseers. Indeed, dressing ostentatiously at popular festivities may itself have come to represent a kind of symbolic defiance similar to that displayed by the political protesters cut down by the Yeomanry Cavalry at Peterloo in 1819, who marched to Manchester from across south-east Lancashire pointedly attired in their best clothes.[28]

The most explicit plebeian advocacy of plain dressing in the eighteenth century came not from rural social protesters, but from those with a religious commitment to material simplicity. From the seventeenth-century Quaker George Fox to the eighteenth-century Methodist John Wesley, Protestant reformers of various persuasions invoked biblical authority to insist on plain, modest dressing. In 1667, Fox had issued 'A Warning to all to keep out of the vain Fashions of the World, which lead them below the Serious Life.'[29] Similarly, Wesley, writing in his *Instructions for Christians* of 1791, declared: 'They that give you fine clothes, are giving your soul to the devil.'[30]

TIGHT LACING, or the COBLER'S WIFE in the FASHION.

The Hoity head & Toighty waift,
   As now they're all the ton,
Ma'am Nell the cobler's wife, in taste
   By none will be outdone,

But, ah! when set aloft her cap,
   Her Boddice while she's bracing,
Jobson comes in, &, with his strap,
   Gives her, a good tight lacing.

Publish'd Nov.r 4.th 1777 by W.m Hitchcock N.o 5 Birchin Lane

91 *Tight Lacing, or the Cobler's Wife in the Fashion*, 1777, coloured engraving, Lewis Walpole Library, Farmington, Conn., 777.11.04 A2 T5. The wife-beating cobbler was the protagonist of numerous popular misogynistic ballads. This print on the same theme emphasises attachment to fashion as the wife's failing. The cobbler is shown wearing an apron to indicate his occupation and working status.

There were profound theological differences between Methodists and Quakers, but where dress was concerned they placed a similar stress on plainness and simplicity. Both issued sartorial regulations, principally itemising what should not be worn. Those issued by the Quakers were especially thorough and precise.[31]

From their origins in the 1650s, Quakers were required to avoid ornament and extravagance in dress. Nothing that suggested vanity or pride was permitted. 'Whatever the flesh takes delight in, and whatever stands in respect of persons, (as saith the Scripture) the lust of the eye, the lusts of the flesh, the pride of life, these are not of God', warned James Naylor in 1658.[32] Robert Barclay explained: 'Seeing the chief end of all Religion is to redeem Man from the Spirit and vain Conversation of this World, and to lead into inward Communion with God . . . therefore, all the vain customs and habits thereof both in word and deed are to be rejected and forsaken.' In particular, 'things meerly superfluous, such as is the use of *Ribbons* and *Lace*, and much more of that kind of stuff' were 'the fruits of the fal[le]n, lustful and corrupt nature, and not of the new Creation'.[33] Rejection of the vain fashions of the world infused every aspect of Quakers' material lives, not just their clothing. In 1660, Ralph Farmer listed unsympathetically 'their *morose* and severe carriage and *conversation*; their *demure* looks; their *abstinences* in meats and drinks, the pulling off their Points, Laces, and Ribons from their *cloaths*, their separating and withdrawing from the society and familiarity of all others, *as unclean and polluted*'.[34] Quakers fought constantly against the power of fashion and ornament to seduce believers into worldliness. Clear lines of battle were crucial. Quakers considered it essential, as Marcia Pointon has commented, to demarcate precisely the functional from the decorative, the necessary from the superfluous.[35] In identifying the clothing they considered improper, they were explicit and ever alert to new fashions. Eighteenth-century secular attacks on plebeian luxury were, by contrast, vague, repetitive and stereotypical in the clothes they cited as evidence of excess.

Throughout the eighteenth century, detailed, constantly updated advice about clothes circulated through the hierarchy of yearly, quarterly, monthly and particular Quaker meetings, to be debated and, if necessary, enhanced at each level. For example, the women's monthly meeting at Knaresborough in Yorkshire recorded in May 1718 that it had received advice from the women's Quarterly Meeting at York

> against the following of fashions as handkerchiefs putting on undecently their necks being bare sometimes behinde and sometimes before as the fashions leads them that are willing to follow likewise some having their petticoats set out at sides in imitation of hooped petticoats with other foolish fashions which are a great trouble to many friends. It is also the advise from this meeting to every particular meeting belonging hereunto that the Quarterly Meeting's advice be not slighted herein.[36]

Over forty years later, in 1762, the Knaresborough meeting was still noting advice from York against fashions that were equally troubling, but different in their particular elements:

> . . . that the present prevailing fashion in the extravagant use of ribbands which too many of our youth especially have fallen into about their hats and elsewhere may be kept clear of.[37]

Such advice had consequences. Those who transgressed faced community discipline. The monthly Quaker meeting at Brighouse, Yorkshire appointed members in 1801 to visit John Flintoft to establish if he was of good moral conduct, as 'his dress and address appears to be very far from a desirable simplicity'. In the same year, Joseph Tatham asked to be re-admitted to the same monthly meeting, having been expelled. 'He owned the principles we profess; acknowledged his inconsistency therewith, both in dress and address, and also in not attending afternoon meetings.'[38] A large proportion of those who enforced and subjected themselves to this sartorial policing were farmers, artisans and labouring people. Urban Quakers often became prosperous in the course of the eighteenth century, but in the countryside many Quakers remained relatively poor. In Lancashire during the second half of the century, for instance, Quakers were described in Anglican visitation returns variously as 'lower class', 'poor farmers', 'lowly' or 'poor'.[39]

The advice about clothing that circulated between Quaker meetings was overwhelmingly concerned with establishing what should not be worn. It never prescribed a fixed, unchanging uniform, although Quaker definitions of plainness became more clearly codified at the end of the seventeenth century, under pressure from the provincial, rural grass roots. Discipline was reinvigorated in the 1760s.[40] Most of the detailed advice was concerned with suppressing exaggerated forms of familiar garments, gaudy colours or modish accessories. In its constituent elements, ordinary Quakers' dress in the eighteenth century broadly shadowed changes in the everyday dress of non-Quakers, although often with a time lag. Hoods for women, seen as a distinctive element of Quaker dress earlier in the century, had all but disappeared among them by its end, replaced by bonnets.[41] Nevertheless, the deliberately unadorned manner in which most Quakers dressed, in combination with other aspects of their self-presentation in public, such as their refusal to doff hats to those in authority, made them highly distinctive and targets for hostility. The yeoman Richard Gough, writing at the start of the eighteenth century about the inhabitants of his Shropshire village of Myddle, recalled that Richard Clarke, a labourer who worked making spinning wheels, joined with 'that phanaticall, selfe-conceited sort of people called Quakers', coming home one day 'a perfect Quaker in appearance, and had gott theire canting way of discourse as readyly as if hee had beene seven years apprentice'.[42] Later in the eighteenth century, newspaper advertisements for stolen goods and runaways could describe hats as 'cocked in Quaker fashion', reflecting the style of hat worn by many male Quakers, who refused to wear them tightly cocked or looped.[43] Quaker plainness became proverbial, at the same time as it prompted accusations of Quaker hypocrisy, whether against gay Quakers for bending the rules, or plain Quakers for spiritual pride.

Eighteenth-century Quakers were a small though widely dispersed sect whose membership was not increasing. Methodism was, by contrast, the most successful religious movement of the century, with a particular appeal to working people. None the less, in his teaching on plainness of dress, John Wesley was profoundly influenced by Quaker ideas.[44] His teaching found its clearest expression in his *Advice to the People Called Methodists, with Regard to Dress*, first published in 1760, which he ordered to be read in every large Methodist society once a year. In it he advised his followers to dress like the Quakers, not in their singularities, such as wearing hats of a particular form, but in their plainness, and their neatness and cleanliness. The clothes worn by Methodists, he insisted, should be cheaper than those worn by non-Methodists in similar walks of life, 'grave, not gay, airy, or showy', and especially 'not on the point of the fashion'. These 'easy rules' were to apply both to materials and to the way those materials were made up into clothing and worn. Like the Quakers, he went on to detail precisely what not to wear.

> Buy no velvets, no silks, no fine linen, no superfluities, no *mere ornaments*, though ever so much in fashion. Wear nothing, though you have it already, which is of a glaring colour, or which is in any kind gay, glistering, showy; nothing made in the very height of the fashion, nothing apt to attract the eyes of the bystanders. I do not advise women to wear rings, ear-rings, necklaces, lace, (of whatever kind or colour,) or ruffles, which by little and little may easily shoot out from one to twelve inches deep. Neither do I advise men, to wear coloured waistcoats, shining stockings, glittering or costly buckles or buttons, either on their coats, or in their sleeves, any more than gay, fashionable, or expensive perukes.[45]

Wesley also followed the Quakers in the reasons he offered for plain dressing. Citing biblical authority, he insisted that preoccupation with appearance diverted attention from true spirituality, as well as reducing the amounts of money available for charitable giving. Subsequently, he expanded on the moral threat posed by fine clothing, emphasising the dangers of pride, vanity, arrogance and lust.[46]

These views were incorporated into Methodist preaching to the poor from the very beginnings of the movement. As early as 1739, John Wesley's brother Charles preached to the members of the newly established Methodist societies at Bristol, many of whom had been drawn by George Whitfield's open-air evangelising among the Kingswood colliers. He reproved the women 'for their lightness, dress, self-indulgence. I then exhorted the men to self-denial'.[47] Methodist advocacy of plain dressing soon became familiar enough to be satirised. A decade after Charles Wesley's preaching at Bristol, Eliza Haywood could quip in her *Epistles for the Ladies* that to become a Methodist 'you have no more to do than to put on a Stuff Gown, – tye your Hair up tight in the Nape of your Neck, – travel two or three times a Week to *Moorfields*, and chaunt out spritual Hymns'.[48] As with Quakers, Methodist plain dressing could provoke accusations of hypocrisy, or expose its wearers to the violent hostility that Methodists sometimes attracted. Nevertheless, many followed Wesley's advice (fig. 92). At a Methodist meeting at Whitby in Yorkshire in 1784, for instance, he was pleased to record: 'They despise all ornaments but good works, together with a meek and quiet spirit. I did not see a ruffle, no, nor a fashionable cap among them; though many of them are in easy circumstances.'[49]

Precise, itemised instructions for plain dressing of this kind were largely confined in the eighteenth century to religious groups like the Quakers and the Methodists, but the sort of moralising vocabulary they used had a much wider purchase as part of the everyday lexicon of terms that people of all kinds employed in describing clothing. If we examine the words witnesses at the Old Bailey used to describe people's clothes, a powerful sense of both propriety and hierarchy emerges. The most frequent response of witnesses when asked how someone was dressed was, not surprisingly, to name the garments worn, their material and their colour. This was the context in which the

92 James Philip de Loutherbourg, *A Midsummer Afternoon with a Methodist Preacher* (detail), 1777, oil on canvas, National Gallery of Canada, Ottawa, 4057. De Loutherbourg contrasts the ostentatious dress of the polite onlookers with the plainer dress of the Methodist preacher and his plebeian audience.

word fashionable was occasionally used, describing an attribute of a garment, rather than a person's overall appearance.[50] Generic descriptions were less frequent, but they were used repeatedly. Some generic descriptions turned on occupation or place. 'He used to change his dress', complained one accused man of a witness in a theft trial in 1761, 'Sometimes he was in a brewer's servant's dress, and sometimes like a sailor.'[51] A witness at another Old Bailey trial in 1771 declared that a suspect 'used to be about the turnpikes, dressed like a countryman'.[52] It was, however, generic descriptions couched in the overlapping evaluative languages of hierarchy and propriety that predominated at the Old Bailey. At one extreme were those whose dress was described as mean, shabby, indifferent, bad or simply ragged. 'The Horse was as ragged and shabby as the Boy', stated a victim of horse theft in 1735.[53] A man accused of stealing money from a Marylebone milk seller was described as having been 'very mean and ragged' prior to the theft.[54] At the other extreme were those who were simply identified as well dressed, or were described as dressing finely, elegantly, smartly, handsomely, or above all genteelly. A man who tried to sell a stolen tankard in 1740 'appeared at that

Time very genteel; he was well dressed, in a powdered Wig, and white Stockings'.[55] A female lodger who stole clothes from her landlord's daughter in 1773 pawned them with a Great Portland Street pawnbroker. He told the Old Bailey that 'she appeared then in a much different manner; she was always very genteelly dressed'.[56]

Genteel versus mean, elegant versus shabby; this was the eighteenth-century language of polite decorum. At the Old Bailey it was employed by rich and poor witnesses alike and was applied to the way both men and women dressed.[57] The rule of decorum decreed that different kinds of dress and different forms of conduct were appropriate to different stations in life, according to social rank, age, sex or occupation. Decorum required at least a nominal acceptance of prevailing social distinctions and hierarchies. It was a keystone of the code of politeness, which prized a genteel agreeableness achieved by means of moderation and simplicity as opposed to exaggeration and excess. In pursuing gentility, polite men and women were expected to respect the rule of decorum, flouting it neither by dressing in ways that were mean or vulgar, nor by indulging in overblown ostentation.[58] Of course, most of those whose dress was described at the Old Bailey as genteel were not actually gentlemen or ladies, even in the loosest eighteenth-century sense of those words. For struggling apprentices like the young William Hutton, saving up in the early 1740s to buy 'a genteel suit of clothes', dressing genteelly was all about distinction within his peer group – 'fully adequate to the sphere in which I moved' as Hutton put it – not about magically moving up to the unattainably distant social rank of gentleman.[59] In a fluid, commercial society, genteel dressing was something to which a man could aspire without ever expecting to be identified as a gentlemen. Like other props in the performances of politeness, genteel clothes could be bought, at a price, but a successful performance also required knowledge of how they should be worn. The gentility embodied in certain ways of dressing carried with it expectations about appropriate behaviour that continued to be conceived in terms of a hierarchical social order. Inappropriate diversions from the rule of decorum were regarded as suspicious, even threatening. Robert Peen, a publican from Ilford, Essex, told the Old Bailey in 1747: 'Seeing the Fellow very indifferently dressed, we wondered to see such a Fellow pull out a Watch.'[60]

Unease at such discrepancies was understandable, because judgements with practical consequences were constantly made on the basis of how people dressed. A pawnbroker who apprehended a woman suspected of theft in 1760 recalled that 'she being genteely dressed, I ordered her not to be put among the common people, but taken up stairs'.[61] A landlady's servant arranging to let a room in 1787 thought a man who 'was very shabbily dressed . . . did not look like a person that wanted a first floor'.[62] A bystander who apprehended a woman suspected of a theft in a West Smithfield draper's shop in 1742 said he 'called her Madam, because she was dressed in a fine damask Gown, and fine Cloaths . . . she was dressed in a very fine Manner'.[63] Time and time again, inappropriate or incongruous dressing aroused suspicion. A brewer's servant expressed surprise at a women he charged with picking his pocket in 1798 because 'when I saw her first, she was very meanly dressed, and when I saw her afterwards, she was very finely dressed'.[64]

Between those who were described as well dressed and those described as badly dressed, there were a few who were literally described as being dressed in a middling way. 'He was dressed middling; not very shabby', said the driver of the Stratford coach describing a highwayman in 1752.[65] More often, however, dress that was adequate but not ostentatious was described in the language of propriety – neat, tight, clean, decent. Neat, when employed to describe dress in the eighteenth century, meant trim, tidy, clean and in good order, implying an agreeable simplicity of form, free from embellishment. 'She was then dressed neat, and in a clean Linnen Gown', said a Clerkenwell publican describing a Hornsey women accused of stealing a brass pottage pot in 1742.[66] A group of men and women caught at work counterfeiting halfpennies in 1781 were described as having 'no clothes on, except in a condition for working. Rebecca Brown was clean and neat, and did not seem to have been at work; but Hannah Trueman was in her working-dress.' Tight, too, meant trim, tidy and smart, with similar connotations of wholesomeness and decency. Three girls said to have been implicated in a rape case were described by a 14-year-old apprentice as 'dressed very tight and neat'.[67] Hannah Sealy, accused in 1732 of stealing velvet from a shop, was described by the shop assistant as 'clean dress'd, and looked like a tight Girl'.[68] Mary Hadlep, accused of stealing a watch from a chairman in 1753, claimed he had 'said he would give her a guinea to get some cloaths to make her look tight and clean'.[69] John Fogg, robbed of his watch in 1789 at night in Bishopsgate by three women, and anxious to deny any illicit dealing with them as over-dressed prostitutes, described them as 'not ragged, but very coarse and homely; their dresses was tight, but that was all'.[70]

The meanings of clean and decent were closer to their modern usages, although clean, like neat and tight, could carry the implication of trim or well put together. 'How was the woman dressed?' a gardener was asked about a woman he had seen in Horse Ferry Road, Westminster in 1761. 'She was dressed clean and decent', he replied.[71] A Grub Street publican who accused his barmaid of stealing money in 1795 denied she had lacked clothes. 'You did not hear me say so', he insisted under questioning, 'She made a decent appearance.'[72] A woman who sold a yellow cotton gown stolen from a day labourer's wife at a Monmouth Street women's clothes shop in 1783 was described by its proprietor as being 'at that time much decenter than she is now'.[73]

The eighteenth-century lexicon of polite decorum was not simply about hierarchy. It also embraced moral propriety. As Amanda Vickery has pointed out in her study of the language of aesthetic discrimination used by well-heeled purchasers of wallpaper, terms like neat and clean could connote either a simple smartness, or an elegance stopping short of fashion and extra adornment, or a respectable plainness of attire.[74] These widely used terms radiated a certain moral assertiveness in their very restraint. Applied to dress, they indicated that the wearer was creditable, not just socially but also morally. Simplicity was a polite virtue. It was also prized by Methodists and Quakers, who otherwise rejected the polite pursuit of an agreeable and inclusive sociability. John Wesley regarded clean, neat clothing as a reflection of a person's inner moral state. At the same time as he lambasted those who wore clothing that was 'gay, glistering or showy', he honoured his wife for her 'uncommon neatness and cleanliness' in her dress and urged Methodists to avoid dirt, slovenliness and raggedness.[75] The words used by Quakers to describe how they should dress were modest, decent and above all plain, but others applied the terms neat and clean to the clothes they wore. When the mother of Essex farmer's wife Jane Farrin asked her to buy material for a stuff gown in the 1750s, she insisted: 'I would not have very dark nor yet gaudey', preferring 'a neat quakers couler', a notion which captured the essence of moderation and self-restraint.[76]

The word gaudy was not used by witnesses at the Old Bailey to describe clothing, but its sense of morally questionable excess was imparted by words such as gay, showy and flashy. A Tower Hill tobacconist considered that a man tried for burglary in 1763 'seemed to be, as most foreigners are, a little gay'.[77] A Strand silversmith described a man who stole earrings from his shop in 1773 as wearing 'one of your showy waistcoats embroidered'.[78] A washerwoman accused of stealing a working man's coat from his lodging room in 1786, had previously 'said she liked it, because it was not made in a flashy manner'.[79] Two women who posed as mistress and maid were suspected of stealing money from a fellow lodger, because 'they flashed away with all new things; the maid had a ring on her finger, new silver buckles, and I saw a ribbon fixed to the bed's-head to hang the watch to'.[80]

When discussing the material aspirations of eighteenth-century plebeian men and women, historians have often reproduced the colourful jeremiads of eighteenth-century elite commentators. In them, plebeian aspirations were portrayed as a fashionable contagion, a plague of luxury contracted by misguided people in the grip of rampant emulative ambition.[81] A different set of plebeian concerns is suggested by the powerful sense of decorum that pervades the language used to evaluate clothes at the Old Bailey. Plebeian judgements embraced not only a keen appreciation of neat, decent and genteel dressing, but also suspicion of showy ostentation and socially inappropriate finery. In practice, the degree of sartorial ostentation Old Bailey witnesses were personally prepared to countenance must have varied considerably, but expectations about moral and social order loomed large in their assessments. Consequently, their choices as consumers were more likely to have been shaped by anxiety about how to dress appropriately than by an uninhibited, materialistic hedonism. We should not treat such anxiety as a guilty hangover from older, sumptuary conceptions of dress. It was not a temporary side-effect of an intermediate, eighteenth-century stage in a transition from traditional, immobile patterns of consumption to modern materialism, individualistic, unconstrained and guilt-free.[82] Anxiety, accompanied by a search for normative justifications, remains central to people's everyday negotiations of fashion in modern Britain, as Alison Clarke and Daniel Miller have demonstrated.[83] It is an inescapable by-product of consumer choice, as it was in the eighteenth century.

Attitudes to clothes among ordinary eighteenth-century people were diverse, variable and often wildly inconsistent. Sullen resistance to fine dressing co-existed with desperate efforts to be genteel. Religious hostility to gaudy show could be encountered alongside idiosyncratic forms of dandyism, associated with particular places or occupations. What they shared was an enthusiasm for judging others by their clothes. Again and again, ordinary people reveal an acute sensitivity to sartorial distinctions, a sensitivity rooted in the language of decorum. It informed their evaluations of social superiors. More importantly for the purposes of this book, it shaped the way they judged each other.

93 James Ward, *A Man in Wiltshire Who was in the Habit of mowing Two Acres of Grass per Day*, c.1810, red and black chalk, heightened with white, British Museum, London, 1885, 0613.55. The labourer is depicted exhausted after a hard day's labour in the fields, but his dress is in good condition, the shirt well made with elaborately pleated sleeves.

13
Budgeting for Clothes

In eighteenth-century England a new way of judging ordinary people's living standards emerged – the household budget. It treated the plebeian household as an accounting unit, detailing family expenditure and family income, and then comparing them in order to gauge material well-being, identify waste and promote improvement. This was a powerful tool for re-conceptualising the behaviour of ordinary people as consumers. It was especially powerful when budgets were collected from different parts of the country to generate a national sample survey, which could then claim to represent the collective experience of the labouring poor as a whole. It helped shift the attention of commentators and administrators away from vague, generalised complaints about the corrosive effects on national productivity of luxury among the poor. Henceforth the material and moral condition of the labouring poor was to be an object of scientific measurement based on data collection at the level of the household. This eighteenth-century innovation remains at the heart of the way we measure standards of living today.

Clothes may not have been a prime stimulus to innovative thinking about plebeian consumption in the eighteenth century, but they featured, none the less, in these household budgets. Indeed, surviving budgets offer one of the few systematic sources for assessing the kinds of clothes worn by the labouring poor and the demands those clothes made on family resources. They have been much used by historians studying ordinary people's living standards, including their clothing. Yet the utility of the budgets is compromised by doubts about their methodology and their accuracy. Clothes were especially hard to accommodate within a framework that assumed a regular pattern of weekly or annual expenditure. What can this new tool of social analysis tell us about everyday dress in the eighteenth century?

In 1734, the merchant economist Jacob Vanderlint published what was almost certainly the first household budget for what he termed a labouring family of the middling sort.[1] It signalled a new interest in the plebeian household and its domestic economy as a unit of accounting.[2] Some 30 years later, the agricultural writer Arthur Young pioneered the systematic economic and social survey in his tours of the north and south of England, designed to assess the state of the rural economy in the aftermath of the grain crisis and riots of 1766.[3] Young occasionally included household budgets for rural labouring people in his findings, but it was the Reverend David

Davies and Sir Frederick Eden who, towards the end of the century, combined the household budget and the sample survey to produce the first systematic, large-scale studies of incomes and expenditures among labouring people. Davies published his *Case of the Labourers in Husbandry* in 1795.[4] It was followed in 1797 by Eden's *State of the Poor*.[5] Both books were written in response to growing concern among ratepayers at the apparently inexorable late eighteenth-century rise in Poor Law expenditure. The methodology adopted by the two authors was groundbreaking. Endeavouring to explain the causes of growing poverty, Davies and Eden collected detailed information on income and expenditure for large numbers of labouring families spread across Britain. Both included information on clothing.

Eden and Davies held strikingly different views on the reasons for increasing poor rates. Davies, concerned specifically with labourers in husbandry, blamed the failure of agricultural wages to keep up with the increasing price of necessities. Eden, reviewing the condition of the labouring poor as a whole, attributed the increase in poverty to an absence of proper household management among the poor and to what he regarded as their excessive luxury and extravagance. In *The Case of the Labourers in Husbandry*, Davies refers to labouring families' clothing mainly to draw attention to its inadequacy. Again and again he points out that agricultural labourers and their families were 'meanly clothed' or 'badly clothed; some children without shoes and stockings'.

> And this is visibly the case of the poor in general. In fact it is but little that in the present state of things the belly can spare for the back. Even such persons as may have been provident enough, when single, to supply themselves with a small stock of clothes, are, after marriage, from inability to buy more, soon reduced to ragged garments. And then the women spend as much time in tacking their tatters together, as would serve for manufacturing new clothing, had they the skill to do it, and materials to do it with.[6]

In *The State of the Poor*, by contrast, the subject of clothing is used by Eden to identify and to condemn a lamentable lack of self-sufficiency he identified among the poor in the south of England, as we have seen in Chapter 8.

Despite these differences, the information provided about clothing in the family budgets collected by the two authors has a number of common features.[7] In both cases, the authors evidently found it difficult to secure precise information from their informants regarding expenditure on clothing. Clothing was, after all, acquired only intermittently. In some cases informants were unable to say how much they spent on clothing or denied that they spent anything at all on clothes.[8] Both authors report that families treated spending on clothes as a residual after other more pressing needs had been fulfilled. Their own calculations often make the same assumption, providing an estimate for the cost of 'clothes, etc.' based on what was left over after a family's other expenditure had been accounted for. Both authors found it difficult to understand how many of the families they studied could afford any clothing whatsoever, given that a large majority of the budgets revealed an excess of spending over income. They repeatedly stress how much families had to rely on the stock of clothes built up before marriage, on charitable gifts of clothing from neighbours, kin, employers or the local gentry and on clothes supplied by the parish overseers of the poor.

Davies's and Eden's difficulties in establishing credible information about labouring families' expenditure on clothing arose because what they were attempting to account was unaccountable, more so indeed than almost any other aspect of the household budget.[9] However much their difficulties reveal about the serendipitous character of clothing acquisition among the poor, as historical evidence for the numbers and cost of clothes their findings should be treated with considerable caution. A close reading of the budgets quickly reveals internal inconsistencies and heavy reliance on inference and conjecture. Davies, despite acknowledging that larger numbers of children required greater expenditure on clothes, compiled his budgets for his own parish of Barkham using a standard estimate of minimum clothing expenditure per family, which took no account of the number or age of children in the family.[10] In this he was followed by a number of the gentlemen and clergy who arranged for budgets to be collected for him in parts of the country distant from his Berkshire home.

The accuracy of both authors' information on clothing may also have been compromised by misrepresentation on the part of the families themselves. Poor families certainly had reason to undervalue their spending on clothes if by doing so they could reinforce their claims to charitable and parochial gifts of clothing. Neither author undertook a statistically representative sampling of families. Eden's budgets, for example, over-represent the Midlands and the north of England and Davies's over-represent the south. There are some indications that each author selected budgets for publication that confirmed his own arguments and prejudices. Davies, anxious to demonstrate the privations experienced by labourers in husbandry, offers a set of budgets which show families earning less and spending less on clothes than the labourers whose budgets are printed by the less sympathetic Eden. Eden, obsessed with the extravagance of the poor in the south of England, provides a set of budgets for southern families that suggests they earned more and spent more on clothes than their equivalents in the north of England. In Davies's budgets the reverse is the case.

Precisely because the budgets were collected to investigate the nature and extent of poverty among the working poor, they suffer from the same disadvantages for students of consumption as the late nineteenth-century surveys of working-class expenditure criticised by Paul Johnson.[11] In their different ways, Eden and Davies were concerned with how money was earned and spent to make ends meet; with addressing the mismatch between expenditure and income that so often had to be made up out of the poor rates. As Johnson points out, this is a narrow and economistic way of looking at expenditure, which ignores the extent to which consumption, even for the very poor, was not just about meeting basic needs, but about defining and asserting identity in the social world. It is this approach to family budgeting that explains why so much of the information on clothing presented by Eden and Davies consists not of details of actual spending, but of imprecise estimates of a family's minimum possible expenditure on clothes.[12] Whether in Davies's laments at impoverishment, or Eden's diatribes against extravagance, what is missing is any real consideration of labouring people's own standards of sartorial decency and of the trade-offs they were prepared to make to achieve them.

Despite these shortcomings, the information on clothing in the family budgets collected by Eden and Davies remains informative, as long as its limitations are recognised. These family budgets were the first to be systematically collected in bulk in England. We have virtually no other information of this sort for the rest of the eighteenth century. The information they offer, despite its flaws, provides an important reference point for judging evidence from other kinds of sources. Some broad, consistent patterns do emerge when the two sets of budgets are analysed together. Most striking is the small proportion of family expenditure that went on clothes: ten percent in Davies's budgets and Eden's. This is significantly lower than the 18 percent estimated by Gregory King for the poorer half of the population a century previously, but markedly higher than the three to seven percent found in urban working-class family budgets a hundred years later.[13] There was no very marked tendency for the proportion of expenditure devoted to clothes to vary according to the overall level of family earnings, except in the case of the poorest third of Davies's families, which came overwhelmingly from only two parishes in Dorset and are probably aberrant.[14] Otherwise expenditure on clothes in the budgets increases broadly in line with increases in total family expenditure, which makes it difficult to categorise clothing as either a luxury or a necessity, at least in the technical sense of those terms employed by economists.[15]

The budgets are detailed enough to enable us to draw some conclusions about the reasons for disparities in total family income. Differences in incomes were related, in part at least, to the amounts earned by wives and children, and, in Eden's occupationally more diverse selection of budgets, to the husband's occupation, with unskilled labourers earning substantially less than men involved in other forms of employment. But the budgets generally fail to provide much sense of how the flow of earnings into spending was managed. They give little sense of who within the family was responsible for decisions about expenditure and of the extent to which income earned by wives and older children gave them authority over such decisions.[16] The only evidence on this issue comes from one of Davies's Berkshire informants, who suggested that the way budgeting was handled within the family could make income earned by wives and children crucial for the acquisition of clothing. 'Her general account was this: that the earnings of her husband and the boys maintained the family in food; and that what she herself and the girls earnt by spinning, and in harvest, found them in clothes, linen and other necessaries.'[17] The budgets certainly demonstrate that the proportion of family income generated by the paid work of wives and children was significant: 25 percent of total family income on average. This was despite the fact that, as Davies pointed out, the wives were restricted in the work they could do for the ten or twelve years after marriage, because they were either pregnant or nursing an infant.[18] Nevertheless, the proportion of income that went on clothes shows very little sensitivity to changes in the proportion of income earned by wives and children.

Detailed breakdown of the information about clothes in the budgets reveals similar internal contradictions and inconsistencies to those that characterise the budgets as a whole. With the exception of an extraordinarily poor 61-year-old woman, whose budget Eden characteristically included as an instructive 'instance of Cumberland economy', the 115 families for whom Eden and Davies provide information on annual clothing expenditures earned between £13 8s. and £63 14s. each year, with an average of over £30.[19] Annual spending on clothes was on average £3 10s., with sums ranging from an improbably low 10s. for a Dorset labourer with three children to the £14 a year estimated by Eden for a Somerset cooper with four working children. The principal problem with this data is that so many of the amounts stated are clearly estimates that depend on assumptions made by those who compiled the budgets about the turnover of clothing and the cost of children's clothes.

Davies's inquiries into labourers' spending in his own parish of Barkham in Berkshire illustrate the difficulty. His first attempt to provide an account of spending on clothes for a typical agricultural labourer's family at Barkham arrived at an annual sum of £3 10s., the same as the average figure for expenditure on clothing that emerges from the Eden-Davies budgets as a whole. Davies made two crucial assumptions in compiling his initial budget, however. First, he assumed (almost certainly correctly) that the parents of young children could not afford to replace their own main garments every year. On that basis he estimated that the cost of what they bought would average out over the years at about £2 10s. per annum. In his list of annual expenditure he used the phrase 'wear of' a suit, a jacket or a gown to indicate that these garments were not bought every year. Second, he made the assumption that the children's clothing was '(usually) partly made up of the parents' old clothes, partly bought at second hand: what is bought (supposing three children to a family) cannot well be reckoned at less that £1'.[20] Davies, however, was not consistent. Later in the book he reconsiders the same families and revises his estimate of spending on clothes downwards. His only justification was that, although the first Barkham clothing budget listed the amount poor families ought rightly to be able to spend, 'as few poor people can every year bestow on themselves the sums here supposed, let the children's clothing (partly made up of the parents' old clothes, partly bought at second-hand) be included, and the whole estimated at £2-10-0.'[21] In other words, he effectively eliminated the sum previously included for the children's clothes.

If Davies was himself inconsistent, his patrician informants were even more so. When we examine the five other English budgets printed in *The Case of the Labourers in Husbandry* which provide a detailed breakdown of expenditure on clothes, it is evident that informants made different assumptions to Davies about the way labouring families spent money on clothes. A Cornish informant followed Davies's use of 'wear of' for outer garments, but the informant from Westmorland assumed that new outer garments were bought each year. The result is that the detailed budget from Westmorland makes the annual cost of adult outer garments a colossal 38 shillings per family, whereas those from Berkshire and Cornwall, which assume a slower rate of renewal, make it only 12 shillings per family, less than a third as much. Because the rest of the budgets do not provide a breakdown of annual clothing costs, we cannot know on which of these assumptions they were based, although we have no reason to be confident that they were consistent.

The inconsistencies in the six detailed budgets may, therefore, have simply arisen from informants adopting different interpretations of Davies's instructions. Equally they could reflect differences in patterns of purchasing between families, or between different parts of the country. The Westmorland informant, clearly aware that the sum allocated to clothes in his budget was exceptionally high, added the excuse that 'if this sum exceeds what is allowed in the more southern counties, such disparity will perhaps be best accounted for, by considering, that in warm dry counties fewer clothes will be required, than in those that are cold and wet.'[22] The important point to stress here is that either explanation for the budgets' inconsistencies is plausible, precisely because spending on clothes was intermittent and often came out of what families had left when more immediate needs had been satisfied. Spending on clothes could be postponed, although there was a cost in the additional time and effort wives and daughters had to put into 'tacking their tatters together'.[23] When times were hard, adult clothes could be coaxed into ever longer service and children's clothes could be further recycled. It is not surprising, therefore, that so many families, faced in the 1780s and 1790s with high prices for foodstuffs and huge fluctuations in those prices, found it hard to answer questions about the precise annual amount they spent on clothes.

These are serious shortcomings in a social survey. Nevertheless, Davies's six detailed budgets do provide information of a kind that is not available anywhere else about the way clothes spending in the late eighteenth century was allocated between different kinds of clothes and different members of agricultural labourers' families.[24] They are therefore worth examining closely, even if we acknowledge that the budgets are best regarded as conjectural estimates based on the experience of individual families and that those families were not in any strict sense typical.[25]

Analysis of the budgets throws up three important issues – first, the costs of clothes and materials, especially the disparity in the amounts spent on husbands and wives; second, the rate of turnover of clothes; and third, the expense of clothing children. Husbands in the six families enjoyed much higher levels of spending on their clothes than their wives. The annual cost of wives' clothing was only two-thirds that of their husbands. It is unlikely that this finding results from the deficiencies in the quality of the data discussed above. The disparity in spending between husbands and wives is too large and there is too much supportive evidence elsewhere in both Eden and Davies.[26] The husbands spent more than twice as much on footwear as their wives and almost twice as much on garments. Only in accessories did the value of wives' purchases exceed that of their husbands (see tables 22, 23 and 24).

In part, these disparities reflect broad differences in the character and therefore cost of men and women's clothing that extended beyond the labouring poor. The basic form of women's outer garments (gown and petticoat) and late eighteenth-century trends in fashion called for lighter materials and less tailoring than were employed in making male outer garments (coat, waistcoat and breeches). For basic working garments both the fabric and the making tended, therefore, to be cheaper. Women's shoes were also smaller and lighter and therefore cheaper.[27] But differences in expenditure between husbands and wives also reflected the fact that adult men in these families, unlike their wives, worked constantly in the open air. They were expected to wear more substantial outer garments and footwear than their wives, and family resources were allocated to meet that expectation. Indeed in three of Davies's six detailed budgets (Berkshire, Cornwall and Durham) it was not so much the annual cost for 'wear' of each individual set of outer garments that accounted for the disparity between husband and wife, but the fact that husbands, unlike their wives, owned two sets of such garments – a working jacket and breeches in addition to a suit of coat, waistcoat and breeches. In other words, husbands were able to sustain a distinction between their working outer garments and their best outer garments. Their wives, who were overwhelmingly mothers with young children, were clearly believed by both Davies and Eden to require less expenditure on outer garments because they pursued lives that were fairly closely confined to their homes. Commenting on the clothes of a Surrey gardener, his wife and their eight children, the youngest aged 16 months, Eden remarked that 'his wife, seldom going out, wears few'.[28] Hence, perhaps, a Somerset vicar's experience on a wet January Sunday in 1809. Few of his parishioners attended church, but 'scarce any females on account of the great rains.'[29]

Wives spent more than their husbands on accessories, but this did not represent an indulgence in stylish ornament. Handkerchiefs, aprons, caps and stockings were essential to sustaining a minimally decent adult female appearance. Their cost – handkerchiefs at 16d., pairs of stockings and aprons at 18d. or less – are consistent with the prices of the cheaper (although not always the very cheapest) such accessories bought by servants in the 1780s and 1790s (see Chapter 17). This is also true of the garments and footwear bought by Davies's wives. The six shillings allocated for a gown in the annual clothes budget of the County Durham family would have been just sufficient to buy and have made up a gown length of cheap camblet costing about 9d. a yard, similar to the cheaper workaday gowns bought by servants. The 3s. 3d. allocated for a petticoat in the same budget was similar to the cost of servants' cheap serge and flannel petticoats. The values given for wives' shoes in several of the budgets are consistent with the cost of the less expensive shoes bought by servants. Phrases in the budgets like 'one pair shoes nailed' and 'one pair strong shoes' make it clear that these were not decorative items, but heavy working shoes.

Comparison of the kind of clothes purchased by servants and Davies's labouring wives demonstrates that the adult women's clothes itemised in Davies's budgets were those needed to put together a minimal, barely decent wardrobe from cheap and coarse materials. This conclusion is confirmed if we examine overseers' accounts from the period, where women are commonly provided with clothing items of approximately the same price (see Chapter 16), or the wholesale prices given in 1789 for clothing a poor woman by the anonymous author of *Instructions for Cutting out Apparel for the Poor*.[30] There are several obvious gaps in Davies's budgets, however. No provision is made for the cloaks or the leather stays that were standard features of working women's wardrobes, but it was probably assumed these items were bought so infrequently that it was not worth entering them in an annual budget. Nor is any mention made of hats. The budgets assume no spending on small, decorative accessories. The fundamental reason for these exclusions and the limited quality and range of the wives' purchases is clear enough. The annual average clothing expenditure of the wives in Davies's six labouring families was less than half that of the female servants in the 1780s and 1790s discussed in Chapter 17.[31] Davies's budgets provide little financial leeway for labourers' wives to afford the petty clothing luxuries which many of the servants bought so enthusiastically. Nevertheless, the shares of the wives' spending that went to garments, to accessories and to footwear do not differ radically from those of the servants, suggesting an underlying consistency across the price range in the relative significance accorded by late eighteenth-century plebeian women to the different elements that went to make up their dress.

It is more difficult to establish from Davies's six budgets the prices and characteristics of many of the individual items of the husbands' clothing. For those outer garments that were not bought every year, the annual sum set down in the budget does not represent the whole cost of the garment. However, the stockings at 1s. 9d. a pair, shoes at 7s. (which probably includes mending), shirts at 3s. and hat and handkerchief at 2s. 6d. are roughly consistent in price and probably quality with those provided to working labourers by overseers of the poor in the 1790s from a general shop in Westoning, Bedfordshire, as well as with the cheaper items bought by labourers themselves at the same shop, and the wholesale costs for clothing a poor man given in *Instructions for Cutting out Apparel for the Poor*.[32] As with the wives, the budgets allow no leeway for these men to afford any decorative accessories. Indeed all but one of the budgets allow nothing for a hat or a handkerchief (fig. 93). There is certainly no provision for the acquisition of the printed cotton and even silk handkerchiefs that were common wear among labouring men, let alone the silver stock buckles and sleeve buttons which labourers occasionally owned.[33] Even more surprising, perhaps, is the complete absence of the smock frocks which were to become from the late eighteenth century the characteristic wear of the southern agricultural labourer. As we have seen, they appear regularly in the Midlands theft records from the 1780s and were acquired by many labouring men from the Westoning shop in the 1780s and 1790s. Instead the husbands' outer garments consisted of either a single suit of coat, waistcoat and breeches, or a suit plus a working jacket and pair of breeches (fig. 94).

It is instructive to compare the proportions of the husbands' spending that went on accessories, garments and footwear with the equivalent proportions for two young

94 George Stubbs, *Labourers Loading a Brick Cart* (detail), 1767, oil on canvas, Philadelphia Museum of Art: The John Howard McFadden Collection, M1928-1-40. The old labouring men putting a tailpiece on a cart were working on a new building at a country estate at Southill in Bedfordshire when Stubbs was commissioned to paint them by the estate's owner. Their outer garments are all in shades of brown. They include coats, a sleeveless waistcoat worn over a white shirt and a short jacket worn with an apron. They wear dark breeches and stockings, and hats cocked in various styles.

male servants employed by the Yorkshire worsted manufacturer Robert Heaton in the 1770s.[34] We know very little about these two servants. Their annual pay was low for an adult male servant, only 55s. in one case, which suggests they were young, probably under fifteen.[35] We do not know what kind of work they did, although they did not receive any kind of livery and were probably not domestic servants. Like their female equivalents, virtually all their spending went on clothes. Their recorded annual expenditure on clothing was greater than that of the average husband in Davies's budgets, although the disparity was not as great as that between female servants and Davies's wives, because the male servants' pay was so low. Much of what they bought was inexpensive – shirts and shoes at prices slightly less than those ascribed to the husbands' purchases, hats and stockings at somewhat higher prices. Like the husbands, the two male servants bought no obviously decorative accessories, apart from a ribbon at 10d. As with the female servants and the wives, the shares of the male servants' spending that went to garments, to accessories and to footwear did not differ radically from those of the husbands. Particularly striking is the small proportion of expenditure, and presumably the low priority, that husbands and servants alike devoted to accessories. The husbands, who were field workers mainly in areas where clogs were not worn, spent proportionately more than the servants on footwear. The servants, who each acquired a new coat and breeches during their year of service, spent proportionately more on garments.

Let us now turn from the cost and quality of Davies's labouring families' clothing to the rate at which they were able to acquire it. As we have seen, it is difficult to evaluate the cost and quality of the outer garments bought by Davies's husbands because several of the budgets assume that their outer garments were not bought every year. Yet, ironically, this feature of the budgets means that, unusually for an eighteenth-century source on plebeian clothing, it is possible for the historian to arrive at an estimate of the rate at which clothes were renewed. Such an estimate depends on heroic assumptions about minimum prices, the accuracy of the budgets, and the consistency of labouring families' spending. Nevertheless, at the very least it serves to indicate the extent to which the rates of renewal for different kinds of clothing could diverge.

The wording of the budgets and the prices they provide suggest that labourers' wives could expect to acquire a minimum of one shift, one pair of shoes, one pair of stockings, two aprons, a handkerchief and a cap each year, although three of the six budgets allow for two shifts and two pairs of stockings. Assuming wives bought the cheapest gowns and petticoats that appear in other sources for the period, which would cost together no less than 8s., three of the budgets (including both those from the north) allow for their purchase once a year, and three for their purchase perhaps every other year. The budgets do not include cloaks, hats or stays, but Eden suggests that a cheap cloak would last two years, a cheap hat two years and a cheap pair of stays six years.[36]

All but one of the budgets provide the husbands with a minimum of two shirts, two pairs of stockings and one pair of shoes each year. Half of them provided two pairs of shoes or more. How quickly shirts, stockings and shoes wore out is unclear, but these rates of renewal were probably sufficient to provide the husbands (and their wives) with changes of linen and stockings. Husbands' outer garments were not renewed anything like as often. The cheapest prices that appear in other contemporary sources for adult labourers' suits consisting of coat, waistcoat and breeches are over 21s., and the cheapest combination of jacket and breeches is at least 11s.[37] At these prices, the husbands who simultaneously owned two sets of outer garments could expect to replace the suit no more than every five to six years and the jacket and breeches every three years.[38] The husbands who owned only one set of outer garments could expect to renew them at least every third year, and in some cases (particularly in the generous Westmorland budget) more often. At their worst, these rates of renewal were seriously inadequate. Eden suggested that a pair of 'stout breeches' bought from the London slop shops would last only a year and 'a good foul-weather coat' two years. Slop shop jackets appear to have lasted no longer than two years.[39] Yet the author of *Cutting out Apparel* claimed that men's outer garments bought from the slop shops were 'of a much better and more durable quality' than those made up in the country from the cheapest cloth, which is what the labouring husbands in the budgets, living deep in rural England, would probably have worn. On the sums allocated to men's outer garments in Davies's six detailed budgets, many labouring husbands had no choice but to keep on wearing outer garments that can have survived only by dint of endless patching and repair by wives, daughters and local tailors.[40]

What emerges from the evidence provided by the budgets on the rate of turnover of clothing is a fundamental distinction in the adult plebeian wardrobe between shirts, shifts, stockings and shoes, which adults even in very poor families could expect to acquire every year, and adult outer garments, which men especially could hope to acquire only intermittently. This distinction also features in several of Eden's budgets.[41] It is a distinction not only between the rates at which clothes were renewed, but also between the ways their acquisition was undertaken. On the one hand, there were those items that had to be acquired regularly to sustain a minimally decent wardrobe. They could be fitted relatively easily into the framework of annual accounting Davies and Eden demanded of their informants. On the other hand, there were outer garments and accessories. Their acquisition was erratic and often opportunistic, resisting incorporation into an annualised accounting framework. The budgets are consequently more credible in what they tell us about rates of turnover for the former than for the latter.

What is most difficult to work out from the detailed budgets is the character and rate of turnover of children's clothes. Only the County Durham budgets itemise the children's clothes. They show a pair of shoes, a pair of stockings, a coat or a gown, and a shirt being bought for each child annually, at a total cost of 34s. 8d. Assuming the family had four children, annual expenditure per child was 8s. 8d. Davies estimated that the annual expenditure per child by the labouring families in his Berkshire parish should average 7s. for that part of their clothing that was bought (usually second-hand). The rest was made up from the parents' old clothes. This figure is consistent with the average expenditure per child in the six Davies family budgets that specify the amount spent on children's clothes and number of children in the family.[42] A budget of less than 7s. would mean that the children had to do without important items of clothing. It was reported of the Holwell, Somerset family that spent only 3s. 3d. per child that 'the children are rather of the diminutive kind, and never wear shoes or stockings'.[43] Similar comments about other families in both Davies and Eden suggest that efforts to cut spending bore especially hard on children's clothing. Of one Dorset family it was commented: 'Clothes they get as they can, and the children go nearly naked.'[44] Nevertheless, the feature of children's clothing that stands out in the budgets remains its expense. In labouring families with several young children, those children accounted for about a third of the family's total annual expenditure on clothes.

The picture presented by David Davies of the clothing of labouring families at the end of the 1780s is a dreary one of shabby clothes made from coarse materials that were worn for too long. We should not, however, exaggerate. Things do not appear to have been so bad that adults were obliged to wear all the clothes they owned at once. Most of the budgets allow for a change of undergarments, stockings and, in some of the more fortunate cases, outer garments and even footwear. Usually adults (although sometimes not their children) appear to have possessed all the basic elements that constituted a decent eighteenth-century English wardrobe, in contrast to some of their Scottish and Welsh equivalents. But for a number of the families it was only with the greatest difficulty that these minimal standards were sustained. Eden's less detailed evidence on clothes collected in the mid-1790s paints a gloomy picture too, despite the fact that on average his occupationally more diverse families spent half as much again on clothing as Davies's.

This bleak impression of the clothing of the labouring poor is in marked contrast to the generally positive evaluations of their dress made by foreign visitors like the Swede Pehr Kalm or the German Karl Philipp Moritz between the 1740s and the 1780s. It is also at odds with the evidence presented elsewhere in this book that during the second half of the eighteenth century servants and other working people were able to acquire petty clothing luxuries. The immediately obvious reason for these inconsistencies is chronological. The researches of both Davies and Eden were prompted by concerns about deterioration in the economic position of the labouring poor in the 1780s and 1790s, as registered in the rising cost of poor relief. The different ways the two authors sought to explain this deterioration may have compromised the quality of the information they collected about clothing. Nevertheless, there is little doubt that the progressive rise in the cost of basic foodstuffs in the second half of the eighteenth century, which does not seem to have been matched by a corresponding improvement in wages in the south at least, meant that Davies's southern agricultural labourers were under considerable financial pressure when their budgets were drawn up at the end of the 1780s. Eden's budgets for labouring families were compiled in the war years between 1794 and 1796, the majority of them in the immediate aftermath of the devastatingly bad harvest of 1795. Many of his families faced a ruinous combination of unprecedently high food prices, falling industrial wages and reduced opportunities for industrial work. In other words, at least some of the deficiencies in the provision of clothing revealed in the budgets can be explained by deteriorating circumstances, either long-term or short-term. Davies's protagonists shared in the progressive squeeze on the disposable incomes of southern agricultural labourers towards the end of the eighteenth century. Eden's occupationally more diverse group of labouring families faced the short-term effects of the century's greatest subsistence crisis, combined with wartime economic dislocation.

There remains, however, another crucial consideration – the family poverty cycle. Almost all of Davies and Eden's budgets are for families, mainly families with large numbers of young dependent children. This was the first of the two stages in the life-cycle of the family when the balance between income and expenditure was at its most precarious (the second being old age).[45] As Davies pointed out, income earned by wives and working children was critical for the acquisition of clothing. Yet mothers with very young children were restricted in the amount of paid work they could undertake, even if it was available, and although children might secure some money income from the age of five or six, their earnings at that early age were very small. This, however, was a limited stage in the life of most parents. Between leaving home and marriage, the majority of labouring people spent a long period during which many of them earned and, at least as far as clothing is concerned, consumed independently. Usually this involved one of the various forms of live-in service or apprenticeship, with adult wages sometimes achieved for men by the age of 19.[46] Typically the majority of late eighteenth-century labouring children left home in their mid-teens, but the average age of first marriage was nearly 26 for men and over 24 for women.[47] Earlier in the century, the period between leaving home and marriage was longer still, because both sexes tended to marry later.

Savings and stocks of clothing accumulated in the financially independent years before marriage might see a couple through the first few years of childbearing, but the need to support several infant children and a nursing mother who could earn little must have progressively impoverished many labouring families. Nevertheless, the heavy initial financial burden of young children began to reduce (assuming both parents remained alive and well) by the time the parents turned 40, as childbearing ended and children grew older. At this stage, older children and wives who did not have to look after infants could provide an increasing contribution to family income (assuming paid work was available for them). At the same time, some of the older children began to leave home (at least semi-permanently), reducing claims on family resources. It is the fact that most of the families in the Eden-Davies budgets were at or near the first trough in the family poverty cycle that accounts for some of the worst deficiencies in their clothing.

The household budget was the single most important eighteenth-century innovation for assessing plebeian living standards. David Davies and Sir Frederick Eden were its most sophisticated exponents. Their implementation of the new technique suffered from many shortcomings, which compromise the usefulness of their budgets as a guide to the clothes labouring people actually acquired. Yet, if used with care, they can provide evidence about expenditure on clothing and rates of turnover that is otherwise wanting. Above all, their budgets demonstrate the critical importance for what people wore of the family poverty cycle. Working people could expect to wear stylish, even fashionable clothing at some stage in their lives, but that stage was unlikely to be the early years of married life.

IV

People and their Clothes

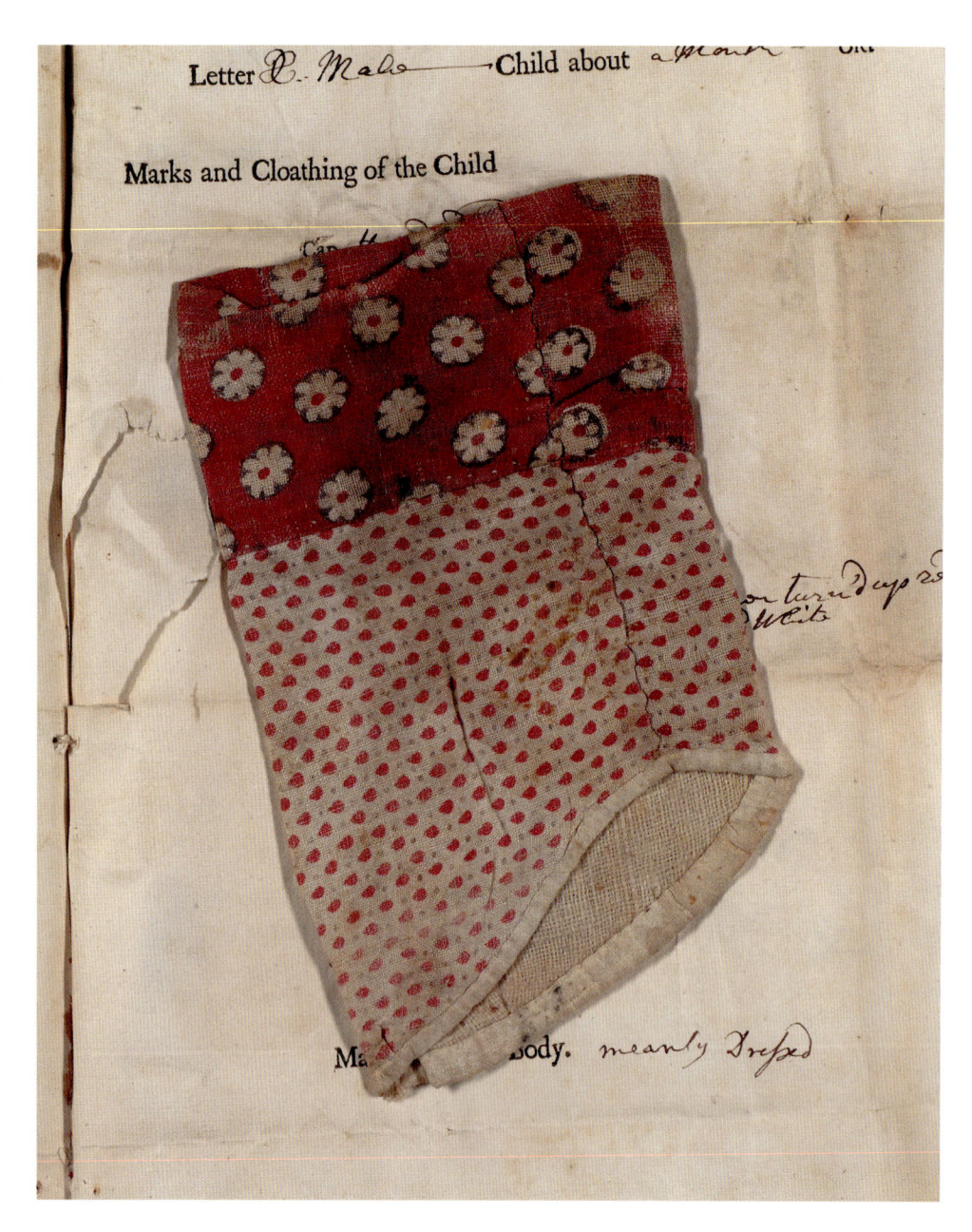

95 'Red and white speckl'd linen turn'd up red spotted with white', 1746, two printed linens, one red on a white ground, the other white on a red ground, made up into a baby's sleeve, London Metropolitan Archives, A/FH/A/9/1/3, Foundling no. 235.

14
Clothes and the Life-cycle

THE PIONEERING HOUSEHOLD BUDGETS PUBLISHED BY David Davies and Sir Frederick Eden in the 1790s provide compelling evidence of the pressure that young children placed on resources in plebeian families. What the Eden-Davies budgets fail to reveal is opportunities enjoyed by members of those families to acquire clothes at other stages in their lives. The stylish, expensive clothing owned by many working people must have been acquired at periods in their lives when they had more financial room for manœuvre. But without detailed, long-term personal accounts, assessment of precisely how much they spent on clothes at each stage in their life-cycle is impossible. Such accounts are extremely rare for families below the level of the gentry, the larger farmers and the mercantile elite. They do not exist at all for labouring families, but a remarkable survival means that it is possible to trace the effects of the family poverty cycle on clothing in one family that was not dramatically better off than those investigated by Eden and Davies – the Lathams of Scarisbrick in south-west Lancashire. They are the poorest family for whom a long run of financial accounts survives from the eighteenth century. Their account book covers the years from 1724 to 1767.[1]

The Lathams enjoyed many economic advantages not available to the Eden-Davies families. They farmed a smallholding of approximately 19 statute acres on fertile land suitable for mixed agriculture in an economically expanding region; they had access to grazing and turbary rights on newly reclaimed common land; they lived in an area where industrial outwork for women was plentiful; they may well have supplemented the income from their farm with carting and dealing.[2] Eighteenth-century polite commentators believed such advantages sustained a more affluent and varied domestic economy than that of the labouring poor. The differences were itemised in a 1766 discussion of why the children of small farmers made better servants.

> The labourer cannot be expected to be able to give his children that learning which is proper to fit them for good places; whilst those who rent small farms have generally wherewithal to give their children learning sufficient to qualify them to read virtuous books, and to know how to behave in a proper and decent manner. Besides, the girls have opportunities of learning at home how to brew, bake, cook, knit, sow, and get up linnen, etc., whereas poor people's children have not such advantages.[3]

The Lathams' annual expenditure as recorded in the account book varied between £10 and £55 per year, averaging £24. Charles Foster has pointed out that while this includes occasional large capital and other exceptional payments, it excludes important aspects of the family's consumption, because some of the food and the textiles they consumed were produced on the farm. He estimates the family's actual income at about £30 a year.[4] This was not especially high. The average annual expenditure of the Eden-Davies labouring families for whom clothes spending is recorded was higher at nearly £35, although we should remember that labourers' money wages rose considerably, by perhaps as much as a quarter, between the 1750s and the 1780s.[5]

If the Lathams were significantly better off than the Eden-Davies labourers in a number of important respects, they remained essentially plebeian. They were in no sense wealthy in the contemporary sense of the word. Unlike most yeoman farmers, they did not employ permanent domestic or farm servants. Indeed, it could accurately have been said of them, just as it was of petty landholders in nearby Cumberland in the 1760s, that 'they work like slaves; they cannot afford to keep a man servant, but husband, wife, sons and daughters all turn out to work in the fields'.[6] Most importantly for our purposes, they did not inhabit an entirely alien world of goods from that of the labouring poor. They bought only a very narrow selection of the small domestic luxuries that spread among the middling sort during the first half of the eighteenth century. Their purchases included books, newspapers, tobacco pipes and knives and forks, but excluded crockery and tea wares. The kind of material existence lived by the Lathams was one to which the hard-pressed agricultural labourers at the end of the eighteenth century often aspired, although increasingly they were forced to recognise that their chances of achieving it had largely disappeared.[7]

There were, however, other ways in which the Lathams were not a typical plebeian family. Their children were disproportionately female and most of them continued to live at home until they were relatively old. Between their marriage in 1723 and the birth of their youngest child in 1741 Richard and Nany Latham produced eight children. Seven of them were daughters. One of the girls died within three months of her birth, but the rest lived to adulthood, leaving home, mainly for service, in their late teens or early twenties, although the youngest may have left home considerably earlier.[8] Their son, Dicy, died aged 20 in 1748, while still living at home. The Latham account book covers the 43 years of their married life from 1724 until Richard Latham's death in 1767, including a period after the children had left home.

Using the Latham account book to gauge expenditure on clothing is not straightforward, as a result of the way the family's activities cultivating and processing textile materials were recorded. We do know, however, that during the whole period covered by the account book the overall proportion of the family's recorded expenditure devoted to clothing was between 10 and 13 percent.[9] But neither the amount nor the proportion of expenditure devoted to clothes remained constant. Richard and Nany Latham's married life, and their spending on clothes, fell into three distinct periods (table 25). During the first, when their children were young, clothes expenditure was limited, both in absolute terms and as a proportion of all spending. The second period, when the children were older and earning more but still largely resident at home, saw spending on clothes rise dramatically, both in absolute terms and as a proportion of total expenditure. In the third period, after the children left home, clothes spending fell back.[10]

The first period consists of the 18 years from 1724 to 1741. For most of these years Richard Latham, who was probably born at the start of the 1690s, was in his thirties and forties, and none of the children was older than 15. This was the trough of the family's poverty cycle. Demands on income were high, not just from an ever-increasing number of small children, but also from the expense of setting up home and the £40 cost of renewing the lease in 1728. The family borrowed heavily, just like the Eden-Davies labourers. Although we have no direct information on income, it appears to have been restricted. Regular purchases of textile fibres indicate Nany Latham was able to undertake some spinning while she looked after her infant children. But this is the only period in the accounts when the family paid for others to spin for them, which suggests Nany (and later perhaps her older children) could barely fulfil the family's own requirements for spun yarn, let alone undertake outwork or market spinning for a money income.

Annual spending on the family's clothes, excluding textile fibres, never exceeded a modest 50s. Clothes spending represented only six percent of all annual expenditure; eight percent if textile fibres are included. Overall expenditure was itself relatively low, averaging less than £23 per year. It is not possible from the accounts to establish the precise proportions of the family's clothes spending that was allocated to the children rather than to the parents, but it is clear that the cost of clothing a fast-increasing number of young children was a heavy one. Three-quarters of the clothing purchases that named a family member were for the children.[11] Relatively few garments are mentioned in the accounts, for either adults or children, but the proportion of clothes spending that went on cloth (mainly woollen and worsted) was high (see table 26). Nevertheless, the amount of woollen or worsted cloth purchased annually was on average well under six yards, enough for a couple of petticoats or a man's coat, but insufficient for an adult gown or suit. The sums laid out on flax fibre, a good part of which was probably made into linen cloth for the family's clothing, were high relative to clothes spending. As we have seen in Chapter 8, the yardage of household-spun fabric used to clothe the family probably exceeded that of cloth bought ready-woven by a large margin. Most striking of all is the very high percentage of clothes spending that went on footwear.

This pattern of purchases between 1724 and 1741 is consistent with low levels of spending on clothes by the adult Lathams. They probably had to rely heavily on clothing, especially main garments, they had acquired before their marriage, in the way Davies and Eden later suggested was common, or on gifts or bartered items. The need to keep having clothes repaired and remodelled, and the fact that Richard Latham evidently owned more than one coat over ten years into his marriage, is indicated by an entry in 1735 for altering his 'best coat'. Payments for tailors' work were made in most of the 18 years. Some of these were for making clothes, but many must have been for mending their increasingly worn garments. The adult Lathams' main garments and at least some of their accessories were renewed infrequently in this period and their range was restricted. Between 1724 and 1741 there were no purchases of gown lengths of cloth, or of stays for Nany Latham.[12] There were only seven purchases of woollen, worsted or linsey-woolsey cloth of more than three yards. This was the minimum length later used to make her petticoats, but it was also the minimum needed for her husband's coats. Of these seven cloth purchases, it is the three that were woollen or worsted that were most likely to have been intended for his use. If we assume that these purchases were divided between them, it seems probable that not only did Nany Latham acquire no new gowns during these 18 years, but only three or four new petticoats. These she probably wore with jackets, like the new one she bought in 1737, dispensing with a gown altogether (fig. 96).[13] We should remember that after 1726 she constantly had at least one child aged under four and, like Eden's Surrey mother, may have led a fairly confined life. Nevertheless, having young children did not prevent her making several visits to her relatives in the Fylde, several miles to the north of Scarisbrick across the Ribble estuary.

A similar picture emerges for her husband's main garments in these years. The lengths of cloth needed for men's outer garments like waistcoats, jackets and breeches were relatively short, so it is difficult to distinguish cloth purchases that might have been intended for these purposes. But, as we have seen, the family bought cloth sufficient for no more than three adult male coats, and Richard certainly did not acquire cloth for a whole new suit of clothes, at least at one purchase. It is also striking that no garment purchases are specifically named as his after a pair of new breeches in 1725, the year before the first child was born. In the whole period, Richard and Nany Latham bought only three hats for themselves, all relatively cheap ones. The only obvious petty clothing luxury they acquired was a new Holland check apron made up for Nany Latham in 1735, which cost 3s.

As with the Eden-Davies families, however, the slow rate of renewal in these hard-pressed years did not extend to all the adult Lathams' clothing. The quantity of flax fibre and linen cloth bought by the family was sufficient to allow them at least one new shirt and shift a year, with enough left over for the children.[14] New handkerchiefs were purchased in nine of the 18 years, in sufficient numbers to provide approximately one every two years for each member of the family.[15] None of them was expensive. Footwear was also bought frequently. At least seven pairs of shoes were bought for Nany, and at least six for Richard. Both adults also wore clogs. Between them they acquired in this period at least seven pairs and possibly as many as 14.

It is particularly difficult to identify in the accounts for these 18 years the clothing acquired for the children. Much of it must have been made up at home either from home-produced cloth, or from cloth that was bought in, or from the parents' old clothes. In the case of the home-produced cloth, it is impossible to identify the member

96 William Hogarth, *The Distressed Poet* (detail), 1736, oil on canvas, Birmingham City Art Gallery, 1934P500. On the right, a truculent milkmaid, holding out her tally to demand payment, wears a short jacket and an apron over a red petticoat, similar to the one Nany Latham bought in 1745. On her feet she has a fashionably shaped pair of shoes tied with ribbons. The poet's wife on the left is sewing a pair of breeches.

of the family for whom it was intended. Unfortunately this is also true of most of the cloth that was purchased. Of all the clothing purchases itemised in the accounts during this period, it is cloth that is least likely to be linked to a name. Nevertheless, the many items of children's clothing that are identified by name do demonstrate that the Latham children were relatively well supplied. They certainly did not go without footwear. In shoes, for example, Betty, the eldest daughter born in 1726, had at least 15 pairs, almost all described as new, before her sixteenth birthday, as well as three pairs of clogs.[16] Her brother Dicy, born in 1727, had at least 13 pairs of shoes and four pairs of clogs in his first 15 years. This rate of purchase – more than one pair of shoes or clogs a year – was sustained for the second daughter, Sara, but not for the third, Rachel, for whom far fewer were bought. She probably had to make do with hand-me-downs from her elder siblings, but the rate of purchase returned to earlier levels for her three younger sisters.

We have already seen that handkerchiefs were bought relatively frequently for all members of the family in this period, but, as with their parents, the children acquired hats far less often. Only two hats each were bought for Betty and Dicy before their fifteenth birthdays, in both cases when they were aged five and ten. As far as outer garments are concerned, we know that Dicy received new sets, consisting either of full suits, or singlet and breeches, at the ages of six (when he was probably breeched), nine, 11, 12 and 15, and it is possible he received more. These garments were made from the most expensive cloth bought by the family in the whole period, varying in price between 16d. and 25d. a yard. For the girls we have very little direct information about outer garments. There are certainly no mentions of gowns for the female children (other than infant ones) in the accounts before 1742 and no purchases of gown lengths of cloth.

Overall, the experience of the Lathams in this period of intense pressure on the family's budget bore many similarities to the Eden-Davies labouring families. The early years of marriage and childbearing imposed heavy financial demands and placed considerable restrictions on family earnings. If a money value is ascribed to the cloth the Lathams made at home and it is added to the rest of their clothes spending, their average annual expenditure on clothing in these years, at just over 50s., was not very different from Davies's most pessimistic calculation for his Barkham families, although it should be remembered that the price of some items, particularly shoes, increased greatly between the 1730s and the 1780s. The Lathams, moreover, lived in an area where clogs were worn, which were relatively cheap. Like several of Davies's labourers, Richard Latham appears to have owned at least two sets of outer garments during this period, but he can have renewed them only very intermittently. Nany Latham appears more abstemious than the labourers' wives in doing without new gowns, but like the adults in the labouring families, both the adult Lathams appear to have been able to acquire footwear and (by their own efforts at manufacturing) undergarments annually. The cost of most of what the adult Lathams bought was low, consistent with prices in northern overseers' accounts for the period, and, as we have seen, they purchased virtually no petty clothing luxuries.

If anything, Richard and Nany Latham spent less on themselves and more on their children than did Davies's labourers. More than a third by value of all clothing purchases (excluding fibres) in this period were for named children. Only half the clothing purchases in the accounts name a family member, and it is inconceivable that all the unnamed purchases were for the two adult Lathams. Consequently, the Lathams must have applied substantially more than a third of the family's clothing expenditure in these years to their children; this was a higher proportion than the average for the Davies families. Certainly the accounts suggest that, unlike the children in some of the Davies families, the Latham children never went without footwear, that the quality of the clothing bought for them was (if their son's case is indicative) high and that hardly any of it was second hand. Apart from five pairs of old shoes, which may have been purchased for the adult Lathams, the only items of clothing described in the accounts as 'old' or 'second hand' during these years were the three pairs of stays bought for the girls.

The second period of the family's clothes spending covers the 13 years from 1742 to 1754. During it, a transformation in the family's spending on clothes took place. Richard Latham was in his fifties for much of the period. The couple had no more children after 1741. Some of the older children left the household in the course of these years. Their two elder daughters went into service, the eldest, Betty, in 1747, aged 22, and Sara in 1748, aged 19. Their son Dicy died in 1748, aged 20. But the rest of the daughters remained at home until the mid-1750s. Throughout this period, therefore, the household always contained a number of older children, mainly female, who were capable of working. At least part of their work consisted of outwork spinning for money wages. The family had bought flax to spin from the beginning of the accounts, but in 1739 and 1740 they acquired three wheels for spinning cotton with accompanying equipment. Surprisingly, only very small amounts of cotton wool were bought during the following decade and a half. It seems likely, therefore, that the new spinning wheels were used by Nany Latham and her elder daughters to spin cotton wool on an outwork basis. The 1740s, 1750s and 1760s were precisely the years when hand cotton spinners were in greatest demand in Lancashire.[17] The income thus generated probably accounts for the fact that the family's overall annual spending was on average 14 percent higher during this second period. The increase in clothes spending was, however, much more spectacular. During the 13 years from 1742 to 1754 the amount the Lathams spent annually on clothes was on average more than three times greater than that of the previous 18 years, although it should be remembered that this represented no more than an extra 1s. 8d. a week, considerably less than the estimated weekly earnings of just one regularly employed outwork cotton spinner in the period.[18]

This leap in spending can be accounted for partly by the fact that the children were older, in some cases young adults, and the cost of clothing them was correspondingly greater. But the figures also bear witness to a massive shift of family resources into more and better quality clothing for children and parents alike, as family income rose and borrowing declined. Much more was spent on every category of clothing than in the previous period, reflecting increases in the number, range and quality of the clothing bought, but at the same time there were shifts in the proportions of expenditure devoted to different categories of clothing (table 26). Most notably, the proportion of clothes spending allocated to footwear declined, while that allocated to garments and accessories rose. As we have seen in Chapter 8, the amount of flax and hemp fibre purchased declined by 20 percent, while the yardage of plain linen bought ready-woven increased more than threefold and the yardage of ready-woven woollen and worsted cloth quadrupled.

The principal beneficiaries of this explosion in the Latham family's expenditure on clothing were those who made it possible: the older children. In the second period the children as a whole accounted for almost 90 percent of named clothing purchases by value, and almost 70 percent of all clothing purchased. We can observe the change in the family's circumstances by examining purchases of two different types of clothing – gowns and accessories. Before 1742, as we have seen, no adult gown lengths of cloth were purchased either for Nany Latham or any of her daughters. Thereafter, as each of the daughters reached their mid-teens, gowns began to be bought for them. Between 1742, when Betty was 16, and 1749, when she was 23 and had already been in service, she acquired four gowns on the family account. Two of these were relatively cheap, with fabric costing 7s. 6d. and 12s. 4d. respectively. They were probably working gowns made from a plain worsted cloth such as camblet at less than 16½ d. a yard. The other two gowns were much more stylish and expensive, made from patterned cloths. Although the word is not used in the accounts, these were almost certainly her 'best' gowns. When she was 16, Betty acquired 11½ yards of blue flowered damask, costing over 20s., which at 20½ d. a yard was probably a mixed worsted-silk fabric. Her plain, workaday gowns used only nine yards of fabric or less, but a gown made from a flowered fabric required a longer (and more costly) length to allow the pattern to repeat harmoniously across the surface of the garment when cut out and assembled. Later, when she was 23, she acquired a printed gown costing 20s., the fabric for which was probably either linen or cotton (figs 95, 97).[19]

A similar pattern emerges for the next daughter, Sara, who acquired six gowns between the ages of 14 and 23. Four of them were cheap and workaday, costing well under 14s. for the fabric. One of them was second hand. But in addition Sara, just like her older sister, secured two expensive, stylish gowns, one of flowered damask and the other of a printed cotton or linen fabric. Gowns were likewise bought for the four younger sisters once they reached their mid-teens, but unlike Betty and Sara, these were all workaday items made mostly of camblet, or mixed cotton-linen cloth locally woven from the family's own yarn and dyed. No dasmask or printed gowns were bought for the younger daughters, although Rachael appears to have acquired two stamped gowns, probably linen or cotton, in 1757. However, it may well be the case that as the older sisters accumulated more clothing and eventually left home, their younger siblings received some of their clothes, including their expensive gowns. This may also have been true of stays, which were an essential foundation if a gown was to be worn in anything approaching a stylish manner. Each of the four older Latham daughters acquired between one and three pairs of expensive whalebone stays during their late teens and early twenties. A process of handing on clothing from sister to sister may explain why, on average, somewhat less was spent each year on clothes for the younger sisters after the age of 15 than had been the case for Betty and Sara.

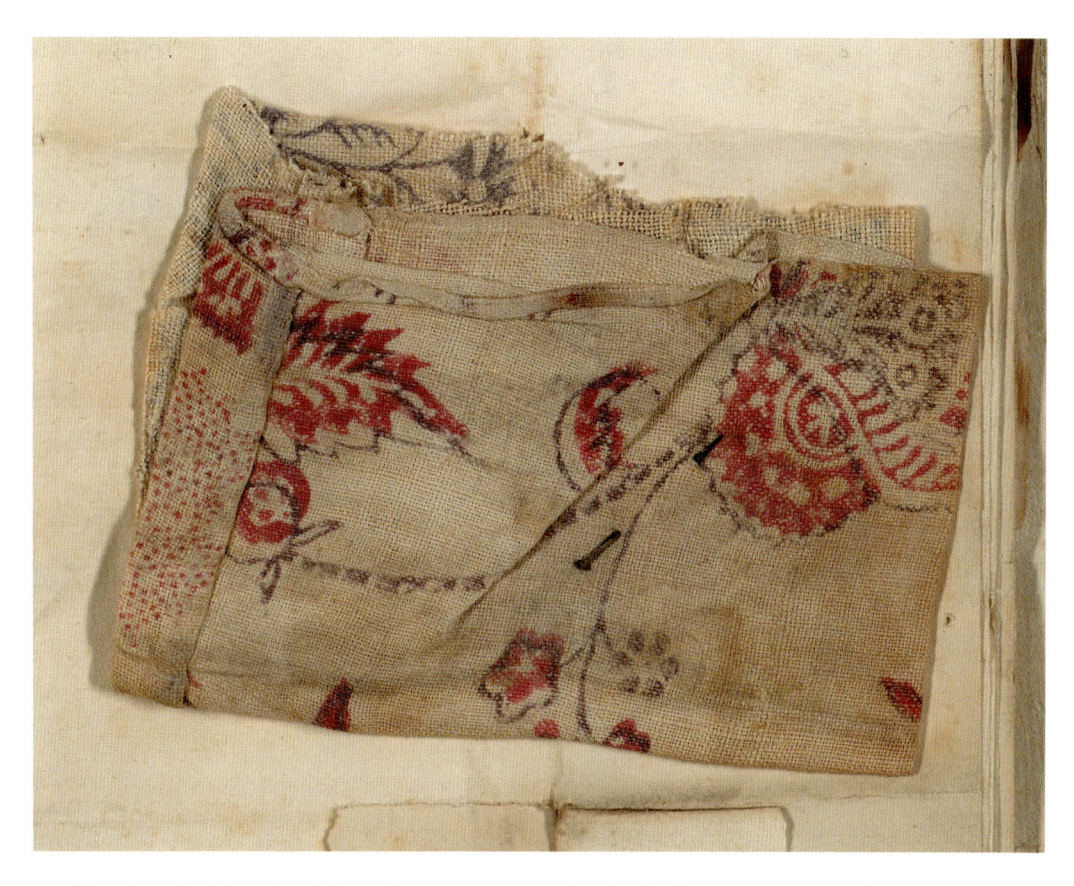

97 'Purple and white printed linen sleeve turned up red and white', 1741, linen printed in red and purple, over linen printed in purple, made up into a baby's sleeve, London Metropolitan Archives, A/FH/A/9/1/1, Foundling no. 27.

Of course, by the standards of the young women of the northern gentry in this period even the most costly, elaborately decorated gowns bought for the daughters of the Latham family were cheap. Young gentlewomen's best gowns were made from much longer lengths of silk fabric that were many times more expensive.[20] Unlike the Lathams, they also bought fashionable hoops to wear under their gowns. In 1749, the 24-year-old Elizabeth Parker of Brownsholme, 25 miles to the north-east of Scarisbrick, had two gown lengths bought for her in London. One, 18 yards in length, was a yellow, unwatered silk tabby at 8s.3d. a yard costing over £7; the other, nearly 16 yards in length, was a checked lutestring at 5s. 11d. a yard which cost over £4 (fig. 98).[21] In 1736 alone, Mary Warde of Hooton Pagnell near Doncaster in Yorkshire bought three silk gown lengths and a second-hand silk gown. She spent over £7 on 18 yards of yellow tabby, nearly £7 on 22 yards of rich white lutestring, and over £4 on a grey lutestring nightgown and accoutrements, as well as buying a gown second-hand from her sister for more than £10.[22] But it is important to bear in mind that, although the sartorial distance between the Lathams and the local gentry was great, there were points of contact. In addition to their expensive tabbys and lutestrings, young gentry women bought cheaper gowns which were closer in cost and character to the better gowns acquired by the Latham girls. In 1735, for example, Mary Warde bought a cherryderry (silk and cotton) gown for only 18s.

The change in the Lathams' clothes purchases after 1742 can also be observed in accessories and footwear. The increase in the number of accessories bought is easily illustrated by hats and handkerchiefs, which between 1742 and 1754 were bought much more frequently than before. In these 13 years, handkerchiefs were purchased in sufficient numbers to provide approximately one every one and a half years for each member of the family, compared with approximately one every two years previously.[23] With hats the contrast is even more marked. The family bought 30 during these 13 years, whereas only eight had been acquired in the previous 18. But it is the increase in the range and the quality of the accessories purchased that is most striking. As we have seen, apart from one Holland check apron, neither Nany Latham nor any of her daughters acquired any petty clothing luxuries before 1742. But thereafter, just as with gowns, when the daughters reached their mid-teens, they each began to acquire relatively costly and decorative accessories, such as shag hats, probably made from silk and costing between 5s. and 8s., silk handkerchiefs and expensive white aprons made from fine fabrics like cambric. It is only in this period, moreover, that there are entries in the account book for expensive bone lace and (with one exception in 1736) for borders for caps and aprons.

It is important to emphasise, however, that the parents as well as the children benefited, at least to some extent, from the increase in family clothes spending. It was not just the Lathams' daughters who began to acquire gowns in the financially buoyant 13 years starting in 1742. In that year their mother, who had not bought a gown in the previous 18 years, purchased nine and a half yards of worsted camblet at 14½d. a yard for a gown costing 11s. 4d. She probably bought another worsted camblet gown in 1749, and in addition, like her daughters, she acquired a pair of whalebone stays, two expensive shag hats and at least one silk handkerchief, none of them items she had bought before. The quality of her garments also improved. Cloth bought by the family before 1742 of the kind that may have been used for her petticoats and cloaks always cost less than 16d. a yard. But after 1742 she bought woollen cloth at 26d. a yard for a petticoat, and at 23d. a yard and 42d. a yard for cloaks.

A superficial reading of the accounts might suggest that the sartorial improvements of these years bypassed Richard Latham, so few are the new garments named as his. But this would be to ignore the fact that after his son Dicy's death in 1748 he was able to wear some and perhaps most of the young man's clothes, albeit with alterations. Dicy had benefited from the family's higher clothes spending in the period from 1742, although the annual sums spent in his name in these years were considerably less than half those spent on the two sisters closest to him in age. In the six years before his

98 A page from Barbara Johnson's album, fabrics from 1752–5, Victoria and Albert Museum, London, T.219-1973. Samples of the fabrics, mainly silks, acquired by Barbara Johnson, the daughter of a Bedfordshire clergyman, between 1752 and 1755, when she was in her teens. The silk in the top left-hand corner is an unwatered yellow tabby, similar to that bought for a gown for the 24-year-old Lancashire gentlewoman Elizabeth Parker in London in 1749.

death aged 20, he acquired in garments alone three new pairs of breeches, two in leather and one in linen twill (one every two years), two coats of expensive woollen cloth costing over 26d. a yard (one every three years), two singlets (one every three years) and a vest. Like Robert Heaton's male servants 30 years later, but in contrast to his sisters, he does not appear to have bought any costly decorative accessories. The hats and handkerchiefs that are named as his were all cheap ones. Yet even if Richard Latham did acquire, as a result of his son's death, more clothing in this second period than is immediately apparent from the accounts, there were strict limits to his acquisitions. Like his son, the accessories he bought were cheap ones, and in contrast to some plebeian men in the period, there is no evidence that he or Dicy bought or owned wigs. By 1749 the family does appear to have had a silver watch – probably Richard's – which they paid to have maintained, although there is no record of its purchase.

The third period in the Latham family's clothes spending covers the 12 years from 1755 to 1766. The last clothes entries in the accounts for the Latham daughters are in 1758, but by 1754 most of them appear to have left home, after which their names appear less and less often. During these years Richard Latham was in his sixties and seventies. Compared to the second period, overall annual expenditure witnessed a modest decline of about ten percent, but clothing expenditure fell by a huge 81 percent, squeezed out by a heavy rent payment and the need to pay for more farm labour as the children departed and the parents grew old. For a short period from 1755 to 1758, Nany Latham kept up her spending, buying gowns, a cloak and expensive accessories. Indeed, the final departure of her daughters was the occasion of an unprecedented spending spree on her part. In 1755 she bought a black and blue gown 'for outside' costing 15s. 8d. and a silk camblet gown costing 15s. 6d.; in 1757 a silk handkerchief for 2s. 6d. and a red cloak for 7s. 9d; in 1758 one and perhaps two black-and-white printed gowns, probably for her, as well as a shag hat and ribbon for 7s. 9d. After 1758, however, spending on clothing for both husband and wife collapsed, although Richard Latham did buy a new coat in 1759 and Nany a costly blue cloak in 1764. In the years 1759 – 66 the lowest levels of annual clothes spending in the whole account book occurred, although a comparison of named purchases suggests Richard and Nany were spending about the same on their own clothes as they had between 1724 and 1741. But the mix of their purchases was different from that earlier period of squeezed budgets, with far less spent on footwear and far more on garments. After 1754, Nany and Richard each bought only one pair of shoes, although these may have been supplemented with clogs. One reason for this distinctive pattern of spending on clothing is that both husband and wife were increasingly infirm, as large numbers of payments for medicines attest. With both husband and wife incapable of doing much heavy work outdoors, labour had to be bought in to work the farm. Richard may also have been concentrating on weaving, an indoor activity.

The Lathams were hardly a typical plebeian family. Nevertheless, in a world where it was normal for plebeian wives and resident older children to contribute to household income, their progression from intense pressure on resources in the early years of parenthood to greater prosperity as the children grew older, followed by a return to restricted budgets in the parents' old age was a familiar one. The shift to a markedly higher proportion of spending on clothes occurred as the children began to reach their late teens. This was exactly the moment when many, perhaps most, plebeian children left home to go into service. The ready availability of spinning work may at least partly explain why most of the Latham children stayed on at home for so long. At the same time, it is the presence in the household of so many young women who otherwise would probably have been servants of one kind or another that accounts for just how much the family spent on clothes from 1742 to 1754. The Latham daughters may have been resident in the parental home, but they strove to sustain a way of dressing that resembled their many peers who entered service (see Chapter 17). Evidently they shared expectations about what constituted best clothes, as well as a desire to acquire them.

A wish to acquire stylish clothes was not only, however, a phenomenon of young adulthood, confined to the Latham children. The Latham evidence suggests that, for plebeian women, stylish clothing retained its importance and its attraction across much of the adult life cycle, although its satisfactions did not necessarily remain the same. Nany Latham had to forgo the pleasures of buying and wearing petty clothing luxuries for her first decade and a half of parenthood, but this was not because those pleasures lost their appeal. As her children grew older and income increased, and particularly about the time the younger ones left home, she bought a number of expensive and showy items of clothing similar to those acquired by her daughters. Yet the satisfactions she derived from them can no longer have been those associated with the key material preoccupations of early female adulthood: courtship and employment.

The Latham accounts, moreover, allow us to observe differences in spending on clothing not only between young and old, but also between women and men. Women in the eighteenth century at all social levels were conventionally believed to be more intensely engaged with clothes, fashion and personal display than men. It comes as a surprise, therefore, to find that, according to the detailed budgets for labouring families collected by David Davies, annual expenditure on wives' clothing was only two-thirds of that on husbands'. The Latham accounts provide some support for the conventional view, while offering an explanation in terms of life-cycle for the different levels of spending by men and women in Davies's budgets.

In the Latham accounts, gender differences characterise spending on clothes for both parents and children. The Lathams' son, Dicy, enjoyed regular purchases of new clothing during his late teens, including all the elements of a suit, but the accounts suggest that more than twice as much was spent on clothing each of his sisters at the same age. Richard Latham too seems to have acquired less than the rest of the family, although the evidence of the accounts is at its weakest in his case, especially if we take into account the fact that he may have worn some of his son's clothes after Dicy's death. Nevertheless, what he acquired was relatively inexpensive, and, unlike his wife, there was no obvious jump in spending as he approached old age. Although named purchases can only be a rough guide, over the whole period of the accounts Richard's purchases were worth only 40 percent of his wife's. In the first period (1724–41), when the Latham's situation was closest to that of Davies's labouring families, the value of Richard and Nany's named purchases was almost equal, but thereafter Richard's share of the couple's named spending fell progressively, until by the third period (1755–66) it was only 20 percent of Nany's. This suggests that the gender division in family clothing expenditure may have been most advantageous to the husband when spending was squeezed in early parenthood, the stage in the family life-cycle captured by Davies's budgets. Thereafter, circumstances permitting, more tended to go to wives, as well as to children. Wives' clothes spending, in other words, displayed greater elasticity than that of their husbands. We should bear in mind, however, that Richard Latham appears to have progressively withdrawn from outdoor farm work and may not have needed to spend as much on clothing as Davies's agricultural labourers later in life. He did not, moreover, go without minor luxuries, such as books and, after 1746, a share in the purchase of a newspaper.

In addition to indicating how spending on clothes differed by gender, the Latham accounts also reveal the descriptive language the family applied to its clothes. Specifically, they enable us to examine the words the family used to identify and evaluate its clothing, or at least the words used by Richard Latham who wrote the accounts. Most striking is the individualised, personal way each family member's purchases of clothes, whether workaday or stylish, were identified. The entries for clothes purchases included the name of a member of the family far more frequently than any other significant group of purchases. If the language of the accounts is any sort of guide, the Lathams invested their individual identities in clothes to the almost complete exclusion of the other goods the family bought, whether perishables or durables. The absence of personal names from entries for food or furniture, for example, suggests that their acquisition was regarded as a communal act on the part of the family as a whole. It is really only in the case of clothes that consumption by the members of the family can be termed individualistic.[24]

The process of identifying clothes with individuals in this way began when they were babies and was constantly reinforced thereafter, because clothes were bought so frequently, with named entries in the accounts appearing nearly 12 times a year on average. Ironically, personalisation at the moment of purchase went hand-in-hand with an unending process of disposal and replacement, because clothing was a semi-durable which deteriorated faster than most household goods. Among non-perishables, clothes were more likely than any other purchase to be identified with a specific family member, but they were quicker to wear out and were replaced more frequently. The rate of turnover may have been slower than that associated with clothes and many other consumer goods in modern western societies; the Lathams' clothes were often bespoke and could be altered and repaired again and again. Nevertheless, the phenomenon is recognisably one that has usually been considered peculiar to modern consumption: heavy initial investment of personal identity in artefacts that are transient and repeatedly replaced.[25]

The language of the accounts also embraced the distinction between working as opposed to best clothes, and old as opposed to new. The terms 'working' or 'for work' were employed, however, infrequently and only for the daughters' shoes. Outdoor agricultural work required a particular kind of heavy shoe, whereas the functional requirements for other working clothes were less exacting. Much more frequently employed in the entries for clothing in the accounts was the distinction between new clothes and those that were old or second-hand. 'New' was used 249 times, which amounts to well over a quarter of the clothing entries in the account book. The frequency with which it was used does not vary markedly between entries for named children and those for named adults. It appeared in 80 percent of footwear entries, 39 percent of garment entries, 21 percent of accessory entries and nine percent of cloth entries. These differences in the rates at which the adjective was used may reflect the family's assumptions about which categories of clothing might be bought second-hand. For instance, while they did buy old shoes, it is most unlikely that they expected to buy cloth that was old or second-hand, particularly as the vast bulk of it was not in any sense fashion fabric which could become rapidly out of date.[26] Much more striking is just how infrequently the word 'old' appeared; it occurred only ten times: six for shoes and four for stays. 'Second hand' was employed only once, for stays. There was, therefore, a huge disparity between the repeated use of the description 'new' and the mere handful of entries in which clothes are described as 'old'. Although a majority of the clothes entries in the accounts used neither of these adjectives, the extent of the disparity suggests that the Lathams purchased relatively little clothing that was second-hand, even for their children. If this was the case, then the Lathams pursued a radically different approach to clothes' purchasing from the one presented by David Davies and Sir Frederick Eden as typical of labouring families later in the century.[27]

Where the Latham accounts are at their weakest is in establishing the sources of the family's clothing. Most obscure is how they purchased made-up accessories and cloth for garments. Beyond a hat and some cloth bought at fairs and some linen cloth bought from 'a cheating traveller', there is no indication of where such items were purchased, of whether more than one outlet was involved, or of the extent to which the Lathams relied on credit provided by shopkeepers or peddlers. That said, the price and character of their purchases were entirely consistent with the goods sold by the generality of drapers and other shopkeepers in the rural north in the period. The account book is much more forthcoming about making and mending. The Lathams were not very loyal to their shoemakers. In the 43 years covered by the account book, they employed 19 different men (and possibly more who are unnamed) to make or repair footwear. In one year, 1745, they employed five different shoemakers. Towards tailors, however, they were more faithful. During the 43 years of the account book they employed eight named tailors, but one, William Gore, appears in more years than the others put together. There is no evidence that the family employed particular individuals for specialised kinds of work.

The division of labour in clothes assembly between men's work and women's work, and between what was made up at home and what was bought in, followed the early eighteenth-century pattern described in Chapter 9. It was tailors who were paid for making the women's as well as the men's outer garments. There is no mention of a mantuamaker or other specialist in assembling women's outer garments. In all the cases where the accounts are explicit, the work was actually done by a male tailor and his male assistants, not by their wives or other women. Tailors also undertook other work for the Lathams that might elsewhere, especially in a town, have been undertaken by specialists. It was tailors who made the women's stays and a tailor who supplied at least one of the pairs of second-hand stays. Linen undergarments and children's clothes were made up almost entirely at home, presumably by the women of the family. There are no payments for making up shifts and shirts, only three for making up little children's clothes and one for making a cap. Stockings were also made up at home. There were 39 entries for purchases of stockings, but the vast majority of these were for infant children. The family bought knitting needles, so it seems likely that stockings for the older children and the adults were knitted in the household. There are frequent payments for dying small quantities of woollen yarn, which were probably intended for stockings. There is no direct evidence that footwear was made by the family, but regular payments for shoe and clog nails indicate that some mending was done at home, although were also payments for this purpose.

On two aspects of the family's clothing the accounts are frustratingly silent: how they came by information to inform their choices of clothing and who in the family controlled decisions about what was spent on clothes. The Latham family, like most others in rural England, could undoubtedly have found out about fashions in clothing by observing their neighbours and the local elite, or by examining the goods offered for sale by peddlers and shopkeepers. In the Lathams' case, we know their observations were not confined to their immediate locality. The parents and the older children regularly visited towns and fairs across south-west Lancashire. In 1747, for example, Sara and Dicy visited Liverpool, while Betty went to Prescot fair. There is also the intriguing possibility that they were able to read fashion news and advertisements placed by drapers, mercers and other retailers in the newspapers Richard Latham had a share in buying, although fashion news did not appear in all newspapers and only infrequently before the 1760s.[28]

On the issue of who had authority over clothes spending, the accounts tell us virtually nothing. Richard Latham made the entries in the account book. Whether that means he dictated what should be bought for each member of the family is impossible to say. Even if his unusually diligent accounting was an exercise in controlling the other members of his family, we should remember that purchases could be concealed. A late eighteenth-century shop ledger from Penmorfa in North Wales includes repeated entries for purchases of clothes on men's credit by wives or maidservants, which use phrases like 'handkerchief . . . wife, not to tell' or 'hat 11s. 6d., to tell 8s'. Evidently, the purchase or its real cost was not to be divulged to the man of the house.[29] All we can say with confidence is that it was the women of the Latham family who benefited disproportionately from its expenditure on clothing. Insofar as the increase in the family's clothes spending after 1742 was funded by the women's paid work, it is not unreasonable to assume that, to some degree at least, it reflected their wishes.

For the Lathams, clothing was a luxury in the technical sense used by economists. As the family's income grew as a consequence of the daughters' industriousness, so did both the amount and the proportion of family spending devoted to clothes. Appropriately, this new spending was led by the unmarried daughters themselves, whose purchases also embraced luxury in a sense more familiar to eighteenth-century social commentators, in that they purchased stylish accessories and garments in addition to practical, workaday items of clothing. Yet it is important to re-emphasise that the increase in family spending required to make all these new luxury purchases did not involve large sums of money. Relatively small shifts in family income could produce dramatic transformations in material culture. Jan de Vries has argued that the Industrial Revolution was preceded by an industrious revolution founded on the kind of waged textile work undertaken in families like the Lathams. If so, it was a revolution that did not have to be especially revolutionary to have a big impact, not only on the material lives of the families where the work was done, but also on patterns of consumption in the wider economy.[30]

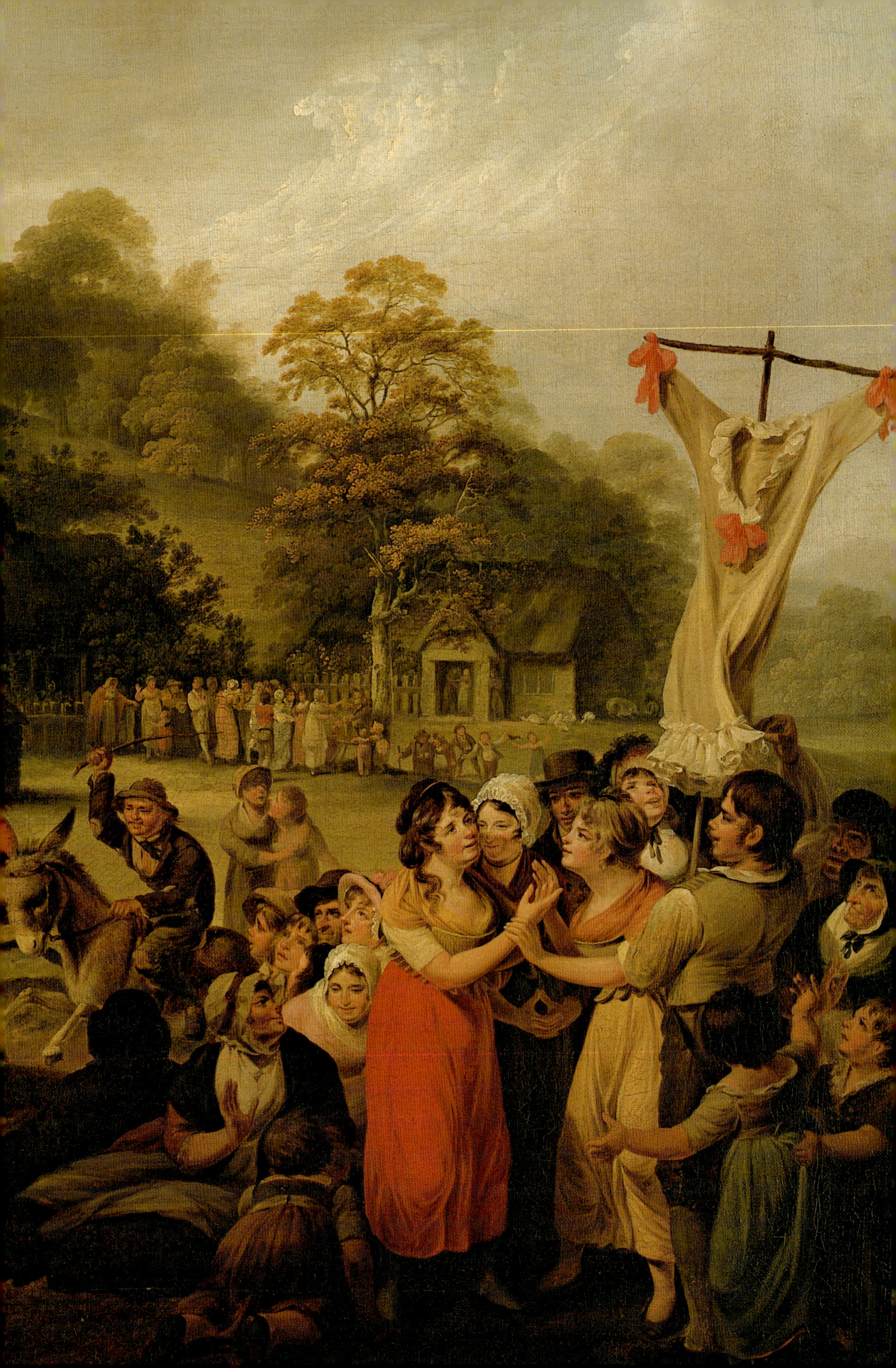

15

Involuntary Consumption? Prizes, Gifts and Charity

THE HISTORY OF CONSUMPTION IN ENGLAND has been written largely in terms of people's capacity to exercise choice. This has been true both of studies which have emphasised progressive expansion in the available range of goods and services from which choices might be made and of studies which have highlighted the many influences – financial, commercial or cultural – that curbed those choices, rendered them illusory or encouraged resistance to them. However, in considering the poorer half of the population before the nineteenth century, the prevailing assumption among historians has been that they enjoyed next to no choice. Either they earned too little to provide access to anything more than the barest of necessities, or they had to make do with what was chosen for them by their social superiors in the form of charity or payment in kind. This book has argued that to portray the predicament of the generality of adult plebeian consumers in this way is too pessimistic, at least as far as clothing in the eighteenth century is concerned. Despite limited resources, most were able and anxious to sustain a minimally decent wardrobe and many were able to choose from a wide and widening range of petty clothing luxuries at some periods in their lives. But very large numbers of plebeian men and women in eighteenth-century England did wear some clothing provided to them by others by means of non-market or semi-market mechanisms, on terms which offered little choice.

Involuntary consumption of at least some items of clothing was a widely shared experience. It took a variety of forms and incorporated many different kinds of people. Gifts and bequests, whether by individuals or by organised charities, accounted for an important and, by the early nineteenth century, a growing proportion of the involuntary consumption of clothing. But clothes were also among the goods used to pay employees as truck. At Colchester during the 1715 depression, retailers claimed that the weavers 'for a long time past have had goods of all sorts imposed upon them by their masters . . . Bread, Butter, Cheese, Candles, Sope, Shoes, Handkerchiefs and Red Herrings etc. for their work instead of British money which said goods we would have sold the poor people at a much cheaper rate.'[1] Clothes were offered by employers as

---

99 *(facing page)* Joseph Parry, *Eccles Wakes: Racing for the Smock* (detail), 1808, oil on canvas, Manchester Art Gallery, 1927.12. A man races on a donkey at the village wake at Eccles, four miles west of Manchester. A prize shift or smock, laced and ribboned, hangs prominently from a frame.

prizes to workers to encourage production. The Edinburgh-trained doctor Sylas Neville noted in 1781 that Richard Arkwright, at his cotton spinning mill at Crompton, Derbyshire, 'not only distributes pecuniary rewards, but gives distinguishing dresses to the most deserving of both sexes, which excites great emulation'.[2] It is not surprising that employers used clothes as incentives in this way, because clothes served as prizes in many kinds of contest. In 1725, for example, an advertisement for horse races at Methley near Leeds was accompanied by an announcement that 'on the same day and same course there will be a holland smock run for by women' (fig. 99).[3] Stone buttons were among the prizes at a mountebank show at Colne, Lancashire in 1773.[4] The various entertainments presented at Astley's Circus in London in 1770 included sack races three times round the arena, for the prize of a silver watch.[5]

For most adults, however, involuntary consumption involved accepting an occasional item of clothing as a gift to add to a stock of clothes that was accumulated mainly by purchase or home production. It is impossible to gauge the frequency of these gifts with any accuracy, as evidence about them comes from occasional, serendipitous references in personal and official documents. Yet we can be confident that they were very common. Donations of clothing by an aunt, a sister, a grandmother or an employer were sufficiently familiar that they were cited over and over again in criminal cases to explain the presence of suspicious clothes. Mary Bell from Thirsk in Yorkshire claimed in 1698 that her sister had given her a white calico hood, two quoifes, a forehead cloth and a hemp linen sheet that turned out to have been stolen from Ampleforth, ten miles away, where the sister lived. Over a century later, in 1811, Mary Brooks insisted that a hempen shift, identified as stolen from Tardebigge in Worcestershire, had been given her by her aunt. George Johnson, a sailor, told an old-clothes dealer at Newcastle upon Tyne in 1789 that 'he had got an account of his grandfather's death and had heard that his grandmother intended to give him his grandfather's clothes'. He broached the subject to the dealer to establish whether she would buy the clothing when he received it. In 1731 Mary Wright, a servant charged with stealing clothes from her mistress at Carleton in the North Riding of Yorkshire, claimed that her employer's daughter had 'told her she could have what odd things she could find in the house' while the family was away in London.[6] Clothing could be a valuable currency in close personal relationships, both emotionally and monetarily, but we should not romanticise these exchanges by assuming that intimacy precluded payment. We know from the accounts kept in the 1770s by Robertl Heaton, a Yorkshire worsted manufacturer, that two of his servants had to pay for gowns which were passed on to them by their aunts.[7]

In addition, clothes were frequently passed on as personal bequests by the dying and the dead. Our knowledge of the practice comes mainly from wills. Wills were rarely left by the labouring poor, but there is every reason to believe that such bequests were made by those who did not write a formal will, as the sailor George Johnson's claims about his grandparents, quoted above, suggest. In surviving wills, bequests of clothing were made most frequently by deceased kin, but sometimes by employers and friends.

This practice was already well established in the sixteenth and seventeenth centuries, although it may have declined among the least affluent testators as the eighteenth century progressed.[8] Women were especially likely to use their wills to make gifts of specific, cherished items of clothing as tokens of affection, but men's wills also included such bequests.[9] Sometimes bequests of this kind even achieved customary status, like the commonly held belief among lady's maids that they had a right to at least some of the clothes of a dead mistress. Lord Bristol wrote to his son in 1741:

> I am glad to find that you have delivered to Williams all the things which were your poor mother's and which by a customary sort of right are now due to every common servant in her place; but as her merit and services for near 18 years have been of the most uncommon kind, that consideration alone would have entitled her to any favour out of the ordinary course of proceedings between executors and residuary legatees.[10]

In addition to these direct, personal forms of gifting, enormous quantities of adult clothing were handed out as charity in ways that were less intimate. This kind of charity took three principal forms: donations by private individuals; charitable bequests to the poor under the terms of wills; and donations by charitable associations. All three forms of charitable giving are difficult to quantify. Evidence about individual donations is recorded only intermittently in private papers, while the records of many local charitable associations do not survive. For charitable bequests, which were repeatedly surveyed by church and parliament in the course of the eighteenth and nineteenth centuries, we often have surprisingly little precise information about the kind of clothing they provided.

Charitable giving by private individuals ranged from regular donations to occasional handouts in times of hardship. Between 1692 and 1719, for example, the sixth Earl of Thanet supplied clothes, including coats, shirts and shifts, to his poor tenants in the Craven area of north-west Yorkshire, particularly 'to the aged and such as have great charge of children'. The clothes were 'to be made soon after Michaelmas as the poor may have them before the weather grows cold'.[11] In 1700, 154 coats were given out; in 1716, 240 garments. The annual cost was between £34 and £58. Thanet's steward at Skipton was responsible for purchasing cloth, usually in Westmorland, and having it made up in Skipton by a poor tailor. On the Egerton estate at Tatton in Cheshire in the second half of the eighteenth century, gifts of clothing, along with money, food and firing, were made to farm and estate workers each year at Christmas. Bedgowns and petticoats were provided for the women, coats and waistcoats for the men, rockets (cloaks) for the girls and wash-leather breeches for the boys.[12] At Brington in Northamptonshire at the end of the 1780s, the Reverend David Davies noted that 'a great many gowns, petticoats, and shifts, are annually distributed by the Countess Spencer to poor families'.[13] In 1796, the owner of a colour manufactory at Hackney, near London, had an old box in the middle of his factory into which he put 'worn out cloaths that I had looked out to give away . . . for the poor and the needy'.[14]

The Thanet, Egerton and Bington donations were made regularly each year, and in the case of the Egerton gifts to estate and farm workers can be regarded as a supplement in kind to wages. But it was also a common practice among the wealthy to make gifts of clothing on an ad hoc basis, especially in response to privation. These acts of charity could be to particular individuals or they could extend more widely. As with regular donations by individuals, it is hard to assess how frequent they were and therefore how important a contribution they made to the stock of clothing worn by the poor. We know about such gifts only when they were recorded in surviving letters or accounts, or from announcements placed in the press in times of hardship to emphasise the paternalistic concern of landowners for the poor, like that in the *London Evening Post* during the harsh winter of 1756–7, when food prices were high: 'We hear that one Day last Week a Quantity of Bread and Beef, with Shifts and Shirts, were distributed by John Gibbons, Esq. of Stanwell Place, Middlesex, to a great Number of the poor Inhabitants.'[15] But not all such giving by the wealthy was a direct response to the hardships of the poor. Clothes were given out to encourage the attendance of mourners at the funerals of the rich, often as an affirmation of the deceased's reputation for charity, although the practice may have been in decline in the eighteenth century.[16] In 1748, for instance, Lady Anne Josephina Wynne had 100 poor women attend her funeral in Denbighshire and provided each with 20 shillings, a gown and petticoat, two shifts, shoes and stockings.[17]

Providing clothes for mourners was not the only, or indeed the most important way that the dead clothed the living. Huge quantities of clothing materials were given away to adults on a regular basis, year after year, under the terms of a multitude of local charitable bequests, many dating from the seventeenth century. Such bequests existed across England, in city, town and village. Bridget Lewis finds that in Northamptonshire, clothes were the third most common form of provision for the poor provided by endowed charities in the early nineteenth century, after money and foodstuffs.[18] Where the type of clothing to be provided was specified in the bequest, outer garments figure prominently, in contrast to the shoes and undergarments that dominated Poor Law provision. In metropolitan Southwark at the start of the eighteenth century there were several such charities, including Mrs Marshall's bequest which provided six poor women with gowns each year from an annual rental income of £6, Mr Buckland's gift which provided ten poor men with gowns from an annual rental income of £5, and Mr Smith's gift with an annual rental income of £28, used partly for clothing poor men and women.[19] At the town of Kendal in Westmorland up to 60 poor men received four yards of kersey (enough to make a coat) annually under the terms of William Janson's will of 1615.[20] In Hampshire in 1725 the village of Hartley Wintney had 'a small charity given for ever by Mr Robert Ray of 60 ells of canvas', at Old Alresford the interest on £15 was 'divided amongst poor families for buying them shoes', while the parish of Overton used 'the interest of £40 left by Mrs Ann Holdripp to buy 6 coats, 3 for widowers and 3 for widows'.[21] At Linton in the West Riding of Yorkshire, the six poor old men and women who lived in the almshouse established under the will of Richard Fountaine in 1721 were provided with a coat or a gown made from blue cloth lined with green each year.[22] As this last example shows, new charitable bequests involving clothing went on being made in the course of the eighteenth century.

Yet in aggregate endowed charities amounted to no more than an uneven, serendipitous patchwork that favoured urban over rural areas and left a majority of parishes unprovided. Hampshire, for example, had far fewer endowed charities than neighbouring Surrey, and they were especially rare in the county's numerous rural parishes.[23] Bridget Lewis finds that in Northamptonshire, 84 percent of the county's 297 rural parishes had some kind of endowed charity by the early nineteenth century, but only 39 of them provided clothing.[24] Moreover, those who benefited from endowed charities tended not to be those who received parish relief. In the West Riding of Yorkshire the overlap between the two groups was limited. Recipients of endowed charity were more likely to be embedded in dense local kinship networks and perhaps, therefore, regarded as more respectable.[25]

Supplying clothes to the needy also played a significant part in the explosion of associative, subscription charity that characterised the eighteenth century.[26] In the Seven Years War of 1756–63, for instance, subscriptions were established specifically to buy clothes for French prisoners of war.[27] But the supply of clothing became an especially prominent element of the work of the charities organised by elite women from the 1770s. The Ladies Charitable Society, otherwise known as the Society for Charitable Purposes, began its activities in London in the early 1770s, supplying clothes to the poor, in addition to pensions, provisions, coals and medicine. According to a published account in 1793, it provided employment and care for the women of the lower classes in the West End of London, especially the old and widowed, mainly by giving clothing and bedding.[28] Where London led, provincial England followed. At Carlisle, a female visiting society for the relief of the aged and indigent was formed in 1803 by philanthropic women, whose members engaged to 'search out the abodes of the wretched'.[29] At Liverpool, a Ladies Benevolent Society was established in 1810 which distributed food and clothing, but not money, to the indigent, paying poor women to sew the clothes.[30]

A slightly different approach was represented by the Dorcas Society set up at Workington in Cumberland in 1818. It provided various articles of clothing to the needy every winter, 'mostly wrought by the fair hands of the contributors to this excellent charity, which distributes yearly about 600 gowns, frocks, petticoats, shirts shifts, caps and stockings'.[31] Dorcas societies, named after the Christian woman of Joppa in the Bible who made coats and garments for the poor, sprang up in many parts of the country from around the time of Waterloo. They consisted of comfortably off women who bought and repaired old clothes, and made up new ones, all for distribution to the poor in their localities. At Wisbech a Dorcas charity was established in 1813 and at

Birmingham a Methodist Dorcasian society in 1818. There were Dorcas societies operating at Mansfield in Nottinghamshire by 1816, at Liverpool by 1818 and at Buckingham by 1820.[32]

These societies combined the work of elite women, often with a strong religious motivation, in making or organising the making-up of clothes and in directly supervising their distribution, with efforts to encourage decency and self-reliance amongst the poor by means of incentives. Each of these features was characteristic of the re-conceptualisation of pauperism and appropriate responses to it that characterised elite thinking in the final decades of the eighteenth century.[33] The objective was neatly summarised by the promoter of an early nineteenth-century clothing charity: 'to connect charity, industry, prudence and morality more intimately together'.[34] The Sunday schools for children set up in large numbers from the 1780s provided crucial models of how charity and self-help might be combined in clothing the poor that were subsequently extended to adults. Sarah Trimmer in her 1787 *Oeconomy of Charity; Or, An Address to Ladies Concerning Sunday-Schools*, one of the founding texts of the Sunday school movement, noted:

> The duty of clothing the naked, ladies will be reminded of while they are hearing the New Testament read in Sunday-schools: and surely the precepts that recommend this branch of charity will strike the mind with double force when the immediate objects of it stand before them in tattered garments, that make silent but powerful claims on their humanity. In such an assembly, what lady can read the account of Dorcas without forming a resolution to imitate her example?[35]

Children's clothing was an issue from the earliest days of the Sunday School movement. Children complained that they did not have clothes good enough to attend school or church, while the schools' patrician patrons were often horrified at the way the children were dressed. At the Sunday schools Sarah Trimmer opened at Brentford in Middlesex in 1786, 'though there were many who made a very neat appearance, such a set of deplorable dirty ragged creatures presented themselves amongst them as it is shocking to recollect'. Her response was to distribute brushes, combs and clothes. Subsequently, 'the young ladies of two boarding schools supplied nearly an hundred caps, and a number of tippets, which, though made of old cloth, greatly improved the appearance of the children; and many articles of clothing were, from time to time, bestowed by the subscribers and others'. One of the chief benefits of the schools, she argued, was that within months, 'many girls, who were deplorably ragged, are now clothed very well, partly by gifts from the school, and partly by the exertions of their parents'.[36] Yet at the same time she was anxious to curb what she regarded as unsuitable and improvident excess in dress. Children of slightly better-off parents were admitted to her schools only on condition 'that all articles of finery should be laid aside'. She took evident pleasure in the discovery that the 'caps, handkerchiefs, pincushions, huswifes, and other gifts (usually the work of young ladies)' dispensed to the most deserving children, were 'in such estimation, that the gauze caps, and other trumpery ornaments so injudiciously purchased by poor people, are readily laid aside for them'.[37]

At Hertingfordbury in Hertfordshire in the 1780s, the Sunday school did not give out clothes, to avoid 'encouraging idleness', which 'is too often the case with *donations* of money or cloathing'.[38] Instead it assisted parents to clothe their children by providing clothing at wholesale prices with a subsidy of a quarter of the cost. At Brentford a similar scheme involved giving 'two-pence in the shilling to all good boys, whose parents should purchase for them any of the following articles; namely, carter's frocks, shirts, swanskin waistcoats, leather-breeches, stout shoes or half boots, worsted or yarn stockings; and in proportion for clothes, etc. well patched and mended'.[39] Early nineteenth-century Dorcas societies provided clothes to adults at reduced cost in the same way. The Liverpool Dorcas society started out in 1818 by giving away the clothes sewn by its members, but by 1827 was asking the poor to pay one shilling towards each item.[40] Ann Adkins, a mother on poor relief at Buckingham in 1820, demonstrated her thriftiness in a begging letter to the Marchioness of Buckingham by pointing out: 'I had saved a trifle which I gave the Ladies here for a warm shawl from the Dorcas charity'.[41]

A further refinement of this kind of assisted self-help scheme was the charitable clothing society. Clothes clubs were, as we have seen in Chapter 8, already a familiar aspect of plebeian associative life, but conventionally they were organised by a draper or a tailor and the adult subscribers were able to select what they wished to buy.[42] The penny clothing clubs set up towards the end of the eighteenth century by Sunday schools, like those at Painswick in Gloucestershire and Sutton Coldfield in Warwickshire in 1786 and at Harborne in Staffordshire in 1799, offered less choice. The children contributed a weekly penny out of their earnings and the honorary members also put in a penny a week. At Harborne in 1801 the membership consisted of 128 boys, 107 girls and 125 honorary members. The first distribution of clothing was made after two years.

> For 82 girls they provided neat cotton gowns, to which two ladies in the neighbourhood added caps and neck handkerchiefs; so that all the girls appeared at church on the following Sunday, uniformly and neatly dressed, presenting a spectacle truly interesting. For the 31 youngest boys there were suits of clothes – for 11 others, coats and waistcoats, and coats for the bigger boys.[43]

Penny clubs, combining self-help and philanthropy along the same lines, were organised for adults in the 1790s, although not specifically to provide clothes. Sir Frederick Eden reported approvingly in 1796 that 'Lord Harcourt has formed a club at Nuneham, in Oxfordshire, to which such of his labourers, as are approved of by him, pay one penny each per week. To this his lordship adds the like sum. This forms a fund which they may have recourse to, upon any exigency'.[44] This was a precursor of the charitable clothing clubs that were to multiply from the end of the Napoleonic Wars. At

Mansfield in Nottinghamshire, a Penny Society to supply clothing on this principle was established in 1815. A Society for Clothing the Indigent was organised at Peckham in the south London suburbs in 1816, and a Clothing Society was formed at Creaton in Northamptonshire in 1817.[45] By 1834, the Reverend Capper of Great Missenden in Buckinghamshire considered such societies required no explanation, 'as this kind of club is so general throughout the country'.[46] The way these clubs operated is illustrated by the Mansfield Penny Society, which in 1816 relieved 102 people, 32 poor women receiving a bedgown, flannel petticoat, chemise and stockings, 32 poor men a hat, shirt and stockings, and others blankets. 'It is hoped, seeing that such beneficial effects result from so trifling a sum as a penny per week, that it will still encourage the benevolent to pursue so laudable an undertaking . . . the clothes were made up by the ladies, and the whole is carried on without any expense.'[47] The implication here is that the depositors could not simply choose the clothes they wanted to buy. This was certainly how the influential Farthinghoe clothing society operated in Northamptonshire in the early 1830s under the direction of the Reverend Francis Litchfield, who policed both quality and style. He insisted on the presence of a draper 'prepared with such useful articles as I considered proper for sale, no flannel but Welch flannel, and nothing tawdry in appearance, being permitted to be bought'.[48] Like the earlier Sunday school clothing schemes and clubs, there was a clear moral agenda which extended to the kinds of clothing supplied. The Farthinghoe rules were widely copied, though we cannot assume that as clothing clubs became ubiquitous in the rural south and Midlands in the 1830s they were always quite so narrowly *dirigiste*.[49]

The strategies adopted towards the end of the eighteenth century by associative charities to encourage self-help among the labouring poor were reflected in private charitable giving of clothes.[50] Once again Sunday schools provided a model. *Instructions for Cutting out Apparel for the Poor*, published in 1789 to publicise the Hertingfordbury Sunday School scheme for supplying children with subsidised clothing, offered advice on how to clothe poor men and women on the same principle, although as 'matters of private charity, only'.[51] At Mongewell in Oxfordshire in the 1790s, the lord of the manor bought flax for poor women and children to spin. It was reported that 'the cloth made from the flax has been sold to the cottager, at about two-pence a yard cheaper, than it can be purchased in the shop'.[52] Writing in her old age, Caroline Wiggett, the daughter of a clergyman, remembered life in the years after Waterloo as a young woman at the Vyne in Hampshire, where she lived with her childless Aunt Elizabeth Chute:

> At Michaelmas we held the Dorcas shop in the Chapel Parlour which lasted a week, having all sorts of unmade clothing from B[asing]stoke. I was shop woman, Aunt C secretary or bill maker. Calico, prints, stockings, sheeting, etc., were sold. They having contributed half the price the people were delighted, thinking the materials so much better, but some of them were very tiresome and particular in choosing. I have stood for 7 hours, yarding off calico, it was very fatiguing and nearly knocked me up, but we led a quiet life and it was change.[53]

Involuntary Consumption? Prizes, Gifts and Charity

Charity, gifts, prizes; for most adults, clothes obtained by these routes were occasional windfalls, although not necessarily unwelcome ones. For many of the poor, the cold and the hungry, any clothing must have been welcome. What local retailers denigrated as truck might, depending on quality, variety and the availability of credit, be welcomed by employees, especially in remote manufactories.[54] Gifts or prizes that were unwelcome or inappropriate could often be sold on the second-hand market or pawned. Simply because clothes were chosen by others did not mean they were automatically disliked by their recipients. Involuntary consumption was not necessarily an unwelcome form of consumption.

100   Poor Law badge with the letters RP for Riccall Parish, East Riding of Yorkshire, 1737, red and black felted woollen cloth, 11.5 × 9.5 cm, Borthwick Institute, University of York, Rom. 60.

16
Involuntary Consumption? The Parish Poor

THOSE WHO RELIED MOST HEAVILY ON CLOTHING chosen by others can legitimately be described as involuntary consumers. In a society with an age distribution heavily skewed towards the young, the largest single group of involuntary consumers was children. They wore clothes chosen and supplied by a variety of adults and institutions – predominantly their parents, but also their kin (living and dead), their masters and mistresses in the course of apprenticeship, charities and the charitable, the parish authorities, and schools of various sorts, most obviously charity schools and, by the end of the century as their numbers rapidly increased, Sunday schools.[1] But it was only a minority, albeit a large minority, of eighteenth-century adults whose clothes were provided mainly by others on terms over which they exercised little or no control. Three categories of eighteenth-century adults were sufficiently reliant on clothing supplied on restrictive terms to merit the description of involuntary consumers: male household and other menial servants, military personnel, and the poor who were clothed by the parish.[2] Of these, the largest single group was the parish poor.

The supply of clothing to adults by charities was extensive and probably growing in the eighteenth century, although it is unlikely to have kept pace with the accelerating population increase of the second half of the century. However, charity was dwarfed by the volume of clothing supplied by parishes under the Poor Law. The number of poor people who received material support from their parishes was huge. Their numbers grew in absolute and probably relative terms as the eighteenth century progressed. By the end of the century, up to a fifth of the population in some areas was receiving assistance from the parish authorities, although elsewhere it was significantly lower.[3] For most of them, however, this was a temporary state of affairs, the result of being orphaned, widowed, deserted, ill or old. The half-century after 1750 did begin to see the emergence of a new group of chronically poor men claiming long-term support, the casualties of growing structural underemployment and unemployment, especially in the south and east of England, but their numbers became really significant only after about 1800. The level of support provided to the poor varied from parish to parish and from region to region. It has been argued that provision tended to be better in the south and east and worse in the north and west, reflecting different living standards, different opportunities for by-employment and different attitudes to relief among ratepayers.[4] Yet irrespective of locality, it was rare for either regular pensions or casual payments to be generous enough to supply everything an individual or a family needed to survive. Consequently, it must have been unusual for anyone to have been clothed entirely by the parish authorities, despite the prominence of clothing among the payments in kind that appear in almost every surviving set of detailed accounts compiled by the overseers of the poor who administered the system in England's ten thousand parishes.

Hundreds of overseers' accounts, originating in every part of England, survive for the eighteenth century. The more detailed among them itemise, with varying degrees of precision, the clothes supplied by the parish, the date they were supplied, their cost, the materials from which they were made, and the people to whom they were given. For some parishes there are receipts or vouchers, indicating the supplier of the clothing; for others, especially from the late eighteenth century, there are pauper letters which include requests to the overseers or the vestry for clothing. Collectively these records constitute an unmatched compendium of clothing practices among a large segment of the eighteenth-century poor.

Yet historians who have worked through these sources, often with the aim of intervening in the long-standing debates about the liberality or otherwise of the Old Poor Law, have had little to say about clothing. Those few who have commented on the clothing supplied by overseers generally portray it as a bare minimum, in terms of both quantity and quality, though acknowledging that what constituted that minimum may have changed in the course of the eighteenth century. 'The worthy poor were never provided with more than the perceived basics in clothing, so as to discourage sloth and a reliance on the parish', suggests Beverly Lemire. At best, 'the clothes provided were adequate, though not elegant', concludes the historian of one Middlesex parish.[5] But a radically different assessment has been offered by Steven King as part of a wider argument for the generosity of elements of Poor Law provision between 1750 and 1840. He argues that overseers supplied clothing that could be superior to that acquired by labouring people from their own resources. 'There is disjointed evidence that some of "the poor" may actually have been as well clothed as some of the comfortable non-elite farming families with whom their situation has sometimes been contrasted in a literary or visual sense'. He argues that 'when compared to the wider population from which they were drawn, the poor on relief were "well clothed" and that clothing the poor "well" became one of the basic tasks of the communal welfare system between 1750 and 1840'. Indeed, he goes further, suggesting that 'some female paupers clearly were fairly fashionable, and even those who were not would apparently have had aprons, gowns, stockings and shoes to match or surpass many working women who were not paupers'.[6]

So did the clothes worn by parish paupers represent a bare minimum of sartorial sufficiency, a baseline on which non-paupers might expect to improve? Or were they superior to the clothes worn by many among the working population, testimony to the generosity of the old Poor Law or, alternatively, to the degradation of the working poor in the half-century after 1750? Two obstacles stand in the way of using the records compiled by parish vestries and overseers to answer these questions. First, as has already been pointed out, it was probably rare for anyone to be clothed entirely by the parish. When instructing the overseer in 1794 on how the poor in the parish workhouse were to be clothed, the vestry at Much Hadham in Hertfordshire stressed that clothes provided by the parish were 'to compleat what may be belonging to each of them in good condition'.[7] The limited evidence that survives about the clothing already owned by those who applied for relief, or the clothes they acquired from sources other than the parish while on relief, confirms that paupers did not necessarily rely wholly on the parish. As we saw in Chapter 3, those who entered St Marylebone workhouse in London in the 1770s brought with them a range of clothing, which could be quite extensive and was certainly not always ragged, and this phenomenon was not restricted to the metropolis. It is possible to identify a number of people in the pledge book of the York pawnbroker George Fettes in the 1770s who pawned clothes during the time they received relief from one of the city's parishes.[8] Robert Turner was receiving a pension of four shillings a week from the parish of St Mary Bishophill in 1778 at the time he pledged a green silk waistcoat for 4s. 2d., which he redeemed after three months. Yet the St Mary Bishophill overseers' accounts for the period show that the parish never provided clothes of this quality.[9] At Cheshunt in Hertfordshire, lists of paupers' clothes drawn up in 1782 distinguished between those provided by the parish and those owned by the pauper. Alice Godfey, for instance, had two pairs of stockings, two pairs of shoes, a pair of pattens, two shifts, one gown, two petticoats, two aprons, one pair of stays and two handkerchiefs provided by the parish, but in addition one gown, one hat and five caps described as 'her own'.[10] Sporadic examples like these are insufficient, however, to establish a typical ratio of parish to non-parish clothing in pauper wardrobes. Consequently, the range of clothing actually worn by paupers remains elusive.

It is almost as difficult, secondly, to establish exactly what clothes parishes paid for and how often they provided them. Overseers' accounts list numerous items of clothing, but we should not assume that all the clothes paid for by the parish were included. Parishes varied in the kinds of assistance they were prepared to offer. Most provided some claimants with regular pensions while other claimants received only casual payments, often in the form of clothes and other goods, but even the regular pensioners might also receive casual payments in cash or kind. The balance between pensions and casual payments varied from one parish to the next, and in any single parish might change over time. Some parishes seem to have assumed that at least part of the cost of clothing was included in the regular pension. Others seem to have provided clothing to those in receipt of pensions mainly by means of intermittent payments in kind. Others again seem to have combined the two approaches, making intermittent payments of part of the cost of an item of clothing.

Take the adjoining townships of Shipton and Leafield in Oxfordshire in the middle of the eighteenth century. Shipton spent more on pensions for its poor and less on payments in kind. Leafield, with a slightly larger population, spent less on regular pensions and much more on benefits in kind, including notably clothing, but also accommodation, on which more was spent than anything else, medical treatment, apprenticeships and funerals. Nevertheless, the total spending per head on the poor in the two townships was similar and ultimately their ratepayers may have paid for roughly the same numbers of clothes per pauper, albeit by different routes. The presence of numerous entries for clothes in the Leafield overseers' accounts does not prove that Leafield's ratepayers paid proportionately more for clothing than Shipton's. It is unlikely that Shipton's poor went barefoot, even though Shipton's overseers' accounts record only two pairs of shoes supplied to paupers between 1740 and 1762, while Leafield's record one hundred and five pairs. More probably Shipton's poor were expected to provide themselves with shoes out of their pensions.[11]

Such discrepancies in the way clothes were supplied pose considerable obstacles to comparisons of the supply of clothing to the poor between different parishes, different regions and different dates. They also raise important questions about who was empowered to choose the clothes and what considerations shaped their choices. Where clothes were supplied on an *ad hoc* basis, usually in response to pauper requests, it is clear from the wording used in the accounts that the overseer generally made the purchase. Parish officers' priorities were not necessarily the same as paupers'. In buying clothing, the parish authorities might privilege considerations as diverse as cheapness, the interests of local retailers who were ratepayers, or quality conceived in terms of warmth and durability. In 1798, for instance, the overseer of Harlington, Bedfordshire wrote a note to the local shopkeeper: 'Mr Jennings desires Mr Flowers will let Jemima Fowler have 2 pair of stockings for her boy good strong stockings'. On another occasion the same year he asked him to 'let Randle have a common waistcoat'.[12] Paupers might have preferred, perhaps, comfort or fashionability in their dress, or might have had different spending priorities altogether, choosing to spend more on food and less on clothing, but it is almost impossible to establish any sense of individual paupers' priorities. Letters from paupers living at a distance from their parishes show them asking for the kinds of fabrics and garments that parishes customarily supplied, but this may simply reflect an awareness that they were more likely to be successful if they asked for what parishes were prepared to give.[13]

A parish policy of providing clothes direct to the poor, as opposed to money, offered vestries and overseers power to impose their priorities. Among late eighteenth-century commentators on the Poor Law there were certainly those who believed it was better to provide relief 'in clothes, or other necessaries, in preference to money'.[14] Yet, as we have seen, parishes varied in the balance they struck between payments in cash and payments in kind. Even where clothing was provided mainly on an *ad hoc* basis, paupers were sometimes given money to buy an item, rather than the item itself. We know very little about the control the parish authorities exercised over the way the poor spent the cash they received as pensions, although a well-organised vestry like that at Wimbledon in Surrey would intervene to ensure propriety. In 1750 it ordered that '2d. a week to be stopped out of [Jo Skinner's] pension by the overseers for washing his linen to keep him clean'. Three years later it allowed Elizabeth Boulter '20s. towards buying her a gown, petticoat, 2 shifts and a pr of shoes', but added 'Mrs Winchester to purchase them for her'. They had already made their preference clear by stipulating in 1751 that 'the churchwardens are to buy all the clothes for the poor for such necessaries as shall be ordered by vestry, and the clothes are to be disbursed as ordered'.[15] At Pyrton in Oxfordshire in the 1780s and 1790s the vestry had an exclusive agreement with one draper and insisted that 'whatever drapery goods be bought without the order or consent of the vestry shall be paid for by the person so ordering the same'.[16] Yet the very fact that these rules had to be imposed suggests previous practice accommodated purchases by paupers. Other parishes may have been less fastidious.

In the light of these difficulties, the analysis presented here focuses not so much on what individual paupers wore, or on the contribution of clothing to total Poor Law expenditure, but rather on the items of clothing supplied, their quality and their cost. To do this, the clothing purchases itemised in the Poor Law accounts of six parishes from different parts of England are examined during two periods, one earlier in the eighteenth century – 1730 to 1760 – and one later – 1770 to 1800. The parishes are Holne, an agricultural village on the edge of Dartmoor in Devon, Leafield, an agricultural village on the edge of Wychwood in Oxfordshire, Spofforth, an agricultural village near Knaresborough in Yorkshire, Theydon Garnon, an agricultural village which included part of the town of Epping in Essex, Thornhill, a village on the southern edge of the Yorkshire woollen manufacturing district, and Ware, a prosperous market town in Hertfordshire.[17] Holne and Spofforth do not appear to have had workhouses for the periods studied; Thornhill, Ware and Theydon Garnon did; Leafield had a workhouse very briefly. These six sets of Poor Law accounts are compared with the acquisitions of non-pauper plebeians, as recorded in private account books and shopkeepers' day books. All these sources are partial and inconsistent, some recording the yardage prices paid for cloth, others recording only the cost of finished garments. To use them to establish the quality and cost of clothing supplied to paupers, the evidence they provide is assessed here in terms of two criteria – price and variety.[18]

Let us consider the prices of fabrics first. In the earlier period, 1730–60, the textiles supplied for clothing by the six parishes were consistent in price with the cheapest, coarsest fabrics acquired by non-paupers for everyday wear (see table 27). Minimum standards were upheld. Paupers were not clothed in the coarsest hardening used for bed ticking, which was bought by overseers at prices from 5d. to 7d. a yard, significantly less than the 10d. a yard average price paid for the various linens bought to make their shirts and shifts.[19] Nevertheless, the paupers' shirts and shifts were hardly luxurious. The six parishes did not all buy the same fabrics for shirting and shifting. There was some geographical variation by type, although all were flaxen or hempen cloths. Spofforth supplied hemp cloth and linen cloth, Ware brown linen cloth, Theydon Garnon brown linen, canvas and dowlas, Holne canvas, dowlas and especially osnaburg. Osnaburg was the standard wear for plantation slaves in the American colonies, in some of them imposed on slaves by law.[20] Despite the different names,

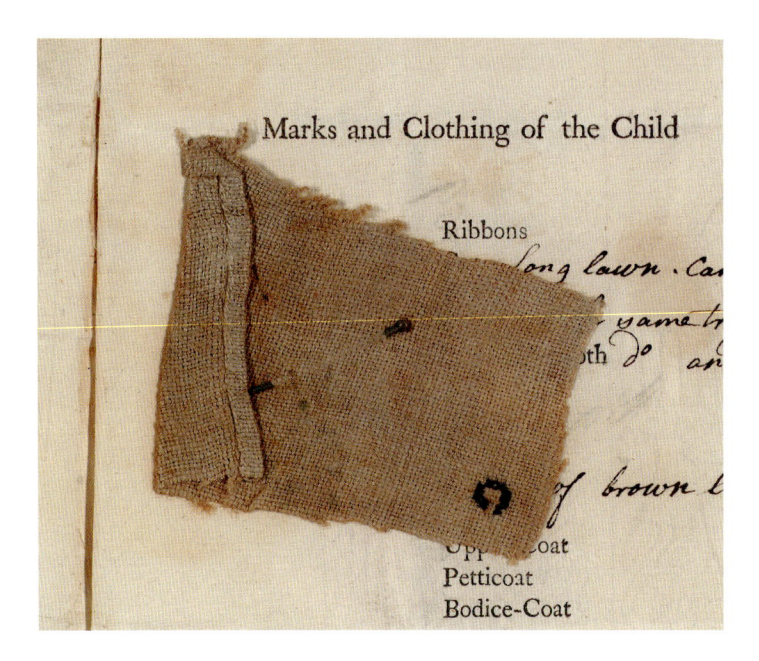

101 'Brown linen', 1759, brown linen with embroidered initial letter, London Metropolitan Archives, A/FH/A/9/ 1/145, Foundling no. 13298.

these fabrics had much in common. They were all coarse, plain and cheap, costing less than 13d. a yard. Often they were unbleached and brown or brownish in colour, sometimes described as 'brown cloth for a shirt', in contrast to the more costly white which was so prized in linens as a sign of cleanliness (fig. 101).[21] Stephen Hudson's shop on the Pennine moors at Fewston sold linens in shirt and shift lengths to his clientele of poor farmers and tradespeople at similar prices, although mainly at 12d. a yard or more.[22] The Latham family also bought linens in shirt and shift lengths at these prices, but it is difficult to judge the overall quality of their wearing linen, because so much of it was manufactured by the family leaving us with no record of its retail value.[23] Strikingly, however, the overseers bought virtually none of the better quality linens at between 14d. and 24d. a yard acquired by Hudson's customers and by the Lathams, even in the early years of their marriage when they were poorest.[24] Sometimes described in both the Latham and the Hudson accounts as 'fine linen' and probably white, these fabrics were acquired in smaller quantities than the cheaper, coarser linens, but purchases included both shirt and shift lengths, and shorter lengths 'for borders'. The holland smocks for which working women competed in races at fairs and other festivities were all the more desirable because they were made from these finer linens.

If we turn to the prices paid for woollens and woollen mixes for outer garments, a similar pattern emerges. The prices paid by overseers for many of these fabrics, including those they bought most frequently, were close to the prices paid by Stephen

Hudson's customers and the Lathams for their coarser cloth. Overseers bought linsey-woolsey for workaday gowns and aprons at 9d. to 16d. yard. The Lathams used linsey-woolsey too, but the majority of it was woven from yarn of their own spinning. However, they also bought some linsey-woolsey to make petticoats at 12d. to 14d. a yard, while Stephen Hudson sold it at 14d. to 19d. a yard. Prices paid by overseers for flannel, serge and shalloon also resembled those in the Latham and Hudson accounts. In buying serge for the stuff gowns that defined 'the parish girl' for the novelist Charlotte Smith, overseers paid 13d. to 16d. a yard.[25] The women of the Latham family paid only a little more for their stuff gowns, which were mostly made of camblet bought at 14d. to 19d. a yard, and the family paid as little as 11¼d. a yard for a worsted gown for the youngest daughter Martha when she was seventeen. But at the same time there were marked differences between the prices paid for some woollens bought by the overseers, especially those for men and boys' outer garments, and those paid by Hudson's customers and the Lathams. Overseers never paid more than 28d. a yard for woollen cloth like kersey for men or boys' garments, and generally paid considerably less, whereas Hudson sold kersey at 36d. a yard and the woollen cloth bought for coats and britches for Dicy, the son of the Latham family, cost between 25d. and 40d. a yard.

In addition, there were several kinds of fabric bought by the Lathams and Hudson's customers that the overseers did not provide at all. The overseers purchased none of the colourful printed cottons, damasks or silk camblets bought by the Lathams for their more expensive gowns and sold by Hudson at prices between 24d. to 48d. a yard for cotton prints, 35d. a yard for damask and 50d. a yard for silk. Nor did they provide any of the short lengths of silk ribbon that added cheap, colourful decoration to the dress of working women, sold by Hudson at 3d. to 9d. a yard to customers like Isabel Gill, clogger and John Wigglesworth, mason. Moreover, the range of cloth provided by each parish was very limited. Although the six sets of overseers accounts from 1730 to 1759 include between them 26 different types of cloth, as many as were bought by the Latham family and nearly as many as the 31 sold by Stephen Hudson, the range of cloth supplied by individual parishes was much narrower. At Leafield three types of fabric are named in the overseers accounts, at Spofforth four, at Ware four, at Thornhill seven, at Holne 12, and at Theydon Garnon 14. In any one parish, therefore, the clothes supplied by the overseers were made from a restricted range of coarse fabrics, predominantly off-white, brown or blue in colour, resulting in a considerable degree of uniformity (figs 102, 103).

The same pattern emerges if we turn our attention from fabrics to garments. A comparison of four items of clothing easily identified in the accounts between 1730 and 1759 – handkerchiefs, aprons, hats and gowns – reveals an overlap towards the bottom of the price range between the acquisitions made by the overseers, the Lathams and Hudson's customers in each case (table 28). These were all items that played an important decorative role in the eighteenth-century wardrobe, not just for women but in the case of hats and handkerchiefs also for men. The overseers never supplied them in anything other than cheap, coarse and minimally decorative varieties – working aprons

102 'Corse blue Linsey', 1759, coarse linsey-woolsey woven in shades of blue, London Metropolitan Archives, A/FH/A/9/1/132, Foundling no. 11772.

103 'Brown and white stript lincey', 1759, linsey-woolsey woven in brown and white stripes, London Metropolitan Archives, A/FH/A/9/1/159, Foundling no. 14464.

in the cheapest check, women's straw hats without ribbons, everyday gowns in linsey-woolsey, serge and drugget (fig. 104). The Lathams and Hudson's customers bought the same items in similar materials and at similar prices, although at eight or nine yards, the adult gown lengths bought in the cheapest materials by the Lathams tended to be longer than those provided by the overseers at six or seven yards. However, in contrast to the overseers, they also bought more expensive, decorative versions of each of these items, such as the new Holland check apron costing 36d. bought for Nany Latham in 1735 at the trough of the family's poverty cycle, the red-and-white linen handkerchiefs retailed by Stephen Hudson at 27d., and the costly decorative silk hats and flowered damask gowns acquired by the female members of the Latham family.

The range of clothes supplied by overseers was, moreover, a narrow one. If we examine the four parishes with sufficiently detailed information (table 29), we discover that the numbers of aprons and handkerchiefs provided was tiny, as were those of cloaks, petticoats, stays and other crucial elements of the eighteenth-century wardrobe. Overseers were hardly more generous with gowns, hats, waistcoats and caps. Stockings, breeches and coats were given rather more frequently, but it was footwear, shirts and shifts that together accounted for more than half the items of clothing supplied in each of the four parishes where it is possible to generate a count. Yet within this broad common pattern, the four parishes varied in their propensity to supply different kinds

104 'Check', 1759, linen or cotton woven in a blue-and-white check pattern, London Metropolitan Archives, A/FH/A/9/1/147, Foundling no. 13169.

of clothing. Footwear accounted for only 12 percent of the 73 items of clothing supplied at Spofforth in Yorkshire (the only parish to provide the cheaper clogs), but 24 percent at nearby Thornhill.

Nevertheless, footwear and undergarments comprised a majority of the clothes supplied in all these parishes, suggesting that across the country the attitudes of overseers, parish vestries and applicants for relief were shaped by the same assumptions about clothing priorities that emerge in the labourers' budgets collected by the Reverend David Davies half a century later. Footwear and undergarments were the items that even the poorest labouring families struggled to acquire regularly in order to sustain a minimally decent wardrobe, along with stockings. Paupers were often expected to knit stockings from yarn provided by the overseer or spun by themselves, and they are consequently not always identifiable in the accounts. For English adults to go barefoot was a sign of utter degradation. A change of undergarments was essential if they were to be washed regularly, which was crucial to eighteenth-century notions of cleanliness. Shoes and clogs, moreover, were a practical necessity for any form of outdoor work. Shoes were expensive. The prices parishes paid for an adult pair of shoes ranged from four shillings in the 1730s to as much as eight shillings by the 1790s. Nevertheless, from the overseers' point of view sturdy footwear represented a form of capital investment, calculated to get the poor into work and reduce their reliance on parish relief. Outer garments, by contrast, were often acquired by the labouring poor intermittently and opportunistically, especially by poor working families with small children, deep in the first trough of the family poverty cycle, like Davies's most impoverished labouring families in the late 1780s, or the Lathams in the early, financially pinched years of their marriage in the 1730s. The pattern of clothing provision that emerges in the overseers' accounts between 1730 and 1759, dominated as it is by what Beverly Lemire terms 'the perceived basics', is entirely consistent with the behaviour of these hard-pressed working families, though it offers few clues as to how the paupers contrived to supply themselves with outer garments.

The character of the clothes provided in these parishes did not change markedly in the final decades of the eighteenth century, despite claims by some historians that what had previously been relatively generous poor relief policies began to be abandoned after 1780.[26] Indeed the range of fabrics supplied by the same six parishes between 1770 and 1799 was wider than in the earlier period and the numbers of different fabrics supplied by each parish expanded (table 30).[27] Despite this expansion, as in the earlier period, the linens and woollens supplied to paupers for clothing were consistent in price with the cheapest, coarsest fabrics acquired by non-paupers for everyday wear. Comparison of parish provision from 1770 to 1799 with the fabrics bought between 1768 and the 1793 by the young, unmarried female servants of Robert Heaton, the Yorkshire worsted manufacturer, who spent their wages on a wide range of clothes as we shall see in Chapter 17, reveals that the parishes did not supply the more expensive, decorative fabrics bought by the servants, such as muslins, lawns, ribbons, printed cottons and silks. If we compare parish purchases with the servants' purchases of four key items of eighteenth-century clothing – handkerchiefs, aprons, hats and adult gowns – we discover that again parishes supplied only cheap, coarse and largely undecorated varieties (table 31). In particular, paupers were never given the expensive gowns, aprons and hats that were regularly bought by the servants. And between 1770 and 1799, as between 1730 and 1759, it was undergarments and footwear that accounted for the majority of the clothing supplied by the parishes (table 32), in contrast to the servants, whose expenditure was weighted towards outer garments and decorative accessories.

Throughout the period from the 1730s to the 1790s, therefore, the mix of clothes supplied by the overseers of the six parishes resembled the acquisitions of poorer working families at the trough of the family poverty cycle.[28] We should bear in mind, however, that the demographic profile of those who received parish clothing was different from the majority of those families. It was dominated by the old, by women and by children. Men of working age were conspicuous by their absence. Care is necessary, therefore, in establishing an appropriate comparison against which to judge the clothes given to paupers. The elderly and mothers of young children, who made up the bulk of the adults on relief, were not the sections of the broader plebeian population from which the sartorially adventurous were predominantly drawn. The 'best' clothes bought by the teenage daughters of the Latham family, or by the young women who worked as servants for Robert Heaton, do not necessarily provide the most appropriate yardstick. Nevertheless, the fact that the purchases of these young working women also embraced mundane, workaday items enables us to establish just how narrow Poor Law provision was in terms of price, range and quality.

Involuntary Consumption? The Parish Poor

The consequences of the distinctive demographic profile of parish paupers for clothing can be observed in vestry minutes from Wimbledon, Surrey in the late 1740s, where it is possible to distinguish between the recipients of clothing by age (table 33).[29] Wimbledon was a prosperous agricultural village near London and a suburban residence for wealthy people from the metropolis. Before 1752 it did not have a workhouse. Eighty-five percent of the 382 items of clothing supplied by the parish in the three years from 1745 to 1748 went to 23 children. The other fifteen percent went to ten adults. Five of the adults were women, who all received regular pensions. They included four widows, but only one was a mother of a child who was clothed by the parish. Of the five men, only two received pensions and none was father to a child clothed by the parish.

The children received on average nearly five items of clothing per year, while the adults received less than two. The children were far more likely than the adults to receive outer garments such as gowns or coats, as well as accessories like handkerchiefs. Undergarments and shoes accounted for only 40 percent of the items supplied to children, but 60 percent of those supplied to adults. The adults, in other words, received at best a skimped version of the adult clothing allocation in David Davies's budgets – regular shirts or shifts and shoes, but other garments very intermittently. The children, on the other hand, were treated more generously than the children in Davies's labouring families, although like them they did occasionally have to accept recycled items. This liberality towards children was rooted in a conscious parish policy. In 1746 the vestry noted that widow Lancaster's three children were to be clothed 'according to the rest of the parish children'.[30] The rate at which the Wimbledon vestry supplied clothing for these children arose partly from the need for children to have clothes replaced as they grew, but also from the vestry's anxiety to get the children apprenticed and off the parish rates. The ages of the children allocated clothes by the vestry between 1745 and 1748 ranged from five to fourteen, but the bulk of the clothes went to those aged from ten to twelve. This was just before the age at which the vestry insisted parish children went to apprenticeship or service, whether or not their parents approved. In March 1748, for example, five widows were denied pensions for their children until they explained 'why they refused to let their children go out apprentice when masters and mistresses ready got for them'. All the children were aged between twelve and fourteen.

Prospective masters and mistresses required parishes to send new apprentices decently clothed. In 1755 a woman living in Clare Market in Westminster was prepared to take into service Elizabeth English, 'a bastard child' from Wimbledon, 'provided the parish will allow her clothes in a decent Christian-like manner'. It was when preparing pauper children for apprenticeship and service that parishes were consequently at their most generous in having them 'clothed out' with full sets of clothing, which might include types of cloth and accessories that were not supplied to paupers under other circumstances. This represented a good investment, because thereafter the master or mistress was responsible for clothing the child. Ann Lewer, one of the five

105 'Red Lincey overcast with Purpel Worsted', 1759, red linsey-woolsey with purple worsted stitching, London Metropolitan Archives, A/FH/A/9/ 1/151, Foundling no. 13624. If the linsey-woolsey given to poor women by the overseers of the poor in Cheshunt, Hertfordshire, for cloaks in the winter of 1783 was the customary red colour, it probably resembled this fabric.

widows' children Wimbledon wanted to have apprenticed in 1748, was subsequently 'allowed 2 shifts, 2 aprons, 2 caps, and a petticoat if [her mother] consent that her daughter be bound out apprentice for 1 year if she likes after a month's trial, but if she will not consent to be bound she is not to be allowed anything'; while £2 was spent on clothing John Brown when he was apprenticed to a London barber and perukemaker in 1755.[31] Providing new sets of clothes to pauper children on their apprenticeship was familiar elsewhere. At Eaton Socon in Bedfordshire in the 1720s boys were often given two sets of clothes on being apprenticed: 'The parish is to double suit him out with apparel both for Holyday and working day.'[32] At Holne in Devon Richard Stranger was paid one pound 'toward cloathing of Anne Beard' when she was bound apprentice to him in 1747. At Spofforth in Yorkshire in 1790 £1 3s. 3d. was spent on clothing for Frank Todd when he was apprenticed, plus 3s. 8d. for making the clothes and an additional 1s. 10d. for stockings, ribbon and buckles. Buckles and ribbons were familiar enhancements to working people's dress, but hardly ever figure in eighteenth-century overseers' accounts.

The pattern of expenditure observed at Wimbledon and elsewhere suggests, therefore, that any liberality in the provision of clothing under the eighteenth-century Poor Law was focused principally on children, often driven by ratepayers' desire to place them in employment. It makes it hard to believe that either the standard to which the adult poor were clothed by their parishes or the rate at which the parishes clothed them did more than barely match, let alone surpass, most non-pauper adults. This is not to suggest that the clothing parishes provided to the adult poor was deliberately inadequate. Policies varied and parishes could often act thoughtfully. Linsey-woolsey to make cloaks was given to 15 women at Cheshunt in Hertfordshire in the course of November and December 1783, at the onset of winter (fig. 105).[33] The overseers' accounts at Thornhill in Yorkshire and Holne in Devon show that widows, in particular, were provided with gowns and petticoats regularly, though not annually. The entries for these items in the accounts are often bunched chronologically in a manner that suggests a strong, and perhaps competitive sense of shared entitlement among the women, to which the overseers responded.

Nevertheless, the clothing schedules for workhouse inmates that are sometimes quoted as evidence of good pauper clothing standards need to be treated with caution. The vestry at Much Hadham in Hertfordshire ordered in 1794 that the inmates of the parish workhouse should have 'good and sufficient clothing', specifying for each woman '2 pair of stockings, 1 pair of shoes, 2 flannel coats, 1 grogram coat, 1 grogram gown, 3 shifts, 2 housewife aprons, 1 pair of stays, 3 neck handkerchiefs. For the men, 1 suit of cloaths, 3 shirts, 1 pair of shoes, 2 pair of stockings, 1 hatt'.[34] We are not told, however, how often any of these items was to be replaced, or whether these rules were consistently enforced. In 1766 at Wethersfield in Essex, only 20 miles from Much Hadham, the vestry compiled 'An Account of the Condition of the Poor in the Workhouse in respect to Clothing'. The number of clothes provided per inmate fell well short of the ideal specified thirty years later at Much Hadham. No items of clothing were available in sufficient numbers to allow three per pauper. The only items available in sufficient quantity to allow two per pauper were shirts and stockings for males, and shifts, petticoats, aprons and caps for females. There was one handkerchief for each female pauper and none for males. The condition of the clothes, moreover, was poor. Out of 249 pieces of clothing for the 20 people in the workhouse (seven male, 13 female), 131 were described as indifferent, bad or old, while only 37 were middling, good or new.[35] Similarly, the surveys of parish workhouses in Bedfordshire undertaken by the magistrate and reformer Samuel Whitbread at the start of the 1800s reveal their inmates to have been frequently in want of clothing.[36]

The limitations of Poor Law provision are confirmed by sporadic evidence about the clothes owned by those who sought relief. We have already seen in Chapter 3 that a significant proportion of the men and women who entered the St Marylebone workhouse in London in 1770 arrived with wigs or stays. Outside London, the pledge book of the York pawnbroker George Fettes shows that among clients who sought parish assistance were a number, including mothers of young children, who had previously owned a range of clothes more extensive than those customarily provided by parishes. Take, for example, Mary Prince, relieved by her York parish with a shilling a week from November 1778, who in the course of the previous year and a half had repeatedly pawned her own clothes and her children's. The adult clothes Mary Prince pawned were hardly luxurious, but they included a cotton gown, a black silk bonnet and hat, plated buckles, two pairs of ruffles and a red cloak, alongside less desirable items like an old coat, a stuff gown and a dirty shift.[37] This is not to suggest that everyone who sought parish relief was accustomed to a higher standard than was available on the parish. Rags were common enough among those who entered the St Marylebone workhouse. Fettes' clients included people like Jane Turpin, who appears to have had only a man's coat and a stuff gown to pawn in the months before she went to her parish for relief. But those who had previously enjoyed a wider range of clothing, not to mention those who aspired to at least some of the petty clothing luxuries that enlivened the wardrobes of many poorer people, had ample reason to disagree with those historians who consider parishes to have clothed paupers well, or even fairly fashionably.

It was neither conservatism nor localism that persuaded parishes to restrict the quality and range of clothing in this way. Parishes were often innovative as consumers, but only within their accustomed limits as to price and quality. At Holne in Devon towards the end of the eighteenth century, canvas increasingly replaced osnaburg for shifts and shirts. Canvas was very slightly cheaper in the 1790s, but it is not clear that price was the decisive consideration here, because at the same time tammy replaced serge for gowns, despite being slightly more expensive. Innovation can also be seen in the types of garments supplied. None of the six parishes provided bedgowns before 1760, but at least three of them did after 1770, reflecting the increasingly popularity of the bedgown among the population at large. Similarly, at least four of the six parishes began to supply men's jackets after 1770, in the case of Theydon Garnon probably ready-made. Nor did the restricted range and quality of clothing reflect an overriding preference for locally made textiles. Only one of the six parishes had cloth woven locally: linsey-woolsey at Thornhill. The overwhelming majority of the textiles supplied to paupers consisted of fabrics manufactured at a distance, sometimes possibly overseas, and sourced commercially through local retailers.[38]

On the rare occasions we find parishes explicitly laying down policy for the quality of the clothing to be supplied to their poor, two priorities emerge which, though not contradictory, were potentially in tension. The first was economy. At Witham in Essex in 1726 it was ordered 'that the poor be clothed in such stuff as is the cheapest and most lasting' and 'that the officers do always seek for such cloth or stuff at the cheapest rate'. At St Austell in Cornwall a parish resolution in 1747 stated 'the Price of Linnen for the poor is not to exceed 8½d. per yard' and 'the price of wollen cloth comonly called Cape cloth, for the Poor, is not to exceed 1s. 6d. per yd'. At Leeds workhouse in Yorkshire in 1764 it was ordered 'that Mr William Cowell buy a low priced broad cloth for the use of the poor in the house'.[39] The second was decency. Clothing paupers decently was an obligation of Christian charity, impelled by the scriptural injunction to clothe the poor and naked, which also reflected on the reputation of the parish. At Finchley near London in 1769 the vestry required the master of the workhouse to 'keep and find the poor in clothing and diet such as is good, wholesome and in every respect fitting for Christians'.[40] Witham combined these two priorities in 1726 by distinguishing between common days and holy days: 'the women's aprons for common days be made of the coarse sixpenny cloth and that each of them have one made of blue for Sundays'.[41] These priorities were made explicit infrequently, but the evidence of overseers' spending suggests they shaped the policies pursued in most parishes. As we have seen, parishes across the country made genuine efforts to address the clothing needs of their poor, but they did so by means of a narrow range of basic clothes made from cheap, coarse fabrics in drab colours, according to a standard set by the most hard-pressed among working families.

Essentially the same priorities were expressed by those who set up the charitable clothing clubs of the early nineteenth century. They, like the eighteenth-century parish overseers, supplied a limited range of cheap, coarse fabrics and basic items of clothing.[42] As far as it is possible to judge, so too did most of the earlier endowed parish charities and those private individuals who provided charity in the form of clothes. Intentions were not necessarily uniform across place, time or institution. In some cases the chief priority was keeping down costs, in others regulating appearance, in others ensuring that the poor had clothes that were wholesome, durable and practical. Yet irrespective of what was intended, the effect of imposing what amounted to local sumptuary regulations on involuntary consumers was to deny the poor who sought relief or charity what Sarah Trimmer belittled in 1787 as 'the gauze caps, and other trumpery ornaments so injudiciously purchased by poor people'.[43] The judgement Isaac Watts offered in 1728 on the clothes given to Charity School children could have been applied to most of the clothing provided as parish relief or as charity: 'The clothes which are bestowed on them once in a year or two are of the coarsest kind, and of the plainest form, and thus they are sufficiently distinguished from children of the better rank . . . there is no ground for charity children to be proud of their raiment when it is but a sort of livery.'[44]

For those who wore parish clothing, parliament added an additional semiotic twist to distinguish them from non-paupers and deny them grounds for pride. An Act of Parliament of 1697, which remained in force until 1810, required those who were on the parish rates and received relief, along with their wives and their children, to be badged. Specifically, the act obliged them to wear a badge or mark 'upon the shoulder of the right sleeve of the uppermost garment of every such person, in an open and visible manner . . . a large Roman P, together with the first letter of the name of the parish or place whereof such poor person is an inhabitant, cut either in red or blew cloth' (fig. 100).[45] The preamble to the badging clause in the Act stated that its purpose was to discourage those who could work from claiming the funds intended for the relief of the impotent poor, who, it was assumed, were in no position to complain. Throughout the eighteenth century patrician commentators continued to regard badging as a tool to stigmatise, humiliate and deter the undeserving poor, but they feared it was a tool parishes were reluctant to use.[46] Sidney and Beatrice Webb in their classic study of the old Poor Law agreed, arguing that badging was enforced neither very extensively nor for very long after the legislation was enacted.[47] The debates that led up to the law's repeal in 1810, which stressed the vulnerability to vexatious prosecutions of the many overseers who were failing to badge a rapidly growing number of paupers, do suggest that it was increasingly ignored by the end of the eighteenth century.[48] Nevertheless, recent research indicates that for the first two-thirds of the century it was widely enforced, although it remains difficult to establish just how consistently.[49] In some parishes it fell into disuse, but was then revived. Sir Frederick Eden reported that as late as 1794 badging was resumed at Newark in Nottinghamshire due to the increase in the numbers of the poor, despite having been laid aside a few years previously.[50] The records of three of the six parishes examined in detail for this chapter – Spofforth, Theydon Garnon and Thornhill – provide evidence of badging in the years between 1720 and 1780. At Thornhill, however, the Act was interpreted as applying only to those who received a regular pension, not to those non-pensioners who received occasional items of clothing. Thornhill was not alone in interpreting the Act in this way and, if this interpretation was common, it must have significantly limited the proportion of adults receiving parish clothing who were actually required to wear badges.[51]

Nevertheless, for those who were obliged to wear them, and they were many, these were literally badges of dependency. Of course, in a social hierarchy like that which characterised eighteenth-century England, dependency was not necessarily synonymous with humiliation. Liveries were worn with pride; badges could be sought-after signs of patronage, belonging and entitlement, whether displayed by illustrious Knights of the Garter, or working London watermen, porters and drovers (fig. 106). Con-

106   *A Scene at Vauxhall Stairs*, 1779, mezzotint, Lewis Walpole Library, Farmington, Conn., 779.01.01 A2 S24. A Thames waterman holds a boat at Vauxhall Stairs. The waterman's badge, showing an anchor, is prominently displayed on his upper right arm.

sequently, as Steve Hindle has argued, what the badge meant to paupers could vary.[52] The deterrent, stigmatising purpose of those who framed the legislation was not lost on many of those who were required to display the badge. Clothing had considerable power to play on feelings both of pride and shame. 'PRIDE', a report on the workhouse at Romford in Essex declared in 1724, 'tho' it does ill become poor Folks, won't suffer some to wear the Badge'.[53] There are numerous examples, from parishes across England, of paupers spurning the badge as a humiliation, even if they had to suffer the loss of their pension as a result. So annoyed was the vestry at Monken Hadley in Middlesex in 1799 at paupers ignoring an order to wear the badge when out of the workhouse, that it required them all in future to wear yellow stockings as well as the badge. In addition, the vestry ordered that the women 'shall all be clothed in the same sort of Garment of the coulour of Blue, and that some regular Uniform shall in like manner be established for the Men and Boys'.[54] This marks an early stage in a new policy of clothing paupers in a 'parish uniform' that gathered pace around the time badging was abolished.[55]

For other paupers, however, the badge could represent a kind of livery, an acknowledgement of their dependence on the parish and their entitlement to its support, albeit as humble subordinates. It was already common for endowed charities to supply outer garments in a colour that identified the charity, like Richard Fountaine's blue and green coats at Linton in Yorkshire. Sometimes they even bore a badge, like the gowns supplied under John Pemel's will at Stepney, in east London, which carried the badge of the London Draper's Company.[56] As with charity clothes, the parish badge marked its wearer as deserving. It could even be employed as a weapon in negotiations over entitlement to relief with overseers, vestries and magistrates. Some paupers, therefore, may have worn a cheap stuff parish gown in brown or blue gratefully, as a kind of parochial livery, even when it bore a red 'P' and the first letter of the name of their parish on its right shoulder. But if the badge represented for some their parish's acknowledgement of its responsibilities, it was an acknowledgement of the most grudging sort. We discover just how grudging when we observe a parish supplying a true livery. In 1750 the vestry at Wimbledon clothed Richard Lowick as its beadle. He was presented with 'a surtout coat, blue turned up with red, the cape and sleeves trimmed round with silver lace, a silver-laced hat, and a pair of buckskin breeches', as well as stockings and a pair of new shoes, at a total cost of over £4, which were replaced every couple of years. There was a stark contrast between Wimbledon's beadle, official representative of the parish, resplendent in a livery that proclaimed its standing and the liberality of its vestrymen, and the clothes Wimbledon provided its adult paupers, who received exactly the kinds of cheap, coarse, drab clothing supplied by other parishes across the country. It shows just how restricted were any notions of reputation or generosity invested in pauper clothing by even a prosperous, well-organised parish. If Wimbledon's adult paupers were 'well dressed' by their parish, it was in waistcoats made from flannel bought for not much more than shilling a yard and the occasional pair of five-shilling canvas breeches.[57]

Wimbledon resembled most eighteenth-century parishes in supplying its paupers, especially its adult paupers, with a narrow range of fabrics and clothes. The clothing provided by parishes was consistently cheap, coarse and undecorated. Paupers received the minimum of sartorial sufficiency, barely matching, let alone surpassing, non-pauper adults at the lowest point of the family poverty cycle. When the range of petty clothing luxuries to which the working poor could realistically aspire is taken into account, it is hard to believe that parishes dressed their paupers well, let alone fashionably.

107 Henry Walton, *Plucking the Turkey*, 1770s, oil on canvas, Tate Gallery, London, N02870. A young woman at work, probably a servant, is dressed in the kind of clothes acquired by Robert Heaton's servants. She wears a printed bedgown with white spots on a lilac ground, a green petticoat, a blue check apron and a laced cap with a pink silk ribbon.

17
Involuntary Consumption? Servants

IN THE EYES OF THE EIGHTEENTH-CENTURY ELITE, no group of working people was more guilty of sartorial extravagance than domestic servants. Frequently rehearsed in pamphlets, magazines, novels, plays and caricatures, the case against servants' pursuit of fashionable and luxurious dress was constructed from three key elements.[1] First, servants were attacked for dressing above their station, so that it was 'a hard matter now to know the Mistress from the Maid by their Dress'.[2] In so doing, servants were blurring what the employing classes regarded as the appropriate hierarchical distinctions in a society where dress was expected to indicate rank. Second, it was argued that servants' determination to acquire expensive, fashionable clothes prevented them from saving, encouraged them to seek increases in wages and inculcated improvident habits which led them into dishonesty and vice. The third argument against servants' indulgence in fashionable dress was that it encouraged a process of emulative competition. Such competition was for many eighteenth-century commentators the force which propelled the spread through the social hierarchy and across the country of luxury, itself regarded as the chief menace to individual morality, national advancement and the balance of trade. Servants, because they were intimate with the fashions adopted by their employers, but socially part of the lower orders, were natural intermediaries. The servants of the great, it was argued, were copied by those of the middling ranks, and likewise London servants by their provincial cousins. The labouring poor copied servants of every kind, of whom it was said 'by their example they spread the contagion of luxury and idleness among the lower ranks of people'.[3] Nor was the sartorial competition stimulated by servants' extravagance in dress believed to be confined to their equals and inferiors. Servants' behaviour was held to contribute to an intensification of rivalry in appearance at every social level.[4]

Historians have generally endorsed these eighteenth-century opinions.[5] Some have gone further and concluded that servants played a decisive role in expanding the markets for fashionable goods, creating a late eighteenth-century consumer boom, and, as a consequence, stimulating the Industrial Revolution.[6] But others, while accepting that servants might dress in clothes resembling those of their masters and mistresses, have argued it does not necessarily follow that servants contributed directly to an expansion of the overall demand for clothing.

Domestic servants were not in a position to purchase newly made clothes in imitation of their employers. On their incomes, they could not possibly contribute to any growth in the effective demand for new fashion goods. Emulative spending emanating from below stairs appears highly improbable. Those clothes worn by servants which echoed upper-class rather than working-class tastes came to them, for the most part, directly from their employers, unmediated by markets of any kind.[7]

In other words, servants were not real waged workers who could choose to emulate their employers and thereby actively contribute to the expansion of a new mass market for fashionable clothes. Their consumption of clothing was involuntary. Because they subsisted on a combination of meagre wages, tips and goods in kind, their access to the expensive fashions worn by their masters and mistresses was only made possible by means of hand-me-downs from their employers. Hand-me-downs did not expand the market for new products. Even when servants purchased their own clothes, the purchase was often made by or under the direction of their employer, with little or no exercise of personal choice. Emulation did not necessarily come into play at all. Eighteenth-century commentators insisted employers at many social levels encouraged their servants to wear finery, or at least dress well, because it reflected favourably on their own status. They claimed that clothing purchased by servants was scrutinised to ensure it was in good taste; gifts of clothes were made on condition that they were worn by the servant herself.[8] These are important issues for plebeian dress in the eighteenth century. If servants were plebeian leaders of fashion, was it because they were precocious consumers, or merely because they were walking displays of their masters' and mistresses' taste? Did they have the means and the desire to exercise choice, or were they involuntary consumers of clothing chosen for them by others?

Service of one kind or another was the experience of vast numbers, perhaps a majority, of adolescents and young adults in early-modern England. It was 'a stage in the progression from child living with parents to married adult living with spouse and children'.[9] A status as much as an occupation, service could involve a variety of different kinds of work. In practice, for most male servants, but also for some female, it was agricultural rather than domestic labour that was demanded. But when eighteenth-century commentators bewailed the excesses of servants' clothing, it was not, of course, to the multitudes of predominantly male servants in husbandry that they referred. Their concern was primarily with female household servants, and to a lesser extent with their much less numerous male colleagues.

Vast numbers of young women entered domestic service. Patrick Colquhoun's 1806 estimate of 910,000 domestic servants in England and Wales, of whom 800,000 were women, in a total population of approximately nine million, may have been exaggerated, but it is suggestive both of the enormous numbers involved and the sex ratio.[10] A large majority of these women were under 25 years of age; in general female domestic servants were expected to be young and unmarried. Most female domestic servants lived in the provinces. Nevertheless, the proportion of the female population represented by household servants was higher in London than in either provincial towns or the countryside.[11] In the metropolis, domestic service was the largest single paid occupation for women both at the start of the eighteenth century and after its close, despite being so heavily concentrated among the young. It probably accounted for between 25 and 40 percent of women employed.[12] In numerical terms, therefore, female domestic servants formed a huge market for clothes, but their capacity to acquire them depended crucially on their incomes, on the kind of control exercised over their consumption and their appearance by their employers, and on the extent to which they treated their usually temporary period in service as a chance to acquire material possessions rather than an opportunity to accumulate savings before marriage.

Female household servants certainly enjoyed a money income. Like young men and women in agricultural service, the usual practice was for them to receive an annual money wage in addition to bed and board. In principle the annual wage was paid at the end of their year's hiring, which could amount to the imposition of compulsory saving on the servant. In practice servants were usually allowed to receive part payments during the course of their hiring, with the balance being settled at the end of the year.[13] The level of wages depended on geography, age, experience and the place of the recipient in the servant hierarchy. Experienced ladies' maids in the houses of the nobility could enjoy annual wages of £10 early in the century and over £15 at its close, but their numbers were small. Maids-of-all-work in less exalted households, who comprised the majority of domestic servants, earned considerably less. In the provinces many of them could expect well under £4 per annum for much of the century, although the wages of lesser female servants appear to have risen, at least in the households of the wealthy, by its end.[14]

Male domestic servants, although on average they received considerably more in money wages than female domestics, were in addition normally provided with a livery on an annual basis. Female servants might receive gifts of clothing from their employers, but in the main these were irregular perquisites, not a formal part of the hiring agreement like male liveries.[15] The normal expectation was that female domestics should acquire their own clothes. Samuel Johnson complained that 'women servants, though obliged to be at the expense of purchasing their own clothes, have much lower wages than men servants, to whom a great proportion of that article is furnished, and when in fact our female house servants work much harder than the male'.[16] The absence of formal livery for female domestics may indicate that they had more sartorial freedom of choice than their male equivalents. Certainly commentators like Daniel Defoe argued in favour of livery for female servants as a means of constraining the extravagance of their dress.[17] But it remains difficult to establish the extent of their freedom of choice without some evidence regarding what clothes the generality of servants could afford to buy out of their meagre money wages (if they spent them at all), how much choice they were allowed in their purchasing decisions, and how much they were forced to rely on their employers' gifts and cast-offs.

This chapter addresses these issues by examining the clothing acquired by the servants of Robert Heaton, a Yorkshire worsted manufacturer and small landowner in the late eighteenth century. Many employers kept a regular record of the money wage they paid their servants, but Heaton was exceptional in systematically recording the goods on which his servants spent their wages.[18] Robert Heaton (1726–1794) lived high in the Yorkshire Pennines near Haworth. His was a medium-sized worsted business with annual sales in the region of £1,000 for most of the 1770s and 1780s.[19] The ambiguity of his social position is suggested by the fact that he was variously styled woolcomber, yeoman and gentleman. His office-holding was confined mainly to his local township.

Heaton was an enthusiastic if somewhat disorganised record keeper. But did his practice of itemising his servants' purchases indicate that he was controlling what they bought? The internal evidence of the accounts suggests this is unlikely. Heaton sometimes headed his lists of each servant's spending with 'paid her in things as follows' or more often 'paid her as follows', indicating he usually paid on his servant's behalf for the items listed. Occasionally he paid cash direct to a named supplier. For instance, in 1778 he noted paying six shillings and sixpence 'cash to Scotchman' for Sarah Earnshaw. On other occasions the servants were given money to make a purchase themselves, as when in 1771 Susanna Robinson was given two shillings and sixpence in 'cash to pay for Bristol stone buttons'. However, the normal arrangement appears to have been for the servants to make their purchases on credit from local retailers and have the transaction charged to Heaton's account.

This arrangement is often found in eighteenth-century retailers' account books and must have been one that was mutually advantageous to master and servant in an economy where cash was in short supply and country shopkeepers had little option but to extend credit to their customers. Heaton was undoubtedly more creditworthy and his credit more extensive than that of his young servants, and they benefited accordingly by being able to make their purchases on his account. Nevertheless, this arrangement does not necessarily mean that Heaton dictated their choices. So varied and inconsistent are the servants' purchases he recorded that it is extremely unlikely he controlled their spending very closely at all. At most, he may have placed some broad limits on their use of their wages. If so, they were not very strict ones. Not only did he advance his servants cash to spend enjoying themselves at Haworth fair and the Bishop Blaize festivities, but he allowed many of them to spend more on credit in the course of their year's hiring than they were due to earn that year. His detailed accounting probably had two main purposes. First, to keep a record of how much he owed local retailers on his servants' behalf. Second, to provide a memorandum of the balance of his account with his servants. It was often only long after they had left his service that he arrived at an eventual settlement with them.

From Heaton's accounts of his servants' spending it appears that for most of the period 1768 to 1793 he employed two live-in female servants, although there are some years in the 1770s when he may have employed three. The precise character of their work is not revealed by the accounts. It is likely that, as with many female servants in smaller households, they were maids-of-all-work. A good part of their time was probably spent on household tasks, although there is evidence that they were also expected to undertake some textile work. There is no indication that Heaton usually expected to employ a household manservant.[20] We do not know the female servants' ages, but, like the generality of live-in servants, they were probably young and drawn from among the local labouring poor. Turnover of servants was high. Only seven out of the 18 women whose precise length of service is recorded served for more than a year, and only three for more than three years. This was the norm in the area and certainly does not indicate that Heaton was a harsh employer.[21] Often servants left in the middle of a year.

In his account book, next to the date of hiring, Heaton noted the money wage he had agreed to pay. There was a general upward trend in his servants' wages from the 1760s to the 1790s. The average annual wage for all hirings of female servants whose clothing purchases are recorded was 59s. Before 1778, however, Heaton never paid any of these servants an annual wage of more than 55s. and some were paid as little as 31s. 6d. This was well below the annual wages of at least 84s. paid to all but one maidservant by a member of the local gentry in the 1760s and early 1770s.[22] From 1778 Heaton never paid less than 52s. and gave as much as 91s. in the 1790s. This rising trend is consistent with what we know about trends in servants' wages elsewhere in Yorkshire and in Lancashire.[23]

It is important to remember that, in addition to a money wage, Heaton provided his servants with payment in kind in the form of accommodation, food, heat, light and soap. The money wage represented, therefore, a form of genuinely disposable income over and above the cost of most (although not all) basic needs. How did Heaton's female servants dispose of this income? The fundamental characteristic of their spending that emerges from Heaton's accounts is that most did not accumulate money savings. On the contrary, as eighteenth-century moralists complained, they spent more than they earned and they did so on Heaton's credit. Heaton balanced his servants' accounts roughly at the end of each hiring year. Out of 32 such balancings recorded by Heaton for 14 servants, in 22 cases the servant owed money to Heaton. The average amount owed (11s.) represented 19 percent of the servants' annual wage and in four cases it represented more than a third of their annual wage. Heaton sometimes allowed these debts to accumulate over several years, although they appear to have been paid off eventually, often some time after the servant had left his employment. It seems unlikely that he wholly disapproved of their overspending when he allowed it to happen time and time again.

The minority of ten servants who saved money was composed disproportionately of the lowest paid, those employed during the first ten years of Heaton's detailed record keeping before 1778, and those who only worked for one year. On average they saved 27 percent of their annual wage (23s.). Three saved more than a third of their annual wage and one nearly two-thirds.

All but one of the 28 female servants employed by Heaton for whom detailed accounts survive devoted the bulk of what they spent out of their wages to the purchase of clothing, irrespective of whether they were in debt or credit at the end of their hiring.[24] Other spending consisted mainly of what Heaton entered in the accounts as 'cash'. If we aggregate the spending of all the 28 servants, 86 percent of what they spent went on clothes, clothing materials and the upkeep of clothing. What did they buy? If we aggregate all their clothing purchases and break them down into broad categories by value (table 34), we discover that garments represented by far the single largest element in their spending. Indeed, if most of the fabric they bought was intended for main garments (as seems likely), then garments accounted for more than half their expenditure on clothes.

Heaton's 28 female servants spent more on gowns than on any other garment (see table 35). At least 21 acquired one or more gowns during their service.[25] Some of the gowns concerned were clearly workaday items, made from cheaper worsted fabrics. Martha Butterfield acquired a second-hand calamanco gown and had it remodelled for 4s. 6d. Mary Greenwood and Nancy Holmes each spent 7s. 6d. on lengths of shalloon for gowns which they had dyed green. Hannah Holmes and Nancy Holmes each bought camblet gown lengths for 11s. 6d.[26] But Heaton's servants also bought gowns that were much more expensive and showy. These were predominantly made not from woollen fabrics, but from cotton or linen, often printed. Eleven servants acquired gowns costing between 15s. and 21s. each. The fabrics, where described, were all cotton or linen, except for a camblet and a crape, both of which could have been pure worsteds, worsted-silk mixes or silks.[27] Four of the gowns were described as painted, by which Heaton probably meant a printed or painted cotton or linen (fig. 108). The cotton and linen gowns appear to have cost Heaton's servants between 2s. 2d. and 3s. per yard, compared with well under 2s. a yard for most of the worsted gowns they bought.[28]

These prices were at the lower end of the range paid for linen and cotton printed fabrics by Barbara Johnson, the Bedfordshire clergyman's daughter who kept an album of the fabrics she acquired for outer garments between the 1740s and the 1820s. They were also in the range paid for most of the cotton gowns acquired in the 1780s and 1790s by Nancy Woodforde, the niece of the Norfolk clergyman and diarist.[29] Evidently a good number of Heaton's servants, although by no means all, were buying gowns made in the cheaper varieties of printed linen and cotton bought by much wealthier provincial women from the 1760s. For the servants, these gowns were major purchases that swallowed up more than a third of their average annual money wages, but they were a perfectly feasible purchase on the income (and credit) they received from Heaton. Nor did they necessarily replace worsted gowns. A number of servants, especially those who served for more than one year, acquired an expensive cotton or linen gown, presumably for best wear, in addition to a cheaper worsted gown for working attire. A letter to the *London Magazine* on the benefits of the wool trade may consequently have exaggerated the impact of cotton and linen garments on the demand for woollen fabrics when in 1783 it criticised servants' desire for cotton gowns. Yet the

108 'Shoolon Bound at the Ends with flowered Cotten', 1759, cotton printed in black; white shalloon, London Metropolitan Archives, A/FH/A/9/1/151, Foundling no. 13668. An undyed shalloon and a printed cotton similar to fabrics bought for gowns by some of Robert Heaton's servants.

picture it offered of at least some servants' sartorial aspirations was probably not wholly misleading, even in a remote Pennine valley:

> Every servant girl has her *cotton* gowns, and her *cotton* stockings, whilst honest grograms, tammeys, linsey woolseys and many other articles of wool, which would be much more becoming their stations, lie to mildew in our mercer's shops, are seldom enquired for but by paupers and parish officers. . . . I believe that luxury in the dress of our female servants, and the daughters of farmers, and many others, in inferior stations, who think that a well-chosen *cotton* gown shall entitle them to the appellation of young ladies, is highly prejudicial both to the land owner, the farmer, and the public.[30]

Linen and cotton gowns were the most obviously fashionable main garments bought by Heaton's servants. Stays, though fundamental to the eighteenth-century female wardrobe and fashionable silhouette, were extremely expensive when made from whalebone and acquired new. Those described as 'new' in Heaton's accounts cost

109 'Striped Linsey cuffed with flowered Cotten', 1759, linsey-woolsey woven in red and cream stripes; cotton printed in blue and black, London Metropolitan Archives, A/FH/A/9/1/148, Foundling no. 13395. The juxtaposition of a linsey-woolsey and a printed cotton shows how a linsey-woolsey petticoat might have appeared under a cotton gown.

110 'Striped flannel', flannel woven in yellow stripes, London Metropolitan Archives, A/FH/A/9/1/125, Foundling no. 11146.

between 16s. and 24s. and only six servants bought them. Eight bought cheaper stays. Two pairs of these were clearly second-hand, being described as 'old', but others may have been the leather stays or 'bodies' sometimes worn by the labouring poor. Cloaks, usually red, were characteristic items of women's wardrobes, especially in the countryside, and were not confined to the labouring classes. They too could be expensive. Only seven servants bought them, at prices ranging from 7s. to 20s. Many of Heaton's servants bought petticoats, all made from the cheaper wool, worsted and wool-mix materials like serge, flannel, linsey-woolsey (sometimes striped), and cloth (figs 109, 110). They were often quilted. Most cost less than 5s. The 'new' quilted petticoat bought by Mary Hartley in 1779–80 was exceptional in costing nearly 12s. Seventeen servants bought cloth for shifts, although Heaton provides almost no information about the fabrics. Heaton was not always consistent in his entries, so many of the numerous purchases of linen and harden cloth listed in the accounts were probably for shifts.

If buying a printed cotton or linen gown was the most spectacular and expensive means by which Heaton's servants could make a show, a less costly one was to buy appropriate accessories. Much fashion innovation in the eighteenth century, especially after 1750, turned on changes in accessories, which comprised the servants' second largest category of expenditure (see table 36). As with gowns, servants' purchases of

111 Paul Sandby, *Band Box Seller*, n.d. [*c*.1759], watercolour, Huntington Library, Art Collections, and Botanical Gardens, San Marino, California, 67.18. A London street seller carries a selection of hat and other boxes, some of them decorated. They include triangular boxes for men's cocked hats and round boxes for women's low-crowned straw hats.

accessories extended from the showy to the resolutely practical. Handkerchiefs and neckcloths were bought by 18 servants, most of whom made more than one purchase.[31] More was spent on them than any other accessory. This is not surprising, because they were relatively inexpensive, but highly conspicuous. A 'common' neckcloth might cost as little as 9d., a handkerchief in a check fabric only 10d. But more fashionable fabrics and styles were costlier. Eight of the eighteen servants bought handkerchiefs costing more than 3s. Betty Mason paid 3s. 6d. for a fashionable shawl neckcloth in 1786. Muslin, fashionable for handkerchiefs in the 1780s, was also expensive, especially early in the decade when Alice Hutchinson paid 3s. 8½d. for a white muslin neckcloth. Silk handkerchiefs bought by the servants were more costly still, most priced at over 4s.

A similar pattern emerges for hats and caps, which were essential wear but also a key focus of fashion between the 1770s and the 1790s, subject to rapid changes in shape, size and trimming. Hats were bought by twelve servants at prices ranging from the 7d. paid in 1783 for a simple chip hat by Nancy Holmes, to the 7s. paid in 1786 by Hannah Kay for a hat made from satin. Seven of the twelve bought hats that cost more than 5s., most of which were described as silk or satin. That these were prized pieces of apparel is suggested by the purchases of three paper hat boxes (fig. 111). Silk ribbons, which could be bought relatively inexpensively at as little as 6d. a yard, were often used to decorate the servants' hats (fig. 107). Caps too were highly visible accessories and, in all cases where fabrics were specified, were made from the finer and more costly varieties of linen or cotton cloth, such as Irish cloth, lawn or even muslin. But not all the 15 servants who acquired caps were prepared to spend the 2s. that Alice Hutchinson paid for a cap in fashionable muslin in 1782, or the 4s. 2d. that Sarah Earnshaw paid out for 'a fine cap' in 1778. Lace edging to decorate a cap could double its cost; Nancy Holmes laid out 5s. 10d. on lace for a cap in 1783.

There was less emphasis on the stylish and the showy in the aprons and stockings acquired by Heaton's servants. Many of the aprons were probably working clothes, although it must be remembered that aprons, at this period, comprised part of fashionable dress and were not necessarily associated with service and the working poor. Nineteen servants bought material for one or more aprons, but these were overwhelmingly in cheaper workaday fabrics costing less than 3s. per apron, like brat, harden, linsey-woolsey, check, blue linen, or in one case wool spun for the purpose by the servant herself. Only three servants bought fine materials like lawn or muslin costing more than 5s. per apron. Stockings bought ready-made were all either worsted or yarn (linen thread). There are no mentions in Heaton's accounts of the cotton stockings condemned by the *London Magazine* in 1783. However, it is striking that there are no entries at all for buying ready-made stockings of any kind after 1777, although there are some payments for worsted for stockings and many for dyeing stockings. The servants probably knitted their own stockings after this date.

Footwear is the most difficult category of the servants' clothing purchases to analyse, except in broad outline, because Heaton included very little descriptive detail in his accounts. Shoes and pumps, bought by at least 22 servants, accounted for two-thirds of their spending on footwear, but we have no means of knowing how stylish or decorative they were. Certainly decoration was an issue when the servants' acquired footwear, because several bought silver-plated shoe buckles. At about 2s. 6d. a pair, plated buckles could increase the final cost of a pair of shoes by more than half. On average the servants paid about 4s. for a pair of shoes or pumps described as 'new' in the accounts (table 37), although prices varied between 3s. and 6s. a pair.[32] Only two pairs of shoes were unambiguously second-hand and they cost 2s. a pair. To protect their shoes in wet, muddy conditions twelve servants bought pattens, which cost about 1s (fig. 112). The alternative for bad weather and perhaps for many everyday uses was to wear ironed, wooden-soled clogs, which were bought by 17 servants. The clogs bought by Heaton's servants were relatively uniform in price, varying between 1s. 8d. and 2s. 6d. a pair, and costing on average 2s. 1d. Yet clogs and shoes were not usually treated as alternatives to each other. At least 18 of the 28 servants appear to have had both clogs and shoes.

Viewed in aggregate, therefore, every significant category of Heaton's servants' expenditure on clothing reveals them to have combined the costly and stylish with the cheap and mundane. However, the aggregate analysis conceals some marked differences between individuals. At one extreme was the parsimonious Hannah Roberts, who

112 Edward Penny, *A Scene from Jonathan Swift's Description of a City Shower*, 1764, oil on canvas, Museum of London, 88.126. A well-dressed London housemaid is shown wearing a white apron over a quilted petticoat and a glazed gown, a printed neckerchief with a red ground, white stockings and pattens. The gentleman is depicted wearing a wig, a sword, ruffles on his sleeve and a laced waistcoat, but no lace on his coat.

served for one year in 1770, saved nearly half of her 54s. wages, and spent most of the rest on visits to Keighley, four miles down the Worth valley from Haworth, perhaps to see her family. She spent only 6s. 3d. on clothing, paying for two cheap caps, a pair of relatively inexpensive shoes and the cost of shoe repair. At the other extreme was the extravagant Alice Hutchinson, who was hired in 1781 at an annual wage of 78s. In her first year of service she actually laid out almost 102s., a 31 percent overspend. All but 10s. of the 102s. went on clothes. She made 28 separate clothing purchases in that year, including expensive, fashionable items like a muslin neckcloth for 3s. 6d., a silk hat for 6s. 10½d. with a paper hat box worth 2s., and a new linen gown for 20s. 6d., as well as shoes, clogs, pattens, other handkerchiefs, a petticoat, a shift, yarn for stockings and various kinds of cloth, including a length of calamanco for 7s. which was probably used to make a gown for everyday use. She went on to serve for another two years, continuing in debt to Heaton but none the less making yet more expensive clothes purchases, including another gown for 21s., lace worth 12s., a cloak, neckcloths in silk and muslin and another hat and hatbox. Most servants fell between the two extremes in their purchasing habits, although the majority resembled profligate Alice Hutchinson more than careful Hannah Roberts in that they acquired at least a couple of expensive, showy items of clothing during each year of service.

Heaton's servants did not maintain this circumscribed but nevertheless active engagement with fashion by buying second-hand clothes, by acquiring fabrics at cost from their cloth-manufacturing master, or by having cloth woven locally. Very few of the clothes purchased by Heaton's servants were second-hand. Heaton sometimes used the words 'new' and 'old' in the accounts to describe items of clothing, although not systematically. Nevertheless, it is striking that 'new' outnumbers 'old' by 81 to six.[33] The accounts make it clear that in acquiring garments the servants' normal practice was to buy new cloth and have it made up. The number of purchases of the kinds of worsted cloth (shalloon before 1783, figured stuffs thereafter) that Heaton himself manufactured was tiny. Moreover, the prices paid by the servants for cloth and other items of clothing are consistent with retail prices in the period. Only two servants had cloth woven on a bespoke basis, one a piece of linsey-woolsey, the other a piece of serge. It is, of course, possible that the servants were assisted in sustaining a more fashionable wardrobe by donations of clothes from Heaton's family or their own relatives, which do not appear in the accounts. But their ability to sustain a stylish wardrobe clearly did not depend on such donations. Nor should we assume these exchanges, insofar as they took place, necessarily took the form of gifts. Often they had to be paid for. Among the few acquisitions of identifiably second-hand clothing that appear in the accounts are Sarah Earnshaw's purchases in 1778 of her recently deceased aunt Martha's gown for 10s. 6d. and a crape gown belonging to Heaton's wife for 19s., and Mary Pighells' purchase of gowns from her aunt and uncle in 1778 and 1779.

With only a handful of exceptions, we do not know precisely where the servants acquired their clothes. Most of their purchases of cloth, accessories and footwear were probably from retailers in the Haworth area with whom Heaton had an account, such as the Stanbury cobler who mended Betty Mason's shoes in 1786. Shops certainly existed in the vicinity that carried the necessary range of goods.[34] Occasionally the accounts mention purchases from further afield or from peddlers. Sarah Heaton bought a new gown at Halifax in 1790, Mary Constantine clogs and pattens at Keighley in 1769 and five servants bought cloth from the ubiquitous 'Scotchman', including Sally Shackleton who bought an expensive gown which appears to have been paid for in instalments. The accounts reveal that it was normal practice for the servants to pay local specialists to make up their gowns and cloaks, although only Mary Hoyle, who was paid for making a gown for Sally Roberts in 1781, was identified by name. Her example suggests that by this date Heaton's servants were using female mantuamakers to cut and sew their outer garments. Specialists (shoemakers, cobblers, staymakers) were also paid to make and repair footwear and stays, and at least two hats were bespoke, although other hats may have been bought ready-made. Making up other garments, such as shifts and petticoats, and accessories, like stockings, caps and handkerchiefs, emerges from the accounts as the responsibility of the servants themselves, drawing on their own skill at cutting out, sewing, knitting and sometimes spinning.

As we have seen, eighteenth-century moralists complained that domestic servants aped 'all the fashions of those they live with'.[35] However, there is no reason to believe that Heaton's servants had to rely on Heaton's female kin for their ideas about fashion. We know that in the early 1760s the female members of the Heaton family dressed well by local standards, owning a range of relatively expensive and probably fashionable items of clothing, such as hats in satin and silk, a silk apron, a silk cloak and gowns in poplin, silk camblet and painted linen.[36] Yet though they lived at the head of a fairly remote Pennine valley, the servants had access to a variety of other sources of information about fashionable dressing, most obviously the retailers and clothes-makers they patronised. Even if shopkeepers and mantuamakers in the immediate locality were not especially well informed or well stocked (and we should not necessarily assume this was the case), retailers in the larger local towns like Halifax, ten miles to the southeast of Haworth, and Colne, six miles to the west, certainly were. These were places Heaton's servants visited for shopping and festivities.

The overall picture that emerges from the accounts kept by Robert Heaton of his servant's spending is one that confirms some, but not all of the conventional stereotypes of female domestics offered by eighteenth-century commentators. A majority of Heaton's servants spent freely, frequently running into debt, in order to acquire clothes that included many of the cheaper varieties of the fashionable garments and accessories worn by their social superiors throughout provincial England. To do this they did not have to rely on hand-me-downs because they could afford to buy clothes with their wages and their borrowings. In their reliance on credit and their reluctance to save they appear to have been guilty of the commentators' charge of improvidence. Is this justified? Undoubtedly a majority of them chose to acquire clothes in preference to accumulating money savings, but it has to be remembered that the clothes the servants bought did represent a form of accumulated capital. Their clothes could be trans-

113 Matthew Darley, *Statute Hall or the Modern Register Office*, 1769, printed engraving, Lewis Walpole Library, Farmington, Conn., 769.4.10.1. Potential employers in a Register Office are shown ogling well-dressed young women seeking work as servants. The young woman in the left foreground is depicted wearing a black silk hat, ruffles at her sleeves and a striped apron. She carries her possessions in a box. The young woman in the centre is shown with ruffles at her sleeves, a laced cap and ribbons in her hair and on her straw hat. Both wear necklaces.

formed into cash by sale or pawning, and they provided a stock which could be drawn on in the early years of marriage, when, as we have seen, working people with young children often found it difficult to spare resources for clothing.[37] Being well dressed was one of the criteria that might in future secure a privileged service in a wealthier household (fig. 113).[38] In addition, for at least some of the servants, buying clothes may have represented an investment in securing a husband and thereby future security.

It is also questionable that in wearing their more stylish and showy purchases Heaton's servants ceased to be identifiable as working women and became indistinguishable from their employer's wife and daughters, as the commentators sometimes claimed. We know that among the fabrics they chose for their more fashionable clothes were some – printed linen for gowns and silk for hats – that resembled items in Heaton's 1763 list of his family's clothes. This is testimony, however, more to the social pervasiveness of certain fashions than evidence of direct emulation. The German visitor Karl Philipp Moritz remarked in 1782 that 'women, in general, from the highest to the lowest wear hats, which differ from each other less in fashion than they do in fineness', and this was not true only of hats.[39] Nevertheless, some of Heaton's servants may have copied female members of Heaton's family in their clothing and may even have been encouraged to do so by their master and mistress. We cannot know. But we do know that they had sufficient sources of information about dress to avoid reliance on Heaton's family for ideas. We also know that many of their more stylish and expensive pieces of clothing were owned by other working women in the area. Insofar as it is appropriate to describe their behaviour as emulative, their aspirations were probably shaped less by the clothes worn by Heaton's family than by ideas about fashionable dressing encountered in the shops and in the street.

Robert Heaton was described in his obituary as 'a most indulgent master'.[40] Should we conclude, therefore, that he was unusually generous and that his servants' sartorial practices were untypical of the generality of domestics? Heaton certainly did not pay his female servants over-generously by local standards: their wages were well below the levels paid by the gentry in the vicinity. His practice of allowing his servants to spend a large part of their wages while they served was not unusual, although it remains unclear whether other masters were prepared to extend their servants credit over and above their annual wage. If Heaton allowed his servants more latitude in their choice of clothing than some masters, he was hardly unique. An examination of servants' purchases of clothing listed in provincial retailers' account books during the second half of the eighteenth century reveals a familiar combination of the showy and the mundane. Female servants to both farmers and gentry in Bedfordshire and Hampshire were regularly buying the same kind of relatively expensive, stylish items as Heaton's servants — printed cotton or linen gown lengths priced from 13s. to 27s., cloth cloaks priced from 11s. to 25s., and silk hats priced at over 3s. 6d. At the same time, like Heaton's servants, they bought gown lengths of workaday worsteds, costing only 5s. to 9s.[41]

It is important to stress that this pattern was as characteristic of the servants of the gentry as it was of the servants of lesser employers. It confirms the evidence of Heaton's accounts that female domestic servants did not have to rely on hand-me-downs and other donations from their employer's family to secure access to the cheaper clothing luxuries. In purely financial terms, this was especially true of the servants of the gentry, who enjoyed higher money wages than Heaton's servants and could therefore afford to spend more on clothes. However, it is possible that gentry employers expected their female servants to sustain sartorial standards that were at one and the same time more elevated and more constrained than those demanded by a Pennine manufacturer, and used a combination of high wages and gifts to sustain those standards.[42] We can observe the practice of one gentry household in the accounts kept by the widowed gentlewoman Elizabeth Shackleton of Alkincoates near Colne, only six miles west of Haworth across the Lancashire border.[43] For four years in the 1770s, Shackleton employed a young maidservant called Nanny Nutter, who was aged between 13 and 17, paying her between 68s. and 80s. a year, on average 74s. This was considerably more than the 59s. Heaton paid his servants on average in the 1770s. Shackleton kept detailed records of Nutter's spending and of any gifts Nutter received. Like Heaton's servants, almost all of Nanny Nutter's income went on clothes. Most of what she bought, whether cloth, garments, accessories or footwear, was broadly comparable in price and character to the acquisitions of Heaton's servants, except that she completely avoided a few of the cheaper fabrics and items of clothing that appear in the Heaton accounts, most noticeably harden cloth and clogs.

Nutter, however, was a particular favourite of her mistress, who showered her with gifts, mainly clothing, on at least 24 occasions during the four years she was employed. The cumulative effect of these gifts was significantly to increase the range of stylish accessories owned by Nutter. We do not know whether Heaton's family made gifts of clothing to their servants, but insofar as they did it is unlikely to have been on anything like the scale of Elizabeth Shackleton's gifts to her cosseted favourite. The combination of gifts and purchases enjoyed by Nanny Nutter left her with a number and variety of stylish accessories that even the most free-spending of Heaton's servants in the 1780s and 1790s could not match out of their combined wages and borrowings. Moreover, as we have seen, Nutter does not appear to have worn the clogs and coarse linens that constituted the everyday wear of Heaton's servants. These were probably crucial distinctions among the young working women of the mid-Pennine valleys. The gifts which Nutter received from her doting employer were fundamental to sustaining these distinctions. Nevertheless, apart from the clogs and the coarse linens, they were distinctions more of quantity than quality. Nutter did not acquire by gift or purchase clothes that were radically superior in price or character to those bought by the more adventurous of Heaton's servants. For instance, she did not wear expensive silk gowns, like those acquired by her mistress. Moreover, almost all of what she bought was bought locally. The gifts Nutter received provided her not with a fundamentally different kind of wardrobe from other, less fortunate servants in the locality, but with more of the petty luxuries to which they could realistically aspire on their wages. Not that we should assume Elizabeth Shackleton's primary purpose in showering Nanny Nutter with gifts of clothing was to render her young maidservant fashionable. Shackleton esteemed servants who were 'proper looking' and 'clean looking', but we know from her diaries that for her the importance of gifts lay less in their precise visual characteristics than in their symbolic capacity to represent and cement interpersonal attachments.[44]

A broadly similar pattern of acquisitions also characterised the spending of non-domestic female servants. Thomas Furber was the tenant of a farm near Nantwich in Cheshire in the second half of the eighteenth century, a much smaller enterprise than Robert Heaton's.[45] His main activity was cheese-making. He employed two or sometimes three women as live-in dairymaids on annual contracts. Like Heaton he advanced them money in the course of their year's hiring and sometimes recorded how they spent it. They were paid less than Heaton's servants and much less than Nanny Nutter.

Their annual money wages were as low as 35 s. in the 1770s, but rose to generally 50s. by the 1790s. Like Heaton's servants, they spent what they earned overwhelmingly on clothes, although their purchases included fewer petty luxury items, reflecting their lower wages. In particular, they bought hardly any full gowns, costly or otherwise. Nevertheless, their purchases in these years did include several of the more expensive, showy pieces of clothing bought by Heaton's servants, such as a 3s. satin hat, ribbons, nuns lace, cloaks, a 16s. petticoat, cotton cloth for bedgowns at 19d. a yard or more, and 30d. handkerchiefs, which were probably printed cotton or cheap silk.

Female service was no idyll. It characteristically involved back-breaking work, long hours, close surveillance from employers and narrow restrictions on behaviour, and could also comprehend corporal punishment and sexual exploitation (fig. 114).[46] Employment was not necessarily continuous. When superior opportunities presented themselves servants often seized them eagerly. In 1798, one Wiltshire servant told her mistress that she intended leaving, 'as she had got a place at spinning, which was better than service'.[47] Earlier in the century, Daniel Defoe had noted the impact on female farm servants of a rise in spinning wages in the woollen textile industries in the 1720s. 'The Farmers's Wives can get no Dairy-Maids . . . and what's the matter? truely the Wenches answer, they won't go to Service at 12d. or 18d. a Week, while they can get 7s. to 8s. a Week at Spinning.'[48]

Of course it is likely that many of the women attracted into spinning by high wages spent just as lavishly on clothes as Heaton's servants. Young female factory workers were certainly believed to do so a century later.[49] Historians have probably laid too much stress on the unique importance of servants as leaders and innovators in plebeian fashionable consumption. After all, the majority of female servants served families of the middling sort on relatively limited wages. Nevertheless, domestic service in the families of the middling sort regularly provided hundreds of thousands of young women in the second half of the eighteenth century with incomes sufficient to acquire a number of decorative, stylish items each year in addition to their cheap, everyday clothes, without having to rely on hand-me-downs. These more fashionable items may not necessarily have been as fine as those owned by their mistresses, but they certainly included, at least as accessories, the silks and muslins complained about by late eighteenth-century critics of servants' behaviour. Not all female servants chose to use their earnings in this way, but, if Robert Heaton's 28 servants were representative, a majority did. In Heaton's case, moreover, they mobilised their master's credit to do so, but with no indication that he exercised any corresponding control over what they bought. Their consumption was not involuntary. They comprised a financially circumscribed but huge and free-spending market for cheaper, but not usually second-hand, fashionable clothing.

It was, moreover, a market that, in the north of England at least, was growing. The wages Robert Heaton paid his servants increased in real terms between the 1760s and the 1790s. The servants he hired at higher wages after 1778 were more likely to spend more on expensive items of clothing and more likely to run into debt to do so. What Heaton's accounts cannot tell us is how far this tendency for servants' spending on

THE MAID OF ALL-WORK'S PRAYER!!

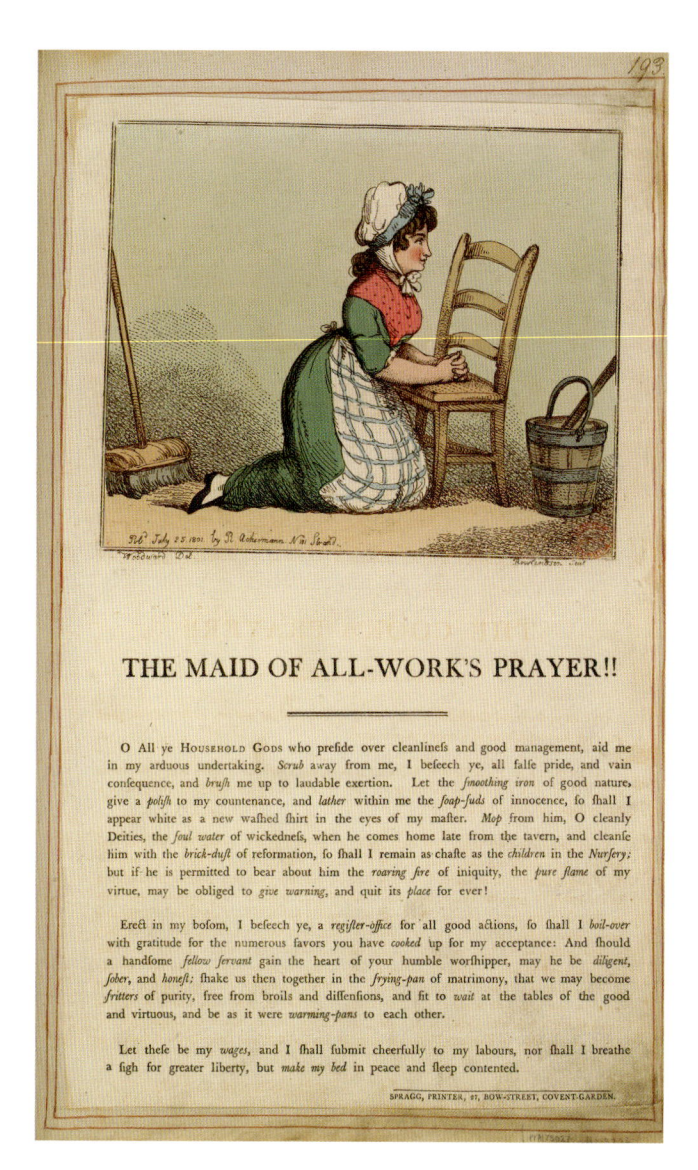

O All ye HOUSEHOLD GODS who preside over cleanliness and good management, aid me in my arduous undertaking. *Scrub* away from me, I beseech ye, all false pride, and vain consequence, and *brush* me up to laudable exertion. Let the *smoothing iron* of good nature, give a *polish* to my countenance, and *lather* within me the *soap-suds* of innocence, so shall I appear white as a new washed shirt in the eyes of my master. *Mop* from him, O cleanly Deities, the *foul water* of wickedness, when he comes home late from the tavern, and cleanse him with the *brick-dust* of reformation, so shall I remain as chaste as the *children* in the *Nursery*; but if he is permitted to bear about him the *roaring fire* of iniquity, the *pure flame* of my virtue, may be obliged to *give warning*, and quit its *place* for ever!

Erect in my bosom, I beseech ye, a *register-office* for all good actions, so shall I *boil-over* with gratitude for the numerous favors you have *cooked* up for my acceptance: And should a handsome *fellow servant* gain the heart of your humble worshipper, may he be *diligent, sober*, and *honest*; shake us then together in the *frying-pan* of matrimony, that we may become *fritters* of purity, free from broils and dissensions, and fit to *wait* at the tables of the good and virtuous, and be as it were *warming-pans* to each other.

Let these be my *wages*, and I shall submit cheerfully to my labours, nor shall I breathe a sigh for greater liberty, but *make my bed* in peace and sleep contented.

SPRAGG, PRINTER, 27, BOW-STREET, COVENT-GARDEN.

114 Thomas Rowlandson, *'The Maid of All-Work's Prayer!!'*, 1801, hand-coloured etching, British Museum, London, BMSat 9792. A housemaid is depicted in a green gown, a check apron, a red neckerchief and a cap tied with a ribbon. The text, like the image, emphasises the many demands of her occupation.

clothing to grow faster than their incomes, resulting in a decline in saving and an increase in borrowing, extended beyond the economically buoyant Pennine valleys of the late eighteenth century. Half a century earlier, Daniel Defoe certainly believed that it did. When servants' wages rose, he complained in 1725, 'this overplus in generally laid out, either in Luxury or Vanity, that is to say, in *Strong-Drink* by the Men-Servants and in *gay things* by the Women-Servants'. High wages meant that 'servants lay up less, *take them one with another*, than they did when they were hir'd at half the Wages'.[50] In the course of the eighteenth century, the money wages of live-in female servants increased, reflecting the growing wealth of the servant-employing classes. Any propensity on the part of these servants to save less and borrow more as their incomes rose can only have provided an additional boost to the market for everyday fashion.

★   ★   ★

If the vast majority of female household servants were not involuntary consumers of clothing, many of their male equivalents certainly were. There were far fewer male household servants than female in eighteenth-century England. Nevertheless, their numbers were considerable. Returns under the tax on servants in 1780 counted 49,475 manservants in England and Wales, some 2.6 percent of males aged over 15. Employing a manservant was a badge of social exclusivity. Employers numbered only 24,553 in 1780, drawn from the highest reaches of the social hierarchy, among the nobility, gentry and the wealthier businessmen and professionals. Only five thousand of them, principally titled landowners, employed more than two manservants. These figures are underestimates, because the definition of a manservant used for the tax was a restricted one and there was every incentive to evade payment. Nevertheless, the underestimate was not necessarily large and the use of a tight definition means that statistics derived from the records of the tax provide a reasonable guide to the numbers of manservants who wore livery.[51]

It was customary for male domestic servants, unlike their female equivalents, to receive clothing in addition to their cash wages as part of their hiring agreement. For most, especially those like footmen who were towards the bottom of the hierarchy of male domestics in larger households, these clothes took the form of a standard livery, usually consisting of a coat, waistcoat, breeches and a hat (fig. 115).[52] A greatcoat, a set of work clothes and other items might also be provided, but were not usually described as livery.[53] Precisely what was given depended on the status of the employer and the rank of the servant. Sometimes an extra sum of money was provided in lieu of an item of clothing that would customarily be provided by an employer, but it was normal for male servants to supply their own shoes, linen, wigs and stockings out of their wages.[54] Livery was usually provided annually, but the frequency varied according to a servant's agreement with his master. At Bell Hall in Yorkshire in 1793 the postillion's agreement provided a 'frock, stable waistcoat and hat in the year and livery and great coat once in two years'.[55] Technically the clothes supplied remained the property of the employer, although often they passed into the servant's ownership when replaced.

The appearance of a livery was in the overwhelming majority of cases determined by the employer. Masters and mistresses often took considerable care over colour and detailing, because a livery, while defining its wearer as a servant, also represented the employing family to the world, often in colours that had family associations. The Buckinghamshire Purefoys in 1743 were not untypical in their concern for exactness as to colour and quality.

> I desire you will make the coachman a frock the same coloured cloth to the pattern as near as you can and a gold coloured serge paduasoy waistcoat. Pray let the serge

115 Arnold Almond, *Two Servants (Daniel Taylor and Elinor Low)*, 1783, oil on canvas, private collection. Taylor and Low were servants at Knole, the Kent country house of the Duke of Dorset. Daniel Taylor is shown in a livery of blue with yellow facings and epaulettes, with a white neckcloth and a ruffled shirt. Elinor Low is well dressed in ordinary clothes, with a laced cap tied with a silk ribbon.

> paduasoy be better than the last was. It must not be a lemon colour but a gold colour, and the lining of the frock must be of the same colour; and let me have it within a week or as soon as you can.[56]

The result of this close attention to detail was that livery garments were clearly recognisable as such. Two features in particular made livery distinctive: first, two-coloured coats with contrasting, often brightly coloured linings and facings, and, second, gold and silver lace trimmings on coats, waistcoats and hats (figs 116, 117). Owen Thomas, who absconded from his service with a Shropshire parson in 1719, wore a grey livery faced with red.[57] Edward Coleman, a runaway postillion advertised in Oxfordshire in 1764 wore a brown livery coat trimmed with blue and blue lace.[58] These characteristics of livery were distinctive enough to mark out a man as a servant at any period in the eighteenth century, but they became increasingly distinctive in the second half of the eighteenth century as lace trimmings ceased to be fashionable and livery came to have an increasingly old-fashioned air.[59] It was with incredulity that a judge asked a

116 Paul Sandby, *Servant to the Duke of Cumberland*, n.d. [early 1750s], pen and watercolour, Royal Collection, RL 14486. The servant wears the Duke's livery of crimson coat with green facings and green waistcoat.

pawnbroker's shopman at the Old Bailey in 1787 how the accused came 'to have a laced hat and a cockade on, if he was a livery servant out of place'. How 'could you possibly believe that a man wearing a livery hat and cockade really kept a shop?'[60]

The trimmings were especially important for advertising the status of the employing family and they accounted for much of the considerable cost of each item of livery. In 1742 the Purefoys bought Caroline hats for their male servants which were trimmed with gold lace, gold loops and gold buttons. Each hat cost nearly eighteen shillings, including the trimming. Yet in 1744, untrimmed men's Caroline hats were valued at under three shillings in the probate inventory of a Suffolk draper. Even if this was a wholesale or second-hand value, it is unlikely these untrimmed hats retailed for more than six shillings.[61] Generally the quality of the materials used for individual items of clothing provided to male servants was high compared with the typical purchases of

117 John Collet, *The Jealous Maids*, 1772, mezzotint, private collection. The scene is below stairs in the kitchen of a grand house. The footman is depicted in a green livery coat with red facings and gold lace on the waistcoat. One of the maids is at work mending a shirt, wearing a check apron. The accompanying verses are on the familiar subject of servants emulating their masters and mistresses (see also fig. 79).

a plebeian man. The Purefoys paid about four shillings a yard for woollen cloth for their servants' frock coats in the 1730s and 1740s; the Latham family never paid more than 2s. 6d. a yard for woollen cloth for any male garment between the 1720s and the 1760s.[62] Moreover, servants' main garments were replaced once every year or two, more frequently than those of many of the labouring poor.

Livery provoked ambivalent reactions among the employing classes and servants alike. For employers, livery was a powerful demonstration of their wealth and status, one that was both ostentatious and personalised. Liveried servants were one of the most potent tools in their employers' equipment of display, constantly exposed to view, whether at home, where the liveried footman served at table, or in the street, where he hung on to the back of his employer's carriage. This visibility provided a powerful incentive for employers to ensure that their livery matched their social pretensions. As a consequence, some employers vied to produce ever more spectacular liveries. Newspapers carried reports of new, sumptuous noble liveries in the same way they reported the new fashions in carriages and women's dress. It was widely believed that competition of this sort resulted in ever more extravagant liveries. The philanthropist Jonas Hanway complained that 'it was a rare thing in my memory to see any gold or silver lace on the clothes of a domestic servant in livery: lace of wool, cotton, or with a mixture of silk, contented us. Now we behold rich vestments, besilvered and begilded, like the servants of sovereign princes.'[63]

Hanway disapproved, revealing a hostility to ostentatious liveries that was widely shared among the employing classes. Critics considered that servants should dress in accordance with their social status, that fine clothes encouraged them in unjustifiable pretensions, and that the employment of large numbers of idle, expensively liveried servants represented a waste of national resources and was a pernicious form of luxury. John Macdonald, the Scots footman whose memoirs were published in 1790, encountered proponents of both views when seeking a position in London in the 1770s. For one interview, he put on 'a gold-laced vest, and other things in form', only to be rejected for being 'more like a gentleman than a servant'. At another, three days later, he 'dressed plain without lace', but was again rejected. The footman of the prospective employer later told him 'I am sorry I did not tell you to dress yourself finer, for Sir Francis is very nice.'[64]

Servants too were ambivalent in their attitudes to the clothes their employers obliged them to wear. We should not, of course, assume that to be identifiable as a servant was necessarily unwelcome. William Austin, an American visitor in 1803, was surprised to discover that London footmen 'wear the appearance of the most perfect contentment. They are pleased with their party coloured clothes, and never seem more happy, than when they expose themselves to the public. Nor is this all; they claim a sort of distinction, and affect to look down on the more respectable man, who cries cat's meat.'[65] Excessive pleasure in fine clothing was considered an occupational hazard for servants. Fine clothes were desirable, regarded by male servants as part of what was due to them. When negotiating with their employers over wages and conditions, servants strove to secure the best possible range of clothing. If customary items of clothing were not provided, money was expected in lieu, often at fairly generous rates. At Bell Hall near York in 1787 a postillion's agreement left the matter undecided, simply stating that he should receive a pair of boots or one guinea, and a pair of leather breeches or one guinea.[66]

An expensive livery could contribute to a servants' sense of his own superiority (fig. 118). The servants of the nobility in particular were noted for an arrogance which was said to reflect their identification with their employers. Servants, complained Vicesimus Knox in 1782, 'assume a share of the grandeur from the rank of their masters, and think themselves intitled to domineer over their equals, and to ridicule their superiors'.[67] The footman John Macdonald took pride in having worn a livery in the late 1760s that he considered 'the genteelest in London'.[68] Indeed, Macdonald's concern for his appearance was such that later, in the 1770s, he was known among his associates as '*Beau Macdonald*, or the *Scotch Frenchman*' for the sword, bag wig, laced ruffles and silk umbrella he sported when off duty.[69] To be demoted from the position of livery servant to that of mere helper in the stables constituted a degradation.[70]

Nevertheless, a livery identified its wearer's servility. Servants, therefore, might have reason to resent it.[71] A correspondent to the *London Chronicle* in 1757 declared: 'I consider an Englishman in livery, as a kind of monster. He is a person born free, with the obvious badge of servility.' The point was reinforced by the writer of a rejoinder in the same paper who, despite arguing that service was neither dishonourable nor disgraceful, had to admit that 'a Livery Suit may indeed be fitly called a Badge of Servility'.[72] It was a view that enjoyed popular currency. In 1751 a Middlesex man replied to an insult from a liveried servant, 'I am not so much like a dog as you, for I wear my own coat, and you wear your master's.'[73] Despite their acute sense of the financial value of livery, servants were often keen to dispense with it. In 1756, William Sayer, a high-class London tailor, wrote to a customer about finding a servant who could dress hair and look after horses: 'you must not expect him to Dress Hair very well, for no servt. which can, will wear a Livery, much less look after Horses'.[74] The clergyman William Freind complained about a manservant in 1740, 'I have just turned off a young fellow I took upon tryal from the Plough because he wants to have Coffee allowed him for breakfast and to be put out of livery.'[75] Over sixty years later the same complaint was still being repeated. A Somerset vicar noted in 1802, 'my man it seems does not chuse to wear a Livery so he is to go at the month's end'.[76]

Yet servants' desire to escape livery does not necessarily offer evidence of a fundamental objection to being involuntary consumers – to wearing clothing chosen and bought for them by an employer, or even to wearing livery as such. Rather it may represent their wish to step up the servant hierarchy, to be treated like the upper manservants of the very rich – butlers and stewards – most of whom did not wear livery. Livery was not just a badge of servitude; it was also a badge of lowly status in the servant hierarchy. The fact that livery performed this distinguishing role in those households where there were enough servants to justify hierarchical distinctions confirms its potency as a sign of subordination. Whether or not it was resented by its wearers, livery marked them out very publicly as menial inferiors, just as having liveried servants serve at table or ride on the back of a carriage identified their employers as superiors of an especially exalted kind. In the course of the eighteenth century, as livery increasingly diverged from everyday dress, these identities became ever more obvious. At the start of the century, the footman's livery was still relatively close to its origins in military and court dress, evocative of the gentlemanly retainer.[77] As the century progressed, fashion changed, while livery ossified. The genteel elements it incorporated at the start of the century were either suppressed, or ceased to be genteel. Until 1701 footmen had been permitted to wear a sword, the distinguishing mark of a gentleman, but they were then forbidden swords in London.[78] In the 1740s, a laced coat and a bag wig were still what a man who was sartorially aspirational, like the highwayman James Maclaine, wore to affect 'the fine Gentleman'.[79] By the 1790s, by contrast, the kind of silver-lace decoration that adorned a velveret livery coat stolen in London in 1795 was almost entirely confined, among civilians at least, to footmen.[80] Livery had become a sartorial fossil, albeit one that, if we are to believe Jonas Hanway, was becoming increasingly

118 Thomas Rowlandson, *Country Characters, No. 4: Footman*, 1799, coloured engraving, Lewis Walpole Library, Farmington, Conn., 799.8.30.4. The conceited London footman on the left is mocked for thinking his ostentatious livery and Frenchified manners will impress 'the Female villagers'. He is shown wearing a red livery coat with gold-lace trim, epaulettes and button loops, and a wig or powdered hair. Seals hang on a chain from his breeches pocket, demonstrating that he carries a watch. The country footman on the right is shown wearing a much less showy livery consisting of a plain blue cloth coat, without facings or epaulettes, and only a shoulder knot to indicate his status.

elaborate and ostentatious in the second half of the century, a trend that may go some way to explain its fossilisation. Lacking parallels in civilian dress, its distinctive features became ever more recognisable as badges of servitude, particularly when worn, as liveries often continued to be, with the wigs that had also disappeared from everyday fashion. By the start of the nineteenth century, the visiting American Benjamin Silliman found the livery worn by the footmen on the noblemen's coaches parading in London for the King's birthday 'gaudy and fantastical to the last degree'.[81]

Eighteenth-century domestic servants, both male and female, displayed a lively interest in their clothes. While liveried male domestic servants were involuntary consumers of clothing, obliged to display their employers' taste on their backs, their far more numerous female equivalents were not. At the start of the century, the lack of choice that wearing a livery entailed was offset by the access it offered to desirable fabrics, styles and identities. By its end, livery had become more limiting and less appealing. Female domestics remained far freer, throughout the eighteenth century, to pursue stylish clothing of the kind that repeatedly annoyed their numerous critics. It would not be until late in the nineteenth century that they, too, were subjected to the limitations of involuntary consumption, when maids' uniforms came to feature in the stock-in-trade of drapers in middle-class residential areas across the land.

119 'A bunch of 4 Ribbons Narrow – Yellow, Blue, Green, & Pink', 1743, silk ribbons, London Metropolitan Archives, A/FH/A/9/1/3, Foundling no. 170.

18
Popular Fashion

Clothes were special. They were distinctive because they had an intimate relationship to the body, at one and the same time protecting it, concealing it, displaying it and representing it. Issues of propriety, identity and reputation were therefore inextricably bound up with clothing, as well as issues of comfort, security and hygiene. Clothes were also distinctive because they were intensely personal. Within large eighteenth-century plebeian families, clothes were among the few things that were conceived as being owned by individual family members, rather than communally, as the frequency of named entries for clothing in the Lancashire husbandman Richard Latham's account book suggests. And clothes were special too because, for many young adults, at the same time as being the only substantial things they owned, they were often the only things in their possession over which they were able to exercise a significant degree of choice. This was in part because many showy, fashionable items of clothing, such as ribbons or handkerchiefs, were relatively inexpensive. There was often a marked contrast in ownership, variety and quality between the clothing owned by working people and the other material things with which they were intimate. When Lydia Harcourt's lodging room in Whitechapel in London was broken into in 1799, some of the goods stolen belonged to her and some to her landlord.[1] Apart from a cheap wooden trunk, Harcourt's stolen goods consisted entirely of clothing. Together they were valued at 3s. 9d. Along with the clothes she stood up in and a pair of white stockings left in the room, they probably represented the best part of her possessions. Far more valuable at £2 6s., but equally familiar to her as an intimate part of her material world, were the stolen furnishings belonging to her landlord. On the March evening Harcourt's lodging room was stripped, she owned enough clothes to leave a number of her choicer and more expensive accessories – her silk hat, her fan, her muslin cap and her silk sash – at home. But her home was a rented room whose furnishings – the bed on which she lay, the chair on which she sat, the table at which she ate – were chosen by her landlord and his wife and, it is important to stress, together were worth considerably more than her clothing. Whereas the list of Lydia Harcourt's clothing suggests a capacity to own, to choose, to duplicate and to differentiate, the list of furnishings reveals a more restricted set of options, dictated by others.

It is no surprise, therefore, that so many plebeian men and women, especially young men and women, yearned to possess at least some stylish clothes alongside their workaday outfits. The sources employed in this book cannot tell us precisely what proportion of the plebeian population actually did possess such clothes. Given the sensitivity of clothes ownership to economic circumstances, that proportion can rarely have been stable. Instead, it must have fluctuated as prosperity waxed and waned. Nevertheless, the available evidence makes it abundantly clear that huge numbers did succeed, at some stage of their lives, in wearing stylish clothes. They identified these clothes by adjectives such as neat, elegant, genteel, even showy. More often than not, they used these words to describe items of clothing that approximated to what was broadly fashionable among the elite. Their choices as consumers of clothing suggest a set of material expectations profoundly influenced by the operation of the fashion system in the commercial marketplace.[2] This is not to say they were able to embrace the fashion of the rich in all its aspects, or that they necessarily sought to do so. But familiarity with the broad trends of high fashion can be observed even among those who lived deep in the countryside. It is unlikely that this familiarity came from reading the stilted descriptions of textiles and clothes encountered in eighteenth-century newspaper advertisements, or from the detailed accounts of the latest London fashions found in expensive periodicals read almost exclusively by the rich. A knowledge of fashion trends was more likely to have been gleaned from seeing goods displayed on the shelves of shopkeepers in market towns, from the professional advice of village tailors and mantuamakers, from watching the local social elite, or from the clothes worn and opinions expressed by the more sartorially adventurous among their peers.

Many ordinary people knew what they wanted and were able to articulate it. They could be adept at formulating preferences and expressing personalised taste. This was true of both men and women. At Christmas 1782, a Furness weaver, Richard Dixon, overtook a man with a large bundle over his shoulder travelling on the road towards Keswick in Cumberland. The man, observing him 'to have on a stript linsey waistcoate . . . asked him whether he would recommend him to a linsey waistcoat of two reds and white, or of blue and white'. Dixon replied: 'of blue and white, but the man seemed to prefer two reds'.[3] When, a decade later Jane Boys, an apprentice in husbandry, went with a friend to the small town of Easingwold in Yorkshire to spend the money she had stolen from her master, she announced to a draper's shopman that 'she would have a ribbon and some gloves for herself'. Later, outside a shop where she bought a pair of silver-plated buckles, she was overheard saying to her companion, 'who seemed inclined to pass by the shop, "come in, this is the house where we can get what we want"'.[4] Some ordinary people, indeed, were confident enough in their own taste to disavow fashion, despite knowing what was fashionable. The wife of a Whitechapel weaver was able to identify a stolen cotton gown in 1790 precisely because it was unfashionable. 'I know it by the old fashioned make; I had it made last year; and I had it made that old fashioned way, because I thought it suited me best.'[5]

Just as people's responses to the current fashion could be intensely personal, so too could their reasons for wearing fine clothing. For instance, a servant who stole a dark cotton gown, a stuff petticoat, a silk capuchin, a scarlet cloth cloak and four silk handkerchiefs in 1755 did so to get her husband back. She had come to London, according to her mistress, 'to look for her husband, and was in great distress. She heard he was in town, and I believe she took the things through vanity, with intent to appear before him, and to return them again.'[6] Evidently, she shared the ancient and persistent belief that clothes could weave a spell. As a generation of cultural theorists has told us over the last quarter-century, consumption is a source of multiple and volatile meanings, which individuals negotiate with various degrees of autonomy and creativity. Meanings vary according to circumstances and are not necessarily coherent. Individual consumers have more than one identity, as do the things they consume.[7] Recent theoretical discussion of these issues has turned on how much a loosening of the bonds of community, place and social class in the West during the late twentieth century enabled consumption of commodities to become increasingly important as a vehicle for developing a sense of identity.[8] Interestingly, the modern morality tale of social bonds weakening as choice and individualisation intensify reproduces many of the anxieties expressed by eighteenth-century elite commentators about the perceived rise of plebeian participation in fashion. Nevertheless, it remains extremely difficult to gauge precisely how much freedom to construct identities through things – to customise lifestyles, free of the shackles of normative constraints – plebeian men and women actually enjoyed in the eighteenth century. If any dimension of their material lives allowed for this kind of freedom, at least at some periods in their lives, it was clothing, but the firm grip of the language of decorum on their judgements about clothes suggests the power of normative expectation.

An alternative approach, also informed by recent theoretical work on consumption, is to ask how fashion was embedded in the practices of everyday life. It requires us to look beyond patterns of individual choice and personal identity, and, instead, approach plebeian clothing – especially the more costly, stylish kinds of plebeian clothing – as a collective, social phenomenon. Rather than searching out the multiple meanings and satisfactions clothing might have afforded the eighteenth-century consumer as an individual, it prompts us to consider the circumstances in which those meanings and satisfactions might typically have been experienced.[9] In particular, it obliges us to ask how clothes were put to use to serve the temporal rhythms and collective routines of plebeian existence. An essential starting point is the distinction between 'best' clothes and 'working' clothes we have already encountered in plebeian autobiographies, Richard Latham's account book, advertisements for runaways and evidence in criminal cases. This distinction, which crops up repeatedly in plebeian and elite sources alike, remained fundamental to the way eighteenth-century men and women ordered their thinking about dress, although it was not new.[10] Some such ordering was inescapable, given that, as we have seen, even working people frequently owned duplicates of many items of dress, often in combinations of new and old, costly and cheap, elegant and indifferent. 'Best' and 'working' were the categories by which that ordering was typically accomplished. When a London apprentice cabinetmaker whose coat and waistcoat were stolen in 1786 was asked by the thief 'if they were my best clothes', he responded: 'Yes, they were my best clothes, I had no other but what was at my friends.'[11] When the officer who arrested a man during the London crimping riots of 1794 was asked in court how the man had been dressed, he simply replied: 'in a working dress; not as he is now'.[12]

Occasionally, however, the distinction between best and working clothes was articulated using words which provide a better sense of the circumstances in which the different categories of clothes were worn. In particular, best clothes were sometimes termed Sunday clothes or holiday clothes. A Westminster carpenter who returned home from work at eight o'clock on a Monday morning in 1780 immediately went out in search of a stonemason he suspected of raping his sister-in-law. 'I put off my working clothes', the carpenter recalled, 'cleaned myself a little, and said I would go after him, I did, and found him in his lodgings; he was putting his Sunday's clothes by'. The woman and the stonemason had been out together most of the previous night.[13] In 1786, the wife of a London publican remembered her surprise when a local linen draper's porter came to her house. 'He came dressed in his best clothes; I says, what, you have a holiday today.'[14] A man whose job was 'water work and engine work' at Execution Dock in London was said by the landlady of the Swan public house at Wapping to have been 'dressed in his holiday dress' when he drank there one Wednesday evening in November 1765, wearing a wig, a hat and silver knee buckles, with a watch in his pocket and a watch chain with a pinchbeck seal hanging out of it.[15] The same distinction crops up in ballads like 'The Coy Lass Dressed up in her Best Commode and Topknot'.

> Do not rumple my topknot,
> I'll not be kissed today.
> I'll not be hauled and pulled about
> Thus on a holiday . . .
> Come upon a working day
> When I have my old clothes on.
> I shall not be so nice nor coy
> Nor stand so much upon.[16]

The use of terms like Sunday clothes or holiday clothes as alternatives for best clothes demonstrates that popular expectations about when such clothes should be worn were rooted in the customary religious and festive calendar. Best clothes were associated with leisure and pleasure, but also with the routines and rituals of religious observance, which themselves continued to shape the festive calendar. It was on high days and holidays that plebeian men and women, especially young men and women, were expected to sport their finery – on Sundays, at Christmas and May Day, at Easter and Whitsuntide, at fairs and hirings, at parish feast and harvest home.

Eighteenth-century English Protestantism prioritised the spoken and the written word, but it also expected regular attendance at Sunday worship. Observing the Sabbath and its rituals was an essential element of religious culture for Anglicans and dissenters alike.[17] An overwhelming majority of the population adhered, at least nominally, to the established church. The church placed a high value on respectable sartorial display by those who attended worship on Sundays. To dress up for church was to show proper respect for the Lord's day and reverence for the Lord's word preached on that day. It marked the status of the Sabbath as a sacred day, set apart for religious observance. Until recently, the received image of eighteenth-century Anglicanism portrayed it as complacent and negligent towards its flock, but recent scholarship suggests the church was moderately successful in sustaining popular participation in Sunday worship, at least until the very last decades of the century. Even in Lancashire, where Protestant dissent and Catholicism were strong and industrialisation and urbanisation rapid, Jan Albers finds that fewer than a quarter of parishes replying to the bishop's visitation questions of 1778 reported 'many absent' from public worship on Sundays, while half reported 'few or none absent'.[18]

Clothes were crucial here. Non-attenders were drawn predominantly from among the poor. The single most common reason given in Lancashire for their non-attendance was a lack of suitable clothes to wear at church. The curate of Turton near Bolton wrote that the reason people were absent was 'rather owing to poverty and want of decent Apparel than Infidelity'.[19] The same was true in neighbouring Cheshire, where the 1778 visitation returns attributed non-attendance among the lower rank to what clergymen identified as false shame or pride in not having decent clothes. As we have seen, inadequate dress was widely considered shameful, and not only on Sundays.[20] Nevertheless, the visitation returns suggest that many, even among the poor, did contrive to dress well enough to attend, even if their Sunday best amounted to precious little. In 1776, an escaped American prisoner of war, Israel Potter, on the loose in the Hampshire countryside and anxious to avoid detection, exchanged his sailor's clothes with a poor agricultural labourer, who gave him what he called his 'church suit' in return. This suit, his best, the labourer had kept at home for use on Sundays. Yet it was no more than 'a coat of very coarse cloth, and containing a number of patches of almost every colour but that of the cloth of which it was originally made'. Potter recalled that the 'man appeared very much pleased with his bargain, and represented to his wife that he could now accompany her to church much more decently clad' in the American's pea jacket and trousers.[21] Arthur Young was told in Devon in 1796 that, thirty years before, the country women around Tiverton 'never wore gowns, except on a Sunday; and then took them off after church'.[22]

The expectation that people should make some effort to dress well on a Sunday was certainly widespread (fig. 120).[23] Significantly, whereas parish vestries hardly ever provided paupers with clothing in the materials or at the prices that distinguished the 'best' clothes bought by either the Latham daughters, Robert Heaton's servants, or the young William Hutton, they did sometimes make a point of requiring paupers to wear 'decent' clothing on Sundays, providing them with garments of a slightly better quality than those intended for wearing on 'common days'.[24] Similarly parish apprentices were often provided with two sets of clothes: in Yorkshire with 'one good and new suit for the Lord's days, and another for the working days', and in Bedfordshire 'with apparel both for Holyday and working day'.[25] In 1799, the niece of the vicar of Over Stowey in Somerset gave a woman in the parish workhouse a new stuff petticoat and a pair of stockings. 'The poor creature was very thankful', the vicar noted. 'She says she will

120 William Bigg, *Sunday Morning, a Cottage Family going to Church*, 1795, stipple and etching with aquatint, printed in colour, British Museum, London, 1941, 1011.15. This family of cottagers is improbably well dressed, but the way they are portrayed emphasises that well-ordered families among the poor were expected to wear their best clothes to attend church.

go down on her knees to Madam to tell her that she will never wear it but on Sundays as long as a rag of it remains.'[26]

The similarity between the words Holyday and holiday is not, of course, coincidental. Sunday was, at least for the less devout, not so much a day devoted single-mindedly to worship as an opportunity to enjoy some leisure, but here again there were powerful expectations about dressing well. When a London carpenter, his wife and some three or four relatives and friends went for a walk after tea on a Sunday afternoon in April 1780, they went from their apartment off Drury Lane to Bagnigge Wells, the spa and tea garden on the northern edge of London opened in 1759 that became a favourite Sunday resort for Londoners, although one frequently criticised for vulgarity and loose morals (fig. 121). They were not allowed into the pleasure garden

121 *The Beauties of Bagnigge Wells*, 1778, mezzotint, Museum of London, A6930. The tea garden and fountain at Bagnigge Wells on the northern edge of London, a favourite Sunday resort for Londoners. It was satirised as the weekend haunt of City shopkeepers and their apprentices, and criticised for vulgarity and loose morals. The behaviour and exaggerated dress of the young woman in the centre of the picture indicate she is a prostitute. Ogling her is a gauche young man with his hands in his pockets. Wearing a round hat and boots, his dress is casual, but smart. At the back of the garden, behind the fountain, people drink tea at tables under cover, while a tea kettle is being heated on a brazier in the left foreground.

because one of their company 'had a silk handkerchief about his neck, and he could not be admitted into the place'. Evidently Bagnigge Well's proprietor, perhaps mindful of its dubious reputation, enforced a dress code that excluded those wearing the typical working man's neckwear. Nevertheless, the story suggests that the carpenter and his other companions, who included a stonemason in his 'Sunday's clothes', were well dressed for their walk, certainly well enough to have secured entry.[27] A decade later, Sunday was the day the Lancashire millwright Benjamin Shaw went a-courting. Having the clothes necessary for going out on a Sunday was already a source of tension between him and his future wife. 'When we courted she had not bonnet, and this was frequently urged as a reason for her not walking out on the Sunday and I therefore bought her one, still she was sometimes short.'[28]

Similar expectations about dressing well attached to most holidays, whether sacred or secular. Eighteenth-century England enjoyed a lively festive calendar. It embraced the principal Christian festivals of Christmas, Easter and Whitsuntide, but also extended to village wakes, rushbearings, feasts, revels, tides and hoppings. There were fairs that retained at best a tenuous relationship with saints days and other holy days, as well as festivities linked to work and occupation, including hiring fairs, harvest festivals, and trade anniversaries such as St Crispin's day for shoemakers and Bishop Blaize for woolcombers. These were not confined to the countryside. In London in the 1730s there were many 'little fairs' in addition to major events like Bartholomew and Southwark Fairs.[29] Edward Thompson and Robert Malcolmson have argued that the late seventeenth and early eighteenth centuries witnessed an efflorescence of this plebeian festive culture in both agricultural and manufacturing communities, encouraged by a reaction against Puritanism after the Restoration and accompanied by many decades of tolerant indifference from the upper classes.[30] At the same time, Malcolmson and others find popular festivities dwindling from the second half of the eighteenth century, faced with the twin onslaughts of industrial urbanisation, which uprooted communities and transformed public spaces, and the evangelical movement for the reform of popular manners, which attacked festivities as nurseries of vice. Yet it is far from clear that popular festivities actually did suffer a general decline. Loud opposition did not necessarily translate into effective suppression. Only a narrow range of events were subjected to systematic assault by the powerful, most obviously those associated with unacceptable cruelty to animals, while industrialisation, far from provoking successful attacks on traditional festivities, saw new communities of workers spending high manufacturing wages on customary forms of leisure, often encouraged by local commercial interests, especially the drink trade.[31]

Eighteenth-century histories and polemics, poems and ballads, diaries and autobiographies all agreed that popular festivities were the occasions when plebeian men and women, in both town and country, showed off their best clothes (fig. 122). The Newcastle clergyman Henry Bourne noted in his pioneering 1725 collection of popular customs and superstitions, *Antiquitates Vulgares*, that it was at wakes (that is, holidays) that the village people 'deck themselves in their gaudiest Clothes'.[32] Indeed,

Voltaire, on his first day in England in 1726, mistook the country people, London servant girls and London apprentices he saw dressed in their holiday clothes at Greenwich fair for 'people of fashion'.[33]

Poets agreed. 'Holyday Gown' was the title of one of John Cunningham's *Poems, Chiefly Pastoral* of 1766. It began:

> In holyday gown and my new-fangled hat,
> Last Monday I tript to the fair:
> I held up my head, and I'll tell you for what,
> Brisk Roger I guess'd wou'd be there.[34]

The same theme was taken up in the broadside ballads produced and reproduced by printers across England for a popular andience. The following version of 'Nelly the Milk Maid' was printed at Kenilworth in Warwickshire:

> Young Nelly the Milk-Maid brisk buxom and gay,
> Oft times with young Roger she'd wantonly play
> One evening of late at a dancing they met,
> And she asked her Dame leave to go to the wake . . .
> She put on her best clothes and away she did steer
> She went to meet Roger, when she came he was there;
> They danc'd at the feast, and had good beer and cake,
> And the best of fine dainties found out at the wake.[35]

Similarly, ballads printed in eighteenth-century London celebrated the holiday finery worn at Greenwich and other metropolitan fairs (fig. 123), sometimes suggesting it might be acquired second-hand at Rag Fair, in Rosemary Lane:

> Come my jolly buxom girls,
> Now the holidays are coming,
> Look spruce about the head & heels
> To Rag Fair all be running;
> A crown my girl from top to toe,
> Will rig you out completely,
> And then to Greenwich you may go
> With your sweetheart so neatly.[36]

122 (*following pages*) Joseph Nollekens, *May Day* (detail), c.1740, oil on panel, private collection. The whole range of activities characteristic of a village festivity are portrayed here: dancing, drinking, competing, courting, retailing. A group of well-dressed gentry is depicted in the left foreground, the men with laced coats and hats, one of the women in a riding habit, but elsewhere in the painting the young women of the village are shown dressed in their best clothes. The hat and breeches hanging from the pole probably represent prizes in the wrestling and cudgelling contests that are in progress.

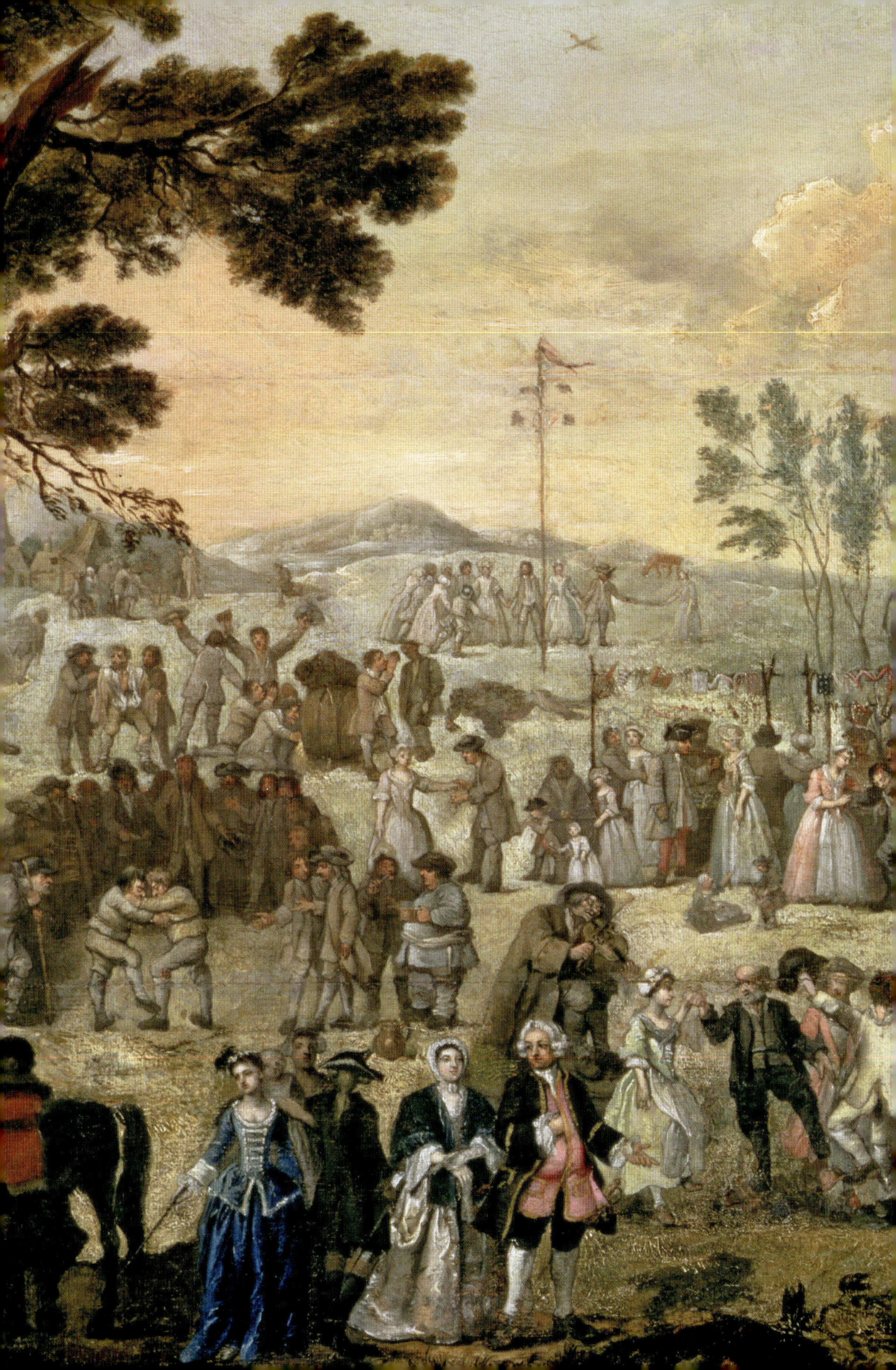

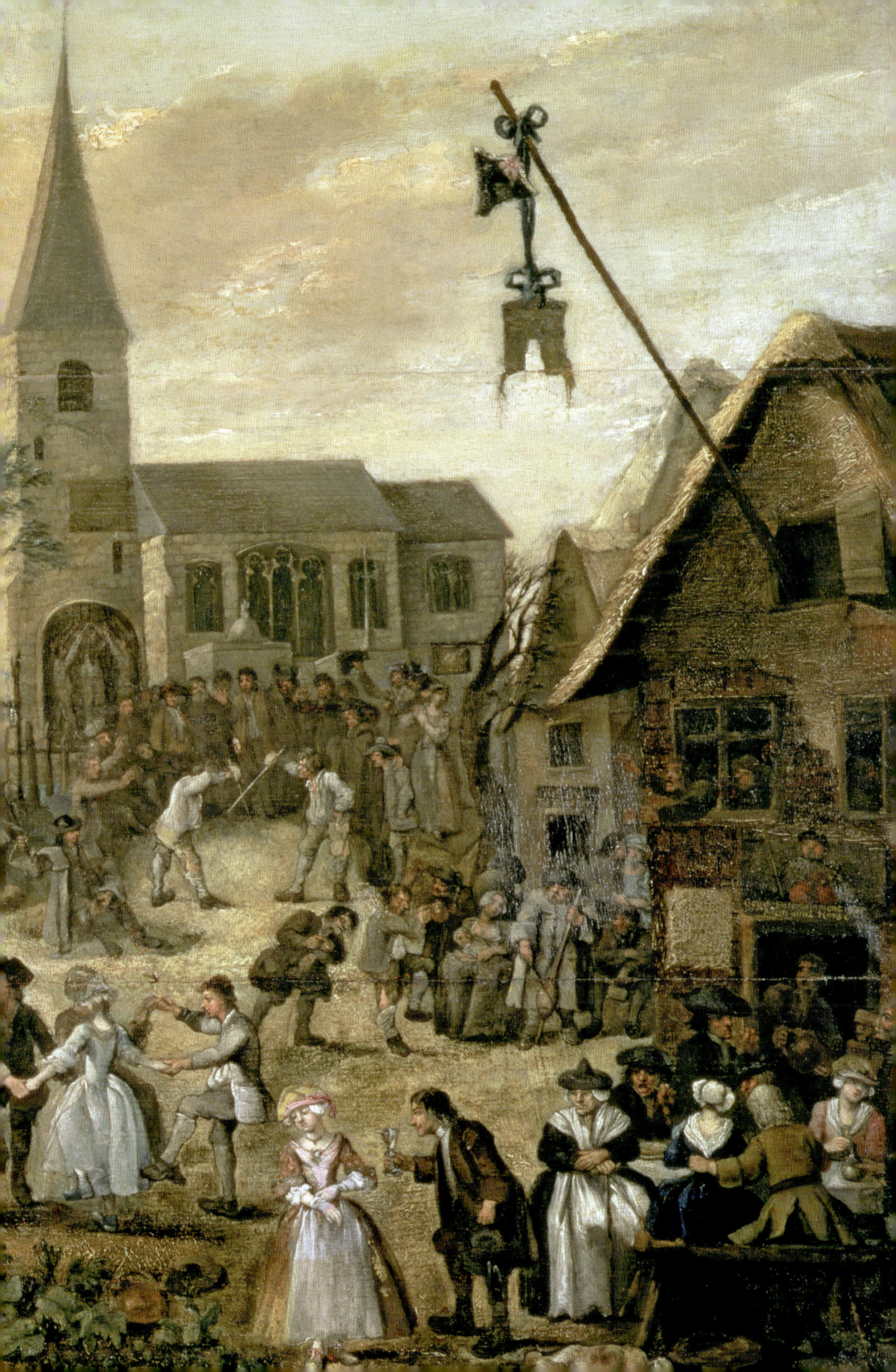

123 *Greenwich Hill or Holyday Gambols*, 1750, printed engraving, British Museum, London, BMSat 3111. A socially mixed company, including a number of sailors wearing trousers, dance, court, drink and sport on the May Day holiday at Greenwich, downriver from London, where couples ran or rolled down the hill. By comparison, asserts the caption, 'the Delights of Assembly and Ball, are . . . just nothing at all'.

    The expectation that those attending wakes and fairs would dress up was so strong that the Oldham weaver William Rowbottom was able to gauge the prosperity of the cotton trade in his diary by how well those attending the local rushbearings were dressed. It did not take long for boom or slump in the local staple industry to manifest itself in the clothes worn by revellers. In 1795, Middleton rushbearing 'was very throngly attended and owing to Nankeens and other light goods being so high in wages the inhabitants appeared in high spirits and well dressed'. At Oldham rushbearing in 1802 there was 'a Deal of Company wich owing to the Goodness of the times where verey weel Dresed', and in 1804 'a vast of forreighn Company who as well as the natives where very well Dresed as usial much Drinking'.[37]

    Displays of finery on these occasions could extend beyond dress. The village rushcarts competitively paraded at Lancashire wakes in the eighteenth century became vehicles for exhibiting plebeian consumer luxuries of all kinds. Samuel Bamford, another Lancashire weaver, recalled that at Middleton wake in the late eighteenth century, it was the custom for the women of each household to contribute to a communal display on the packsheet which covered the cart:

> [There were] silver watches, trays, spoons, sugar-tongs, tea-pots, snuffers, or other fitting articles of ornament and value; and the more numerous and precious the articles were, the greater was the deference which the party which displayed them expected from the wondering crowd.[38]

Fairs, wakes and other festivities were, moreover, not just events where best clothes were worn, but also places where they could be acquired. Retailers of cloth and clothing of every kind set up their stalls in large numbers at fairs, taking advantage of the crowds and providing them with an unusually wide choice of merchandise. The Latham family bought cloth and a new hat at local fairs. The cheesemaking Cheshire farmer Thomas Furber advanced one of his female dairymaids 15s. 6d. from her wages to purchase clothes at Wrenbury Wakes in 1789.[39] To give or buy presents at fairs was so familiar that such gifts were known as fairings. They were particularly associated with courtship, for which the local calendar of wakes and fairs was crucial, as popular ballads tell us. Samuel Bamford courted his future wife at Middleton Wakes.[40] Courtship must have been one of the attractions of fairs for young women like Robert Heaton's servants and Richard Latham's daughters, who occasionally received small amounts of money to spend there. Ribbons were especially common as fairings, famously so in the song 'Oh dear! What can the matter be':

> Oh dear! What can the matter be?
> Dear, dear, what can the matter be?
> O dear, what can the matter be?
> Johnny's so long at the fair?
>
> He promised to buy me a fairing should please me,
> And then for a kiss, oh! he vowed he would tease me,
> He promised he'd buy me a bunch of blue ribbons
> To tie up my bonnie brown hair.[41]

Often ribbons served as the first in a sequence of courtship presents that could become steps on the way to a customary binding or promise of marriage (figs 119, 124, 125).[42]

Clothing also featured prominently among the prizes offered to the winners of the sporting contests that proliferated at fairs and other recreations. Smock races by women were the most common, in both town and country, usually involving a prize of a smock made from a fine linen such as Holland. Values for these smocks mentioned in advertisements ranged from 11 shillings to 15 shillings, more than three times the cost of the coarse shifts of rawlin or harden bought by Robert Heaton's servants.[43] Sometimes their desirability was further enhanced by decoration with lace, ruffles or ribbons (figs 126, 127). The Hertfordshire farmer John Carrington attended the fair at Birch

124 George Morland, *Valentine's Day, The Fairing*, 1787, oil on canvas, Victoria and Albert Museum, London, 541-1882. A young woman sitting at a cottage door holds up a length of blue ribbon she has been given as a fairing.

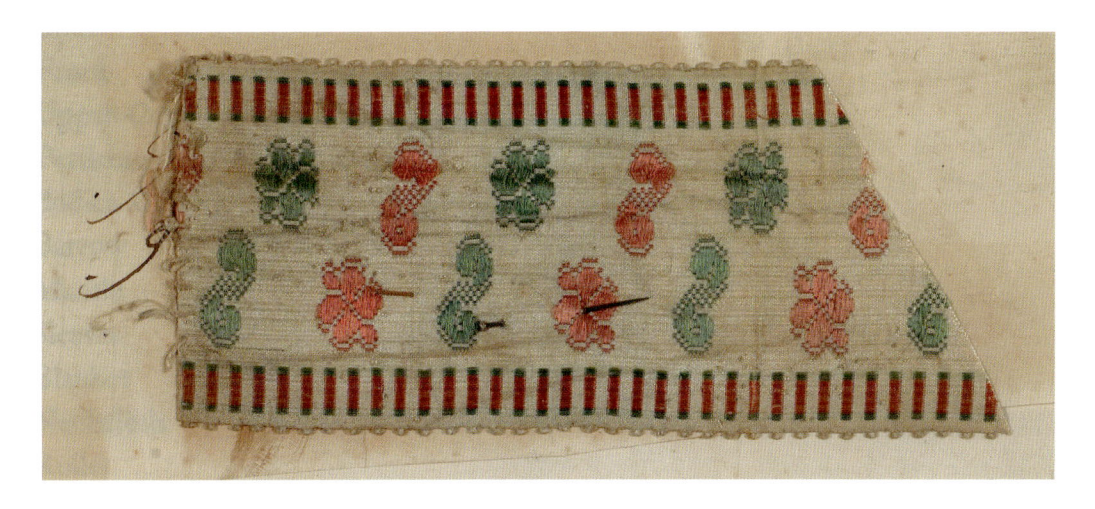

125 'Ribbon', 1754, polychrome silk ribbon with a repeat pattern of woven figures in pink and green on a white ground, London Metropolitan Archives, A/FH/A/9/1/16, Foundling no. 1177.

Green in April 1805, where he saw a race by 'Young girls for a shift deckerated with Ribons'.[44]

Other prizes included silver-laced hats, silver shoe and coat buckles, ribbons, cambric handkerchiefs and aprons, kid gloves, caps of fine linen, waistcoats trimmed with gold lace, breeches, petticoats and gowns, amounting to a checklist of the desirable clothing accessories and smaller garments worn by plebeian men and women as their best clothes.[45] At Weston in Norfolk in 1788, the clergyman James Woodforde recorded 'Merry doings at the Heart to day being Whit Monday, plowing for a Pair of Breeches, running for a Shift, Raffling for a Gown etc.'[46] At Boughton Green fair in Northamptonshire in 1721, the prize for men fighting with cudgels was a hat worth a guinea, and for wrestling, a similar hat and six pairs of buckskin gloves, each worth five shillings.[47]

We know that a local landowner provided the prizes at this Northamptonshire fair, because he was identified as the benefactor in a newspaper report of the event, but such prizes were more typically a form of commercial sponsorship by publicans, who supported festivities to encourage the consumption of drink. Publicans, unlike gentry, were rarely feted as sponsors by the local press, but they were in the lead when it came to introducing organised races and competitions at customary festivities.[48] At the wake at Didsbury near Manchester in the summer of 1791, Thomas Wood, the proprietor of the Ring o' Bells, laid out four shillings to provide a hat to be run for, as well as paying for a fiddler, rushes for the rush cart, and drink for bell-ringers and morris dancers. Wood's account book makes it clear that he regularly supported a whole programme of wakes' attractions at his public house, including races, sports, shows, musicians and morris dancers.[49] It was reported to be customary in Lancashire and Cheshire for the

126 John Collet, *An Holland Smock to be run for, by any Woman born in this County: The best Woman in three Heats*, 1770, printed engraving, Lewis Walpole Library, Farmington, Conn., 770.0.38. A smock race at a country fair. The prize shift or smock, decorated with a ribbon, hangs in the tree, along with be-ribboned hats, the prizes in other contests. A sailor dressed in a jacket and trousers examines the smock. The pervasive innuendo emphasises the reputation of fairs as places for sexual encounters.

prizes to be offered by publicans at wakes, such as hats and tea kettles, to be displayed beforehand at their windows.[50]

The significance that customary festivities held for plebeian consumers of clothing can, finally, be registered in the attitude of the Quakers. Not only were the best clothes worn by young plebeian adults at these festivities precisely those that bore the brunt of the sect's internal discipline, such as 'the superfluous use of ribbands' condemned by the York Quarterly Women's meeting in 1757, but Quakers were also consistently hostile to attendance at fairs, as were Methodists.[51] Plebeian Quakers who persisted in wearing fashionable holiday clothes to attend fairs risked exclusion. Dorothy Garbutt, a young Quaker from the village of Rounton in Yorkshire, was expelled in 1797 for having been 'very inconsistent particularly in respect to dress, being accustomed to have two sorts of dress, one to attend meetings, the other fairs, markets, etc'. Yet so ingrained was the customary distinction between workaday and holiday clothes that it was reported: 'she don't think there is any rong in it'.[52]

127 J. Pitts, *A Smock Race at Tottenham Court Fair*, 1784, printed engraving, British Museum, London, BMSat 9668. The prize shift or smock at this London fair is hanging from the pole on the right and is decorated with a ribbon. The fair is portrayed as a site of disorder and dissipation.

The unfortunate Dorothy Garbutt was one of a large number of young plebeian men and women who enjoyed disposable incomes sufficient to acquire petty luxuries, especially clothing that was broadly fashionable. The distinction they made between their best clothes and their work clothes was rooted in a fashion system that was an integral component of eighteenth-century commercial expansion. Yet the timing and location of the occasions when their best clothes were worn were shaped by a festive calendar that found its legitimacy in emphatically customary usage, and sometimes had to be defended against attack by local elites. It was through dress that working people were most likely to realise their material ambitions, yet opportunities to flaunt their fashionable finery were subject to a customary calendar that controlled many of their most important life decisions, in particular courtship, marriage and employment. Popular consumption and popular custom were inextricably entwined.

128 Paul Sandby, *Dancing outside a Public House on Lambeth Marsh* (detail), *c.*1770, watercolour, Lambeth Archives, LP12/170/IAM. M.1. A couple dance to music provided by a man playing a barrel organ outside a pub on the southern edge of London.

Conclusion

In the eighteenth century, material abundance helped define what it was to be English for ordinary people. All sorts of new consumer goods insinuated themselves into everyday life, not least new kinds of clothing. Yet eighteenth-century England was not a consumer society of the kind which has, since the early Cold War era, evoked enthusiasm and distaste in equal measure. Advocates and opponents alike have seen retail choice as the defining characteristic of modern consumer society, irrespective of whether they celebrate that choice as a vehicle for freedom and self-realisation, or dismiss it as an illusion inflicted on supine, brainwashed consumers by hidden persuaders in the mass media. Whatever its merits as a characterisation of modern western societies, this notion of a consumer society, with its emphasis on whole populations affluent enough to exercise choice, retail supply tightly integrated with commercial propaganda, and material abundance combined with rapid turnover of material possessions, is inappropriate to the eighteenth century.

The difficulty here is not simply one of degree. Doubtless, in the eighteenth century most people's choices were constrained by limited disposable incomes, reflected in a correspondingly low incidence of retail purchases and material possessions. But in addition, many of the things people used, treated and spoke of as their own were supplied to them on terms which removed choice. Goods reached eighteenth-century consumers, especially plebeian consumers, not just as retail purchases, but through a diversity of other channels over which they exercised widely differing degrees of control. Often these involved non-market, semi-market or indirect mechanisms, as when landlords furnished lodgings for their tenants, or employers fed their workers, or vestries clothed parish paupers, or small items of clothing were made up in the wearer's family.[1] Plebeian consumers, as we have seen, were frequently involuntary consumers. In characterising their relationship with the world of goods, we need to take into account not simply what they owned, but what they had in their possession and how it came to them. In other words, we need to recognise the diversity of means by which they sustained an engagement with things.

We also need to remember that the material characteristics of the things in their possession, whether wholly owned or not, were significantly different from the artefacts conventionally associated with a modern consumer society. Modern consumer goods are cheap, disposable, infrequently repaired and quickly worthless. Eighteenth-century artefacts, by contrast, tended to be costly, durable, much repaired and readily marketable second-hand. For working people whose lives could be precarious and unpredictable, consumer goods were as much a store of capital to realise in times of hardship as they were physical comforts, emblems of emulative self-advancement, markers of social distinction or badges of personal identity.

Clothes shared many of these distinguishing characteristics. Nevertheless, if any component of the material lives of plebeian men and women in the eighteenth century can bear comparison with modern consumer goods, it is their clothing. Everyone had to dress. Even those driven by poverty or ill health into the Marylebone workhouse in London in the 1770s were clothed, and only a minority arrived in rags. A good number brought changes of some items of clothing with them. Similarly, the poorer victims of the fire at Brandon in Suffolk in 1789 owned spare clothes which they kept at home, while many working people who lived in cheap London lodgings had changes of clothing stored in boxes in their rooms that were vulnerable to theft when they were out at work. In July 1756, for instance, a deal box, two cloth coats, two flannel waistcoats, one shag waistcoat, one dimity waistcoat, seven linen shirts and a guinea and a half belonging to John Jones, drawer at the Gentleman and Porter public house in Leicester Fields, were stolen from his lodging room while he was at work.[2] Plebeian men and women could realistically expect to own duplicates of many items of clothing, including undergarments, such as shirts or shifts, and outer garments, such as gowns and petticoats, coats and waistcoats. Duplication is not, of course, evidence for unfettered choice, but it suggests that clothing was an area of consumption where relative abundance prevailed and the exercise of discrimination was a possibility, even among the working poor.

Opportunities for exercising discrimination presented themselves with some frequency, because, as semi-durables rather than durables, clothes had to be replaced regularly. Most clothing was sourced commercially. Even in the rural north of England, with perhaps a lower density of shops than the south-east, replacement was predominantly by means of retail purchase. It required engagement with a host of specialist commercial suppliers, from shoemakers and hatters to mercers and drapers. Indeed, as self-provisioning of woollen and especially linen fabrics declined, purchases from drapers must have become ever more frequent, although cutting out and sewing linen clothes went on being undertaken by the women of many families. Because personal identity and reputation were so tied up with the way clothes looked, even poor people expected to have their outer garments made up by professionals. As a result, replacing those garments required commercial transactions not just to acquire fabric, but also to have it cut out and assembled by tailors and mantuamakers.

While many ordinary people owned duplicate items of clothing, they often had few other belongings. Insofar as their material lives revolved around what they owned, clothing loomed large. In cases tried at the Old Bailey involving working people's property stolen from their lodgings, the stolen goods consisted almost exclusively of clothes, often accompanied by a cheap deal box and occasionally by some money.[3]

This pattern was especially characteristic of young, single adults. Among the victims of the 1789 Brandon fire, clothing accounted for two-thirds or more of the value of the goods lost by the three servants, who are likely to have been young and single. For two of them – Sarah Holmes and William Eagle – it accounted for virtually everything they lost. By contrast, for the blacksmith Mark Palmer and the cordwainer John Neel, both of whom had families, as well as for the mantuamaker Elizabeth Cooper, clothes accounted for less than two-thirds of their losses. Their missing goods included significant quantities of domestic furnishings and equipment. Nevertheless, in none of their cases did clothes account for less than a third of their losses.[4] Clothes remained prominent even among the goods owned by older, married householders.

It was on clothes, therefore, that plebeian consumer expectations focused, far more than on other durable or semi-durable consumer goods. It was entirely realistic for ordinary people to assume that at some point in their lives they would own stylish, fashionable clothing. For most, that opportunity came in young adulthood, when apprentices saved to buy genteel coats, high-earning miners and sailors flourished their silver watches, and serving maids ran into debt so they could walk out in printed cotton gowns. It was a brief gaudy hour, when fine clothes celebrated life's early achievements and initiated sexual possibilities. The exigencies of the family poverty cycle meant that, for most, such opportunities narrowed in the early years of marriage. And of course there were some who refused them, preferring the solace of the alehouse or the religious meeting. Others were denied them by the hazards of eighteenth-century plebeian life: ill health, unemployment and single motherhood.

In analysing plebeian fashion, *The Dress of the People* has focused on how it was embedded in the practices of everyday life, not on the issues of meaning and identity which have often engaged those who study dress. In particular, the book has stressed the distinction between best and working clothes and the way that distinction was articulated through the customary religious and festive calendar. Custom and consumption, this book has argued, were intertwined in ways that have important implications for the debates about consumer goods with which this chapter began. One implication is for the notion of emulation. Modern historians have been as keen as elite eighteenth-century commentators to treat changes in plebeian taste as the outcome of a process of emulation. It is true that whole new categories of goods, including muslins, tea wares, watches and cotton counterpanes, were acquired first by the rich and the fashionable and only subsequently trickled down into the receptive hands of plebeian men and women. Although not all clothing fashions originated among the *beau monde*, moving subsequently down the social scale, plebeian dress did, in its basic components, broadly follow the trends of high fashion. Many plebeian men and women shared a longing to acquire clothes that aped specific fashions worn by the better-off, whether it was a genteel laced hat in the 1740s, a sprigged cotton gown in the 1750s or the large metal buttons fashionable in the 1780s. Yet the everyday fashion worn by ordinary people amounted to more than just an effort to emulate the taste of the rich, 'the mill girl who wanted to dress like a duchess', as Neil McKendrick puts it.[5] We should beware of reproducing eighteenth-century snobberies by portraying such behaviour as an attempt at emulation that inevitably misfired.

It is important to remember that as new fashions moved through the social hierarchy, they changed. They were made from different materials, they joined different assemblages of clothes, and, most importantly, they were worn in different circumstances, acquiring different meanings in the process. Even the most stylish plebeian clothes were usually worn not at the balls and assemblies frequented by the genteel, but, as we have seen, at popular festivities of a kind that often provoked hostility as inducements to profligacy, insobriety and immorality, sometimes, indeed, because of the way clothes were worn. When the Reverend William Holland, no evangelical firebrand, attended festivities at Stowey in Somerset in May 1800, he witnessed 'so terrible a race, petticoats tucked up to the knees and stays open, or taken off, that I began to think it became almost indecent. I don't think I shall stand by to countenance such exhibitions in future for I hate to see the female character let down.'[6] At the Lancashire wakes in the 1790s and early 1800s described by the Oldham weaver William Rowbottom, high wages and full employment for the cotton workers meant well-dressed revellers, but also an orgy of drunkenness and fighting.[7] And, of course, the rich and fashionable were terrified when the Lancashire wakes tradition of wearing best clothes to process with banners behind a rush cart to a neighbouring town was reworked in the years after Waterloo to serve radical political ends. Among the men and women who walked peaceably in procession from towns all over south-east Lancashire to Manchester in August 1819, only to be cut down by the Yeomanry Cavalry at Peterloo, 'the majority were young persons, in their best Sunday's suits', reported an eye-witness, the journalist Archibald Prentice.[8] The cut and decoration of the clothes donned for these events may often have descended to their plebeian wearers from the *beau monde* by a process that can be termed emulative, but the same cannot be said of the uses to which the clothes were put or the ways they were understood.

The intertwining of plebeian custom with stylish clothing also has broader implications for the way we conceptualise the history of consumption in the eighteenth century. It demonstrates that custom and consumption could be allies, not enemies. The customary assumptions and practices that ordered many aspects of plebeian life in early-modern England were symbiotically entwined with the development of the early-modern market economy. Contrary to Edward Thompson's insistence that in the eighteenth century 'capitalist process and non-economic customary behaviour are in active and conscious conflict, as in resistance to new patterns of consumption', customary practices often flourished precisely because they provided opportunities and legitimising excuses to participate in attractive forms of commercialised consumption.[9] As Hans Medick has pointed out, 'Thompson's work lacks an analysis of those quieter but equally "communal" characteristic manifestations of the everyday life of the plebeian lower orders, which developed – to a considerable extent in harmony with the growth of capitalistic markets – in consumption, fashions and especially in drinking culture.'[10]

Even Medick, however, puts too much stress on the elements of resistance and picaresque 'irrationality' in everyday plebeian consumption, so concerned is he to distinguish communal plebeian life from the stereotype of an emerging rational, individualistic 'bourgeois' culture. Such cultural stereotypes, often derived uncritically from eighteenth- and nineteenth-century models, can be profoundly misleading in the study of eighteenth-century consumption. The stereotypical view of eighteenth-century plebeian culture as unremittingly collectivist, anti-individualistic, immune to rational economic calculation and overwhelmingly short-term in its time horizons ignores the obvious variations of plebeian experience which grew out of differences of gender, age, location and employment. Even among single adult working men, who were perhaps the group in the plebeian population most likely to fall into unpredictable, picaresque lives, attitudes to consumption varied considerably. They embraced the disdain for clothes exhibited by the hard-drinking Tyneside collier Johnny Chapman, but they also included the craving for a genteel suit of clothes that drove the aspirational Nottingham apprentice William Hutton. Yet life was not all work and no play for Hutton. Having laboriously assembled his genteel suit of clothes in 1741, he took time off to enjoy the customary festivities during Nottingham race week, along with his fellow apprentices.[11]

In the sphere of clothing at least, plebeian custom embraced the market as often as it resisted it. Customary practice was uniquely receptive to dressing well, which in the context of the eighteenth-century commercial fashion system meant dressing in ways that drew heavily on the modes of the elite. Affordable, new fashions readily insinuated themselves into popular ways of dressing precisely because wearing special, fashionable clothes fitted customary expectations about how the distinction between Sundays and weekdays, holidays and workdays should be marked. Even if, as Hans-Joachim Voth has argued, working people enjoyed fewer and fewer days of leisure as the eighteenth century progressed, the consequence may simply have been an intensification of the commercialised opportunities for leisure in the free time that remained: cock and hen clubs, hops and dances at public houses, ever more elaborate entertainments at fairs, all requiring their participants to don their best clothes (fig. 128).[12] Custom was not immutable; commerce helped it change.

Edward Thompson famously insists that the 'share of the "average" working man in the "benefits of economic progress"' was paltry, consisting of more potatoes, soap and candles, some tea and sugar, and a few articles of cotton clothing for his family.[13] This book has argued that for many ordinary eighteenth-century men and women, new kinds of fashionable clothing, especially those made of cotton, represented a far more important benefit than Thompson allows, one that was implicated in the fundamental temporal ordering of everyday life. Yet clothing remained a precarious benefit, however prized, fashionable or hard-won it may have been.

The last decade of the eighteenth century and the first two decades of the nineteenth were an economic switchback ride for ordinary people. Periods of exceptionally high wages and full employment, reflecting a context of burgeoning economic opportunity, were tempered by times of devastating slump and near-famine food prices against a background of general inflation. No group of workers felt the violence of these economic oscillations more than those in the Lancashire cotton industry, as Thompson himself describes so vividly in his *Making of the English Working Class*.[14] The Oldham weaver William Rowbottom registered the industry's prosperous peaks during these tumultuous years by noting in his diary the large numbers of well-dressed people at the local wakes. During its poverty-striken troughs, references to clothes are notably absent from his diary. In times of hardship, such as New Year 1799, when Rowbottom found it 'imposable fully to describe the wretchedness of the poor of this once happy country', his yardstick was hunger. 'Roast beff pyes and ale are not to be seen on the poor mans table on the conterary it is graced with misery and want and a universal lowness of spirits and dejected countinance appear in every one.'[15] Hard times meant that clothes, including best clothes, had to be pawned, sold or simply worn to rags. With starvation imminent, clothing ceased to be an immediate priority. That did not mean it ceased to be important. In 1819, another hard year, the working people of the Lancashire cotton towns wore their Sunday best to march to St Peter's Field, Manchester, on the occasion of what became known as the Peterloo Massacre. Wearing their best clothes to demand parliamentary reform demonstrated self-respect, invoked the collective power of a vibrant customary culture, and suggested a quasi-religious seriousness of purpose. It served, at the same time, to show they considered themselves people of substance. They may not have lived in a consumer society, but they had things to lose.

Appendix 1
Sources

WRITTEN SOURCES

This book brings together a multiplicity of written sources from the eighteenth century to rediscover the consumer habits of ordinary people.[1] They range from the handful of surviving autobiographies written by working men and women to the lists of expenditure laboriously compiled in parishes across the land by overseers of the poor. Many of the sources have not previously been employed for this purpose; others have been almost entirely overlooked by historians. Two neglected sources are particularly important for their capacity to provide quantitative as well as qualitative information: the records of the criminal courts and newspaper advertisements for fugitives.

The need to employ a wide range of sometimes neglected written sources is a consequence of the major evidential obstacles that confront historians of clothing worn by ordinary people. The principal source employed by historians of early-modern England to explore other aspects of the history of consumer behaviour – the probate inventory – is of limited assistance here.[2] There are three principal reasons. First, probate inventories rarely survive after 1740, other than in Yorkshire and a few peculiar jurisdictions. Second, inventories for working people are relatively rare, because the compilation of inventories was heavily biased towards the wealthier half of the population who had more property to bequeath. Third, after 1660, it was only very occasionally that probate inventories included an itemised list of the deceased's clothes. In the vast majority of inventories after this date, clothing is aggregated under the headings 'apparel' or 'purse and apparel', and accorded a valuation that is a suspiciously round figure, in Yorkshire often £1.

Yet there is a shortage of alternative sources.[3] No one set of written records can provide the historian of plebeian clothing with the combination of quantitative and qualitative evidence that the probate inventory, despite its limitations, offers the study of other aspects of everyday material life. The history of plebeian clothing has, therefore, to be compiled from a patchwork of sources, all of them to some degree obdurate, flawed and incomplete. Assembling the evidence they provide to throw light on the kinds of clothing characteristically worn by plebeian men and women involves a process of triangulation reminiscent of the work of the eighteenth century's pioneering map-makers. In the case of criminal records and newspaper advertisements for fugitives, it also involves the negotiation of some thorny technical issues.

Criminal records[4]

Theft of clothes and clothing materials was one of the most frequently prosecuted offences in the eighteenth-century criminal courts. The process of prosecution generated a sequence of documents that survive in large numbers in the court records.[5] For the historian of clothing, three types of documents are especially useful: the deposition, the recognizance and the indictment. Depositions (otherwise known as informations and examinations) were a precis of the spoken testimony offered to magistrates by witnesses to explain the circumstances of the case. They were written down by the magistrate's clerk, usually soon after the accused was apprehended, and represent the evidence on which the decision was initially made to send the accused for trial. A recognizance was a formal document drawn up by the magistrate, usually at the same time as a deposition, to bind the prosecutor (usually the victim) or witnesses to appear in court. The indictment was the formal charge on which the accused was tried, drawn up by the clerk of the court shortly before the trial. Among other things, it listed and valued the stolen property.

Depositions, recognizances and indictments can often be found together among the official records of the criminal courts. Transcripts of the evidence actually given in court are much more unusual. They were, however, compiled and printed throughout the eighteenth century for trials at the Old Bailey in London and are known as the Old Bailey Proceedings. The Old Bailey dealt with cases of theft from the City of London and the County of Middlesex, which together accounted for most of the urban population of the metropolis. By the eighteenth century a majority of London's population north of the River Thames lived in Middlesex.

Two groups of criminal records dating from the 1670s to the 1820s are employed in this book. First, manuscript records of trials at the courts of Quarter Sessions and Assizes from a number of counties in the North of England, including both towns and rural areas, industrial districts and agricultural regions. Second, the manuscript and printed records of trials at the Old Bailey.

Two linked but distinct sets of data have been extracted from the criminal records. The first is based on indictments from Yorkshire and London, and is used mainly quantitatively. The Yorkshire sample is drawn from all the surviving indictments at Quarter Sessions and Assizes for cases of theft of clothing from unambiguously plebeian owners in the North and West Ridings of Yorkshire during the decades 1730–9, 1750–9 and 1780–9 and their corresponding recognizances.[6] It comprises 205 indictments which list 852 individual items of clothing.[7] The London sample is drawn from all the surviving Middlesex manuscript indictments at Gaol Delivery at the Old Bailey for clothes thefts from unambiguously plebeian owners at all eight sittings of the court in 1756 and at four of the eight sittings in 1785 (January, February, June and September), and their corresponding recognizances.[8] It comprises 103 indictments, which list 657 individual items of clothing.[9] It was decided not to use the indictments for clothes theft at the Middlesex and Westminster Sessions of the Peace because their numbers were relatively small and, in the case of the Westminster quarter sessions, their survival is poor.[10]

The second set of data extracted from the criminal records draws on witness statements in the north of England and London, and is used mainly to supply qualitative evidence. The northern sample is based on an examination of all the surviving depositions for cases of murder, rape, and theft of money, cloth, clothing and textile raw materials for the years 1680–99, 1730–9, 1750–9 and 1780–99 in the Assize records for York, Kingston-upon-Hull, Yorkshire, Newcastle-upon-Tyne, Northumberland, Cumberland and Westmorland, and in the Quarter Sessions records for the North and West Ridings of Yorkshire.[11] A different approach is adopted for London. Taking advantage of the word-search facilities available for the printed Old Bailey trial transcripts digitised at Old Bailey Online (www.oldbaileyonline.org), trials for both the City of London and Middlesex between 1674 and 1820 were searched by means of a variety of keyword combinations for evidence about clothing and clothing materials. Because the printed Old Bailey Proceedings are fewer in number and less detailed before 1740, these searches were supplemented by an examination of all the surviving manuscript depositions from the Old Bailey for thefts of cloth and clothing in Middlesex during the decade 1690–9.[12]

Criminal indictments in cases of theft usually itemise the stolen goods, often describing the materials from which they were made and sometimes their other characteristics, including their colour, although at the Old Bailey the materials from which clothes were made cease to be regularly identified soon after 1800. Indictments also value the goods and identify their owners. In this book, information about clothes gathered from indictments has been used principally to establish quantitative patterns of ownership. To use indictments for this purpose a number of difficulties have to be addressed, in particular establishing the social status of owners, interpreting the monetary values ascribed to stolen goods, and allowing for the selectivity of thieves and victims.

It was an eighteenth-century legal convention that criminal indictments should use a narrow range of status and occupational descriptions to identify victims of theft. They bore little relationship to the actual occupations of those victims. This study is concerned specifically with plebeian owners of stolen clothing. It requires, therefore, that plebeian victims be distinguished from victims with a higher social status. This cannot be done with any confidence using the indictments alone. Instead, it is necessary to draw status descriptions from the corresponding recognizance or deposition. In contrast to indictments, they employed the whole range of status and occupational designations in common use during the eighteenth century.[13]

Even here, it is sometimes difficult to distinguish between, for example, master and man in the same occupation, or between larger and smaller farmers. For female owners, who are almost always identified only as widow or single woman, it is especially difficult to establish status distinctions. In ambiguous cases like these, this study only treats owners as plebeian if ancillary evidence about their work or type of residence is available in the corresponding depositions or trial transcripts. Unfortunately, recognizances and depositions change in their propensity to identify occupations, with occupations mentioned less often, and in some jurisdictions not at all, before 1750. For Middlesex, it was only after the 1740s that occupations were recorded in Old Bailey recognizances. For Yorkshire, there survive very few recognizances at all in the Assize records before 1720, while occupational information in both recognizances and depositions was more likely to be recorded in the 1780s than in the 1730s or 1750s. It is for this reason that this book confines its indictment-based analysis of quantitative patterns of plebeian clothes ownership to the last two-thirds of the eighteenth century, specifically the 1730s, 1750s and 1780s for Yorkshire and 1756 and 1785 for London.

The descriptions of stolen goods in indictments were written by the court clerk at the start of the court session, probably in consultation with the prosecutor, who was usually the victim of the theft and the owner of the goods. In most cases, the stolen goods itemised in the indictment correspond closely to the goods described in the depositions compiled by the committing magistrate shortly after the accused was apprehended. Valuations are not usually found in depositions, however. The valuations given in indictments have to be used with caution, because they were subject to manipulation to serve legal priorities. At Quarter Sessions in the West and North Ridings of Yorkshire in the 1780s, stolen goods on any one indictment were always valued to add up to 12d. or less, irrespective of their actual value. This was to ensure that the charge remained that of petty larceny, which was defined as theft of goods worth 12d. or less. The same practice seems to have been frequently followed at Quarter Sessions in the 1730s and 1750s. Consequently, indictment valuations at Quarter Sessions are not used in this book.

At the superior criminal courts such as the Yorkshire Assizes and the Old Bailey, where more serious offences were tried, indictment valuations also appear occasionally to have been manipulated, when the definition of an aggravated theft such as shoplifting turned on the value of the stolen goods. Normally, however, such manipulation was undertaken by the jury when giving a verdict. The jury had discretion to find the accused guilty to a value below the threshold that would trigger a more severe punishment. Indictment valuations at Assizes and the Old Bailey are, therefore, much more credible than those at Quarter Sessions, especially when used in aggregate. In the small minority of cases where valuations were provided by owners in depositions or in court, indictment valuations almost always follow them, suggesting that indictment values represent the valuations supplied by owners to the court clerks. It is possible that owners inflated valuations of stolen goods, although in most cases there was no obvious advantage to the prosecutor in doing so. Yet there are examples where it is clear that realism prevailed. Among the clothing stolen from a Burniston, Yorkshire widow in 1780, for example, was a silk and cotton handkerchief. She described it in her deposition as being 'of little or no value', in contrast to her red spotted silk handkerchief and her muslin neckcloth, each of which she valued at one shilling. The indictment followed suit. Her silk and cotton handkerchief was valued at one penny, her other two handkerchiefs at a shilling each.[14] In the bulk of Assize and Old Bailey cases, we can therefore assume that the values on the indictments represent the owner's estimation, accurate or otherwise, of the resale value of the goods. It is on this assumption that indictment valuations from these courts are used in this book.

The clothes listed in criminal indictments do not, of course, offer a representative sample of the clothes owned or worn by eighteenth-century plebeian men and women. Large numbers of plebeian victims, including many labourers, did prosecute in cases of clothes theft, if only because there was no other way to retrieve their property once it had been sold or pawned, or because the involvement of officials such as constables or magistrates in the detection and apprehension of a suspect made it difficult to avoid being bound over to prosecute.[15] Yet thieves were probably selective in what they stole, tending to take more desirable, expensive and easily disposed items, in addition to those that were especially vulnerable as they dried on country hedges or lay unattended in boxes in multi-occupied urban lodging houses. Equally, owners may have been more willing to prosecute when it was their best clothes that were stolen, as opposed to their oldest, workaday garments. The poorest among the poor are probably under-represented among the indictments as they had fewer clothes to steal and less desirable clothes at that. The time and cost of prosecution were, moreover, likely to have been especially discouraging to the very poorest, despite the lure of statutory rewards and new provision during the second half of the eighteenth century for the payment of costs.[16]

If the aggregated patterns of ownership that emerge from the indictments do not provide a balanced sample of the different elements in the typical plebeian wardrobe, they do, nevertheless, enable us to observe the range of what was owned, the relative values of the various items of clothing worn, and the trends of changes in ownership over time. In other words, indictments allow us to map the different types of clothes the poorer half of the population managed to acquire, as well as their capacity to respond to clothing innovations. It is, however, a form of mapping that lacks the contours that would enable us to measure ownership of one variety of a garment as opposed to another with any precision. We always have to bear in mind that the costlier, more desirable and more fashionable varieties of any item may well be over-represented, as well as those clothes that were easiest to steal. Nevertheless, the indictments enjoy a great advantage as evidence over newspaper advertisements for fugitives because, unlike the advertisements, they include large numbers of women's clothes and of the undergarments worn by both sexes.

Witness statements are the other kind of evidence drawn from the criminal records used in this book. Witness statements do not just provide information about how clothes and clothing materials were stolen and how those thefts were investigated. They can also tell us an enormous amount about the unremarkable, everyday lives of clothes and their wearers; about the ways in which clothing and clothing materials were valued, marketed, acquired, made, worn, cleaned, repaired, stored, recycled and disposed of. The usefulness of witness statements for the study of eighteenth-century clothing derives from the interest of the courts in two issues: first, in confirming that the goods were owned by the person named as their owner in the indictment and, second, in following the chain of events leading from the period before the clothes were stolen to the apprehension of the accused, in order to establish how the person concerned came to be the object of suspicion. In addressing these issues, witnesses throw light on almost every aspect of eighteenth-century clothing. Witnesses, of course, sometimes lied. More than two centuries later, it is usually impossible to distinguish truth from falsehood, but lies had to be plausible if they were going to convince the court. It is likely that even concocted evidence offers a reasonably accurate account of prevailing clothing practices.

There was, however, no obligation to provide or record such information. It is not available for all cases. The printed Old Bailey Proceedings did not always detail the evidence offered in court by witnesses. The proportion of cases in the Proceedings which simply state the charge and the verdict is higher in the 1750s than in the 1780s, while before 1740 the majority of trials lack the detailed question-by-question format that increasingly became the norm thereafter. Before 1740, too, there are many Old Bailey sittings for which Proceedings do not survive at all. Similarly, depositions do not necessarily survive, although for the North and West Ridings of Yorkshire they survive for a majority of clothing cases during the eighteenth century at both Assizes and Quarter Sessions. There are no surviving Assize depositions for the years 1700 to 1724 for the northern counties studied.

Newspaper advertisements for fugitives[17]

Two samples of advertisements for fugitives are used systematically in this book to generate quantitative information about the ownership of clothing. One, for the north of England, draws on newspapers from Leeds in Yorkshire and comprises 441 advertisements, which include 1,530 individual items of clothing. The other, for the English Midlands, draws on Worcester and Oxford newspapers and comprises 708 advertisements, which include 2,189 individual items of clothing. Both samples include advertisements originating in towns as well as the countryside, and in areas that were predominantly industrial as well as in areas that were predominantly agricultural. Similar advertisements appeared in London newspapers, but, compared with provincial newspapers, the number of such advertisements was very small relative to the overall numbers of advertisements. This made extracting them too time-consuming for this study.

There are many more surviving advertisements for fugitives in provincial newspapers later in the eighteenth century than earlier. There are three principal reasons. First, the number of provincial newspapers grew markedly. Second, the number of advertisements per edition increased as the century progressed. Third, the survival of provincial newspapers is patchy and this is especially so among those published earlier in the century. Nevertheless, by combining advertisements from different newspapers in the sample areas, it is possible to generate sufficient numbers of advertisements after 1740 to allow comparison of the middle decades of the century with those towards its end. For Leeds, the *Leeds Mercury* was used for the years 1739–45, 1749 and 1789–99, and the *Leeds Intelligencer* for 1754–89. For the Midlands, *Jackson's Oxford Journal* was used for the years 1753–1800, the *Worcester Postman* for 1714–23, the *Weekly Worcester Journal* for 1736–80, *Berrow's Worcester Journal* for 1782–7 and the *Worcester Herald* for 1794.

Most eighteenth-century newspapers carried advertisements for a variety of fugitives. They included apprentices or servants advertised by their masters, husbands or wives advertised by their spouses or their parish overseers of the poor, deserters from the army advertised by their officers, escaped prisoners advertised by gaolers and escaped criminals advertised by their victims. Occasionally suspects already in custody were advertised by gaolers or magistrates to establish their guilt or innocence. Apprentices, criminal offenders and deserters from the army predominated among these advertisements, which are therefore heavily biased towards young men in their teens and twenties. Those advertised appear to have been overwhelmingly plebeian. The soldiers were drawn from the ranks. They were mainly new recruits escaping from recruiting parties and often, therefore, were not in uniform. The apprentices, who were bound, for a fixed period, under contract to their masters, came mainly from the provincial working trades, although masters may have had a greater propensity to advertise the more valuable apprentices in the skilled trades. It is striking that virtually no female apprentices were advertised. The criminal suspects probably shared the overwhelmingly plebeian social profile of criminal offenders who were brought to trial.[18] They too were overwhelmingly male.

Describing the fugitive's appearance was crucial to the success of these advertisements. Height was usually noted and, occasionally, distinguishing physical features, but it was the fugitive's clothing that was described most consistently and in the greatest detail.[19] Advertisements most frequently described the clothing the fugitives ran away wearing. We might assume runaways would have tended to wear their newest, most valuable items, but we should remember that William Hutton ran away from his apprenticeship in 1741 with his best clothes in two bags.[20] Colour and pattern were itemised more frequently in the advertisements than in the indictments, but values were not given. Because the advertisements were designed to enable third parties to identify fugitives in public places, it was overwhelmingly their outer garments that were described, especially main outer garments such as coats, breeches and waistcoats. Accessories and undergarments were mentioned far less often.

VISUAL AND MATERIAL SOURCES

Very few pieces of eighteenth-century clothing have survived that can be identified with any confidence as having belonged to plebeian owners.[21] Plebeian clothes were worn and re-worn by a succession of owners until they fell into rags, or they were cut up and reused for quilts, baby clothes and the like. If, by chance, they outlived the eighteenth century, they were unlikely to excite the attention of collectors or museums. Nineteenth- and twentieth-century museum collections of costume were built up primarily from the clothes worn by the rich, which had comprised the cutting edge of fashion. Museums have, until very recently, largely ignored the clothes worn by the poor, unless they could be construed as a kind of regional folk costume, something that hardly existed in England. This book, consequently, makes little use of surviving garments or accessories to provide evidence about the visual and material characteristics of eighteenth-century plebeian clothing. It does, however, employ a number of alternative visual and material sources as evidence, in particular, eighteenth-century textiles and visual representations of dress in eighteenth-century prints and paintings.

Textiles

The principal group of surviving textiles employed in this book comes from the records of the London Foundling Hospital. The Hospital's billet or admission books from 1741 to 1760 contain what is probably the world's largest collection of everyday eighteenth-century fabrics.[22] From the opening of the Hospital in March 1741, each child left in its care was registered with an identifying number. On the registration forms or billets, initially written but subsequently printed, the sex of the child was entered and often his or her clothing itemised. These forms were subsequently bound up into the billet books. In the cases of more than 10,000 admissions between 1741 and the end of the period of general entry in March 1760, a piece of fabric was pinned to the billet.[23] Sometimes, especially in the period of selective entry from 1741 to 1756, these pieces of fabric were provided as a token to identify the child by whoever left the baby, often with an accompanying letter or statement. Sometimes, especially in the period of general entry from 1756 to 1760, they were cut, presumably by the Hospital's clerk, from one of the items of clothing the baby was dressed in when it arrived, such as a sleeve, a ribbon, or most frequently a gown. These pieces of fabric appear to have been retained in the expectation that they could subsequently be used to identify the child.

Whether supplied as a token by whoever left the child, or cut from the child's clothing by a Hospital official, the tendency was to choose a patterned fabric that would be identifiable. The majority of the fabrics in the billet books are colourful and decorated. Most were not described in words, but a large minority were, because the Hospital's clerks often added descriptions with details of the fabric to the printed list of clothing on the billet. This enables the surviving textiles to be cross-referenced to other kinds of written sources in which the same kinds of fabric are named, such as criminal records and newspaper advertisements.[24] This book uses a survey of all surviving textiles in the Foundling Hospital billet books during the period of selective entry, 1741–56, and during one year, 1759, of the period of general entry.[25]

It was believed in the eighteenth century that the majority of the mothers of infants taken in by the Foundling Hospital were poor. The Foundling collection represents, therefore, textiles that were available to poor women, mainly, but not exclusively, in London. The collection as a whole is heavily skewed towards patterned and colourful fabrics, but it is so large that also includes examples of many of the more mundane, plain fabrics that we know ordinary people wore. Most of the textiles had previously been made up into items of infant clothing. Nevertheless, they can tell us a great deal about the textiles worn as clothes by plebeian adults. Not only were the same kinds of fabric used in clothing infants and adults, but infants' clothing was often made up from old adult garments.

Paintings and prints

This is first and foremost a book about eighteenth-century plebeian clothing, not about its visual representations. Eighteenth-century paintings and prints are used as evidence throughout the book, sometimes to identify particular items of clothing mentioned in the text and sometimes to develop arguments about the way clothes were differentiated or interpreted. Irrespective of precisely how these kinds of visual evidence are employed, it is with a recognition that they do not offer a straightforward, uncomplicated representation of the way people dressed. Visual images of plebeian men and women were rarely portraits of actual individuals, whose opinions might have influenced the kind of clothes shown and the way they were portrayed. Nor were they simple snapshots of clothes actually worn in particular places. Instead, we find artists trading largely in stereotypes. Portrayals could be comical or moralistic, celebratory or hostile, sentimental or brutally realist. Nevertheless, they were inescapably shaped by eighteenth-century preoccupations about art and about ordinary people, especially the preoccupations that exercised the image-buying classes. That said, much of the effectiveness of these stereotypical portrayals turned on the typicality of the clothes they depicted. Artists exaggerated and manipulated the way ordinary people dressed, but their point of departure remained the kind of clothes such people were expected actually to wear. The way eighteenth-century priorities and preoccupations shaped particular images used as illustrations in the book is discussed, where appropriate, in the captions.

Appendix 2
Tables

1 Clothes lost in the fire at Brandon, Suffolk in 1789

	Number of clothes itemised	Value of clothes	Value per item (shillings)
Mr Webb, postmaster (married with 5 children)	199*	£88 17s. 3d.	n/a
Mr Shanley, surgeon (married with children)	221*	£75 14s. 0d.	n/a
George Warner, tailor (married)	228	£37 18s. 6d.	3s. 4d.
Mark Palmer, blacksmith (married with children)	72	£16 6s. 0d.	4s. 6d.
John Neel, cordwainer (married with children)	41	£7 5s. 3d.	3s. 6d.
Sarah Holmes, servant	69	£10 4s. 6d.	3s. 0d.
Mary Cooper, servant	37	£4 18s. 8d.	2s. 9d.
William Eagle, servant	17	£4 16s. 0d.	5s. 8d.
Elizabeth Cooper, mantuamaker	22	£2 13s. 0d.	2s. 5d.

Only those who lost substantial numbers of clothes are included. Pairs of shoes, buckles, etc., are counted as one item. The valuations given varied according to the age of the clothes and were therefore probably second-hand rather than replacement values.

*For Shanley and Webb the numbers of clothes are gross underestimates, as many of the clothes listed, especially the children's, were not itemised.

Source: Suffolk Record Office (Bury St Edmunds), FL 536/1/47: Brandon Parish, Brandon Fire, 'Estimation of the Goods and Chattles, Wearing Apparel, etc., destroyed and damaged by fire at Brandon in Suffolk on Thursday, 14 May 1789'.

2 Gowns lost in the fire at Brandon, Suffolk in 1789

	All	Silk/silk mix	Cotton/linen	Stuff
William Webb, postmaster (married with 5 children)	16	7	9	–
Francis Shanley, surgeon (married with children)	12	2	9	1
George Warner, tailor (married)	6	2	2	2
Mark Palmer, blacksmith (married with children)	4	–	2	2
John Neel, cordwainer (married with children)	1	–	1	–
Sarah Holmes, servant	4	–	3	1
Mary Cooper, servant	4	–	2	2
William Eagle, servant	–	–	–	–
Elizabeth Cooper, mantuamaker	3	–	3	–

Source: Suffolk Record Office (Bury St Edmunds), FL 536/1/47: Brandon Parish, Brandon Fire, 'Estimation of the Goods and Chattles, Wearing Apparel, etc., destroyed and damaged by fire at Brandon in Suffolk on Thursday, 14 May 1789'.

3 Shirts and shifts lost in the fire at Brandon, Suffolk, in 1789

	Number
William Webb, postmaster (married with 5 children)	18
Francis Shanley, surgeon (married with children)	16
George Warner, tailor (married)	35
Mark Palmer, blacksmith (married with children)	9
John Neel, cordwainer (married with children)	9
Sarah Holmes, servant	5
Mary Cooper, servant	4
William Eagle, servant	1
Elizabeth Cooper, mantuamaker	1

Source: Suffolk Record Office (Bury St Edmunds), FL 536/1/47: Brandon Parish, Brandon Fire, 'Estimation of the Goods and Chattles, Wearing Apparel, etc., destroyed and damaged by fire at Brandon in Suffolk on Thursday, 14 May 1789'.

4 Handkerchiefs lost in the fire at Brandon, Suffolk, in 1789

	All	Silk	Muslin
William Webb, postmaster (married with 5 children)	52	8	20
Francis Shanley, surgeon (married with children)	36	4	18
George Warner, tailor (married)	35	2	–
Mark Palmer, blacksmith (married with children)	5	–	–
John Neel, cordwainer (married with children)	5	–	–
Sarah Holmes, servant	10	–	–
Mary Cooper, servant	8	1	–
William Eagle, servant	–	–	–
Elizabeth Cooper, mantuamaker	1	–	1

Source: Suffolk Record Office (Bury St Edmunds), FL 536/1/47: Brandon Parish, Brandon Fire, 'Estimation of the Goods and Chattles, Wearing Apparel, etc., destroyed and damaged by fire at Brandon in Suffolk on Thursday, 14 May 1789'.

5 Pairs of stockings lost in the fire at Brandon, Suffolk, in 1789

	All	Cotton	Worsted	Thread	Silk
William Webb, postmaster (married with 5 children)	21	15	6	–	–
Francis Shanley, surgeon (married with children)	13	1	3	5	4
George Warner, tailor (married)	16	7	9	–	–
Mark Palmer, blacksmith (married with children)	11	3	8	–	–
John Neel, cordwainer (married with children)	4	1	3	–	–
Sarah Holmes, servant	7	n/a	n/a	n/a	n/a
Mary Cooper, servant	3	1	2	–	–
William Eagle, servant	3	n/a	n/a	n/a	n/a
Elizabeth Cooper, mantuamaker	3	3	–	–	–

Source: Suffolk Record Office (Bury St Edmunds), FL 536/1/47: Brandon Parish, Brandon Fire, 'Estimation of the Goods and Chattles, Wearing Apparel, etc., destroyed and damaged by fire at Brandon in Suffolk on Thursday, 14 May 1789'.

6 Clothes lost by poorer adult victims in the fire at Brandon, Suffolk, in 1789

Men's clothes	John Neel, cordwainer	William Eagle, servant	Mark Palmer, blacksmith
Shirts	3	1	5
Coats	1	4	6
Waistcoats	4	2	3
Breeches	2	2	4
Shoes/boots (pairs)	–	2	2
Buckles (pairs)	–	1	1
Stockings (pairs)	2	3	4
Hats	1	2	1
Neckcloths	3	–	2
Total number	16	17	28
Total value	£3 5s. 0d.	£4 16s. 0d.	£11 3s. 6d.

Women's clothes	John Neel's wife	Elizabeth Cooper, mantuamaker	Mark Palmer's wife	Mary Cooper, servant	Sarah Holmes, servant
Shifts (+sleeves)	2	1	6	7	5#
Stays	1	1	–	–	1
Petticoats	2	3	1	3	5
Gowns	1	3	2	4	6
Shoes (pairs)	–	1	2	3★	6★
Buckles (pairs)	–	1	–	–	–
Stockings (pairs)	2	3	3	3	7
Aprons	2	3	3	4	9
Caps	4	4	8	3	11
Hats	1	–	1	1	3
Handkerchiefs	2	1	5	8	10
Cloaks	–	1	–	1	5
Pockets (pairs)	–	–	–	–	1
Total number	17	22	31	37	69
Total value	£2 13s. 9d.	£2 13s. 0d.	£3 18s. 0d.	£4 18s. 8d.	£5 4s. 6d.

\# includes 2 bedgowns

★ includes pattens

Source: Suffolk Record Office (Bury St Edmunds), FL 536/1/47: Brandon Parish, Brandon Fire, 'Estimation of the Goods and Chattles, Wearing Apparel, etc., destroyed and damaged by fire at Brandon in Suffolk on Thursday, 14 May 1789'.

7 Clothes worn by runaways described in advertisements in the Leeds and the Oxford and Worcester newspapers, 1780–1789

	Leeds	Oxford and Worcester
Women		
Gowns	4	3
Bedgowns	2	–
Petticoats/skirts	3	–
Handkerchiefs	1	2
Cloaks	2	–
Hats/bonnets	2	2
Stockings (pairs)	2	–
Shoes (pairs)	2	–
All women's clothes	18	7
Number of female runaways	4	2
Men		
Breeches	67	76
Coats	65	78
Waistcoats	56	62
Hats	44	35
Stockings (pairs)	19	17
Neckcloths/handkerchiefs	11	5
Jackets	9	17
Buckle/buckles (pairs)	9	1
Suits of clothes/clothes	7	–
Singlets	4	–
Shoes (pairs)	4	5
Aprons	3	–
Shirts	2	5
Frocks	2	2
Trousers	1	–
Capes	1	–
Smocks/waggoners' frocks	1	6
Caps (regimental)	1	–
Garters	–	1
Pumps (pairs)	–	2
Boots (pairs)	1	6
Regimentals	1	–
All men's clothes	308	318
Number of male runaways	87	101

Sources: see Appendix 1.

8   **Clothes stolen from plebeian owners listed in indictments for theft, Yorkshire, North and West Ridings, Assizes and Quarter Sessions, 1780–1789, and London, Old Bailey, Middlesex cases, 1785**

	Yorkshire	London
Women		
Gowns	19	29
Bedgowns	4	6
Petticoats	10	20
Cloaks	9	12
Bonnets	4	1
Caps	23	11
Pattens (pairs)	1	–
Hoods	2	–
Shifts	15	39
Shawls	–	2
Sleeves (pairs)	6	2
Stays	4	2
Stomachers	–	2
Wrappers	1	–
Safeguards [protective garment]	–	1
Robins [trimmings]	–	1
Pockets (pairs)	1	2
Total women's clothes	99	130
Men		
Breeches	17	20
Coats	24	26
Waistcoats	23	22
Jackets	5	8
Shirts	58	91
Trousers	3	1
Smocks/waggoners' frocks	1	–
Button/s	4	1
Boots (pairs)	1	1
Stocks	–	8
Total men's clothes	136	178

[*Table 8 continued*]

Wearer/owner's sex unclear		
Aprons/brats	35	56
Handkerchiefs/neckcloths/cravats	60	52
Hats	10	5
Shoes/pumps (pairs)	20	5
Stockings (pairs)	32	61
Buckles (pairs)	13	12
Watches	10	14
Frocks (child's)	6	9
Gloves/mits (pairs)	2	2
Ribbons	5	1
Ruffles	2	–
Rings	2	1
Total, wearer/owner's sex unclear	197	218
All clothes	432	526
Owners	113	65

Sources: see Appendix 1.

9 Items of clothing mentioned 20 times or more in runaway advertisements in newspapers in the Midlands, 1714–1799

	1714–99	1714–69	1770–99
Breeches	479	232	247
Buckles (pairs)	34	15	19
Cloaks/Cardinals/Josephs/mantles	21	15	6
Coats	529	254	275
Frocks	109	77	32
Gowns	36	24	12
Neckwear	37	15	22
Hats	143	44	99
Jackets	32	3	29
Shirts	25	12	13
Shoes (pairs)	53	25	28
Smock frocks	20	4	16
Stockings (pairs)	121	58	63
Waistcoats	468	235	233
Wigs	82	69	13
All items of clothing	2,271	1,137	1,134
People advertised	708	366	342

Sources: see Appendix 1.

10 Items of clothing mentioned 20 times or more in runaway advertisements in newspapers in Yorkshire, 1739–1799

	1739–99	1739–69	1770–99
Breeches	315	78	237
Buckles (pairs)	25	5	20
Coats	351	104	247
Gowns	20	6	14
Neckwear	32	5	27
Hats	145	22	123
Jackets	43	2	41
Shoes (pairs)	22	1	21
Stockings (pairs)	109	29	80
Waistcoats	312	83	229
Wigs	35	31	4
All items of clothing	1,565	416	1,149
People advertised	441	128	313

Sources: see Appendix 1.

11 Wearers of wigs mentioned in runaway advertisements in newspapers in the Midlands and Yorkshire, 1714–1799

	Wearing a wig	Wearing own hair	All whose hair is described	% wearing wigs
Midlands				
Pre-1770	69	219	288	24
Post-1770	13	239	252	5
Yorkshire				
Pre-1770	31	70	101	31
Post-1770	4	249	253	1.5

Sources: see Appendix 1.

12 Owners of stolen watches in the Northern Circuit Assize depositions, 1660–1799

	Gentry	Middling	Plebeian	Unknown/retail	All
1660–1750	3	–	1	3	7
1750s	2	3	4	1	10
1760s	2	4	5	5	16
1770s	–	4	12	4	20
1780s	–	11	17	5	33
1790s	–	15	13	3	31
Total	7	37	52	21	117

Source: PRO, ASSI 45/1/2 to 45/40/1: Assizes Northern Circuit depositions, 1640–1799. 'Retail' indicates that the watch was stolen from a watchmaker.

13 Old Bailey trials that involved stolen watches, 1674–1834, all owners

	A	B	C	D	
	Silver watches	Gold watches	All trials with watches★	All trials	Ratio C:D
1670s	1	0	9	408	1:45
1680s	5	1	54	2,369	1:44
1690s	19	16	76	3,166	1:42
1700s	10	7	21	776	1:37
1710s	57	23	87	2,854	1:33
1720s	128	49	233	4,811	1:21
1730s	192	46	271	4,697	1:17
1740s	148	32	238	3,935	1:17
1750s	210	37	284	4,061	1:14
1760s	259	43	374	4,102	1:11
1770s	396	76	665	6,155	1:9
1780s	409	76	707	7,320	1:10
1790s	234	43	450	5,563	1:12
1800s	310	56	535	7,058	1:13
1810s	24	28	1,008	10,908	1:11
1820s	11	16	1,321	16,445	1:12
1830–4	4	6	584	8,482	1:15

★These figures slightly over-estimate the number of prosecutions involving stolen watches as they include a handful of cases of theft of watch chains or keys, without accompanying watches.

Source: Old Bailey Proceedings Online, keyword search of offence descriptions, 28 October 2006.

14 Occupations of plebeian owners of stolen watches in the Northern Circuit Assize depositions, 1749–1799

Working trade	33
Servant	7
Labourer	6
Husbandman	4
Soldier	2
Total	52

Source: PRO, ASSI 45/1/2 to 45/40/1: Assizes Northern Circuit depositions, 1640–1799.

15 Old Bailey trials that involved stolen gowns, 1674–1759, all owners

	All gowns	silk gowns	worsted gowns	cotton gowns	linen gowns
1670s	9	0	1	0	0
1680s	95	17	7	0	0
1690s	181	45	32	2	0
1700s	53	8	20	7	0
1710s	184	25	44	34	3
1720s	267	31	27	16	21
1730s	280	44	42	33	29
1740s	278	47	54	74	41
1750s	253	45	67	72	70

All of these are underestimates, owing to the varied nature of the nomenclature for fabrics, especially silk fabrics, which are restricted here to those described as 'silk'. Cotton gowns are cotton, calico, calicoe, callico, callicoe, fustian, muslin, chintz, chints and chince (although note that chintzes could be linen). Linen gowns are linen, linnen, flaxen, Holland and lawn. Worsted gowns are stuff, serge, camblet, camlet and calimanco.

Source: OBP, keyword search in offence descriptions, 15 November 2006.

16 Old Bailey trials that mentioned printed/painted fabrics, 1674–1834, all owners

	Printed cotton	Printed linen	All trials
1670s	–	–	408
1680s	1	–	2,369
1690s	1	–	3,166
1700s	1	1	776
1710s	13	7	2,854
1720s	3	11	4,811
1730s	10	22	4,697
1740s	18	21	3,935
1750s	11	9	4,061
1760s	20	16	4,102
1770s	68	40	6,155
1780s	181	27	7,320
1790s	164	4	5,563
1800s	185	3	7,058
1810s	211	1	10,908
1820s	182	–	16,445
1830–4	90	–	8,482

For cottons keyword searches were made under cotton, calico, calicoe, callico, callicoe, muslin, chintz, chints and chince (although note that chintzes could be linen); for linens keyword searches were made under linen, linnen, flaxen, harden, hempen, cambrick, holland and lawn. For both fabrics keyword searches were made under printed and painted.

Source: OBP, keyword searches, 30 September 2006.

17 Average value of gowns stolen from plebeian owners in Yorkshire Assize indictments, 1780–1789

	Value	Number
Silk gowns	11s.	2
Cotton gowns	10s.	4
Linen gowns	3s.	3
Worsted stuff gowns	5s. 6d.	2

Source: see Appendix 1.

18 Average value of gowns stolen from plebeian owners in Old Bailey, Middlesex indictments, 1785

	Value	Number
Silk gowns	16s. 10d.	5
Cotton gowns	8s.	17
Linen gowns	2s. 4d.	3
Worsted stuff gowns	–	0

Source: see Appendix 1.

19 Average pledge value of gowns pawned to George Fettes, York, 1777–1778

	Value	Number
Silk gowns	4s. 5d.	11
Cotton gowns	4s. 5d.	20
Linen gowns	4s.	4
Worsted stuff gowns	2s. 5d.	14

Source: York City Archives, Accession 38: Pledge book of George Fettes, pawnbroker, York, 1777–8, sample of four weeks, 29 December 1777 to 3 January 1778; 30 May 1778 to 4 April 1778; 29 June 1778 to 4 July 1778; 28 September 1778 to 3 October 1778. Pledges of single items only.

20 Old Bailey trials that mentioned shirts or shifts, 1674–1834, all owners

	Cotton shirt/s	Cotton shift/s	Linen shirt/s	Linen shift/s	All shirt/s	All shift/s	All trials
1670s	–	–	1	–	3	9	408
1680s	1	–	14	1	47	21	2,369
1690s	1	–	25	12	66	36	3,166
1700s	–	–	25	1	37	3	776
1710s	1	–	66	13	118	52	2,854
1720s	1	–	75	25	257	90	4,811
1730s	4	1	110	38	384	169	4,697
1740s	3	1	187	59	416	213	3,935
1750s	8	–	210	122	365	222	4,061
1760s	6	–	193	112	437	225	4,102
1770s	8	2	422	234	588	290	6,155
1780s	28	–	384	159	827	355	7,320
1790s	29	3	285	130	543	235	5,563
1800s	17	2	10	1	646	252	7,058
1810s	4	–	5	–	851	293	10,908
1820s	3	–	9	2	1,098	446	16,445
1830–4	5	–	6	1	638	231	8,482

For cottons keyword searches were made under cotton, calico, calicoe, callico, callicoe and muslin; for linens keyword searches were made under linen, linnen, flaxen, harden, hempen, cambrick, holland, lawn, dowlas and canvas.

Source: Old Bailey Proceedings Online, keyword search 30 September 2005.

21 Fabrics of stolen shirts and shifts, West Riding of Yorkshire Quarter Sessions indictments, 1750–1759, 1780–1789, 1821–1825, all owners

	Cotton	Linen
1750–9	0	28
1780–9	0	62
1821–5	8	42

Source: WYAS (Wakefield), QS1/89–97, /119–38, /160–4: West Riding of Yorkshire Quarter Sessions Rolls, 1750–9, 1780–99 and 1821–5; QS4/31–3, /39–42, /55–8: West Riding of Yorkshire Quarter Sessions Indictment Books, 1750–9, 1780–9, 1821–5.

22 Breakdown by family member of annual clothes spending in the six of David Davies's budgets that provide itemised information on clothing

	%	Average sum per family
Husband	42	£1 17s. 7d.
Wife	28	£1 4s. 10d.
Children	30	£1 7s. 5d.
Total	100	£4 9s. 10d.

Source: David Davies, *The Case of the Labourers in Husbandry*, London, 1795.

23 Breakdown of wives' annual clothes spending by type of clothes in the six of David Davies's budgets that provide itemised information on clothing

	%	Average sum per family
Accessory	32	£0 7s. 10d.
Footwear	19	£0 4s. 8d.
Garment	49	£0 12s. 4d.
Total	100	£1 4s. 10d.

Source: David Davies, *The Case of the Labourers in Husbandry*, London, 1795.

24 Breakdown of husbands' annual clothes spending by type of clothes in the six of David Davies's budgets that provide itemised information on clothing

	%	Average sum per family
Accessory	13	£0 5s. 0d.
Footwear	31	£0 11s. 5d.
Garment	56	£1 1s. 2d.
Total	100	£1 17s. 7d.

Source: David Davies, *The Case of the Labourers in Husbandry*, London, 1795.

25 Latham family's average annual expenditure on clothing, 1724–1766

	Period 1 1724–41 (18 years)	Period 2 1742–54 (13 years)	Period 3 1755–66 (12 years)	All years 1724–66 (43 years)
Clothes	£1 5s. 11d.	£5 10s. 7d.	£1 0s. 8d.	£2 10s. 0d.
Clothes + fibres	£1 16s. 10d.	£6 4s. 3d.	£1 19s. 6d.	£3 4s. 0d.
All spending	£22 18s. 0d.	£26 2s. 4d.	£23 8s. 11d.	£24 0s. 6d.
Clothes as % of all spending	6%	21%	4%	10%
Clothes plus fibres as % of all spending	8%	24%	8%	13%

Source: Lorna Weatherill, ed., *The Account Book of Richard Latham, 1724–1767*, London, 1990.

26 Latham family's clothing purchases, 1724–1766, percentage breakdown by cost

Category	Period 1 1724–41 (18 years) %	Period 2 1742–54 (13 years) %	Period 3 1755–66 (12 years) %	All years 1724–66 (43 years) %
Accessory	15	21	11	18
Cloth and weaving	32	14	17	18
Dyeing	3	3	1	3
Footwear	26	15	5	16
Garment	8	36	54	32
Making	12	8	8	9
Mending clothes	0	2	3	2
Mending footwear	2	1	2	2
Raw materials	3	5	3	4

Totals come to more than 100% because some purchases involved more than one category.

Source: Lorna Weatherill, ed., *The Account Book of Richard Latham, 1724–1767*, London, 1990.

27 Price range of linen and woollen fabrics for clothes in the accounts of six parish overseers, 1730–1759, the Latham family and the Hudson shop, pence per yard

	Six overseers' accounts 1730–59	Latham account book 1724–67	Hudson shop book 1758–9
Linens	5–17	7–24	4–126
Woollens	7–28	8–34	6–48
All	7–28	8–34	6–50
Number of cloth types named	26	26	31

Only those fabrics for which yardage prices are given in the accounts are included. Ribbon, materials for bedding and notions such as binding, brade, buckram and galloon are excluded.

Sources: for parishes see Chapter 16, note 17; Lorna Weatherill, ed., *The Account Book of Richard Latham, 1724–1767*, London, 1990; WYAS (Bradford), 33D80/6/7: Shop book of Stephen Hudson of Fewston, 1751–9.

28 Price range of selected items of clothing in the accounts of six parish overseers, 1730–1759, the Latham family and the Hudson shop, pence

	Six overseers' accounts 1730–59	Latham account book 1724–67	Hudson shop book 1758–9
Aprons			
Fine cloth	–	76	–
Check	x	27–36	–
Linsey-woolsey	9–13	–	–
Russia	10	–	–
All adult	6–29	9–76	–
Gown lengths			
Flowered damask	–	244–312	–
Silk camblet	–	186	–
Printed	–	140–240	144–288
Camblet	–	136–163	112
Worsted	–	135	–
Cotton	–	–	114–168
Stuff	–	–	98–105
Linsey-woolsey	95–105	–	90
Serge	84–96	–	–
Drugget	147	–	–
All adult	84–147	90–312	114–288
Handkerchiefs			
Silk	–	12–54	51–54
Silk and muslin	–	–	24–33
Cotton	–	–	18–20
Linen	–	–	14–27
Check	–	–	11–20.5
All	7–15	4–54	6.5–54
Hats			
Leghorn	–	–	7–16
Satin	–	–	42–60
Silk	–	–	57
Shag	–	59–102	–
All adult	9–20	9–102	7–62

x indicates that the fabric is named but the cost of the item is not given.

Sources: for parishes see Chapter 16, note 17; Lorna Weatherill, ed., *The Account Book of Richard Latham, 1724–1767*, London, 1990; WYAS (Bradford), 33D80/6/7: Shop book of Stephen Hudson of Fewston, 1751–9. For gowns these sources differ in the nature of the information they provide. In the overseers' accounts it is possible to identify fabrics used for gowns and their yardage prices. In the Hudson book, the use of the fabric is not given. In the Latham book, a price is often given for a finished gown, not a yardage price. To allow a comparison, fabrics from the Hudson book have been included that were used for gowns in the other sources. An adult gown length is taken to be six yards or more.

29 Numbers of named items of clothing supplied by four parishes, 1730–1759

	Spofforth, Yorkshire 1730–59	Thornhill, Yorkshire 1730–59	Leafield, Oxfordshire 1740–59	Holne, Devon 1746–59
Aprons	2	3	3	5
Boots (pairs)	–	–	2	–
Breeches	3	35	40	9
Caps	2	8	7	7
Cloaks	–	–	–	1
Clogs (pairs)	3	–	–	–
Coats	13	19	20	16
Frocks	–	2	7	–
Gowns	1	1	10	17
Handkerchiefs	–	–	1	8
Hats	1	8	11	4
Pattens (pairs)	–	–	1	–
Petticoats	1	3	4	1
Pockets (pairs)	–	–	1	1
Shifts	24	21	24	27
Shirts	10	99	65	35
Changes (i.e., a shirt or shift)	–	–	–	15
Shoes (pairs)	6	71	96	82
Stays	–	–	5	1
Stocks	–	–	1	–
Stockings (pairs)	7	34	51	15
Suits	–	–	–	1
Waistcoats/vests	–	11	14	12
Total	73	315	363	257
Shirts and shifts	47%	38%	25%	30%
Shoes and clogs	12%	23%	26%	32%

Sources: see Chapter 16, note 17.

30 Price range of linen and woollen fabrics for clothes in the accounts of six parish overseers, 1770–1799, and Robert Heaton's female servants, 1768–1792, pence per yard

	Six overseers' accounts 1770–99	Robert Heaton's female servants 1768–92
Linens	6–26	14–120
Woollens	8–42	10–24
All	6–42	9–120
Number of cloth types named	38	27

Only those fabrics for which yardage prices are given in the accounts are included. Ribbon, materials for bedding and notions such as binding, brade, buckram and galloon are excluded. The woollens bought by Heaton's female servants were mainly cheap varieties for workaday gowns and petticoats.

Sources: for parishes see Chapter 16, note 17; for Heaton's servants see WYAS (Bradford), B149: Heaton of Ponden MSS, account book of Robert Heaton, 1764–92.

31 **Price range of selected items of clothing in the accounts of six parishes, 1770–1799, and for Robert Heaton's female servants, 1768–1792, pence**

	Six overseers' accounts 1770–99	Robert Heaton's female servants 1768–92
Aprons		
Barras	10–16	–
Brat	–	8
Brown roll	x	–
Check	15–21	30–43
Eagep cloth	12	–
Harden	9	24
Linen	19.5–23.5	12–24
Linsey-woolsey	19	–
Lawn	–	60–174
Muslin	–	74
Serge	12–20	–
Woollen	15–18	–
All adult	8–33	8–174
Gown lengths (not bedgowns)		
Camblet	48–77	76–184
Cotton	95–105	198–216
Crape	–	228
Linen	–	246
Linsey-woolsey	123	–
Painted/printed cotton/linen	–	180–216
Serge	84–128	–
Shalloon	–	93–108
Stuff	84	135
Wildbore	96	99
All adult	48–147	93–252
Handkerchiefs		
Gauze	–	8–11
Check	15	10
Muslin	–	24–45
Shawl	–	42
Silk	–	75–78
All	6–44	6–78
Hats		
Chip	–	7–8
Silk	–	60–71
Satin	–	84
All adult	9–36	7–84

[*Table 31 continued*]

x indicates the fabric is named but the cost of the item is not given.

Sources: for parishes see Chapter 16, note 17; for Heaton's servants see WYAS (Bradford), B149: Heaton of Ponden MSS, account book of Robert Heaton, 1764–92. For gowns these sources differ in the nature of the information they provide. In the overseers' accounts it is possible to identify fabrics used for gowns and their yardage prices, but in the Heaton servants' account book a price is sometimes given for the finished gown, not a yardage price. Fabric lengths of six yards or more are assumed to be for gowns.

32 Numbers of named items of clothing supplied by four parishes, 1770–1799

	Spofforth, Yorkshire 1770–99	Thornhill, Yorkshire 1770–99	Leafield, Oxfordshire 1792–99	Holne, Devon 1770–9, 1790–9
Aprons	17	60	2	48
Bedgowns	4	26	–	2
Breeches	31	13	3	26
Buckles (pairs)	4	1	–	–
Caps, dowds	5	39	8	60
Cloaks, mantles, whittles	2	–	–	4
Clogs (pairs)	16	3	–	–
Coats	24	9	3	47#
Frocks	6	4	–	4
Gowns	8	12	1	32
Handkerchiefs	13	41	1	35
Hats	19	10	2	10
Jackets	2	3	–	5
Petticoats	13	49	5	–
Pockets	1	–	–	2
Shifts, smocks	61	172	4	82
Shirts	83	98	13	57
Changes (i.e., either shift or shirt)	–	–	–	41
Shoes (pairs)	128	90	14	x★
Stays, jumps	3	10	–	1
Stockings (pairs)	43	31	2	81
Waistcoats	14	14	2	12
Total	497	685	60	>549
Shirts, shifts and smocks	29%	39%	28%	n/a
Shoes and clogs	29%	14%	23%	n/a

\# at Holne, coats were mostly petticoats for women.

★ at Holne, shoes were not itemised later in the period, when only the total value of the shoemaker's bill for shoes is given.

Sources: see Chapter 16, note 17.

33 Number of named items of clothing supplied to paupers by the vestry at Wimbledon, Surrey, December 1745 to November 1748

Clothes supplied to girls and women:	Girls (n=15)	Women (n=5)
Aprons	15	3
Bodice leather	1	0
Caps	22	0
Clogs	0	1
Gowns	19	1
Handkerchiefs	13	0
Petticoats	19	2
Shifts	46	11
Shoes (pairs)	39	5
Stockings/yarn for stockings (pairs)	50	3
Total	224	26
Clothes supplied to boys and men:	Boys (n=8)	Men (n=5)
Breeches	9	3
Caps	0	1
Coats	15	2
Drawers	0	1
Hats	1	0
Shirts	25	15
Shoes (pairs)	19	4
Stockings (pairs)	28	3
Waistcoats	4	2
Total	101	31

Source: F. M. Cowe, ed., *Wimbledon Vestry Minutes, 1736, 1743–1788* (Guilford, Surrey Record Society, vol. 25, 1964). Girls and boys are defined as those aged 14 or younger.

34 Percentage breakdown by value of the clothing purchases made by all 28 of Robert Heaton's female servants for whom detailed accounts survive, 1768–1792

Category of clothing	%
Garment	43
Accessory	22
Fabric	14
Footwear	13
Mending footwear	4
Dyeing	1
Making clothes	1
Raw materials	1
Mending clothes	1
Total	100

The total amount spent was £110 11s 4d.

Source: WYAS (Bradford), B149: Heaton of Ponden MSS, account book of Robert Heaton, 1764–92.

35 Percentage breakdown by value of the types of garment purchased by all 28 of Robert Heaton's female servants for whom detailed accounts survive, 1768–1792

Type of garment	%
Gown	44
Stays	22
Shift	12
Cloak	12
Petticoat	10
Total	100

The total amount spent was £47 11s 7d.

Source: WYAS (Bradford), B149: Heaton of Ponden MSS, account book of Robert Heaton, 1764–92.

36 Percentage breakdown by value of the types of clothing accessories purchased by all 28 of Robert Heaton's female servants for whom detailed accounts survive, 1768–1792

Type of accessory	%
Handkerchief/neckcloth	31
Apron	21
Cap	17
Hat	13
Miscellaneous	8
Stockings	7
Ribbon	3
Total	100

The total amount spent was £25 9s 10d.

Source: WYAS (Bradford), B149: Heaton of Ponden MSS, account book of Robert Heaton, 1764–92.

37 Percentage breakdown by value of the types of footwear purchased by all 28 of Robert Heaton's female servants for whom detailed accounts survive, 1768–1792

Type of footwear	%
Shoes and pumps	67
Clogs	19
Pattens	7
Other	7
Total	100

The total amount spent was £14 6s 5d.

Source: WYAS (Bradford), B149: Heaton of Ponden MSS, account book of Robert Heaton, 1764–92.

Notes

Introduction

1. William Hutton, *The Life of Willam Hutton F.A.S.S.* (London, 1816), 30–1.
2. E. P. Thompson, quoted on the dust jacket of Peter Linebaugh, *The London Hanged: Crime and Civil Society in the Eighteenth Century* (London, 1991); Neil McKendrick, 'The Consumer Revolution of Eighteenth-Century England', in Neil McKendrick, John Brewer and J. H. Plumb, *The Birth of a Consumer Society* (London, 1982), 9–33.
3. E. P. Thompson, *Customs in Common* (London, 1991), 12.
4. Thompson, *Customs*, 14.
5. Robert W. Malcolmson, *Life and Labour in England, 1700–1780* (London, 1981), 149.
6. Adrian Randall and Andrew Charlesworth (eds), *Markets, Market Culture and Popular Protest in Eighteenth-Century Britain and Ireland* (Liverpool, 1996), 8.
7. For the most influential study of British consumption patterns based on probate inventories, see Lorna Weatherill, *Consumer Behaviour and Material Culture in Britain, 1660–1760* (London, 1988); and for the most sophisticated recent quantitative analysis, see Mark Overton and others, *Production and Consumption in English Households, 1600–1750* (London, 2004). Detailed probate inventories do survive in large numbers for Yorkshire in the 1780s and 1790s; see Chapter 8 below.
8. Neil McKendrick, 'The Commercialisation of Fashion', in Neil McKendrick, John Brewer and J. H. Plumb, *The Birth of a Consumer Society* (London, 1982), 60.
9. E. P. Thompson, *The Making of the English Working Class* (London, 1963), 318.
10. There is a vast specialist literature on this subject, but for useful overviews see Pat Hudson, *The Industrial Revolution* (London, 1992), chapter 6; Steven King and Geoffrey Timmins, *Making Sense of the Industrial Revolution: English Economy and Society, 1700–1850* (Manchester, 2001), chapter 5; Jane Humphreys, 'Household Economy', Hans-Joachim Voth, 'Living Standards and the Urban Environment', and Maxine Berg, 'Consumption in Eighteenth- and Early Nineteenth-Century Britain', in Roderick Floud and Paul Johnson, *The Cambridge Economic History of Modern Britain*, vol. 1: *Industrialization, 1700–1860* (Cambridge, 2004).
11. Although even in the 1790s, working people's household budgets suggest over ten percent of their expenditure went on non-essentials, especially clothing; see Sarah Horrell, 'Home Demand and British Industrialization', *Journal of Economic History*, 56 (1996), 580. The reliance on the late 1780s and 1790s as a baseline is a particular problem with studies based on household budgets, which survive in any numbers only from those decades. Household budgets from the period are an especially unreliable source for the consumption of clothes, which were acquired only intermittently; see Chapter 13 below.
12. Robert C. Allen, 'The Great Divergence in European Wages and Prices from the Middle Ages to the First World War', *Explorations in Economic History*, 38 (2001), 411–47; Peter Earle, 'The Economics of Stability: The Views of Daniel Defoe', in D. C. Coleman and A. H. John (eds), *Trade, Government and Economy in Pre-Industrial England*, (London, 1976), 274–94.
13. Carole Shammas, *The Pre-Industrial Consumer in England and America* (Oxford, 1990), 77–86.
14. *Manchester Mercury*, 14 November 1786.
15. Jan de Vries, 'Between Purchasing Power and the World of Goods: Understanding the Household Economy in Early Modern Europe', in John Brewer and Roy Porter (eds), *Consumption and the World of Goods* (London, 1993), 85–132, and, espe-

cially, 'The Industrial Revolution and the Industrious Revolution', *Journal of Economic History*, 54 (1994), 249–70. Also see Neil McKendrick, 'Home Demand and Economic Growth: A New View of the Role of Women and Children in the Industrial Revolution', in Neil McKendrick (ed.), *Historical Perspectives: Studies in English Thought and Society in Honour of J. H. Plumb* (Cambridge, 1975).

16 Daniel Defoe, *The Complete English Tradesman, in Familiar Letters* (London, 1726), 400.

17 J. M. Price, 'The Transatlantic Economy', in J. P. Greene and J. R. Pole (eds), *Colonial British America* (Baltimore, 1984), 32.

18 McKendrick, 'Commercialisation of Fashion' argues that the intensity and social reach of fashion-driven change in the eighteenth century was unprecedented.

19 Rev. Richard Warner, *A Tour through Cornwall in the Autumn of 1808* (Bath, 1809), 342.

20 Beverly Lemire, 'Consumerism in Preindustrial and Early Industrial England: The Trade in Secondhand Clothes', *Journal of British Studies*, 27 (1988), 1–24; 'The Theft of Clothes and Popular Consumerism in Early Modern England', *Journal of Social History*, 24 (1990), 256, 264. In fact, stolen clothes were mostly sold or pawned, not worn by those prosecuted for stealing them.

21 Horrell, 'Home Demand', 568.

22 For prices paid for black silk hats by servants, see WYAS (Bradford), B149, Heaton of Ponden MSS, account book of Robert Heaton, 1764–92, and Chapter 17 below. For the debate over Stubbs's paintings of labouring people, see John Barrell, *The Dark Side of the Landscape: The Rural Poor in English Painting, 1730–1840* (Cambridge, 1980), 25–31; McKendrick, 'Commercialisation of Fashion', 60–2; and more recently Richard Wendorf, *After Sir Joshua: Essays on British Art and Cultural History* (London, 2005), chapter 6, and Robert Blake, *George Stubbs and the Wide Creation: Animals, People and Places in the Life of George Stubbs, 1724–1806* (London, 2005), chapter 48. If we choose to assess Stubbs's portrayal of farm labourers' dress by comparing it with the range of clothing actually worn by labouring people in the period, it is not the women's headwear that emerges as implausible (although it is noticeable how many of them wear hats covered with black silk, rather than the cheaper plain straw hats), but the men's breeches and stockings in his 1794 enamel *Haymakers* (fig. 6). In contrast to the earlier paintings in the series, all the men wear white stockings, while their breeches are in a variety of light colours, including blues and greys. Breeches worn by runaways advertised in the 1780s and 1790s were predominantly dark in colour, very rarely blue or grey, while their stockings were mainly coloured (see Appendix 1 for sources).

23 Sue Bowden and Avner Offer, 'Household Appliances and the Use of Time: The United States and Britain since the 1920s', *Economic History Review*, new series, 47 (1994), 725.

24 There is no single major study of ordinary people's clothing in eighteenth-century England. Beverly Lemire, *Fashion's Favourite: The Cotton Trade and the Consumer in Britain, 1660–1800* (Oxford, 1991), and *Dress, Culture and Commerce: The English Clothing Trade before the Factory, 1660–1800* (London, 1997), deal with cotton textiles and the clothing trades respectively. They do not focus exclusively on the plebeian experience and deal first and foremost with supply and marketing, rather than patterns of ownership or meaning. Her essay 'Second-hand Beaux and "Red-armed Belles": Conflict and the Creation of Fashions in England, *c.*1660–1800', *Continuity and Change*, 15 (2000), 391–417 comes closest to the issues addressed in this book. Dress history has produced no significant major study of plebeian clothing in the period. Anne Buck's two chapters on the clothing of working people in her indispensable *Dress in Eighteenth-Century England* (London, 1979) remain the best treatment of the subject from a dress history perspective.

25 The most comprehensive statement of the pessimists' position with regard to clothing is to be found in John Rule, *The Labouring Classes in Early Industrial England, 1750–1850* (London 1986), 66–71, which mainly addresses a later period than this book. Based chiefly on the evidence of contemporary commentators, it notes that little is known about actual plebeian consumption patterns. For a more recent and trenchant re-statement, see Peter King, 'Social Inequality, Identity and the Labouring Poor in Eighteenth-Century England', in Jonathan Barry and Henry French (eds), *Identity and Agency in England, 1500–1800* (London, 2004). The optimists' position on clothing is set out most fully in Lemire, *Fashion's Favourite*; Lemire, *Dress, Culture and Commerce*; and Lemire, 'Second-hand Beaux'.

26 A notable exception is N. B. Harte, 'The Economics of Clothing in the Late Seventeenth Century', *Textile History*, 22 (1991), 277–96, which uses the data assembled by Gregory King at the

end of the seventeenth century to offer a systematic breakdown of English consumption of clothing at that period. As Harte points out, the evidence King assembled was exceptional; there is no equivalent for the eighteenth century.

27 Hannah Greig, 'Leading the Fashion: The Material Culture of London's *Beau Monde*', in John Styles and Amanda Vickery (eds), *Gender, Taste and Material Culture in Britain and North America, 1700–1830* (London and New Haven, 2006).

28 McKendrick, 'Commercialisation of Fashion'; Lemire, *Fashion's Favourite*, 8, 197–200.

29 John Hustler, *The Occasion of the Dearness of Provisions, and the Distress of the Poor* (London, 1767), 24.

30 E. P. Thompson, 'Patrician Society, Plebeian Culture', *Journal of Social History*, 7 (1974), 382–405.

31 There is now a huge literature on this subject. The single most important intervention is Peter King, 'Edward Thompson's Contribution to Eighteenth-Century Studies: The Patrician-Plebeian Model Re-Examined', *Social History*, 21 (1996), 215–28. For a review of the literature which usefully links social-structural and cultural issues over a long timescale, see H. R. French, 'The Search for the "Middle Sort of People" in England, 1600–1800', *The Historical Journal*, 43 (2000), 277–93.

32 Weatherill, *Consumer Behaviour*.

33 Robert Malcolmson estimates these people, whom he variously terms 'plebeian' or 'labouring men and women', were sufficiently numerous to comprise more than three-quarters of the population, but this may be excessive; Malcolmson, *Life and Labour*, 19. For useful tabulations of a variety of eighteenth-century estimates see Douglas Hay and Nicholas Rogers, *Eighteenth-Century English Society: Shuttles and Swords* (Oxford, 1997), 19–21, although significantly the authors decline to provide a single figure. See also Roy Porter, *English Society in the Eighteenth Century* (London, 1990), chapter 2.

34 Lady Maria Theresa Villiers Lister Lewis (ed.), *Extracts of the Journals and Correspondence of Miss Berry from the Year 1783–1852*, 3 vols (London, 1866), 2: 400.

35 For an interpretation of the three-piece suit that emphasises its broader cultural significance, see David Kuchta, *The Three Piece Suit and Modern Masculinity: England 1550–1850* (London, 2002).

36 N. B. Harte, 'State Control of Dress and Social Change in Pre-Industrial England', in Coleman and John, *Trade, Government and Economy*, 132–65. See also Hans Medick, 'Une culture de la considération: les vêtements et leurs couleurs à Laichingen entre 1750 et 1820', *Annales: Histoire, Sciences Sociales*, 50 (1995), 753–74.

37 Stephen Dowell, *A History of Taxation and Taxes in England*, 4 vols (London, 1884), 3:305–9, 4:343–9, 401–6. Often these excises were graduated in order to advantage poorer consumers, with a higher rate of duty on more expensive items. Thus the excise on hats introduced by the Act of Parliament 24 Geo. III, c. 51 (1783) imposed a stamp duty of three pence on hats sold for less than four shillings, six pence on hats sold for between four and seven shillings, one shilling on hats sold for between seven and 12 shillings, and two shil-lings on those sold for more than 12 shillings. The Clock and Watch Act of 1797 (37 Geo. III, c. 108), imposed an annual duty of two shillings and sixpence on metal and silver watches, and ten shillings on gold watches, to be paid by the owner.

38 See Chapter 7 below.

1 Travellers' Tales: Nation and Region

1 K. Morgan (ed.), *An American Quaker in the British Isles: The Travel Journals of Jabez Maud Fisher, 1775–1779* (Oxford, 1992), 60–1.

2 Henri Misson, *M. Misson's Memoirs and Observations in his Travels over England*, trans. John Ozell (London, 1719), 364.

3 Madame du Boccage, *Letters Concerning England, Holland and Italy*, 2 vols (London, 1770), 1: 61, letter dated 4 June 1750.

4 Pehr Kalm, *Kalm's Account of his Visit to England on his Way to America in 1748*, trans. Joseph Lucas (London, 1892), 326, 52–3.

5 Charles P. Moritz, *Travels, Chiefly on Foot, through Several Parts of England, in 1782*, (London, 1795), 23–4, 182.

6 Johann Wilhelm von Archenholz, *A Picture of England: Containing a Description of the Laws, Customs and Manners of England*, 2 vols (London, 1789), 2: 135–6.

7 Friedrich August Wendeborn, *A View of England towards the Close of the Eighteenth Century*, 2 vols (London, 1791), 1: 115.

8 Moritz, *Travels*, 215, 242.

9 Arthur Young, *A Tour in Ireland: With General Observations on the Present State of that Kingdom. Made in the Years 1776, 1777, and 1778*, 2 vols (Dublin, 1780), 2: Part II, 35, Part I, 177. For important qualifications to the view presented by Young, see Mairead

Dunlevy, *Dress in Ireland* (Cork, 1999), 111–14, 135–42.

10 Morgan, *American Quaker*, 69, 74, and also see 60–1, 64.

11 Corita Myerscough (ed.), *Uncle John Carr: The Diaries of his Great-nieces, Harriet and Amelia Clark* (York, 2000), 13.

12 Susan Sibbald, *The Memoirs of Susan Sibbald (1783–1812)*, ed. Francis Paget Hett (London, 1926), 112.

13 For extended discussions of the dress of the common people in eighteenth-century Wales, see F. G. Payne, 'Welsh Peasant Costume', *Folk Life*, 2 (1964), 42–57; Anne Buck, *Dress in Eighteenth-Century England* (London, 1979), 149–51; Jacqueline Lewis, 'Passing Judgements – Welsh Dress and the English Tourist', *Folk Life*, 33 (1994–5), 29–47; Christine Stevens, 'Welsh Peasant Dress – Workwear or National Costume?' *Textile History*, 33 (2002), 63–78. For an unusual focus on men, see Rev. Richard Warner, *A Walk through Wales in August 1797* (Bath, 1799), 32, 184.

14 Henry Wigstead, *Remarks on a Tour to North and South Wales in the Year 1797* (London, 1799), 32.

15 Mrs Morgan, *A Tour to Milford Haven in the Year 1791* (London, 1795), 272–3, 138.

16 Christine Stevens identifies the term 'jacket' used by tourists as referring to a kind of short bedgown or over-bodice; Stevens, 'Welsh Peasant Dress', 66. Also see Warner, *Walk through Wales*, 183.

17 Catherine Hutton, *Reminiscences of a Gentlewoman of the Last Century: Letters of Catharine Hutton*, ed. C. H. Beale (London, 1891), 52, 120, 125. For the absence of aprons, see Morgan, *Tour to Milford Haven*, 278.

18 See, for example, Hutton, *Reminiscences*, 120; Warner, *Walk through Wales*, 183.

19 Morgan, *Tour to Milford Haven*, 268, 273.

20 Arthur Young, *Tours in England and Wales, selected from the Annals of Agriculture* (London, 1932), 9, also 14.

21 Gilbert White, *The Natural History and Antiquities of Selborne* (London, 1789), 222. White uses the phrase 'comparatively modern' to refer to his preceding discussion of leprosy during the Middle Ages, not to suggest that wearing linen undergarments in England had only begun earlier in the eighteenth century. Some naval doctors were, however, beginning to question the health benefits of linen undergarments; see B. McL. Ranft, *The Vernon Papers* (London, Navy Record Society, vol. 99, 1958), 329–33 and C. Lloyd, *The Health of Seamen* (London, Navy Record Society, vol. 107, 1965), 246. Cornish miners wore woollen shirts underground; see Chapter 2, note 26.

22 University College of North Wales, Bangor, Dept. of MSS, MS 82: Penmorfa, Caernarvonshire, shop ledger, *c.*1788–*c.*1803, ff. 20, 24, 38, 95, 311.

23 Anne Buck, 'Variations in English Women's Dress in the Eighteenth Century', *Folk Life*, 9 (1971), 5.

24 Sibbald, *Memoirs*, 112.

25 Basil Cozens-Hardy (ed.), *The Diary of Sylas Neville, 1767–1788* (London, 1950), 281. The published text of the diary names Wiltshire rather than Warwickshire, but the context makes it clear that it is Warwickshire to which Neville is referring.

26 Andrew Oliver (ed.), *The Journal of Samuel Curwen Loyalist*, 2 vols (Cambridge, Mass., 1972), 2: 628.

27 Christopher Morris (ed.), *The Journeys of Celia Fiennes* (London, 1949), 243.

28 James Brome, *Travels over England, Scotland and Wales* (London, 1700), 234.

29 Devon RO, 1249A/PO2-4: Overseers' payments for Holne, 1746–1799 (transcribed by Brian Brassett at *http://genuki.cs.ncl.ac.uk/DEV/Holne/Overseers/index.html*, examined May 2005). Shag was provided for whittles for Grace Roland, an adult, in 1772 and for Mary Ford, a child, in 1778. Cloaks made from Penistone were provided for Elizabeth Easterbrook and Eleanor Jarman in 1776.

30 James Joel Cartwright (ed.), *The Travels through England of Dr Richard Pococke*, 2 vols. (London, 1888), 1: 44.

31 Quoted in Angus Winchester, 'Travellers in Grey: Quaker Journals as a Source for Local History', *The Local Historian*, 21 (1991), 73.

32 Overseers' accounts examined from England south of the Trent do not include payments for clogs. See Chapter 16.

33 WYAS (Leeds), RDP17/84: Calverley parish officers' accounts, 1692–1822.

34 See Chapter 17.

35 Sir Frederick Eden, *The State of the Poor*, 3 vols (London, 1797), 2: 309, 1: 555, 2: 434, 3: 709. Others suggested a pair of clogs would last a year; J. Bailey and G. Culley, *General View of the Agriculture of the County of Westmorland* (Newcastle, 1797), 266.

36 *The Gentleman's Magazine*, 1 (December 1731), 527.

37 J. H. Campboll, 'Answers to Queries Relating to the Agriculture of Lancashire', *Annals of Agriculture*, 20 (1793), 138–9.

38 For Robert Heaton, see Chapter 17; for Spofforth and Thornhill parish overseers, see Chapter 16; for Westmorland, see Loraine Ashcroft, *Vital Statistics: The Westmorland 'Census' of 1787* (Kendal, 1992). It is possible that at least some of the discrepancy between numbers of clogs purchased and numbers of shoes reflects the fact that clogs were easier to repair at home. The family of husbandman Richard Latham of Scarisbrick in Lancashire, whose accounts survive for the years 1724–67, bought far more shoes than clogs, but additionally made many purchases of clog nails. For the Latham account book, see Chapter 14.

39 'Survey of the Parish of Wilmslow' by Samuel Finney of Fulshaw, Esq., in T. Worthington Barlow (ed.), *The Cheshire and Lancashire Historical Collector*, 2 (May, 1853), 5–6.

40 WYAS (Leeds), RDP18/114: Carleton-in-Craven overseers' accounts, 1751–1820. For rising prices, see Giorgio Riello, *A Foot in the Past: Consumers, Producers and Footwear in the Long Eighteenth Century* (Oxford, 2006), 28–9.

41 Anne Buck, 'The Countryman's Smock', *Folk Life*, 1 (1963), 16–34.

42 OBP, April 1785, John Barlow (t17850406-104).

43 Thomas Pennant, *A Journey from London to the Isle of White*, 2 vols (London, 1801), 2: 103.

44 E. M. Forster, *Marianne Thornton, 1797–1887* (London, 1956), 49.

45 OBP, February 1788, John Bishop (t17880227-106).

46 The smock was, however, already being employed in the 1740s to signify the country bumpkin on stage in productions of John Hippisley's opera *Flora*, as well as in the accompanying engravings. See Judith Milhous, 'Gravelot and Laguerre: Playing Hob on the Eighteenth-Century English Stage', *Theatre Survey*, 43 (2002), 149–75.

47 See Chapter 13.

48 William Cobbett, *Rural Rides*, ed. Ian Dyck (London, 2001), 78.

49 University of London, Senate House Library, Manuscripts, MS 625: Account books of L. Cottchin and R. Flowers, grocer and draper, Westoning, Bedfordshire, 1785–1800.

50 Buck, *Eighteenth Century*, 142.

2 What the People Wore

1 John E. Basham, *Brandon 1789: Village Fire* (Ipswich, 1986).

2 Suffolk RO (Bury St Edmunds), FL 536/1/47: Brandon Parish, Brandon Fire, 'Estimation of the Goods and Chattles, Wearing Apparel, etc. destroyed and damaged by fire at Brandon in Suffolk on Thursday May the 14th 1789'. The lists were compiled for the purpose of compensation. In them, clothes tend to be grouped by type for valuation purposes, so it is not always possible to provide unit valuations. The information on personal clothing used here excludes clothing items listed under stock in trade.

3 *The Universal British Directory of Trade, Commerce and Manufacture*, 4 vols, (London, 1793), 2: 355.

4 Pairs of drawers were occasionally worn as undergarments in the eighteenth century, but appear only very rarely in the sources used for this book. Where they do appear, it is among the clothing worn by older men, like George Warner, the wealthy Brandon tailor, and Joseph Skinner, a Wimbledon parish pensioner in 1748. Even in these cases, the drawers may have been an outer garment, like the ticking drawers worn by some deserters advertised in the *Leeds Intelligencer* in the 1770s. For Wimbledon, see F. M. Cowe (ed.), *Wimbledon Vestry Minutes, 1736, 1743–1788* (Guilford, 1964), 25: 10.

5 OBP, September 1751, Ad [sic], widow (t17510911-54); OBP, January 1787, Sophia Pringle (t17870112-1).

6 OBP, September 1784, Joseph Hewlett and John Stockdale (t17840915-47).

7 Nesta Evans, *The East Anglian Linen Industry: Rural Industry and Local Economy, 1500–1850* (Aldershot, 1985).

8 Charlotte Smith in her novel *The Old Manor House* (London, 1793), 29–31, emphasised the unacceptability of women going without a cap. The orphan heroine is not allowed to have her hair 'flaring without a cap', which her mistress thought 'monstrously indecent for a female at any age'.

9 Though often thought of as a typically plebeian garment, the bedgown was not confined to poorer women. The family of Francis Shanley, the surgeon, also lost two bedgowns. They were made from cotton and lined and valued at 4s. 6d. each, much more than Sarah Holme's two bedgowns valued at 1s. 9d. each. Bedgowns were considered no substitute for proper gowns, at least in winter.

The wife of an old clothes seller in Saffron Hill, London told a woman who came in mid-February intending to sell the only gown she owned: 'she had better try to save the gown, as she had only a bed-gown on'; OBP, February 1777, Sarah Tongue (t17770219-33).

10. For the conventional lengths of cotton fabric for bedgowns and gowns in the 1780s, see OBP, April 1785, Sarah Whitehead (t17850406-49) and OBP, April 1780, David Davis (t17800405-27).
11. OBP, February 1808, Martha Smith (t18080217-90), for red cloaks not being 'genteel'. Red cloaks were also made in London for sale; see OBP, December 1773, Elizabeth Tugwell (t17731208-51).
12. OBP, May 1795, Alice Burroughs and Amelia Evans (t17950520-34).
13. LMA, OB/SR.238: September 1785, Elizabeth Bland; PRO, ASSI 44/96: Yorkshire, summer 1781, Ann Kelly; WYAS (Wakefield), QS 1/121/9: 1782, Martha Beckett.
14. P. and R. A. Mactaggart, 'Some Aspects of the Use of Non-Fashionable Stays', in *Strata of Society*, Proceedings of the Seventh Annual Conference of the Costume Society (London, 1973), 20–8; Lynn Sorge-English, ' "29 Doz and 11 Best Cutt Bone": The Trade in Whalebone and Stays in Eighteenth-Century London', *Textile History*, 36 (2005), 20–45.
15. OBP, July 1770, John Pursel (t17700711-37). 'Want of stays' could be taken as evidence that a woman was a common prostitute; [Edward Ward,] *The London-Spy Compleat* (London, 1703), 259.
16. Andrew Oliver (ed.), *The Journal of Samuel Curwen Loyalist*, 2 vols (Cambridge, Mass., 1972), 1: 948.
17. OBP, July 1759, Anne Bennet (t17590711-14).
18. OBP, October 1749, Charles Mosely (t17491011-15).
19. PRO, ASSI 45/37/1/183: Newcastle 1790, Fletcher Rennison.
20. OBP, December 1741, Hannah Rossiter (t17411204-55).
21. OBP, February 1749, Archibald Blare (t17490222-51). Interestingly, the dead man was also wearing a wig.
22. Anon., *An Apology for the Ministerial Life and Actions of a Celebrated Favourite* (London, 1766), 18.
23. See Phillis Cunnington and Catherine Lucas, *Occupational Costume in England from the Eleventh Century to 1914* (London, 1967).
24. *Leeds Intelligencer*, 5 February 1788, *Jackson's Oxford Journal*, 13 November 1756, 29 October 1763.
25. OBP, May 1766, Robert Morton (t17660514-33).
26. George Symes Catcott, *A Descriptive Account of a Descent Made into Penpark-Hole, in the Parish of Westbury-upon-Trim, in the County of Gloucester, in the year 1775* (Bristol, 1792), 26; Edward Clarke descended a tin mine near Truro in Cornwall wearing 'a miner's wardrobe' consisting of 'a woollen shirt, trowsers, night cap, and jacket'. Edward Daniel Clarke, *A Tour through the South of England, Wales and Part of Ireland, Made during the Summer of 1791* (London, 1793), 90.
27. For examples, see OBP, October 1782, William Clarke (t17821016-33); OBP, January 1780, Thomas Cantrell (t17780115-24); OBP, January 1788, George Green (t17880109-5); OBP, May 1725, John Plant (t17250513-1).
28. In OBP 1674 to 1820, sailor's jacket appears in 36 cases, soldier's/regimental jacket in 17, brewer's jacket in three, butchering jacket in one.
29. See, for example, LMA, MJ/SP, Middlesex Sessions Papers, 1695 October/20-1: William Newarke, charged with stealing five new calamanco jackets from John Holmes, mariner.
30. Nathan Bailey, *An Universal Etymological English Dictionary* (London, 1733), unpaginated. The difference between the loose breeches and the trousers worn by sailors is not always very clear. Trousers were defined in a nautical dictionary in 1769 as 'a sort of loose breeches of canvas worn by common sailors'; William Falconer, *An Universal Dictionary of the Marine* (London, 1769), unpaginated. For seamen's dress see Dudley Jarrett, *British Naval Dress* (London, 1960); N. A. M. Roger, *The Wooden World* (London, 1986); Brian Lavery, *Nelson's Navy: The Ships, Men and Organisation, 1793–1815* (London, 1989); Peter Earle, *Sailors: English Merchant Seamen, 1650–1775* (London, 1998).
31. OBP, April 1801, Richard Harnell (t18010415-39).
32. PRO, ASSI 45/36/3/198: Northumberland 1789, John Dixon; ASSI 45/19/1/32-33A: Yorkshire 1731, Raper.
33. Iain Bain (ed.), *A Memoir of Thomas Bewick Written by Himself* (Oxford, 1979), 31.
34. *Jackson's Oxford Journal*, 23 December, 1797.
35. For military uniform, see especially Scott Myerly, *British Military Spectacle from the Napoleonic Wars through the Crimea* (Cambridge, Mass., 1996); C. Walton, *History of the British Standing Army, 1660–1700* (London, 1894); C. C. P. Lawson, *A History of the Uniforms of the British Army*, 2 vols (London, 1940), 1; H. C. B. Rogers, *The British Army of the Eighteenth Century* (London, 1977); Sylvia R. Frey, *The British Soldier in America: A*

Social History of Military Life in the Revolutionary Period (Austin, Texas, 1981).
36. A. Pleat (ed.), '*The Most Dismal Times*': *William Rowbottom's Diary. Part 1: 1787–1799* (Oldham, 1996), 56.
37. T. S. Ashton, *Economic Fluctuations in England, 1700–1800* (London, 1959), 187.
38. C. Bruyn Andrews (ed.), *The Torrington Diaries*, 4 vols (London, 1934–8), 3: 236.
39. Leonard Schwarz, 'English Servants and their Employers during the Eighteenth and Nineteenth Centuries', *Economic History Review*, new series, 52 (1999), 239–44.
40. *Leeds Intelligencer*, 21 July 1789; *Berrow's Worcester Journal*, 25 March 1784, 25 May 1786.
41. Alexander Smith, *The History of the Lives of the Most Notorious Highway-men, Foot-pads, House-breakers, Shop-lifts, and Cheats* (London, 1714), 191.
42. Robert Owen, *The Life of Robert Owen, written by Himself* (London, 1857), 19.
43. OBP, Ann the wife of John Smith, April 1754 (t17540424-46); for a similar case, see OBP, September 1758, Judith Riley (t17580913-26).

3 *Clothing Biographies*

1. William Hutton, *The Life of Willam Hutton F.A.S.S.* (London, 1816), 26–7.
2. Hutton, *Life*, 30–1, 35–6, 38.
3. Hutton, *Life*, 50, 56, 62, 64, 83, 87.
4. Mary Thale (ed.), *The Autobiography of Francis Place (1771–1854)* (Cambridge, 1972), 102, 106, 111, 116–17.
5. Thale, *Autobiography of Francis Place*, 124, 128, 158.
6. James Lackington, *Memoirs of the Forty-five First Years of the Life of James Lackington* (London, 1794), 128, 204, 354.
7. Mary Saxby, *Memoirs of a Female Vagrant Written by Herself* (London, 1806), 11, 17, 18, 22, 26–7.
8. Walsall Local History Centre, 'The Life and Times of James Gee of Walsall, 1746–1827', unpaginated typescript, chapter 4.
9. Thale, *Autobiography of Francis Place*, 62.
10. Thale, *Autobiography of Francis Place*, 106.
11. Thale, *Autobiography of Francis Place*, 63.
12. For an analysis of Shaw's life, see Alan G. Crosby (ed.), *The Family Records of Benjamin Shaw Mechanic of Dent, Dolphinholme and Preston, 1772–1841* (Stroud, 1991), introduction. Also Shani D'Cruze, 'Care, Diligence and "Usfull Pride" [*sic*]: Gender, Industrialisation and the Domestic Economy, c.1770 to c.1840', *Women's History Review*, 3 (1994), 315–46.
13. Crosby, *Benjamin Shaw*, 77.
14. Crosby, *Benjamin Shaw*, 76.
15. Crosby, *Benjamin Shaw*, 44.
16. Crosby, *Benjamin Shaw*, 77.
17. P. H. E. Hair (ed.), *Coals on Rails, or The Reason of my Wrighting. The Autobiography of Anthony Errington from 1778 to around 1825* (Liverpool, 1988); Ann Kussmaul (ed.), *The Autobiography of Joseph Mayett of Quainton (1783–1839)* (Aylesbury, 1986), 23. For an assessment of plebeian memoirs which offers a pessimistic interpretation of material life, see Peter King, 'Social Inequality, Identity and the Labouring Poor in Eighteenth-Century England', in Jonathan Barry and Henry French (eds), *Identity and Agency in England, 1500–1800* (Palgrave, 2004).
18. Iain Bain (ed.), *A Memoir of Thomas Bewick Written by Himself* (Oxford, 1979), 28–9.
19. Woodes Rogers, *A Cruising Voyage round the World* (London, 1718), 11.
20. For Sandby, see Sean Shesgreen, *Images of the Outcast: The Urban Poor in the Cries of London* (Manchester, 2002), chapter 5. For the ragged poor of the London streets, see also Tim Hitchcock, *Down and Out in Eighteenth-Century London* (London, 2004), chapter 5.
21. Richard Chenevix Trench (ed.), *The Remains of the Late Mrs. Richard Trench, Being Selections from Her Journals, Letters, and Other Papers* (London, 1862), 367.
22. LMA, P89/MRY 1/618: St Marylebone Workhouse admissions register, 1769–1772, admissions for January, April, July and October 1770. The main concern here is adult clothing, so the analysis that follows is confined to those aged 15 years old and above. Numbers of children were small.
23. OBP, January 1789, Mary Wade (t17890114-58).
24. Again and again, those applying for relief to the Refuge for the Destitute in the 1810s tell how they had to sell off or pawn all their clothes as they spiralled into destitution. Alysa Levene (ed.), *Narratives of the Poor in Eighteenth-Century Britain*, 5 vols (London, 2006), 4.
25. OBP, April 1780, Mary Hatfield (t17800510-6); June 1785, Ann Icorn (t17850629-99).
26. Saxby, *Memoirs*, 11, 18. Francis Place, recalling the London of the 1790s, noted that the gowns worn by barrow-women were made either from printed linen, or from 'printed cotton generally a large chintz pattern, and these patterns sold in the shops from about 4s. to 12s. the yard; a gown of this sort

was therefore an expensive article, many however were no doubt purchased at second hand from ladies maids or dealers.' British Library, Additional MSS 27827, f. 137, Francis Place collection.

4 Keeping Up Appearances

1. NYCRO, QSB/1730, Thomas Banks.
2. PRO, ASSI 45/34/4/89: Cumberland 1783, William Gill.
3. Anon., *The Reports of the Society for Bettering the Condition and Increasing the Comforts of the Poor*, 4 vols (London, 1798), 1: 178.
4. Lorna Weatherill (ed.), *The Account Book of Richard Latham, 1724–1767* (London, 1990), xxvii.
5. Richard Gough, *The History of Myddle* (London, 1981), 139.
6. William Hutton, *The Life of Willam Hutton F.A.S.S.* (London, 1816), 87.
7. OBP, September 1793, Mary Bryan (t17930911-85).
8. Sir Frederick Eden, *The State of the Poor*, 3 vols (London, 1797), 1: 557. For the view that suits bought in London slop shops were of superior durability, see Anon., *Instructions for Cutting out Apparel for the Poor; Principally intended for the Assistance of the Patronesses of Sunday Schools, and other Charitable Institutions* (London, 1789), 56.
9. David Davies, *The Case of the Labourers in Husbandry* (London, 1795), 15–16. Also Eden, *State of the Poor*, 3:cccxliii. For the basis of this calculation and a more detailed discussion of what the labouring people's budgets collected by David Davies and Sir Frederick Eden can tell us about rates of replacement, see Chapter 13.
10. [Simon Smith] *The Golden Fleece: Or the Trade, Interest, and Well-Being of Great Britain Considered* (London, 1736), 25.
11. Eden, *State of the Poor*, 1:557. Stays were long-lasting and replaced only infrequently among the rich as well as the poor; see Lynn Sorge-English, '"29 Doz and 11 Best Cutt Bone": The Trade in Whalebone and Stays in Eighteenth-Century London', *Textile History*, 36 (2005), 34.
12. Peter Jones, 'Clothing the Poor in Early Nineteenth Century England', *Textile History*, 37 (2006), 23.
13. Eden, *State of the Poor*, 1: 557, 2: 434, 3: 709.
14. Esther Hewlett, *Cottage Comforts with Hints for Promoting them Gleaned from Experience, Enlivened with Anecdotes* (London, 1825), 51–2. I would like to thank Barbara Burman and Jonathan White for alerting me to this book.
15. OBP, May 1786, John Jackson (t17860531-21).
16. OBP, January 1771, Ann Banks (t17710116-19).
17. OBP, December 1793, James Turner (t17931204-10).
18. OBP, September 1793, Mary Bryan (t17930911-85).
19. OBP, April 1794, Diana Young (t17940430-84).
20. OBP, July 1779, James Barrett (t17790707-49).
21. Edward Miles Riley (ed.), *The Journal of John Harrower, an Indentured Servant in the Colony of Virginia, 1773–1776* (Williamsburg, Va., 1963), 14; OBP, October 1740, John Loppenburg (t17401015-66).
22. Davies, *Labourers in Husbandry*, 14–15.
23. Eden, *State of the Poor*, 3: 710; also 2: 76.
24. See, for examples, Suffolk RO (Bury St Edmunds), FL 668/13/1: Daybook of Short Smith, cordwainer, Wattisfield, Suffolk, 1797–1821; East Riding Archives Service, DDBD/87/17: Bird MSS, Account book of Thomas Hewson of Market Weighton, tailor, 1800–1801; Hampshire RO, Mansbridge, 8M62/8: Account Book of Robert Mansbridge of Basing, Hampshire, tailor, 1811–20.
25. OBP, October 1793, Ann Banks (t17931030-42).
26. OBP, July 1784, Thomas Porter (t17840707-113).
27. OBP, December 1789, John Keys (t17891209-21).
28. OBP, September 1780, Benjamin Kinder (t17800913-97).
29. OBP, October 1814, James Topping (t18141026-62).
30. OBP, April 1808, William Shepherd (t18080406-72).
31. WYAS (Wakefield), QS 1/97/8: 1758, Richard Caradice.
32. OBP, September 1757, Ann Lucas (t17570914-17).
33. OBP, February 1785, David Jones (t17850223-4).
34. WYAS (Wakefield), QS 1/122/4: 1783, William Cotter.
35. WYAS (Wakefield), QS 1/122/4: 1783, William Cotter; QS 1/122/7: 1783, Sarah Rowen. For use of the phrase 'washing gown' at the same period, see PRO, ASSI 44/97: Northern Circuit Assizes Indictments, Yorkshire 1783, George Davison, and PRO, ASSI 45/34/1/23–30, 60 and 92: Yorkshire 1780, Elizabeth Ellerington.
36. OBP, June 1783, Sophia Owen (t17830604-37).
37. WYAS (Wakefield), QS 1/121/10: 1782, Hannah Higgs.
38. Catherine Davidson, *A Woman's Work is Never*

Done: A History of Housework in the British Isles, 1650–1950 (London, 1982), 160.
39 OBP, May 1761, David Morgan (t17610506-15). For a dirty cloth coat being sent to a tailor to be cleaned, see OBP, September 1787, Charles Knowland (t17870912-70).
40 Mary Thale (ed.), *The Autobiography of Francis Place (1771–1854)* (Cambridge, 1972), 51.
41 OBP, May 1793, Jane Field (t17930529-46).
42 OBP, December 1732, Hannah Sealy (t17321206-1). 'Tight' in this context meant trim, tidy or smart.
43 OBP, December 1789, John Keys (t17891209-21).
44 PRO, ASSI 45/25/2/100: Yorkshire 1754, Elizabeth Green and Richard Smith.
45 OBP, October 1771, Joseph Wade (t17711023-4).
46 Charles P. Moritz, *Travels, Chiefly on Foot, through Several Parts of England, in 1782* (London, 1795), 23–4.
47 Mrs [Sarah] Trimmer, *The Oeconomy of Charity* (London, 1787), 85.
48 Georges Vigarello, *Concepts of Cleanliness: Changing Attitudes in France since the Middle Ages* (Cambridge, 1988), chapters 4–6; Virginia Smith, 'Cleanliness: Idea and Practice in Britain, 1770–1850' (PhD dissertation, London School of Economics, 1985), chapter 4. Also see Daniel Roche, *The Culture of Clothing: Dress and Fashion in the 'Ancien Régime'* (Cambridge, 1994), chapter 7.
49 Just how important an attribute whiteness was, before and after washing, for judging the quality of both linens and cottons emerges in many of the entries in 'J. F.', *The Merchant's Warehouse Laid Open or the Plain Dealing Linen Draper* (London, 1696).
50 OBP, October 1760, John Hughes (t17601022-16).
51 Sylvia R. Frey, *The British Soldier in America: A Social History of Military Life in the Revolutionary Period* (Austin, Tex., 1981), 34–5.
52 OBP, December 1792, Joseph Edwards (t17921215-118). See also OBP, January 1727, Elizabeth Travers (t17270113-6).
53 Basil Cozens-Hardy (ed.), *Mary Hardy's Diary*, Norfolk Record Society, vol. 37 (Norwich, 1968), 31.
54 PRO, ASSI 45/36/2/130: Westmorland 1788, Esther Nicholson. For the same frequency of washing in London, see OBP, December 1784, Thomas Wood (t17841208-2).
55 OBP, July 1762, Sarah Metyard (t17620714-30).
56 Trimmer, *Oeconomy of Charity* (1787), 63–4.
57 OBP, October 1740, John Loppenburg (t17401015-66).
58 For different methods of washing, see Davidson, *Woman's Work*, 138–53. For washing and the working poor, see Howlett, *Cottage Comforts*, 86–9. For women washing in an English river, at Morpeth in Northumberland in 1673, see James Raine (ed.), *Depositions from the Castle of York relating to Offences Committed in the Northern Counties in the Seventeenth Century* (Durham, 1861), 202–3.
59 Henri Misson, *M. Misson's Memoirs and Observations in his Travels over England*, trans. John Ozell (London, 1719), 303.
60 WYAS (Wakefield), QS 1/96/2: 1757, Margaret Wilson.
61 Stephen Hudson's shop high in the Yorkshire Pennines sold blue, starch and some soap to his clientele of poor farmers and tradespeople; see Chapter 7.
62 Synthetic chemical soda was first produced from salt by the Leblanc process, patented in France in 1791. It became available only slowly in Britain prior to the repeal of the salt duty in 1825. Thereafter, the Leblanc soda industry grew very rapidly and displaced vegetable alkalis in soap making. The first mention of soda as a cleaning agent in the Old Bailey trials is in 1809, when 40 pounds of soda were stolen from a soap factory at Bethnal Green, along with 30 pounds of the much cheaper pearl ash (a form of vegetable alkali, like lye); OBP, February 1809, Thomas Harris (t18090215-69). Soaps continued to carry a heavy excise duty until 1853.
63 Alan G. Crosby (ed.), *The Family Records of Benjamin Shaw Mechanic of Dent, Dolphinholme and Preston, 1772–1841* (Stroud, 1991), 97.
64 WYAS (Wakefield), QS 1/93/2: 1754, Elizabeth Hartley; QS 1/125/3: 1786, Fanny Curtis.
65 PRO, ASSI 45/35/1/85-92: Northumberland 1784, William Graham; ASSI 45/37/1/16-26A: Northumberland 1790, Dennis Banks. A similar rinsing house was operated in the 1770s at Ruswarp, near Whitby; see ASSI 45/33/2/18-23: Yorkshire 1778, Elizabeth Bower. It is probably significant that both these examples of commercial washing facilities were in places with large populations of seamen.
66 Eden, *State of the Poor*, 3: 874, 2: 621–2.
67 George Parker, *A View of Society and Manners in High and Low Life; Being the Adventures in England, Ireland, Scotland, Wales, France &c. of Mr G. Parker. In which is comprised a History of the Stage Itinerant*, 2 vols (London, 1781), 1: 225.
68 OBP, May 1785, Worley Walmslay (t17850511-23).
69 OBP, May 1811, Mary Little (t18110529-98).
70 Eden, *State of the Poor*, 3:cccxli.

5 Changing Clothes

1. OBP, September 1756, Elizabeth Rivers (t17561020-50).
2. Neil McKendrick, 'Home Demand and Economic Growth: A New View of the Role of Women and Children in the Industrial Revolution', in Neil McKendrick (ed.), *Historical Perspectives: Studies in English Thought and Society in Honour of J. H. Plumb*, (Cambridge, 1975), 209.
3. Pehr Kalm, *Kalm's Account of his Visit to England on his Way to America in 1748*, trans. Joseph Lucas (London, 1892), 52–3. The advertisements in the Oxford newspaper are drawn from an area near Little Gaddesdon in Hertfordshire where Kalm stayed.
4. Anne Buck, *Dress in Eighteenth-Century England* (London, 1979), 30; C. Willett Cunnington and Phillis Cunnington, *Handbook of English Costume in the Eighteenth Century* (London, 1957), 241–7. It is noticeable, however, that among the wealthy victims of the Brandon fire in 1789, only one lost a wig to the flames, and he was George Warner, a wealthy tailor, who appears to have been old.
5. These fustian frocks appear to have been different from the fustian jackets that came to symbolise the working man of the Chartist era. Fustian jackets became common at the Old Bailey only from the 1810s. From the 1770s to the 1800s, there are very few Old Bailey cases that mention men's upper garments made of fustian, although fustian breeches appear with some regularity. For fustian jackets and their symbolic significance for working-class identity in the 1840s, see Paul A. Pickering, 'Class without Words: Symbolic Communication in the Chartist Movement', *Past and Present*, 112 (1986), 144–62.
6. Francis Place dated the collapse of the leather breeches trade in which he was trained to the 1790s, but leather breeches were evidently already in decline before that; Mary Thale (ed.), *The Autobiography of Francis Place (1771–1854)* (Cambridge, 1972), 110.
7. *Weekly Worcester Journal*, 19 June 1766. For Gee, see Chapter 3.
8. Buck, *Dress in Eighteenth-Century England*, 58.
9. The exceptions were a handful of coats made from fustian, suggesting that what were described as fustian coats in the indictments may be the fustian frocks of the advertisements.
10. OBP, June 1785, John Scott (t17850629-90).
11. The terms cloak and hood appear to have overlapped in Yorkshire, sometimes being used to describe the same garment. A short cloak owned by a Yorkshire labourer in 1738 was also referred to as a hood. Hoods were mainly silk, never cloth, and usually black, associated with mourning. Cloaks were either woollen cloth, usually red, or silk, usually black. The term hood was not used in the London sources employed here.
12. The provincial newspaper advertisements after 1770 confirm this trend, although in a muted way. Cottons and linens accounted for nearly half the gowns worn by runaways at this period, with woollens continuing to comprise most of the rest. The continuing high proportion of gowns made from woollen materials in the advertisements, often worn by younger runaways in their teens, may result from a number of them having been parish apprentices, clothed to a basic standard by overseers of the poor, who virtually never supplied cottons for gowns before the end of the eighteenth century (see Chapter 16).
13. It should be remembered that the accessories listed in the trial records and those listed in the advertisements cannot be directly compared. The advertisements listed mainly men's clothes, while the trial records failed to distinguish between men's and women's clothing.
14. At the Old Bailey, the number of cases involving swords fell continuously relative to the total number of cases each decade from the 1700s to the 1750s, suggesting that sword ownership (and the use of swords in murder cases) was declining rapidly. In the decade 1700–9 the ratio was 1:77; by 1750–9 it was 1:677; OBP, keyword searches on sword. None of the wealthier victims of the Brandon fire in 1789 lost a sword. See Robert Shoemaker, 'Male Honour and the Decline of Public Violence in Eighteenth-century London', *Social History*, 26 (2001), 205.
15. Buck, *Dress in Eighteenth-Century England*, 59, 203–4.
16. Oliver Goldsmith, *The Works of Oliver Goldsmith*, 3 vols, ed. Arthur Friedman (Oxford, 1966), 3: 305–6; John Eglin, *The Imaginary Autocrat: Beau Nash and the Invention of Bath* (London, 2005), 75; Buck, *Dress in Eighteenth-Century England*, 22, 43–4.

6 Fashioning Time: Watches

1. William Hutton, *The Life of Willam Hutton F.A.S.S.* (London, 1816), 64.
2. For a similar story from London of a fifteen-year-old servant in a public house who saved up his

money to buy a silver watch, probably second-hand, for 23 shillings, see OBP, December 1792, Eleanor Hollwell (t17921215-107).

3   PRO, ASSI 45/1/2 to 45/40/1: Assizes Northern Circuit depositions, 1640–1799.

4   PRO, ASSI 5/20 to 5/119: Assizes Oxford Circuit indictments, 1700–1799.

5   OBP, July 1745, Thomas Ford (t17450710-19).

6   At the time of the debate over the clock and watch tax in 1797–8, official (and not necessarily very accurate) estimates of the expected yield from the tax put the number of watches in Britain at 800,000 silver and 400,000 gold, for a population of under 11 million, more than a third of whom were children under 15. If these figures were only approximately accurate, they would allow for watch owners amongst plebeian men. E. P. Thompson, 'Time, Work-discipline and Industrial Capitalism', *Past and Present*, 38 (1967), 67–8.

7   Maxwell Cutmore, *The Pocket Watch Handbook* (London, 1985), chapter 2.

8   York City Archives, Accession 38: Pledge book of George Fettes, pawnbroker, York, 1777–8. Also see Alison Backhouse, *The Worm-Eaten Waistcoat* (York, 2003). It is possible, of course, that London makers' names had been put on watches made elsewhere; see *House of Commons Sessional Papers*, volume 6 (1817), Report from the Committee on the Petitions of Watchmakers of Coventry, etc., 11 July 1817, 15.

9   York City Archives, Accession 38: Pledge book of George Fettes, pawnbroker, York, 1777–8. Also see Backhouse, *The Worm-Eaten Waistcoat*.

10 The Record Office for Leicestershire, Leicester and Rutland, 9D 51/ii/2 and 8: Papers of Samuel Deacon of Barton in the Beans, clockmaker and Baptist, 1806 and 1803.

11 See, for example, Suffolk RO (Ipswich), P616:8566: Account book of John Spore, shoemaker, Chediston, Suffolk, 1768–84.

12 OBP, June 1780, Leonard Sullivan (t17800628-49).

13 Thompson, 'Time, Work-discipline and Industrial Capitalism', 56–97.

14 Thompson, 'Time, Work-discipline and Industrial Capitalism', 69.

15 Paul Glennie and Nigel Thrift, 'Reworking E. P. Thompson's "Time, Work-discipline and Industrial Capitalism"', *Time and Society*, 5 (1996), 275–300; Paul Glennie and Nigel Thrift, 'The Spaces of Clock Times', in Patrick Joyce (ed.), *The Social in Question: New Bearings in History and the Social Sciences* (London, 2002), 151–74.

16 Glennie and Thrift, 'Spaces of Clock Times', 173.

17 In particular, he dismisses too easily Dorothy George's contention that labouring men owned watches in London in the mid-eighteenth century as indefinite and inadequately documented; Thompson, 'Time, Work-discipline and Industrial Capitalism', 66–7, Dorothy George, *London Life in the Eighteenth Century* (London, 1925), 170.

18 Thompson, 'Time, Work-discipline and Industrial Capitalism', 69.

19 Thompson, 'Time, Work-discipline and Industrial Capitalism', 70.

20 *House of Commons Sessional Papers*, volume 6 (1817), Report from the Committee on the Petitions of Watchmakers of Coventry, etc., 11 July 1817, 15.

21 OBP, February 1734, William Collins (t17340227-55).

22 York City Archives, Accession 38: Pledge book of George Fettes, pawnbroker, York, 1777–8. These conclusions are based on a sample consisting of all the items pawned during four weeks in January, April, July and October 1778. For other pawnbrokers with large stocks of watches, see, for examples, City of London, Guildhall Library Archives, MS 9174/46, inventory of Joseph Gun, St Brides London, pawnbroker, 1727 and PRO, PROB 3/48/30, inventory of Francis Shipley, St Mary's, Whitechapel, chandler, 1749.

23 Peter Earle points out that merchant seamen often possessed a range of silver objects, including watches, citing a mid-eighteenth-century inventory; Peter Earle, *Sailors: English Merchant Seamen, 1650–1775* (London, 1998), 57.

24 See, for example, WYAS (Wakefield), QS 1/130/9: 1791, Peggy Dearden.

25 In the Yorkshire trial records for the 1730s, 1750s and 1780s, ten percent of named owners of stolen clothes were female.

26 York City Archives, Accession 38: Pledge book of George Fettes, pawnbroker, York, 1777–8. Information about watches is drawn from the whole book; information about women's pledges is based on a sample consisting of all the items pawned during four weeks in January, April, July and October 1778.

27 The Record Office for Leicestershire, Leicester and Rutland, 9D 51/ii/2 and 8: Papers of Samuel Deacon of Barton in the Beans, clockmaker and Baptist, 1806 and 1803. For a discussion of a range of possible reasons for women owning fewer watches than men in the period, see Moira

28 By the start of the eighteenth century the vast majority of parish churches in towns and nearly half of those in the countryside had clocks; Glennie and Thrift, 'Spaces of Clock Times', 164.

Donald, '"The Greatest Necessity for Every Rank of Men": Gender, Clocks and Watches', in Moira Donald and Linda Hurcombe (eds), *Gender and Material Culture in Historical Perspective* (Basingstoke, 2000), 54–75.

29 PRO, ASSI 45/36/3/59: Yorkshire 1789, Thomas Clayton; ASSI 45/24/3/68G: Northumberland 1751, Mary Smith; W. Williamson, *The Trials at Large of the Felons in the Castle of York at the Lent Assizes, 1777* (York, 1777), 17; ASSI 45/36/2/67–9: Yorkshire 1788, Duncan Graham. See E. Gillet and K. A. MacMahon, *A History of Hull* (Oxford, 1980), 228–30, for the high earnings of seamen in the whale fishery.

30 PRO, ASSI 45/40/1/32–7: Westmorland 1799, William Denison; ASSI 45/36/3/230: Northumberland 1789, Thomas Young.

31 PRO, ASSI 45/34/1/38: Westmorland 1780, William Fowler; ASSI 45/38/3/115: York City 1795, John Smith.

32 PRO, ASSI 45/29/1/69: Yorkshire 1768, George Greenbank; ASSI 45/34/3/108–10: Yorkshire 1782, Bailey Wall; ASSI 45/32/1/35–7: Yorkshire 1775, George Brodwell; ASSI 45/32/1/208: Yorkshire 1775, John Raper.

33 PRO, ASSI 45/36/2/67–9: Yorkshire 1788, Duncan Graham; ASSI 45/32/1/208: Yorkshire 1775, John Raper; ASSI 45/37/3/125: Yorkshire 1792, Matthew Little. The Foundling Museum, London holds two watch seals that were left with infants as tokens in the mid-eighteenth century; one has an anchor engraved on it, the other the head of a man.

34 See Elisabeth Bogdan, 'An Investigation of Eighteenth-Century Iconography: Sir Kenrick Clayton's Revolving Seal', Victoria and Albert Museum/Royal College of Art M.A. Course essay, 1991. I would like to thank Elisabeth Bogdan for allowing me to use her essay.

35 PRO, ASSI 45/33/2/134: Yorkshire 1778, Nicholas Todd.

36 It is not clear for most stolen watches whether they were single or double cased.

37 OBP, Feb. 1787, James Johnson (t17870221-89).

38 David Roberts, *Lord Chesterfield: Letters* (Oxford, 1992), 132.

7 Fashion's Favourite? Cottons

1 11 and 12 W. III, c. 10 (1700), *An Act for the more effectual employing the Poor, by encouraging the Manufactures of this Kingdom*, and 7 Geo. I, c. 7 (1720), *An Act to preserve and encourage the Woollen and Silk Manufactures of this Kingdom, and for more effectual employing the Poor, by prohibiting the Use and Wear of all printed, painted, stained or dyed Callicoes in Apparel, Houshold Stuff, Furniture, or otherwise, after the twenty-fifth Day of December one thousand seven hundred and twenty-two*. For the broader significance of this legislation, see Patrick O'Brien, Trevor Griffiths and Philip Hunt, 'Political Components of the Industrial Revolution: Parliament and the English Cotton Textile Industry, 1660–1774', *Economic History Review*, new series, 44 (1991), 395–423.

2 Beverly Lemire, *Fashion's Favourite: The Cotton Trade and the Consumer in Britain, 1660–1800* (Oxford, 1991), 4, 14, 20. For an earlier expression of the view that the taste for Indian cottons reached 'epidemic proportions' in the later seventeenth century, see Neil McKendrick, 'The Consumer Revolution of Eighteenth-Century England', in Neil McKendrick, John Brewer and J. H. Plumb (eds), *The Birth of a Consumer Society* (London, 1982), 14.

3 David MacPherson, *Annals of Commerce, Manufactures, Fisheries and Navigation*, 4 vols (Edinburgh, 1805), 4: 81.

4 K. N. Chaudhuri, *The English East India Company: A Study of an Early Joint Stock Company, 1600–1640* (London, 1965), 199; John Styles, 'Product Innovation in Early Modern London', *Past and Present*, 168 (2000), 133.

5 John Pollexfen, *A Discourse of Trade and Coyn* (London, 1700), 99.

6 Similarly, only one gown made from cotton appears in the manuscript Old Bailey examinations for Middlesex in the 1690s, although there are numerous mentions of clothing accessories in calico and muslin. In the criminal records for the North and West Ridings of Yorkshire in the same decade no gowns made from cotton appear and only one cotton accessory. Indeed, in the North Riding quarter sessions rolls between 1691 and 1730, there are only two mentions of calico gowns, one in 1715 belonging to the wife of the deputy clerk of the peace and one in 1718 belonging to the wife of a surgeon, both well-off women.

7 The number of cases that identify the status of owners of clothing accessories made from Indian

fabrics is too small to draw conclusions about the social depth of the market, but it was clearly assumed that cheaper Indian fabrics were commonly worn in this form by working people, at least in London. A man who claimed to be a provincial Member of Parliament in 1692 was suspected of deceit by his landlady's daughter because his handkerchief was coarse and dirty, 'and not fit for his Quality (as she thought) it being made of ordinary Indian stuff, like her Mothers Maids Apron'. See OBP, April 1692, Andrew Clenche (t16920406-1).

8 Alfred P. Wadsworth and Julia de Lacy Mann, *The Cotton Trade and Industrial Lancashire, 1600–1780* (Manchester, 1931), 133–9.

9 Commissioners for Trade and Plantations, 'Account of the trade of this Kingdom', in Historical Manuscripts Commission, *The Manuscripts of the House of Lords, 1702–1704* (London, 1910).

10 Wadsworth and Mann, *Cotton Trade*, 133.

11 Styles, 'Product Innovation', 132–6.

12 Quoted in Wadsworth and Mann, *Cotton Trade*, 133. As always in the debates over calico, the view that large numbers of poorer people wore printed fabrics at this date was disputed; see Anon., *A Further Examination of the Weavers Pretences* (London, 1719), 19–20. The number of cases at the Old Bailey that provide occupational information at this date is insufficient to draw firm conclusions. Nevertheless, the rise in the number of cases involving such fabrics is striking.

13 Natalie Rothstein, 'The Calico Campaign of 1719–1721', *East London Papers*, 7 (1964), 3–21.

14 This pattern is broadly consistent with the account of linen and cotton imports in the 1720s and 1730s in O'Brien, Griffiths and Hunt, 'Political Components of the Industrial Revolution', 414.

15 In the billet books of the London Foundling Hospital from 1741, these printed fabrics are always described as cotton, never as fustian; see Appendix 2. The exemption for printing on fabrics with linen warps and cotton wefts was confirmed in 1736 by Act of Parliament 9 Geo. II, c. 4 (1736).

16 OBP, April 1744, Jane Morris (t17440404-28).

17 OBP, June 1758, Elizabeth Rice (t17580628-6).

18 Anon., *A Further Examination of the Weavers Pretences*, 20.

19 Fayrer Hall, *The Importance of the British Plantations in America to this Kingdom* (London, 1731), 10–11.

20 See, for examples, 'T.S.', *England's Danger by Indian Manufactures* (?London, 1701), 3; Anon. [Daniel Defoe], *The Female Manufacturers Complaint: Being the Humble Petition of Dorothy Distaff, Abigail Spinning-Wheel, Eleanor Reel, &c. Spinsters* (London, 1720), 8, 9, 14. For an exception, which identifies fashion in printed calicoes with the patterns printed on the cloth, see *The Case of the Linnen Drapers and other Dealers in Printed Callicoes and Linnens* (?London, 1711).

21 The foundling textiles also include striped cottons, very similar in appearance to the striped linens and again woven mainly in blue and white, which do not appear in the criminal records or the advertisements.

22 *Weekly Worcester Journal*, 20 March 1766.

23 Gown lengths of camblet sold to servants by a Hampshire draper in the 1760s cost between 11 d. and 13 d. per yard, such a low price that it is most unlikely the material had any silk content. Hampshire RO, 96M82 PZ25: Account book of Mary Medhurst and Thomas North, drapers, 1762–81.

24 LMA, A/FH/A/9/1/125: Foundling Hospital Billet Book, January 1759, 30 monochrome, 14 polychrome; A/FH/A/9/1/149: July 1759, 20 monochrome, 13 polychrome.

25 Natalie Rothstein (ed.), *Barbara Johnson's Album of Fashions and Fabrics* (London, 1987).

26 Monochrome prints in Barbara Johnson's album between 1746 and 1769 were cheaper than polychrome prints.

27 By Acts of Parliament 10 Anne, c. 19 (1712) and 12 Anne, c. 9 (1714), which also placed a duty of 6 d. a yard on prints on pure cottons.

28 WYAS (Bradford), 33D80/6/7: Shop book of Stephen Hudson of Fewston, 1751–9. Prices are based on an analysis of the shop accounts for 1759.

29 WYAS (Bradford), 33D80/6/7: Shop book of Stephen Hudson of Fewston, 1751–9, 19 June 1752.

30 There are, however, insufficient cases that distinguish between printed and non-printed linen and cotton gowns to enable the historian to generate average values for the two types.

31 OBP, January 1753, Sarah Steele (t17530111-5).

32 OBP, May 1753, Mary Brown (t17530502-36).

33 OBP, September 1758, William More, (t17580913-64).

34 WYAS (Wakefield), QS 1/95/8: West Riding Quarter Sessions Rolls, October 1756, Elizabeth Miller.

35 OBP, February 1758, William Coupeland (t17580222-6); May 1755, Elisabeth Wills (t17550409-8); February 1758, William Coupeland (t17580222-6).

36 Lemire, *Fashion's Favourite*, 112.

37. MacPherson, *Annals of Commerce*, 4: 81. Others have agreed with MacPherson; see O'Brien, Griffiths and Hunt, 'Political components of the industrial revolution', 415. Similarly Michael Edwards suggests that cottons had a slight price advantage over linens and woollens at the start of the 1780s and that from 1780 'the increased demand for cotton goods was due to their relative cheapness compared with other fabrics'. Michael M. Edwards, *The Growth of the British Cotton Trade, 1780–1815* (Manchester, 1967), 28 and 31. This view is not supported by a Lancashire author in 1780, who suggested that cotton yarn remained slightly more expensive than linen yarn. 'A Friend of the Poor', *Thoughts on the Use of Machines in the Cotton Manufacture* (Manchester, 1780), 16.
38. Act of Parliament 14 Geo. III, c. 72 (1774).
39. Bedfordshire and Luton Archives and Record Service, M10/4/34: Williamson Muniments, correspondence, letters to Mary Williamson, 1775–8, Margaret Cater to Mrs Mary Williamson, 17 October 1776,
40. For a brief period between 1784 and 1787, prints on pure linens enjoyed a slight tax advantage over prints on cotton and cotton-linen mixes; thereafter all printed fabrics paid the same excise duty of three and a half pence a yard. See Acts of Parliament 24 Geo. III, c. 40 (1784), 25 Geo. III, c. 72 (1785) and 27 Geo. III, c. 13 (1787).
41. See Chapter 16.
42. M. C. Buer, *Health, Wealth and Population in the Early Days of the Industrial Revolution* (London, 1926), 60.
43. J. D. Chambers, *Population, Economy, and Society in Pre-Industrial England* (Oxford, 1972), 104.
44. David Landes, 'The Fable of the Dead Horse; or, the Industrial Revolution Revisited', in Joel Mokyr (ed.), *The British Industrial Revolution: An Economic Perspective* (Boulder, Colo., 1999), 152, note 27.
45. Woodruff D. Smith, *Consumption and the Making of Respectability, 1600–1800* (London, 2002), 61.
46. Buer, *Health, Wealth and Population*, 196; Chambers, *Population, Economy, and Society*, 104–5.
47. Mary Thale (ed.), *The Autobiography of Francis Place (1771–1854)* (Cambridge, 1972), 51. Also Dorothy George, *England in Transition: Life and Work in the Eighteenth Century* (London, 1931), 98.
48. For detailed discussion of the East India Company's trade in cotton shifts and shirts, see John Styles, 'Product Innovation', 124–69; also Beverly Lemire, 'Transforming Consumer Cus-tom: Linens, Cottons and the English Market, 1660–1800', in Brenda Collins and Philip Ollerenshaw (eds), *The European Linen Industry in Historical Perspective* (Oxford, 2003), and 'Fashioning Cottons: Asian trade, Domestic Industry and Consumer Demand, 1660–1780', in David Jenkins (ed.), *The Cambridge History of Western Textiles*, vol. 1 (Cambridge, 2003).
49. Shirts of this kind were not an entirely untested commodity. Six hundred and thirty-one, probably ready-made from cotton, had been offered for sale at one of the Company's auctions in 1676. However, shirts did not feature regularly at the Company's auctions in the 1670s and the Company's surviving Surat and Madras correspondence does not refer to them in that decade. Moreover, the number offered for sale at the 1676 auction was tiny compared with the scale of the Company's orders in the subsequent decade. See 'A Particular of the Goods to be Exposed to Sale by the East India Company, in September, 1676', printed bill, Bodleian Library, John Johnson Collection, East India Company, Box 1; also 'For Sale at the East India House, November 10, 1673', printed bill, British Library, c.136.g.43.
50. These are very approximate orders of magnitude, but register the fact that the proportion of children in London's population was relatively low. See Roger Finlay and Beatrice Shearer, 'Population Growth and Suburban Expansion', in A. L. Beier and Roger Finlay (eds), *London, 1500–1700: The Making of the Metropolis* (London, 1986), 47.
51. See N. B. Harte, 'The Economics of Clothing in the Late Seventeenth Century', *Textile History*, 22 (1991), 293. The East India Company correspondence initially refers mainly to 'shifts', the term used for women's linen undergarments, but references elsewhere make it clear that both shirts and shifts were being ordered. King uses the term 'smock' to refer to shifts.
52. H. Dodwell (ed.), *Records of Fort St George: Despatches from England, 1681–1686* (Madras, 1916), 15: Josiah Child, London, to William Gifford, Agent and Governor at Fort St George, 9 October 1682.
53. Dodwell, *Records of Fort St George*, 112: London to Fort St George, 26 November 1684.
54. Dodwell, *Records of Fort St George*, 15: Child to Gifford, 9 October 1682.
55. The 1682 order for ready-made cotton shifts and shirts has been noted by a large number of historians, but the problems the Company subsequently faced in selling the new product have been over-

looked. See, for example, P. J. Thomas, *Mercantalism and the East India Trade* (London, 1926), 46; Chaudhuri, *Trading World of Asia*, 287; A. W. Douglas, 'Cotton Textiles in England: The East India Company's Attempt to Exploit Developments in Fashion, 1660–1721', *Journal of British Studies*, 8 (1968), 32; Lemire, *Fashion's Favourite*, 180; J. E. Wills, 'European Consumption and Asian Production in the Seventeenth and Eighteenth Centuries', in John Brewer and Roy Porter (eds), *Consumption and the World of Goods in the Seventeenth and Eighteenth Centuries* (London, 1993), 137.

56 Dodwell, *Records of Fort St George. Despatches from England, 1681–1686*, 112, 140, 174–5: London to Fort St George, 26 November 1684; ibid., 140, London to Fort St George, 19 March 1684–5. An account of what Coast and Bay goods are remaining in the Company's warehouse unsold, 29 December 1685.

57 Information from Anthony Farrington based on his comprehensive survey of the manuscript records of the East India Company's London auctions. Many of the shirts and shifts sent from India may have ended up being sold by private treaty when they failed to sell well at auction. A small number (about 4,000) was bought by the Hudson's Bay Company between 1684 and 1694, although this may have been simply a case of benefiting from the East India Company's failure in the domestic market; see Beverly Lemire, *Dress, Culture and Commerce* (London, 1997), 36.

58 A. V. Venkatarama Ayyar (ed.), *Records of Fort St George. Despatches from England, 1686–1692* (Madras, 1929), 144, List of Coromandel Coast goods to be provided for the year 1690.

59 OBP, September 1802, Sarah Powell (t18020918-27).

60 C. Knick Harley, 'Cotton Textile Prices and the Industrial Revolution', *Economic History Review*, new series, 51 (1998), 49–83.

61 W. G. Rimmer, *Marshalls of Leeds, Flax-Spinners, 1788–1886* (Cambridge, 1960), 73–4, 128, 144.

62 Michael Edwards argues, however, that in the later eighteenth century workers 'were probably more impressed by low prices than any claims about durability'. Edwards, *Growth of the British Cotton Trade*, 31–2.

63 Anon., *The Trade of England Revived* (London, 1681), 16–17.

64 Daniel Defoe, *A Brief Deduction of the Original, Progress, and Immense Greatness of the British Woollen Manufacture* (London, 1727), 50.

65 Esther Hewlett, *Cottage Comforts with Hints for Promoting them Gleaned from Experience, Enlivened with Anecdotes* (London, 1825), 36.

66 Arthur Young, *General View of the Agriculture of the County of Suffolk* (London, 1794), 150–1.

67 Thomas Jones, *Clothing Societies* (Northampton, 1822), 4, 17; Francis Lichfield, *Three Years' Results of the Farthinghoe Clothing Society* (Northampton, 1832), 8. At Farthinghoe the purchases were for the years 1829 to 1831; the club's members also bought 1,072 yards of sheeting at 8d. a yard, but the fibre is not specified.

68 Edwards, *The Growth of the British Cotton Trade*, 36.

69 Quoted in Rimmer, *Marshalls of Leeds*, 164–5.

70 Rimmer, *Marshalls of Leeds*, 239.

71 Mark Overton et al., *Production and Consumption in English Households, 1600–1750* (London, 2004), 108–11; Christopher Husbands, 'Standards of Living in North Warwickshire in the Seventeenth Century', *Warwickshire History*, 4, 6 (1980–1), 203–15.

8 Clothing Provincial England: Fabrics

1 Sir Frederick Eden, *The State of the Poor*, 3 vols (London, 1797), 1: 554–5. For examples of the use of this passage by a variety of historians (not just those concerned with dress) see Anne Buck, *Dress in Eighteenth-Century England* (London, 1979), 146; Aileen Ribeiro, *Dress in Eighteenth-Century Europe* (London, 1984), 63; Ivy Pinchbeck, *Women Workers and the Industrial Revolution, 1750–1850* (London, 1969), 50–1; Asa Briggs (ed.), *How They Lived*, 3 vols (Oxford, 1969), 3: 254–5.

2 Eden, *State of the Poor*, 1: 555.

3 The proportion of the population living in towns grew substantially during the eighteenth century, but it remained less than a third. It rose from just under 20 percent of the total population of England and Wales in 1700 to just over 30 percent by 1800. London's population grew in absolute terms, but not as a proportion of the country's growing population, remaining at about 11 percent. Urban growth was concentrated in the provinces, especially the Midlands and the north. P. J. Corfield, *The Impact of English Towns, 1700–1800* (Oxford, 1982), 9–11.

4 Eden, *State of the Poor*, 1: 491.

5 Eden, *State of the Poor*, 1: 245.

6 See Carole Shammas, *The Pre-Industrial Consumer in England and America* (Oxford, 1990), 137, note 24.

7 Lorna Weatherill, *Consumer Behaviour and Material*

Culture in Britain, 1660–1760 (London, 1988), chapter 3.
8. Shammas, *Pre-Industrial Consumer*, 248–60; H. Mui and L. H. Mui, *Shops and Shopkeeping in Eighteenth-Century England* (London, 1989), chapter 2.
9. Anne Buck, 'Variations in English Women's Dress in the Eighteenth Century', *Folk Life*, 9 (1971), 5–28.
10. For a discussion of these phenomena and their typicality, see John Styles, 'Manufacturing, Consumption and Design in Eighteenth-Century England', in John Brewer and Roy Porter (eds), *Consumption and the World of Goods in the Seventeenth and Eighteenth Centuries* (London, 1993), 535–42, and 'Product Innovation in Early Modern London', *Past and Present*, 168 (2000), 124–69.
11. The most powerful claim for the central importance of these issues to the history of consumption in the early-modern period has been made by Jan de Vries in his 'Between Purchasing Power and the World of Goods: Understanding the Household Economy in Early Modern Europe', in Brewer and Porter, *Consumption and the World of Goods*, 85–132, and 'The Industrial Revolution and the Industrious Revolution', *Journal of Economic History*, 54 (1994), 249–70. For three rather different discussions of the same theme see Pinchbeck, *Women Workers and the Industrial Revolution*, Shammas, *Pre-Industrial Consumer*, chapter 2, and Mick Reed, '"Gnawing it Out": A New Look at Economic Relations in Nineteenth-Century Rural England', *Rural History*, 1 (1990), 83–94.
12. See, for examples of work that discusses some of these issues, Maxine Berg, 'Markets, Trade and European Manufacture', in Maxine Berg (ed.), *Markets and Manufacture in Early Industrial Europe* (London, 1991) and Julian Hoppit, 'Income, Welfare and the Industrial Revolution in Britain', *The Historical Journal*, 31 (1988), 721–31.
13. Borthwick Institute for Archives, University of York: Exchequer and Prerogative Courts of York, wills, 1689–1800 and Dean and Chapter of York, wills, 1660–1800. I would like to thank John Moore for bringing the existence of these inventories to my attention.
14. Borthwick Institute for Archives, University of York: Exchequer and Prerogative Courts of York, wills, 1689–1800 and Dean and Chapter of York, wills, 1660–1800. The first sample consists of all the surviving inventories for textile and clothing suppliers in the main Yorkshire wills series for two three-year periods, 1715–1717 and 1780–1782. The second is a four-year-per-decade sample, 1690 to 1789, of surviving inventories in the same series of wills for textile and clothing suppliers from Halifax, a large manufacturing parish with a major town. The third sample consists of all surviving inventories 1660–1800 for textile and clothing suppliers for the Dean and Chapter liberty, which covered a large number of mainly rural parishes throughout Yorkshire and the adjacent counties of Nottinghamshire and Lancashire. In combination, the three samples contain 200 inventories. In view of generally recognised problems of using inventories and as yet unresolved questions about how representative the later eighteenth-century Yorkshire probate material can be taken to be, the samples are used here to establish only very broad patterns. I would like to thank John Smail for making his list of Halifax probate inventories available to me.
15. Mui and Mui, *Shops and Shopkeeping*, 289.
16. Shammas, *Pre-Industrial Consumer*, 259–60.
17. Nancy Cox, *The Complete Tradesman: A Study of Retailing, 1550–1820* (Aldershot, 2000), chapter 2. Weatherill, *Consumer Behaviour*, 203, acknowledges that some of the northern inventories, particularly those for Cumbria and Lancashire, are less detailed than those elsewhere, and therefore, perhaps, less reliable. Carole Shammas's figures for the numbers of shops in 1785, which indicate extreme regional disparities in the distribution of non-urban retailers, derive from the records of a tax that applied only to those shops paying an annual rent of more than £5 a year. The usefulness of these figures is called into question by the fact that shop rents were often much lower than this, perhaps particularly so in the north. If a two-room lock-up haberdasher's shop in the borough of Richmond, Yorkshire, with a diverse stock worth over £50, paid an annual rent of only £2 12s. 6d., it is unlikely that most smaller shops in northern rural parishes paid the 1785 shop tax. Shammas, *The Pre-Industrial Consumer*, 248–60; PRO, ASSI 45/37/3/35: Yorkshire, 1792, Mary Blake.
18. It is impossible to establish from this material whether the rise of the small general store was at the expense of chapmen and other itinerant traders, as the Muis imply but Shammas has disputed. Mui and Mui, *Shops and Shopkeeping*, 99–100; Shammas, *Pre-Industrial Consumer*, 255.
19. This phrase 'system of provision' is taken from Ben Fine and Ellen Leopold, *The World of Consumption* (London, 1993), chapters 1 and 2, whose approach

20 Although all the references in the criminal depositions to yarn produced for use by the household identify women as the spinners, it would be wrong to assume that hand spinning was an exclusively female activity. In the Yorkshire Pennines north of Skipton, men accounted for about a quarter of outwork hand spinners in the late eighteenth century. See WYAS (Wakefield), QE 15/39-40: Convictions for false reeling of worsted yarn by Thomas Garforth and Charles Knowlton, JPs, 1795 and 1797.

21 NYCRO, QSB/1694: George Waud.

22 These cases derived disproportionately, however, from north-east Yorkshire, an area with a linen weaving industry producing for distant markets. This may indicate that having the household's hempen or flaxen yarn woven up for family use was more prevalent in areas where there was an established large-scale linen manufacture. See R. Hastings, 'The North Riding Linen Industry', *North Yorkshire County Record Office Journal*, 7 (1980), 67–85.

23 NYCRO, QSB/1734: John Pinckney. Spinning woollen yarn for this purpose may have been more widespread earlier in the eighteenth century. H. E. Strickland in *A General View of the Agriculture of the East Riding of Yorkshire* (York, 1812), 283–4, says 'the domestic manufacture of coarse gray woollen cloths, from a mixture of black and white wool, for the clothing of the farmer and his family, which was formerly not unusual, has now long ceased.'

24 PRO, ASSI 45/35/2/61B: Yorkshire 1785, Joseph Eastwood.

25 PRO, ASSI 45/34/4/89: Cumberland 1783, William Gill; also see WYAS (Wakefield), QS 1/93/10: 1754, John Myers. Myers was a Barnsley weaver, who 'being charged by and upon the oath of Mary the wife of John Walker with imbezling ten pounds weight of linen yarn of the value of eleven shillings to him delivered to be manufactured confesses that he made up the same in woolsey for his own use.'

26 PRO, ASSI 45/24/3/40: Yorkshire 1751, Mary Holdforth.

27 WYAS (Wakefield), QS 1/74/1: 1735, Jane Milner.

28 PRO, ASSI 45/35/2/13-15: Yorkshire 1785, Ellin Bayston.

29 NYCRO, Z.371: 'The Weaver's Guide', linen designs of Ralph Watson of Aiskew, late eighteenth century.

30 Both suffer from deficiencies. Few household accounts survive for families below the level of the gentry and, when they do, they are usually inconsistent and incomplete. Poor Law accounts also suffer from inconsistency and incompleteness, while we cannot be sure that the provisioning policies pursued by overseers of the poor always followed the patterns of acquisition that characterised the independent labouring poor. Nevertheless, these two sources, used in combination with the criminal depositions, can offer a useful guide to plebeian practice.

31 Lorna Weatherill, *The Account Book of Richard Latham, 1724–1767* (London, 1990). The analysis that follows is based on this printed edition of the accounts, which contains inaccuracies; see the review by S. Harrop and P. Perrins in *Transactions of the Historic Society of Lancashire and Cheshire*, 140 (1991), 234–6 and Charles F. Foster, *Seven Households: Life in Cheshire and Lancashire, 1582–1774* (Northwich, 2002), 142. In using the accounts for this study, inconsistencies within the printed text have been corrected, but it has not been possible to check the whole of the printed text against the original manuscript. As most of the inaccuracies are minor, and arise especially in the jottings on the endpapers, it is unlikely that they substantially alter the findings drawn here from the printed edition. For an extended discussion of the family and their household economy, see Chapter 13 below. For another example of cloth making from home-spun yarn, see Cumbria RO (Carlisle), DX1182/4: Diary of Jonathan Williamson, tailor of Haltcliffe, Cumberland, 1797–8.

32 A. Wadsworth and J. de L. Mann, *The Cotton Trade and Industrial Lancashire, 1600–1780* (Manchester, 1965), 79; John James, *History of the Worsted Manufacture* (London, 1857), 324.

33 We know that the family used more linen than this between 1724 and 1741 because there are payments for dyeing approximately forty-two yards of plain linen – considerably more than was bought ready-woven – despite the fact that most plain linen worn as clothing would not have been dyed.

34 For a useful discussion of household textile requirements in the period, in a colonial context, see Adrienne D. Hood, 'The Material World of Cloth: Production and Use in Eighteenth-Century Rural Pennsylvania', *William and Mary Quarterly*, 53 (1996), 48.

35 David Davies, *The Case of the Labourers in Hus-*

bandry (London, 1795), 84–5, suggests that if an adult woman 'sits closely to her wheel the whole day, she can spin 2 lbs. of coarse flax for ordinary sheeting and toweling.' Other authorities suggested an adult woman could spin more than this; for example, John Claridge in his *General View of the Agriculture of the County of Dorset* (London, 1793), 38, gives a figure of four pounds a day.

36 Calculated on the assumption that one pound of flax or hemp would make about one yard of relatively coarse cloth; see Joseph Plymley, *General View of the Agriculture of Shropshire* (London, 1803), 177–8 for hemp, and Hood, 'The Material World of Cloth', 52–3 for wool.

37 Between 1724 and 1741 the family bought only 35½ lbs of wool. They do not appear to have owned sheep during this period, and only did so on a small scale thereafter. Sheep did not figure prominently among the livestock owned by other small farmers in the area. The amount of raw cotton purchased was even less at 15½ lbs.

38 See, for examples, Eden, *State of the Poor*, 2: 98, 107, 204–5.

39 For an extended discussion of the sacrifices made by the Latham family in their clothing during these early years of marriage, see Chapter 14 below.

40 Flax seed was bought only in 1745. There are payments for braking, swingling or dressing flax from 1745 to 1748, but they then cease. It is therefore questionable whether the family went on growing its own flax thereafter.

41 It is impossible to estimate the relative quantities of ready-woven and household-spun fabric used in the last twelve years of the account book from 1755 to 1767 when the children had left home. Purchases of ready-woven cloth declined, while those of flax increased. However, a large but unknowable proportion of this flax was probably intended for sale as yarn or cloth, rather than for the elderly couple's own use.

42 For the gentry, see Cumbria Record Office (Carlisle), D/Sen.: Bridget Hudleston and Humphrey Senhouse cash books, 1700–3 and 1709–20, and Senhouse rental and account book, 1762–82; Cumbria Record Office (Kendal), WD/TE: Browne of Troutbeck MSS, Boxes 8/1/4 and 8/2/1-3; Norman Penney (ed.), *The Household Account Book of Sarah Fell of Swarthmore Hall* (Cambridge, 1920); Hull University Archives, DDCA (2)48/1-19: Stapleton of Carlton MSS, Household account books of Sir Miles Stapleton, 1656-1705; WYAS (Bradford), SSt. 6/2/1/2: Spencer Stanhope MSS, Household account books of the Stanhope family of Horsforth, 1734–88; Cheshire Record Office, DAR/B/14 and 20: Arderne Collection, Household accounts and vouchers of Sarah Arderne, 1741–52; Amanda Vickery, 'Women of the Local Elite in Lancashire, 1750–c.1825' (PhD dissertation, University of London, 1991), 266–9; Foster, *Seven Households*, esp. 79 and 199–201. For contemporary comment on the narrowing of the quantity and range of home-produced cloth in plebeian households in the north, see Strickland, *East Riding of Yorkshire*, 283–4; Thomas West, *The Antiquities of Furness* (London, 1774), xvii; William Hutchinson, *The History and Antiquities of Cumberland*, 2 vols (Carlisle, 1794), 1: 661.

43 We should bear in mind, however, that sporadic attempts were made by some Poor Law authorities, especially those with workhouses, to force the dependent poor into sartorial self-sufficiency. Eden's *State of the Poor* cites examples of such policies from workhouses across the country approvingly.

44 WYAS (Leeds), RDP18/108-114: Carleton-in-Craven, Overseers' accounts 1713–1841. WYAS (Kirklees): Mirfield, Township accounts, 1717–1795. WYAS (Leeds), RDP17/84: Calverley, Officers' accounts, 1692–1822. Also see Cumbria RO (Kendal), WPR 83/1: Hawkshead, Overseers' Accounts, Hawkshead Quarter, 1691–1750 and WPR 83/2: Overseers' miscellaneous vouchers, 1749–1825; Cumbria RO (Carlisle), PC/44/2/53: Dalton, workhouse account book, 1746-1775.

45 For the evidence of decline, see J. H. Clapham, *An Economic History of Modern Britain: The Early Railway Age, 1820–1850* (Cambridge, 1930), 159–62.

46 Eden, *State of the Poor*, 1: 555 and 2: 84.

47 Of course raw materials did not necessarily have to be bought. Where small plots of land were available they could be grown. For growing raw materials for yarn, see Weatherill, *Account Book of Richard Latham*, xxvi.

48 For the decline in household-spun woollens, see the chronological series of case studies in Foster, *Seven Households*.

49 Barbara Pidcock, 'The Spinners and Weavers of Swarthmore Hall, Ulverston, in the Late 17th Century', *Transactions of the Cumberland and Westmorland Antiquarian and Archeological Society*, 95 (1995), 153–67; Foster, *Seven Households*, chapter 4.

50 Margaret Spufford, *The Great Reclothing of Rural England: Petty Chapmen and their Wares in the Seventeenth Century* (London, 1984).

51 WYAS (Bradford), 33D80/6/7: Shop book of Stephen Hudson of Fewston, 1751–9. Prices are based on an analysis of the shop accounts for 1759. For Hudson, see Chapter 7.

52 PRO, ASSI 45/35/2/57-8: Cumberland 1785, John Donichery; ASSI 45/39/2/4B: Westmorland 1798, Ellinor Berry; ASSI 45/36/1/280: Yorkshire 1787, Henry Wood.

53 PRO, ASSI 45/20/2/26: Yorkshire 1736, Mary Clay.

54 See, for example, Neil McKendrick, 'The Commercialisation of Fashion', in Neil McKendrick, John Brewer and J. H. Plumb, *The Birth of a Consumer Society* (London, 1982), 86.

55 See, for example, Martha Olney, 'Demand for Consumer Durable Goods in 20th-Century America', *Explorations in Economic History*, 27 (1990), 322–49.

56 PRO, ASSI 45/36/2/178-81: Newcastle 1788, William Towns. Clothing clubs were not, of course, a development that was restricted either to the north of England or to the largest towns; see for Birmingham, William Hutton, *An History of Birmingham* (Birmingham, 1783), 138, and for Kent, Centre for Kentish Studies, Maidstone, U 1823/35/A3: daybook of a Maidstone draper, 1768–1773, ff. 103–4. For an overview, see Peter Clark, *British Clubs and Societies: The Origins of an Associational World* (Oxford, 2000), esp. 129.

57 Mui and Mui, *Shops and Shopkeeping*, 98.

58 Stuart Henry, *The Hidden Economy: The Context and Control of Borderline Crime* (Oxford, 1978).

59 PRO, ASSI 45/34/3/27-29: Cumberland 1782, John Byers.

60 PRO, ASSI 45/34/1/15-7: Cumberland 1780, Ann Brown.

61 PRO, ASSI 45/37/2/208-9: Yorkshire 1791, Thomas Tunstall.

62 See, for example, Northumberland Collections Service, 808/1: Account books and papers of Messrs. Dodds and Co., drapers of Alnwick, daybook of sales, 1790–1.

63 Like an anonymous retailer in the north Tyne valley in Northumberland whose account book of sales to fairly humble customers survives for the 1770s; Northumberland Collections Service, 1619/1: account book of a tailor in North Tynedale, 1772–5.

64 Cox, *Complete Tradesman*, 57–8.

65 Arthur Young, *General View of the Agriculture of the County of Suffolk* (London, 1794), 49–50; Plymley, *Agriculture of Shropshire*, 123; Arthur Young, *General View of the Agriculture of the County of Lincolnshire* (London, 1813), 455. Also see J. Pilkington, *A View of the Present State of Derbyshire*, 2 vols (Derby, 1789), 2: 52.

66 W. Pitt, *General View of the Agriculture of the County of Stafford* (London, 1794), 162–3.

67 F. G. Emmison, 'The Relief of the Poor at Eaton Socon, 1706–1834', *Publications of the Bedfordshire Historical Record Society*, 15 (1933), 17; Geoffrey C. Edmonds, 'Accounts of Eighteenth-Century Overseers of the Poor of Chalfont St Peter', *Records of Buckinghamshire*, 18 (1966–70), 11–12; Essex RO, D/P 16/12/2: Thaxted overseers' accounts, 1696–1716. These do not appear to have been cases of newly opened parish workhouses embarking on schemes to cut the poor rates by becoming self-sufficient. For Holne, see Devon RO, 1249A/PO2-4: Overseers' payments for Holne, 1711–27, 1746–1799 (transcribed by Brian Brassett at http://genuki.cs.ncl.ac.uk/DEV/Holne/Overseers/index.html, examined May 2005).

68 Huntington Library, HM 31192: William Smedley's executors, account book of farm receipts and disbursments, Derbyshire 1741–52.

69 Suffolk RO (Ipswich), P616:8566: Account book of John Spore, shoemaker, Chediston, Suffolk, 1768–84. For the industry, see Nesta Evans, *The East-Anglian Linen Industry: Rural Industry and Local Economy, 1500–1850* (Aldershot, 1985).

70 Suffolk RO (Bury St Edmunds), FL 536/1/47: Brandon Parish, Brandon Fire, 'Estimation of the Goods and Chattles, Wearing Apparel, etc. destroyed and damaged by fire at Brandon in Suffolk on Thursday May the 14th 1789'.

71 R. W. Blencowe (ed.), 'Extracts from the journal and account book of Timothy Burrell ... from 1683 to 1714', *Sussex Archeological Collections*, 3 (1850), 122, 128; Paul Brassley, Anthony Lambert and Philip Saunders (eds), *Accounts of the Reverend John Crakanthorp of Fowlmere, 1682–1710* (Cambridge, 1988), 168; British Library, Additional MSS 45204, 45208, 45210: Household accounts kept by Ann Brockman, of Beachborough, Kent, 1701–24.

72 Writing in the late eighteenth century, the Chichester, Sussex Baptist minister James Spershott recalled that early in the century 'spinning of

73 Eden, *State of the Poor*, 3: 704, 847.
74 The exception is Stanhope in Weardale, county Durham. 'The women spin jersey and can earn 3d. or 4d. a day; many of them manufacture their own woollen and linen apparel.' Eden, *State of the Poor*, 2: 169.
75 For the boom in topographical writing on the Lake District, see Peter Bicknell, *The Picturesque Scenery of the Lake District* (Winchester, 1990).
76 West, *Antiquities of Furness*, xvii; Hutchinson, *History and Antiquities*, 1: 661; John Housman, *A Topographical Description of Cumberland, Westmorland, Lancashire and a part of the West Riding of Yorkshire* (Carlisle, 1800), 58.
77 See, for progress, Hutchinson, *History and Antiquities*, 1: 659–664 and, for simplicity, Housman, *Topographical Description*, 104–5. For the sentimentalisation of the Cumbrian 'statesman', see J. D. Marshall, *Old Lakeland: Some Cumbrian Social History* (Newton Abbot, 1971), chapter 2.
78 *The Gentleman's Magazine* (1766), 582.
79 See T. C. Smout, *A History of the Scottish People* (London, 1969), 305; H. G. Graham, *The Social Life of Scotland in the Eighteenth Century* (London, 1969), 180–1, 214–15; M. Swain, 'The Linen Supply of a Scottish Household, 1777–1810: Extracts from the Accounts of Thomas Hog of Newliston', *Textile History*, 13 (1982), 77–89.
80 K. Morgan (ed.), *An American Quaker in the British Isles: The Travel Journals of Jabez Maud Fisher, 1775–1779* (Oxford, 1992), 76.
81 For Eden on Scottish clothing, see *State of the Poor*, 1: 558–9.

9 Clothing Provincial England: Garments

1 Sir Frederick Eden, *The State of the Poor*, 3 vols (London, 1797), 1: 554–5.
2 For pre- and post-eighteenth-century examples, see Anon., *Per una Storia della Moda Pronta* (Florence, 1990); Pamela Sharp, '"Cheapness and Economy": Manufacturing and Retailing Ready-Made Clothing in London and Essex, 1830–50', *Textile History*, 26 (1995), 203–13; Stanley Chapman, 'The Innovating Entrepreneurs in the British Ready-Made Clothing Industry', *Textile History*, 24 (1993), 5–25.
3 Neil McKendrick, 'The Commercialisation of Fashion', in Neil McKendrick, John Brewer and J. H. Plumb, *The Birth of a Consumer Society* (London, 1982), 53.
4 John Styles, 'Manufacture, Consumption and Design in Eighteenth-Century England', in John Brewer and Roy Porter (eds), *Consumption and the World of Goods* (London, 1993), 529–35, and, more broadly, John Styles, 'Dress in History: Reflections on a Contested Terrain', *Fashion Theory*, 2 (1998), 383–90.
5 Beverly Lemire, 'Consumerism in Preindustrial and Early Industrial England: The Trade in Secondhand Clothes', *Journal of British Studies*, 27 (1988), 12; 'Peddling Fashion: Salesmen, Pawnbrokers, Taylors, Thieves and the Second-Hand Clothes Trade in England, c.1700–1800', *Textile History*, 22 (1991), 71. Also see her *Dress, Culture and Commerce: The English Clothing Trade before the Factory, 1660–1800* (London, 1997), esp. chapters 3 and 4.
6 Borthwick Institute for Archives, University of York: Exchequer and Prerogative Courts of York, wills, 1689–1800 and Dean and Chapter of York, wills, 1660–1800. Shoemakers and cordwainers are treated here together, because the inventories reveal few marked differences between the two.
7 The mean total value of tailors' inventories before 1740 was £33 (n = 29), after 1740 it was £47 (n = 37).
8 The mean total value of shoemakers' inventories before 1740 was £42 (n = 27), after 1740 it was £59 (n = 34).
9 Chester shoemakers held large stocks of finished boots and shoes in the late sixteenth century. See D. M. Woodward, 'The Chester Leather Industry, 1558–1625', *Transactions of the Historic Society of Lancashire and Cheshire*, 119 (1967), 75–6.
10 Margaret Spufford, *The Great Reclothing of Rural England* (London, 1984), 123–4 and 210–11. I follow Carole Shammas here in using the word garment to designate both what Spufford terms 'heavy-weight garments' – gowns, suits, breeches, jackets, waistcoats, coats – and lighter garments like shifts, petticoats and shirts, but to exclude shoes, stockings, hats, gloves, shawls, ribbons and the like, which I refer to as accessories. See Shammas, *The Pre-Industrial Consumer in England and America* (Oxford, 1990), 235.
11 In 1749 two Leeds women were charged with receiving goods stolen from a chapman, which

were described in the deposition as '4 doz. worsted and cotton stockings, 1 worsted cap, 4 doz. chequered linen handkerchiefs, 9 doz. white Scotch Kentish handkerchiefs and 3 lbs. Scotch white sewing thread'. One of the women confessed that 'after they had bought the said goods... they carried 'em upstairs into a chamber where... Hannah Smith cut off some handkerchiefs from the webb or piece'. PRO, ASSI 45/24/1/78-80: Yorkshire 1749, Margaret Russel.

12   See, for example, Beverly Lemire's discussion of ready-made gowns in her 'Developing Consumerism and the Ready-made Clothing Trade in Britain, 1750–1800', *Textile History*, 15 (1984), esp. 36–8. I would not dispute that selling cloth in pre-determined, garment-sized or even garment-shaped units represented an important innovation.

13   Lorna Weatherill, ed., *The Account Book of Richard Latham, 1724–1767* (London, 1990); Northumberland Collections Service, 1619/1: account book of a tailor in North Tynedale, 1772–5. In the case of the Northumberland tailor-shopkeeper it is not clear precisely who undertook the cutting and sewing.

14   Madeleine Ginsburg, 'The Tailoring and Dressmaking Trades, 1700–1850', *Costume*, 6 (1972), 64; Janet Arnold, 'The Dressmakers Craft', *Strata of Society*, Proceedings of the Seventh Annual Conference of the Costume Society (London, 1974), 30–3.

15   Bernard Johnson, *The Acts and Ordinances of the Company of Merchant Tailors in the City of York* (York, 1949), 84–9. Also see Michael Walker, 'The Extent of the Guild Control of Trades in England, c.1660–1820' (PhD dissertation, University of Cambridge, 1985), 235–9; Mary Prior, 'Women and the Urban Economy: Oxford, 1500–1800', in Mary Prior (ed.), *Women in English Society, 1500–1800* (London, 1985), 110–113; Beverly Lemire, *Dress, Cutlure and Commerce: The English Clothing Trade before the Factory, 1660–1800* (London, 1997), chapter 2.

16   For Wigglesworth, see WYAS (Bradford), 33D80/6/7: Sales ledger of Stephen Hudson of Thruscross, shopkeeper, 1751–1759; for Crosthwaite, see PRO, ASSI 45/26/1/7-32: Cumberland 1766, Margaret Davison.

17   Loraine Ashcroft, *Vital Statistics. The Westmorland 'Census' of 1787* (Kendal, 1992). There were more tailors than mantuamakers (by a ratio of nearly four to one), but evidently they were not more widely distributed.

18   For a critical discussion of these issues, see Amanda Vickery, 'Golden Age to Separate Spheres? A Review of the Categories and Chronology of English Women's History', *The Historical Journal*, 36 (1993), especially 401–5.

19   PRO, ASSI 45/34/2/15-16: Cumberland 1781, David Dixon. For women and shirt making, see Amanda Vickery, 'His and Hers: Gender: Consumption and Household Accounting in Eighteenth-Century England', *Past and Present*, Supplement 1 (2006), 12–38.

20   NYCRO, QSB/1753:, George Fenkell.

21   PRO, ASSI 45/39/3/101: Newcastle 1798, Joseph Irving; ASSI 45/37/3/162-172: Northumberland 1792, John Penfold.

22   WYAS (Leeds), RDP 18/114: Carleton-in-Craven, Overseers' accounts 1751–1820; /109: Various accounts, bills, vouchers, etc., 1739–1841. WYAS (Kirklees): Mirfield, Township accounts, 1717–1795. WYAS (Leeds), RDP 17/84: Calverley, Officers' accounts, 1692–1822.

23   Anon., *The Reports of the Society for Bettering the Condition and Increasing the Comforts of the Poor*, 4 vols (London, 1798–1800), 2: 198–9.

24   PRO, ASSI 45/37/3/224-240: Northumberland 1792, William Winter.

25   PRO, ASSI 45/37/3/224-240: Northumberland 1792, William Winter.

26   Ashcroft, *Vital Statistics*.

27   PRO, ASSI 45/37/1/161-170: Yorkshire 1790, Luke Normington.

28   Aileen Ribeiro, *Dress in Eighteenth-Century Europe, 1715 to 1789* (London, 1984), 54.

29   WYAS (Wakefield), QS 1/125/3: 1786, Mary Boardell.

30   PRO, ASSI 45/25/4/177-8: Yorkshire 1756, William Wilson.

31   PRO, ASSI 45/38/1/18-23A: Yorkshire 1793, Jane Boys.

32   PRO, ASSI 45/38/1/183-193: Northumberland 1793, Mark Thornton.

33   PRO, ASSI 45/38/3/8-11: Yorkshire 1795, William Bramley.

34   By Act of Parliament 30 Geo. II, c. 24 (1757) and subsequent legislation.

35   WYAS (Wakefield), QS 1/30/1: 1691, William Holden.

36   Miles Lambert, '"Cast-off Wearing Apparel": The Consumption and Distribution of Second-hand Clothing in Northern England during the Long Eighteenth Century', *Textile History*, 35 (2004), 1–26.

37 PRO, ASSI 45/37/3/162-172: Northumberland 1792, John Penfold.
38 York City Archives, Accession 38: Pledge book of George Fettes, pawnbroker, York, 1777–8. Also see Alison Backhouse, *The Worm-Eaten Waistcoat* (York, 2003).
39 Margot Finn, 'Debt and Credit in Bath's Court of Requests, 1829–39', *Urban History*, 21 (1994), 230 makes a similar observation for the second quarter of the nineteenth century.
40 York City Archives, Accession 38: Pledge book of George Fettes, pawnbroker, York, 1777–8. The average pledge values are based on gowns pawned as single items during four weeks in January, April, July and October 1778.
41 For a resumé of the evidence for second-hand dealers in directories, see Beverly Lemire, 'Consumerism in Preindustrial and Early Industrial England: the Trade in Secondhand Clothes', *Journal of British Studies*, 27 (1988), 12 and 'Peddling Fashion: Salesmen, Pawnbrokers, Taylors, Thieves and the Second-Hand Clothes Trade in England, c. 1700–1800', *Textile History*, 22 (1991), 71.
42 Lambert, '"Cast-off Wearing Apparel"', 3–8.
43 For studies of the clothing trades in one southern county, see Anne Buck, 'Buying Clothes in Bedfordshire: Customers and Tradesmen, 1700–1800', *Textile History*, 22 (1991), 211–38 and 'Mantua-makers and Milliners: Women Making and Selling Clothes in Eighteenth Century Bedfordshire', *Bedfordshire Historical Miscellany: Essays in Honour of Patricia Bell* (Bedford, 1993), 142–55.
44 Spufford, *Great Reclothing*, 123–4 and 210–30.
45 Ursula Priestley and Alayne Fenner, *Shops and Shopkeepers in Norwich, 1660–1730* (Norwich, 1985), 24.
46 Lemire, *Dress, Culture and Commerce*, 59; Jasmine S. Howse, *Index the Probate Records of the Court of the Archdeacon of Berkshire, 2: 1653–1710* (London, 1975).
47 Lemire, 'Consumerism in Preindustrial and Early Industrial England', 12.
48 Surrey History Centre, Mortlake Parish Records, 2397/6/31: Workhouse accounts 1768–87.
49 Anon., *Instructions for Cutting out Apparel for the Poor; Principally intended for the Assistance of the Patronesses of Sunday Schools, and other Charitable Institutions, But useful in all Families* (London, 1789), 56–9.
50 Essex RO, D/P 152/12/14: Theydon Garnon, overseers' bills and vouchers, 1785–1848.
51 British Museum, Banks Collection, D.2-4140 and D.2-4152, handbills for James Mills and Co., 1789.
52 OBP, April 1784, Mary Nash (t17830430-14).
53 Except where the Poor Law authorities, usually those with workhouses, adopted a deliberate policy of enforcing sartorial self-sufficiency on the dependent poor.

10   Clothing the Metropolis

1 Many aspects of the supply of clothing in eighteenth-century London have been explored by historians, starting with Dorothy George's *London Life in the Eighteenth Century* (London, 1925). See, in particular, Madeleine Ginsburg, 'The Tailoring and Dressmaking Trades 1700–1850', *Costume*, 6 (1972), 64–9; Madeleine Ginsburg, 'Rags to Riches: The Second-hand Clothes Trade 1700–1978', *Costume*, 14 (1980), 121–35; David Corner, 'The Tyranny of Fashion: The Case of the Felt-Hatting Trade in the Late Seventeenth and Eighteenth Centuries', *Textile History*, 22 (1991), 153–78; Leonard Schwarz, *London in the Age of Industrialisation: Entrepreneurs, Labour Force and Living Conditions, 1700–1850* (Cambridge, 1992); Beverly Lemire, *Dress, Culture and Commerce: The English Clothing Trade before the Factory, 1660–1800* (London, 1997); Giorgio Riello, *A Foot in the Past: Consumers, Producers and Footwear in the Long Eighteenth Century* (Oxford, 2006).
2 For London's population and wealth at the start of the eighteenth century, see Roger Finlay and Beatrice Shearer, 'Population Growth and Suburban Expansion', in A. L. Beier and Roger Finlay (eds), *London, 1500–1700: The Making of the Metropolis* (London, 1986), 37–59; also J. A. Chartres, 'Food Consumption and Internal Trade', Beier and Finlay, *London, 1500–1700*, 168–96.
3 Claire Walsh, 'Shops, Shopping and the Art of Decision Making in Eighteenth-Century England', in John Styles and Amanda Vickery (eds), *Gender, Taste and Material Culture in Britain and North America, 1700–1830* (London and New Haven, 2006), 154.
4 OBP, April 1790, George Wakeman (t17900424-8).
5 See John Styles, 'The Goldsmiths and the London Luxury Trades, 1550 to 1750', in David Mitchell (ed.), *Goldsmiths, Silversmiths and Bankers: Innovation and the Transfer of Skill, 1550–1750* (Gloucester, 1995), 112–20; Riello, *A Foot in the Past*, chapter 6.

6 Riello, *Foot in the Past*, 96.
7 Anon., *Low-Life: Or One Half of the World Knows not how the Other Half Live* (London, 1764), 6.
8 OBP, February 1808, Martha Smith (t18080217-90).
9 OBP, February 1785, Ann Mott (t17850223-100).
10 OBP, October 1785, James Worthy (t17851019-28); LMA, OB/SR 239: Middlesex Gaol Delivery Roll, October 1785, James Worthy.
11 For examples, see OBP, February 1730, John Rich (t17300228-34) and OBP, September 1771, James May (t17710911-37).
12 Chandlers were among the dozen most numerous male occupations among Westminster householders in both 1749 and 1784, rarer than tailors or shoemakers, but much more numerous than drapers; Charles Harvey, Edmund M. Green and Penelope J. Corfield, 'Continuity, Change, and Specialization within Metropolitan London: The Economy of Westminster, 1750–1820', *Economic History Review*, new series, 52 (1999), 483.
13 Mary Thale (ed.), *The Autobiography of Francis Place (1771–1854)* (Cambridge, 1972), 106–7. See Peter Clark, *British Clubs and Societies: The Origins of an Associational World* (Oxford, 2000), esp. 129.
14 OBP, February 1787, James Johnson (t17870221-89); OBP, January 1767, William Taylor (t17670115-2); OBP, January 1795, Elizabeth Salvel (t17950114-17); OBP, January 1782, John Morgan (t17820109-23); OBP, December 1784, William Astill (t17841208-10); OBP, December 1782, Mary White (t17821204-48).
15 OBP, November 1796, Samuel Smith (t17961130-25).
16 Riello, *Foot in the Past*, 102.
17 See, for example, *Exeter Mercury*, 25 May 1781, advertisement for Morgan's printed linen and cotton warehouse, and 2 July 1789, advertisement for Tribe's cheap clothing warehouse. For a general discussion of this development, see Nancy Cox, *The Complete Tradesman: A Study of Retailing, 1550–1820* (Aldershot, 2000), 102–7.
18 For a thorough treatment of this development in London, see N. V. Sleigh-Johnson, 'The Merchant Taylor's Company of London, 1580–1645, with Special Reference to Government and Politics' (PhD Dissertation, University of London, 1989), 366–7, 370–1. Beverley Lemire addresses some of these developments in *Dress, Culture and Commerce*, especially chapters 1 and 2.
19 Anon., *The Trade of England Revived* (London, 1681), 36; Peter Earle, *The Making of the English Middle Class* (London, 1989), 21–2, 286–8.
20 For clothing the Civil War armies see Peter Edwards, *Dealing Death: The Arms Trade and the British Civil Wars, 1638–52* (Stroud, 2000), chapter 6; for plantation clothing see Richard Ligon, *A True and Exact History of the Island of Barbadoes* (London, 1673), 109–10; for style see Ginsburg, 'Tailoring and Dressmaking Trades', 67.
21 For a London salesmen in the provinces, see PRO, PROB 32/67/129: Probate Inventory of Samuel Dalling of Southwark, salesman, 1699; for stock from London, see *Norwich Mercury*, 13 May 1758, advertisement for C. Kett; also Lemire, *Dress, Culture and Commerce*, chapter 2.
22 OBP, June 1783, Sarah Harrison (t17830604-73).
23 R. Campbell, *The London Tradesman* (London, 1747), 202.
24 For London sale shop stocks, see the examples in Lemire, *Dress, Culture and Commerce*, 63–4, and for the development of the trade in the late eighteenth century, Beverly Lemire, *Fashion's Favourite: The Cotton Trade and the Consumer in Britain, 1660–1800* (Oxford, 1991), chapter 5. For examples of street sellers offering clothes for sale, see OBP, February 1730, Thomas Adderley (t17300228-54); OBP, September 1791, Ann Burton (t17910914-53).
25 OBP, June 1785, Ann Icorn (t17850629-99); see also OBP, February 1755, Elizabeth Williams (t17550226-23).
26 OBP, January 1753, Sarah Steel (t17530111-5).
27 Anon., 'The Humours of Rag Fair, or the Countryman's Description of their several Trades and Callings' (n.d.), Harding Collection B3 (75), Bodleian Library Oxford.
28 London Guildhall Library, MS 2642/1: St Botolph Aldgate Vestry Minutes, 1730. I would like to thank Janice Turner for supplying this information.
29 OBP, February 1787, James Johnson (t17870221-89).
30 Gerald I. Mungeam, 'Contracts for the Supply of Equipment to the "New Model" Army in 1645', *Journal of the Arms and Armour Society*, 6 (1968–70), 109. The lack of precision in the specifications for garment sizes for the New Model Army may simply indicate that it had already adopted the practice that was to be followed by eighteenth-century army regiments of having the clothing supplied ready-made by the contractors taken apart and re-made by the tailors serving with the regiment in order to ensure a correct fit. See

H. Strachan, *British Military Uniforms, 1766–1796* (Lon-don, 1975), 27; also J. R. Western, *The English Militia in the Eighteenth Century* (London, 1965), 354. For shoes, see D. M. Woodward, 'The Chester Leather Industry, 1558–1625', *Transactions of the Historic Society of Lancashire and Cheshire*, 119 (1967), 76.

31 PRO, E140/85/2: Exchequer Masters Exhibits, Smith v. Goater, 1745, Books A and B.

32 Anon., *Instructions for Cutting out Apparel for the Poor; Principally intended for the Assistance of the Patronesses of Sunday Schools, and other Charitable Institutions, But useful in all Families* (London, 1789), 56, 58 and 59.

33 PRO, E140/85/2: Exchequer Masters Exhibits, Smith v. Goater, 1745, Books A and B.

34 I would like to thank Edmund Green for providing these figures derived from Westminster voting records. For details, see Harvey, et al., 'Continuity, Change, and Specialization'. The ratio of tailors to salesmen for 1749 was 120 : 1, and for 1818, 13 : 1.

35 Peter Earle, in his occupational analysis of female witnesses in the church courts, found large numbers of manutamakers already present in London between 1695 and 1725; Peter Earle, 'The Female Labour Market in London in the Late Seventeenth and Early Eighteenth Centuries', *Economic History Review*, new series, 42 (1989), 339–40. Also see Nicola Phillips, *Women in Business, 1700–1850* (Woodbridge, 2006), 177–8.

36 OBP, April 1755, Mary Kettle (t17550409-20).

37 OBP, February 1785, Christopher Webb (t17850223-112).

38 For the various female needle trades, see Earle, 'The Female Labour Market', 340–1.

39 OBP, June 1785, Ann Icorn (t17850629-99).

11 The View from Above

1 See, for a recent example, Jennie Batchelor, *Dress, Distress and Desire: Clothing and the Female Body in Eighteenth-Century Literature* (London, 2005), 2–18, which usefully outlines debates among literary scholars.

For a discussion of some of the problems associated with reading clothes in this way, see Colin Campbell, 'The Meaning of Objects and the Meaning of Actions: A Critical Note on the Sociology of Consumption and Theories of Clothing', *Journal of Material Culture*, 1 (1996), 93–105.

2 John Eglin, *The Imaginary Autocrat: Beau Nash and the Invention of Bath* (London, 2005), 64, 75.

3 William Darrell, *A Gentleman Instructed in the Conduct of a Virtuous and Happy Life* (London, 1704), 37.

4 Lawrence Klein, 'Politeness and the Interpretation of the British Eighteenth Century', *The Historical Journal*, 45 (2002), 869–98.

5 Edward Chamberlayne, *Angliae Notitia: Or the Present State of England* (London, 1704), 319. The book was first published in 1669.

6 Bernard Mandeville, *The Fable of the Bees; Or, Private Vices Publick Benefits* (London, 1714), 105.

7 Daniel Defoe, *Everybody's Business, is Nobody's Business* (London, 1725), 4.

8 *The Annual Register, or a View of the History, Politicks, and Literature, of the Year 1761* (London, 1762), 201.

9 *The European Magazine and London Review*, 5 (1784), 245.

10 Mrs [Sarah] Trimmer, *The Two Farmers, an Exemplary Tale* (London, 1787), 111.

11 For example, Thomas Andrews, *An Enquiry into the Causes of the Encrease and Miseries of the Poor of England* (London, 1738), 24: 'It would make greatly for the Benefit of our *Meaner People*, and for the Honour and Distinction of *Persons of Quality*, and likewise be no small Incitement to *Virtue and Industry*, if *Laws* were made and duly executed, to regulate the *Equipages, Servants, Liveries, Entertainments, Apparel*, etc. of all People, according to their *Quality, Office,* or *apparent Substance*.'

12 C. Bruyn Andrews (ed.), *The Torrington Diaries* 4 vols (London, 1934–8), 1: 6. The 'Strand misses' were the well-dressed prostitutes who paraded the Strand in London.

13 Huntington Library, MO 3450, Elizabeth Robinson Montagu Collection: Elizabeth Montagu to Sarah Scott, 16 June 1778.

14 For my understanding of this issue I am indebted to the work of Jonathan White. See Jonathan White, '"The Slow Sure Poyson": Representing Gin and Its Drinkers in Eighteenth-Century England, 1736–1751', *Journal of British Studies*, 42 (2003), 35–64; 'The Laboring-Class Domestic Sphere in Eighteenth-Century British Social Thought', in John Styles and Amanda Vickery (eds), *Gender, Taste and Material Culture in Britain and North America, 1700–1830* (London, 2006), 247–63; 'Luxury and Labour: Ideas of Labouring-Class Consumption in Eighteenth-Century England' (PhD dissertation, University of Warwick,

2001). The conclusions drawn here remain my own. Also see E. S. Furniss, *The Position of the Laborer in a System of Nationalism: A Study in the Labor Theories of the Later English Mercantilists* (New York, 1965); A. W. Coats, 'Changing Attitudes to Labour in the Mid-Eighteenth Century', *Economic History Review*, new series, 11 (1958), 35–51; John Hatcher, 'Labour, Leisure and Economic Thought before the Nineteenth Century', *Past and Present*, 160 (1998), 64–115, and, for the way debates around enclosure and the Poor Law focused attention on the cottage, Sarah Lloyd, 'Cottage Conversations: Poverty and Manly Independence in Eighteenth-Century England', *Past and Present*, 184 (2004), 69–108.

15 A Country Farmer, *Cursory Remarks on Inclosures*, (London, 1786), 21–2. These criticisms are remarkably similar to those offered by Mrs Montagu in her letter to her sister eight years earlier (note 13 above). They are characteristic of the genre.

16 See, for example, William Green, *Plans of Economy; Or A Guide to Riches and Independence* (London, 1800), 9; *The Gentleman's Magazine* (1801), 587–9.

17 Arthur Young, *The Farmer's Letters to the People of England* (London, 1768), 282. A rare example at this date of clothing being included among the inappropriate luxuries consumed by working people is found in Anon., *Considerations on Taxes: As they are Supposed to Affect the Price of Labour and our Manufactures* (London, 1765), 53, which includes printed linens in a long list of the 'luxuries the poor manufacturers consume, such as brandy, gin, tea, sugar, tobacco, foreign fruit, strong beer, printed linens, snuff, etc'. However, it should be remembered that printed fabrics had been subject to an excise duty since 1712, which for many eighteenth-century commentators necessarily defined them as a luxury.

18 Samuel Johnson, *A Journey to the Western Islands of Scotland* (London, 1775), 44–5.

19 Andrew Hooke, *An Essay on the National Debt, and National Capital* (London, 1750), 33.

20 Mrs Godfrey Clark (ed.), *Gleanings from an Old Portfolio, Containing some Correspondence between Lady Louisa Stuart and her Sister Caroline, Countess of Portarlington, and other Friends and Relations*, 3 vols (Edinburgh, 1895–8), 1: 19.

21 Tobias Smollett, *Launcelot Greaves*, 2 vols (London, 1762), 1: 57.

22 'Survey of the Parish of Wilmslow', by Samuel Finney of Fulshaw, Esq., in T. Worthington Barlow (ed.), *The Cheshire and Lancashire Historical Collector*, 2 (May, 1853), 5–6.

23 John Smith, *The Necessity, Advantages, and Amiableness of Beneficence. A Sermon Preached in the Parish Church of Bury, In the County of Lancaster, on Sunday, September 29, 1765* (Manchester, 1766), 12. See Jan Albers, 'Seeds of Contention: Society, Politics and the Church of England in Lancashire, 1689–1790' (PhD dissertation, Yale University, 1988), chapter 5.

24 F. M. Cowe (ed.), *Wimbledon Vestry Minutes, 1736, 1743–1788* (Guildford, 1964), 29.

25 Young, *Farmer's Letters*, 279–80. Also John Hustler, *The Occasion of the Dearness of Provisions, and the Distress of the Poor* (London, 1767), 27–8.

26 Andrews, *Enquiry into the Causes of the Encrease and Miseries of the Poor*, 9.

27 Hatcher, 'Labour, Leisure and Economic Thought', 104–11.

28 Thomas Bernard, 'Extract from an account of the late improvements in the house of industry, at Dublin', *The Reports of the Society for Bettering the Condition and Increasing the Comforts of the Poor*, 4 vols (London, 1798–1800), 2: 104–5.

29 For sensibility and simplicity, see Batchelor, *Dress, Distress and Desire*, especially chapter 4. For the earlier appeal of plebeian and rural modes among the fashionable, see Anne Buck, *Dress in Eighteenth-Century England* (London, 1979), especially 48–59 and 138–9.

30 Madame du Boccage, *Letters Concerning England, Holland and Italy*, 2 vols (London, 1770), 1: 7–8, letter dated 8 April 1750. For an earlier foreigner's comment in 1727 on the wearing of straw hats by ladies of the highest rank, see Madame van Muyden, *A Foreign View of England in the Reigns of George I and George II: The Letters of Monsieur César de Saussure to his Family* (London, 1902), 204.

31 Jean Bernard Le Blanc, *Letters on the English and French Nations*, 2 vols (London, 1747), 1: 18 and 1: 20.

32 *The Gentleman's Magazine*, 9 (1739), 28.

33 David Roberts, *Lord Chesterfield: Letters* (Oxford, 1992), 128.

34 Andrew Oliver (ed.), *The Journal of Samuel Curwen Loyalist*, 2 vols (Cambridge, Mass., 1972), 2: 930.

35 See Robert W. Jones, *Gender and the Formation of Taste in Eighteenth-Century Britain* (Cambridge, 1998).

12 The View from Below

1. Peter Linebaugh, *The London Hanged: Crime and Civil Society in the Eighteenth Century* (London, 1991), 257. The importance of clothes as markers of social distinction extended, of course, beyond the materials they were made from, to how they were worn; see, for example, Penelope J. Corfield, 'Dress for Deference and Dissent: Hats and the Decline of Hat Honour', *Costume*, 23 (1989), 64–79.
2. Joyce Ellis, 'Urban Conflict and Popular Violence: The Guildhall Riots of 1740 in Newcastle upon Tyne', *International Review of Social History*, 25 (1980), 344.
3. [Hannah More] *The Shepherd of Salisbury Plain*, 2 vols (London, 1795), 1: 15.
4. OBP, June 1751, Richard Holland and Daniel Thoroughgood (t17510703-42).
5. OBP, October 1750, George Anderson (t17501017-19).
6. Georg Simmel, 'The Philosophy of Fashion', in David Frisby and Mike Featherstone (eds), *Simmel on Culture* (London, 1997), 187–205.
7. Robert Shoemaker, 'The Street Robber and the Gentleman Highwayman: Changing Representations and Perceptions of Robbery in London, 1690–1800', *Cultural and Social History*, 3 (2006), 381–405.
8. OBP, Ordinary of Newgate's Account, October 1750, James Maclean (oa17501003); *Public Advertiser*, 29 February and 1 March, 1764, quoted in Shoemaker, 'The Street Robber and the Gentleman Highwayman', 399.
9. OBP, October 1726, Anthony Drury (t17261012-38); James Guthrie, *The Ordinary of Newgate, his Account of the Behaviour, Confession, and Dying Words, of the Malefactors, who were executed at Tyburn, on Wednesday the 16th of September 1741* (London, 1741), 10. By no means all mounted highwaymen dressed in this way, however. A highwayman on horseback who assaulted the Stratford coach between Whitechapel and Bow in 1751 was described as 'shabbily dressed'; OBP, January 1752, William Williams (t17520116-10).
10. OBP, February 1716, Elizabeth Wild (t17160222-41).
11. See Chapter 3.
12. Mary Thale (ed.), *The Autobiography of Francis Place (1771–1854)* (Cambridge, 1972), 63. The highwayman John Rann, executed in 1774, famously affected a similar style. He was known as 'Sixteen-String Jack' because he was accustomed to wearing eight silver-tipped laces in his breeches at each knee; see Shoemaker, 'The Street Robber and the Gentleman Highwayman', 401–2. At the scaffold, the ways in which condemned men dressed ranged from those who defiantly wore white suits like bridegrooms to those who wore mourning and were considered by their social superiors to have dressed decently; see Andrea McKenzie, 'God's Tribunal: Guilt, Innocence and Execution in England, 1675–1775', *Cultural and Social History*, 3 (2006), 140–2.
13. Thomas Trotter, *Medicina Nautica*, 2 vols (London, 1797), 1: 38.
14. PRO, ASSI 45/24/3/16C-D: Cumberland 1751, James Clark; OBP, February 1749, Archibald Blare (t17490222-51).
15. N. A. M. Roger, *The Wooden World* (London, 1986), 15 and 64.
16. Henry Thursfield (ed.), *Five Naval Journals* (London, 1951), 129; Brian Lavery, *Nelson's Navy: The Ships, Men and Organisation, 1793–1815* (London, 1989), 204.
17. Ian Dyck, *William Cobbett and Rural Popular Culture* (Cambridge, 1992), 54. For women, see the early eighteenth-century ballad, 'What though I am a London dame', replying to the earlier 'What though I am a country lass?' in John Wardroper, *Lovers, Rakes and Rogues: A New Garner of Love-Songs and Merry Verses, 1580 to 1830* (London, 1995), 258–9.
18. Anon., 'The New-Fashioned Farmer', [n.d.] Madden Collection of Ballads, Cambridge University Library.
19. Anon., 'My Old Hat' (Ledbury, n.d.), Madden Collection of Ballads, Cambridge University Library.
20. For the popularity of these ballads, see Dyck, *William Cobbett*.
21. E. P. Thompson, *Customs in Common* (London, 1991), 14.
22. Jeanette Neeson, *Commoners: Common Right, Enclosure and Social Change in England, 1700–1820* (Cambridge, 1993), 41. There is, of course, a close parallel in Pierre Bourdieu's argument that the working class develops a 'taste of necessity', which validates consumption patterns forced on them by limitations of economic resources and cultural capital, and rebuffs as wasteful and extravagant the taste of the rich and cultured; Pierre Bourdieu, *Distinction: A Social Critique of the Judgement of Taste* (London, 1984), 178. For a discussion of this issue which

takes up the themes addressed here, but suggests rather different conclusions, see Peter Jones, 'Clothing the Poor in Early Nineteenth Century England', *Textile History*, 37 (2006), 32–3.

23 For an excellent discussion of the campaigns on these issues mounted by the labourers' greatest advocate, William Cobbett, see Dyck, *William Cobbett*.

24 For tensions between men and women in urban working-class households in the early nineteenth century, see Anna Clark, *The Struggle for the Breeches: Gender and the Making of the British Working Class* (London, 1995), especially chapters 3 and 5.

25 Edwin Gray, *Cottage Life in a Hertfordshire Village* (Harpenden, 1977), 39. For parish clothing clubs, see Chapter 15.

26 Alan G. Crosby (ed.), *The Family Records of Benjamin Shaw Mechanic of Dent, Dolphinholme and Preston, 1772–1841* (Stroud, 1991). See above, Chapter 3.

27 A. Pleat (ed.), *'The Most Dismal Times': William Rowbottom's Diary. Part 1. 1787–1799* (Oldham, 1996), 41. Elsewhere in his diary, however, Rowbottom takes pleasure in the presence of well-dressed young men and women at the local wakes.

28 Donald Read, *Peterloo: The 'Massacre' and its Background* (Manchester, 1958), 130–1. There was, of course, a countervailing tendency in early nineteenth-century radicalism, especially among the early socialists influenced by William Godwin's writings in the 1790s, who sought a simplification of desire, a limitation of consumption to natural wants, and the elimination of useless superfluities. Its implications for clothing emerge most clearly in the dress codes promulgated by Robert Owen for his co-operative communities. See Gregory Claeys, 'The Origins of the Rights of Labor: Republicanism, Commerce, and the Construction of Modern Social Theory in Britain, 1796–1805', *Journal of Modern History*, 66 (1994), 249–90 and Noel Thompson, 'Social Opulence, Private Asceticism: Ideas of Consumption in Early Socialist Thought', in Martin Daunton and Matthew Hilton (eds), *The Politics of Consumption: Material Culture and Citizenship in Europe and America* (Oxford, 2001), 51–68.

29 George Fox, *A Collection of Many Select and Christian Epistles, Letters and Testimonies*, 2 vols (London, 1698), 2: 249.

30 John Wesley, *Instructions for Christians* (London, 1791), 20.

31 For Quaker dress, see, in particular, Joan Kendall, 'The Development of a Distinctive Form of Quaker Dress', *Costume*, 19 (1985), 58–74; Marcia Pointon, 'Quakerism and Visual Culture, 1650–1800', *Art History*, 20 (1997), 297–431; Nicholas Morgan, *Lancashire Quakers and the Establishment, 1660–1730* (Edinburgh, 1993), chapter 7.

32 James Nayler, *The Lambs Warre Against the Man of Sinne* (London, 1658), 3.

33 Robert Barclay, *An Apology For the True Christian Divinity, As the Same is Held Forth, and Preached by the People, Called, in Scorn, Quakers* (London, 1678), 'The Fifteenth Proposition' [unpaginated] and 364–5.

34 Ralph Farmer, *The Lord Cravens Case Stated* (London, 1660), 2.

35 Pointon, 'Quakerism and Visual Culture', 401.

36 Brotherton Library, Leeds University, Special Collections, Quaker Records, A21: Knaresborough Women's Monthly Meeting, Minute Book, 1694–1723, f. 149: 1718.

37 Brotherton Library, Leeds University, Special Collections, Quaker Records, A23: Knaresborough Women's Monthly Meeting, Minute Book, 1747–1784, f. 100: 1762.

38 Brotherton Library, Leeds University, Special Collections, Quaker Records, R1: Brighouse Monthly Meeting, Minute Book, 1797–1804, ff. 289 and 298: 1801.

39 Jan Albers, 'Seeds of Contention: Society, Politics and the Church of England in Lancashire, 1689–1790' (PhD dissertation, Yale University, 1988), 383–4.

40 Morgan, *Lancashire Quakers*, 252–60. Morgan disputes the view of earlier Quaker historians that an original, inspirational form of Quakerism was replaced towards the end of the seventeenth century by uniformity, discipline and a narrow obsessiveness about outward appearance.

41 Kendall, 'Distinctive Form of Quaker Dress', 65–6.

42 Richard Gough, *The History of Myddle* (London, 1981), 172.

43 *Jackson's Oxford Journal*, 21 January 1761; see also *Weekly Worcester Journal*, 4 August 1774. Kendall, 'Distinctive Form of Quaker Dress', 63.

44 For Wesley and dress, see Edwina Ehrman, *Dressed Neat and Plain: The Clothing of John Wesley and his Teaching on Dress* (London, 2003).

45 John Wesley, *Advice to the People Called Methodists, with Regard to Dress* (London, 1780), 5.

46 Ehrman, *Dressed Neat and Plain*, 16.

47 Thomas Jackson (ed.), *The Journal of the Rev. Charles Wesley*, 2 vols (London, 1849), 1: 169. For

48 Eliza Haywood, *Epistles for the Ladies*, 2 vols (London, 1749–50), 1: 30. Moorfields was the site of the first Methodist chapel in London, opened in 1739.
49 Luke Tyerman, *The Life and Times of John Wesley*, 3 vols (London, 1871), 3: 413.
50 See, for examples, OBP, July 1771, Stephen Clements (t17710703-45); OBP, May 1780, Thomas Humphreys (t17800510-33).
51 OBP, January 1761, Thomas Manton (t17610116-2).
52 OBP, February 1771, Thomas Harvey (t17710220-36).
53 OBP, September 1735, George Holloway (t17350911-92).
54 OBP, October 1786, John Cloud (t17861025-117).
55 OBP, January 1740, Paul Kyte (t17400116-5).
56 OBP, February 1773, Mary Catherine Cameron (t17730217-16).
57 For some witnesses, use of this terminology may have represented an attempt to tailor their language to the expectations of judges and lawyers in court, but it seems unlikely that this was generally the case, given that it was used so frequently, in so many different contexts and by such a wide range of people. Witnesses employed it not just to express their own judgements, but when quoting the words of other people involved in a case. They used it not only in court, but in their examinations before magistrates. They employed it not just in London, but in the provinces. It was even used by convicts condemned to death in the accounts of their lives in their own words published by the Ordinary of Newgate, who had every incentive to provide readers with at least an impression of veracity, even if the words had not always actually come from the prisoner's mouth.
58 The word polite was not used by Old Bailey witnesses to describe dress, although it was used to describe behaviour; genteel appears to have remained the equivalent word for dress throughout the eighteenth century.
59 William Hutton, *The Life of Willam Hutton F.A.S.S.* (London, 1816), 30–1.
60 OBP, January 1747, Daniel Harvey (t17470116-40).
61 OBP, December 1760, William Harrison (t17601204-4).
62 OBP, April 1787, Joseph Cook (t17870418-77). The first floor was the most prestigious in an eighteenth-century London house and the most expensive on which to rent a room.
63 OBP, July 1742, Mary Shirley (t17420714-18).
64 OBP, July 1798, Elizabeth Starenaugh (t17980704-5).
65 OBP, January 1752, William Williams (t17520116-10).
66 OBP, December 1742, Jane Grice (t17421208-32).
67 OBP, December 1745, John Baynham (t17451204-29).
68 OBP, December 1732, Hannah Sealy (t17321206-1).
69 OBP, September 1753, Mary Hadlep (t17530906-32).
70 OBP, January 1790, John Hyams (t17900113-81).
71 OBP, January 1761, Nicholas Campbell (t17610116-29).
72 OBP, May 1795, Helena Holman (t17950520-57).
73 OBP, June 1783, Sarah Harrison (t17830604-73).
74 Amanda Vickery, '"Neat and Not too Showey": Words and Wallpaper in Regency England', in John Styles and Amanda Vickery, *Gender, Taste and Material Culture in Britain and North America, 1700–1830* (New Haven and London, 2006), 201–22.
75 Wesley, *Advice to the People Called Methodists*, 5; Frederick C. Gill (ed.), *Selected Letters of John Wesley* (London, 1956), 120; Ehrman, *Dressed Neat and Plain*, 16.
76 Essex RO D/DZg/33: Correspondence to and from Mary Farrin and her husband, William White of Bulphan, Essex, 1744–1791: Jane Farrin to Poll [Mary Farrin], n.d. [1750s].
77 OBP, January 1763, William Autenreith (t17630114-23).
78 OBP, September 1773, William Williamson (t17730908-7).
79 OBP, May 1786, Elizabeth Connelly (t17860531-34).
80 OBP, February 1768, Anne Robinson (t17680224-65).
81 See, for example, Neil McKendrick, 'The Commercialization of Fashion', in Neil McKendrick, John Brewer and J. H. Plumb (eds), *The Birth of a Consumer Society* (London, 1982), 50–1, 94–6.
82 Such a trajectory is implied in Beverley Lemire's recent application to eighteenth-century England of Gilles Lipovetsky's account of the emergence of

fashion. See Beverley Lemire, 'Second-hand Beaux and "Red-armed Belles": Conflict and the Creation of Fashions in England, c.1660–1800', *Continuity and Change*, 15 (2000), 400–3; Gilles Lipovetsky, *The Empire of Fashion: Dressing Modern Democracy* (Princeton, 1994).

83 Alison Clarke and Daniel Miller, 'Fashion and Anxiety', *Fashion Theory*, 6 (2002), 191–214.

13 Budgeting for Clothes

1. Jacob Vanderlint, *Money Answers all Things: Or, An Essay to Make Money Sufficiently Plentiful Amongst all Ranks of People* (London, 1734), 75.
2. For the development and significance of plebeian household budgets as an object of social scientific enquiry, see Jonathan White, 'The Laboring-Class Domestic Sphere in Eighteenth-Century British Social Thought', in John Styles and Amanda Vickery (eds), *Gender, Taste and Material Culture in Britain and North America, 1700–1830* (London, 2006), 247–63.
3. Liam Brunt, 'The Advent of the Sample Survey in the Social Sciences', *Journal of the Royal Statistical Society: Series D*, 50 (2001), 179–89.
4. David Davies, *The Case of the Labourers in Husbandry* (London, 1795).
5. Sir Frederick Eden, *The State of the Poor*, 3 vols (London, 1797).
6. Davies, *Labourers in Husbandry*, 6, 28.
7. The following analysis is based on the 115 budgets for English families in Davies, *Labourers in Husbandry* and Eden, *State of the Poor* where the sum set down for expenditure on clothing is unique to the family concerned and is not a standard figure used for every family from that parish. Because the main purpose of this analysis is to explore what the budgets reveal about clothing, families for whom no expenditure on clothing is recorded are excluded. It is possible that some of these excluded families genuinely did not buy any clothing, and their absence from the analysis should be borne in mind.
8. For example, Davies, *Labourers in Husbandry*, 146–7, 148–50.
9. Thomas Sokoll, 'Early Attempts at Accounting the Unaccountable: Davies' and Eden's Budgets of Agricultural Labouring Families in Late Eighteenth-century England', in Toni Pierenkemper (ed.), *Zur Ökonomik des privaten Haushalts: Haushaltsrechnungen als Quellen historischer Wirtschafts- und Sozialforschung* (Frankfurt and New York, 1991), 34–58.
10. See, for example, Davies, *Labourers in Husbandry*, 136–7.
11. Paul Johnson, 'Conspicuous Consumption and Working-Class Culture in Late-Victorian and Edwardian Britain', *Royal Historical Society Transactions*, fifth series, 38 (1988), 28–9.
12. See Davies, *Labourers in Husbandry*, 156 for use of the word 'estimate' regarding the Durham budgets.
13. N. B. Harte, 'The Economics of Clothing in the Late Seventeenth Century', *Textile History*, 22 (1991), 292; Johnson, 'Conspicuous Consumption', 31.
14. These low-spending families spent under £23 a year in total and devoted only seven percent of their total expenditure to clothes. They came overwhelmingly from two parishes in Dorset and these aberrant figures may reflect peculiar local conditions or, much more likely, idiosyncratic estimates by those who reported from Dorset to Davies. Eden's low-spending families tended, if anything, to devote a slightly higher proportion of their expenditure to clothing.
15. The distinction economists usually make is between luxuries, on which spending increases faster than total income, and necessities, on which spending increases more slowly.
16. For some suggestive evidence that wives controlled family expenditure, see Keith Snell, *Annals of the Labouring Poor: Social Change and Agrarian England, 1660–1900* (Cambridge, 1985), 357.
17. Davies, *Labourers in Husbandry*, 84–5. This is similar to the way income was allocated in the early eighteenth-century families where the women undertook paid work described by Daniel Defoe: 'The Father gets them Food, and the Mother gets them Clothes.' Daniel Defoe, *A Plan of the English Commerce* (London, 1728), 91.
18. Davies, *Labourers in Husbandry*, 14–15.
19. Eden, *State of the Poor*, 2: 75.
20. Davies, *Labourers in Husbandry*, 15–16.
21. Davies, *Labourers in Husbandry*, 136–7.
22. Davies, *Labourers in Husbandry*, 184–5.
23. Davies, *Labourers in Husbandry*, 28.
24. The six detailed budgets cover the years 1787–9.
25. Two of the six families lived in the north of England (Marton, Westmorland and Auckland, County Durham), three in the south-west

26. See, for example, Eden, *State of the Poor*, 2: 434, 3: 734; Davies, *Labourers in Husbandry*, 170–1.
27. Other information on the cost of clothing confirms this. The costings of clothes for a poor man and a poor woman provided in 1789 by the anonymous Hertfordshire author of *Instructions for Cutting out Apparel for the Poor* show the man's shoes costing more than twice as much as the woman's, and the man's outer garments costing more than the woman's, even though the woman's includes a cloak (unlike the wives in the Davies budgets) and the cost of making is not included for either man or woman. Similarly, in Eden's costing of clothes from the London slop shops in the 1790s, basic outer garments for a man are more expensive than those for a woman. Anon., *Instructions for Cutting out Apparel for the Poor; Principally intended for the Assistance of the Patronesses of Sunday Schools, and other Charitable Institutions* (London, 1789), 68, 72; Eden, *State of the Poor*, 1: 557–8.
28. Eden, *State of the Poor*, 2: 709–10.
29. Jack Ayres (ed.), *Paupers and Pig Killers: The Diary of William Holland, a Somerset Parson, 1799–1818* (Gloucester, 1984), 172.
30. Anon., *Cutting out Apparel*, 68.
31. It is difficult to establish the precise annual amount spent on clothing by the servants of the Yorkshire manufacturer, Robert Heaton, discussed in Chapter 17, because of the way his accounts were organized, but there is little doubt that their annual expenditure was at least twice as high as Davies's wives.
32. University of London MSS, MS 625/3: Account books of L. Cottchin and R. Flowers, grocers and drapers in Westoning, Bedfordshire, 1785–1800, Servants' Book, entries for purchases by local overseers 1793–5. For a discussion of this shop, its owners, and its customers see Anne Buck, 'Buying Clothes in Bedfordshire: Customers and Tradesmen, 1700–1800', *Textile History*, 22 (1991), 229–32. See also Anon., *Cutting out Apparel*, 72.
33. For examples, see PRO, ASSI 44/96: Northern Circuit Assize Indictments, Yorkshire Summer 1781, Tate Lawson, for a silver stock buckle stolen in 1781 from Richard Houseman, labourer of Grimston in the West Riding of Yorkshire, and ASSI 45/35/2/95-6: Yorkshire 1785, William Johnson, for silver shirt buttons stolen in 1785 from Thomas Todd, labourer of Heworth in the North Riding.
34. WYAS (Bradford), B149: Heaton of Ponden MSS, account book of Robert Heaton, 1764–92. For Heaton and his servants, see Chapter 17 below.
35. Ann Kussmaul, *Servants in Husbandry in Early-Modern England* (Cambridge, 1981), 38.
36. Eden, *State of the Poor*, 1: 558, 3: cccxliii.
37. University of London MSS, MS 625: Account books of L. Cottchin and R. Flowers, grocers and drapers in Westoning, Bedfordshire, 1785–1800; Anon., *Cutting out Apparel*; WYAS (Bradford), B149: Heaton of Ponden MSS, account book of Robert Heaton, 1764–92.
38. The breeches of the suit would wear out much quicker than the coat and waistcoat, but Davies's figures do not allow for such fine distinctions.
39. Eden, *State of the Poor*, 1: 557. For slop-shop jackets see Lois Mulkearn (ed.), *George Mercer Papers Relating to the Ohio Company of Virginia* (Pittsburgh, 1954), 215–16, J. Mercer to George Mercer in London, 28 January 1768. I would like to thank Ann Smart Martin for bringing my attention to this reference. Anon., *Cutting out Apparel*, 56.
40. University of London MSS, MS 625: Account books of L. Cottchin and R. Flowers, grocers and drapers in Westoning, Bedfordshire, 1785–1800, has numerous entries for mending labourers' clothes.
41. Eden, *State of the Poor*, 2: 15, 107, 246–7, 585–6, 621–2, 660–1; 3: cccxliii.
42. Davies, *Labourers in Husbandry*, families from Barkham, Berkshire, Holwell, Somerset, and Great Eccleston, Barton, and Kirkland, Lancashire. The average is 7s. 2d. per child.
43. Davies, *Labourers in Husbandry*, 178–9.
44. Davies, *Labourers in Husbandry*, 148–50.
45. See Snell, *Annals of the Labouring Poor*, 358–9. Also Tim Wales, 'Poverty, Poor Relief and the Life-cycle: Some Evidence from Seventeenth-Century Norfolk', in Richard M. Smith (ed.), *Land, Kinship and Life-Cycle* (Cambridge, 1984), 351–404.
46. Snell, *Annals of the Labouring Poor*, 333.
47. E. A. Wrigley and R. S. Schofield, *The Population History of England, 1541–1871* (Cambridge, 1981), 424.

14 Clothes and the Life-cycle

1. The following discussion is, unless otherwise indicated, based on Lorna Weatherill, *Account Book of Richard Latham, 1724–1767* (London, 1990). See Chapter 8, note 31 for the problems that arise in using this printed edition of the account book.
2. Charles F. Foster, *Seven Households: Life in Cheshire and Lancashire, 1582–1774* (Northwich, 2002), 150–1.
3. Anon., *An Address to the P-t in Behalf of the Starving Multitude* (London, 1766), 39.
4. Foster, *Seven Households*, 152.
5. For a distillation of research on agricultural labourers' wages in the second half of the eighteenth century, see G. E. Mingay (ed.), *The Agrarian History of England and Wales, 1750–1850* (Cambridge, 1989), 701.
6. *The Gentleman's Magazine* (1766), 582.
7. Ian Dyck, *William Cobbett and Rural Popular Culture* (Cambridge, 1992), chapter 5, and J. M. Neeson, 'An Eighteenth-Century Peasantry', in John Rule and Robert Malcolmson (eds), *Protest and Survival* (London, 1993), 51–8.
8. There are very few entries in the Latham accounts after 1752 for their daughter Martha, born in 1741.
9. As with the Eden-Davies labouring families, we have no information on clothing the Lathams received as gifts. It is not unlikely that they received gifts of clothes on the death of relatives.
10. The figures for total spending used here are those provided by Lorna Weatherill, not the revised expenditure figures computed by Charles Foster that take into account capital and other exceptional spending. Both sets of figures show marked differences between the three periods. Foster, *Seven Households*, 168–9.
11. 76 percent of named clothing purchases by number, 71 percent by value. Named purchases accounted for 36 percent of all clothing purchases in this period by number and 47 percent by value.
12. The Lathams had 16 yards of linsey-woolsey woven and dyed in 1727. There are also two payments for dyeing lengths of linen cloth which exceeded seven yards. This cloth might have been made into gowns for Nany, but this seems unlikely as there are no mentions of linsey-woolsey or linen gowns anywhere in the account book. Linsey-woolsey was widely used for petticoats, aprons and waistcoats, but even in overseers' accounts it hardly ever appears as a fabric for gowns, nor does linen.
13. The Cunningtons suggest this combination of jacket and petticoat was commonly adopted by working women in the first half of the eighteenth century, although Anne Buck asserts that later it was much less common than the combination of petticoat and bedgown. C. Willett Cunnington and Phillis Cunnington, *Handbook of English Costume in the Eighteenth Century* (London, 1957), 130–1; Anne Buck, *Dress in Eighteenth-Century England* (London, 1979), 144.
14. See above, Chapter 8.
15. Calculation based on the average cost of handkerchiefs bought between 1724 and 1741, the total sum spent on handkerchiefs, and the number of family members alive in each year.
16. Although if, as Charles Foster suggests, another Betty, the daughter of Richard Latham's dead brother, also lived with the family for part of this period, this may be an overestimate. Foster, *Seven Households*, 147.
17. Ivy Pinchbeck, *Women Workers and the Industrial Revolution, 1750–1850* (London, 1981), 139–40.
18. See John James, *History of the Worsted Manufacture* (London, 1857), 239, for an estimate of worsted spinning earnings in the 1730s at 2s. 3d. a week. Cotton spinners in south Lancashire and north Cheshire in the 1750s and 1760s appear to have earned slightly more; Pinchbeck, *Women Workers*, 139–40. Davies estimated later in the century that the mother of a Berkshire labouring family could earn 1s. 8d. a week at spinning flax if regularly employed, in addition to spinning yarn for her family's use; David Davies, *The Case of the Labourers in Husbandry* (London, 1795), 84–5.
19. Shopkeepers' inventories for the period 1720 to 1750 often include cloth described as printed linen and printed cotton. Occasionally printed flannel and printed linsey-woolsey also occur.
20. In addition, gentry women spent a great deal on trimmings.
21. Lancashire RO, DDB 7886: Parker of Brownsholme MSS, Wallet 7, no. 278, Miss Parker's dress bills.
22. WYAS (Bradford), Sp St 6/2/1/1: Spencer Stanhope MSS, Account book of Mary Warde, 1734–7.
23. Based on the average cost of handkerchiefs between 1742 and 1754, the total sum spent on handkerchiefs, and the number of family members alive and resident in each year.
24. Other goods that were sometimes named for a family member included medicines, books, boxes

(significantly these were probably for storing the daughters' clothes when they went to service) and spinning wheels.

25 It is this immersion of personal identity in artefacts that are transient and insubstantial that has constituted one of the key objections offered by critics to modern consumption in general, and especially to fashion in dress. It was also, of course, of concern to many eighteenth-century moralists.

26 Drapers' probate inventories do, however, occasionally contain cloth that was moth-eaten or had otherwise deteriorated. Almost all the uses in the accounts of the word 'new' in connection with cloth are for linen. The distinction Latham was making by using the word 'new' in these cases may have been between ready-made cloth and the cloth the family had woven from yarn of its own spinning. 'Old' is never used in connection with cloth.

27 There were some parallels with the Eden-Davies families, however. Almost all the few purchases identifiable as second-hand were for children under 15. They occurred during the period of greatest pressure on budgets, 1724 to 1741, and the two subsequent years.

28 Proprietary medicines were the items consumed by the Lathams that appeared most frequently in newspapers. See John Styles, 'Product Innovation in Early Modern London', *Past and Present*, 168 (2000), 124–69.

29 University College of North Wales, Bangor, Dept. of MSS, MS 82: Penmorfa, Caernarvon, shop ledger, *c.*1788–*c.*1803, f. 4, account of Harry Evan of Tyddynfilin, 14 May 1792; f. 13, account of William Evans of Wern, 15 August 1793.

30 Jan de Vries, 'The Industrial Revolution and the Industrious Revolution', *Journal of Economic History*, 54 (1994), 249–70 and 'Between Purchasing Power and the World of Goods: Understanding the Household Economy in Early Modern Europe', in John Brewer and Roy Porter (eds), *Consumption and the World of Goods* (London, 1993), 85–132.

15 Involuntary Consumption? Prizes, Gifts and Charity

1 Quoted in K. H. Burley, 'A Note on a Labour Dispute in Early Eighteenth-century Colchester', *Bulletin of the Institute of Historical Research*, 29 (1956), 224.

2 B. Cozens-Hardy (ed.), *The Diary of Sylas Neville, 1767–1788* (Oxford, 1950), 279.

3 *Leeds Mercury*, 21 September, 1725

4 Lancashire RO, DDB/81/15: Parker of Brownsholme MSS, Nanny Nutter account book, 1772–5.

5 Marius Kwint, 'Astley's Amphitheatre and the Early Circus in England, 1768–1830' (DPhil thesis, Oxford University, 1994), 25.

6 NYCRO, QSB/1698, Mary Bell; Worcestershire RO, Worcestershire Quarter Sessions, Summer 1811, Mary Brooks; PRO, ASSI 45/36/3/8–203: Northumberland 1789, George Johnson; NYCRO, QSB/1732, Mary Wright. Gifting and material mutuality among the plebeian classes could give rise to ambiguity concerning rights of ownership and control. See Lynn MacKay, 'Why They stole: Women in the Old Bailey, 1779–1789', *Journal of Social History*, 32 (1999), 623–39.

7 WYAS (Bradford), B149: Heaton of Ponden MSS, account book of Robert Heaton, 1764–92. For Heaton's servants see Chapter 17.

8 J. A. Johnston, 'The Family and Kin of the Lincolnshire Labourer in the Eighteenth Century', *Lincolnshire History and Archeology*, 14 (1979), 51.

9 Amy L. Erickson, *Women and Property in Early Modern England* (London, 1993), 65, 216; W. Coster, *Kinship and Inheritance in Early Modern England: Three Yorkshire Parishes* (York, 1993), 21–2.

10 John Hervey, *Letterbooks of John Hervey, first Earl of Bristol*, ed. Sydenham H. A. Hervey, 3 vols (London, 1894), 3:272–3.

11 Yorkshire Archaeological Society, DD 121/91/4, Skipton Castle MSS. See R. W. Hoyle (ed.), *Lord Thanet's Benefaction to the Poor of Craven in 1685* (Giggleswick, 1978), ix, on which the following discussion of Thanet's activities is based.

12 C. Stella Davies, *The Agricultural History of Cheshire, 1750–1850* (Manchester, 1960), 89.

13 David Davies, *The Case of the Labourers in Husbandry* (London, 1795), 174–5.

14 OBP, Samuel Jackson, May 1796 (t17960511–30).

15 *London Evening Post*, 1 January 1757. Newspaper announcements of this kind were most common in times of dearth. They tended to emphasise gifts of foodstuffs more than clothing. Such announcements often pointed out that these gifts were evidence of practical compassion on the part of the wealthy, which removed any justification for the poor to riot.

16 For the argument that this practice was already in

17. *London Evening Post*, 22 March 1748.
18. Bridget Lewis, 'Charitable Provision for the Rural Poor: A Case Study of Policies and Attitudes in Northamptonshire in the First Half of the Nineteenth Century' (PhD dissertation, University of Leicester, 2003), 145.
19. LMA, P92/SAV/1412: Southwark, St Saviour, Account book and rental of Richard Bliss, Warden of the General Poor, 1697–8.
20. Cumbria RO (Kendal), WD/AG/Box 31: Janson's charity, Kendal, 1712–1798.
21. W. R. Ward, *Parson and Parish in Eighteenth-Century Hampshire: Replies to Bishops' Visitations* (Winchester, 1995), 68, 102, 104.
22. Copy of the will of Richard Fountaine of Enfield, Middlesex, Esq., 1721, at Fountaine's Hospital, Linton-in-Craven, North Yorkshire.
23. Ward, *Parson and Parish in Eighteenth-Century Hampshire*, xxix.
24. Lewis, 'Charitable Provision', 42.
25. Sam Barrett, 'Kinship, Poor Relief and the Welfare Process in Early Modern England', in Steven King and Alannah Tomkins (eds), *The Poor in England, 1700–1850: An Economy of Makeshifts* (Manchester, 2003), 218. At Wimbledon in Surrey in the mid-eighteenth century the four coats provided annually from Henry Smith's bequest virtually never went to those in receipt of parish pensions; see F. M. Cowe (ed.), *Wimbledon Vestry Minutes, 1736, 1743–1788* (Guilford, 1964). Private charitable donors of clothing also sometimes gave preference to those who were not receiving parish relief; for a Hertfordshire example from the 1790s see Anon., *The Reports of the Society for Bettering the Condition and Increasing the Comforts of the Poor*, 4 vols (London, 1798–1800), 1: 63.
26. Donna Andrew, *Philanthropy and Police: London Charity in the Eighteenth Century* (Oxford, 1989); Joanna Innes, 'The "Mixed Economy of Welfare" in early modern England: Assessments of the Options from Hale to Malthus (c.1683–1803)', in Martin Daunton (ed.), *Charity, Self-interest and Welfare in the English Past* (London, 1996), 139–80.
27. Anon., *Proceedings of the Committee Appointed to Manage the Contributions begun at London Dec. 18, 1759 for Cloathing French Prisoners of War* (London, 1760).
28. Society for Charitable Purposes, *The governors of the Society for charitable purposes think it their duty to give the following general view of the manner in which the fund has been applied* (London, 1774), 7; Donna Andrew, 'Noblesse Oblige. Female Charity in an Age of Sentiment', in John Brewer and Susan Staves (eds), *Early Modern Conceptions of Property* (London, 1995), 292–3.
29. W. Parson and W. White, *History, Directory and Gazetteer of the Counties of Cumberland and Westmorland* (Leeds, 1829), 142.
30. Anon., *The Fifth Annual Report of the Ladies' Benevolent Society, Liverpool, Instituted, January 1810* (Liverpool, 1815).
31. Parson and White, *Cumberland and Westmorland*, 286.
32. R. B. Pugh (ed.), *Victoria History of the County of Cambridge and the Isle of Ely*, vol. 4 (London, 2002), 271; Birmingham City Archives, MC 21/37: Minute book of the Dorcasian Society, 1824–61; *The Nottingham Review*, 19 January 1816; Anon., *First Report of the Liverpool Dorcas Society* (Liverpool, 1818); Huntington Library, Stowe, Grenville, Accounts, Box 169: General charity accounts, 1740s–1860s.
33. See, for a recent discussion of parallel developments focused on pauper housing, Sarah Lloyd, 'Cottage Conversations: Poverty and Manly Independence in Eighteenth-Century England', *Past and Present*, 184 (2004), 69–108.
34. Rev. Francis Lichfield, *Three Years' Results of the Farthinghoe Clothing Society* (Northampton, 1832), 3.
35. Mrs [Sarah] Trimmer, *The Oeconomy of Charity* (London, 1787), 47.
36. Mrs [Sarah] Trimmer, *The Oeconomy of Charity*, 2 vols (London, 1801), 2: 302, 304; Trimmer, *Oeconomy of Charity* (1787), 158.
37. Trimmer, *Oeconomy of Charity* (1801), 2: 301; Trimmer, *Oeconomy of Charity* (1787), 156.
38. Anon., *Instructions for Cutting out Apparel for the Poor; Principally intended for the Assistance of the Patronesses of Sunday Schools, and other Charitable Institutions, But useful in all Families* (London, 1789), v.
39. Trimmer, *Oeconomy of Charity* (1787), 159.
40. Anon., *Tenth Report of the Liverpool Dorcas and Spinning Society* (Liverpool, 1827), 6.
41. Huntington Library, Stowe, Grenville, Accounts, Box 169: Ann Adkins to Marchioness of Buckingham, 14 January 1820.
42. See, for London, M. Thale (ed.), *The Autobiography of Francis Place (1771–1854)* (Cambridge, 1972),

106–7; for Birmingham, William Hutton, *An History of Birmingham* (Birmingham, 1783), 138; for Newcastle on Tyne, PRO, ASSI 45/36/2/178–81: Newcastle 1788, William Towns; for Kent, Centre for Kentish Studies, Maidstone, U 1823/35/A3: daybook of a Maidstone draper, 1768–1773, ff. 103–4.
43 Anon., *The Reports of the Society for Bettering the Condition and Increasing the Comforts of the Poor*, 4 vols (London, 1798–1800), 3: 243.
44 Sir Frederick Eden, *The State of the Poor*, 3 vols (London, 1797), 1: 615.
45 *Nottingham Review*, 27 December, 1816; *The Philanthropist*, 7 (1819), 173–4; Thomas Jones, *Clothing Societies* (Northampton, 1822), 3.
46 Rev. D. Capper, *Practical Results of the Workhouse System, as Adopted in the Parish of Great Missenden, Bucks., during the Year 1833–4*, second edition (London, 1834), 81.
47 *Nottingham Review*, 27 December 1816.
48 Lichfield, *Farthinghoe Clothing Society*, 21. Also see *House of Commons Sessional Papers*, vol. 28 (1834), Reports from Commissioners on the Poor Laws, Appendix A, Assistant Commissioners' Reports, Part I: 21, 410.
49 See Lewis, 'Charitable Provision', chapter 4 and Tina Vivienne Richmond, '"No Finery": the Dress of the Poor in Nineteenth-Century England' (PhD Dissertation, University of London, 2004), chapter 5.
50 Some of these strategies had been employed much earlier by private individuals, such as the writer Sarah Scott in her schemes for employing poor women at Bath in the 1750s; see Eve Tavor Bannet, 'The Bluestocking Sisters: Women's Patronage, Millennium Hall, and "The Visible Providence of a Country"', *Eighteenth-Century Life*, 30 (2005), 25–55.
51 Anon., *Instructions for Cutting out Apparel*, 62.
52 *The Reports of the Society for Bettering the Condition and Increasing the Comforts of the Poor*, 4 vols (London, 1798–1800), 4: 72.
53 Trevor Lummis and Jan Marsh, *The Woman's Domain: Women and the English Country House* (London, 1990), 106.
54 See Frances Collier, *The Family Economy of the Working Classes in the Cotton Industry, 1784–1833* (Manchester, 1965), 40, for purchases of fashionable and presumably desirable accessories, often on credit, by employees at the mill shop at Styal in Cheshire in the 1820s.

16 Involuntary Consumption? The Parish Poor

1 For charity school clothing, see Phillis Cunnington and Catherine Lewis, *Charity Costumes* (London, 1978). For Sunday schools see T. Laqueur, *Religion and Respectability: Sunday Schools and Working Class Culture, 1780–1850* (Berkeley, California, 1976), 170–4; and specifically for the late eighteenth century, Mrs [Sarah] Trimmer, *The Oeconomy of Charity* (London, 1787), 156–9.
2 There were, of course, other categories of involuntary consumers, like beadles, watchmen and petty officials who were clothed in large part by their employers, but their numbers were much smaller.
3 Steven King, *Poverty and Welfare in England* (Manchester, 2000), 84. Proportions of the population receiving poor relief were generally under 10 percent in north Lincolnshire at the end of the eighteenth century; see R. Dyson, 'The Experience of Poverty in a Rural Community: Broughton, north Lincolnshire, 1760–1835', *Local Population Studies*, 70 (2003), 13–14. But in Ardleigh, Essex in the near-famine year of 1796 they reached 43 percent; see Thomas Sokoll, *Household and Family among the Poor* (Bochum, 1993), 150.
4 King, *Poverty and Welfare, passim*.
5 Beverly Lemire, *Fashion's Favourite: The Cotton Trade and the Consumer in Britain, 1660–1800* (Oxford, 1991), 108; David Pam, *A Parish Near London: A History of Enfield, Volume 1*, (Enfield, 1990), 194.
6 Steven King, 'Reclothing the English Poor, 1750–1840', *Textile History*, 33 (2002), 46, 38, 45.
7 Hertfordshire Archives and Local Studies., DP/44/12/1: Much Hadham Overseers' accounts, 1778–99.
8 Alannah Tomkins, 'Pawnbroking and the Survival Strategies of the Urban Poor in 1770s York', in Steven King and Alannah Tomkins (eds), *The Poor in England, 1700–1850: An Economy of Makeshifts* (Manchester, 2003), 184–91.
9 York City Archives, PR/Y/M/Bp.S/22: St Mary Bishophill, overseers' accounts, 1759–89.
10 Hertfordshire Archives and Local Studies, DP/29/9/1: Cheshunt constables' book, 1669–1785.
11 Joan Howard-Drake, 'The Poor of Shipton under Wychwood Parish, 1740–62', *Wychwood's History*, 5 (1989), 4–44.
12 University of London MSS, MS 625/3: Account book of L. Cottchin and R. Flowers, grocer and

draper, Westoning, Bedfordshire, 1785–1800, labelled 'Servants Book'.

13 For examples of letters of this kind from Essex parishes in the first two decades of the nineteenth century see Thomas Sokoll (ed.), *Essex Pauper Letters, 1731–1837* (Oxford, 2001), 561, 564, 583.

14 Anon., *The Reports of the Society for Bettering the Condition and Increasing the Comforts of the Poor*, 4 vols (London, 1798–1800), 1: 26. Such comments suggest the poor preferred money. 'By indulging each family in the liberty to purchase of their own tradesman, all was harmony, gratitude, and content' admitted one author discussing subsidised purchases of meal; Anon., *Instructions for Cutting out Apparel for the Poor; Principally Intended for the Assistance of the Patronesses of Sunday Schools, and other Charitable Institutions, But Useful in all Families* (London, 1789), xii.

15 F. M. Cowe (ed.), *Wimbledon Vestry Minutes, 1736, 1743–1788* (Guilford 1964), 18, 27, 21.

16 Quoted in Edward Newbold, 'The Geography of Poor Relief Expenditure in Late Eighteenth-century and Early Nineteenth-century Rural Oxfordshire' (DPhil dissertation, University of Oxford, 1995), 230.

17 Devon RO, 1249A/PO2–4: Overseers payments for Holne, 1746–1799 (transcribed by Brian Brassett at http://genuki.cs.ncl.ac.uk/DEV/Holne/Overseers/index.html, examined May 2005); Oxfordshire RO, Leafield Parish, b1 and b2: Leafield overseers' accounts, 1740–62 and 1792–1811 (transcribed by Joan Howard-Drake); WYAS (Leeds), RDP 96/71 and 75: Spofforth overseers' accounts, 1707–67 and 1767–1807; WYAS (Wakefield), WDP 14/5/1–2: Thornhill Township Books, 1673–1801; Essex RO, D/P 152/12/14: Theydon Garnon, overseers' bills and vouchers, 1685–1848; Hertfordshire Archives and Local Studies, DP/116/5–12: Ware overseers' accounts, 1753–97. These sources vary in character. Those used for Holne, Leafield, Spofforth and Thornhill are itemised accounts of overseers' expenditure entered in parish books. Those used for Ware are lists of cloth purchased and clothes issued at the workhouse, entered in parish books. Those used for Theydon Garnon are loose bills submitted to the parish by suppliers. The precise years covered are Holne: 1746–59, 1770–9, 1790–9; Leafield: 1742–59, 1792–99; Spofforth: 1730–59, 1770–99; Theydon Garnon: 1730–9, 1755–59, 1770–74, 1795–99; Thornhill: 1730–59, 1770–99; Ware: 1753–57, 1770–84. Spofforth and Thornhill were technically townships, the normal unit of Poor Law administration in the north of England. This chapter uses the word parish to denote both parishes and townships.

18 It is difficult to establish whether overseers paid normal retail prices for cloth and garments, whether they secured reduced prices as regular, bulk buyers, or whether they paid premium prices to suppliers who were privileged as ratepayers or who bribed parochial officials. Bulk buying may have secured price reductions for large workhouses like that at Ware, with 60 resident paupers in 1756, but this seems less likely in small, rural parishes like Spofforth with only 7 pensioners in 1740, or Thornhill with 18 in 1776, especially when, as at Thornhill, many clothing purchases required journeys to retailers outside the parish. Accusations of corrupt collusion between overseers and retailers were made in the 1830s; see *House of Commons Sessional Papers*, vol. 28 (1834), Reports from Commissioners on the Poor Laws, Appendix A, Assistant Commissioners' Reports, Part 1:21. Given the possibility that Poor Law prices may have been manipulated either upwards or downwards, caution is required in drawing conclusions from small differentials between the prices paid by parishes and the prices paid by independent consumers.

19 The other cheap cloth bought by some of the overseers was Russia cloth, which seems to have been provided exclusively for children, though it is not clear for what use.

20 Linda Baumgarten, *What Clothes Reveal: The Language of Clothing in Colonial and Federal America* (Williamsburg, Va., 2003), 135. John Faucheraud Grimke, *The Public Laws of the State of South-Carolina* (Philadelphia, 1790), 137, 'An Act for the better Ordering and Governing Negroes and other Slaves in this Province, 1740', XL, 'Be it enacted, That no owner or proprietor of any negro slave or other slave (except livery-men and boys) shall permit or suffer such negro or other slave, to have or wear any sort of apparel whatsoever, finer, other, or of greater value than negro cloth, duffels, kerseys, oznabrigs, blue linen, check linen or coarse garlix, or calicoes, checked cottons, or Scots plaids.'

21 Essex RO, D/P 152/12/14/1: Theydon Garnon, overseers' bills and vouchers, 1685–1755, bill for 1734; John Holroyd, Earl of Sheffield, *Observations on the Commerce of the American States* (London, 1784), 37: 'the white linens, which are chiefly used

for general purposes, such as shirting, sheeting, etc. are from 2s. 9d. to 10d. per yard [wholesale] in Great Britain or Ireland. Linens under that price are either brown or whited brown, particularly Osnaburghs.'

22 For Hudson's shop and its clients see Chapter 7. The exception was the cheap Russia cloth that the overseers supplied only for children's use.
23 For the Lathams see Chapter 14.
24 Only three purchases of linens were made by the overseers at 14d. a yard and none at prices higher than that.
25 Charlotte Smith, *The Old Manor House* (London, 1793), 29–31.
26 K. D. M. Snell, *Annals of the Labouring Poor: Social Change and Agrarian England, 1660–1900* (Cambridge, 1985), 104–7.
27 At Leafield 1 type of fabric is named in the overseers' accounts, at Spofforth 7, at Ware 8, at Thornhill 11, at Holne 21, and at Theydon Garnon 17.
28 And the evidence of surviving overseers' accounts from different parts of the country suggests that this was true earlier in the eighteenth century. See, for examples, WYAS (Leeds), P18/108: Carleton-in-Craven, overseers' accounts, 1713–34; Essex RO, D/P 16/12/2: Thaxted overseers' accounts, 1696–1716; F. G. Emmison, 'The Relief of the Poor at Eaton Socon 1706–1834', *Publications of the Bedfordshire Historical Record Society*, 15 (1933), 1–98.
29 Cowe, *Wimbledon Vestry Minutes*, 2–11. The three years 1745–8 were chosen because thereafter the clothes provided were not itemised as consistently.
30 Cowe, *Wimbledon Vestry Minutes*, 6.
31 Cowe, *Wimbledon Vestry Minutes*, 9, 29, 17, 9, 29.
32 Quoted in Emmison, 'Eaton Socon', 69.
33 Hertfordshire Archives and Local Studies, DP/29/9/1: Cheshunt constables' book, 1669–1785.
34 Hertfordshire Archives and Local Studies., DP/44/12/1: Much Hadham overseers' accounts, 1778–1799. The numbers of clothes ordered to be provided for boys and girls was similar.
35 Essex RO, D/P 119/8/3: Wethersfield vestry minutes, 1763–81, ff. 58–9.
36 Joyce Godber, *History of Bedfordshire, 1066–1888* (Bedford, 1969), 427–8.
37 York City Archives, Accession 38: Pledge book of George Fettes, pawnbroker, York, 1777–8. Other examples from the pledge book are Mary Budd, and Joseph Armitage and his wife. For identification of Fettes' clients who sought parish relief I have relied on Tomkins, 'Pawnbroking and the Survival Strategies'.

38 This was generally true elsewhere, although new workhouse schemes often proposed reducing costs by putting the inmates to work spinning and having the yarn woven into cloth to clothe them. Such attempts at institutional self-sufficiency were widely promoted, but in practice rarely answered expectations either financially or in terms of an adequate supply of clothing. See, for an example of such a scheme, Sir Frederick Eden, *The State of the Poor*, 3 vols (London, 1797), 2: 625–33, Shrewsbury House of Industry.
39 Essex RO, D/P 30/18/1–7: Witham, overseers' miscellanea; Joseph Hammond, *A Cornish Parish* (London, 1897), 89; WYAS (Leeds), LO/M5: Leeds Workhouse Minutes, 1762–70, f. 83.
40 Alan B. Coolins, *Finchley Vestry Minutes, 1768 to 1840*, part 1 (London, 1957), 37.
41 Essex RO, D/P 30/18/1–7: Witham, overseers' miscellanea.
42 See, for lists of club purchases, Thomas Jones, *Clothing Societies* (Northampton, 1822), 4 and 17; Rev. Francis Lichfield, *Three Years' Results of the Farthinghoe Clothing Society* (Northampton, 1832), 8. By the 1830s, of course, what constituted cheap fabric and basic clothing was changing, as the price of cottons of all kinds continued to decline.
43 Trimmer, *Oeconomy of Charity* (1787), 156.
44 Isaac Watts, *An Essay Towards the Encouragement of Charity Schools* (1728) in *The Works of the Rev. Isaac Watts, D.D., in Seven Volumes*, 7 vols (Leeds, n.d.), 4: 548.
45 8 & 9 Will. III c. 30 (1697), *An Act For supplying some Defects in the Laws for the Relief of the Poor*. The badging provisions of this Act were repealed by the Act of Parliament 50 Geo. III, c.52 (1810).
46 *The Times*, 25 November 1801, commenting on a proposal to repeal the act, identified it as having been designed to 'throw a stigma' on those who received parish relief in order to encourage industry. It described the badge as 'a humiliating distinction'.
47 Sidney Webb and Beatrice Webb, *English Local Government*, 7, *English Poor Law History*, part 1, *The Old Poor Law* (London, 1927), 161.
48 *The Times*, 25 November 1801, argued that badging had become inappropriate and ineffective at a time when high prices were forcing so many on to the parish. Also see John, Lord Somerville, *The System Followed during the Two Last Years by the Board of Agriculture Further Illustrated* (London, 1800), 125–6.
49 See the excellent discussion in Steve Hindle, 'Dependency, Shame and Belonging: Badging the

Deserving Poor, c.1550–1750', *Cultural and Social History*, 1 (2004), 6–35.

50 Eden, *State of the Poor*, 2: 571. In Yorkshire, printed forms used for appointing overseers of the poor in the 1730s included a section reminding them to enforce badging; Borthwick Institute for Archives, University of York, Rom, 60: Romans Deeds, Appointment of overseer of Riccall, 29 April 1737.

51 Restricting badges to paupers who received regular pensions was also the policy adopted at Fyfield in Essex in 1708, at Chigwell in Essex in 1745 and at Bitton in Gloucestershire in 1769; see W. R. Powell (ed.), *A History of the County of Essex*, (London, 1956), 4: 55–6, 37–8; Bristol RO, P/B/V/1/c: Bitton vestry order book, 1761–81.

52 Hindle, 'Dependency, shame and belonging', on which the following paragraph draws for sources, unless otherwise stated.

53 Anon., *Account of Workhouses in Great Britain in the Year 1732* (London, 1786), 110.

54 LMA, DRO/17/B1/1: St Mary the Virgin Monken Hadley, Vestry Minute Book, 1794–1820, 13 January 1799.

55 For the use of the phrase 'parish uniform' at this period, see the rules for the new workhouse at Laleham, Middlesex, January 1805; LMA, DRO 21/64: All Saints Laleham, Vestry Minute Book, 1803–1848. Although some workhouses, like that at St Marylebone in London, had long followed the practice of reclothing inmates on entry, often for reasons of health, it was only at this period that visually distinctive uniforms began to proliferate, prefiguring the hated workhouse uniforms of the New Poor Law. At Laleham in 1805, significantly, the order that workhouse inmates should wear the parish uniform, consisting of clothes of the same colour for men and women, was combined with punishments for bad behaviour which included 'Distinction of Dress'.

56 Copy of the will of Richard Fountaine of Enfield, Middlesex, Esq., 1721, at Fountaine's Hospital, Linton-in-Craven, North Yorkshire; T. F. T. Baker (ed.), *History of the County of Middlesex*, 11 (1998), 83–6.

57 Cowe, *Wimbledon Vestry Minutes*, 2–11.

17 Involuntary Consumption? Servants

1 For examples of the range of criticism applied to servants' clothing in the period, see J. Jean Hecht, *The Domestic Servant Class in Eighteenth-Century England* (London, 1956), chapter 8; Anne Buck, *Dress in Eighteenth-Century England* (London, 1979), chapter 4; Anne Buck, 'The Dress of Domestic Servants in the Eighteenth Century', in *Strata of Society*, Proceedings of the Seventh Annual Conference of the Costume Society (London, 1973), 10–16.

2 Daniel Defoe, *Every-Body's Business, is No-Body's Business* (London, 1725), 4.

3 Anon., *Manufactures Improper Subjects of Taxation* (London, 1785), 12.

4 Defoe, *Every-Body's Business*, 13.

5 See the works referred to in note 1; Beverly Lemire, *Fashion's Favourite: The Cotton Trade and the Consumer in Britain, 1660–1800* (Oxford, 1992), 96; Neil McKendrick, John Brewer and J. H. Plumb, *The Birth of a Consumer Society* (London, 1982), 21–2, 60.

6 Neil McKendrick, 'The Commercialisation of Fashion', in McKendrick et al., *The Birth of a Consumer Society*, 60.

7 Ben Fine and Ellen Leopold, 'Consumerism and the Industrial Revolution', *Social History*, 15 (1990), 169. The same argument is restated in their *The World of Consumption* (London, 1993), 123–30. Similar lines of reasoning are developed in John Rule, *The Labouring Classes in Early Industrial England, 1750–1850* (London, 1986), 67, Pat Hudson, *The Industrial Revolution* (London, 1992), 178, and Carole Shammas, *Pre-Industrial Consumer in England and America* (Oxford, 1990), 210–4 (although see 293–4 for the view that the general trend after 1650 was away from payment in kind).

8 Hecht, *Domestic Servant Class*, 121–3.

9 Ann Kussmaul, *Servants in Husbandry in Early Modern England* (Cambridge, 1981), 31.

10 Patrick Colquhoun, *A Treatise on Indigence* (London, 1806), 253.

11 L. D. Schwarz, *London in the Age of Industrialisation: Entrepreneurs, Labour Force and Living Conditions, 1700–1850* (Cambridge, 1992), 11–18.

12 Peter Earle, 'The Female Labour Market in London in the Late Seventeenth and Early Eighteenth Centuries', *Economic History Review*, new series, 42 (1989), 328–53, esp. 342, note 39.

13 Kussmaul, *Servants in Husbandry*, 38–9. Also see

C. Stella Davies, *The Agricultural History of Cheshire, 1750–1850* (Manchester, 1960), 80.

14. See Hecht, *Domestic Servant Class*, 141–53, Kussmaul, *Servants in Husbandry*, 37, and Jane Holmes, 'Domestic Service in Yorkshire, 1650–1780' (DPhil dissertation, University of York, 1989), 74–84 and 163–9.

15. New clothes were occasionally provided to female servants as part of the hiring agreement, but this was unusual. Certain women servants might also have the right to at least some of their employers' cast-off clothes and it came to be regarded as customary for lady's maids to receive some of their mistress's clothing if she died. See Buck, 'The Dress of Domestic Servants', 12–14. However, bequests to maidservants in the wills of mainly the middling sort in three Yorkshire parishes between 1500 and 1650 were relatively few, appearing in only 11 percent of wills. Interestingly, female servants were much more likely to receive bequests of clothing than their male equivalents. See W. Coster, *Kinship and Inheritance in Early-Modern England* (York, 1993), 22.

16. George Birkbeck Hill (ed.), *Boswell's Life of Johnson*, 4 vols (Oxford, 1934), 2: 217.

17. Defoe, *Every-Body's Business*, 15.

18. WYAS (Bradford), B149, Heaton of Ponden MSS, account book of Robert Heaton, 1764–92. All the information on Heaton's servants used in the rest of this chapter derives from this account book, unless otherwise stated.

19. For Heaton's business see Eric Sigsworth, 'William Greenwood and Robert Heaton: Two Eighteenth-Century Worsted Manufacturers', *Journal of the Bradford Textile Society* (1951–2), 61–72.

20. All except two of the 30 live-in servants for whom detailed accounts survive were women. The two male exceptions both served for the same single year in 1774–5, when they worked alongside two female servants. The nature of these young men's duties is unclear, but they were probably industrial or agricultural. For particulars of their expenditure, see Chapter 13 above.

21. Holmes, 'Domestic Service in Yorkshire', 102 and 153–4.

22. Amanda Vickery, *The Gentleman's Daughter: Women's Lives in Georgian England* (London, 1998), 137. For Elizabeth Shackleton, the gentlewoman concerned, see below.

23. For Yorkshire see Holmes, 'Domestic Service in Yorkshire', 74–84; for Lancashire see Sir Frederick Eden, *The State of the Poor*, 3 vols (London, 1797), 2: 294, note 1.

24. The exception was Hannah Roberts, hired in 1770, who saved nearly half her wages, and spent most of the rest on visits to Keighley.

25. I have not included bedgowns in the category gown, as they were substantially cheaper than a full-length gown. Four servants bought items described as bedgowns, at an average price of just under 4s. Each of the four also bought at least one full-length gown.

26. These were the prices for the cloth from which the gown was made. Heaton often noted separately the cost of having the gown made up, which was an additional 1s. to 2s. The lower price of the worsted cloths is not a result of the servants buying wholesale from Heaton. Only three servants bought gowns made from the type of cloth Heaton was producing at the time.

27. Heaton's wording is ambiguous, but the servant concerned appears to have bought the camblet gown from Heaton's wife. It was not necessarily unusual for a servant to own a silk camblet gown. For example, in 1783, a red and yellow silk camblet gown was stolen from Elizabeth Beck, a servant to a husbandman at Newsham in the North Riding of Yorkshire, along with other relatively expensive possessions like a red painted handkerchief, a silk handkerchief, a pair of plated buckles and a muslin apron; PRO, ASSI 45/34/4/2–3: Yorkshire 1783, Jane Bell.

28. The average length of fabric for a gown mentioned in Heaton's accounts was seven yards, although the accounts specify the length only occasionally.

29. Natalie Rothstein (ed.), *Barbara Johnson's Album of Fashions and Fabrics* (London, 1987); Woodforde diaries quoted in Buck, *Eighteenth Century*, 177.

30. *London Magazine* (1783), 128–9.

31. Heaton used both terms, but, as was usual in the eighteenth century, there was no very clear distinction in his usage. Handkerchiefs and neckcloths were both worn round the neck.

32. Pumps were low-heeled shoes, slightly less expensive than other shoes, and were bought by only six servants, mainly in the 1770s.

33. Significantly, the few items described as old or otherwise identifiable as second-hand were mainly gowns and stays, the most expensive garments.

34. See Chapter 8 above.

35. *London Chronicle*, 15–17 February, 1791.

36 WYAS (Bradford), B 144: Account book of Heaton of Haworth, 1728–78, list of clothes, etc. in various drawers, in Robert Heaton's hand, 1763.
37 See Chapters 13 and 14 above.
38 For example, Margaret Edwards, confessing to the theft of table linen, a spoon and two silver buckles, in 1698 said she 'intended to dispose of the same to buy herself clothes to put herself into a service'. LMA, MJ/SP, Middlesex Sessions Papers, 1699 Jan/46–7, Margaret Edwards.
39 Charles P. Moritz, *Travels, Chiefly on Foot, through Several Parts of England, in 1782*, (London, 1795), 182.
40 WYAS (Bradford), A501, manuscript obituary of Robert Heaton.
41 Hampshire County RO, 96M82 PZ25, Account book of Mary Medhurst and Thomas North, drapers, 1762–81; University of London Library, MSS 625/3: account book of L. Cottchin and R. Flowers, grocer and draper, Westoning, Bedfordshire, labelled 'Servants Book'. It is not possible to reconstruct individual servant's clothes purchases as a whole from these books, because they must almost always have bought clothing from more than one supplier. For similar purchases of clothing accessories by the maids of the Paglesham, Essex oyster merchant, James Wissman, in the 1780s and 1790s, see Pamela Horn, *The Rise and Fall of the Victorian Servant* (Gloucester, 1986), 7–8.
42 For a discussion of this issue see Hecht, *Domestic Servant Class*, 121–2.
43 Lancashire RO, DDB/81/15: Parker of Brownsholme MSS, Nanny Nutter account book, 1772–5. For Elizabeth Shackleton's gifts to her servants, see Vickery, *Gentleman's Daughter*, 144–5, 184, 192.
44 Amanda Vickery, 'Women and the World of Goods: A Lancashire Consumer and her Possessions', in John Brewer and Roy Porter (eds), *Consumption and the World of Goods* (London, 1993), 247–301.
45 Cheshire RO, DDX 150 and 223: Copies of account books of Thomas Furber, of Austerson, near Nantwich, Cheshire, 1767–1796 and 1796–1820; W. B. Mercer, 'Thomas Furber: An Eighteenth-century Cheesemaker', *The Reaseheath Review: A Journal of Cheshire Agriculture*, 5 (1933), 5–14; Davies, *Agricultural History of Cheshire*, 80–2, 95–6.
46 Tim Meldrum, *Domestic Service and Gender, 1660–1750* (London, 2000), chapters 4 and 5.
47 Wiltshire and Swindon RO, A1/110: Wiltshire Quarter Sessions roll, Easter 1798. I would like to thank Gail Bancroft for bringing this reference to my attention.
48 Daniel Defoe, *The Great Law of Subordination Consider'd* (London, 1724), 84.
49 Female factory workers were widely criticised in the first half of the nineteenth century for excessive spending on clothes; see W. F. Neff, *Victorian Working Women* (New York, 1929), 51–5. For the elasticity of factory workers' spending on clothes in the 1820s see Francis Collier, *The Family Economy of the Working Classes in the Cotton Industry, 1784–1833* (Manchester, 1965), 40.
50 Defoe, *Great Law of Subordination*, 81.
51 Leonard Schwarz, 'English Servants and their Employers during the Eighteenth and Nineteenth Centuries', *Economic History Review*, new series, 52 (1999), 239–44.
52 Newspaper advertisements for runaways used the word livery to describe suits, coats, waistcoats and breeches.
53 See, for example, Hull University Archives, DDBH 24/6: Baines of Bell Hall, Servants' wages book, 1787–1874.
54 Hecht, *Domestic Servant Class*, 117–18 and Holmes, 'Domestic Service in Yorkshire', 90–2.
55 Hull University Archives, DDBH 24/6: Baines of Bell Hall, Servants' wages book, 1787–1874.
56 G. Eland (ed.), *The Purefoy Letters*, 2 vols (London, 1931), 2: 310.
57 *Worcester Postman*, 23 October 1719.
58 *Jackson's Oxford Journal*, 14 April 1764.
59 It was the increasingly fossilised, old-fashioned character of livery that probably lay behind the difficulty of selling it second-hand in Britain by the mid-nineteenth century. See Beverley Lemire, 'Consumerism in Preindustrial and Early Industrial England: The Trade in Secondhand Clothes', *Journal of British Studies*, 27 (1988), 17. Earlier it had been possible to make it appear more like ordinary clothing by removing distinguishing decorations.
60 OBP, September 1787, William Grant (t17870912-99).
61 Eland, *The Purefoy Letters*, 309; Suffolk RO (Ipswich), FE 1/28/27: Archdeaconry of Suffolk Probate Inventories, James Laing, Woodbridge, draper, 1744.
62 Eland, *The Purefoy Letters*, 302; for the Lathams, see Chapter 14 above.
63 Jonas Hanway, *Letters on the Importance of the Rising Generation of the Laboring Part of our Fellow-subjects*, 2 vols (London, 1767), 2: 173.
64 John Macdonald, *Travels in various Parts of Europe,*

     Asia, and Africa, during a Series of Thirty Years and Upwards (London, 1790), 288–9.
65 William Austin, *Letters from London written during the Years 1802 and 1803* (Boston, Mass., 1804), 274.
66 Hull University Archives, DDBH 24/6: Baines of Bell Hall, Servants' wages book, 1787–1874.
67 Vicesimus Knox, *Essays Moral and Literary*, 2 vols (London, 1782), 1: 303.
68 Macdonald, *Travels*, 152.
69 Macdonald, *Travels*., 293, 382–4.
70 OBP, Ordinary of Newgate's Account, October 1751, Robert Steel (oa17511023).
71 Holmes, 'Domestic Service in Yorkshire', 92; Hecht, *Domestic Servant Class*, 210.
72 *London Chronicle*, 12–15 Nov., 1757 and 24–27 Dec., 1757.
73 *Bristol Weekly Intelligencer*, 15 June 1751, quoted in Beverly Lemire, *Dress, Culture and Commerce: The English Clothing Trade before the Factory, 1660–1800* (London, 1997), 7.
74 PRO, C108/30: Chancery Masters Exhibits, letterbook of William Sayer, tailor, 1756–63, William Sayer to Abel Doltin, junior, Esq., English, near Nettlebed, Oxfordshire, 27 July 1756.
75 Huntington Library, MO 981: Elizabeth Robinson Montagu Collection, Montagu Papers, William Freind to Elizabeth Robinson, 1740.
76 Jack Ayres (ed.), *Paupers and Pig Killers: The Diary of William Holland, a Somerset Parson, 1799–1818* (Gloucester, 1984), 74.
77 Tim Knox, 'Enter a Footman in Plush Breeches', *Country Life*, 192, 10 (5 March 1998), 50–3.
78 James Peller Malcolm, *Anecdotes of the Manners and Customs of London during the Eighteenth Century* (London, 1808), 426–7.
79 OBP, Ordinary of Newgate's Account, October 1750, James Maclean (oa17501003).
80 OBP, May 1795, Robert Mansfield (t17950520–1).
81 Benjamin Silliman, *A Journal of Travels in England, Holland, and Scotland, and of Two Passages over the Atlantic, in the Years 1805 and 1806*, 2 vols (Boston, Mass., 1812), 1: 170.

18 Popular Fashion

1 OBP, April 1799, Susannah Priest (t17990403–30).
2 The reference here to Roland Barthes, *The Fashion System* (London, 1985) is deliberate, embracing the distinction Barthes suggests is fundamental to the fashion system in capitalist societies between the real garment and the garment as it is imagined or represented. It is, perhaps, more useful to conceive this as a three-fold distinction between, first, clothes as material objects in the process of manufacture, second, clothes as imagined objects that undergo a process of meaning-making through words and images in the course of their distribution and purchase, and, third, clothes as material objects that are worn after purchase. This chapter places less emphasis than Barthes on representation, and more on use.
3 PRO, ASSI 45/34/4/89: Cumberland 1783, William Gill.
4 PRO, ASSI 45/38/1/18–23A: Yorkshire 1793, Jane Boys.
5 OBP, April 1790, William Morse (t17900424–90).
6 OBP, December 1755, Jane Fowls (t17551204–46).
7 For a recent review of this literature that is admirably thoughtful and concise, perhaps because it is written by an outsider, see Ben Fine, 'Addressing the Consumer', in Frank Trentmann (ed.), *The Making of the Consumer: Knowledge, Power and Identity in the Modern World* (Oxford, 2006), 291–311.
8 Anthony Giddens, *Modernity and Self-Identity: Self and Society in the Late Modern Age* (London 1991), chapter 3.
9 The following discussion has benefited greatly from reading Mark Harvey, Andrew McMeekin, Sally Randles, Dale Southerton, Bruce Tether and Alan Warde, *Between Demand & Consumption: A Framework for Research*, ESRC Centre for Research on Innovation and Competition, Discussion Paper No. 40 (Manchester, 2001) and Alan Warde, 'Consumption and Theories of Practice', *Journal of Consumer Culture*, 5 (2005), 131–53.
10 For the use of the same distinction in sixteenth-century wills made principally by people of middling rank or below, see Jane E. Huggett, 'Rural Costume in Elizabethan Essex: A Study Based on the Evidence from Wills', *Costume*, 33 (1999), 75–6. For its use in eighteenth-century wills, see Maxine Berg, 'Women's Consumption and the Industrial Classes of Eighteenth-Century England', *Journal of Social History*, 30 (1996), 421. Another fundamental distinction, which is not explored here, was that between ordinary clothes and clothes worn for mourning. The presence of a number of crape gowns and black handkerchiefs among clothes stolen from or pawned by plebeian owners suggests that some were able to follow the sartorial conventions of mourning.

11 OBP, July 1786, William Robinson (t17860719-10).
12 OBP, September 1794, James Rainbow (t17940917-5).
13 OBP, May 1780, James Purse (t17800510-57).
14 OBP, October 1786, Edward Evans (t17861025-134).
15 OBP, January 1766, Brian Swinney (t17660116-2).
16 John Wardroper, *Lovers, Rakes and Rogues: A New Garner of Love-Songs and Merry Verses, 1580 to 1830* (London, 1995), 240.
17 For a useful discussion of some of these issues in early America, see Leigh Eric Schmidt, '"A Church-Going People are a Dress-Loving People": Clothes, Communication, and Religious Culture in Early America', *Church History*, 58 (1989), 36–51.
18 Jan Albers, 'Seeds of Contention: Society, Politics and the Church of England in Lancashire, 1689–1790' (PhD dissertation, Yale University, 1988), 134. Michael Snape has recently interpreted the evidence of the Lancashire visitation returns in a more pessimistic light, but, unlike Albers, he offers an impressionistic rather than a statistical reading; Michael Snape, *The Church of England in Industrialising Society: The Lancashire Parish of Whalley in the Eighteenth Century* (Woodbridge, 2003), 24 and 194. For a review of recent scholarship re-assessing the eighteenth-century established church, see Mark Goldie, 'Voluntary Anglicans', *The Historical Journal*, 46 (2003), 999–1004.
19 Quoted in Albers, 'Seeds of Contention', 139, although she points out that at least one clergyman, the curate of Peel, was more sceptical, reporting that 'I am persuaded it cannot be altogether owing to the want of Stockings and Shoes to come in, which is sometimes made a Plea for such Negligence', believing instead that their non-attendance was due to 'a thoughtless, careless Disposition'.
20 J. Howard Hudson, *Cheshire, 1660–1780: Restoration to Industrial Revolution* (Chester, 1978), 47.
21 Israel R. Potter, *The Life and Remarkable Adventures of Israel R. Potter* (Providence, R.I., 1824), 28.
22 [Arthur Young] 'A Farming Tour in the South and West of England, 1796; by the Editor', *Annals of Agriculture*, 28 (1797), 632.
23 After telling the Old Bailey in 1744 that, when he and his associates went thieving, 'some were dressed clean, and some were in a ragged dress', a London pickpocket was then asked: 'Did you make any difference between a Sunday, and a working-day?' He replied 'I never did.' OBP, December 1744, William Tarbutt (t17441205-49).
24 Essex RO, D/P 30/18: Witham overseers' miscellanea, / 1: Agreement between the Parish of Witham and John Darby for running the workhouse, 1790, and / 7: Orders for regulating the workhouse, 1726.
25 For Yorkshire, see WYAS (Wakefield), QS 1/72/3: 1733, Doncaster, printed apprenticeship indenture for Samuel Smith, 25 August 1725; also QS 1/75/9: 1736, Halifax, printed apprenticeship indenture for Michael Dyson, 23 December 1729. For Bedfordshire, see F. G. Emmison, 'The Relief of the Poor at Eaton Socon 1706–1834', *Publications of the Bedfordshire Historical Record Society*, 15 (1933), 69.
26 Jack Ayres (ed.), *Paupers and Pig Killers: The Diary of William Holland, a Somerset Parson, 1799–1818* (Gloucester, 1984), 19.
27 OBP, May 1780, James Purse (t17800510-57). Such dress codes were not unusual. The gate to a London tea garden shown in Henry Bunbury's 1772 satirical etching 'The Fish-Street Macaroni' displays the notice: 'THE NEW PARADISE NO GENTLEMAN OR LADIES to be admitted with NAILS in their SHOES. RECREATION AND ENTERTAINMENT at 6d. pr. HEAD,' British Museum, BMSat, 4713.
28 Alan G. Crosby (ed.), *The Family Records of Benjamin Shaw Mechanic of Dent, Dolphinholme and Preston, 1772–1841* (Stroud, 1991), 77.
29 Dorothy George, *London Life in the Eighteenth Century* (London, 1925), 419.
30 E. P. Thompson, 'Patrician Society, Plebeian Culture', *Journal of Social History*, 7 (1974), 393–4; Robert W. Malcolmson, *Popular Recreations in English Society, 1700–1850* (Cambridge, 1973), 13. More generally, see Ronald Hutton, *The Stations of the Sun: A History of the Ritual Year in Britain* (Oxford, 1996), esp. 426.
31 See, for example, John K. Walton and Robert Poole, 'The Lancashire Wakes in the Nineteenth Century', in Robert D. Storch (ed.), *Popular Culture and Custom in Nineteenth-Century England* (London, 1982), 100–24 and, more generally, Emma Griffin, *England's Revelry: A History of Popular Sports and Pastimes, 1660–1830* (Oxford, 2005).
32 Henry Bourne, *Antiquitates Vulgares; or the Antiquities of the Common People* (Newcastle, 1725), 225.
33 J. Churton Collins, *Voltaire, Montesquieu and*

34 John Cunningham, *Poems, Chiefly Pastoral* (London, 1766), 117.
35 Anon., 'Nelly the Milkmaid', printed by Thornton of Kenilworth, Warwickshire in an eighteenth-century or very early nineteenth-century typeface, Bodleian Library, Firth Collection, b.33 (47). See Roy Palmer, 'Some Warwickshire Ballads', *Warwickshire History*, 6 (1986), 152.
36 Anon., 'Holiday Song', printed and sold by J. Pitts, 14 Great Andrew Street, Seven Dials, London, in an eighteenth-century or very early nineteenth-century typeface, Bodleian Library, Johnson Ballads, 861. A 1794 London ballad on the same theme suggested that when the holidays were over, the fine clothes would have to be pawned. Anon., 'Whitsun Holidays', printed June 1794, sold at No. 42, Long Lane, London, Bodleian Library, Firth Collection, c.19 (147).
37 A. Pleat (ed.), *'The Most Dismal Times': William Rowbottom's Diary. Part 1. 1787–1799* (Oldham, 1996), 76; Oldham Local Studies and Archives, D-M54, Rowbottom Diaries, entries for 28 August 1802 and 30 August 1806.
38 Samuel Bamford, *The Autobiography of Samuel Bamford*, 1: *Early Days* (London, 1967), 150. Robert Poole dates the emergence of rush carts, which were peculiar to the cotton manufacturing districts in and around south-east Lancashire, to the years 1660 to 1720; Robert Poole, 'Wakes Holidays and Pleasure Fairs in the Lancashire Cotton District, c.1790–1890' (PhD dissertation, University of Lancaster, 1985), 59.
39 Cheshire RO, DDX 150: Copy of account book of Thomas Furber, of Austerson, near Nantwich, Cheshire, 1767–1796.
40 Bamford, *Early Days*, 222–5.
41 First published in this version about 1792; Iona and Peter Opie, *The Oxford Dictionary of Nursery Rhymes* (Oxford, 1997), 292–3.
42 John R. Gillis, *For Better or For Worse: British Marriages, 1600 to the Present* (Oxford, 1985), 30–3.
43 Dennis Brailsford, *A Taste for Diversions: Sport in Georgian England* (Cambridge, 1999), 149–53. Also see Daniel Lysons, *Collectanea: or, a Collection of Advertisements and Paragraphs from the Newspapers, relating to Various Subjects: Publick Exhibitions and Places of Amusement*, 5 vols (London, 1840), 4: 233–71.
44 Hertfordshire Archives and Local Studies, DE/X3/8: diary of John Carrington, 1805, entry for 15 April 1805.
45 John Goulstone, *The Summer Solstice Games: A Study of Early English Fertility Religion* (Bexleyheath, 1985), 32–7.
46 John Beresford (ed.), *Diary of a Country Parson: The Reverend James Woodforde*, 5 vols (London, 1924–31), 3: 24.
47 *Northampton Mercury*, 5 June 1721.
48 For publicans' promotion of events like organised races and competitions at popular festivals, see Brailsford, *Taste for Diversions*, 108–13. Arthur Young noted that in competitions involving Suffolk ploughmen, the prize for the straightest furrow was 'a hat, or pair of breeches, given by alehouse keepers, or subscribed among themselves'. Arthur Young, *General View of the Agriculture of the County of Suffolk* (London, 1797), 32.
49 Poole, 'Wakes Holidays and Pleasure Fairs', 97–8.
50 Robert Walmsley, *Peterloo: The Case Reopened* (Manchester, 1969), 252.
51 Brotherton Library, Leeds University, Special Collections, Quaker Records, B9: Rounton Women's Preparatory Meeting, Minute Book, 1762–94, f. 42. The Moravians also discouraged their members from attendance at fairs and feasts; Joyce Godber, *History of Bedfordshire, 1066–1888* (Bedford, 1969), 386.
52 Brotherton Library, Leeds University, Special Collections, Quaker Records, F4.2: Thirsk Women's Monthly Meeting, Minute Book, 1761–1801, f. 191.

Conclusion

1 See, for example, John Styles, 'Lodging at the Old Bailey: Lodgings and their Furnishing in Eighteenth-Century London', in John Styles and Amanda Vickery (eds), *Gender, Taste and Material Culture in Britain and North America, 1700–1830* (New Haven and London, 2006), 61–80.
2 OBP, September 1756, James Scott (t17560915-24).
3 See, for example, OBP, February 1797, John Smith (t17970215-30); OBP, April 1798, Moses Knott (t17980418-73); OBP, February 1798, Alexander Elder (t17930220-61).
4 Suffolk RO (Bury St Edmunds), FL 536/1/47: Brandon Parish, Brandon Fire, 'Estimation of the Goods and Chattles, Wearing Apparel, etc. destroyed and damaged by fire at Brandon in Suffolk on Thursday May the 14th 1789'.

5. Neil McKendrick, 'Home Demand and Economic Growth: A New View of the Role of Women and Children in the Industrial Revolution', in Neil McKendrick (ed.), *Historical Perspectives: Studies in English Thought and Society in Honour of J. H. Plumb* (Cambridge, 1975), 209.
6. Jack Ayres (ed.), *Paupers and Pig Killers: The Diary of William Holland, A Somerset Parson, 1799–1818* (Gloucester, 1984), 35–6.
7. Oldham Local Studies and Archives, D-M54: Rowbottom Diaries, entries for 28 and 29 August 1802 and 30 August 1806.
8. Archibald Prentice, *Historical Sketches and Personal Recollections of Manchester* (London, 1970), 159. I thank Robert Poole for bringing this point to my attention. Earlier, rush carts had sometimes been associated with the anti-radical politics of Paine burnings; see Samuel Bamford, *The Autobiography of Samuel Bamford*, I: *Early Days* (London, 1967), 44.
9. E. P. Thompson, *Customs in Common* (London, 1991), 14.
10. Hans Medick, 'Plebeian culture in the transition to capitalism', in Raphael Samuel and Gareth Stedman Jones (eds), *Culture, Ideology and Politics* (London, 1982), 89.
11. William Hutton, *The Life of Willam Hutton F.A.S.S.* (London, 1816), 30–1.
12. Hans-Joachim Voth, *Time and Work in England, 1750–1830* (Oxford, 2000), especially 118–33.
13. E. P. Thompson, *The Making of the English Working Class* (London, 1963), 318.
14. Thompson, *Making of the English Working Class*.
15. Oldham Local Studies and Archives, D-M54, Rowbottom Diaries, entry for January 1799.

Appendix 1

1. In interpreting written sources, three books have proved invaluable: C. Willett Cunnington and Phillis Cunnington, *Handbook of English Costume in the Eighteenth Century* (London, 1957), C. Willett Cunnington, Phillis Cunnington and Charles Beard, *A Dictionary of English Costume* (London, 1960), and Anne Buck, *Dress in Eighteenth-Century England* (London, 1979).
2. For the most sophisticated recent quantitative analysis of consumption using probate inventories, see Mark Overton et al., *Production and Consumption in English Households, 1600–1750* (London, 2004).
3. The probate accounts used by Margaret Spufford suffer from many of the same social and chronological limitations as probate inventories, and deal mainly with the clothing of children. See Margaret Spufford, 'The Cost of Apparel in Seventeenth-century England and the Accuracy of Gregory King', *Economic History Review*, new series, 53 (2000), 677–705 and 'Fabric for Seventeenth-Century Children and Adolescents' Clothes', *Textile History*, 34 (2003), 47–63.
4. The records of the criminal courts have been used previously to study eighteenth-century clothing, first by Madeleine Ginsburg and subsequently by Beverly Lemire, but neither used them quantitatively. See Madeleine Ginsburg, 'Rags to Riches: The Second-Hand Clothes Trade, 1700–1978', *Costume*, 14 (1980), 121–35 and Beverly Lemire, *Fashion's Favourite: The Cotton Trade and the Consumer in Britain, 1660–1800* (Oxford, 1991).
5. For an excellent overview of the whole prosecution process, see Peter King, *Crime, Justice and Discretion in England, 1740–1820* (Oxford, 2000).
6. PRO, ASSI 44/45–54, /65–74, /95–104: Assizes Northern Circuit indictments, 1730–9, 1750–9 and 1780–9; NYCRO, QSB/1630–39, /1750–9, /1780–99: North Riding of Yorkshire, Quarter Sessions Bundles, 1730–39, 1750–9, 1780–99; WYAS QS1/69–78, /89–97, /119–128: West Riding of Yorkshire, Quarter Session Rolls, 1680–99, 1730–9, 1750–9 and 1780–9.
7. 718 indictments survive for thefts of clothing from owners of all social backgrounds, which list 2,609 individual items of clothing.
8. LMA, OB/SR 1–8: Middlesex Gaol Delivery Rolls, 1756; OB/SR 233–4 and 236–7: Middlesex Gaol Delivery Rolls, 1785.
9. 233 indictments survive for thefts of clothing from owners of all social backgrounds, which list 1,140 individual items of clothing.
10. LMA, WJ/SR and MJ/SR: Westminster Sessions of the Peace, MJ/SR: Middlesex Sessions of the Peace. I would like to thank Norma Landau for allowing me to consult her survey of indictments and recognizances in the Middlesex and Westminster sessions records for selected years.
11. In addition, the typescript subject index to the Northern Circuit Depositions compiled by David Clark and James Cockburn and held at the Public Record Office allowed all cases of stolen watches to be surveyed from 1640 to 1799. The typescript calendars at NYCRO allowed all cloth and cloth-

ing cases to be surveyed from 1685 to 1736. PRO, ASSI 45/12/4–40/1: Northern Circuit Assizes, depositions, 1680–1799; NYCRO, QSB/1685–39, /1750–9, /1780–99: North Riding of Yorkshire, Quarter Sessions Bundles, 1685–39, 1750–9, 1780–99; WYAS QS1/19–37, /69–78, /89–97, /119–138: West Riding of Yorkshire, Quarter Session Rolls, 1680–99, 1730–9, 1750–9 and 1780–99.

12 LMA, MJ/SP 1690–9, Old Bailey Sessions Papers (Middlesex), 1690–9.
13 For this issue, see King, *Crime, Justice and Discretion*, 35–42.
14 PRO, ASSI 45/34/1/80–2: Yorkshire 1780, Margaret Shepherd; ASSI 44/95: Assizes Northeastern Circuit Indictments, Yorkshire Summer 1780, Margaret Shepherd.
15 For a comparison of the social profile of felony prosecutors in Essex with that of the county's population as a whole, see King, *Crime, Justice and Discretion*, 36. For cases where prosecution resulted from the refusal of pawnbrokers to return stolen goods to their owners, see OBP, December 1756, William Freeman (t17561208-8) and OBP, October 1756, Elizabeth Rivers (t17561020-50).
16 King, *Crime, Justice and Discretion*, chapter 3.
17 Newspaper advertisements for fugitives have not been used systematically in the study of plebeian clothing in eighteenth-century England, in contrast to colonial British North America where, unlike in England, black slaves and indentured white servants figured prominently among the runaways. For America, see, in particular, Jonathan Prude, 'To Look upon the "Lower Sort": Runaway Ads and the Appearance of Unfree Laborers in America, 1750–1800', *Journal of American History*, 78 (1991), 124–59 and David Waldstreicher, 'Reading the Runaways: Self-Fashioning, Print Culture and Confidence in Slavery in the Eighteenth-Century Mid-Atlantic', *William and Mary Quarterly*, third series, 56 (1999), 243–72. For a general assessment of eighteenth-century crime advertising in England, see John Styles, 'Print and Policing. Crime Advertising in Eighteenth-Century Provincial England', in Douglas Hay and Francis Snyder (eds), *Police and Prosecution in Britain in the Eighteenth and Nineteenth Centuries* (Oxford, 1989), 55–111.
18 King, *Crime, Justice and Discretion*, chapter 6.
19 For the kind of distinguishing physical features occasionally found in advertisements, see Gwenda Morgan and Peter Rushton, 'Visible Bodies: Power, Subordination and Identity in the Eighteenth-Century Atlantic World', *Journal of Social History*, 39 (2005), 39–64.
20 See Chapter 3.
21 This point is made in a number of the contributions to *Strata of Society* (Proceedings of the Seventh Annual Conference of the Costume Society, London, 1973).
22 For the Foundling Hospital, see Ruth K. McClure, *Coram's Children: The London Foundling Hospital in the Eighteenth Century* (London, 1981). For the foundling textiles, see Gillian Clarke, 'Infant Clothing in the Eighteenth Century: A New Insight', *Costume*, 28 (1994), 47–59.
23 LMA, A/FH/A/9/1/1–178, Foundling Hospital Billet Books, 1741–1760.
24 Florence Montgomery, *Textiles in America, 1650–1870* (London and New York, 1984) has been invaluable for this process of cross-referencing.
25 LMA, A/FH/A/9/1/1–18 and /125–64, Foundling Hospital Billet Books, 1741–56 and 1759.

Select Bibliography

MANUSCRIPTS AND ARCHIVAL SOURCES

Bedfordshire and Luton Archives and Record Service
M10/4/34: Williamson Muniments, correspondence, letters to Mary Williamson, 1775–8

Bristol Record Office
P/B/V/I/c: Bitton vestry order book, 1761–81

Birmingham City Archives
MC 21/37: Minute book of the Dorcasian Society, 1824–61

Borthwick Institute for Archives, University of York
Exchequer and Prerogative Courts of York, wills, 1689–1800
Dean and Chapter of York, wills, 1660–1800
Testamentary cause papers, 1700–99
Rom. 60: Romans Deeds, Appointment of overseer of the poor of Riccall, 29 April 1737

British Library, London
Add. MSS 27827: Francis Place collection
Add. MSS 45204, 45208, 45210: Household accounts kept by Ann Brockman, of Beachborough, Kent, 1701–24

British Museum, London
Banks Collection, D.2-4140 and D.2-4152: Handbills for James Mills and Co., 1789

Cheshire Record Office
DAR/B/14 and 20: Arderne Collection, Household accounts and vouchers of Sarah Arderne, 1741–52
DDX 150 and 223: Copies of account books of Thomas Furber, of Austerson, near Nantwich, Cheshire, 1767–96 and 1796–1820

Cumbria Record Office, Carlisle
DX1182/4: Diary of Jonathan Williamson, tailor of Haltcliffe, Cumberland, 1797–8
D/Sen: Bridget Hudleston and Humphrey Senhouse cash books, 1700–3 and 1709–20, and Senhouse rental and account book, 1762–82
PC/44/2/53: Dalton workhouse account book, 1746–75

Cumbria Record Office, Kendal
WD/AG/Box 31: Janson's charity, Kendal, 1712–98
WD/TE: Browne of Troutbeck MSS, Boxes 8/1/4 and 8/2/1-3
WPR 83/1: Hawkshead overseers' accounts, Hawkshead Quarter, 1691–1750
WPR 83/2: Hawkshead overseers' miscellaneous vouchers, 1749–1825

Devon Record Office
1249A/PO2-4: Overseers' payments for Holne, 1746–99 (transcribed by Brian Brassett at http://genuki.cs.ncl.ac.uk/DEV/Holne/Overseers/index.html, examined May 2005)

East Riding Archives Service
DDBD/87/17: Bird MSS, Account book of Thomas Hewson of Market Weighton, tailor, 1800–1

Essex Record Office
D/DZg/33: Correspondence to and from Mary Farrin and her husband, William White of Bulphan, Essex, 1744–91
D/P 16/12/2: Thaxted overseers' accounts, 1696–1716
D/P 30/18/1-7: Witham, overseers' miscellanea
D/P 119/8/3: Wethersfield vestry minutes, 1763–81
D/P 152/12/14: Theydon Garnon, overseers' bills and vouchers, 1685–1848

Fountaine's Hospital, Linton-in-Craven, Yorkshire
Copy of the will of Richard Fountaine of Enfield, Middlesex, Esq., 1721

Guildhall Library Archives, City of London
MS 2642/1: St Botolph Aldgate Vestry Minutes, 1730
MS 9174/46: Inventory of Joseph Gun, St Brides London, pawnbroker, 1727

Hampshire Record Office
96M82 PZ25: Account book of Mary Medhurst and Thomas North, drapers, 1762–81
Mansbridge, 8M62/8: Account Book of Robert Mansbridge of Basing, Hampshire, tailor, 1811–20

Hertfordshire Archives and Local Studies
DE/X3/1-13: Diaries of John Carrington, 1797–1810
DP/29/9/1: Cheshunt constables book, 1669–1785
DP/44/12/1: Much Hadham overseers' accounts, 1778–99
DP/116/5-12: Ware overseers' accounts, 1753–97

Huntington Library, San Marino, California
HM 31192: William Smedley's executors, account book of farm receipts and disbursements, Derbyshire, 1741–52
MO 981: Elizabeth Robinson Montagu Collection, 1740
MO 3450: Elizabeth Robinson Montagu Collection, 1778
Stowe, Grenville, Accounts, Box 169: General charity accounts, 1740s to 1860s

Centre for Kentish Studies, Maidstone
U 1823/35/A3: Daybook of a Maidstone draper, 1768–1773

Lancashire Record Office
DDB 7886: Parker of Brownsholme MSS, Wallet 7, no. 278, Miss Parker's dress bills
DDB/81/15: Parker of Brownsholme MSS, Nanny Nutter account book, 1772–5

The Record Office for Leicestershire, Leicester and Rutland
9D 51/ii/2 and 8: Papers of Samuel Deacon of Barton in the Beans, clockmaker and Baptist, 1806 and 1803

London Metropolitan Archives
A/FH/A/9/1/1-178: Foundling Hospital Billet Books, 1741–60
DRO/17/B1/1: St Mary the Virgin Monken Hadley, Vestry Minute Book, 1794–1820
DRO 21/64: All Saints Laleham, Vestry Minute Book, 1803–48
MJ/SP 1690-9: Old Bailey Sessions Papers (Middlesex), 1690–9
MJ/SR/1847: Old Bailey Gaol Delivery Rolls (Middlesex), 1695
MJ/SR/2629, 2647: Old Bailey Gaol Delivery Rolls (Middlesex), 1735

MJ/SR/2710: Old Bailey Gaol Delivery Rolls (Middlesex), 1745
OB/SR 1-8: Middlesex Gaol Delivery Rolls, 1756
OB/SR 233-4 and 236-7: Middlesex Gaol Delivery Rolls, 1785
P89/MRY 1/618: St Marylebone workhouse admissions register, 1769–72
P92/SAV/1412: Southwark, St Saviour, Account book and rental of Richard Bliss, Warden of the General Poor, 1697–8

National Archives, Public Record Office
ASSI 5/1-119: Assizes Oxford Circuit indictments, 1662–1799
ASSI 44/45-54, /65-74, /95-104: Assizes Northern Circuit indictments, 1730–9, 1750–9, 1780–9
ASSI 45/1/2-40/1: Assizes Northern Circuit depositions, 1640–1799
C108/30: Chancery Masters Exhibits, letterbook of William Sayer, tailor, 1756–63
E140/85/2: Exchequer Masters Exhibits, Smith v. Goater, 1745
PROB 32/67/129: Inventory of Samuel Dalling of Southwark, salesman, 1699
PROB 3/48/30: Inventory of Francis Shipley, St Mary's, Whitechapel, chandler, 1749

Northumberland Record Office
808/1: Account books and papers of Messrs. Dodds and Co., drapers of Alnwick, daybook of sales, 1790–1
1619/1: Account book of a tailor in North Tynedale, 1772–5

North Yorkshire County Record Office
QSB/1685-1739, /1750-9, /1780-99: North Riding of Yorkshire, Quarter Sessions Bundles, 1685–1739, 1750–9, 1780–99
Z.371: The weaver's guide. Linen designs of Ralph Watson of Aiskew, late eighteenth century

Oldham Local Studies and Archives
D-M54: Rowbottom diaries, 1787–1830

Oxfordshire Record Office
Leafield Parish, b1 and b2: Leafield overseers' accounts, 1740–62 and 1792–1811

Suffolk Record Office, Bury St Edmunds
FL 536/1/47: Brandon Parish, Brandon Fire, 'Estimation of the Goods and Chattles, Wearing Apparel, etc. destroyed and damaged by fire at Brandon in Suffolk on Thursday 14 May 1789'

Suffolk Record Office, Ipswich
FE 1/28/27: Archdeaconry of Suffolk Probate Inventories, James Laing, Woodbridge, draper, 1744
FL 668/13/1: Daybook of Short Smith, cordwainer, Wattisfield, Suffolk, 1797–1821
P616:8566: Account book of John Spore, shoemaker, Chediston, Suffolk, 1768–84

Surrey History Centre
Mortlake Parish Records, 2397/6/31: Workhouse accounts 1768–87

West Yorkshire Archive Service, Bradford
A501: Heaton of Ponden MSS, obituary of Robert Heaton
B144-9: Heaton of Ponden MSS, account books of Robert Heaton, 1764–92
33D80/6/7: Shop book of Stephen Hudson, of Fewston, 1751–9
SpSt 6/2/1/1: Spencer Stanhope MSS, Account book of Mary Warde, 1734–7
SpSt 6/2/1/2: Spencer Stanhope MSS, Household account books of the Stanhope family of Horsforth, 1734–88

West Yorkshire Archive Service, Kirklees
Mirfield township accounts, 1717–95

West Yorkshire Archive Service, Leeds
LO/M5: Leeds workhouse minutes, 1762–70
RDP17/84: Calverley parish officers' accounts, 1692–1822
RDP18/108-14: Carleton-in-Craven overseers' accounts, 1713–1841
RDP 96/71 and 75: Spofforth overseers' accounts, 1707–67 and 1767–1807

West Yorkshire Archive Service, Wakefield
QS1/19-37, /69-78, /89-97, /119-138, /160-164: West Riding of Yorkshire Quarter Sessions Rolls, 1680–99, 1730–9, 1750–9, 1780–99, 1821–5
QS4/16-91, /27–9, /31-3, /39-42, /55-8: West Riding of Yorkshire Quarter Sessions Indictment Books, 1690–9, 1730–9, 1750–9, 1780–9, 1821–5
QE 15: Convictions for false reeling of worsted yarn, 1777–1800
WDP 14/5/1-2: Thornhill township books, 1673–1801

Wiltshire and Swindon Record Office
A1/110: Wiltshire Quarter Sessions Rolls, Easter 1798

Worcestershire Record Office
Worcestershire Quarter Sessions, 1811

University College of North Wales, Bangor, Department of Manuscripts
MS 82: Penmorfa, Caernarvonshire, shop ledger, c.1788–c.1803

University of Hull, Hull University Archives
DDBH 24/6: Baines of Bell Hall, Servants' wages book, 1787–1874
DDCA (2)48/1-19: Stapleton of Carlton MSS, Household account books of Sir Miles Stapleton, 1656–1705

University of Leeds, Brotherton Library, Special Collections, Quaker Records
A21: Knaresborough Women's Monthly Meeting, Minute Book, 1694–1723
A23: Knaresborough Women's Monthly Meeting, Minute Book, 1747–84
B9: Rounton Women's Preparatory Meeting, Minute Book, 1762–94
F4.2: Thirsk Women's Monthly Meeting, Minute Book, 1761–1801
R1: Brighouse Monthly Meeting, Minute Book, 1797–1804

University of London, Senate House Library, Manuscripts
MS 625: Account books of L. Cottchin and R. Flowers, grocers and drapers, Westoning, Bedfordshire, 1785–1800

Walsall Local History Centre
'The Life and Times of James Gee of Walsall, 1746–1827', unpaginated typescript

York City Archives
Accession 38: Pledge book of George Fettes, pawnbroker, York, 1777–8
PR/Y/M/Bp.S/22: St Mary Bishophill, overseers' accounts, 1759–89

Yorkshire Archaeological Society
DD 121/91/4: Skipton Castle MSS

Select Bibliography

PRIMARY SOURCE WEBSITES

Old Bailey Online, www.oldbaileyonline.org

PRINTED WORKS BEFORE 1850

A Country Farmer, *Cursory Remarks on Inclosures* (London, 1786)
A Friend of the Poor, *Thoughts on the Use of Machines in the Cotton Manufacture* (Manchester, 1780)
Thomas Andrews, *An Enquiry into the Causes of the Encrease and Miseries of the Poor of England* (London, 1738)
Anon., *Account of Workhouses in Great Britain in the Year 1732* (London, 1786)
Anon., *An Address to the P-t, in Behalf of the Starving Multitude* (London, 1766)
Anon., *An Apology for the Ministerial Life and Actions of a Celebrated Favourite* (London, 1766)
Anon., *A Further Examination of the Weavers Pretences* (London, 1719)
Anon., *Considerations on Taxes: As they are Supposed to Affect the Price of Labour and our Manufactures* (London, 1765)
Anon., *First Report of the Liverpool Dorcas Society* (Liverpool, 1818)
Anon., 'Holiday Song,' (London, n.d.), Johnson Ballads, Bodleian Library, Oxford
Anon., 'The Humours of Rag Fair, or the Countryman's Description of their several Trades and Callings,' (n.d.), Harding Collection, Bodleian Library, Oxford
Anon., *Instructions for Cutting out Apparel for the Poor; Principally Intended for the Assistance of the Patronesses of Sunday Schools, and other Charitable Institutions* (London, 1789)
Anon., *Low-Life: Or One Half of the World Knows not how the Other Half Live* (London, 1764)
Anon., *Manufactures Improper Subjects of Taxation* (London, 1785)
Anon., 'My Old Hat' (Ledbury, n.d.), Madden Collection of Ballads, Cambridge University Library
Anon., 'Nelly the Milkmaid' (Kenilworth, n.d.), Firth Collection, Bodleian Library Oxford
Anon., *Proceedings of the Committee Appointed to Manage the Contributions begun at London Dec. 18, 1759 for Cloathing French Prisoners of War* (London, 1760)
Anon., *Tenth Report of the Liverpool Dorcas and Spinning Society* (Liverpool, 1827)
Anon., *The Case of the Linnen Drapers and other Dealers in Printed Callicoes and Linnens* (?London, 1711)
Anon., *The Fifth Annual Report of the Ladies' Benevolent Society, Liverpool, Instituted, January 1810* (Liverpool, 1815)
Anon, 'The New-Fashioned Farmer', (n.d.), Madden Collection of Ballads, Cambridge University Library
Anon., *The Reports of the Society for Bettering the Condition and Increasing the Comforts of the Poor*, 4 vols (London, 1798)
Anon., *The Trade of England Revived* (London, 1681)
Anon., 'Whitsun Holidays' (London, 1794), Firth Collection, c.19 (147), Bodleian Library, Oxford
Johann Wilhelm von Archenholz, *A Picture of England: Containing a Description of the Laws, Customs and Manners of England*, 2 vols (London, 1789)
William Austin, *Letters from London written during the Years 1802 and 1803* (Boston, Mass., 1804)
Nathan Bailey, *An Universal Etymological English Dictionary* (London, 1733)
J. Bailey and G. Culley, *General View of the Agriculture of the County of Westmorland* (Newcastle, 1797)
Robert Barclay, *An Apology For the True Christian Divinity, As the same is held forth, and preached by the People, Called, in Scorn, Quakers* (London, 1678)

Thomas Bernard, 'Extract from an Account of the Late Improvements in the House of Industry, at Dublin', *The Reports of the Society for Bettering the Condition and Increasing the Comforts of the Poor*, 4 vols (London, 1798–1800), 2: 99–107

Jean Bernard Le Blanc, *Letters on the English and French Nations*, 2 vols (London, 1747)

Madame du Boccage, *Letters Concerning England, Holland and Italy*, 2 vols (London, 1770)

Henry Bourne, *Antiquitates Vulgares; or the Antiquities of the Common People* (Newcastle, 1725)

James Brome, *Travels over England, Scotland and Wales* (London, 1700)

R. Campbell, *The London Tradesman* (London, 1747)

J. H. Campboll, 'Answers to Queries Relating to the Agriculture of Lancashire', *Annals of Agriculture*, 20 (1793), 109–53

Rev. D. Capper, *Practical Results of the Workhouse System, as Adopted in the Parish of Great Missenden, Bucks., during the Year 1833–4*, second edition (London, 1834)

George Symes Catcott, *A Descriptive Account of a Descent Made into Penpark-Hole, in the Parish of Westbury-upon-Trim, in the County of Gloucester, in the Year 1775* (Bristol, 1792)

Edward Chamberlayne, *Angliae Notitia: or the Present State of England* (London, 1704)

John Claridge, *General View of the Agriculture of the County of Dorset* (London, 1793)

Edward Daniel Clarke, *A Tour through the South of England, Wales and Part of Ireland, Made during the Summer of 1791* (London, 1793)

Patrick Colquhoun, *A Treatise on Indigence* (London, 1806)

John Cunningham, *Poems, Chiefly Pastoral* (London, 1766)

William Darrell, *A Gentleman Instructed in the Conduct of a Virtuous and Happy Life* (London, 1704)

David Davies, *The Case of the Labourers in Husbandry* (London, 1795)

[Daniel Defoe], *The Female Manufacturers Complaint: Being the Humble Petition of Dorothy Distaff, Abigail Spinning-Wheel, Eleanor Reel, &c. Spinsters* (London, 1720)

Daniel Defoe, *The Great Law of Subordination Consider'd* (London, 1724)

Daniel Defoe, *Every-body's Business, is No-body's Business* (London, 1725)

Daniel Defoe, *The Complete English Tradesman, in Familiar Letters* (London, 1726)

Daniel Defoe, *A Brief Deduction of the Original, Progress, and Immense Greatness of the British Woollen Manufacture* (London, 1727)

Daniel Defoe, *A Plan of the English Commerce* (London, 1728)

Sir Frederick Eden, *The State of the Poor*, 3 vols (London, 1795)

'J.F.', *The Merchant's Warehouse Laid Open or the Plain Dealing Linen Draper* (London, 1696)

William Falconer, *An Universal Dictionary of the Marine* (London, 1769)

Ralph Farmer, *The Lord Cravens Case Stated* (London, 1660)

George Fox, *A Collection of Many Select and Christian Epistles, Letters and Testimonies*, 2 vols (London, 1698)

William Green, *Plans of Economy; or A Guide to Riches and Independence* (London, 1800)

John Faucheraud Grimke, *The Public Laws of the State of South-Carolina* (Philadelphia, 1790)

James Guthrie, *The Ordinary of Newgate, his Account of the Behaviour, Confession, and Dying Words, of the Malefactors, who were executed at Tyburn, on Wednesday the 16th of September 1741* (London, 1741)

Fayrer Hall, *The Importance of the British Plantations in America to this Kingdom* (London, 1731)

Jonas Hanway, *Letters on the Importance of the Rising Generation of the Laboring Part of our Fellow-Subjects*, 2 vols (London, 1767)

Eliza Haywood, *Epistles for the Ladies*, 2 vols (London, 1749–50)

John Holroyd, Earl of Sheffield, *Observations on the Commerce of the American States* (London, 1784)

Andrew Hooke, *An Essay on the National Debt, and National Capital* (London, 1750)

John Housman, *A Topographical Description of Cumberland, Westmorland, Lancashire and a part of the West Riding of Yorkshire* (Carlisle, 1800)

Esther Hewlett, *Cottage Comforts with Hints for Promoting them Gleaned from Experience, Enlivened with Anecdotes* (London, 1825)
John Hustler, *The Occasion of the Dearness of Provisions, and the Distress of the Poor* (London, 1767)
William Hutchinson, *The History and Antiquities of Cumberland*, 2 vols (Carlisle, 1794)
William Hutton, *An History of Birmingham* (Birmingham, 1783)
William Hutton, *The Life of William Hutton F.A.S.S.* (London, 1816)
Thomas Jackson (ed.), *The Journal of the Rev. Charles Wesley*, 2 vols (London, 1849)
Samuel Johnson, *A Journey to the Western Islands of Scotland* (London, 1775)
Thomas Jones, *Clothing Societies* (Northampton, 1822)
Vicesimus Knox, *Essays Moral and Literary*, 2 vols (London, 1782)
James Lackington, *Memoirs of the Forty-five First Years of the Life of James Lackington* (London, 1794)
Rev. Francis Lichfield, *Three Years' Results of the Farthinghoe Clothing Society* (Northampton, 1832)
Richard Ligon, *A True and Exact History of the Island of Barbadoes* (London, 1673)
Daniel Lysons, *Collectanea: or, a Collection of Advertisements and Paragraphs from the Newspapers, relating to Various Subjects: Public Exhibitions and Places of Amusement*, 5 vols (London, 1840)
John Macdonald, *Travels in various Parts of Europe, Asia, and Africa, during a Series of Thirty Years and Upwards* (London, 1790)
David MacPherson, *Annals of Commerce, Manufactures, Fisheries and Navigation*, 4 vols (Edinburgh, 1805)
James Peller Malcolm, *Anecdotes of the Manners and Customs of London during the Eighteenth Century* (London, 1808)
Bernard Mandeville, *The Fable of the Bees; or, Private Vices Publick Benefits* (London, 1714)
Henri Misson, *M. Misson's Memoirs and Observations in his Travels over England*, transl. John Ozell (London, 1719)
[Hannah More], *The Shepherd of Salisbury Plain*, 2 vols (London, 1795)
Mrs Morgan, *A Tour to Milford Haven in the Year 1791* (London, 1795)
Charles P. Moritz, *Travels, Chiefly on Foot, through Several Parts of England, in 1782* (London, 1795)
James Nayler, *The Lambs Warre Against the Man of Sinne* (London, 1658)
George Parker, *A View of Society and Manners in High and Low Life; Being the Adventures in England, Ireland, Scotland, Wales, France &c. of Mr G. Parker. In which is Comprised a History of the Stage Itinerant*, 2 vols (London, 1781)
W. Parson and W. White, *History, Directory and Gazetteer of the Counties of Cumberland and Westmorland* (Leeds, 1829)
Thomas Pennant, *A Journey from London to the Isle of White*, 2 vols (London, 1801)
J. Pilkington, *A View of the Present State of Derbyshire*, 2 vols (Derby, 1789)
W. Pitt, *General View of the Agriculture of the County of Stafford* (London, 1794)
J. Plymley, *General View of the Agriculture of Shropshire* (London, 1803)
John Pollexfen, *A Discourse of Trade and Coyn* (London, 1700)
Israel R. Potter, *The Life and Remarkable Adventures of Israel R. Potter* (Providence, R. I., 1824)
Woodes Rogers, *A Cruising Voyage round the World* (London, 1718)
'T.S.', *England's Danger by Indian Manufactures* (?London, 1701)
Mary Saxby, *Memoirs of a Female Vagrant Written by Herself* (London, 1806)
William Sheldrake, *A Picturesque Description of Turton Fair, and its Pernicious Consequences: A Poem* (Bolton, 1789)
Benjamin Silliman, *A Journal of Travels in England, Holland, and Scotland, and of Two Passages over the Atlantic, in the Years 1805 and 1806*, 2 vols (Boston, Mass., 1812)
Alexander Smith, *The History of the Lives of the Most Notorious Highway-men, Foot-pads, Housebreakers, Shop-lifts, and Cheats* (London, 1714)
Charlotte Smith, *The Old Manor House* (London, 1793)

John Smith, *The Necessity, Advantages, and Amiableness of Beneficence: A Sermon Preached in the Parish Church of Bury, In the County of Lancaster, on Sunday, September 29, 1765* (Manchester, 1766)

[Simon Smith], *The Golden Fleece: Or the Trade, Interest, and Well-Being of Great Britain Considered* (London, 1736)

Society for Charitable Purposes, *The governors of the Society for Charitable Purposes think it their duty to give the following general view of the manner in which the fund has been applied* (London, 1774)

John, Lord Somerville, *The System Followed during the Two Last Years by the Board of Agriculture Further Illustrated* (London, 1800)

H. E. Strickland, *A General View of the Agriculture of the East Riding of Yorkshire* (York, 1812)

Mrs [Sarah] Trimmer, *The Oeconomy of Charity* (London, 1787)

Mrs [Sarah] Trimmer, *The Two Farmers: An Exemplary Tale* (London, 1787)

Mrs [Sarah] Trimmer, *The Oeconomy of Charity*, 2 vols (London, 1801)

Thomas Trotter, *Medicina Nautica*, 2 vols (London, 1797)

The Universal British Directory of Trade, Commerce and Manufacture, 4 vols, (London, 1793)

Jacob Vanderlint, *Money Answers all Things: Or, An Essay to Make Money Sufficiently Plentiful Amongst all Ranks of People* (London, 1734)

[Edward Ward], *The London-Spy Compleat* (London, 1703)

Rev. Richard Warner, *A Walk through Wales in August 1797* (Bath, 1799)

Rev. Richard Warner, *A Tour through Cornwall in the Autumn of 1808* (Bath, 1809)

Isaac Watts, *An Essay towards the encouragement of Charity Schools* (1728) in *The works of the Rev. Isaac Watts, D.D., in Seven Volumes*, 7 vols (Leeds, n.d.)

Friedrich August Wendeborn, *A View of England towards the Close of the Eighteenth Century*, 2 vols (London, 1791)

John Wesley, *Advice to the People Called Methodists, with Regard to Dress* (London, 1780)

John Wesley, *Instructions for Christians* (London, 1791)

Thomas West, *The Antiquities of Furness* (London, 1774)

Gilbert White, *The Natural History and Antiquities of Selborne* (London, 1789)

Henry Wigstead, *Remarks on a Tour to North and South Wales in the Year 1797* (London, 1799)

W. Williamson, *The Trials at Large of the Felons in the Castle of York at the Lent Assizes, 1777* (York, 1777)

Arthur Young, *The Farmer's Letters to the People of England* (London, 1768)

Arthur Young, *A Tour in Ireland: with General Observations on the Present State of that Kingdom. Made in the Years 1776, 1777, and 1778*, 2 vols (Dublin, 1780)

Arthur Young, *General View of the Agriculture of the County of Suffolk* (London, 1794)

[Arthur Young], 'A Farming Tour in the South and West of England, 1796; by the Editor', *Annals of Agriculture*, 28 (1797), 620–40

Arthur Young, *General View of the Agriculture of the County of Lincolnshire* (London, 1813)

NEWSPAPERS AND PERIODICALS BEFORE 1850

Berrow's Worcester Journal, 1782–7
Jackson's Oxford Journal, 1753–1800
Annual Register, or a View of the History, Politicks, and Literature, of the Year 1761
European Magazine and London Review, 1784
Exeter Mercury, 1763–1800
Gentleman's Magazine, 1731–1801
Leeds Intelligencer, 1754–89
Leeds Mercury, 1739–45, 1749, 1789–99
London Chronicle, 1757 and 1791
London Evening Post, 1756–7
London Magazine, 1783
Manchester Mercury, 1786
Northampton Mercury, 1721
Norwich Mercury, 1758
Nottingham Review, 1816
Philanthropist, 1819
The Times, 1785–1810
Weekly Worcester Journal, 1736–80
Worcester Herald, 1794
Worcester Postman, 1714–23

PARLIAMENTARY PAPERS

House of Commons Sessional Papers, vol. 6 (1817), Report from the Committee on the Petitions of Watchmakers of Coventry, etc., 11 July 1817
House of Commons Sessional Papers, vol. 28 (1834), Reports from Commissioners on the Poor Laws, Appendix A, Assistant Commissioners' Reports, Part 1

PRINTED WORKS AFTER 1850

Robert C. Allen, 'The Great Divergence in European Wages and Prices from the Middle Ages to the First World War', *Explorations in Economic History*, 38 (2001), 411–47
Donna Andrew, *Philanthropy and Police: London Charity in the Eighteenth Century* (Oxford, 1989)
Donna Andrew, 'Noblesse Oblige. Female Charity in an Age of Sentiment', in John Brewer and Susan Staves (eds), *Early Modern Conceptions of Property* (London, 1995), 275–300
C. Bruyn Andrews (ed.), *The Torrington Diaries*, 4 vols (London, 1934–8)
Anon., *Per una Storia della Moda Pronta* (Florence, 1990)
Janet Arnold, 'The Dressmaker's Craft', in *Strata of Society* (Proceedings of the Seventh Annual Conference of the Costume Society, London, 1974), 29–40
Loraine Ashcroft, *Vital Statistics. The Westmorland 'Census' of 1787* (Kendal, 1992)
T. S. Ashton, *Economic Fluctuations in England, 1700–1800* (London, 1959)
Jack Ayres (ed.), *Paupers and Pig Killers: The Diary of William Holland, a Somerset Parson, 1799–1818* (Gloucester, 1984)
A. V. Venkatarama Ayyar (ed.), *Records of Fort St George. Despatches from England, 1686–1692* (Madras, 1929)
Alison Backhouse, *The Worm-Eaten Waistcoat* (York, 2003)

Iain Bain (ed.), *A Memoir of Thomas Bewick Written by Himself* (Oxford, 1979)

T. F. T. Baker (ed.), *History of the County of Middlesex*, 11 (1998)

Samuel Bamford, *The Autobiography of Samuel Bamford, Vol. 1: Early Days* (London, 1967)

Eve Tavor Bannet, 'The Bluestocking Sisters: Women's Patronage, Millennium Hall, and "The Visible Providence of a Country"', *Eighteenth-Century Life*, 30 (2005), 25–55

T. Worthington Barlow (ed.), *The Cheshire and Lancashire Historical Collector*, 2 (May, 1853)

John Barrell, *The Dark Side of the Landscape: The Rural Poor in English Painting, 1730–1840* (Cambridge, 1980)

Sam Barrett, 'Kinship, poor relief and the welfare process in early modern England', in Steven King and Alannah Tomkins (eds), *The Poor in England, 1700–1850: An Economy of Makeshifts* (Manchester, 2003), 199–227

Roland Barthes, *The Fashion System* (London, 1985)

John E. Basham, *Brandon 1789: A Village Fire* (Ipswich, 1986)

Jennie Batchelor, *Dress, Distress and Desire: Clothing and the Female Body in Eighteenth-Century Literature* (London, 2005)

Linda Baumgarten, *What Clothes Reveal: The Language of Clothing in Colonial and Federal America* (Williamsburg, Virginia, 2003)

A. L. Beier and Roger Finlay (eds), *London, 1500–1700: The Making of the Metropolis* (London, 1986)

John Beresford (ed.), *Diary of a Country Parson: the Reverend James Woodforde*, 5 vols (London, 1924–31)

Maxine Berg, 'Markets, Trade and European Manufacture', in Maxine Berg (ed.), *Markets and Manufacture in Early Industrial Europe* (London, 1991), 3–26

Maxine Berg, 'Women's Consumption and the Industrial Classes of Eighteenth-Century England', *Journal of Social History*, 30 (1996), 415–34

Maxine Berg, 'Consumption in Eighteenth- and Early Nineteenth-Century Britain', in Roderick Floud and Paul Johnson, *The Cambridge Economic History of Modern Britain*, vol. 1: *Industrialization, 1700–1860* (Cambridge, 2004), 357–87

Peter Bicknell, *The Picturesque Scenery of the Lake District* (Winchester, 1990)

Robert Blake, *George Stubbs and the Wide Creation: Animals, People and Places in the Life of George Stubbs, 1724–1806* (London, 2005)

R. W. Blencowe (ed.), 'Extracts from the journal and account book of Timothy Burrell . . . from 1683 to 1714', *Sussex Archaeological Collections*, 3 (1850), 117–72

Pierre Bourdieu, *Distinction: A Social Critique of the Judgement of Taste* (London, 1984)

Sue Bowden and Avner Offer, 'Household Appliances and the Use of Time: The United States and Britain since the 1920s', *Economic History Review*, new series, 47 (1994), 725–48

Dennis Brailsford, *A Taste for Diversions: Sport in Georgian England* (Cambridge, 1999)

Paul Brassley, Anthony Lambert and Philip Saunders (eds), *Accounts of the Reverend John Crakanthorp of Fowlmere, 1682–1710* (Cambridge, 1988)

Asa Briggs (ed.), *How They Lived*, 3 vols (Oxford, 1969)

Liam Brunt, 'The Advent of the Sample Survey in the Social Sciences', *Journal of the Royal Statistical Society: Series D*, 50 (2001), 179–89

Anne Buck, 'The Countryman's Smock', *Folk Life*, 1 (1963), 16–34

Anne Buck, 'Variations in English Women's Dress in the Eighteenth Century', *Folk Life*, 9 (1971), 5–28

Anne Buck, 'The Dress of Domestic Servants in the Eighteenth Century', in *Strata of Society*, Proceedings of the Seventh Annual Conference of the Costume Society (London, 1973), 10–16

Anne Buck, *Dress in Eighteenth-Century England* (London, 1979)

Anne Buck, 'Buying Clothes in Bedfordshire: Customers and Tradesmen, 1700–1800', *Textile History*, 22 (1991), 211–38

Anne Buck, 'Mantuamakers and Milliners: Women Making and Selling Clothes in Eighteenth Century Bedfordshire', *Bedfordshire Historical Miscellany: Essays in Honour of Patricia Bell* (Bedford, 1993), 142–55

M. C. Buer, *Health, Wealth and Population in the Early Days of the Industrial Revolution* (London, 1926)

K. H. Burley, 'A Note on a Labour Dispute in Early Eighteenth-century Colchester', *Bulletin of the Institute of Historical Research*, 29 (1956), 220–30

Colin Campbell, 'The Meaning of Objects and the Meaning of Actions: A Critical Note on the Sociology of Consumption and Theories of Clothing', *Journal of Material Culture*, 1 (1996), 93–105

James Joel Cartwright (ed.), *The Travels through England of Dr Richard Pococke*, 2 vols (London, 1888)

J. D. Chambers, *Population, Economy, and Society in Pre-Industrial England* (Oxford, 1972)

Stanley Chapman, 'The Innovating Entrepreneurs in the British Ready-Made Clothing Industry', *Textile History*, 24 (1993), 5–25

J. A. Chartres, 'Food Consumption and Internal Trade', in A. L. Beier and Roger Finlay (eds), *London, 1500–1700: The Making of the Metropolis* (London, 1986), 168–96

K. N. Chaudhuri, *The English East India Company: A Study of an Early Joint Stock Company, 1600–1640* (London, 1965)

Gregory Claeys, 'The Origins of the Rights of Labor: Republicanism, Commerce, and the Construction of Modern Social Theory in Britain, 1796–1805', *Journal of Modern History*, 66 (1994), 249–90

J. H. Clapham, *An Economic History of Modern Britain: The Early Railway Age, 1820–1850* (Cambridge, 1930)

Alison Clark and Daniel Miller, 'Fashion and Anxiety', *Fashion Theory*, 6 (2002), 191–214

Anna Clark, *The Struggle for the Breeches: Gender and the Making of the British Working Class* (London, 1995)

Mrs Godfrey Clark (ed.), *Gleanings from an Old Portfolio, Containing some Correspondence between Lady Louisa Stuart and her Sister Caroline, Countess of Portarlington, and other Friends and Relations*, 3 vols (Edinburgh, 1895–8)

Peter Clark, *British Clubs and Societies: The Origins of an Associational World* (Oxford, 2000)

Gillian Clarke, 'Infant Clothing in the Eighteenth Century: A New Insight', *Costume*, 28 (1994), 47–59

A. W. Coats, 'Changing Attitudes to Labour in the Mid-Eighteenth Century', *Economic History Review*, new series, 11 (1958), 35–51

William Cobbett, *Rural Rides*, ed. Ian Dyck (London, 2001)

Frances Collier, *The Family Economy of the Working Classes in the Cotton Industry, 1784–1833* (Manchester, 1965)

J. Churton Collins, *Voltaire, Montesquieu and Rousseau in England* (London, 1908)

Alan B. Coolins, *Finchley Vestry Minutes, 1768 to 1840*, part 1 (London, 1957)

P. J. Corfield, *The Impact of English Towns, 1700–1800* (Oxford, 1982)

Penelope J. Corfield, 'Dress for Deference and Dissent: Hats and the Decline of Hat Honour', *Costume*, 23 (1989), 64–79

David Corner, 'The Tyranny of Fashion: The Case of the Felt-Hatting Trade in the Late Seventeenth and Eighteenth Centuries', *Textile History*, 22 (1991), 153–78

W. Coster, *Kinship and Inheritance in Early Modern England: Three Yorkshire Parishes* (York, 1993)

F. M. Cowe (ed.), *Wimbledon Vestry Minutes, 1736, 1743–1788* (Guilford, Surrey Record Society, vol. 25, 1964)

Nancy Cox, *The Complete Tradesman: A Study of Retailing, 1550–1820* (Aldershot, 2000)

Basil Cozens-Hardy (ed.), *The Diary of Sylas Neville, 1767–1788* (London, 1950)
Basil Cozens-Hardy (ed.), *Mary Hardy's Diary* (Norwich, Norfolk Record Society vol.37, 1968)
Alan G. Crosby (ed.), *The Family Records of Benjamin Shaw Mechanic of Dent, Dolphinholme and Preston, 1772–1841* (Stroud, 1991)
Shani D'Cruze, 'Care, Diligence and "Usfull Pride" [sic]: Gender, Industrialisation and the Domestic Economy, c.1770 to c.1840', *Women's History Review*, 3 (1994), 315–46
C. Willett Cunnington and Phillis Cunnington, *Handbook of English Costume in the Eighteenth Century* (London, 1957)
C. Willett Cunnington, Phillis Cunnington and Charles Beard, *A Dictionary of English Costume* (London, 1960)
Phillis Cunnington and Catherine Lucas, *Occupational Costume in England from the Eleventh Century to 1914* (London, 1967)
Phillis Cunnington and Catherine Lewis, *Charity Costumes* (London, 1978)
Maxwell Cutmore, *The Pocket Watch Handbook* (London, 1985)
Catherine Davidson, *A Woman's Work is Never Done: A History of Housework in the British Isles, 1650–1950* (London, 1982)
C. Stella Davies, *The Agricultural History of Cheshire, 1750–1850* (Manchester, 1960).
H. Dodwell (ed.), *Records of Fort St George: Despatches from England, 1681–1686* (Madras, 1916).
Moira Donald, '"The Greatest Necessity for Every Rank of Men": Gender, Clocks and Watches', in Moira Donald and Linda Hurcombe (eds), *Gender and Material Culture in Historical Perspective* (Basingstoke, 2000), 54–75.
W. Douglas, 'Cotton Textiles in England: the East India Company's Attempt to Exploit Developments in Fashion, 1660–1721', *Journal of British Studies*, 8 (1968), 28–43.
Mairead Dunlevy, *Dress in Ireland* (Cork, 1999).
Ian Dyck, *William Cobbett and Rural Popular Culture* (Cambridge, 1992).
R. Dyson, 'The Experience of Poverty in a Rural Community: Broughton, North Lincolnshire, 1760–1835', *Local Population Studies*, 70 (2003), 11–28.
Peter Earle, 'The Economics of Stability: The Views of Daniel Defoe', in D. C. Coleman and A. H. John (eds), *Trade, Government and Economy in Pre-Industrial England* (London, 1976), 274–92.
Peter Earle, *The Making of the English Middle Class* (London, 1989).
Peter Earle, 'The Female Labour Market in London in the Late Seventeenth and Early Eighteenth Centuries', *Economic History Review*, new series, 42 (1989), 339–40.
Peter Earle, *Sailors: English Merchant Seamen, 1650–1775* (London, 1998).
Geoffrey C. Edmonds, 'Accounts of Eighteenth-Century Overseers of the Poor of Chalfont St Peter', *Records of Buckinghamshire*, 18 (1966–70), 3–23.
Michael M. Edwards, *The Growth of the British Cotton Trade, 1780–1815* (Manchester, 1967).
Peter Edwards, *Dealing Death: The Arms Trade and the British Civil Wars, 1638–52* (Stroud, 2000).
John Eglin, *The Imaginary Autocrat: Beau Nash and the Invention of Bath* (London, 2005).
Edwina Ehrman, *Dressed Neat and Plain: The Clothing of John Wesley and his Teaching on Dress* (London, 2003).
G. Eland (ed.), *The Purefoy Letters*, 2 vols (London, 1931).
Joyce Ellis, 'Urban Conflict and Popular Violence: The Guildhall Riots of 1740 in Newcastle upon Tyne', *International Review of Social History*, 25 (1980), 332–49.
F. G. Emmison, 'The Relief of the Poor at Eaton Socon 1706–1834', *Publications of the Bedfordshire Historical Record Society*, 15 (1933), 1–98.
Amy L. Erickson, *Women and Property in Early Modern England* (Routledge, 1993).
Nesta Evans, *The East Anglian Linen Industry: Rural Industry and Local Economy, 1500–1850* (Aldershot, 1985).

Ben Fine and Ellen Leopold, 'Consumerism and the Industrial Revolution', *Social History*, 15 (1990), 151–79.
Ben Fine and Ellen Leopold, *The World of Consumption* (London, 1993).
Ben Fine, 'Addressing the Consumer', in Frank Trentmann (ed.), *The Making of the Consumer: Knowledge, Power and Identity in the Modern World* (Oxford, 2006), 291–311.
Roger Finlay and Beatrice Shearer, 'Population Growth and Suburban Expansion', in A. L. Beier and Roger Finlay (eds), *London, 1500–1700: The Making of the Metropolis* (London, 1986), 37–59.
Margot Finn, 'Debt and Credit in Bath's Court of Requests, 1829–39', *Urban History*, 21 (1994), 211–36.
Roderick Floud and Paul Johnson, *The Cambridge Economic History of Modern Britain*, vol. 1: *Industrialization, 1700–1860* (Cambridge, 2004).
E. M. Forster, *Marianne Thornton, 1797–1887* (London, 1956).
Charles F. Foster, *Seven Households: Life in Cheshire and Lancashire, 1582–1774* (Northwich, 2002).
H. R. French, 'The Search for the "Middle Sort of People" in England, 1600–1800', *The Historical Journal* 43 (2000), 277–93.
Sylvia R. Frey, *The British Soldier in America: A Social History of Military Life in the Revolutionary Period* (Austin, Texas, 1981).
E. S. Furniss, *The Position of the Laborer in a System of Nationalism: A Study in the Labor Theories of the Later English Mercantalists* (New York, 1965).
Dorothy George, *England in Transition: Life and Work in the Eighteenth Century* (London, 1931).
Dorothy George, *London Life in the Eighteenth Century* (London, 1925).
Anthony Giddens, *Modernity and Self-Identity: Self and Society in the Late Modern Age* (London 1991).
Frederick C. Gill (ed.), *Selected Letters of John Wesley* (London, 1956).
E. Gillet and K. A. MacMahon, *A History of Hull* (Oxford, 1980).
John R. Gillis, *For Better or For Worse: British Marriages, 1600 to the Present* (Oxford, 1985).
Madeleine Ginsburg, 'The Tailoring and Dressmaking Trades, 1700–1850', *Costume*, 6 (1972), 64–9.
Madeleine Ginsburg, 'Rags to Riches: The Second-hand Clothes Trade 1700–1978', *Costume*, 14 (1980), 121–35.
Clare Gittings, *Death, Burial and the Individual in Early Modern England* (London, 1984).
Paul Glennie and Nigel Thrift, 'Reworking E. P. Thompson's "Time, work-discipline and industrial capitalism"', *Time and Society*, 5 (1996), 275–300.
Paul Glennie and Nigel Thrift, 'The Spaces of Clock Times', in Patrick. Joyce (ed.), *The Social in Question: New Bearings in History and the Social Sciences* (London, 2002), 151–74.
Joyce Godber, *History of Bedfordshire, 1066–1888* (Bedford, 1969).
Mark Goldie, 'Voluntary Anglicans', *The Historical Journal*, 46 (2003), 999–1004.
Oliver Goldsmith, *The Works of Oliver Goldsmith*, 3 vols, ed. Arthur Friedman (Oxford, 1966).
Richard Gough, *The History of Myddle* (London, 1981).
John Goulstone, *The Summer Solstice Games: A Study of Early English Fertility Religion* (Bexleyheath, 1985).
H. G. Graham, *The Social Life of Scotland in the Eighteenth Century* (London, 1969).
Edwin Gray, *Cottage Life in a Hertfordshire Village* (Harpenden, 1977).
Hannah Greig, 'Leading the Fashion: The Material Culture of London's *Beau Monde*', in John Styles and Amanda Vickery (eds), *Gender, Taste and Material Culture in Britain and North America, 1700–1830* (New Haven and London, 2006).
Emma Griffin, *England's Revelry: A History of Popular Sports and Pastimes, 1660–1830* (Oxford, 2005).
P. H. E. Hair (ed.), *Coals on Rails, or The Reason of my Wrighting: The Autobiography of Anthony Errington from 1778 to around 1825* (Liverpool, 1988).
Joseph Hammond, *A Cornish Parish* (London, 1897).

C. Knick Harley, 'Cotton Textile Prices and the Industrial Revolution', *Economic History Review*, new series, 51 (1998), 49–83.
S. Harrop and P. Perrins, review of Lorna Weatherill, *The Account Book of Richard Latham, 1724–1767*, *Transaction of the Historic Society of Lancashire and Cheshire*, 140 (1991), 234–6.
N. B. Harte, 'State Control of Dress and Social Change in Pre-Industrial England', in D. C. Coleman and A. H. John (eds), *Trade, Government and Economy in Pre-Industrial England* (London, 1976), 132–65.
N. B. Harte, 'The Economics of Clothing in the Late Seventeenth Century', *Textile History*, 22 (1991), 277–96.
Charles Harvey, Edmund M. Green and Penelope J. Corfield, 'Continuity, Change, and Specialization within Metropolitan London: The Economy of Westminster, 1750–1820', *Economic History Review*, new series, 52 (1999), 469–93.
Mark Harvey, Andrew McMeekin, Sally Randles, Dale Southerton, Bruce Tether and Alan Warde, *Between Demand and Consumption: A Framework for Research*, ESRC Centre for Research on Innovation and Competition, Discussion Paper no. 40 (Manchester, 2001).
R. Hastings, 'The North Riding Linen Industry', *North Yorkshire County Record Office Journal*, 7 (1980), 67–85.
John Hatcher, 'Labour, Leisure and Economic Thought before the Nineteenth Century', *Past and Present*, 160 (1998), 64–115.
Douglas Hay and Nicholas Rogers, *Eighteenth-Century English Society: Shuttles and Swords* (Oxford, 1997).
J. Jean Hecht, *The Domestic Servant Class in Eighteenth-Century England* (London, 1956).
Stuart Henry, *The Hidden Economy: The Context and Control of Borderline Crime* (Oxford, 1978).
John Hervey, *Letter-books of John Hervey, First Earl of Bristol*, ed. Sydenham H. A. Hervey, 3 vols (London, 1894).
George Birkbeck Hill (ed.), *Boswell's Life of Johnson*, 4 vols (Oxford, 1934).
Steve Hindle, 'Dependency, Shame and Belonging: Badging the Deserving Poor, c.1550–1750', *Cultural and Social History*, 1 (2004), 6–35.
Tim Hitchcock, *Down and Out in Eighteenth-Century London* (London, 2004).
Adrienne D. Hood, 'The Material World of Cloth: Production and Use in Eighteenth-Century Rural Pennsylvania', *William and Mary Quarterly*, third series, 53 (1996).
Julian Hoppit, 'Income, Welfare and the Industrial Revolution in Britain', *The Historical Journal*, 31 (1988), 721–31.
Pamela Horn, *The Rise and Fall of the Victorian Servant* (Gloucester, 1986).
Sarah Horrell, 'Home Demand and British Industrialization', *Journal of Economic History*, 56 (1996), 561–604.
Joan Howard-Drake, 'The Poor of Shipton under Wychwood Parish, 1740–62', *Wychwood's History*, 5 (1989), 4–44.
Jasmine S. Howse, *Index of the Probate Records of the Court of the Archdeacon of Berkshire*, vol. 2, 1653–1710 (London, 1975).
R. W. Hoyle (ed.), *Lord Thanet's Benefaction to the Poor of Craven in 1685* (Giggleswick, 1978).
J. Howard Hudson, *Cheshire, 1660–1780: Restoration to Industrial Revolution* (Chester, 1978).
Pat Hudson, *The Industrial Revolution* (London, 1992).
Jane E. Huggett, 'Rural Costume in Elizabethan Essex: A Study Based on the Evidence from Wills', *Costume*, 33 (1999), 74–88.
Jane Humphreys, 'Household Economy', in Roderick Floud and Paul Johnson, *The Cambridge Economic History of Modern Britain*, vol. 1: *Industrialization, 1700–1860* (Cambridge, 2004), 238–67.
Christopher Husbands, 'Standards of Living in North Warwickshire in the Seventeenth Century', *Warwickshire History*, 4, 6 (1980–1), 203–15.

Select Bibliography

Catherine Hutton, *Reminiscences of a Gentlewoman of the Last Century: Letters of Catharine Hutton*, ed. C. H. Beale (London, 1891).

Ronald Hutton, *The Stations of the Sun: A History of the Ritual Year in Britain* (Oxford, 1996).

Joanna Innes, 'The "Mixed Economy of Welfare" in Early Modern England: Assessments of the Options from Hale to Malthus (c.1683–1803)', in Martin Daunton (ed.), *Charity, Self-interest and Welfare in the English Past* (London, 1996), 139–80.

John James, *History of the Worsted Manufacture* (London, 1857).

Dudley Jarrett, *British Naval Dress* (London, 1960).

Bernard Johnson, *The Acts and Ordinances of the Company of Merchant Tailors in the City of York* (York, 1949).

Paul Johnson, 'Conspicuous Consumption and Working-Class Culture in Late-Victorian and Edwardian Britain', *Royal Historical Society Transactions*, fifth series, 38 (1988), 27–42.

J. A. Johnston, 'The Family and Kin of the Lincolnshire Labourer in the Eighteenth Century', *Lincolnshire History and Archeology*, 14 (1979), 47–52.

Peter Jones, 'Clothing the Poor in Early Nineteenth Century England', *Textile History*, 37 (2006), 17–37.

Robert W. Jones, *Gender and the Formation of Taste in Eighteenth-Century Britain* (Cambridge, 1998).

Pehr Kalm, *Kalm's Account of his Visit to England on his Way to America in 1748*, trans. Joseph Lucas (London, 1892).

Joan Kendall, 'The Development of a Distinctive Form of Quaker Dress', *Costume*, 19 (1985), 58–74.

Peter King, 'Edward Thompson's Contribution to Eighteenth-Century Studies: The Patrician-Plebeian Model Re-Examined', *Social History*, 21 (1996), 215–28.

Peter King, *Crime, Justice and Discretion in England, 1740–1820* (Oxford, 2000).

Peter King, 'Social Inequality, Identity and the Labouring Poor in Eighteenth-Century England', in Jonathan Barry and Henry French (eds), *Identity and Agency in England, 1500–1800* (London, 2004).

Steven King, *Poverty and Welfare in England* (Manchester, 2000).

Steven King and Geoffrey Timmins, *Making Sense of the Industrial Revolution: English Economy and Society, 1700–1850* (Manchester, 2001).

Steven King, 'Reclothing the English Poor, 1750–1840', *Textile History*, 33 (2002), 37–47.

Lawrence Klein, 'Politeness and the Interpretation of the British Eighteenth Century', *The Historical Journal*, 45 (2002), 869–98.

Tim Knox, 'Enter a Footman in Plush Breeches', *Country Life*, 192, 10 (5 March 1998), 50–3.

David Kuchta, *The Three Piece Suit and Modern Masculinity: England 1550–1850* (London, 2002).

Ann Kussmaul, *Servants in Husbandry in Early-Modern England* (Cambridge, 1981).

Ann Kussmaul (ed.), *The Autobiography of Joseph Mayett of Quainton (1783–1839)* (Aylesbury, 1986).

Miles Lambert, '"Cast-off Wearing Apparel": The Consumption and Distribution of Second-hand Clothing in Northern England during the Long Eighteenth Century', *Textile History*, 35 (2004), 1–26.

David Landes, 'The Fable of the Dead Horse; or, the Industrial Revolution Revisited', in Joel Mokyr (ed.), *The British Industrial Revolution: An Economic Perspective* (Boulder, Colo., 1999), 128–59.

T. Laqueur, *Religion and Respectability: Sunday Schools and Working Class Culture, 1780–1850* (Berkley, Calif., 1976).

Brian Lavery, *Nelson's Navy: The Ships, Men and Organisation, 1793–1815* (London, 1989).

C. C. P. Lawson, *A History of the Uniforms of the British Army*, 2 vols (London, 1940).

Beverly Lemire, 'Developing Consumerism and the Ready-made Clothing Trade in Britain, 1750–1800', *Textile History*, 15 (1984), 21–44.

Beverly Lemire, 'Consumerism in Preindustrial and Early Industrial England: The Trade in Secondhand Clothes', *Journal of British Studies*, 27 (1988), 1–24.

Beverly Lemire, 'The Theft of Clothes and Popular Consumerism in Early Modern England', *Journal of Social History*, 24 (1990), 255–76.

Beverly Lemire, 'Peddling Fashion: Salesmen, Pawnbrokers, Taylors, Thieves and the Second-Hand Clothes Trade in England, c.1700–1800', *Textile History*, 22 (1991), 67–82.

Beverly Lemire, *Fashion's Favourite: The Cotton Trade and the Consumer in Britain, 1660–1800* (Oxford, 1991).

Beverly Lemire, *Dress, Culture and Commerce: The English Clothing Trade before the Factory, 1660–1800* (London, 1997).

Beverly Lemire, 'Second-hand beaux and "Red-armed Belles": Conflict and the Creation of Fashions in England, c.1660–1800', *Continuity and Change*, 15 (2000), 391–417.

Beverly Lemire, 'Transforming Consumer Custom: Linens, Cottons and the English Market, 1660–1800', in Brenda Collins and Philip Ollerenshaw (eds), *The European Linen Industry in Historical Perspective* (Oxford, 2003), 187–207.

Beverly Lemire, 'Fashioning Cottons: Asian Trade, Domestic Industry and Consumer Demand, 1660–1780', in David Jenkins (ed.), *The Cambridge History of Western Textiles*, vol. 1 (Cambridge, 2003), 493–512.

Alysa Levene (ed.), *Narratives of the Poor in Eighteenth-Century Britain*, 5 vols (London, 2006).

Jacqueline Lewis, 'Passing Judgements: Welsh Dress and the English Tourist', *Folk Life*, 33 (1994–5), 29–47.

Lady Maria Theresa Villiers Lister Lewis (ed.), *Extracts of the Journals and Correspondence of Miss Berry from the Year 1783–1852*, 3 vols (London, 1866).

Peter Linebaugh, *The London Hanged: Crime and Civil Society in the Eighteenth Century* (London, 1991).

Gilles Lipovetsky, *The Empire of Fashion: Dressing Modern Democracy* (Princeton, 1994).

C. Lloyd, *The Health of Seamen* (London, Navy Record Society, vol. 107, 1965).

Sarah Lloyd, 'Cottage Conversations: Poverty and Manly Independence in Eighteenth-Century England', *Past and Present*, 184 (2004), 69–108.

Trevor Lummis and Jan Marsh, *The Woman's Domain: Women and the English Country House* (London, 1990).

Ruth K. McClure, *Coram's Children: The London Foundling Hospital in the Eighteenth Century* (London, 1981).

Lynn MacKay, 'Why they Stole: Women in the Old Bailey, 1779–1789', *Journal of Social History*, 32 (1999), 623–39.

Neil McKendrick, John Brewer and J. H. Plumb, *The Birth of a Consumer Society* (London, 1982).

Neil McKendrick, 'The Consumer Revolution of Eighteenth-Century England', in Neil McKendrick, John Brewer and J. H. Plumb (eds), *The Birth of a Consumer Society* (London, 1982), 9–33.

Neil McKendrick, 'The Commercialization of Fashion', in Neil McKendrick, John Brewer and J. H. Plumb (eds), *The Birth of a Consumer Society* (London, 1982), 34–99.

Neil McKendrick, 'Home Demand and Economic Growth: A New View of the Role of Women and Children in the Industrial Revolution', in Neil McKendrick (ed.), *Historical Perspectives: Studies in English Thought and Society in Honour of J. H. Plumb* (Cambridge, 1975), 152–210.

Andrea McKenzie, 'God's Tribunal: Guilt, Innocence and Execution in England, 1675–1775', *Cultural and Social History*, 3 (2006), 121–44.

P. and R. A. Mactaggart, 'Some Aspects of the Use of Non-Fashionable Stays', in *Strata of Society* (Proceedings of the Seventh Annual Conference of the Costume Society, London, 1973), 20–8.

Robert Malcolmson, '"A Set of Ungovernable People": The Kingswood Colliers in the Eighteenth Century', in John Brewer and John Styles (eds), *An Ungovernable People: The English and their Law in the Seventeenth and Eighteenth Centuries* (London, 1980), 85–127.

Robert W. Malcolmson, *Life and Labour in England, 1700–1780* (London, 1981).

J. D. Marshall, *Old Lakeland: Some Cumbrian Social History* (Newton Abbot, 1971).

Hans Medick, 'Plebian Culture in the Transition to Capitalism', in Raphael Samuel and Gareth Stedman Jones (eds), *Culture, Ideology and Politics* (London, 1982), 84–112.

Hans Medick, 'Une Culture de la considération: les vêtements et leurs couleurs à Laichingen entre 1750 et 1820', *Annales: Histoire, Sciences Sociales*, 50 (1995), 753–74.

Tim Meldrum, *Domestic Service and Gender, 1660–1750* (London, 2000).

W. B. Mercer, 'Thomas Furber: An Eighteenth-century Cheesemaker', *The Reaseheath Review: A Journal of Cheshire Agriculture*, 5 (1933), 5–14.

Judith Milhous, 'Gravelot and Laguerre: Playing Hob on the Eighteenth-Century English Stage', *Theatre Survey*, 43 (2002), 149–75.

G. E. Mingay (ed.), *The Agrarian History of England and Wales, 1750–1850* (Cambridge, 1989).

Florence Montgomery, *Textiles in America, 1650–1870* (London and New York, 1984).

Gwenda Morgan and Peter Rushton, 'Visible Bodies: Power, Subordination and Identity in the Eighteenth-Century Atlantic World', *Journal of Social History*, 39 (2005), 39–64.

K. Morgan (ed.), *An American Quaker in the British Isles: The Travel Journals of Jabez Maud Fisher, 1775–1779* (Oxford, 1992).

Nicholas Morgan, *Lancashire Quakers and the Establishment, 1660–1730* (Edinburgh, 1993).

Christopher Morris (ed.), *The Journeys of Celia Fiennes* (London, 1949).

H. Mui and L. H. Mui, *Shops and Shopkeeping in Eighteenth-Century England* (London, 1989).

Lois Mulkearn (ed.), *George Mercer Papers Relating to the Ohio Company of Virginia* (Pittsburgh, 1954).

Gerald I. Mungeam, 'Contracts for the Supply of Equipment to the "New Model" Army in 1645', *Journal of the Arms and Armour Society*, 6 (1968–70), 53–115.

Madame van Muyden, *A Foreign View of England in the Reigns of George I and George II: the Letters of Monsieur César de Saussure to his Family* (London, 1902).

Scott Myerly, *British Military Spectacle from the Napoleonic Wars through the Crimea* (Cambridge, Mass., 1996).

Corita Myerscough (ed.), *Uncle John Carr: The Diaries of his Great-nieces, Harriet and Amelia Clark* (York, 2000).

Jeanette Neeson, *Commoners: Common Right, Enclosure and Social Change in England, 1700–1820* (Cambridge, 1993).

J. M. Neeson, 'An Eighteenth-Century Peasantry', in John Rule and Robert Malcolmson (eds), *Protest and Survival* (London, 1993), 51–8.

W. F. Neff, *Victorian Working Women* (New York, 1929).

Patrick O'Brien, Trevor Griffiths and Philip Hunt, 'Political Components of the Industrial Revolution: Parliament and the English Cotton Textile Industry, 1660–1774', *Economic History Review*, new series, 44 (1991), 395–423.

Andrew Oliver (ed.), *The Journal of Samuel Curwen Loyalist*, 2 vols (Cambridge, Mass., 1972).

Martha Olney, 'Demand for Consumer Durable Goods in 20th Century America', *Explorations in Economic History*, 27 (1990), 322–49.

Iona and Peter Opie, *The Oxford Dictionary of Nursery Rhymes* (Oxford, 1997).

Mark Overton et al., *Production and Consumption in English Households, 1600–1750* (London, 2004).

Robert Owen, *The Life of Robert Owen, written by Himself* (London, 1857).

Roy Palmer, 'Some Warwickshire Ballads', *Warwickshire History*, 6 (1986), 148–60.

David Pam, *A Parish Near London: A History of Enfield, Volume 1* (Enfield, 1990).

F. G. Payne, 'Welsh Peasant Costume', *Folk Life*, 2 (1964), 42–57.

Norman Penney (ed.), *The Household Account Book of Sarah Fell of Swarthmore Hall* (Cambridge, 1920).
Nicola Phillips, *Women in Business, 1700–1850* (Woodbridge, 2006).
Paul A. Pickering, 'Class without Words: Symbolic Communication in the Chartist Movement', *Past and Present*, 112 (1986), 144–62.
Barbara Pidcock, 'The Spinners and Weavers of Swarthmore Hall, Ulverston, in the Late Seventeenth Century', *Transactions of the Cumberland and Westmorland Antiquarian and Archeological Society*, 95 (1995), 153–67.
Ivy Pinchbeck, *Women Workers and the Industrial Revolution, 1750–1850* (London, 1969).
A. Pleat (ed.), *'The Most Dismal Times': William Rowbottom's Diary. Part 1. 1787–1799* (Oldham, 1996).
Marcia Pointon, 'Quakerism and Visual Culture, 1650–1800', *Art History*, 20 (1997), 297–431.
Roy Porter, *English Society in the Eighteenth Century* (London, 1990).
W. R. Powell (ed.), *A History of the County of Essex*, vol. 4 (London, 1956).
Archibald Prentice, *Historical Sketches and Personal Recollections of Manchester* (London, 1970).
J. M. Price, 'The Transatlantic Economy', in J. P. Greene and J. R. Pole (eds), *Colonial British America* (Baltimore, 1984), 18–42.
Ursula Priestley and Alayne Fenner, *Shops and Shopkeepers in Norwich, 1660–1730* (Norwich, 1985).
Mary Prior, 'Women and the Urban Economy: Oxford, 1500–1800', in Mary Prior (ed.), *Women in English Society, 1500–1800* (London, 1985), 93–117.
Jonathan Prude, 'To Look Upon the "Lower Sort": Runaway Ads and the Appearance of Unfree Laborers in America, 1750–1800', *Journal of American History*, 78 (1991), 124–59.
R. B. Pugh (ed.), *Victoria History of the County of Cambridge and the Isle of Ely*, vol. 4 (London, 2002).
James Raine (ed.), *Depositions from the Castle of York relating to Offences Committed in the Northern Counties in the Seventeenth Century* (Durham, 1861).
Adrian Randall and Andrew Charlesworth (eds), *Markets, Market Culture and Popular Protest in Eighteenth-Century Britain and Ireland* (Liverpool, 1996).
B. McL. Ranft, *The Vernon Papers* (London, Navy Record Society, vol. 99, 1958).
Donald Read, *Peterloo: The 'Massacre' and its Background* (Manchester, 1958).
Mick Reed, '"Gnawing it Out": A New Look at Economic Relations in Nineteenth-Century Rural England', *Rural History*, 1 (1990).
Aileen Ribeiro, *Dress in Eighteenth-Century Europe* (London, 1984).
Giorgio Riello, *A Foot in the Past: Consumers, Producers and Footwear in the Long Eighteenth Century* (Oxford, 2006).
Edward Miles Riley (ed.), *The Journal of John Harrower, an Indentured Servant in the Colony of Virginia, 1773–1776* (Williamsburg, Va., 1963).
W. G. Rimmer, *Marshalls of Leeds, Flax-Spinners, 1788–1886* (Cambridge, 1960).
David Roberts, *Lord Chesterfield: Letters* (Oxford, 1992).
Daniel Roche, *The Culture of Clothing: Dress and Fashion in the 'Ancien Régime'* (Cambridge, 1994).
N. A. M. Roger, *The Wooden World* (London, 1986).
H. C. B. Rogers, *The British Army of the Eighteenth Century* (London, 1977).
Natalie Rothstein, 'The Calico Campaign of 1719–1721', *East London Papers*, 7 (1964), 3–21.
Natalie Rothstein (ed.), *Barbara Johnson's Album of Fashions and Fabrics* (London, 1987).
John Rule, *The Labouring Classes in Early Industrial England, 1750–1850* (London, 1986).
Leigh Eric Schmidt, '"A Church-Going People are a Dress-Loving People": Clothes, Communication, and Religious Culture in Early America', *Church History*, 58 (1989), 36–51.
Leonard Schwarz, *London in the Age of Industrialisation: Entrepreneurs, Labour Force and Living Conditions, 1700–1850* (Cambridge, 1992).

Leonard Schwarz, 'English Servants and their Employers during the Eighteenth and Nineteenth Centuries', *Economic History Review*, new series, 52 (1999), 239–44.

Carole Shammas, *The Pre-Industrial Consumer in England and America* (Oxford, 1990).

Pamela Sharp, '"Cheapness and Economy": Manufacturing and Retailing Ready-Made Clothing in London and Essex, 1830–50', *Textile History*, 26 (1995), 203–13.

Sean Shesgreen, *Images of the Outcast: The Urban Poor in the Cries of London* (Manchester, 2002).

Robert Shoemaker, 'Male Honour and the Decline of Public Violence in Eighteenth-century London', *Social History*, 26 (2001), 190–208.

Robert Shoemaker, 'The Street Robber and the Gentleman Highwayman: Changing Representations and Perceptions of Robbery in London, 1690–1800', *Cultural and Social History*, 3 (2006), 381–405.

Susan Sibbald, *The Memoirs of Susan Sibbald (1783–1812)*, ed. Francis Paget Hett (London, 1926).

Eric Sigsworth, 'William Greenwood and Robert Heaton: Two Eighteenth-Century Worsted Manufacturers', *Journal of the Bradford Textile Society* (1951–2), 61–72.

Georg Simmel, 'The Philosophy of Fashion', in David Frisby and Mike Featherstone (eds), *Simmel on Culture* (London, 1997), 187–205.

Woodruff D. Smith, *Consumption and the Making of Respectability, 1600–1800* (London, 2002).

T. C. Smout, *A History of the Scottish People* (London, 1969).

Michael Snape, *The Church of England in Industrialising Society: The Lancashire Parish of Whalley in the Eighteenth Century* (Woodbridge, 2003).

Keith Snell, *Annals of the Labouring Poor: Social Change and Agrarian England, 1660–1900* (Cambridge, 1985).

Thomas Sokoll, 'Early Attempts at Accounting the Unaccountable: Davies' and Eden's Budgets of Agricultural Labouring Families in Late Eighteenth-century England', in Toni Pierenkemper (ed.), *Zur Ökonomik des privaten Haushalts: Haushaltsrechnungen als Quellen historischer Wirtschafts- und Sozialforschung* (Frankfurt and New York, 1991), 34–58.

Thomas Sokoll, *Household and Family among the Poor* (Bochum, 1993).

Thomas Sokoll (ed.), *Essex Pauper Letters, 1731–1837* (Oxford, 2001).

Lynn Sorge-English, '"29 Doz and 11 Best Cutt Bone": The Trade in Whalebone and Stays in Eighteenth-Century London', *Textile History*, 36 (2005), 20–45.

Margaret Spufford, *The Great Reclothing of Rural England: Petty Chapmen and their Wares in the Seventeenth Century* (London, 1984).

Margaret Spufford, 'The Cost of Apparel in Seventeenth-century England and the Accuracy of Gregory King', *Economic History Review*, new series, 53 (2000), 677–705.

Margaret Spufford, 'Fabric for Seventeenth-Century Children and Adolescents' Clothes', *Textile History*, 34 (2003), 47–63.

F. W. Steer (ed.), *The Memoirs of James Spershott* (Chichester, 1962).

Christine Stevens, 'Welsh Peasant Dress: Workwear or National Costume?' *Textile History*, 33 (2002), 63–78.

H. Strachan, *British Military Uniforms, 1766–1796* (London, 1975).

John Styles, 'Print and Policing: Crime Advertising in Eighteenth-Century Provincial England', in Douglas Hay and Francis Snyder (eds), *Police and Prosecution in Britain in the Eighteenth and Nineteenth Centuries* (Oxford, 1989), 55–111

John Styles, 'Manufacturing, Consumption and Design in Eighteenth-Century England', in John Brewer and Roy Porter (eds), *Consumption and the World of Goods in the Seventeenth and Eighteenth Centuries* (London, 1993), 527–54.

John Styles, 'Clothing the North: The Supply of Non-Elite Clothing in the Eighteenth-Century North of England', *Textile History*, 25 (1994), 139–66.

John Styles, 'The Goldsmiths and the London Luxury Trades, 1550 to 1750', in David Mitchell (ed.), *Goldsmiths, Silversmiths and Bankers: Innovation and the Transfer of Skill, 1550–1750* (Gloucester, 1995), 112–20.

John Styles, 'Dress in History: Reflections on a Contested Terrain', *Fashion Theory*, 2 (1998), 383–90.

John Styles, 'Product Innovation in Early Modern London', *Past and Present*, 168 (2000), 124–69.

John Styles, 'Involuntary Consumers? The Eighteenth-Century Servant and her Clothes', *Textile History*, 33 (2002), 9–21.

John Styles, 'Custom or Consumption? Plebeian Fashion in Eighteenth-Century England', in Maxine Berg and Elizabeth Eger (eds), *Luxury in the Eighteenth Century: Debates, Desires and Delectable Goods* (London, 2003), 103–15.

John Styles, 'Lodging at the Old Bailey: Lodgings and their Furnishing in Eighteenth-Century London', in John Styles and Amanda Vickery (eds), *Gender, Taste and Material Culture in Britain and North America, 1700–1830* (New Haven and London, 2006), 61–80.

John Styles and Amanda Vickery (eds), *Gender, Taste, and Material Culture in Britain and North America, 1700–1830* (New Haven and London, 2006).

M. Swain, 'The Linen Supply of a Scottish Household, 1777–1810: Extracts from the Accounts of Thomas Hog of Newliston', *Textile History*, 13 (1982), 77–89.

Mary Thale (ed.), *The Autobiography of Francis Place (1771–1854)* (Cambridge, 1972).

P. J. Thomas, *Mercantilism and the East India Trade* (London, 1926).

E. P. Thompson, *The Making of the English Working Class* (London, 1963).

E. P. Thompson, 'Time, Work-discipline and Industrial Capitalism', *Past and Present*, 38 (1967), 56–97.

E. P. Thompson, 'Patrician Society, Plebeian Culture', *Journal of Social History*, 7 (1974), 382–405.

E. P. Thompson, *Customs in Common* (London, 1991).

Noel Thompson, 'Social Opulence, Private Asceticism: Ideas of Consumption in Early Socialist Thought', in Martin Daunton and Matthew Hilton (eds), *The Politics of Consumption: Material Culture and Citizenship in Europe and America* (Oxford, 2001), 51–68.

Alannah Tomkins, 'Pawnbroking and the Survival Strategies of the Urban Poor in 1770s York', in Steven King and Alannah Tomkins (eds), *The Poor in England, 1700–1850: An Economy of Makeshifts* (Manchester, 2003), 166–98.

Henry Thursfield (ed.), *Five Naval Journals* (London, 1951).

Richard Chenevix Trench (ed.), *The Remains of the Late Mrs Richard Trench, Being Selections from Her Journals, Letters, and Other Papers* (London, 1862).

Luke Tyerman, *The Life and Times of John Wesley*, 3 vols (London, 1871).

Amanda Vickery, 'Golden Age to Separate Spheres? A Review of the Categories and Chronology of English Women's History', *The Historical Journal* (1993), 383–414.

Amanda Vickery, 'Women and the World of Goods: A Lancashire Consumer and her Possessions', in John Brewer and Roy Porter (eds), *Consumption and the World of Goods* (London, 1993), 247–301.

Amanda Vickery, *The Gentleman's Daughter: Women's Lives in Georgian England* (New Haven and London, 1998).

Amanda Vickery, '"Neat and Not too Showey": Words and Wallpaper in Regency England', in John Styles and Amanda Vickery, *Gender, Taste and Material Culture in Britain and North America, 1700–1830* (New Haven and London, 2006), 201–22.

Amanda Vickery, 'His and Hers: Gender, Consumption and Household Accounting in Eighteenth-century England', *Past and Present*, Supplement 1 (2006), 12–38.

Georges Vigarello, *Concepts of Cleanliness: Changing Attitudes in France since the Middle Ages* (Cambridge, 1988).

Hans-Joachim Voth, *Time and Work in England, 1750–1830* (Oxford, 2000).

Hans-Joachim Voth, 'Living Standards and the Urban Environment', in Roderick Floud and Paul Johnson, *The Cambridge Economic History of Modern Britain*, vol. 1: *Industrialization, 1700–1860* (Cambridge, 2004), 268–94.

Jan de Vries, 'Between Purchasing Power and the World of Goods: Understanding the Household Economy in Early Modern Europe', in John Brewer and Roy Porter (eds), *Consumption and the World of Goods* (London, 1993), 85–132.

Jan de Vries, 'The Industrial Revolution and the Industrious Revolution', *Journal of Economic History*, 54 (1994), 249–70.

Alfred P. Wadsworth and Julia de Lacy Mann, *The Cotton Trade and Industrial Lancashire, 1600–1780* (Manchester, 1931).

David Waldstreicher, 'Reading the Runaways: Self-Fashioning, Print Culture, and Confidence in Slavery in the Eighteenth-Century Mid-Atlantic', *William and Mary Quarterly*, third series, 56 (1999), 243–72.

Tim Wales, 'Poverty, Poor Relief and the Life-cycle: Some Evidence from Seventeenth-century Norfolk', in Richard M. Smith (ed.), *Land, Kinship and Life-Cycle* (Cambridge, 1984), 351–404.

Robert Walmsley, *Peterloo: The Case Reopened* (Manchester, 1969).

Claire Walsh, 'Shops, Shopping and the Art of Decision Making in Eighteenth-Century England', in John Styles and Amanda Vickery (eds), *Gender, Taste and Material Culture in Britain and North America, 1700–1830* (New Haven and London, 2006), 151–77.

C. Walton, *History of the British Standing Army, 1660–1700* (London, 1894).

John K. Walton and Robert Poole, 'The Lancashire Wakes in the Nineteenth Century', in Robert D. Storch (ed.), *Popular Culture and Custom in Nineteenth-Century England* (London, 1982), 100–24.

W. R. Ward, *Parson and Parish in Eighteenth-Century Hampshire: Replies to Bishops' Visitations* (Winchester, Hampshire Record Series vol. 13, 1995).

Alan Warde, 'Consumption and Theories of Practice', *Journal of Consumer Culture*, 5 (2005), 131–53.

John Wardroper, *Lovers, Rakes and Rogues: A New Garner of Love-Songs and Merry Verses, 1580 to 1830* (London, 1995).

Lorna Weatherill, *Consumer Behaviour and Material Culture in Britain, 1660–1760* (London, 1988).

Lorna Weatherill (ed.), *The Account Book of Richard Latham, 1724–1767* (London, 1990).

Sidney Webb and Beatrice Webb, *English Local Government*, 7, *English Poor Law History*, Part 1, *The Old Poor Law* (London, 1927).

Richard Wendorf, *After Sir Joshua: Essays on British Art and Cultural History* (London, 2005).

J. R. Western, *The English Militia in the Eighteenth Century* (London, 1965).

Jonathan White, '"The Slow Sure Poyson": Representing Gin and Its Drinkers in Eighteenth-Century England, 1736–1751', *Journal of British Studies*, 42 (2003), 35–64.

Jonathan White, 'The Laboring-Class Domestic Sphere in Eighteenth-Century British Social Thought', in John Styles and Amanda Vickery (eds), *Gender, Taste and Material Culture in Britain and North America, 1700–1830* (London, 2006), 247–63.

J. E. Wills, 'European Consumption and Asian Production in the Seventeenth and Eighteenth Centuries', in John Brewer and Roy Porter (eds), *Consumption and the World of Goods in the Seventeenth and Eighteenth Centuries* (London, 1993), 133–47.

Angus Winchester, 'Travellers in Grey: Quaker Journals as a Source for Local History', *The Local Historian*, 21 (1991), 70–76.

D. M. Woodward, 'The Chester Leather Industry, 1558–1625', *Transactions of the Historic Society of Lancashire and Cheshire*, 119 (1967), 65–111.

E. A. Wrigley and R. S. Schofield, *The Population History of England, 1541–1871* (Cambridge, 1981).

Arthur Young, *Tours in England and Wales, Selected from the Annals of Agriculture* (London, 1932).

UNPUBLISHED DISSERTATIONS AND ESSAYS

Jan Albers, 'Seeds of Contention: Society, Politics and the Church of England in Lancashire, 1689–1790' (PhD dissertation, Yale University, 1988).

Elisabeth Bogdan, 'An Investigation of Eighteenth-Century Iconography: Sir Kenrick Clayton's Revolving Seal', Victoria and Albert Museum/Royal College of Art MA Course essay, 1991.

Jane Holmes, 'Domestic Service in Yorkshire, 1650–1780' (DPhil dissertation, University of York, 1989).

Marius Kwint, 'Astley's Amphitheatre and the Early Circus in England, 1768–1830' (DPhil thesis, University of Oxford, 1994).

Bridget Lewis, 'Charitable Provision for the Rural Poor: A Case Study of Policies and Attitudes in Northamptonshire in the First Half of the Nineteenth Century' (PhD dissertation, University of Leicester, 2003).

Edward Newbold, 'The Geography of Poor Relief Expenditure in Late Eighteenth Century and Early Nineteenth Century Rural Oxfordshire' (DPhil dissertation, University of Oxford, 1995).

Robert Poole, 'Wakes Holidays and Pleasure Fairs in the Lancashire Cotton District, $c.$1790–1890' (PhD dissertation, University of Lancaster, 1985).

Tina Vivienne Richmond, '"No Finery": The Dress of the Poor in Nineteenth-Century England' (PhD Dissertation, University of London, 2004).

N. V. Sleigh-Johnson, 'The Merchant Taylor's Company of London, 1580–1645, with Special Reference to Government and Politics' (PhD Dissertation, University of London, 1989).

Virginia Smith, 'Cleanliness: Idea and Practice in Britain, 1770–1850' (PhD dissertation, London School of Economics, 1985).

Amanda Vickery, 'Women of the Local Elite in Lancashire, 1750–$c.$1825' (PhD dissertation, University of London, 1991).

Michael Walker, 'The Extent of the Guild Control of Trades in England, $c.$1660–1820' (PhD dissertation, University of Cambridge, 1985).

Jonathan White, 'Luxury and Labour: Ideas of Labouring-Class Consumption in Eighteenth-Century England' (PhD dissertation, University of Warwick, 2001).

Photograph Credits

NOTE References are to figure numbers

Ashmolean Museum, University of Oxford: 23
Birmingham Museums and Art Gallery: 96
© The Trustees of the British Museum: 31, 74, 85, 93, 114, 120, 123, 127
Reproduced from an original in the Borthwick Institute for Archives, University of York: 100
The Colonial Williamsburg Foundation: 32, 75
The Colonial Williamsburg Foundation. Gift of Mrs Cora Ginsburg: 79
© The Fitzwilliam Museum, University of Cambridge: 15, 16
Guildhall Library or Guildhall Art Gallery, City of London: 72, 73
© Chalmers Bequest, Hackney Art Gallery, UK / The Bridgeman Art Library: 22
Photograph reproduced with the permission of the Herbert Art Gallery and Museum, Coventry: 19.
Courtesy of the Huntington Library, Art Collections, and Botanical Gardens, San Marino, California: 111
Reproduced by permission of London Borough of Lambeth, Archives Department: 128
© Lady Lever Art Gallery, National Museums Liverpool: 6
© Leeds Museums and Art Galleries (Temple Newsam House) UK / The Bridgeman Art Library: 87
Library of Congress, Prints & Photographs Division: 24
London Metropolitan Archives: frontispiece, 37, 43, 44, 45, 46, 47, 48, 49, 50, 51, 52, 53, 54, 55, 56, 57, 58, 59, 60, 61, 62, 64, 65, 68, 69, 70, 95, 97, 101, 102, 103, 104, 105, 108, 109, 110, 119, 125

Courtesy of the Lewis Walpole Library, Yale University: 1, 3, 8, 9, 12, 14, 17, 23, 35, 36, 42, 71, 78, 80, 81, 86, 88, 89, 90, 91, 106, 113, 118, 126
© Manchester Art Gallery: 99
Museum of English Rural Life, University of Reading: 40
© Museum of London: 39, 112, 121
© National Museum of Wales: 11
National Gallery of Canada, Ottawa: 92
National Gallery of Scotland: 83, 84
National Gallery of Victoria, Melbourne, Felton Bequest, 1921: p. viii
© National Maritime Museum, London: 20
National Portrait Gallery, London: 38, 41
Upton House, The Bearstead Collection (The National Trust), © NTPL / Angelo Hornak: 5
North Yorkshire County Record Office: 67
Courtesy Nottingham City Museums and Galleries: 76, 77
Philadelphia Museum of Art: The John Howard McFadden Collection, 1928: 94
Private collection: 7, 10, 115, 117
© Private Collection / The Bridgeman Art Library: 122
© Private Collection / © Agnew's, London, UK / The Bridgeman Art Library: 34
The Royal Collection © 2007 Her Majesty Queen Elizabeth II: 30, 116
© Tate Gallery London: 18, 107
V&A Images / Victoria and Albert Museum, London: 2, 4, 13, 63, 66, 82, 98, 124
Yale Center for British Art, Paul Mellon Collection: 21, 25, 26, 28, 29, 33

Index

NOTE   Page numbers in *italic* refer to illustrations

advertisements, 11
Aiskew, Yorkshire, 140, *141*
Albers, Jan, 307
Allan, Robert, 5
Almond, Arnold, *296*
Andrews, Reverend Thomas, 188
Annals of Agriculture, 26
Annual Register, 183
apprenticeship, parish, 267–9, 307
Arkwright, Richard, 127, 248
associations, *see* clubs
Astley's circus, London, 248
Austin, William, 299
autobiography, 57–63

badges, 51, *256*, 272–4, *273*, 300
Bagnigge Wells, London, 308–9, *309*
Baines, Edward, 131
ballads, 60, 199–201, 306, 311, 315
Bamford, Samuel, 314–15
Barclay, Robert, 202
bare feet, a sign of poverty, *18*, 20–3, *21*, 65, 195, 224, 235, 265
Barker, Thomas, *76*
Barkham, Berkshire, 72, 215, 217, 234
Barnard, Thomas, 188, 201
Barthes, Roland, 398 n.2
Berrow's Worcester Journal, 52, 332
Berry, Mary, 14
Bewick, Thomas, 49, 197
    Memoir, 63
Bigg, William, *2*, *7*, *189*, *308*
Birmingham, Warwickshire, 1, 20, 58–9
Blaize, Bishop, 280, 310
Board of Agriculture, 149
Boccage, Madame du, 19, 190
Bourdieu, Pierre, 384 n.22

Bourne, Henry, *Antiquitates Vulgares*, 310
Bowden, Sue, 10
Brandon, Suffolk, 31–8, 322–3, 335–7
Bristol, Lord, 249
Brome, James, 25
Buck, Anne, 24, 28
Buckingham, Buckinghamshire, 63
Buer, M. C., *Health, Wealth and Population in the Early Days of the Industrial Revolution*, 128
Bunbury, Henry, *3*, *193*
Byng, John, 51, 184

calico craze, 111
Calverley, Yorkshire, 25
Campbell, R., *The London Tradesman*, 174
Capper, Reverend D., 254
Carlisle, Cumberland, 21, *134*, 147–8
Carrington, John, 315–16
Catcott, George, 45
Chamberlayne, Edward, *Angliae Notitia: or the Present State of England*, 182
Chambers, J. C., 128
Chapman, Johnny, 63, 197, 325
Charing Cross, London, *172*
Charlotte, Queen, 95
Cheshunt, Hertfordshire, 259, *268*, 269
Chesterfield, Earl of, 107
Child, Josiah, 128, 131
children, 14, 223–4
Chute, Elizabeth, 254
Clark, Harriet, 21
Clarke, Alison, 210
clocks, 99–100
clothes
    as charity, 249–55, 271
    as gifts, 248, 288, 315
    as prizes, *246*, 248, *312–13*, 315–18, *318*, *319*
    children's, 14, 223–4, 232–4, 241, 252–3, 267–9, 271–2, 356

cleaning and cleanliness of, 70, 71, 77–82, 81, 99, 114, 130, 209
distinctions in, between rich and poor, xii, 31–8, 33, 34, 46, 94–5, 127, 189–93, 192, 193, 195–202, 207, 237–8, 277–8, 289, 399 n.27
female, 33, 34, 35–7, 41–3, 90–3, 218–20, 241–2, 244, 277–95, 356–8
home-made, 137–46, 149, 153–60, 177–8, 194, 199–202, 322
in criminal records, 40–44, 89–93, 97–8, 101, 139–41, 327–31, 340–1, 343–7
in newspaper advertisements, 28, 38–40, 86–9, 331–2, 339, 341–2
in visual sources, 333–4
language used to describe, 206–10, 242–3, 305–6, 398 n.10
making-up, 148–9, 153–60, 165, 177–8, 243–4
male, 35, 39–41, 86–93, 220–2, 238–9, 241–2, 356
materials for, 31–3, 39–40, 41–4, 88, 90–3, 98–9, 109–32
mourning, 34–5, 59, 250, 398 n.10
national
   English, 19–20
   French, 3, 180
   Irish, 20–1
   Scottish, 21, 21, 224
   Welsh, 18, 22–4, 23, 29, 224
occupational, 27, 28, 45–6, 52–4, 207
pauper, 127, 144–5, 149, 165, 176, 256, 257–75, 307, 350–6
ragged, 56, 63–7, 64, 71, 83, 191, 207, 326
ready-made, 153, 161–5, 169, 169, 173–7
regional variations in, 24–9, 39–44, 86–94, 97–8, 134–51, 153–65, 167–78
repair, 73–5, 74, 75, 76, 84, 194, 231, 232, 242, 243, 244, 288, 289, 349, 357
replacement rates for, 71–3, 82–3, 222–4, 231–2, 322
second-hand, 82–3, 99, 107, 162–4, 168, 169, 173, 174–6, 175, 243, 288
simplicity in, 22–3, 94, 182, 189–93, 192, 193
sizing of, 176–7
socialists, early, and, 385 n.28
types of, examined in detail
   aprons, 31–8, 39–44, 94–5, 182, 285, 351–6
   bedgowns, 22, 39, 41, 75, 84, 90, 276, 355, 363 n.9
   breeches, 31–8, 39–44, 86–95, 352–6
   buckles, 31–8, 39–44, 86–95
   caps, 31–8, 39–44, 86–95, 285–6, 352–6
   cloaks, 31–8, 36, 42, 90, 284, 352–6
   clogs, 3, 25–6, 286
   coats, 31–8, 39–44, 86–95, 352–6
   court dress, 13
   frocks, 86–7, 352–5
   gowns, 31–8, 39–44, 86–95, 110–27, 236–8, 282–3, 336, 344, 346, 351–6
   handkerchiefs, 31–8, 39–44, 86–95, 351–6
   hats, 8, 9, 10, 11, 31–8, 39–44, 39, 86–95, 89, 285–6, 297, 351–6
   jackets, 27, 30, 45–9, 47, 75, 87, 106, 172, 355, 368 n.5
   Macaroni, 169
   mantuas, 159–60
   pattens, 286, 287
   petticoats, 31–8, 39–44, 86–95, 233, 287, 352–6
   pumps, 286
   ribbons, 285–6, 302, 315, 316, 317
   rockets, 25
   shifts, shirts, smocks, 31–8, 39–44, 86–95, 127–32, 212, 246, 315–16, 318, 319, 336, 347, 352–6, 362 n.21
   shoes, 31–8, 39–44, 86–95, 352–6
   slops, 27, 47, 49, 172
   smock frocks, 26–8, 27, 36, 45, 86, 94, 104, 186, 200, 220
   stays, 31–8, 42–3, 47, 70, 283–4, 352–6
   stockings, 31–8, 39–44, 86–95, 75, 172, 195, 285, 337, 352–6
   swords, 93, 182, 300
   trousers, 45, 87, 89, 106
   waistcoats, 31–8, 39–44, 86–95, 352–6
   watches, 8, 58, 60, 62, 96, 97–107, 173, 208, 240, 315, 343–4
   watch seals, 104, 105, 106, 103–5
   whittles, 24
   wigs, 19, 32, 58, 65, 86, 198, 240, 300, 342
   see also fashion; livery; occupations; shops; uniforms
clubs, 99, 101, 130, 147, 173, 202, 251, 253–4, 271, 400 n.48
Cobbett, William, 28
Collet, John, 50, 75, 84, 89, 180, 183, 298, 318
Colquhoun, Patrick, 278
consumers, consumption, 3, 6, 210, 247, 257, 277–8, 305, 321–6
Cornwall, 6, 25
courting, 312–13, 315, 316
courts of law, 11, 327–31
Cox, Nancy, 138
Cumberland, Duke of, 297
Cunningham, John, *Poems, Chiefly Pastoral*, 311
Curwen, Samuel, 24, 43
custom, plebeian, 4, 5, 310, 319, 323–6

dancing, *312–13*, *320*, 325
Darley, Matthew, *290*
Darrell, William, 182
Davies, Reverend David, 72–3, 80, 214–26, 229, 234, 243, 249, 265, 267, 348
 The Case of the Labourers in Husbandry, 214, 217
De Loutherbourg, James Philip, *207*
De Vries, Jan, 7, 245
decorum, 208–10
Defoe, Daniel, 5, 6, 130, 183, 279, 293–4
Derby, 57–8
Devon, 25
Dibdin, Charles, 27
Dorcas societies, 251–3, 254
Dorset, Duke of, *296*
Draper's Company, London, 274
dress, *see* clothes
drink, drunkenness, 6, 7, 15, *30*, 63, 66, *66*, 103, 184, *312–13*, 314, 317, 324

East India Company, 110, 112, 128–9
Eccles, Lancashire, *246*
Economic History Review, 5
economy, domestic, 185–8, *189*, *190*, *191*, 199–202, *200*, *201*, 213–26, 229–45
Eden, Sir Frederick, 72–3, 80, 82, 138, 145–6, 150–1, 202, 214–26, 229, 243, 253, 272
 The State of the Poor, 25, 135, 150, 153, 161, 214
Eden Treaty (1786), 15
embroidery, *see* sewing
emulation, 181–4, *180*, *183*, 186, *187*, 188, 198, 210, 248, 277, 283, 291, *298*, 323–4
enclosure, 182–4, 199–202
Errington, Anthony, 63
European Magazine, 183

factories, 5, 7, 99, 101, 109, 293
fairs, fairings, 202, 243, 244, *246*, 306, 310–19, *312–13*, 314, 316, 318, 319, 324–5
family poverty cycle, 225–6, 229–45, 323
Farmer, Ralph, 204
fashion, 6, 11–13, *13*, *30*, *33*, 85–6, 89, 93–5, 98, 110, 114, 122, 127, 167–8, 180, *192*, 196–8, *200*, *201*, 203, 244, 258, 289, 304, 305, 323–6
Fettes, George, 98–9, 100–1, 163, 176, 259, 270, 346
Fewston, Yorkshire, *see* Hudson, Stephen
Fiennes, Celia, 25
Finney, Samuel, 26, 187
Fisher, Jabez, 19, 21
food, *2*, 67, 136, 167, *189*, 326, 390
Foster, Charles, 230,

Foundling Hospital, London, ii, 93, 108, 114–22, *115*, *116*, *117*, *118*, *119*, *120*, *121*, 123, *124*, 125, 152, 158, 159, 228, 237, 262, 264, 265, 268, 283, 284, 302, 317, 333
Fox, George, 202
France, 3, 159, 191
Freind, William, 300
Furber, Thomas, 292-3, 315

Gay, John, *The Shepherd's Week*, 193
Gee, James, 61, 198
gentility, *see* politeness
Gentleman's Magazine, 26, 150, 192
Gillray, James, 186, *187*, 192
Glennie, Paul, 100–1
Godwin, William, 385 n.28
Gough, Richard, 72, 205
Green, Valentine, *104*
Greenwich, Surrey, 311, *314*
Greig, Hannah, 12
gypsies, 61

Hall, Fayrer, 114
Hanway, Jonas, 299, 300
hat boxes, 285, *285*, 288
Haworth, Yorkshire, *see* Heaton, Robert
Haywood, Eliza, *Epistles for the Ladies*, 206
Head, Guy, *105*
Heaton, Robert, 25–6, 222, 240, 248, 266, 280–95, 307, 315, 353–4, 357–8
Hewlett, Esther, *Cottage Comforts with Hints for Promoting them Gleaned from Experience*, 73, 130
Highmore, Joseph, *viii*
highwaymen, 196, *197*
Hindle, Steve, 274
Hogarth, William, *233*
holidays, 187, 306–14, *311*, *312–13*, 325
Holland, Reverend William, 324
Holne, Devon, 25, 149, 261–6, 350–5
Hooke, Andrew, 186
Houndsditch, London, 167, *169*, 177, 178
household budgets, 213–26
Housman, John, *Topographical Description of Cumberland, Westmorland, Lancashire and a part of the West Riding of Yorkshire*, 150
Hudson, Stephen, 124, 146, 262–5, 350–1
Hustler, John, 13
Hutchinson, William, *History and Antiquities of Cumberland*, 150
Hutton, Catherine, 22, 24
Hutton, William, 1, 57–9, 72, 97, 98, 100, 196, 208, 325

Ibbetson, Julius Caesar, 23, *81*
India, 109–12
Industrial Revolution, 4, 5, 6, 8, 11, 15, 99–101, 109, 128, 132, 136, 277
Instructions for Cutting out Apparel for the Poor, 220, 223, 254
inventories, 4, 136, 137–9, 153–4, 327
Ireland, 20–1, 188
itinerant selling, 62, 147–8, 173, 280, 289
  see also occupations

Jackson's Oxford Journal, 332
Jervas, Charles, *94*
jewellery, 107
Johnson, Barbara, 122, *123*, 126, *239*, 282
Johnson, Paul, 215
Johnson, Samuel, 185, 279
Jones, Peter, 72, 384 n.22

Kalm, Pehr, 19, 224
King, Gregory, 128, 216
King, Steven, 258
knitting, 140, 244, 265, 286
Knole, Kent, *296*
Knox, Vicesimus, 299

Lackington, James, 59–60, 136
Lambeth Marsh, Surrey, *320*
Landes, David, 128
Latham family, 141–4, 155, 229–45, 262–5, 266, 298, 303, 307, 315, 349–51
Le Blanc, Jean Bernard, 190
Leafield, Oxfordshire, 165, 259–6, 350–5
Leblanc process, 132, 367 n.62
Leeds Intelligencer, 52, 332
Leeds Mercury, 131, 332
leisure, 102–3
  see also holidays
Lemire, Beverly, 8, 109–10, 153, 258, 266
Lewis, Bridget, 250–1
Linebaugh, Peter, 195
Lipovetsky, Gilles, 386 n.82
Litchfield, Reverend Francis, 254
livery, 51–2, *180*, *183*, *187*, 272–4, 279, 295–301, *296*, *297*, *298*, *301*
Llanrwst Bridge, Denbighshire, *81*
Locke, John, 136
London Chronicle, 300
London Evening Post, 250
London Magazine, 282, 286
Low Countries, 5

Luxury, 181–4, *194*, 210, 245, 277, 283, 383 n.17
Lyon, France, 110

Macdonald, John, 299
McKendrick, Neil, 3, 4, 6, 14, 153, 323–4
Maclaine, James, 196, *197*, 300
MacPherson, David, 110, 126
Malcolmson, Robert, 310
Mandeville, Bernard, *The Fable of the Bees*, 182
Marine Society, 199
mass production, 153
Mayett, Joseph, 63
Medick, Hans, 324–5
Merchant Tailors Company, London, 174
Merchant Tailors Company, York, 155
Miller, Daniel, 210
misogyny, 202, *203*
Misson, Henri, 19, 80
Monmouth Street, London, *166*, 167, 174
Montagu, Elizabeth, 184
More, Hannah, *The Shepherd of Salisbury Plain*, 195
Morgan, Mary, 22–3
Moritz, Karl Philipp, 20, 78, 224, 291
Morland, George, 24, *34*, *36*, *48*, *190*, *191*, *316*
Much Hadham, Hertfordshire, 269

Nash, Richard 'Beau', 94, 182
Naylor, James, 203
Neeson, Jeanette, 201
Nelson, Admiral Horatio, *105*
Neville, Sylas, 24, 248
Newcastle Emlyn, Carmarthenshire, *23*
nobles, 192, 301
Nollekens, Joseph, *312–13*
North, Dudley, 188
novels, vii, *viii*, 187, 263, 363 n.8

occupations, examined in detail
  apothecary, 31–8
  beadle, 51, 274
  blacksmith, 31–8
  bookbinder, 58
  bookseller, 58, 60
  breeches-maker, 59, 61–2
  brewer, 45
  bucklemaker, 61
  butcher, 45, *180*
  clogger, 26
  coach driver, 102–3
  cobbler, *see* shoemaker
  collier, 45, 63

cordwainer, *see* shoemaker
farmer, 185, *186*, *187*, *192*, 199–200, *200*, *201*, 229–245
hairdresser, 167
labourer, agricultural, 9, *10*, 14, *27*, *39*, *104*, 199–202, *212*, *221*, 360 n.22
mantuamaker, 31–8, 148, 155–60, 165, 177–8, 244, 289, 322
mechanic, 62–3
milkmaid, *94*, *233*
milliner, 52, *53*
pawnbroker, *see* pawning
pitman, *see* collier
porter, *46*
postman, 51
postmaster, 31–8
prostitute, 37, 52–4, *54*, *309*
sailor, *27*, 45–9, *47*, 63, 87, *105*, *106*, 198–9, *172*,
salesmen, *see* shops and shopping: ready-made clothes shops
servant, 31–8, 51–2, *180*, *183*, 187, 222, 229, 240, 248–9, 257, *276*, 277–301, *287*, *290*, *294*, *296*, *297*, *298*, *301*, 307
shoemaker, 26, 31–8, 59–60, 73, *74*, 153–4, *203*, 243, 289
shop assistant, 52
soldier, *see* uniforms
stocking frame knitter, 1, 57–9
streetseller, 56, 60–1, *64*, 66, *66*, *67*, *68*, *69*, *84*, *89*, *172*, *175*, *285*
  see also itinerant selling
surgeon, 31–8
tailor, 31–8, 59, 61–2, 73, *74*, 148, 153–4, 165, 177, 243–4, 300, 322
waggonway wright, 63
washerwoman, 81–2
waterman, *273*
Offer, Avner, 10
Oldknow, Samuel, 131
Owen, Robert, 52, 385 n.28

Paine, Thomas, 401
Parker, Elizabeth, 237, *239*
  see also Shackleton, Elizabeth
Parker, George, 82
Parry, Joseph, *246*
pawning, 59, 60, 62, 98–9, 100, 101, 163–4, 173, 259, 290, 326, 346, 400 n.36, 402 n.15
Pennant, Thomas, 28
Penny, Edward, *287*
Peterloo, 202, 324, 326
petit-maître, 191

Pinchbeck, 99
Pitts, J., *319*
Place, Francis, 59, 61–2, 128, 196, 198
pleasure gardens, *272*, 308–10, *309*, 399 n.27
plebeian, definition of, 13–14
Pococke, Dr Richard, 25
poems, *194*, 311
Pointon, Marcia, 204
politeness, 1, 181–2, *197*, 208, 386 n.58
Pollexfen, John, 111
Potter, Israel, 307
Prentice, Archibald, 324
prohibition on printed calicoes, 15, 109–113, 127
Purefoy family, 295, 297–8

Queensberry, Duchess of, 94, *94*, 182

Rag Fair, London, *168*, 176, 312
Rann, John, 384 n.12
Register Office, 290
religion, 188, 205–9, 306–8, 326, *308*
  Christian social thought, 188
  Methodists, 205–6, *207*, 208–10
  Moravians, 400 n.51
  Quakers, 19, 25, 202–5, 208–10, 318–19
Riccall, Yorkshire, 256
Richardson, Samuel, *Pamela*, vii, *viii*
Riello, Giorgio, 173
rococo, 122
Rogers, Woodes, 63
Rosemary Lane, London, 167, *168*, 176, 312
Rowbottom, William, 51, 202, 314, 324, 326
Rowlandson, Thomas, *294*, *301*

St Marylebone, London, 64–9
Salte, Samuel, 131
Sandby, Paul, 56, 64, *64*, 66, *67*, *67*, 70, *172*, *175*, *285*, *297*, *320*
Sandpit Gate, Windsor, Berkshire, *70*
Saxby, Mary, 60–1, 69
  Memoirs of a Female Vagrant Written by Herself, 60
Sayer, William, 300
Saye's law, 109
Scotchman/Scotsman [itinerant seller], 62, 280, 289
Scotland, 20–1, 151
second-hand goods, 8
sensibility, 182, 189
sewing, 152, 157–60, *158*, *159*, *233*, *298*
Shackleton, Elizabeth, 291–2
  see also Parker, Elizabeth
Shammas, Carole, 138

Shaw, Benjamin, 62–3, 81, 202, 310
Shipton, Oxfordshire, 259–60
Shoemaker, Robert, 196
shops and shopping, 24, 52, *53*, 83, 124, 136, 138, 146–7, 149, 153–4, 167–77, *171*, 200, 244, 261, 288–9, 304, *312–13*, 322
    pawnbrokers, *see* pawning
    ready-made clothes shops, 154, 162–5, *166*, 167, *168*, *170*, 174–7
    sale shops, salesmen, *see above* ready-made clothes shops
    shop account books, 28, 124, 146, 220, 262–5, 280, 291, 350–1
    slop shops, 72, 165, 174
    warehouses, 167, 169, *170*, 173
Sibbald, Susan, 21, 24
Silliman, Benjamin, 301
Simmel, Georg, 196
Singleton, Henry, *30*
slaves, 261, 402 n.17
Smith, Adam, 188
Smith, Charlotte, 263, 363 n.8
Smith, Reverend John, 188
Smith, Woodruff D., 128
Smollett, Tobias, *Launcelot Greaves*, 187
soap, 80, 131–2
societies, *see* clubs
Southill, Bedfordshire, *221*
Spencer, Countess, 249
spinning, 139–40, 142–3, 149, *193*, 199–200, 202, 216, 231, 235, 289, 293, 375 n.20
Spitalfields, London, 110
Spofforth, Yorkshire, 26, 165, 261–6, 350–5
standard of living, 5, 11, 213, 325
Stuart, Lady Louisa, 186
Stubbs, George, 8, *9, 10, 39, 221*, 360 n.22
sugar, 2, 5, 8, 185, 188, *189*
sumptuary laws, 15, 184, 271
Sunday schools, 165, 252, 254, 257
Swift, Jonathan, *Description of a City Shower*, 287
system of provision, 139

taxes, 15, 51, 112, 127, 295, 361 n.37
tea, 2, 5, 6, 8, 15, 19, 184, 185, 188, *189*, 230, *309*, 315, 325
textiles, examined in detail
    cottons, 93, 95, 109–32, *115*, 117, 118, *123*, 124, 134–51, *265*, *283*, *284*, 345, 350–4
    designs for, *134, 141*
    domestic self-sufficiency in, 139–40, 142–5, 149, 199–202, 231

    linens, ii, 93, 95, *108*, 109–32, *115*, 117, *119*, *123*, 134–51, *228*, *237*, 261–2, *262*, *265*, *268*, 350–4, 362 n.21
    printed, ii, *84*, 93, *108*, 110–27, *115*, *116*, 117, *118*, *123*, *124*, *125*, *134*, 148, *228*, *237*, *283*
    silks, 95, *120*, *121*, 122, *123*, 195, *239*
    surviving, 333
    woollens and worsteds, ii, 95, 118–22, *119*, *120*, *123*, 134–51 *152*, 159, 262–3, *264*, *268*, *283*, *284*, 350–4
Thanet, Earl of, 249
The Trade of England Revived, 130
Theydon Garnon, Essex, 165, 261–6, 350–5
Thompson, Edward, 4, 5, 13, 99–101, 107, 201, 310, 324–6
    The Making of the English Working Class, 326
Thornhill, Yorkshire, 26, 165, 261–6, 350–5
Thornton, Marianne, 28
Thrift, Nigel, 100–1
tobacco, 6, 7, 230
Tottenham Court, London, *319*
Townley, James, *High Life below Stairs*, 180
Trench, Melissa, 64
Trimmer, Mrs Sarah, 80, 271
    Oeconomy of Charity; Or, An Address to Ladies Concerning Sunday-Schools, 252
    The Two Farmers, 184
Trotter, Thomas, 198
truck [payment of wages in kind], 247, 255

uniforms
    army, 45, *48*, 49–51, *50*, 63, 79, 381 n.30
    navy, 49
    parish, 51, 274, 395 n.55
    post office, 51
    servants', 301

Vanderlint, Jacob, 213
Vauxhall, Surrey, *272*
Vickery, Amanda, 209
Voltaire, 311
Von Archenholz, Johann Wilhelm, 20
Voth, Hans Joachim, 325

wakes, *see* fairs
Wales, *18*, 22–24, *23*, *81*
Walton, Henry, *11*, 276
Ward, James, *212*
Warde, Mary, 237–8
Ware, Hertfordshire, 261–6, 350–5
washhouse, public, 82
watchmaking, 98
Watson, Ralph, 140, *141*

Watts, Isaac, 271
weaving, 140, *141*, 142–3, 149, 240, 288
Webb, Beatrice and Sidney, 272
Wedgwood, Josiah, 136
Weekly Worcester Journal, 332
Wenderborn, Friedrich August, 20
Wesley, Charles, 206
Wesley, John, 205–6, 209
    Advice to the People Called Methodists, with Regard to Dress, 205
    Instructions for Christians, 202
West, Thomas, *The Antiquities of Furness*, 150
Wethersfield, Essex, 269–70
Wheatley, Francis, *47*, *194*
Whitbread, Samuel, 270
White, Reverend Gilbert, 24
Whitfield, George, 206
Wiggett, Caroline, 254
Wigstead, Henry, *xii*, 22

Wilkes, John, *141*
Wilmslow, Cheshire, 26
Wiltshire, *212*
Wimbledon, Surrey, 267–9, 274–5, 356
Wood, Thomas, 317
Woodforde, James, 317
Woodforde, Nancy, 282
Worcester Herald, 332
Worcester Postman, 332
workhouses, 63–9, 71, 257–75
Wycombe, Lord, *192*
Wynne, Lady Anne Josephina, 250

xenophobia, 2, *3*, *190*, 193

Young, Arthur, 20, 24, 130, 185, 188, 213, 307

Zoffany, Johan, *46*